FIRST & SECOND
CORINTHIANS

Recived as a gift from.
Brother John Watson.
J Ritchie Kilmarnock
19/4/96.

FIRST & SECOND CORINTHIANS

JOHN HEADING

JOHN RITCHIE LTD.
KILMARNOCK, SCOTLAND

Published by John Ritchie Ltd, 40 Beansburn, Kilmarnock, Scotland
KA3 1RH.

First published in two volumes
1st Corinthians – 1965
2nd Corinthians – 1966
Revised and combined edition published 1995

Cover Photograph
Temple Ruins at ancient Corinth.
Photograph supplied by Global Scenes.

ISBN 0 946351 47 3

Printed by the Bath Press, Avon
Typeset by Newtext Composition Ltd, Glasgow.

PUBLISHERS' INTRODUCTION

This commentary on First and Second Corinthians, first published in two volumes in 1965 and 1966, brings to a new generation of Bible students the benefit of the written ministry of the late Professor John Heading of Aberystwyth.

The Publishers considered that such valuable material ought to be made available once again, and they gratefully acknowledge the co-operation of Mrs Margaret Heading and her son, Peter, in making this possible.

This book is a careful verse by verse exposition of these important but often neglected New Testament epistles. In it you will find scholarly attention to the exact meaning of words, combined with practical applications to everyday circumstances in individual life, home life, and assembly life.

Familiar passages and more difficult ones are treated with thoroughness, fairness, and consistency. The author shows that the meaning of a passage is best understood from the context in which it is found.

The original helpful subdivisions into sections and subjects are again highlighted in this edition, while the presentation and style have been modified for the present day reader.

The Publishers wish to place on record their deep appreciation for the help of Dr Bert Cargill, St Monans, who so willingly undertook the task of editing and overseeing the production of this combined volume.

John Ritchie Ltd

November 1995   Kilmarnock

Contents

Page

SECOND CORINTHIANS

PREFACE

During the years 1975 to 1978 while studying Law at Aberystwyth, Wales, it was my privilege to become acquainted with Professor John Heading. All too rarely does one encounter a person who is destined to have such a profound influence for good upon one's life. Yet for many residents of Aberystwyth, and for some of the students who studied there, John Heading's influence was out of all proportion to his shy personality.

John Heading was born in the city of Norwich, where he was also saved and baptised. He studied in Cambridge, was Reader of Mathematics in Southampton University, and eventually became Professor of Pure Mathematics in University College of Wales, Aberystwyth. Not long after his arrival in Aberystwyth he became the catalyst which brought a number of believers from the area to gather to the Name of the Lord Jesus using the premises of the Red Cross Hall, Vulcan Street, as the venue for their meetings. During term-time the numbers in fellowship in the little assembly were swelled by students.

I can still picture Professor Heading sitting in the Red Cross Hall at the Thursday night Bible Reading. His feet were invariably planted, side by side, firmly on the floor, his knees together. Balanced on those knees was his Bible; on a chair at his side was his Greek New Testament. After the brother who was responsible for opening the Bible Reading had finished his introduction, the discussion began. And what discussions we had! Seldom was there a question asked which "Prof", as he was affectionately known, failed to answer. His knowledge of the Scriptures was encyclopaedic, his enthusiasm and love of them infectious, his expositions careful and reasoned. To open a Bible Reading with such a learned brother sitting opposite was not an easy thing for many of us students to do. Yet he never put us off. He was not a hard man. Correction was given, whenever and wherever necessary, but always courteously and with feeling. We were encouraged, edified, corrected, and nurtured.

He gave to many of us something invaluable and irreplaceable—an experience of verse-by-verse expositions of Scripture which has left us dissatisfied with much that passes for exposition today. Notes of his expositions, some from the Thursday night studies and some from his Sunday afternoon Bible Classes, were subsequently published in book form so that others would benefit from them. They have gone around the world to the edification of many. He also demonstrated a willingness to address any problems or difficulties of interpretation in the Scriptures without avoiding them, whilst his teaching and example instilled in us a deep love for and commitment to the assembly and to New Testament church principles. He has left us with many fragrant memories as has his dear, kind, gentle, and hospitable wife, Margaret.

In this new and revised edition of this exposition of First and Second Corinthians you will find that meticulous treatment of the Word of God for which John Heading became well known. You will also find his willingness to address problems of interpretation. Frequently you will come across originality of thought and expression. Throughout the whole, you will find a warm love for the Lord and for the Scriptures. I hope you will be as enthused as many others have been.

Francistown, Botswana   Ian Rees

AUTHOR'S NOTE ON THE EXPOSITION OF
FIRST AND SECOND CORINTHIANS

The first Epistle of Paul to the Corinthians is recognised by all believers as being the "Charter of the Church", but apart from many familiar passages, the Epistle as a whole is not properly known or appreciated. The subject matter in the second Epistle follows on from the first, but its structure and its doctrine are also largely unknown by believers today.

This verse-by-verse exposition is designed to be understood only when read in conjunction with the actual verses of Scripture. The following points should be noted:

1. The first object has been to show the structure of the Epistles, and to show their position in the divine unfolding of truth.

2. Secondly, the arguments that the apostle uses to prove his points are traced in detail. A number of passages give difficulty because readers fail to realise that there is a trend of thought involved in these passages. Slight repetitions occur occasionally, to make each chapter self-contained.

3. Old Testament references are followed up in detail.

4. The author has sought to write impersonally — not seeking to commend certain companies of Christians or methods that he agrees with, and not seeking to criticise other companies and methods that he disagrees with. The exposition has thus been written for all, to help many to gain a better understanding of the Epistles.

5. In a detailed exposition of this character, it cannot be expected that every thought expressed will coincide exactly with thoughts of other writers who have also studied the Epistles in detail. Dogmatism has been avoided as far as possible, with a spirit of kindness adopted when suggestions of other writers are known not to coincide exactly with those expressed here. This observation should, of course, only apply to explanations of words and phrases, not to the broad outlines of church truth and practice.

6. The book is intended for individual study and reference. The style using subsidiary paragraphs throughout the text has been adopted to break up the lengthy arguments for easier understanding. The book may also provide many ideas for believers preparing for ministry, Bible study meetings, or young believers' classes.

Finally, the author would commend the exposition to the Lord, that He may use it for the building up of the saints and for His glory. The exposition has been written solely with this in view.

J. HEADING
Southampton, 1965

OUTLINE MAP

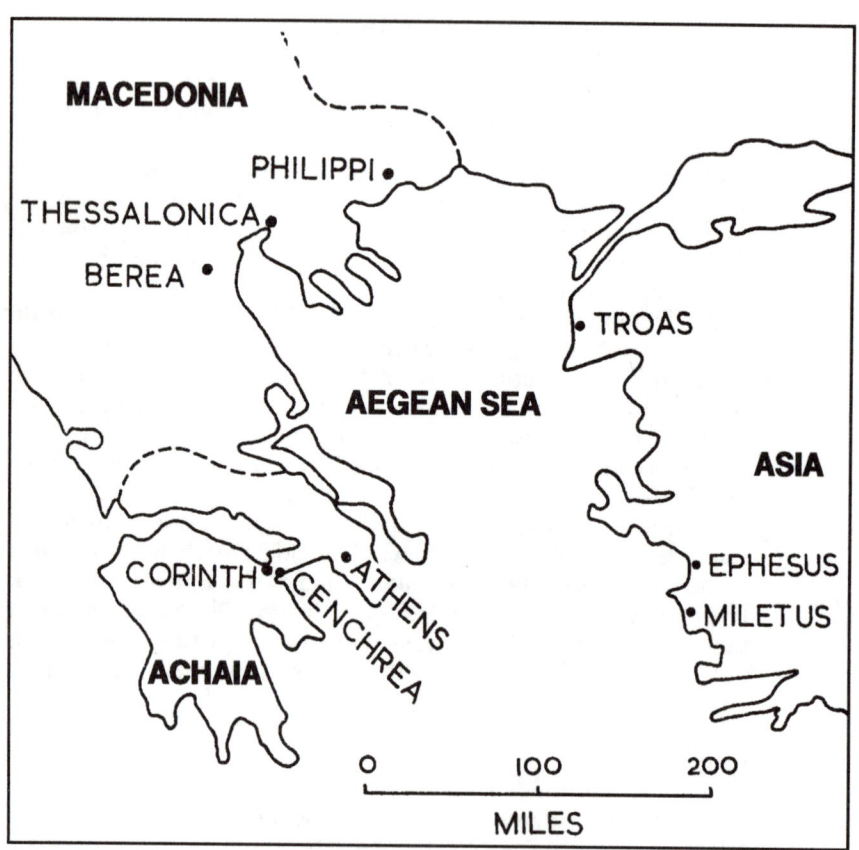

PAUL'S VISITS AND LETTERS TO CORINTH

1. The City of Corinth

The background of these Epistles is best understood by considering the historical, geographical, and spiritual background of the city of Corinth.

Prior to 196 B.C. the Macedonians had held Corinth, but after a period of liberation, the city was destroyed in 146 B.C. Julius Caesar rebuilt Corinth in 46 B.C. as a Roman colony, and Augustus Caesar established Corinth as the capital city of Achaia. Corinth became the commercial centre for Greece, and its population of four hundred thousand was exceeded only by Rome, Alexandria and Antioch of Syria. Its population included Romans, Greeks and Jews, these latter possessing a synagogue, Acts 18. 7. The city was noted for its wealth and luxury, and for its gross sensuality.

The place-names in the O.T., the Gospels, the Acts and the Epistles are not meant to be passed over in mystery and ignorance. The original readers knew where they were, and so should we. The spiritual interpretation of the wanderings of Israel in the wilderness, the capture of the promised land by Joshua, the life and kingdom of David, the Babylonian captivity, the ministry of the Lord Jesus in Galilee and Jerusalem, and Paul's journeys in the Acts, all demand the use of a map. In our outline map, it will be seen that Asia (in its N.T. meaning and not in its modern meaning) is on the right, while Greece (separated into the two provinces of Macedonia and Achaia) is on the left.

During his second missionary journey, Paul was guided in an anticlockwise direction around the coast from Philippi to Athens, having crossed the sea from Troas. Corinth was separated from Athens by a narrow isthmus about forty miles in length. Nearby was Cenchrea, Rom. 16. 1, a town serving as a port for Corinth. At the end of this journey, he crossed the sea again into Asia, to the city of Ephesus. His third journey effectively started at Ephesus, after which he went to Troas and thence around the coast again in the same anticlockwise direction to Corinth. He returned by a similar route into Macedonia, from whence he departed to Jerusalem via Troas and Miletus, Acts 20. 6, 17. We shall see that these blunt facts provide the choicest of spiritual lessons for all those who desire to be guided by God in their life and service.

2. Movements of Paul

The movements of a servant of God should always be under the divine control. Hence the recognition of God's mind is so important in every aspect of service. In 1 Corinthians 12. 4–6 we find that the Spirit selects the particular gifts given to each man, that the Lord selects the particular spheres of service of His servants, and that God accomplishes the outworking of service in the souls of men. Otherwise, the flesh chooses its own interests and activity, its own sphere of service, and its own achievements in the resulting fruit. The flesh is still in the believer, although the believer is not in the flesh, Rom. 8. 9, so we must take heed to all aspects of our service.

The movements of the apostle Paul provide a grand example of the divine control of service. His journeys to and from Corinth are therefore full of spiritual principles for service. Superficial reading of the Acts will not show exactly what took place, so it is a healthy spiritual exercise to piece together all the information in order to ascertain the facts. No doubt many readers are familiar with a map showing Paul's journeys. This is but a means to an end. The underlying motives, intents, impulses, exercises, discouragements and encouragements must be discerned, for we all travel that way. We can take sides with Paul who said, "We also are men of like passions with you", Acts 14. 15. Such similarity in our nature ensures that we can share his experiences at God's hand, for he was a pattern to all who would believe, 1 Tim. 1. 16. We have only to think of the pathway of the Saviour as Man here below; He had ever moved according to the Father's will. Yet He was distinct, since He, as divine, moved in contact with the Father in a way that neither Paul nor we can ever do.

3. Paul's Second Missionary Journey

This started from Antioch in Syria, Acts 15. 30. Paul was no new teacher in this assembly. His first service was achieved there at the instigation of Barnabas, 11. 25, 26, where they "taught much people". Again, just prior to his first missionary journey, he had been recognised amongst the "prophets and teachers" in Antioch, 13. 1. From this service, he was called by the direct intervention of the Spirit of God, "for the work whereunto I have called them", v. 2. After this first journey, it was in Antioch that he "abode long time with the disciples", 14. 28, "teaching and preaching the word of the Lord", 15. 35.

The second journey was a result of Paul's own exercise, "Let us go again and visit our brethren in every city where we have preached the word of the Lord, and see how they do", 15. 36. It is good to have plans like this for service, bringing commendation by the brethren to "the grace of God", v. 40. Here we have the secret of being in the divine will. Servants should expect *their* plans to be altered if His will is being worked out. This took place in outstanding ways on both Paul's second and third journeys. An original plan, doggedly adhered to against all circumstances and signs, can result in work of the flesh. The Lord Jesus would not remain in a city of unbounding unbelief, Matt. 10. 14. This was a sign to move on, except, of course, from Jerusalem where unbelief was a pointer to His sacrifice.

God's plans soon overruled those of Paul, thus preparing the way for the apostle's further service. But God quietly made other preparations as well. In Acts 16. 1, we read of Timothy, a young man saved either during the first journey or else shortly afterwards. This young convert had not rushed immediately into service; his character and devotion to Christ led him to be "well reported of by the brethren", v. 2. Such a proving by a good report is a necessary qualification prior to any sort of deacon service, 1 Tim. 3. 10. Paul chose this young man to be a fellow labourer, one who would play a conspicuous part in the apostle's movements to and from Corinth. Paul's selection of an *equipped* servant should be emulated today by brethren who have the responsibility for inviting speakers to local assemblies.

After this, Paul journeyed westwards, forbidden of the Spirit to preach until he came to Troas. There was need everywhere of course, but this could be no direct criterion for service everywhere and anywhere without exercise. The Lord of the harvest would send forth His labourers to follow His directions, Matt. 9. 38. Hence even in Troas, Paul accomplished no work, although there were souls waiting to be saved. Indeed they were saved later, and an assembly established. In Paul's case, the Lord was ordering His own purpose that the Gospel should be taken to "the uttermost part of the earth", Acts 1. 8. Hence the Lord gave to Paul only, the vision to go over into Macedonia, 16. 9. Had not Elihu said, "In a dream, in a vision of the night, . . . He openeth the ears of men, and sealeth their instruction", Job. 33. 15, 16? The effect of Paul's vision is given in verse 10; "after he had seen the vision, immediately *we* endeavoured to go into Macedonia, *assuredly gathering* that the Lord had called *us* to preach the gospel unto them". This was a blending of minds in mutual confidence and fellowship of service; they recognised that *they* had all been called by one vision.

4. The Second Journey Continued

God would not have His servants stay in one place for too long a time. When life has been formed, it will be selfsustaining when the true Life dwells in them. Moreover, God's final destination for Paul on this second journey was Corinth. God works out His purposes step-by-step, often in ways that His servants cannot immediately understand. The various cities visited on the way to Corinth were as follows:

> *Philippi.* Souls were saved and an assembly formed, so God would have His people move on. The hatred of the message by the people was disguised under the cloak of political rightness, Acts 16. 21. This led to them leaving the city. Had not Caiaphas treated the Lord in a similar manner? "The Romans shall come and take away both our place and nation . . . it is expedient for us, that one man should die for the people, and that the whole nation perish not", John 11. 48, 50.

Thessalonica. Here Paul preached in the synagogue the sufferings and resurrection of Christ. An assembly was formed through persecution, but the hatred of the message was disguised (a) by an uproar caused by "lewd fellows of the baser sort", Acts 17. 5, as if Paul had started it by turning "the world upside down", and (b) by an appeal to politics in verse 7, saying that "these all do contrary to the decrees of Caesar". Paul was there only for a short time. He had to go, and could not immediately return.

Berea. The people "received the word with all readiness of mind" and they "searched the scriptures daily", 17. 11. This encouragement came to an end when the Jews "stirred up the people". God used this to cause His servants to move on.

Athens. Here Paul proved the value of Timothy in a way that was to be so valuable later regarding the Corinthians. Anxious about the persecution in Thessalonica, Paul sent Timothy "our brother, and minister of God, and our fellow labourer in the gospel of Christ", 1 Thess. 3. 2, to Thessalonica to "know your faith", v. 5. He brought back news of their faith and charity, v. 6. Paul wrote the first Epistle to the Thessalonians upon hearing this. Meanwhile, as Paul waited in Athens, his spirit was stirred in him as he saw the city "wholly given to idolatry", Acts 17. 16. He preached Jesus and the resurrection, v. 18, but there was no point in labouring long where mockery and unbelief reign unbroken. He was a "savour of death unto death" to them, 2 Cor. 2. 16. The Lord had given instructions not to remain where men would receive neither the preacher nor his words, Matt. 10. 14. It would be "more tolerable for the land of Sodom and Gomorrha in the day of judgment" that for such a city, v. 15. Paul's sermon on Mars' hill in Acts 17. 22–31, usually regarded as a failure, was really his *last* sermon, designed to place the responsibility firmly upon the men of Athens, and to prepare for his departure. God was calling His servant to Corinth, and it was to this city that Timothy returned from Thessalonica, 18.5.

5. Paul's Work at Corinth

Arriving in Corinth, Paul located a married couple, Aquila and Priscilla, Acts 18. 2. A life long friendship in the service of the Lord was thus formed, lasting to the time when Paul was ready to be offered, 2 Tim. 4. 6, 19. No doubt we are right in thinking that this couple was already converted when Paul met them; perhaps they had been converted in Rome prior to their expulsion from that city. In Corinth they would have heard of the stirring of the Spirit of God northward in Macedonia. It would appear that they refrained from evangelical activity themselves, awaiting the arrival of the apostle. Their record shows that they were more gifted as teachers. Hence there was fellowship from the start. Upon removal to a new town, whether to live or for holiday, it is good to seek out those who are like-minded in the faith. In his work for the Lord, Paul maintained himself financially. He worked as a tentmaker together with Aquila and Priscilla. This side of Paul's life is dealt with more fully in 1 Corinthians 9.

The faith of the Thessalonians some two hundred miles to the north had sounded out to Macedonia and Achaia, where Corinth was, 1 Thess. 1. 8. Many hearts were already prepared to hear Paul's reasonings and persuadings in the synagogue every sabbath, Acts 18. 4, while the next verse shows that the return of Timothy and Silas from Macedonia brought about a more powerful joint testimony for Christ.

Paul's evangelistic methods appear to have been the same in almost every place he visited. Although he realised that he was called an apostle for the Gentiles, Gal. 2. 7–8, he knew that God's order was "to the Jew first, and also to the Greek", Rom. 1. 16; 2. 10; Acts 13. 46. This had been the order commanded by the Lord Jesus prior to His ascension; His witnesses would embrace Jerusalem, Samaria, and the uttermost part of the earth, Acts 1. 8. This order was peculiar to the beginning of the testimony. Throughout the O.T. and the life of the Lord Jesus, the voice of God had been essentially to the Jews; they possessed "the adoption, and the glory, and the covenants, and the giving of the law, and the service of God, and the promises", Rom. 9. 4. This would only be broken by their rejection of the Gospel message, Rom. 11. 11–12; Matt. 21. 43; then the Gentiles would be fully brought in. It cannot therefore be properly said today that the order of testimony in any unevangelised place is "to the Jew first, and also to the Greek". This has already been accomplished, and today every saint has his or her individual service given from the Lord. Hence if someone is called to work, say, among old people, it would be improper for another servant called to work among the Jews, to come and interfere saying that they should rather work first among the Jews and leave the old people until afterwards.

Paul knew the sphere in which God would have him work, and he went where the people were, namely into the synagogue. He had done this in Cyprus, Acts 13. 5, in Antioch, 13. 14, in Iconium, 14. 1, in Thessalonica "as his manner was", 17. 2, in Berea, 17. 10, but not in Athens. This was not formal preaching, but was accomplished under great exercise of soul— "Paul was pressed in the spirit, and testified to the Jews that Jesus was Christ", 18. 5. Because of immediate opposition and blasphemy, Paul would not remain in such strongholds of unbelief, and he went "unto the Gentiles", 18. 6. But the nucleus of the Corinthian church was already there. Stephanas, 1 Cor. 16. 15, is named as the "firstfruits of Achaia" implying that the rest of the harvest of souls was waiting to be gathered in. Justus, whose house joined hard to the synagogue building, was saved, Acts 18. 7, followed by Crispus the chief ruler of the synagogue, v. 8. Paul recalls these early days in 1 Corinthians 1. 14–17; 2. 1–5. Right from the beginning he foresaw dangers, so he avoided baptising many himself, and determined in his testimony to know nothing else than Jesus Christ and Him crucified, to avoid criticism that he had in any way been taken up with the wisdom of this world. By this means, the Lord brought blessing to many souls: "the Corinthians hearing, believed, and were baptised", Acts 18. 8.

With blessing manifested, no doubt Paul recalled similar experiences on his first missionary journey. Then there had been fierce persecutions, and he had been stoned and left as dead, 14. 19. Would the same happen in Corinth? But the Lord sustained His servant by a vision in the night, 18. 9, for "where there is no vision, the people perish", Prov. 29. 18. Paul had several visions of the Lord:

1. on the Damascus road, Acts 9. 3; 26. 13–20;
2. in the temple speaking of his testimony, 22. 17–21;
3. as caught up into the third heaven, 2 Cor. 12. 1–4 (referring perhaps to Acts 14. 19 when he had been stoned and left as dead);
4. in Troas relating to his movements in service, 16. 9;
5. this vision in Corinth referring to a peaceful harvest in that city, 18. 9;
6. later when a prisoner, the Lord appeared to him saying that he had to testify in Rome, 23. 11;
7. on the ship during the storm relating to this journey to Rome, 27. 23–24;
8. finally, he would see the Lord "face to face" when his journeys and service would be ended.

Having this certainty about the purposes of God in Corinth, Paul remained for a year and six months teaching the Word of God, 18. 11. During this period, he was *planting*, 1 Cor. 3. 6, and laying the one foundation even Jesus Christ, v. 10. His teaching, for example, would embrace the Lord's supper, 1 Cor. 11. 23.

The Jews attempted to cause trouble, but the deputy, Gallio by name, took no interest in these matters, Acts 18. 12–17. The assembly, being safe from persecution, was now endued with every spiritual gift, 1 Cor. 1. 5. So Paul could leave them, sailing from the port of Cenchrea to Ephesus, with Priscilla and Aquila, Acts 18. 18. Later, Apollos came to Corinth, 18. 27, 28; 19. 1 and helped the believers, an occupation that Paul describes as *watering*, 1 Cor. 3. 6.

After this, however, weaknesses set in at Corinth. Paul learned of these while he was at Ephesus on his third missionary journey. The Corinthians had written to Paul about certain difficulties, 1 Cor. 7. 1, and Paul, in his reply, not only deals with these difficulties, but also deals with the weaknesses that had come to his notice. The structure of the first Epistle to the Corinthians revolves around these difficulties and weaknesses. Many of Paul's letters were written, not as doctrinal treatises, but to correct error that had appeared in various churches. In this way, God chooses to instruct us regarding church truth, showing us the dangers of going astray. At the same time the practical nature of the Epistles is emphasised.

Exactly how many letters Paul wrote to Corinth, the contents of those not left on record in Holy Scripture, how many times Paul visited Corinth, and the purposes and results of those visits not recorded in the N.T., are a matter of speculation. The interpretation of the Epistles does not rest upon possessing an answer to these questions, else one would be questioning the wisdom of divine inspiration. Interested readers may find discussions of these questions in more formal works on the Epistles.*

6. Paul's Departure fom Corinth

First Corinthians shows the enormous range of teaching that the apostle engaged in during his stay in Corinth. He dealt with morality and mutual conduct, with the doctrine behind the Gospel, with assembly order (baptism and the Lord's supper), and with the service of the saints. In everything they were enriched by Christ, "in all utterance, and in all knowledge", 1 Cor. 1. 5. Seeing the assembly on its own spiritual feet, Paul was exercised to return to Antioch and Jerusalem, Acts 18. 18–22. The Jewish insurrection in Corinth against Paul, v. 12, did not contribute to his departure, since he tarried there "yet a good while", v. 18.

Paul sailed eastwards to Ephesus, a suitable place to board a ship for Caesarea. He could not stop in Ephesus, although he opened a testimony there by reasoning in the synagogue, v. 19. But he promised to return on his third journey, "if God will", v. 21. That is, a plan was made, but its outworking was subject to the over-ruling of God. We shall see more of this later. If we are faithful in service, and if plans have to be changed, that is for the good. But if the flesh is manifest in service and then plans change, that is merely the result of the servant's own folly.

Priscilla and Aquila remained in Ephesus while Paul was away. No recorded testimony is given, and no converts, since they were not public evangelists. Meanwhile, Apollos arrived and gained disciples (in Acts 19. 1) by teaching the baptism of John. Aquila and Priscilla, being teachers, corrected Apollos by expounding unto him the way of God more perfectly, 18. 26. Only after this Apollos is sent with a letter of commendation to Corinth to help them there, v. 27.

7. Paul's Work in Ephesus

A few phases of the work may be noticed:
1. He corrected men who may have been converts of Apollos, Acts 19. 1–7. We note that faith in Christ, the reception of the Spirit, and baptism are all linked together. These men, now converts to Christ, formed the nucleus of the assembly at Ephesus, and obviously met in the house of Priscilla and Aquila, 1 Cor. 16. 19.
2. The Word of God mightily grew and prevailed, 19. 20. Paul declared to them "all the counsel of God", 20. 27, and he warned them all "with tears" night and day for three years, v. 31. The

---

* See, for example, the article "Corinthians, Epistle to the" on pages 252-257 of The New Bible Dictionary, published by the I.V.F.

success of the work in the gospel was followed up with teaching all the Word of God.

3. Persecution did not drive the apostle from Ephesus. The Lord ensured a period of stability for the laying of the foundation of the heavenly position in Christ.

4. Paul often refers to his trials in Ephesus, by which he was wholly cast upon God. In Acts 20. 19 R.V. we read of the "trials which befell me by the plots of the Jews"; previously he had written that he had "fought with beasts at Ephesus", 1 Cor. 15. 32. No doubt these were not real beasts, refering rather to the holders of false doctrine and to the "many adversaries", 16. 9. Again, he could write, "our trouble which came to us in Asia, that we were pressed out of measure, above strength", 2 Cor. 1. 8. Here, he appears to refer to the physical and mental strain of overwork. Finally, we have the uproar about the goddess Diana, Acts 19. 23–41. God allowed these trials so that he could appreciate divine comfort, and be able later to comfort the Corinthians in their own afflictions.

8. Corinth was not Forgotten – The First Epistle Sent

Amidst all this busy evangelistic and pastoral work in Ephesus, Paul did not forget the fruitful field of Corinth. How could he, when he had the "care of all the churches" daily at heart, 2 Cor. 11. 28?

1. He thanked God *daily* on their behalf for all the grace given them in Christ, 1 Cor. 1. 4.

2. A letter had been sent from Corinth to Paul regarding certain problems, such as the liberty of marriage in service, 1 Cor. 7. 1.

3. The verse "when ye are gathered together, *and my spirit*, with the power of our Lord Jesus Christ", 1 Cor. 5. 4, suggests that Paul regarded his apostolic authority as present with them.

4. 1 Corinthians 16. 1–4 and 2 Corinthians 8–9 show that Paul was arranging a collection for the poor saints in Jerusalem.

5. The house of Chloe had told Paul of the contentions in Corinth, 1 Cor. 1. 11. There was certainty in these reports, no gossip as from "tattlers also and busybodies", 1 Tim. 5. 13.

6. A few men had come from Corinth with a personal gift for the apostle, 1 Cor. 16. 17.

Hence Paul was constantly in touch with the situation in Corinth, and it was from Ephesus that he wrote the first Epistle to the Corinthians as a means of correction. From that time, he determined to visit Corinth again. He wrote, "I will come to you shortly, if the Lord will", 1 Cor. 4. 19, a plan showing up Paul's devotion in being subject to the superior will. Yet he would not visit Corinth until he had heard of their repentance.

9. The Brethren Sent to Corinth

With the first Epistle, Paul sent various brethren with duties to perform.

Timothy. This young man had previously served in a similar way by being sent to Thessalonica. Paul wrote, "I sent unto you Timotheus, who is my beloved son, and faithful in the Lord, who shall bring you into remembrance of my ways which be in Christ, as I teach everywhere in every church", 1 Cor. 4. 17. Timothy was faithful because God could trust him to represent the teaching of the apostle Paul. At the end of the first Epistle, Paul said of him, "he worketh the work of the Lord, as I also do", 16. 10, adding that he looked for him "with the brethren", showing that others were sent besides.

Apollos. Paul had desired Apollos to go also, but "his will was not at all to come at this time", 16. 12, no doubt because of the party spirit that existed in Corinth both for and against him.

Titus. He was sent to deal with the collection for the poor in Jerusalem, and to bring back news to Paul of the repentance of the Corinthians, 2 Cor. 7. 7; 8. 16–17. Paul regarded him as "my partner and fellowhelper concerning you", 8. 23.

"The brother" and *"our brother"*, 2 Cor. 8. 18, 22. The former had deep spiritual qualifications, since his praise was in the gospel throughout all the churches. Because of this, he was chosen to travel with the collection. The latter also had a commendation direct from Paul himself, "whom we oftentimes proved diligent in many things".

10. The Results of the First Epistle

In this letter written from Ephesus, Paul partially outlined his future plans. He would tarry there at least until Pentecost, 1 Cor. 16. 8, since a great door and effectual was opened to him. A careful reading of 1 Corinthians 16. 5–7; 2 Corinthians 1. 16 (particularly); Acts 19. 21; Romans 15. 25, 26, 28 will demonstrate Paul's detailed plans. "If the Lord permit", 1 Cor. 16. 7, Paul intended to go straight to Corinth after which he would pass into Macedonia. Then he would return to Corinth, visit Jerusalem, cross to Rome and thence to Spain. Paul did not know how God would allow these plans to work out. Certainly he avoided the type of attitude quoted by James, "To day or to morrow we will go into such a city, and continue there a year, and buy and sell, and get gain", James 4. 13. Rather James continues, "ye ought to say, If the Lord will, we shall live, and do this, or that", v. 15.

The news of their reaction to the letter took a long time to reach Paul in Ephesus. He longed to visit the saints in Macedonia, but he would not visit Corinth until he had heard of the repentance of the assembly. Hence Paul came straight to Troas, 2 Cor. 2. 12–13, where he could not take advantage of an open door. He had no rest in his spirit because Titus had not returned from Corinth. Under such pressure of soul, Paul could do no work. Nevertheless, at some time, an assembly had been formed in Troas, and later Paul broke bread there, Acts 20. 6–7. Paul then sailed directly over to Macedonia, 2 Cor. 2. 13, giving the believers in those parts "much exhortation", Acts 20. 1–2. The apostle's spirit had evidently revived since he left Troas. How was this? At first in Macedonia, Paul recalled "our flesh had no rest, but we were troubled on every side; without were fightings, within were fears", 2 Cor. 7. 5. But then he was comforted of God. Titus arrived from Corinth telling him of the Corinthian repentance and of their regained respect for his apostolic authority, v. 7. Titus also had been received by them "with fear and trembling", v. 15.

The next events were as follows:

1. Paul boasted of them to the Macedonians among whom he was staying, 2 Cor. 9. 2, and of the Macedonians to the Corinthians, 8. 1.
2. He engaged in the daily care of all the churches within his reach in Macedonia, 11. 28.
3. From Macedonia, he would now go to Corinth with joy and relief; "the third time", 12. 14; 13. 1, refers to this. He had been ready the second time when he was in Ephesus, but had instead passed directly into Macedonia.
4. He wrote the second Epistle to prepare the ground. Obviously Timothy had also returned from Corinth, and joined Paul in writing it, 1. 1. He wrote to comfort those who had repented, and to warn any others who still would not accept his authority, 13. 2.

11. Paul Accused of Vacillation – the Second Epistle Sent

We have seen that his original plan was to visit Corinth, journey to Macedonia and return to Corinth. In the event, he visited Macedonia, visited Corinth and returned to Macedonia, Acts 20. 3. In other words, Paul did things exactly the other way round and was accused of vacillation. Unjust charge indeed, so Paul deals with this in 2 Corinthians 1. 16–20.

What does "yea yea, and nay nay" mean in verse 17? Paul defines it in the verse. Taking a "yea yea, and nay nay" attitude means to use lightness, to plan according to the flesh, to have no settled plans, to plan without weighing the consequences, to have a helter-skelter mind. As James writes, "A double minded man is unstable in all his ways", James 1. 8. Paul answers the charge by observing that his "word" (or preaching) is "not yea and nay", 2 Cor. 1. 18 (not "was", as in the A.V.). His service is not haphazard, but it is in keeping with God's overruling will. We should not be uncertain in our service—taking up first one thing and then another. In the early days, the apostles would not act like that; it was "not reason" for them to leave the Word of God and do something else, such as "serve tables", Acts 6. 2.

Paul continues the second Epistle by further showing his motives for not going straight to Corinth; see 2 Cor. 1. 23; chapters 2 and 7. The example of Christ was certain, "in Him was yea. For all the promises of God in Him are yea, and in Him Amen", 1. 20. Indeed God's plans were wholly accomplished by the Son of God:

> *John's Gospel* shows the devotion of the Son to the Father's purposes. He treasured the Father's Word, John 14. 10, the Father's will, 5.30; 6. 38, the Father's works, 5. 36, the Father's witness, 5. 37; 8. 18.

> *Luke's Gospel* traces the Lord's progress to Jerusalem, showing that the divine purposes "in Him are yea". See Luke 9. 31, 51; 13. 22; 17. 11; 18. 31; 19. 1, 28, 41.

12. Paul's Departure from Corinth

The apostle followed the second Epistle down the coast to Corinth where he abode three months, Acts 20. 2. Scripture gives no hint concerning the effects both of this visit and of the second Epistle. The purpose of inspiration is served by preserving only what is recorded; anything else would merely satisfy curiosity. But it is certain that the Spirit intends second Corinthians to affect every believer in every church.

Paul went to Cenchrea, the port of Corinth, Rom. 16. 1, intending "to sail into Syria", Acts 20. 3, but because of the Jews he went on foot back into Macedonia and Philippi, vv. 3–6. Luke accompanied Paul, note the use of the words "us" and "we" in verses 5 and 6. Paul's other "companions in travel", 19. 29, sailed directly to Troas, 20. 5. These men originated from Paul's three missonary Journeys:

> Gaius of Derbe, and Timotheus, from churches founded on the *first* journey.

> Sopater of Berea, and Aristarchus and Secundus of the Thessalonians, churches founded on the *second* journey.

> Tychicus and Trophimus of Asia (Ephesus), where Paul founded the church on his *third* journey.

In other words, fellowship in the things of Christ lasts. At Miletus Paul finally gave his long discourse to the elders from Ephesus, with many warnings, Acts 20. 17–35. Then he sailed to Caesarea, 21. 8, and "went up to Jerusalem", v. 15, with the collection for the poor saints there.

Later the apostle had hoped to visit Rome and Spain, but in the event how differently God worked out His own plan in the service and experience of His servant.

Summary of the First Epistle

An overall picture is as follows. Chapters 1–10 deal essentially with what is individual, regarding conduct, service and responsibilities. Chapter 11. 17 to chapter 14 deals with collective assembly experience. Chapter 11. 1–16 shows the individual response to the Headship of Christ manifest both outside and inside the local assembly.

Different expositors divide the Epistle into various sections, these variations being consequent upon the particular point of view adopted by the individual expositors. The freshness of the Word and its living character are demonstrated by the fact that any sub-division into sections and paragraphs is not unqiue.

We divide the first Epistle up into seven *sections*, most consisting of several *subjects*.

Section 1 consists of the first nine verses of chapter 1, and forms the *"Introduction"*. The one subject here is *"The grace of correction"*.
Paul makes no reference to the errors at all, but his greetings and commendations provide a basis for dealing with the errors later.

Section 2 is from chapter 1. 10 to the end of chapter 4, and may be entitled *"Divisions amongst the saints"*. There are four subjects as follows:
   Subject 1: *"Principles of service"*, chapter 1. 10–31.
   Subject 2: *"Discourse on preaching"*, chapter 2.
   Subject 3: *"Spiritual work"*, chapter 3.
   Subject 4: *"The preacher and his converts"*, chapter 4.
The Corinthians were divided among themselves, in that various groups elevated some preachers and debased others. Since all true service is of God, Paul shows that there can be no legitimate grounds for such a state of affairs. He develops the proper relationship that should exist between the Lord's servants and those served.

Section 3, embracing chapters 5 and 6, may be called *"The saints' conduct"*. There are two subjects:
   Subject 1: *"Unsanctified conduct"*, chapter 5.
   Subject 2: *"Sanctified conduct"*, chapter 6.
The sin of fornication that existed in the church brought forth sharp rebuke and correction. At the same time, Paul develops wholesome truth for the proper conduct of the Lord's people.

Section 4 consists of chapters 7, 8, 9 and 10; its overall subject matter relates to *"Christian liberty"*. The four subjects are:
   Subject 1: *"Marriage and service"*, chapter 7.
   Subject 2: *"Partaking of meats"*, chapter 8.
   Subject 3: *"Living of the gospel"*, chapter 9.
   Subject 4: *"Partaking of tables"*, chapter 10.

In many phases of Christian living and service, there is liberty granted by the Lord. Yet liberty is not automatic and unwise; rather it calls for wise exercise as the expediency of one's action is discerned by the individual. Paul would not take advantage of any of the four forms of liberty discussed in this section.

Section 5 runs from chapter 11 to chapter 14, where Paul takes up the theme of *"Assembly service"*. The five subjects are:
Subject 1: *"Christ manifested in authority"*, chapter 11. 2–16.
Subject 2: *"The Lord's supper"*, chapter 11. 17–34.
Subject 3: *"Variety and unity in the purpose of God"*, chapter 12.
Subject 4: *"The influence of love"*, chapter 13.
Subject 5: *"Principles of edification"*, chapter 14.
The order of these subjects is important, the main principle being that the Lord's position and portion come first. The saints' position and portion come afterwards, and the recognition of this affects all true service for the Lord.

Section 6 embraces chapter 15 only, and may be called *"Pay attention to doctrine"*. The one subject is *"The resurrection"*.
Paul deals with certain mental difficulties regarding this event, and, by showing the great truth of the resurrection of Christ and its consequences, overcomes the difficulties of the Corinthians regarding the resurrection of believers.

Section 7 closes the Epistle. This section *"Concluding remarks"* may be summarised by the title *"Brotherly love"*, chapter 16.
With the corrective part of the Epistle written, Paul closes with thoughts on the mutual fellowship among the Lord's people. This happy close would give even greater authority to the many previous corrective sections.

The reader should not think that every church matter is dealt with in this Epistle. For a full exposition, we have discusssed other topics outside the general scope of the above sections and subjects, in places where their brief appearance seemed most suitable.

Summary of the Second Epistle

Although Paul rejoiced that many had repented, he was afraid that not everyone had accepted his corrections or his apostolic authority. Hence the letter was written to comfort those who had repented, and to warn those who did not accept his authority. In this Epistle, Paul unburdens his own heart, with numerous references to the state of the Corinthians. He provides grounds for the approval of
   his teaching, chapters 1–7;
   their liberality, chapters 8–9;
   his apostleship, chapters 10–13.
The Spirit provides, as it were, two grand letters of commendation for the apostle.
   Letter 1: chapters 3–6, written about *Paul and his ministry* to those who would gladly accept him.
   Letter 2: chapters 10–13, written about *Paul as a minister* to those who would not receive him.

As in the first Epistle, we divide this second letter into four *sections*, each with various *subjects*. It is of little use examining individual verses in detail if the overall structure has not first been perceived. That would be similar to trying to hang coats up when there are no pegs to hang them on!

Section 1 embraces chapters 1–2, and may be entitled "*Historical: Paul's grief.*" Two subjects arise,
   Subject 1: "*Apostolic sufferings*", chapter 1.
   Subject 2: "*Apostolic exercises*", chapter 2.
The outcome of Paul's sufferings in Ephesus and Troas was comfort from God, enabling Paul to comfort the Corinthians in a deeper way.

Section 2 takes in chapters 3–6, and deals with "*The service of the true minister*". The four subjects discussed are
   Subject 1: "*The ministry of the minister*", chapter 3.
   Subject 2: "*The vessel of the minister*", chapter 4.
   Subject 3: "*The object of the minister*", chapter 5.
   Subject 4: "*The character of the minister*", chapter 6.
Throughout this section, Paul uses the plural form "we". The ministry described in such detail is characteristic of all who seek to serve their Lord.

Section 3 reverts to historical considerations again, following on the end of chapter 2. It may be called "*Historical: Paul's rejoicing*", taking in chapters 7–9. This section contrasts with section 1, as rejoicing contrasts with grief. The subjects are
   Subject 1: "*Encouragement after discouragement*", chapter 7.
   Subject 2: "*The Corinthian collection*", chapters 8–9.

The former subject arises from Paul's exercises in Macedonia when Titus returned from Corinth. The latter subject also arises from the news that Titus brought back to Paul.

Section 4, concluding the Epistle with chapters 10–13, describes *"The example of the true minister"*. Four subjects arise:
Subject 1: *"Apostolic humility"*, chapter 10.
Subject 2: *"True and false apostles"*, chapter 11.
Subject 3: *"Preparation for service"*, chapter 12.
Subject 4: *"Approval of the apostle"*, chapter 13.
Throughout this section, Paul uses the singular form "I". The Spirit would bring Paul's letter of commendation before all men today, so that once again the authority of this servant of Christ may be recognised by all.

Outstanding ideas concerning the Lord Jesus Christ should be noticed in this second Epistle:
The sufferings of Christ in Paul, 1. 5.
The unalterable promises of God in Him, 1. 20.
All faithful service is a sweet savour of Christ, 2. 15.
Saints are an epistle of Christ, 3. 3.
Christ alone preached as the Light of God, 4. 5–6.
The dying of the Lord Jesus in the servant's vessel, 4. 10.
The judgment seat of Christ, 5. 10.
The constraining love of Christ, 5. 14.
Believers a new creation in Christ, 5. 17.
He was made sin for us, 5. 21.
Christ a complete contrast to Belial, 6. 15.
The rich One who became poor, 8. 9.
Christ the unspeakable gift of God, 9. 15.
Every thought to the obedience of Christ, 10. 5.
Espoused as a chaste virgin to Christ, 11. 2.
The simplicity that is in Christ, 11. 3.
The power of Christ upon Paul, 12. 9.
Paul's testimony before God in Christ, 12. 19.
The proof of Christ speaking in Paul, 13. 3 .
Crucified through weakness, yet He liveth, 13. 4.

FIRST
CORINTHIANS

1 CORINTHIANS 1. 1–9

Section 1.   Introduction
Subject: The Grace of Correction

General Relationships and Background of this Section

Corinth was a city with a population of four hundred thousand, standing on the principal trade routes of the world as it then was known. Paul continued there for a year and six months, teaching the Word of God, Acts 18. 11. After that, he spent three years at Ephesus across the Aegean Sea, some two hundred miles away, Acts 19; 20. 31. A delegation had been sent from Corinth to Ephesus, seeking help from the apostle regarding difficulties, weaknesses and errors that had arisen in Corinth. Paul, having already heard news of the situation in Corinth, 1. 11, had previously written one letter to the assembly, 5. 9. By return, it appears that the delegation from Corinth had brought with them a letter to the apostle, 7. 1, raising points upon which they desired the apostle's advice.

The whole Epistle suggests that there was little godly order in the Corinthian assembly, that almost everything (including motive, conduct, service and doctrine) needed apostolic correction. Yet the remarkable thing is that this introduction, 1. 1–9, contains no hint of the disorder at all. In the Epistle to the Galatians, the introduction, 1. 1–5, is what may be termed "short and sweet", the apostle hastening to plunge into his constructive criticism. But here in 1 Corinthians, Paul lingers upon the work of the blessed Lord Jesus, this being an encouragement to Paul before he begins the painful process of examination and correction. It was calculated to gain the ear of the Corinthians with grace, so that nothing harsh should detract from the corrective process.

These early assemblies had no central meeting-place; they used the believers' homes for the purpose, being divided into small groups (as was done also in Ephesus, 16. 19). These groups evidently developed into rivals, instead of being spiritually co-operating units.

The two Epistles to the Corinthians view the assembly as a practical fellowship on earth, the living expression of the fellowship stated in 1. 9; "God is faithful, by whom ye were called unto the fellowship of His Son Jesus Christ our Lord". The assembly is also seen as the body of Christ, being subject to its living Head, with the Spirit taking possession to work out the divine will. Similarly, it is seen as His corporate witness; they were "the epistle of Christ", 2 Cor. 3. 3, a word in the singular. Yet *all* the saints were needed to grow into a singular manifestation; Eph. 4. 13–16. To achieve these great spiritual ends, the process of correction in this Epistle appears to be somewhat negative in character. Hence the second Epistle follows, being ministerial in character, presenting a positive approach to the building up of the saints.

There are two large subdivisions in this Epistle, with additional subsidiary chapters:

1. Chapters 1–10 refer to the *conduct of the fellowship*.
    Christ is made unto the saints wisdom, 1. 30, but the opposite was manifested at Corinth. This opposite wisdom "descendeth not from above, but is earthly, sensual, devilish", James 3. 15. These three types are found in:
    the errors of chapters 1 to 4 – *earthly;*
    the errors of chapters 5 to 7 – *sensual;*
    the errors of chapters 8 and 10 – *devilish;*
    John also noticed these modes of departure, 1 John 2. 14–17.
2. Chapters 11–14 refer to the *service of the fellowship,* and deal with corrections to assembly service, both God-ward and saint-ward in the matter of spiritual gifts.

The introduction fittingly introduces these great themes.

Exposition of 1 Cor 1. 1–9: The Introduction

1 Paul called *to be* an apostle of Jesus Christ through the will of God, and Sosthenes *our* brother,
2 Unto the church of God which is at Corinth, to them that are sanctified in Christ Jesus, called *to be* saints, with all that in every place call upon the name of Jesus Christ our Lord, both theirs and ours:
3 Grace *be* unto you, and peace from God our Father, and *from* the Lord Jesus Christ.
4 I thank my God always on your behalf, for the grace of God which is given you by Jesus Christ ;
5 That in every thing ye are enriched by him, in all utterance, and *in* all knowledge;
6 Even as the testimony of Christ was confirmed in you :
7 So that ye come behind in no gift; waiting for the coming of our Lord Jesus Christ:
8 Who shall also confirm you unto the end *that ye may be* blameless in the day of our Lord Jesus Christ.
9 God *is* faithful, by whom ye were called unto the fellowship of his Son Jesus Christ our Lord.

1. Paul draws attention to his apostolic calling right at the outset. This gives character and authority to this corrective Epistle. Though some of the Corinthians were calling into question his apostleship, he does not dwell on the matter in the introduction, rather leaving it until later in the letter (see chapter 9). In another Epistle, Paul commences by enlarging upon his apostleship, "Paul, an apostle, (not of men, neither by man, but by Jesus Christ, and God the Father, who raised Him from the dead)", Gal. 1. 1. The authority of the apostle derives from the divine origin of his apostolic calling, and that his teaching had been received from the Lord. He who gainsays this is preaching "another gospel, which is not another", Gal. 1. 6. In himself, Paul realised that he was not meet to be called an apostle, on account of his pre-conversion conduct in persecuting the church of God, but after his conversion and his calling to divine service he knew "by the grace of God I am what I am", 1 Cor. 15. 10. Conversion, the call to service, and the ability to serve are all of grace, leaving no room for boasting.

Paul regarded apostleship as a particular service based upon a special divinely given gift. We may note the Scriptures:

> 1 Corinthians 12. 28: "God hath set some in the church, first apostles, secondarily prophets, thirdly teachers, . . .";
>
> Ephesians 4. 11: The risen Lord "gave some, apostles; and some, prophets; and some, evangelists . . .".

The apostles had the "first" position, since it was to them particularly that God gave the authority necessary for the original establishment of the assemblies. Peter was essentially the apostle of the circumcision while Paul was the apostle of the Gentiles, Gal. 2. 8.

Paul used his apostleship in different ways in the various Epistles. Restricting ourselves to the church Epistles, we may note:

> Romans: in exposition of fundamental doctrine;
>
> 1 Corinthians: in correction of assembly matters;
>
> 2 Corinthians: in ministerial edification;
>
> Galatians: in correction of fundamental doctrine;
>
> Ephesians: in revealing the counsels of God regarding the assembly;
>
> Philippians: the title was not used, since the Epistle declares the bondservant's joy in Christ;
>
> Colossians: in correction of false doctrine regarding Christ Himself;
>
> 1 Thessalonians: the title was not used, since he was writing in love and tender affection to those who accepted his authority without it being mentioned.

The apostleship of Paul was through the "will of God", as indeed are all gifts and local charges in the assemblies. It is presumption for a man to engage in any sort of spiritual work as a vocation, similar in standing to any other in daily life. Gifts and local charges do not arise by one's birth, by acquisition, by the normal processes of education (spiritual education in the school of God is not implied here) or by the election of men. The Lord alone calls men to His service, and those faithful to Him must repudiate whatever is inconsistent with such a divine calling.

The mention of Sosthenes as Paul's writing-companion, brings to mind Acts 18. 12–17. When Paul was in Corinth, Sosthenes became chief ruler of the synagogue after the conversion of Crispus the original ruler. Sosthenes made insurrection against Paul, but the Greeks took him and beat him while the deputy Gallio cared not to interfere. Admittedly, Sosthenes was a common name at that time, but it may well be that this man was now converted and a brother in Christ. Being associated with Paul would show the power of conversion, and the reality of departure from synagogue service to the blessings of assembly fellowship.

2. Paul writes to the "church of God" at Corinth. Paul is not referring here to the great universal church consisting of all believers saved in the dispensation of grace. Rather, he addresses a local company of believers. It is remarkable that the same name "church" or "assembly" is used in Scripture to denote both a local company and the universal company throughout time and space. The local company should manifest the same character as the universal gathering, but alas, this is not usually the case. The local company can be guilty of grave departure, but the universal company is for ever suited to be the bride of Christ. In the N.T., the name of a particular local assembly is always associated with the place in which the believers were found; hence, "the church of God which is at Corinth". There was no church named after a country — see Galatians 1. 2, where there was a plurality of churches in the country of Galatia. The local company is the property of God, a habitation for God in a place where there can be little else for Himself. In those days, of course, there was nothing else for Himself at all in these cities. Nowadays, there may well be many other believers who do not gather with a local company. Clearly such are members of the universal church, but are outside the local fellowship according to the N.T. pattern. One cannot make a local church merely by gathering to patterns and according to rules that are outside the scope of the N.T. revelation. A local church is such, not merely because men and women are saved by grace, but because of the Spirit's presence amongst those who value the N.T. pattern of gathering.

Paul observes that the individual members are "sanctified in Christ Jesus". This is the past act of God, and must be distinguished from any present aspect of sanctification in growth. The basic root of the word "sanctify" is the same as that of the word "holy". The former is of Latin derivation and the latter is Germanic. English— and hence the A.V.—is rich in duplicated words (such as Spirit, Ghost; just, righteous), but one must not try and read differences of meaning into such pairs. Such pairs are merely a phenomenon of translation, originating from single words in the Greek. Sanctified, or rendered holy, means "set apart" for God in Christ Jesus. (See 1 Cor. 6. 11; Heb. 10. 10; 1 Pet. 1. 2.)

These Christians were also "called saints", or "holy ones". "Sanctified" implies their standing before God; "saints" denotes the name God gives to those possessing this standing. The same distinction is found in the experience of the Lord Jesus: He was "the Holy One", Acts 3. 14, as to His title, and He said in prayer "I sanctify myself", John 17. 19, as to His blessed conduct amongst men. Some feel that the description "holy" relates more particularly to the priestly character of the Lord's people, since they are a "holy priesthood", 1 Pet. 2. 5.

Paul also sends the letter to "all that in every place call upon the name of Jesus Christ our Lord". This links together all believers everywhere, and it shows the universal appeal of the Epistle. None can deny the relevance of its teaching; none can tamper with it today, since it is for us. "One Lord, both theirs and ours" denotes one central authority, a divine centre, far removed from central organisations of men. The universality of the Epistle can also be found in the following references:

"as I teach every where in every church", 4. 17;

"so ordain I in all churches", 7. 17;

"we have no such custom, neither the churches of God", 11. 16;

"came the word of God . . . unto you only? . . . the things that I write unto you are the commandments of the Lord", 14. 36, 37;

"as I have given order to the churches in Galatia, even so do ye", 16. 1.

3. This verse contains the usual apostolic greeting; it appeared first in Romans 1. 7, while it even occurred in Galatians 1. 3. It formed a suitable greeting to an individual as well as to an assembly, 1 Tim. 1. 2. A similar greeting terminated many of the Epistles, Rom. 16. 24; 1 Cor. 16. 23.

"Grace" suggests the continued manifestation of the free gifts of God under doubtful circumstances. The introduction is full of references to the free supply of grace to His people:

"sanctified in Christ Jesus", v. 2;

"grace of God which is given you by Jesus Christ", v. 4;

"in everything ye are enriched by Him", v. 5;

"the testimony of Christ was confirmed in you", v. 6;

"ye come behind in no gift", v. 7;

"who shall confirm you unto the end", v. 8;

"God is faithful, by whom ye were called", v. 9.

All these quotations contain references to the unmerited favours of God. It goes without saying that these things should be manifested rather than any activity of the flesh. But no mention is made of this in the introduction.

Peace is a form of greeting: "Peace I leave with you, My peace I give unto you: not as the world giveth, give I unto you", John 14. 27. The world gave that sort of greeting, but the Lord would not use it as a mere word as from the world. He elevated the greeting, placing it as His blessing upon those whose hearts might have been troubled and afraid, v. 1, v. 27. Paul re-iterates this peace from the divine source, a peace that had its origin in justification by faith, Rom. 5.1, and that passes into practical experience, Phil. 4. 7.

"From God our Father, and from the Lord Jesus Christ" suggests the divine unity, linking with Christian unity at the end of the previous verse.

4. Here we find Paul's usual thanksgiving for the saints, found in most Epistles. For example, in Romans 1. 8 he gives thanks for their faith, the subject of the Epistle; in Ephesians 1. 16 his thanksgiving and prayer are for their appreciation of the heavenly subject matter of the Epistle. But in 1 Corinthians 1. 4, he gives thanks for their spiritual enrichment, although the outworking of it was clouded with error.

Paul's introductory thanskgivings and prayers should be an example for us. Do we ever thank God for our possessions in the local assembly? Is this

ever the subject and theme of the prayer meeting? The translation here
should read "in" and not "by Christ Jesus". This suggests "as a result of",
or "in virtue of" His person and work. It may also suggest identity with
Christ, 2 Cor. 1. 21.

5. This verse is a remarkable catalogue of enrichment. Notice the wide
extent of the riches, "*all* utterance", "*all* knowledge", "ye come *behind in no
gift*", v. 7. This expanse of blessing is characteristic of the two Epistles:

"all are yours; and ye are Christ's", 3. 22;
"that ye through His poverty might be enriched", 2 Cor. 8. 9;
"God is able to make all grace abound toward you", 2 Cor. 9. 8;
"being enriched in every thing", 2 Cor. 9. 11.

These latter verses imply temporal as well as spiritual blessings. Note
also

"all that is in the heaven and in the earth is Thine, . . ., all things
come of Thee", 1 Chron. 29. 11, 14.

The reference to "utterance" means ability in discourse. The principles
governing the various gifts involving discourse are given in chapter 12,
and the weaknesses associated with discourse are dealt with in chapter 14.
Here, in the introduction, Paul does not mention that weaknesses are
associated with this enrichment of gift. "Knowledge" is singled out in
chapter 12 as one of the gifts of the Spirit, "to another the word of
knowledge by the same Spirit", v. 8. These gifts are means to spiritual ends,
but they have their practical outcome as well, "As ye abound in every
thing, in faith, in utterance, and knowledge . . . see that ye abound in this
grace also", 2 Cor. 8. 7, where the apostle is referring to the grace of
ministering financial gifts. Spiritually, Paul owns that all enrichment is "by
Him"; the source is divine, and it is "given to every man to profit withal",
1 Cor. 12. 7. The realisation that the source is divine adds dignity and
responsibility to the service of those possessing the gifts.

6. The testimony of Christ (or the testimony of God, 2. 1) was the
spiritual material that Paul preached when he had been in Corinth first of
all. It is one thing for such a testimony to be *believed* unto salvation, 2
Thess. 1. 10, but it is another for the testimony to be *confirmed*. Here, the
confirmation to testimony means that God added to faith the ability to
serve—an outward spiritual manifestation by means of gifts. In the
assembly, faith thus gave rise to works of divine origin, faith dressed in
outward form. The particular gifts that God gives at any time, to confirm
the testimony, depend upon present need. For example, immediately after
the ascension of the Lord, we read "the Lord working with them, and
confirming the word with signs following", Mark 16. 20, these signs being
listed in verses 17 and 18. Such miraculous outward displays
of power suited the introductory period of the church; it is not clear
whether all those gifts were even operative at Corinth. Certainly today,
owing to differing circumstances, such outward displays of power are more

limited, and gifts reach rather to the heart than to the body.

7. "So that ye come behind in no gift" implies that the Corinthians possessed all that God would give them for adequate service. Gifts—the ability to serve—had been given at Pentecost. They had been distributed among men as one and another had come to believe on the Lord Jesus for salvation. Having been given, they had to be recognised by the possessors and then to be developed. Such gifts should not lie dormant (compare the hidden talent and the pound, Matt. 25. 25; Luke 19. 20), but they should be stirred up by development and exercise, 2 Tim. 1. 6.

It is important to note that Paul regarded the assembly at Corinth as complete. In a gathering of reasonable size, the multiplicity of gifts should make the assembly self-supporting. There should be no need for constant looking *without* with no looking *within*. An assembly that feels it is lacking in gift really disbelieves God who makes a local gathering a complete functioning unit. A small assembly may well have to seek gift from elsewhere. The saints at Joppa had to send to Lydda for help on one occasion, Acts 9. 38, and Barnabas introduced Paul to the church in Antioch , Acts 11. 26.

Because He is the Giver of every perfect gift, saints must hold their gifts in the light of a day yet to come. The A.V. reads "waiting for the coming of our Lord Jesus Christ". Such a rendering suggests the *rapture*, His coming *for* His saints, 1 Thess. 4. 17. But the correct translation should be "waiting for the revelation of our Lord Jesus Christ", R.V. This refers to His manifestation in glory, to the time when He comes forth *with* His saints, 2 Thess. 1. 7-10. The *rapture* relates to His counsels in grace for His own, the beginning of the great processes by which He will draw things to a close in this scene. His *revelation* relates to responsibility. When He comes in glory He will take control of this scene, but believers will be manifested with Him in that day as overcomers in assembly matters. After the *rapture*, there will take place the judgment seat of Christ (see our comments on 3. 13; 4. 5). Saints will then receive the great variety of rewards that He has for those who display faithful conduct and service. The display of these rewards will occur at His revelation, when the saints, blessed after the judgment seat of Christ, will be united to Him in glory and in rule over the earth. Hence, one's heart waits for Himself at the *rapture*, but as far as gifts are concerned, it is His return in glory one waits for, since our rewards and our close association with Him then will enhance His own glory.

8. By the grace of God eternal security is never in question . The failure in Corinth could never nullify the truth of this verse, that the saints would be confirmed unto the end of the period of their responsible testimony here, and that they would be "blameless in the day of the Lord Jesus Christ". The day of the Lord Jesus Christ relates to the period commencing at the rapture and embracing the advent of the Lord to earth. The judgment seat of Christ takes place in this period, as well as the distribution of reward. The word "blameless" means that sins will not and cannot be called into question judicially. Rather motives, conduct and service will be examined as when a race is run, with blessings being freely distributed. The "day" associated with the name of the Lord Jesus always refers to this period and to the saints, slight variations of meaning being discerned in the various titles ascribed to the Lord:

day of Christ, Phil. 1. 10; 2. 16;
day of the Lord Jesus, 1 Cor. 5. 5; 2 Cor. 1. 14;
day of Jesus Christ, Phil. 1. 6;
day of our Lord Jesus Christ, 1 Cor. 1. 8.

The oft-repeated phrase "day of the Lord", or the "day of Jehovah", first mentioned in Isaiah 2. 12, refers to times of judgment, having nothing to do with saints of the Church period. It has to do with the earth, beginning immediately after the rapture, continuing through the millennium and terminating shortly afterwards, 2 Pet. 3. 8–10.

To be blameless in that day should thrill every believer who senses his own weakness. We shall be presented "faultless before the presence of His glory with exceeding joy", Jude 24, being able to return with Him without shame or blushing, reigning with Him over a scene which had previously witnessed our own failures. See Colossians 1. 22. "When Christ, who is our life, shall appear, then shall ye also appear with Him in glory", Col. 3. 4.

9. All this rests upon the faithfulness of God; "He is faithful that promised", Heb. 10. 23. In spite of the divisions in Corinth, the party spirit, the service manifesting wood, hay and stubble, the open fornication, the apparent idolatry, the disputing about sisters' head coverings, the mockery of the Lord's supper, the theatrical use made of spiritual gifts and the false doctrines held regarding the resurrection, in spite of all this, God remains faithful.

They had all been called unto "the fellowship of His Son", to a living spiritual partnership with Him. This did not refer to the local assembly in Corinth. The fellowship was all embracing, a common basis for all saints to be linked together because they are thus linked to Him. This is no organisation; it represents a living organism controlled by the living Head of the fellowship.

As we come to the end of this introduction, we note that where sin abounded, grace has superabounded. One would think that no failure existed in Corinth at all. But Paul now turns his attention to the practical details of failure, responsibility and correction, necessary for every local assembly.

1 CORINTHIANS 1. 10–31

Section 2.   Divisions amongst the Saints
Subject 1.   Principles of Service

Relationships of this Section

The first subject that Paul deals with in this Epistle illustrates important principles for effective Bible study. We should never plunge into the first verse of a paragraph or chapter without knowing just why that paragraph or chapter is there. False exposition or fictitious interpretation may easily be the result if one is ignorant of the direction of one's study. We should notice the position of any chapter occurring in any connected argument. There is little point in examining verses independently, out of context and out of the order in which the Spirit originally chose to inspire them. A haphazard study of verses, either privately or in a public Bible reading, can provide little profit for the soul. So we have divided the Epistle into "sections", the second of which, from 1. 10 to 4. 20, consists of a lengthy connected argument.

These first four chapters deal with a certain type of division amongst the saints at Corinth. Paul therefore shows that true servants and true service are all of God. There is no room for boasting either in oneself or in others. A party-spirit based on the achievements of individual workers is thereby excluded.

The four chapters may be summarised as follows:
Chapter 1. 10–31: After preliminary statements, Paul gives many general principles of service. The wisdom of God is pre-eminent in preaching Christ crucified; the wisdom of man is destroyed. This *doctrine* is placed *before* its later *application* in chapter 4. (Similarly, *doctrine* associated with spiritual gifts in chapter 12 comes *before* its *application* in chapter 14.)
Chapter 2: These principles are now applied to Paul's service. Paul shows that the *power* is from God, that *revelation* is from God and that *Spirit-given understanding* is from God.
Chapter 3: Paul discusses his specific work in Corinth under various figures. The husbandry and the building are all of God.
Chapter 4. 1–20: In the conclusion of this section the proper relationship that should exist between Paul and his converts is shown, thereby avoiding a party spirit.

Exposition of 1 Cor. 1. 10–31: Principles of Service

This subject opens by brief remarks on Corinth and Paul's service among them. But from verse 18, Paul and Corinth are put on one side, so that the

Spirit can develop wholesome teaching concerning the preaching and reception of the Gospel. A summary is as follows:

Verses 10–13: the error at Corinth;
Verses 14–17: Paul minimises himself—the argument of
                     baptism;
Verse 18:   the preaching of the cross;
Verses 19–21: the wisdom of the world is useless to affect a
                     soul;
Verses 22–25: what the Jews and Gentiles want naturally;
Verses 26–29: those whom God calls to spiritual service;
Verses 30–31: the work of God accomplished in a soul;

Verses 10–17: Corinth and Paul

10 Now I beseech you, brethren, by the name of our Lord Jesus Christ, that ye all speak the same thing, and *that* there be no divisions among you; but *that* ye be perfectly joined together in the same mind and in the same judgment.

11 For it hath been declared unto me of you, my brethren, by them *which are of the house* of Chloe, that there are contentions among you.

12 Now this I say, that every one of you saith, I am of Paul; and I of Apollos; and I of Cephas; and I of Christ.

13 Is Christ divided? Was Paul crucified for you or were ye baptized in the name of Paul?

14 I thank God that I baptized none of you, but Crispus and Gaius;

15 Let any should say that I had baptized in mine own name.

16 And I baptized also the household of Stephanas: besides, I know not whether I baptized any other.

17 For Christ sent me not to baptize, but to preach the gospel; not with wisdom of words, lest the cross of Christ should be made of none effect.

10. Paul opens his first corrective section by beseeching the brethren that they "all speak the same thing". The full title of the Lord is brought to bear upon the subject. Paul hides himself behind the person of the Lord. The responsibility of the Corinthians is towards the Lord and not towards Paul. To speak the same thing means that all must be subject to the same teaching Spirit. Only the ideas of men can bring in differences of opinion. God has forged an absolute unity in Christ, Eph. 4. 4–6, but the practical demonstration of this unity has been marred since the days of the Corinthians onwards. The saints do not create or form the unity, they endeavour only "to keep the unity of the Spirit in the bond of peace", Eph. 4. 3. There can be no unity with what is not of God, in spite of the popular religious and political clamour of the present day.

Paul often called attention to this great principle of unity in thought and utterance:

Romans 15. 5 "The God of patience and consolation grant you to be *likeminded* one toward another according to Christ Jesus". This is followed by being one in worship, v. 6, and one in the fellowship of reception, v. 7.

Philippians 2. 2: "Fulfil ye my joy, that ye be *likeminded*, having the same love, being of *one accord*, of *one mind*". This is followed by the exhortation to let the mind of Christ in sacrificial service abide in the saints.

Philippians 3. 16: "Let us walk by the same rule, let us *mind the same thing*". Paul refers to his mind in service, seeking the prize of the high calling of God in Christ Jesus, v. 14, and not the earthly things sought by the enemies of the cross of Christ, vv. 18–19.

Paul would have the Corinthians to "be perfectly joined together". There are various aspects of unity. In Ephesians 4. 16, "the whole body fitly joined together", Paul deals with growth in Christ under the outworking of gifts that He gave unto men. Here, Paul is concerned with "the same mind" and "the same judgment".

Mind refers to a faculty of heart, to a spiritual state whereby doctrine is appreciated. The depth of implication behind such a word may be seen in 2. 16, "But we have the mind of Christ".

Judgment refers to the faculty whereby one recognises the appropriate application of truth to practical matters. For example, "I give my judgment", 7. 25.

There can obviously be no unity in this sense if brethren are full of biassed private interpretations and have different applications of Scripture to assembly service and problems.

11. Paul's knowledge of the error of division at Corinth rested upon the certainty of reports he received from a sister's house, namely the house of Chloe. This may have been a house in Corinth, from whence the reports were brought to Paul. On the other hand, it may have been a house in the district where Paul was writing the Epistle, whose inhabitants had contact with Corinth. The thing stressed is that this was no gossip in a sister's house, no foolish talking, Eph. 5. 4, no hearsay. Rather it was with grief that the information was brought to the attention of Paul. This was the opposite to those whom Paul describes as "wandering about from house to house; and not only idle, but tattlers also and busybodies, speaking things which they ought not", 1 Tim. 5. 13. Gossip against the Lord's people and the local assembly shows the barren state of heart of those who engage in it.

Contentions or strifes were reported to Paul. This word is translated "debates" in 2 Corinthians 12. 20 and "variance" in Galatians 5. 20 referring to the works of the flesh. Even immediately after the institution of the Lord's supper, there was a strife amongst the disciples which of them "should be accounted the greatest", Luke 22. 24. This weakness can characterise even the most holy occasions. We may but contrast the blessed Lord, of whom we read, "He shall not strive", Matt. 12. 19. Such a sin leads to the divisions (schisms) in the previous verse, and to heresies (sects) in 11. 9. Strife is a sin within, tending to spoil the holy harmony of the people of God.

12. These contentions and divisions led to the manifestation of party-spirit. The adherents to hero-personalities, to the various preferred teachers who had laboured among them or of whom they had heard, were to be found everywhere in Corinth. Then the assembly could not meet under one roof, as would be the case today when a hall is owned. The various suitable homes of the believers were used, and this grouping tended to foster adherence to preferred teachers, namely Paul, Apollos, Cephas and even Christ. Nothing was wrong with those named ! The error lay in the spirit adopted by the Corinthians. Again there is nothing wrong with recognising special ability in some teachers of the Word, but this must not develop into sectarianism.

Those who said "I of Christ" appeared to quote "One is your Master, even Christ; and all ye are brethren", Matt. 23. 8, thereby forsaking altogether the Lord's sent servants. The question in this context is, do teachers make a claim to fame? No servant should be elevated either by himself or by others, but they should be recognised by those who are taught. In any case, the position "I of Christ" appears to be rather amiss. "In Christ" is more appropriate, 1. 30, for God places us there. Such a position is of grace alone.

Regarding the order of these names, Paul had been in Corinth the longest, Apollos next, Peter would only be known by name as labouring in Jerusalem, while Christ had not been there at all in the days of His flesh.

We should notice an important contrast. Here, the *disciples* sin, by falsely following certain teachers. In Acts 20. 30, the *elders* at Ephesus may sin by drawing away disciples after them. In each case, the results are approximately the same.

13. To touch the conscience of the Corinthians, Paul asks questions without providing immediate answers. See, similarly, 9. 4–13; 12. 29–30. "Is Christ divided?" is a question, although the R.V. margin suggests it is a statement "Christ is divided". The proper translation would be "Is *the* Christ divided?". The definite article is placed before "Christ" in the Greek text. The same idea appears in 12. 12, "so also is *the* Christ". Paul refers not only to the exalted Lord on high, but also to His universal body, to His members, representing the extension of His name throughout the whole Gospel dispensation. This universal body is not divided. The unity is absolute, a spiritual creation of God.

The answer Paul wants to the question is "no". Conscience would immediately contrast this aspect of unity with the one displayed locally in Corinth, where the local manifestation of the body was divided. But if the saints walk in truth and light, then since His body is not divided, neither should a local assembly be divided. In any case, only One was crucified efficaciously to bring about such unity, John 11. 52; 10. 16. Moreover, it would be illegitimate to adhere to Paul, since they were not baptized into his name. The apostle was but human and subsidiary.

In these days of popular religious clamour for unity, believers loving the Lord and His Word should abide by the beautiful words of Mrs. Peters in the hymn :*

> O Lord, what hast Thou wrought!
>> How full of power Thy name !
> Subdue in us each differing thought,
>> And light up love's pure flame.
>
> One judgment and one mind
>> We seek in all our ways,
> One heart to God's own truth inclined,
>> One mouth to speak His praise.

14. This verse forms the beginning of Paul's argument to deliver the Corinthians from themselves. Paul knew before the Lord that he was right and the Corinthians wrong, but he did not brandish this before them. Rather he minimized himself, in order that only the work of God in him should be recognised. It requires grace and humility for a servant of God to take such a position, since some may take unfair advantage of it. But in exhortation or in rebuke, Paul still loved his children in Christ, even though their love might be adversely affected: "the more abundantly I love you, the less I be loved", 2 Cor. 12. 15.

The whole of these first four chapters is occupied with Paul taking a lowly position:

Chapter 1. 14–17: Paul did no baptising.

Chapter 1. 17–31: Paul would demonstrate no wisdom in order that the preaching of the cross should alone be of value.

Chapter 2: The truth is ultimately known by revelation, not by Paul.

Chapter 3: "Let no man glory in men", v. 21, since true service is subsidiary to God's work; the gardening, vv. 6–9, and the building, vv. 9–17, are God's.

Chapter 4. 1 6: God is Judge of the standard of service, not men; hence one should be humble as before Him.

Chapter 4. 7–13: In his lowly stand for the truth, Paul is as the offscouring of all things. Yet he is their spiritual father, and as such will come to correct.

In Corinth, baptism was associated with faith, Acts 18. 8. Paul had at least baptised Crispus, the chief ruler of the synagogue, v. 8, and apparently one of the first converts. Later, Sosthenes, the next chief ruler of the synagogue, was converted and baptised (see Acts 18. 17 and 1 Cor. 1. 1 if these refer to the same person). Gaius, the other one whom Paul names, was host to Paul in Corinth when he wrote to the Romans, Rom. 16. 23.

It is obvious that Silas and Timothy did the baptising in Corinth, Acts 18. 5. There was thus joint fellowship in following the requests of the Lord

---

* Hymns of Light and Love, 295.

Jesus, Matt. 28. 19. Paul did the teaching, while others did the baptising.

15. Even when Paul was at Corinth on his second missionary journey, he anticipated danger by foreseeing the future developments of the local assembly. He could sense that some might say that he had baptised in his own name. He thanked God, therefore, that he had restrained himself from the act of baptising. Paul did not rush into every kind of service without weighing the consequences. Paul might have done everything, leaving nothing for the others. No doubt, he was the "chief speaker", Acts 14. 12, but others took their place beside him in the service of the Gospel.

16. Paul recalls one other name, Stephanas, and adds "besides, I know not whether I baptised any other". Some would use this to argue against the doctrine of inspiration. But the writers were not infallible in their memory; inspiration does not depend on memory. Rather inspiration refers to the Spirit of God using what He wills in the experience of a writer. The historical matter here is not a question of doctrine, to which John 14. 26 applies, "He shall teach you all things, and bring all things to your remembrance".

The baptising of the household of Stephanas has led to strange doctrines. Households contain infants, some would argue, so infant baptism is deduced from this verse. This doctrine, however, is contrary to the order "many of the Corinthians hearing believed, and were baptised", Acts 18. 8. It is certainly refuted by Romans 6. 1–11, where a definite stand is taken before the Lord in baptism, something an infant could never do. If some still are not convinced, a consideration of the composition of the households referred to will refute the doctrine.

> Acts 16. 33: Referring to the Philippian keeper of the prison, "he and all his" were baptised. But the next verse goes on to say that both he and "all his house" rejoiced and believed in God. Only adults are therefore included.
>
> 1 Corinthians 1. 16: The household of Stephanas was baptised, but we read of them that they "addicted themselves to the ministry of the saints", 16. 15. Only adults could engage in such service.
>
> Acts 16. 15: Referring to Lydia, we read, "when she was baptised, and her household". No further information is provided about this household, so some postulate that Lydia had a baby in her household. It is this one pathetic assumption that provides the basis on which the false doctrine and practice of infant baptism are founded.

Further verses alleged to refer to infant baptism are 7. 14 and 10. 1–2. Once a mind rests upon this doctrine, all sorts of strange verses out of context may be used to try and prove it. Happy is the soul who knows the truth of baptism of those who believe in Jesus. All these strange verses then fit properly into their context. We return to this subject in chapters 7 and 10.

17. Paul's argument rests upon the fact that he preached the Gospel, not that he baptised. The character of this preaching is described in the words, "not with wisdom of words, lest the cross of Christ should be made of none effect". Today, men would judge that this is a strange kind of preaching. The motive behind it was that all glorying should be in God and not in man. Moreover, it was the Lord who had sent him thus to preach. Paul had received the commission from the living Head, Acts 26. 16–19; see also Matthew 10. 5. All true service originates from the divine Originator, and recognition is due to Him. Often times much is made of a popular preacher's results, even though he may desire to remain quietly unknown, 2 Cor. 6. 9.

Paul feared the "wisdom of words". That is, he had no desire for eloquence and natural ability, since this might well displace the power of the cross of Christ through the preaching. This shows up the distinction between natural theology and spiritual power. It appears that natural ability in preaching was another of the fears of the apostle. Certainly Paul was not an able orator, as was Tertullus before Felix, Acts 24. 1–8. He had no "excellency of speech" or "enticing words of (man's) wisdom", 1 Cor. 2. 1, 4. Notice the verse: "For his letters, say they, are weighty and powerful; but his bodily presence is weak, and his speech contemptible", 2 Cor. 10. 10. Paul delighted that this should be so; yet the Lord could use him. On the other hand, not all evangelists are like Paul in that respect. Some may well possess natural ability sanctified by the Spirit's power. We deal with this in chapter 12. In Gospel service, however, natural ability must not displace the Spirit's power.

Verses 18–31: The Preaching of the Cross and its Effects

18 For the preaching of the cross is to them that perish foolishness; but unto us which are saved it is the power of God.

19 For it is written, I will destroy the wisdom of the wise, and will bring to nothing the understanding of the prudent.

20 Where is the wise? where is the scribe? where is the disputer of this world? hath not God made foolish the wisdom of this world?

21 For after that in the wisdom of God the world by wisdom knew not God, it pleased God by the foolishness of preaching to save them that believe.

22 For the Jews require a sign and the Greeks seek after wisdom:

23 But we preach Christ crucified, unto the Jews a stumblingblock, and unto the Greeks foolishness;

24 But unto them which are called, both Jews and Greeks, Christ the power of God, and the wisdom of God. ·

25 Because the foolishness of God is wiser than men; and the weakness of God is stronger than men.

26 For ye see your calling, brethren, how that not many wise men after the flesh, not many mighty, not many noble *are called*:

27 But God hath chosen the foolish things of the world to confound the wise; and God hath chosen the weak things of the world to confound the things which are mighty;

28 And base things of the world, and things which are despised, hath God chosen, *yea*, and things which are not, to bring to nought things that are:

29 That no flesh should glory in his presence.

30 But of him are ye in Christ Jesus, who of God is made unto us wisdom,
   and righteousness, and sanctification, and redemption;
31 That, according as it is written, He that glorieth, let him glory in the Lord.

18. All reference to Paul, his service and the Corinthians now ceases.
A basis of wholesome doctrine is now necessary if later correction is to be
effective. Paul outlines two distinct effects of the preaching of the cross:
     to them that perish – foolishness;
     to those who are saved – it is the power of God.
These verbs are continuous. Paul writes of those who were actively
walking on the broad road that leads to destruction, and of those who
were walking the narrow way to life, Matt. 7. 13–14.
   We should notice the characteristic difference between the blood, the
death and the cross of the Lord:
   His blood: this is associated with the truth of cleansing from sin, 1
     John 1.7.
   His death: this is associated with the truth of separation from sin,
     Rom. 6. 1–12; Gal. 1. 4.
   His cross: this is associated with the stigma attached to a believer
     because he trusts in Christ, Gal. 6. 12–14.
To unbelievers today, the cross means but one thing. It is merely a
theological term, rooted in history and tradition, and concerns only a few
religious folk. In Paul's day, unbelievers would think quite differently.
Then, it was a common method of putting men to death. Shame, stigma
and a criminal's name was attached to it. Unbelievers, who were perishing,
would think it foolish to value the death of a man, whom they would know
as Jesus. They would not treat it as men would today, namely as a curious
piece of theology.
   To believers, however, the *preaching of the cross* is the power of God. In
verse 24, *Christ* is named as the power of God. In chapter 2 verse 5, the
faith of believers does not stand even in the ability of a preacher to explain
the cross. The power of the cross is something outside its mode of
explanation. Lack of appreciation of this may explain the weakness of
some preaching today. It is not the word but the power that must be
manifested, 4. 20. Elsewhere, Paul declared that the *Gospel* was the power
of God unto salvation, Rom. 1. 16. The work is a miraculous work, outside
the ability of man. The cross is so vital, because therein God is glorified,
Satan is defeated, and man is put in his right position.

19. As we explained earlier, verses 19–31 divide into four paragraphs:
Verses 19–21: the wisdom of the world is useless to affect a soul.
Verses 22–25: what the Jews and Gentiles want naturally.
Verses 26–29: those whom God calls to spiritual service.
Verses 30–31: the work of God accomplished in a soul.
   Compared with spiritual truth, the wisdom and knowledge of the
unsanctified mind is ripe for destruction. Paul quotes in this verse Isaiah
29. 14 to prove his point. The context of this verse is remarkable. In verse

10, the Lord had poured out the spirit of deep sleep so that the prophets, rulers and seers could not understand. In verse 11, the vision of God had been made a book that was sealed, so unlike the work of the Spirit of God in a believer who unfolds to the heart the truth of God's book. Such a promise is made in verse 18, "And in that day shall the deaf hear the words of the book, and the eyes of the blind shall see out of obscurity, and out of darkness". Again, referring to the context, verse 13 is quoted in Matthew 15. 8–9, showing the uselessness of the unsanctified mouth to seek to honour Him.

Finally, verse 14 follows; God would do a "marvellous work" in that He would blind the understanding of unbelievers. How often this principle emerges in Scripture; it is something that Gospel preachers must sense today in the hearts of those to whom they preach. For example, in the chapter dealing with the parables of the kingdom of the heavens, the Lord explained, ". . . but whosoever hath not, from him shall be taken away even that he hath", Matt. 13. 11–12. God cannot be trifled with, nor can He be mocked by unbelievers; what a man sows in this connection, that shall he also reap. Many things have been hidden from the wise and the prudent, but revealed to babes, Matt. 11. 25. See also, Isaiah 6. 10; Matthew 13. 14–15; John 12. 40; Acts 28. 25–27. These verses reflect upon the common activity of God, the Son and the Holy Spirit.

20. Paul asks, "Where is the wise? where is the scribe? where is the disputer of this world?". The question he asks is: since they have no understanding, what status have they before God? Paul refers to the wisdom of the Greeks, to the scribes amongst the Jews and to men generally who can engage in a logical argument (see Luke 24. 15; Acts 28. 29 for words possessing the same root as in "disputer"). "Where is the scribe?" is quoted from Isaiah 33. 18. The prophet describes the king in his beauty, the land very far off, Zion the city of solemnities, Jerusalem a quiet habitation, and the glorious Lord. But these precious things are "very far off" to the scribe; he is outside of it all. Paul implies that the wise, the scribe and the disputer are very far off from the blessings of the cross. The word of the cross is foolishness to them, so God has rendered foolish their own understanding also. This was Paul's position, *as a man*. He had been numbered with such a company once. Only God could transform a soul by taking him out of such unholy conditions and setting him apart for service.

21. The wisdom of God had brought about this distinction of which the apostle speaks. His wisdom implies His divine knowledge applied critically and practically. By it He put everything on earth in its proper place and in its proper perspective.

There are two classes in this verse:
1. "The world by wisdom knew not God." God has decreed that man's knowledge cannot lead him to God. Zophar had said, "Canst thou by searching find out God? Canst thou find out the

Almighty unto perfection?", Job 11 . 7. Only in the Scriptures can one find out the Lord. We may seek Him while He may be found, but materialism and earthly wisdom lead away from God down the broad way.

2. "It pleased God by the foolishness of preaching to save them that believe". The "foolishness of preaching" would be man's estimation of that holy activity, but this saves! In Corinth, they had heard and then believed. God's order is: sending forth, preaching, hearing, believing, calling upon His name, Rom. 10. 14. It is God's good pleasure to use this method, His sure way to salvation. Any other methods that men may introduce today must be judged in the light of the pleasure that they bring to Him.

Paul, as a man, would be in the first class unless called by God into the second. Well might he be lowly in his service, knowing these great principles that govern the preaching of the Gospel!

22. In verses 22–25, Paul discusses what men desire in contrast to the provision that God makes through preaching. In those days, men would not have God's method.

The Jews sought a sign in order to touch their materialistic intellect. In the Lord's day, they had sought a sign, but none was granted save the sign of the temple destroyed and raised again, John 2. 18–21, and the sign of the prophet Jonah, Matt. 12. 39–40; 16. 1. The Jews had sought a miraculous sign from heaven, but the Lord told them parables of His death and resurrection instead.

The Gentiles sought wisdom. Paul had to contend with the philosophers of the Epicureans and of the Stoicks, Acts 17. 18. They thought that Paul preached two new gods, namely Jesus and the resurrection. Paul took them up on their own ground, but the mention of the resurrection brought mockery from their own hearts.

23–24. The preaching of Christ crucified replaces all the desires of men. In these two verses we find the differing effects on the three classes of men listed in 10. 32, namely the Jews, the Gentiles and the church of God.

To the Jews, this is a stumbling-block. This idea is common in Scripture. They walk in the dark and fall whenever they contact the person of Christ. In Isaiah 8. 14, the Lord is "a stone of stumbling and . . . a rock of offence . . . And many among them shall stumble, and fall, and be broken, and be snared, and be taken". Later, Isaiah writes for believers, "Behold, I lay in Zion for a foundation a stone, a tried stone, a precious stone, a sure foundation: he that believeth shall not make haste", Isa. 28. 16. Paul quotes both these verses in Romans 9. 33, where he is contrasting faith with unbelief. Neither of the two verses contains the thought he really requires, so motivated by the Spirit of God, the apostle mingles the two verses

so as to fit the sense he desires in Romans 9. Needless to say, such a
mixing of verses is not permitted today in exact exposition. We read,
"For they stumbled at that stumbling-stone; as it is written, Behold,
I lay in Sion a stumbling-stone and rock of offence: and whosoever
believeth on Him shall not be ashamed". These two verses in Isaiah
are also quoted in 1 Peter 2. 6–8.

To the Greeks, such preaching was foolishness. This was their approach
to God's greatest work. Today, apart from what modern theology
may say, the world would approach the cross with indifference,
believing it to be irrelevant to modern life.

To the church of God—believing Jews and Gentiles alike—Christ is the
power of God, and the wisdom of God, v. 24. Jew and Gentile are
united according to the truth of Ephesians 2. 11–22. He has
reconciled "both unto God in one body by the cross, having slain
the enmity thereby", v. 16. The middle wall of partition has been
broken down, and both have access by one Spirit unto the Father.
The power of God in Christ contrasts with the signs desired by the
Jews, while Christ as the wisdom of God contrasts with the wisdom
of the Greeks. God will make sure that His spiritual principles differ
completely from men's.

25. By this we understand that the foolishness of God (as judged by
man) has substituted something of power (namely, Christ raised) in place
of man's wisdom. Similarly, the weakness of God (as judged by man) has
raised the stone that the builders disallowed, Ps. 118. 22. See Matthew 21.
42–44. Through apparent temporary defeat at the hands of men, God has
wrought an infinite victory in Christ, and one day this victory will be
manifested openly.

26–29. Paul now lists those whom God calls to Himself. He argues that
the world, the flesh, natural ability, and status are hindrances to the
formation of faith. Hence, salvation seems to pass by certain men,
although the Gospel is directed to "whosoever will".

Paul first gives three categories of people, not many of whom are called:

Wise men after the flesh: These are those who have any pretensions
that God may be found by argument and natural reasoning. This is
further developed at the end of chapter 2. The peak of such wisdom
was found in Athens, Acts 17. 16–34. Their efforts merely brought
in idolatry and an altar to the unknown god.

Mighty: This refers to men with strength, see Rev. 6. 15. In a holy and
spiritual sense, the word is used of the Lord, Luke 24. 19, and of
Paul, 2 Cor. 12. 10.

Noble: The word means "high-born—well-born—of good birth".
These are the best of those born of blood, or of the will of the flesh,
or of the will of man, John 1. 13. These would be "clothed in soft
raiment . . . in kings' houses", Matt. 11. 8, but John the Baptist was

not one of these. Mary had sung, "He hath put down the mighty from their seats, and exalted them of low degree. He hath filled the hungry with good things; and the rich He hath sent empty away", Luke 1. 52–53. See also Luke 16. 19. Conversely, the Bereans were "more noble" since they searched the Scriptures, Acts 17. 11. These were of good birth because they had experienced the second birth and were showing signs of spiritual life immediately after their conversion.

Five cases are now given, of those who are chosen. They are named according to the impression gained by the world, but the effects worked out by God are exactly the opposite to what the world would expect.

Foolish things: those who make no claims that natural wisdom can seek out God. The apostles were "unlearned and ignorant men", Acts 4. 13, but they had been with Jesus. Paul was foolish, even to the Corinthians, 2 Cor. 11. 16–19. The parable in Matthew 25. 1–13 may be consulted for the use of these words in the opposite senses.

Weak things: these contrast to the mighty in verse 26. This word is used of the "impotent" man in Acts 4. 9. His testimony in verse 14 as he stood with the apostles foiled the arguments of the priests. Paul used this word of himself, 2 Cor. 10. 10.

Base things: these contrast to the high-born, since the word means low-born. For example, "He raiseth up the poor out of the dust, and lifteth up the beggar from the dunghill, to set them among princes, and to make them inherit the throne of glory", 1 Sam. 2. 8. In effect, these are those who are born "of God", John 1. 13.

Things despised: that is, things made light of. The publican in the parable was such a man, Luke 18. 9; he was despised by the self-righteous Pharisee. Christ as the Stone had been set at naught (despised) by the builders, and yet had been exalted on high. Moreover, Paul's speech was contemptible (despised), 2 Cor. 10. 10.

Things which are not: implies those who have no status in this world at all. By their testimony, God will eventually bring to naught (disannul) the things that are, namely those who have status in this world.

29. The object of all this is that "no flesh should glory in His presence". In the great matter of justification by faith, self-glorying is excluded. Paul asks the question, "Where is boasting then?", and provides the answer, "It is excluded", Rom. 3. 27. Paul would only boast in the cross of the Lord Jesus Christ, Gal. 6. 14. All glory and boasting is in Christ. This leaves no room to elevate either oneself, or one's own works, or somebody else on a pedestal of glory. God resists the proud but gives grace to the humble whom He will exalt in due time, 1 Pet. 5. 5–6.

30–31. Hence the position of the believer is not one of being in the flesh. Rather we are in Christ, and all that Christ is becomes real to us in our blessings and spiritual status.

> *The mind of Christ in wisdom* is ours, so different from the wisdom of the world.
>
> *The righteousness of Christ* is ours, so different from the righteousness of works which would give rise to self-glory, Rom. 4. 2.
>
> *The sanctification of Christ* is ours. He set Himself apart to accomplish God's will in order that we might be sanctified by the truth, John 17. 19.
>
> *Redemption in Christ* is ours, so different from any ceremonial redemption with corruptible things, 1 Pet. 1. 18. Rather, we are redeemed with the precious blood of Christ.

Paul concludes by quoting Jeremiah 9. 23–24. We have nothing of ourselves, so "let him that glorieth glory in this, that he understandeth and knoweth Me, that I am the Lord which exercise loving-kindness, judgment, and righteousness, in the earth: for in these things I delight, saith the Lord".

1 CORINTHIANS 2

Section 2.   Divisions amongst the Saints
Subject 2.   Discourse on Preaching

Relationships of this Section

Chapter two continues the great theme commenced in chapter one. There, we have seen that the wisdom of the world and the natural desires of Jew and Gentile are quite incapable of bringing a soul into contact with God. The choice of true servants and the direction of true service are all of God, leaving no room for believers to take sides with servants of their own choosing. The chapter concluded with the exhortation to glory only in the Lord; see also 1 Cor. 3. 21; 2 Cor. 10. 17.

Throughout these first four chapters, Paul seeks to develop the proper relationship that should exist between believers and able servants of the Lord. "And they glorified God in me", Gal. 1. 24, would appear to be the proper conclusion, namely a recognition of divinely given ability, yet all praise and glory being ascribed to God who gives and directs such service.

In chapter 1 verse 18, Paul suddenly stopped writing about his own service, in order to deal with general principles. In these next three chapters, the service of Paul comes more into focus. Yet the apostle is not merely speaking of himself. He is applying principles to himself and to Apollos for the sake of the Corinthians, 4. 6, in order that they should the better understand. The same remarks apply to all servants who had ever laboured in Corinth.

The four chapters may roughly be summarised as follows:
    Chapter 1: methods of service;
    Chapter 2: character of service;
    Chapter 3: types of service;
    Chapter 4: application of service.

In chapter two, Paul deals with the subject of preaching—the service that he had mostly accomplished in Corinth. This chapter should form the spritual handbook of all believers who seek to speak in the Lord's name today. It is divided into three paragraphs:
    Verses 1–5: The delivery of the message—the servant's side in weakness.
    Verses 6–10: The contents of the message—God's side in revelation.
    Verses 11–16: The reception of the message—man's side in spiritual or natural understanding.

Exposition of 1 Cor. 2: Discourse on Preaching

Verses 1–5: The Delivery of the Message

1 And I, brethren, when I came to you, came not with excellency of speech or of wisdom, declaring unto you the testimony of God.

2 For I determined not to know any thing among you, save Jesus Christ, and him crucified.

3 And I was with you in weakness and in fear, and in much trembling.

4 And my speech and my preaching *was* not with enticing words of man's wisdom, but in demonstration of the Spirit and of power.

5 That your faith should not stand in the wisdom of men, but in the power of God.

1. Paul recalls his original stay in Corinth. In chapter one he had recalled the question of baptism during his stay; here, he dwells on the fact that he exhibited no "excellency of speech or of wisdom". There can be nothing worse than listening to a speaker indeed exhibiting no excellency of speech, but at the same time demonstrating no spiritual power either. The demonstration of spiritual power fills every gap apparently caused by the absence of excellency of speech. But this gives no licence for carelessness in speech or in prior preparation of a message. A message prepared and delivered in spiritual detail is more valuable for edification than a message roughly prepared and then delivered with a multiplicity of words to fill in time. The motive of preaching should be the manifestation of spiritual power under the good hand of God; any ability in speech or in preparation is but ancillary when sanctified in service. The record of Paul's preaching shows capability with power, as many quoations bear out:

1. In Corinth, he "reasoned" in the synagogue. He "persuaded the Jews and the Greeks", and he "testified" that Jesus was Christ, Acts 18. 4–5.

2. On another occasion, Paul was the "chief speaker", Acts 14. 12.

3. Acts 13. 16–43 shows that he was an orderly, able speaker in the synagogue at Antioch. The fact that the rulers asked him to speak, v. 15, shows that they recognised him as a teacher. This selection of able speakers by the rulers was characteristic of the synagogue service.

4. Yet ability was mingled with inability. His speech was contemptible, 2 Cor. 10. 10; he had a "thorn in the flesh", 2 Cor. 12. 7; he preached in much infirmity of the flesh, Gal. 4. 13. By this means, he had a right perspective, maintaining a balance between natural ability and its abuse in spiritual things.

It suffices to say that all of Paul's speeches and all his letters show order in their development. Are we able to follow Paul in this, yet realising at the same time the insufficiency of the flesh?

2. Paul determined to know nothing save Jesus Christ and Him crucified. It is good to have such a resolution both prior to service and also when engaged in it. This would remove a lot of effort which does not have

the glory of Christ in view. Paul resolved to have nothing to do with the prevalent idolatrous sins around him. Jesus Christ and Him crucified were alone before his gaze, forming the substance of his preaching. He was like Anna before him, who "spake of Him", Luke 2. 38, while others were looking for national redemption from the Roman yoke. Similarly he was like Philip before him, who "preached unto him Jesus", Acts 8. 35, instead of engaging in a discussion concerning the barrenness of worship in Jerusalem.

Paul did not restrict himself to "Jesus Christ crucified", namely to the Man and the cross. Rather, the phrase "and Him crucified" would suggest the stigma of association with One crucified yet risen again.

3. Paul recalls that he had been in Corinth in weakness, fear and much trembling. On the Damascus road, it was with power he had breathed out threatenings and slaughter against the disciples, Acts 9. 1, but shortly afterwards he fell to the ground, trembling and astonished, v. 6. This was an outward demonstration of a heart struck down before the Lord.

But we suggest that here Paul is not recalling physical weakness and fear when he had been in Corinth. Indeed, he had been encouraged by the Lord in a vision, "Be not afraid, . . . I am with thee, and no man shall set on thee to hurt thee", Acts 18. 9–10. Admittedly, he was weak in the flesh, but elsewhere he had not been despised nor rejected on that account; rather he had been received as an angel of God, Gal. 4. 14.

Instead of refering to this physical weakness, we suggest that he was in fear and trembling lest his inborn natural ability should tend to displace the spiritual power of God working through him. The next verse provides support for this suggestion.

4. *Note:* the word "man's" before "wisdom" should be omitted, according to the various editors of the Greek text. Paul would not preach with "enticing (or persuasive) words of wisdom".

All forms of persuasion are not bad. In Corinth itself, Paul had persuaded the Jews and the Greeks, Acts 18. 4. There is an improper use of persuasion and a proper use of it.

> *Improper use of persuasion.* This implies using human logic and reasoning, with no regard to the Word or to the power of the Spirit. We have already discussed this in chapter 1 verses 19–21. Such would employ "cunningly devised fables", 2 Pet. 1. 16; they would be "false teachers", and many would "follow their pernicious ways", 2. 1–2, since they would speak "great swelling words of vanity", 2. 18. These would be "false prophets", almost able to deceive the very elect, Matt. 24. 24.

> *Proper use of persuasion.* Spiritual persuasion is good and proper. Paul had used it in Corinth in the Gospel. The spiritually minded would always know the difference between natural persuasion and spiritual persuasion. Preachers who seek to persuade their hearers after having preached the Gospel need great care in this matter, lest they

mar the work of the Spirit of God. Knowing the terror of the Lord, Paul sought to "persuade men", 2 Cor. 5. 11. King Agrippa realised that Paul had almost persuaded him to be a Christian, Acts 26. 28.

Paul did not want anything to distract from the work of the Spirit of God. In Zerubbabel's day, there was opposition to the rebuilding of the house of God, Ezra 4. But he had the promise that his hands would complete the work, "Not by might, nor by power, but by My spirit, saith the Lord of hosts", Zech. 4. 6, 9. Our sufficiency is of God, 2 Cor. 3. 5, but this is often a hard lesson to learn.

We may note that we

worship in Spirit and in truth, John 4. 24;

preach in Spirit and in power, 1 Cor. 2. 4;

walk in Spirit and in light, Gal. 5. 16; 1 John 1. 7.

The word "power" suggests something *dynamic* and not *static* in the service of God. The word must not be confused with another Greek word often given the same translation; for example, in Matthew 28. 18 the "power" given to the Lord Jesus means "authority". See also 1 Cor. 11. 10. As far as preaching is concerned, Paul declares that the results are miraculous, outside the natural ability of man.

5. Faith comes through hearing the Word and it stands in the power of God, whatever the preacher might be. The basis of faith is not wisdom, neither can it be light emotionalism nor a multiplicity of choruses however popular they may be. Faith on such a basis seldom yields converts who can stand on their own spiritual feet. The difference is about as wide as those who build on the rock or on the sand, Matt. 7. 24–27. True faith is absolute; it is like "an anchor of the soul, both sure and stedfast, and which entereth into that within the veil", Heb. 6. 19.

This is the reason why Paul could obtain, not simply converts, but converts built into a local assembly so quickly. They could stand on their own feet, so that he could afterwards leave them. The power of God both produces and maintains the faith delineated in Hebrews 11. It preserves saints from being drawn away into the faithlessness of the last days, 2 Tim. 3. 1–9; 4. 1–4.

Verses 6–10: The Contents of the Message

6 Howbeit we speak wisdom among them that are perfect: yet not the wisdom of this world, nor of the princes of this world, that come to nought:

7 But we speak the wisdom of God in a mystery, *even* the hidden *wisdom*, which God ordained before the world unto our glory:

8 Which none of the princes of this world knew: for had they known *it*, they would not have crucified the Lord of glory.

9 But as it is written, Eye hath not seen, nor ear heard, neither have entered into the heart of man, the things which God hath prepared for them that love him.

10 But God hath revealed *them* unto us by his Spirit: for the Spirit searcheth all things, yea, the deep things of God.

6. If the ability in proclaiming the message is all of God, so, too, are the contents of the message preached. Paul, therefore, now discusses God's side giving revelation through the message. Paul rejects as unsatisfactory the wisdom of this world and of the princes of this world, but he does not reject the wisdom that comes from God. There is, after all, a natural wisdom and a spiritual wisdom. Often wisdom implies the critical and practical application of knowledge, but here, the thought goes far deeper, since Christ as the wisdom of God is brought in. Since Paul preached Christ, he is able to regard his own teaching as being wisdom to those that are perfect (that is, complete, or mature). This contrasts with the philosophy of men, which is not "after Christ", Col. 2. 8. Christ is eternal, and the Word revealing Him is likewise eternal. The world, its princes, and their wisdom come to nought in that coming day of judgment when only that which is of Christ will remain.

James 3. 13–18 very appropriately contrasts the wisdom that is earthly and the wisdom that is heavenly: "Who is a wise man and endued with knowledge among you? let him shew out of a good conversation (conduct) his works with meekness and wisdom. But if ye have bitter envying and strife in your hearts, glory not, and lie not against the truth. This wisdom descendeth not from above, but is earthly, sensual, devilish. For where envying and strife is, there is confusion and every evil work. But the wisdom that is from above is first pure, then peaceable, gentle, and easy to be entreated, full of mercy and good fruits, without partiality, and without hypocrisy. And the fruit of righteousness is sown in peace of them that make peace".

7. This is the crux of the matter; the wisdom of God that Paul preached was wrapped up in mystery. That is, it is a secret truth of God made known only by revelation and spiritual enlightenment. Paul had received such enlightenment through grace, so he sought to pass it on to others (see Jonah 3. 2). To believers today, the truth of this mystery is revealed indirectly through the written Word. To Paul and the prophets there was a direct revelation from the Spirit apart from the written Word.

This wisdom is hidden. In Christ "are hid all the treasures of wisdom and knowledge", Col. 2. 3. Christ and Him crucified are found in the O.T. Scriptures, but they are concealed there until a spiritual exposition enlightens the reader through faith. Much was revealed to the O.T. prophets, who searched diligently concerning the sufferings and glory of Christ. It was revealed to them so that they could pass it on to us through their ministry, 1 Pet. 1. 10–12. A knowledge of the O.T. without true exposition produces men like the Jews of old. They knew the word of the law, but they could not see Christ therein. Their ignorance led them to crucify the Lord of glory. His death was the fulfilment of the hidden mystery in the O.T., and in turn this has brought to light the Father's heart towards His own.

There are many mysteries recorded in Holy Scripture, some being entirely absent from the O.T. Scriptures and revealed only in the N.T. The reader may care to meditate on them.

> Matthew 13. 11: The mysteries of the kingdom of heaven. These were hidden in parabolic form, later explained by the Lord to His disciples, vv. 18, 36.
>
> Romans 11. 25: The mystery that blindness is happened to Israel during this present period of grace until the fulness of the Gentiles comes in.
>
> 1 Corinthians 15. 51: The mystery that we shall not all sleep, but that all believers will be changed at His coming.
>
> Ephesians 3. 3, 4, 9: The mystery of the union of Jew and Gentile in the same body, but hidden during the period of O.T. history and prophecy.
>
> Colossians 1. 27: The mystery of Christ amongst the Gentiles, the hope of glory.
>
> Revelation 10. 7: The mystery of God as declared to the prophets, namely the final overthrow of mystery Babylon, 17. 5, and the establishment of the kingdom of Christ in this world.

In our verse, Paul declares that this mystery was ordained by God *before* the world (ages) unto our glory. This does not mean that it was wholly hidden *since* the foundation of the world. It was made known in the O.T. Scriptures, but hidden to the blind eyes of unbelief. The fact that it was predetermined by God *before* the ages means that the whole purpose of God for salvation through Christ was no afterthought. Salvation's plan was not arranged *after* sin came in; God had been ready *before* sin came in. We have eternal life, and are thus connected to the eternal days of the future, but this great thought connects us with the eternal past as well.

Christ in the eternal ages of the past is a theme for worship, as well as one of holy dignity and grace for the saints. We may notice other similar verses:

> 1 Peter 1. 20: ". . . Christ, as of a lamb without blemish and without spot: who verily was foreordained *before* the foundation of the world".
>
> John 17. 5–24: "the glory which I had with Thee before the world was"; "Thou lovedst Me *before* the foundation of the world".
>
> Ephesians 1. 4: "He hath chosen us in Him *before* the foundation of the world".

This word *before* must always be distinguished from the thought of *since* or *from*. The difference is one of dispensational truth, and shows clearly where the assembly fits into the purposes of God. The assembly is connected with heaven and eternal things; so the word *before* is used in connection with its blessings in Christ. The kingdom and God's earthly people are connected with earth and with O.T. prophecies; and so the word *from* is used in connection with their blessings. Here are two examples,

> Matthew 25. 34: This refers to the judgment of the "quick", namely

the living nations when the Lord comes in glory: "Inherit the kingdom prepared for you *from* the foundation of the world".

Revelation 13. 8: This refers to the remnant on earth faithful during the tribulation after the assembly has been taken to be with the Lord: "All that dwell upon the earth shall worship him (the first beast), whose names are not written in the book of life of the Lamb slain from the foundation of the world". This does not mean that the Lamb was slain from the foundation of the world. Some alter the words to read "the Lamb slain from before the foundation of the world", and ascribe this to the purpose of God before its accomplishment at the cross. This, however, is just not the meaning of the verse, as a glance at Revelation 17. 8 will show. The phrase refers to names written in the book from the foundation of the world. The *names* of the subjects to enter the kingdom are associated with the past creatorial period but not with the past heavenly eternal period.

8. Paul declares that none of the princes of this world knew of Christ revealed in the O.T. The word "princes" means "rulers of this age". The thought links with Psalm 2. 2, "The kings of the earth set themselves, and the rulers take counsel together, against the Lord, and against His anointed". See also Acts 4. 26. The revelation of the O.T. was a closed book to such men. The chief priests and scribes had been able to quote the very O.T. passage containing the place of birth of the King of the Jews, Matt. 2. 5–6, but this was merely quoting according to the letter and not of the spirit, 2 Cor. 3. 6. If they had known the truth of the Christ spoken by the prophets, then they would have been enlightened men of faith, and they could not then have been party to the evil deed of the cross. Wisdom and understanding are hidden "from the eyes of all living", Job 28. 21, so we cannot trust anyone who is not in contact with God for spiritual enlightenment. This is the testimony of the apostles concerning those who crucified the Lord Jesus:

Acts 3. 17: "I wot that through ignorance ye did it, as did also your rulers".

Acts 13. 27: "For they that dwell at Jerusalem, and their rulers, because they knew Him not, nor yet the voices of the prophets which are read every sabbath day, they have fulfilled them in condemning Him".

9. The very O.T. Scriptures, which these princes knew after the letter, were against them. In their state of sin and unbelief, they could not understand. Isaiah 64. 4, with slight alterations, is quoted to show the wretchedness of their position: "For since the beginning of the world men have not heard, nor perceived by the ear, neither hath the eye seen, O God, beside Thee, what He hath prepared for him that waiteth for Him". The confession of Isaiah in verses 6–7 shows sin abounding; this sin prevented men from seeing, hearing and understanding in the heart. In chapter one, we have already quoted similar verses in Isaiah 6. 9–10; Matthew 13. 14–15; John 12. 40; Acts 28. 26–27. Unbelief, prevalent in all from birth, is hardened by God at a certain stage. This hardening cannot be overcome by natural effort; rather, it can be removed by God using revelation through the Word.

It should be stressed that this verse 9 does not apply to believers today. They may feel their faith is weak, and that their understanding is limited, but this is not because God is deliberately withholding something from them. They have every opportunity of growing in grace and in the knowledge of the Lord Jesus Christ.

10. The position of the saints today is that "God hath revealed them unto us by His Spirit", that is, the precious truth relating to the person and work of Christ. Paul had a special revelation of these things, since he was an apostle. Today, the Spirit makes known to our hearts truth already contained in the written Word. We cannot expect to be vessels full of truth if we neglect the Word. Ignorance is a measure of our neglect, but knowledge is a measure of the Spirit's grace.

The content of the written Word or of the preached word can only be made acceptable to faith by the Spirit, since He searcheth all things, yea, the deep things of God. The Spirit of God knows all things, so He can be the only effectual teacher. He is the Spirit of truth, John 14. 17; He teaches all things and brings all things to remembrance, v. 26; He guides us into all truth, 16, 13. Paul declares that the Spirit "*searcheth* all things". This refers to John 16. 13, "whatsoever He shall *hear*, that shall He speak". This is a inexplicable exercise in the Godhead, but it shows that the Spirit (and not man) is eminently suited to teach. What divine dovetailing unity of purpose! In 1 Corinthians 2, it is the Spirit who reveals; in Matthew 11. 27, the Son reveals the Father, while in Matthew 16. 17, the Father reveals the Son.

"The deep things of God" refer to things that are properly the province of the Godhead, things which surpass natural understanding, but may be made known to faith. The thoughts of God are very deep, Ps. 92. 5; the knowledge of the searching power of God is too wonderful, "it is high", Ps. 139. 6. The ultimate in Christ necessitates the understanding of "the breadth, and length, and depth, and height; and to know the love of Christ, which passeth knowledge", Eph. 3. 18–19. Yet these things can be the substance of our preaching, with the prayer that the Spirit may make them real to many hearts.

Verses 11–16: The Reception of the Message

11 For what man knoweth the things of a man, save the spirit of man which
   is in him? even so the things of God knoweth no man, but the Spirit of
   God.
12 Now we have received, not the spirit of the world, but the spirit which is
   of God; that we might know the things that are freely given to us of God.
13 Which things also we speak, not in the words which man's wisdom
   teacheth, but which the Holy Ghost teacheth; comparing spiritual things
   with spiritual.
14 But the natural man receiveth not the things of the Spirit of God: for they
   are foolishness unto him: neither can he know *them*, because they are
   spiritually discerned.
15 But he that is spiritual judgeth all things, yet he himself is judged of no
   man.
16 For who hath known the mind of the Lord, that he may instruct him? But
   we have the mind of Christ.

11. We have noticed that verses 1–5 deal with the preacher's side,
verses 6–10 with God's side, and verses 11–16 with man's side.

Paul argues that no man knows the things of a man except the spirit of
man which is in him. He asks this in the form of a question, demanding
therefore a considered reply. Paul means that no one can know what exists
in another's mind; only the man himself can know that. (Jesus, being
divine, was of course an exception; He knew their thoughts on many
occasions, Matt. 9. 4; 12. 25; Luke 5. 22; 6. 8; 9. 47; 11. 17.) The thoughts
of a man can only be made known by what he says or does. These are
conveyed to another by means of the senses. For example, a school teacher
passes on only that which is known by the intellect.

What about the mind of God? The same observations apply. No man
can know the things of God if revelation is absent. The natural man is not
in contact with the Spirit, unlike believers, who are the temple of the Holy
Spirit, 6. 19. The mind of God can only be known by the Godhead, but
this can be expressed through communications from the Godhead by His
servants. Hence, when preaching the Gospel, evangelists should realise
that they present truth that represents the mind of God expressed in
words. These are solemn observations indeed!

12. *Note*: "the spirit which is of God" refers to the Holy Spirit, else the
verse does not fit into Paul's argument.

This verse represents the believer's privilege; we have received "the
Spirit which is of God". The reception of the Teacher *inwardly* is our only
means of knowing the truth. This is exactly the opposite to the spirit of the
world, which manifests natural understanding. This may well have its
rightful place in academic and business matters, but is quite impotent in
the understanding of divine things.

Elsewhere, Paul declares that "the Spirit beareth witness with our spirit,
that we are the children of God", Rom. 8. 16. It is this witness that gives
conviction and certainty within. This is why the world can never
understand the source and the reality of our faith; it is external to

ourselves and foreign to their own comprehension. Hence we may conclude that, if anyone seeks to contradict the Word, then the Spirit of God is not working in that soul. Such would be the spirit of anti-Christ, 1 John 4. 3.

One object of this divine visitation of the Spirit in our souls is that "we might know the things that are freely given to us of God". The reception and perception of blessing are all of grace. The hymn exhorts saints to "Count your blessings, name them one by one"; this can only be done according to His ability. A brief list would appear invidious, but we may mention some:

Roman blessings: predestinated, called, justified, glorified, 8. 30.

1 Corinthian blessings: "the manifestation of the Spirit is given to every man to profit withal", 12. 7.

2 Corinthian blessings: "that ye through His poverty might be enriched", 8. 9.

Galatian blessings: "the liberty wherewith Christ hath made us free", 5. 1.

Ephesian blessings: "blessed with all spiritual blessings in heavenly places in Christ", 1. 3.

Philippian blessings: the possession of the mind of Christ to walk as He walked, 2. 5.

The Spirit is ready to make these blessings known to our souls, but there is a danger that we may quench the Spirit within.

13. Not only is the Spirit instrumental in the reception of divine truth, but Paul would ensure that his preaching was on the same basis. He was an agent of the Spirit. "Which things" would refer to the blessings freely given (at the end of the previous verse), things that are entirely spiritual. Since Paul would speak only of such spiritual things, we may well beware of the many pronouncements on current political problems made in high religious circles. Moses could have expounded at length the wisdom of the Egyptians, but instead he declared the Word of God. The desire to speak the words "which the Holy Ghost teacheth" is characteristic of the apostles, prophets, teachers and evangelists. The proper exercise of spiritual gifts is to ensure that only spiritual things are treasured and passed on to others; see Ps. 48. 13; 2 Tim. 2. 2.

The fact that Paul used words "which the Holy Ghost teacheth" means that Paul used divine words! This is a great claim, but is in keeping with the Lord's own promises, John 14. 26; 16. 13. The promise extends even to the Spirit showing us "things to come", so prophecy should not be neglected in the assembly. This teaching of the Spirit is either directly to the prophet or indirectly through the Word to a teacher. The same power that inspired the Word is still present with the saints; He continues to make the Word real and precious to faith. The apostle John explains this, "But the anointing which ye have received of Him abideth in you, and ye need not that any man teach you: but as the same anointing teacheth you of all things, and is truth, and is no lie, and even as it hath taught you, ye shall abide in Him", 1 John 2. 27. John does not mean that there is no need for teachers obviously. Rather he means that the natural man is not operative. Saints can be taught by the Spirit through a gifted spiritual man.

"Comparing spiritual things with spiritual" involves a great principle. Translations of this phrase differ, but the whole argument of the apostle supports the translation given by J.N.D. and the interlinear translation of Bagster's Greek N.T., namely "communicating spiritual things by spiritual means". That is what Paul is writing about: the reception of truth and the method God uses for passing it on. Spiritual means are various; for example, the foolishness of preaching, 1. 21, individual testimony, Acts 18. 26; searching the Word, Acts 17. 11, conduct without the word, 1 Pet. 3. 1. "Search the Scriptures; . . . they are they which testify of Me", said the Lord Jesus, John 5. 39; this is a spiritual method. With all its various forms, this method is alone blessed by God to young and old alike. Can we afford to dilute the method that God *will* use with His own power? Can we afford to use both natural and spiritual means? Entertainment may appeal to the emotions of the flesh, but spiritual methods enable the Spirit to witness to the spirits of men unto salvation and growth in grace. Moreover, these *means* themselves do not convert a soul, rather they provide opportunity for the Spirit to do His gracious work. How he depends upon the faithful labours of the people of God! It may well be that expediency may argue against spiritual means, but anything else endangers the soul to the extent that "having begun in the Spirit, are ye now made perfect in the flesh?", Gal. 3. 3.

14. Having dealt with the reception of truth by spiritual men, Paul now briefly touches upon the effect of such truths and methods upon the natural man. A natural man is a man of one birth, namely one born of blood, of the will of the flesh and of the will of man, John 1. 13. There is no common point of contact between such a man and the teaching of the Spirit, so he regards the preaching of the cross as foolishness. It is like listening to something in a foreign language that is not understood, Acts 2. 13.

Only spiritual discernment can appreciate spiritual things. Such a man is possessed of a mind which understands the language! The Lord Himself had said, "It is the Spirit that quickeneth; the flesh profiteth nothing: the words that I speak unto you, they are spirit, and they are life", John 6. 63. How wonderful is the provision of God: gifts, the servants, the message and the reception are *all* of the Spirit of God. This leaves no room for any boasting either in the servant or in his work.

15. This is a difficult verse together with verse 16. Paul has in mind the situation in Corinth. They were discerning the servants of the Lord and placing false emphasis upon them, but this could be only carnal discernment.

The word twice translated "judge" in this verse should read "discern". A spiritual man discerns all things taught by the Spirit of God; he cannot go outside this holy range, else he would cease to be spiritual. Moreover he should not be discerned by anyone else, namely he should not be raised upon a party pedestal by other believers. Certainly the Spirit does not teach anyone to take sides in this fashion. Only good things can be discerned through the Spirit. Hence a believer doing such a thing ceases to be *spiritual*, rather he is *carnal* (see verse 1 of the next chapter). If anyone tends to think of any servant of God above that which is written, then he is puffed up, 4. 6, and this is not of the Spirit of God.

16. If such a man thinks that his point of view is correct, he can never justify himself by asserting that the Spirit prompted such an attitude. He cannot "instruct" God regarding his point of view. He does not know God's mind in order to do such a thing.

The party-spirit remains a demonstration of the flesh working in a believer; he is *carnal* not *spiritual*. "We have the mind of Christ" means that our minds should be formed by His mind. We cannot change His holy mind into ours, His holy will into our will.

1 CORINTHIANS 3

Section 2.   Divisions amongst the Saints
Subject 3.   Spiritual work

Background of this Subject

This subject follows immediately after chapter 2. Up to this point in his argument, the apostle has outlined general principles concerning
the call to service, 1. 27–28;
the attitude in service, 2. 4;
the substance of service, 2. 7;
the method of service, 2. 13.
All point to one conclusion, namely that the Lord has all power in service and all control of service.

Paul now returns to the state of affairs in Corinth, the manifestation of party spirit described originally in chapter 1 verses 10–13. He continues his argument by showing in more detail the shortcomings in Corinth, and by outlining the actual work accomplished in Corinth no doubt by Paul and Apollos but ultimately by the Lord. His conclusion again is, "Let no man glory in men", v. 21. Chapter 4 ends the section, where Paul develops the proper relationship that should exist between the Lord's servants and those served in order that party-spirit should be avoided.

This chapter divides into four paragraphs:
Verses 1–5: divisions in Corinth;
Verses 6–9: God's husbandry;
Verses 10–17: God's building;
Verses 18–23: let no man glory in men.

In verses 10–11, Paul makes reference to the foundation that is laid, even Jesus Christ. We expound this in due course, but in order not to break into the argument at that point, it would be helpful to bring together here various foundations occurring elsewhere in Holy Scripture. By themselves, they form an interesting subject for careful study.

Foundation of the tabernacle. The forty-eight boards overlaid with *gold* and the four pillars supporting the vail rested in one hundred sockets of silver, Exod. 26. 19, 21, 25, 32. These were made of the atonement money gathered from all who were numbered, 30. 13; 38. 25–27. These sockets separated the boards from the desert soil. But the articles of furniture within the tabernacle—overlaid with *pure gold* – were not separated from the soil by silver sockets. This *pure gold* speaks of the deity and righteousness of the Lord; He was ever undefiled and separate from sinners because of His own nature, Heb. 7. 26. But *gold* (by itself) speaks of the imputed righteousness of the saints. They need to be separated from the world, so the foundation of redemption not only supports but also delivers, Gal. 1. 4.

Foundation of the temple. The pattern of the temple was given by David to Solomon, 1 Chron. 28. 11, 19. With this in mind, Solomon prepared for the laying of the foundation, 2 Chron. 8. 16, bringing "great stones, costly stones, and hewed stones, to lay the foundation of the house", 1 Kings 5. 17. We should likewise own that the foundation of the assembly (the house of the living God, 1 Tim. 3. 15), is not of our own design. All is precious because it is His design. We rest upon truth established in our hearts as a result of deep exercise and the labours of brethren who have gone before.

Foundation Stone of prophecy. Christ is the foundation, centre and glory of all prophecy. In the latter half of 1 Peter 2. 7 (quoted from Psalm 118. 22), He is viewed as a Stone with reference to unbelievers. In verse 8 (quoted from Isaiah 8. 14), He again is viewed as a Stone with reference to the disobedient. But in verse 6 (quoted from Isaiah 28. 16), He is viewed as a Stone laid in Zion with reference to believers. This is in complete contrast to Babylon, of whom it is written "They shall not take of thee a stone for a corner, nor a stone for foundations; but thou shalt be desolate for ever" , Jer. 51. 26.

Foundation of the assembly. Apart from 1 Corinthians 3. 11, we may mention the following references.

1. "Upon this rock I will build My church", Matt. 16. 18. The church should never be referred to as "our" church, either referring to the saints or the hall they meet in. "My church" implies the Lord's possession. "This rock" cannot refer either to Peter or to the Lord. Men build a new bridge on a natural rock formation, but the rock is not part of the bridge that is built. Similarly, since Peter as a member and Christ as the Head are part of the church, they cannot be the Rock on which the church is built. The reference is to the foundation formed by the confession of the person of Christ as the Son of the living God. The reader should also note Matthew 7. 24; the rock refers to one's adherence to the sayings of the Lord.

2. "Built upon the foundation of the apostles and prophets, Jesus Christ Himself being the chief corner stone", Eph. 2. 20. This does not mean that the church is built *on these men*; rather it is built on *what they laid*. To suggest that it is built on these men contradicts 1 Corinthians 3. 11, where Jesus Christ is the only foundation. They laid this precious foundation in the beginning, and it exists today. As the foundation, Christ is the basis, strength and protection of the church. Christ as the chief corner stone would refer to His pre-eminent position of glory and headship.

Foundation of the wall of the new Jerusalem. Revelation 21. 14, 19–20 shows that the names of the apostles will be in the foundations of this holy city. They will be the Lord's representatives in government over the millennial earth.

Exposition of 1 Cor. 3: Spiritual Work

Verses 1–5: Divisions in Corinth

1 And I, brethren, could not speak unto you as unto spiritual, but as unto carnal, *even* as unto babes in Christ.

2 I have fed you with milk, and not with meat; for hitherto ye were not able to *bear it*, neither yet now are ye able.

3 For ye are yet carnal: for whereas *there is* among you envying, and strife, and divisions, are ye not carnal, and walk as men?

4 For while one saith, I am of Paul; and another, I *am* of Apollos; are ye not carnal?

5 Who then is Paul, and who *is* Apollos, but ministers by whom ye believed, even as the Lord gave to every man?

1. Scripture often subdivides men into classes. Later in the Epistle we shall see the implications of God's division of men into Jews, Gentiles and the church of God, 1 Cor. 10. 32. The Lord often distinguished between those who believe and those who believe not, John 3. 18. In the present verse, Paul finds it impossible to call his brethren spiritual; instead he uses the description "carnal". In the present context, Paul uses three descriptions of men, namely *natural, spiritual* and *carnal*. The latter two names refer to Christians.

> *The natural man.* Paul has used this name in 2. 14. Such a man can know only those things known by the spirit of man which is in him, 2.11. He has natural understanding only, because he is a man of one birth. He walks by sight and by sense, not by faith. The name does not distinguish his actual character; he is unregenerate, whether refined or gross.

> *The spiritual man.* Such a man is a believer. He has received the things of the Spirit of God, and he seeks to walk in the light of God's Word. Such a man is God's ideal for testimony having "the mind of Christ", 2. 16. A man who is spiritual will acknowledge that the things that Paul has written are "the commandments of the Lord", 14. 37.

> *The carnal man.* In the present context, this refers to a believer who is not walking in the light of the Word of God. Such introduce their own tastes into the assembly, and sadly others can be affected.

2. Brethren who are carnal are really "babes in Christ". This description is used, not because they are young in the faith, but because they are undeveloped in the spiritual sphere. This idea should be distinguished from the following references to babes and children in the N.T.

> Ephesians 2. 2: "Children of disobedience" refers to the unconverted, the children of wrath among whom Paul and the Ephesians were once found; see Col. 3. 6; 2 Pet. 2. 14.

> Hebrews 5. 13: "He is a babe" refers to those who should be teachers, but still needed to be taught because they valued Jewish ceremony more than Christ. At least, they were Christians.

> 1 Peter 2. 2: "As newborn babes" refers to the perpetual innocence of

those "born again, not of corruptible seed, but of incorruptible, by the word of God", 1. 23 . These are the only commendable form of babes.

Paul recalls that he had fed them with "milk, and not with meat". This is the first of the three great figures in this chapter, namely feeding, planting and building. It refers to the time when Paul had been present with these young converts for one and a half years, Acts 18.11. This was commendable, corresponding to 1 Peter 2. 2. But he then adds that they are *still not able* to partake of meat. The fact that they *still* needed milk was *not* commendable. After several years of Christian life and experience they should be able to partake of meat, namely truth provided by God for a more mature spiritual assembly.

In Hebrews 5. 12, the "babes" needed milk, and could not partake of strong meat. This seems to refer to the fact that these Hebrews were unable to appreciate Christ revealed in the types and prophecies of the O.T. The N.T. only approves of "babes" and "milk" under one condition, namely for newly born young believers in Christ. If one's appetite remains at this elementary stage for many years, then one must seriously question whether one is growing in grace or whether teachers are providing the right spiritual food for the soul. In daily school life, there is a progression through classes and lessons over the years; should we expect anything less when the Spirit of God is working?

3. The carnality of the Corinthians was manifested by the envying, strife and divisions among them. Such conduct reflected in the lives of the saints meant that they were walking according to the fashion of men in the world. Strife, envying and divisions are characteristic of the political life of a nation, in which rivalry for power can stifle legitimate progress. These weaknesses that Paul mentions do not refer to the gross moral sin dealt with in chapter 5, but to weaknesses in assembly practice.

Envying: Saints were not satisfied with the position and service to which God had called them and for which He had equipped them with spiritual gifts. Hence they envied the status and ability of others, refusing to recognize that they themselves were necessary members of the body.

Strife: Chapter 14 shows that the saints were striving one against the other in the exercise of gift in the assembly. The true outworking of gift should be characterised by the virtues of the ascended Lord. Gifts are not for show nor for rivalry; they are held by the saints so that the Spirit can use them for the edification of the assembly.

Divisions: The Corinthians were taking sides with the original evangelists and teachers who had been used by God to establish the assembly in Corinth; 1. 12; 3. 4.

4. This verse represents the crux of the chapter. The state of disunity that Paul is dealing with was caused by adhering to particular servants of

God. The Corinthians were carnal because one and another said "I am of Paul; I am of Apollos". As an apostle, Paul had special authority, and in a certain sense he could even be imitated, see 11. 1. But he could not be elevated by the saints to a status of a particular party leader. He and Apollos would be judged and rewarded by the Lord as every other believer would be, 4. 1–6. So there could be no ground for glorying in them, 3. 21, neither for thinking of them above that which is written, 4. 6. In the latter half of chapter 4 Paul finally deals with the true relation that should exist between the Lord's servants and those who are served.

The status of party leader can unwittingly be attained, unless special care is taken to avoid it. The introduction of some new mode of service into a gathering may often produce this danger, particularly if some of the Lord's people interpret this new form of service as violating N.T. principles. If one brother is particularly forthright in opposition to this form of service, there is the danger that other saints will immediately take sides with him. The position "I am of Paul; I am of Apollos" will be attained and may split the assembly. Such a brother may be falsely accused by other members that he is obstructing the onward progress and development of service. Mere self-justification in such circumstances can be very dangerous, again tending to produce a situation where many would adhere to him. This would be a greater disunity than that caused by the introduced service itself. The truth of 1 Peter 3. 8 bears upon the subject, "Finally, be ye all of one mind, having compassion one of another, love as brethren, be pitiful, be courteous: not rendering evil for evil, or railing for railing: but contrariwise blessing". The Lord will justify through His Word, and will ensure that what ultimately stands is His own work, even though the novelty, change and expediency may become very popular on occasions. See Exodus 14. 14.

5. Paul and Apollos would be as *nothing in themselves* before the saints. They would be regarded as the filth and the offscouring of all things, 4. 13; they would be unknown and yet well known, 2 Cor. 6. 9. They were but ministers by whom the Corinthians believed. The Lord gives the call and the commission to every one of His servants. For example, Paul was called in Acts 9, and received a typical commission in Antioch to the work whereunto the Spirit had called him, Acts 13. 2. Apollos had been equipped at Ephesus in the home of Aquila and Priscilla where they taught him the way of God more perfectly, Acts 18. 26. Men such as these could teach the saints. But a man not so equipped by the Lord should not seek to teach the saints. Also the saints should not side for or against any brother who ministers faithfully according to the call received from the Lord.

Verses 6–9: God's Husbandry

6 I have planted, Apollos watered; but God gave the increase,
7 So then neither is he that planteth any thing, neither he that watereth; but God that giveth the increase.

8 Now he that planteth and he that watereth are one: and every man shall receive his own reward according to his own labour.

9 For we are labourers together with God: ye are God's husbandry, *ye are* God's building.

6. Paul now makes use of the idea of God's husbandry, namely of the cultivated field of God. In the previous verse, Paul had placed the ministers in their proper perspective—the calling and the equipping are of God. Now he places their ministry in its proper perspective, showing that it is God who accomplishes true results in a soul. Our own service has eternal value only when God has been allowed to accomplish His own will in a soul through the channel of His servant.

The metaphor that Paul uses goes back to the beginning. In Genesis 1, the Lord made all things; man had no part in that great work of God. After that, man may cast seed into the ground, and it grows up, "he knoweth not how", Mark 4. 27. In other words, the miraculous still works today. The secret of life which none can explain is still in the hands of God. So, too, in the spiritual realm: any result in service is a spiritual miracle. Man has no part except in humbly being a channel through which God works.

This verse "I have planted, Apollos watered; but God gave the increase" is often misquoted in a Gospel context. It is suggested that the planting and the watering refer to the preaching of the Gospel, and that God alone can give life to a soul. This is perfectly true from other Scriptures, but this cannot be the meaning of the verse here. It refers to what was actually accomplished in Corinth:

I have planted: This refers to the ministry of Paul in Corinth during his original stay there of eighteen months, Acts 18. 1–18. During that time, "he reasoned in the synagogue", v. 4; he "testified to the Jews that Jesus was Christ", v. 5; he preached to the Corinthians the Gospel by which they were saved, 1 Cor. 15. 1 . As a result of this, many of them "hearing believed, and were baptized", Acts 18. 8. God had much people in that city who were converted, and Paul stayed for a long time "teaching the word of God among them", v. 11. The assembly was formed locally. He had fed them with milk,1 Cor. 3. 2, and he "delivered" to them the truth of the Lord's supper, 11. 23 . By this means, Paul enabled the young assembly to stand on its own spiritual feet. This whole procedure of Paul would form an ideal treatment of young converts today. All this is embraced by the idea of planting.

Apollos watered: In Acts 18. 24–28, Apollos was instructed in the way of God more perfectly; then "when he was disposed to pass into Achaia, the brethren wrote, exhorting the disciples to receive him: who, when he was come, helped them much which had believed through grace: for he mightily convinced the Jews, and that publickly, showing by the scriptures that Jesus was (is) Christ". Corinth was the seat of government for Achaia, and Apollos nourished the assembly formed locally by Paul. This spiritual process

of nourishing corresponds to "watering". Growth is fostered, and
the public preaching of the Gospel is included in the idea. Paul
apparently visited the saints again later for about three months,
Acts 20. 3.

God gave the increase: The intention of God is that we should "bring
forth more fruit", John 15. 2. Fruit would be everything of Christ-
likeness that rises from the saints individually, and collectively as an
assembly. Only the Spirit can make effective in a soul a ministry
which yields a sweet savour of Christ.

7. This is no mere metaphor that Paul is using; there is an exact parallel
in spiritual service. The status of the one who plants and of the one who
waters diminishes to zero when the miraculous resulting work of God is
viewed. John the Baptist had said before, "He must increase, but I must
decrease", John 3. 30. Paul extends this status of humility and nothingness
still further. The words of Paul exalt the Giver of gift and the Giver of
spiritual life through the work of the Lord's servants.

Our own service would be deeply influenced if we realised that God was
going to follow on. Are our acts of planting and watering really suitable for
God to follow on? Is it true that sometimes some of us are more careful
with our gardens than in assembly service? We readily follow the
instructions given on the seed packet or those contained in a gardening
handbook. Nature will work when we give the seeds or plants a right start.
But if we use the wrong soil, the wrong depth or the wrong time of
planting, can we expect the methods of nature to take over where we leave
off? The same applies to the service of God. We have the handbook of His
Word to guide in all planting. He will then take over, provided what we
have done fits in with His methods. This will happen if we know His
methods beforehand, so that our service will blend with His holy working
later.

8. Planting and watering are different kinds of service, yet Paul now
argues that all servants are on the same footing before God. There is a
unity even in the variety of service. Hence an assembly should never seek
to distinguish between the Lord's servants, siding with them for
partisanship. All are one, in that they are nothing in themselves, and that
they are the mere preliminaries to the great work of God. This touches
directly on the fault in Corinth which Paul is dealing with: the saints had
no right to choose.

But choice and reward belong to God. "Every man shall receive his own
reward according to his own labour". The reward from God is given to an
individual, according as he takes up the particular work of God's choice and
distribution. This reward refers primarily to the judgment seat of Christ, of
which we shall speak in detail in verses 13–15. Hence where is boasting on
the behalf of the partisans? It is excluded since God is all in all in our
service.

9. In the concluding remark, "We are labourers together with God; ye are God's husbandry", the "we" refers to Paul and Apollos, while the " ye" refers to the assembly in Corinth. The unity of service with the Lord takes us to Mark 16. 20, "And they went forth, and preached every where, the Lord working *with* them, and confirming the word with signs following". In such a holy fellowship in service, there can be no sense in bringing God down to our standard or to our methods; rather we are raised to the standard and to the methods of Christ Himself. We, as members, are in living relationship with the Head, as is expounded in chapter 12. Such knowledge would elevate the standard and the sanctity of our work. It would provide us with a real incentive to watch for the Lord to bless with signs following.

Moreover, such service takes place in the property of God. We labour in "God's husbandry". It is not *our* field, so the Lord must be all in all in the direction of service. We must sow the seed of the Word that He has provided.

Whereas verses 6–9 deal with the Lord's servants *placing the Word* in God's field, verses 10–17 now deal with His servants *placing the Lord* as the foundation of God's building.

Verses 10–17: God's Building

10 According to the grace of God which is given unto me, as a wise masterbuilder, I have laid the foundation, and another buildeth thereon. but let every man take heed how he buildeth thereupon.

11 For other foundation can no man lay that that is laid, which is Jesus Christ.

12 Now if any man build upon this foundation gold, silver, precious stones, wood, hay, stubble;

13 Every man's work shall be made manifest: for the day shall declare it, because it shall be revealed by fire; and the fire shall try every man's work of what sort it is.

14 If any man's work abide which he hath built thereupon, he shall receive a reward.

15 If any man's work shall be burned, he shall suffer loss: but he himself shall be saved; yet so as by fire.

16 Know ye not that ye are the temple of God, and *that* the Spirit of God dwelleth in you?

17 If any man defile the temple of God, him shall God destroy; for the temple of God is holy, which *temple* ye are.

10. The idea of the temple, vv. 16–17 arises from the O.T. God would dwell amongst His people, so the tabernacle was constructed for wilderness use, Exod. 25. 8, and the temple for the more permanent conditions in the land, 2 Sam. 7. 1–7; 1 Kings 9. 3. The temple that Herod built later had no divine authority behind it at all. Herod built it merely for pomp and display, a craftsman's masterpiece. But the original ceremony introduced by God had as its purpose a spiritual object. It looked forward to "the house of God, which is the church of the living God", 1 Tim. 3. 15. There is both a *local* and a *universal* thought behind this idea. In Ephesians

2. 21–22, we have the universal thought, "In whom all the building fitly framed together groweth unto an holy temple in the Lord: in whom ye also are builded together for an habitation of God through the Spirit". In 1 Corinthians 3, we have the thought of the work of the local builders. In no way does this diminish the promise of the Lord Jesus that He Himself would build His church, Matt. 16. 18.

As with the previous paragraph dealing with the husbandry, Paul joins himself with Apollos in this work. They are seen in the first stage of local building. Paul is deliberately transferring these things to himself and Apollos, 4. 6, in order to bring out his lesson. Paul states that the grace of God "is given unto me". He stresses that he did not originate his own service. The hasty plan, perhaps following tradition or being the product of a fertile imagination, cannot be of God. In this work, Paul regards himself as a "wise master-builder". The actual Greek word used here is *architect*. He was God's head-worker on earth, used by God to introduce full assembly principles. The one whom Paul describes as "another" (that is, *another of the same kind,* see our exposition of chapter 12 verses 8–10) is Apollos; he followed Paul in this faithful act of building. But after that, every saint who engages in service in the assembly continues to build on the one foundation defined in the following verse. Paul and Apollos, the original founders, would not always be there. Ultimately gifted converts had to continue the building. Such must be the process (and progress) taking place in every local gathering. Saints are built up in themselves when they are equipped to build up the assembly around them.

11. The foundation of a building must be suitable in strength and in shape for the structure intended to be built upon it. As the builder of the author's present house said, "If you start right, you can keep right, but if you start wrong, it is almost impossible to get right afterwards". It is the same spiritually. The only foundation that men can lay in a new testimony is Jesus Christ. (Compare the various foundations discussed at the beginning this chapter.) This is true, whether for a local testimony or in a more universal sense. In Ephesians 2. 20, we read, "And are built upon the foundation of the apostles and prophets, Jesus Christ Himself being the chief corner stone". This refers to the foundation laid by the apostles and prophets, namely Jesus Christ. Yet at the same time He is the chief corner Stone. He has the pre-eminent position, and yet a miraculous position. It is miraculous because He occupies the position of the top-most Stone before the rest of the building is constructed. It would almost appear that the foundations were on top and not at the bottom. These would be heavenly roots indeed.

Various heretical sects are built upon the doctrines of their founders, and various orthodox groups are built upon traditional concepts. But a N.T. local assembly should be built on Christ alone, and the faith of the individual members should also rest upon Him alone. Evangelists should take heed in their zeal and in their methods that their converts enter upon the christian pathway according to the N.T. pattern. Any other start implies that it is almost impossible to re-orientate the outlook and desires of the converts to fit in with the building of God.

12. Even in Paul's day, men were not building properly upon the one foundation that God had enabled him to lay. "Gold, silver, precious stones, wood, hay, stubble" characterised the work. Certainly the work of Paul and Apollos was good, represented by gold, silver and precious stones. Their work was of spiritual value before God.

In verse 1, we distinguished between the spiritual, carnal and natural man. This same distinction may be discerned in the verses before us.

The spiritual man is a good workman who, at the same time, accomplishes good work, characterised by gold, silver and precious stones.

The carnal man is a believer, saved by grace and in assembly fellowship, one who should be able to accomplish good work, but who, alas, is doing bad work. Such were many of the Corinthians; they were producing wood, hay and stubble. These represent things useless in service, things that have no lasting value, produced by a carnal mind. In chapter 14, Paul exhorts that all be done for edification, for such work is precious. Instead, the Corinthians were using certain gifts merely for show and pride, such work being valueless. Moreover, an individual worker must not judge his own work according to his own tastes. In that case all work would be judged of value. Zeal can be gravely misplaced, and service could be judged as good when really it is bad. The Word provides the test to those who will be exercised according to its truth.

The natural man is an unbeliever outside assembly fellowship. Such can only accomplish bad work. Sometimes unregenerate men seek to touch the holy things of the assembly. It would appear that Paul deals with this in verse 17.

13–15. The day of the future shall show God's true estimate of all work supposedly done in His name. The fire that tries and reveals the character of the work, stands for Christ's most holy discernment at the judgment seat of Christ before which all believers will appear. Even now, as walking amongst His assemblies, His eyes are as a flame of fire, Rev. 1. 14. How much more in that day, when we shall see Him as He is.

Salvation unto eternal life depends upon the *faith* of the workman, not on the *work* he has sought to do. In spite of their work, the Corinthians were saved. They would be "blameless in the day of our Lord Jesus Christ", 1. 8. But rewards will depend on God's estimate of our work. If our work is valued, ours will be the special reward. At the same time, we should seek by grace to do good work, not because of the promise of rewards, but because we seek His glory in taking heed how we build on the one foundation.

Some further remarks on the judgment seat of Christ may be of value. It represents Christ's assessment of the race which we have run. It is a judgment of acceptance, and takes place in heaven *after* the rapture (see 1 Cor. 4. 5) and *before* His glorious advent to this earth, coming forth with His own. The four main references to this judgment seat are as follows:

Romans 14. 10–12: assessment *of motives for conduct*. Reasons will be probed as to why we engaged in such-and-such an activity where a certain amount of liberty is allowed. In the context, our liberty may stumble another brother, and this will be examined.

1 Corinthians 4. 5: assessment of *motives for service*. It is required in stewards that they be found faithful, so when the Lord comes, He will manifest the counsels of all hearts. It is not for us now to elevate or discredit a brother in service.

1 Corinthians 3. 13–15: assessment of *service* — of everything that we do to build upon the one foundation.

2 Corinthians 5. 9–10: assessment of *conduct*. We shall "receive the things done in the body". For example, the virtues in 2 Peter 1. 5–11 lead to an abundant entrance into the everlasting kingdom of the Lord Jesus Christ.

As far as rewards are concerned, "one star differeth from another star in glory", 1 Cor. 15. 41. We may mention the principles contained in Matthew 25. 21; the crown of rejoicing, 1 Thess. 2. 19; the incorruptible crown, 1 Cor. 9. 25; the crown of righteousness, 2 Tim. 4. 8; the shepherd's crown, 1 Pet. 5. 4; the various blessings for overcomers in Revelation 2–3; and Christ admired in all believers through these rewards, 2 Thess. 1. 10.

16. The truth that "ye are the temple of God, and that the Spirit of God dwelleth in you" is another impetus to good work. The saints build locally, but God uses this work in order to fuse together in spiritual growth a temple in the Lord, Eph. 2. 21. This is a great thought, and this knowledge would sanctify all we do. The *Spirit of God* would dwell within, a habitation for *God* would thus be formed, Eph. 2. 22, and the *Lord Jesus* would always be with His own, Matt. 28. 20. The Triune God would be found amongst the saints. What a glorious thought to motivate our service! But alas, much service sometimes has no thought of God in it at all.

17. "If any man defile the temple of God, him shall God destroy; for the temple of God is holy, which temple ye are". In the Greek text, the two words "defile" and "destroy" are identical. It was merely the style of the A.V. translators that used two different English verbs here. The word is usually translated "corrupt", as in Ephesians 4. 22 referring to the old man, in Jude 10 referring to "brute beasts", and in Revelation 19. 2 referring to the great whore, mystery Babylon. Some expositors explain this verse by implying that the act of defiling or corrupting is the work of the *carnal* believer, but the present author feels that this is incorrect. It is suggested rather that the act of corruption brought into the assembly is the work of the *natural* man, "false brethren unawares brought in, who came in privily to spy out our liberty which we have in Christ Jesus, that they might bring us into bondage", Gal. 2. 4. Paul states that God visits them with the same corruption that they seek to introduce into the temple. This is altogether too strong a term to describe the corrective action that God takes now, when some of His servants bring forth wood, hay and stubble. Rather, it represents the final judgment upon the unsaved who seek to tamper with the holy temple of God. See also Zech. 12. 3 in a similar situation referring to Jerusalem.

At the same time, this in no way minimises the gravity of a believer seeking to mar the holy temple of God. But God deals in a different way with such misguided folk.

Verses 18–23: Let no Man Glory in Men

18 Let no man deceive himself. If any man among you seemeth to be wise in this world, let him become a fool, that he may be wise.
19 For the wisdom of this world is foolishness with God. For it is written, He taketh the wise in their own craftiness.
20 And again, The Lord knoweth the thoughts of the wise, that they are vain.
21 Therefore let no man glory in men. For all things are yours;
22 Whether Paul, or Apollos, or Cephas, or the world, or life, or death, or things present, or things to come; all are yours;
23 And ye are Christ's; and Christ is God's.

18. Paul now returns to the Corinthians, as he had done previously in the paragraphs 1. 10–17; 2. 1–5; 3. 1–5. "Let no man deceive himself" means that some were convinced that things were right when really they were wrong. Similar uses of the word may be found in Romans 16. 17–18 and 2 Thessalonians 2. 2–3. The Corinthians thought that the wisdom of this world was sufficient for appreciation of the things of the Spirit of God. The wisdom of this world may be legitimate in the affairs of daily life, but for spiritual wisdom one must "become a fool", that is, as judged by man. Concerning the attitude and outlook that believers must take, men "think it strange", 1 Pet. 4. 4.

19–20. Men may regard believers as fools when they take up spiritual things. Similarly God regards men as foolish when they take up the wisdom of this world, for such is "foolishness with God". Paul gives two quotations from the O.T. to support this:
    1. Paul firstly quotes Job 5. 13. Job 4–5 forms the first reply of Eliphaz the Temanite to Job's first discourse when he desires never to have been born. Eliphaz tries to prove that Job in his suffering is reaping the rewards of his own unrighteousness, 4. 8; 5. 12, 13, 17, 18, whereas these sufferings were really demonstrating his uprightness (see 1. 11, although Job later humbled himself, 42. 6). For being so biased against Job, Eliphaz reaped the anger of the Lord kindled against him, 42. 7. Yet the Holy Spirit could take the statement in

5. 13 "He taketh the wise in their own craftiness" (where the word "wise" is wrongly meant by Eliphaz to refer to Job), and use it in 1 Corinthians 3. 19 making it apply to an *exactly opposite* case, namely to the natural wisdom of the unregenerate man or of the carnal believer.

2. The second quotation, "The Lord knoweth the thoughts of the wise, that they are vain" is from Psalm 94. 11, "The Lord knoweth the thoughts of man, that they are vanity". In this Psalm, the people of God are viewed under the oppression of the wicked, vv. 3–7. But verse 12 regards this as the chastening of the Lord (the same situation may be found in Hebrews 12. 1–11). At the same time, the oppression of man is not overlooked. The Lord knoweth the thoughts of man, that they are vanity.

Hence the natural man is useless in his achievements of mind. Carnal believers have no excuse for following such an outlook; the only lasting wisdom comes from the Lord who controls and brings to fruition all service. Man is nothing; even the most refined and spiritual of believers is impotent in himself .

21. Hence we cannot glory in any kind of man, natural, carnal or spiritual. We cannot take sides with any man since all calling, ability and results are of God. Moreover, it would be odd to take sides with the ones and the twos, since everything belongs to the Corinthians, "For all things are yours", although ultimately all belongs to God.

22–23. Believers have great possessions. None should be minimised and none should be elevated. The servants of the Lord are theirs, given by God to work amongst them. The world is theirs, meaning no doubt their ordinary possessions here below; these too are really given by the Lord, "All things come of Thee", 1 Chron. 29. 14. Life and death are theirs, referring, one would assume, to the possession of mortal life in the physical body. Things present and things to come would refer to spiritual blessings both now and in the future day.

But there can be no boasting in our possessions. Firstly they come from God, secondly, we ourselves belong to Christ. He calls His own, John 13. 1, the following names, which imply that we belong to Him:

My sheep, John 10. 14–15;
My servant, John 12. 26; 18. 36;
My disciples, John 15. 8;
My friends, John 15. 14;
My brethren, John 20. 17.

At the same time, Paul concludes that "Christ is God's". We suggest that this goes beyond the thought in 1 Corinthians 11. 3, "the head of Christ is God". Rather it would refer to the Son, as the burnt offering, alive again from among the dead, received back by the Father into heavenly glory. The infinite possession of the Father is His well-beloved Son.

1 CORINTHIANS 4

Section 2.   Divisions amongst the Saints
Subject 4.   The Preacher and his Converts

Background of this Subject

We have seen that chapters 1–4 form a connected argument. The apostle Paul is seeking to demonstrate the proper relation that should exist between the Lord's servants and those served, between Paul and his converts. A misdirected relationship leads to the development of party-spirit, thereby dividing an assembly into factions. Paul has dealt with the subject by showing that God is all in all in service. This includes the call of the servants, the wisdom granted them, their ability to serve, the uselessness of natural ability, the choice of the cross as the subject matter of testimony, the reception of the message, and following up the original work achieved.

In this chapter, Paul concludes the argument at verse 20, verse 21 properly belonging to chapter 5. The three main paragraphs are as follows:

Verses 1–7: faithful service cannot be examined critically by other brethren;
Verses 8–13: Paul's nothingness in the world;
Verses 14–20: the relationship between Paul and the Corinthian converts.

Exposition of 1 Cor. 4. 1–20: The Preacher and His Converts

Verses 1–7: Faithful Service

1 Let a man so account of us, as of the ministers of Christ, and stewards of the mysteries of God.
2 Moreover it is required in stewards, that a man be found faithful.
3 But with me it is a very small thing that I should be judged of you, or of man's judgment: yea, I judge not mine own self.
4 For I know nothing by myself; yet am I not hereby justified: but he that judgeth me is the Lord.
5 Therefore judge nothing before the time, until the Lord come, who both will bring to light the hidden things of darkness, and will make manifest the counsels of the hearts: and then shall every man have praise of God.
6 And these things, brethren, I have in a figure transferred to myself and *to* Apollos for your sakes; that ye might learn in us not to think *of men* above that which is written, that no one of you be puffed up for one against another.
7 For who maketh thee to differ *from another?* and what hast thou that thou didst not receive? now if thou didst receive *it,* why dost thou glory, as if thou hadst not received *it?*

1. "Let a man so account of us" means that the Corinthians had to recognise the position of Paul in service, even though he was nothing in himself. Absence of party-spirit does not imply that one should neglect the Lord's call to service in others. In fact, we should know the position of each servant in Christ by reason of their work.

Paul uses two names in connection with his service, namely "ministers"and "stewards". In order to ascertain the meanings of these words, wise use of a concordance is necessary, otherwise one may be tempted to link this verse to other Scriptures where no connection really exists.

Minister. This is not the usual word *diakonos*, also translated *deacons*, 1 Tim. 3. 8, which refers to one serving in the assembly using spiritual gifts; for example, "*ministers* by whom ye believed", 1 Cor. 3. 5, "Who hath made us able *ministers* of the new testament", 2 Cor. 3. 6. Neither is it the less common word *litourgos*, twice used as *minister* referring to the saints, Rom. 15. 16; Phil. 2. 25, which means priestly service, implying an offering up to God. This word is used of Christ Himself, "a *minister* of the sanctuary, and of the true tabernacle", Heb. 8. 2.

Rather, it is the word *hupeeretees*, which occurs many times in the Gospels, but only a few times in a spiritual sense. It usually refers to an *officer* of the Sanhedrin, "and sat with the *servants*, to see the end", Matt. 26. 58, or to an *attendant* in the synagogue, "and He gave it again to the *minister*", Luke 4. 20. Hence Paul means that he is an *attendant* to Christ, that the real service is done by Another. The word is used in Luke 1. 2, "eyewitnesses, and *ministers* of the word", and in Acts 26. 16, "to make thee a *minister* and a witness". In this sense, all saints are called upon to wait on the divine Worker; see 1 Cor. 3. 9.

Steward. This refers to a manager of a household. All saints are included, "as every man hath received the gift . . . as good *stewards* of the manifold grace of God", 1 Pet. 4. 10. In the Gospels, this word *oikonomos* occurs only in Luke. The Lord spoke of "that faithful and wise *steward*", Luke 12. 42, who would give the portion of meat in due season to the Lord's household. Such a servant would be blessed when the Lord comes and finds him thus doing. He would enter into the blessing that the Lord provides. In this sense, the parable links with the present Epistle, 1. 7; 4. 8. Today, the Lord's stewards feed the saints with "the mysteries of God". While the Lord is away, the building (chapter 3. 9) is regarded as a house managed in a spiritual sense by His stewards.

2. The ultimate responsibility of such stewards is to God; they must be faithful, that is, faithful to His will, Luke 12. 42–43. It is good to examine the work and character of those who are designated faithful in the N.T. Faith is the means of *acquiring* salvation; faithfulness is a *result* of salvation.

If we trust God, that is faith; if God trusts us, that is faithfulness. Faith produces devotion to Christ that is expressed in faithfulness.

Certainly God is faithful in His promises, Tit. 1. 2; He "is faithful that promised", Heb. 10. 23; "He is faithful and just to forgive us our sins,"1 John 1. 9; He is faithful to set us up and to equip us for life, 2 Thess. 3. 3; He is "the faithful witness", Rev. 1. 5.

Paul was faithful in his service: "I thank Christ Jesus our Lord, who hath enabled me, for that He counted me faithful, putting me into the ministry", 1 Tim. 1. 12. Apart from that, there are five men named in the N.T. as "faithful".

> *Timothy.* This young man had known the Holy Scriptures from his youth, and had been saved during Paul's first missionary journey. He quickly matured, and Paul had him accompany him on his second journey, Acts 16. 3. As such, he was Paul's "beloved son, and faithful in the Lord", 1 Cor. 4. 17. In this verse we find that God trusted Timothy to teach Paul's ways in Christ in every church. Today, the Lord would count brethren as faithful, if He can trust them to minister every aspect of assembly truth in the same way as Paul ministered it.

> *Tychicus.* Whom could God trust to report correctly to others all the state of the apostle Paul? Tychicus was chosen, "a beloved brother and faithful minister in the Lord", Eph. 6. 21–22; Col. 4. 7. He would neither elevate nor disparage Paul. He would not exaggerate, and would report only those things that are Christ-like. Holy conversation about servants engaged in holy things is required by God.

> *Epaphras.* This man was dear to Paul's heart when he wrote to the Colossians. Epaphras told them that Paul always prayed for them, 1. 7, and he told Paul of their love in the Spirit, 1. 8. This was holy mutual conversation about the well-being of the assembly. God could use this "faithful minister of Christ", 1. 7, who had zeal and prayerful exercise towards the assembly, 4. 12–13.

> *Onesimus.* If we cannot aspire to the heights of these three men, on the grounds that we started life badly, then we may learn from Onesimus. As a thief, having wronged Philemon, he contacted Paul in prison in Rome. The slave was converted, becoming profitable to Paul and to his master Philemon as a brother beloved. Hence Paul was able to write of him as "a faithful and beloved brother", Col. 4. 9.

> *Silvanus.* Peter in his first Epistle calls him "a faithful brother", 1 Pet. 5. 12. He wrote at Peter's dictation, with latitude for introducing his own expressions. He is thought to be the Silas of Paul's second missionary journey. Silvanus was associated with Paul in the writing of the two Epistles to the Thessalonians. In other words, God used this faithful brother both in the process of divine inspiration of Holy Scripture and also in the spreading abroad of such truth. Today, faithfulness adheres to the inspired Word.

3. The verb twice translated *judge* in this verse really means *to examine*. The same applies to the verb *judge* in verse 4, whereas in verse 5 judicial judgment is implied. The Corinthians were in effect subjecting the apostle to a critical examination of his motives and his ability, but not according to the Word of God. They were taking note neither of his faithfulness nor of any possible weakness and failure. These things will always be noticed by a spiritual brother.

Paul counted it but a small thing that he should be thus examined by the Corinthians. Paul's faithful stewardship was under false inspection. Their examination consisted either of seeking out the bad when there was nothing but good in his service, or of raising the useful service of the apostle to the level of man's achievement rather than God's. Some were against and some were for the apostle, but the evil was that they were either elevating man or abasing Christ.

"Or of man's *judgment*" should be translated "or of man's *day*". Paul appears to refer to the methods of unregenerate men before the Lord's return. Throughout the period of the church dispensation, Paul has had his critics. Man is still in his "day" with apparent liberty to criticise. He was often criticised on his missionary journeys. In Acts 13. 45 they contradicted and blasphemed the holy things spoken by Paul, while in Philippi he was accused of having exceedingly troubled the city, 16. 20.

Finally, Paul would not judge himself in this fashion. This has nothing to do with the legitimate examination of oneself demanded in other Scriptures, such as 1 Cor. 11. 28; 2 Cor. 13. 5, where other words are used. Rather Paul would not engage in any false elevation or commendation of himself. This can never be approved, since the commendation of the Lord is the only thing that matters, 2 Cor. 10. 18.

4. Paul continues: "I know nothing by myself". Paul is not referring to his past life, nor to any sense of his own faithfulness, 2 Tim. 4. 7, nor to any sense of his own weakness, 1 Cor. 2. 3. Rather he means that he possessed no spiritual competence *thus* to examine himself or anyone else.

Moreover, ignorance in any form does not allow justification. The men of the world are ignorant of the exceeding sinfulness of sin according to the standards of God, but this does not clear the guilty. Paul's refusal to examine himself according to the strange whims of the Corinthians did not justify him, since only the Lord may examine His servants. Such are accountable to Him alone. He sees the service done for Himself, and He rewards in that day.

5. Moreover, Paul continues "Therefore judge nothing before the time". Here this word *judge* means judicial judgment, not a critical examination. If brethren engage in the latter unhealthy activity, it would be even more foolish to engage in the former, since believers cannot come into condemnation (judgment), John 5. 24. But unfortunately, if brethren entertain false thoughts in examining the motives and service of another, then this can lead to deeper thoughts with respect to guilt as the mind feeds on these things.

But when the Lord comes, He will not *judge* in this sense, rather He will *examine* at His judgment seat. He "will bring to light the hidden things of darkness, and will make manifest the counsels of the hearts". This verse is sufficient to show that the judgment seat of Christ takes place when He has come for His own. It dispels the thought that there is an individual judgment seat for each believer soon after his natural death.

In 3. 13, one's *service* is examined for bad or good; here one's *heart* is examined by the Lord. (See our exposition of 3. 13–15 for a fuller account of the judgment seat of Christ.) The hidden things of darkness would correspond to the chaff in the heart while the counsels of the heart would refer to the wheat. None is perfect now, but in that day the great principles of judgment will separate the wheat from the chaff. Even now, every heart is naked and opened unto His eyes, Heb. 4. 13, which are as a flame of fire, Rev. 1. 14. But there is no fear, neither now nor then. Perfect love casts out fear. Rather every believer shall have praise of God in that day. The degree of the reward will depend upon Christ's faithfulness in recognising that which stands the test of the fire.

6. Paul now arrives at the conclusion of this paragraph. He observes that he had "transferred" these things to himself and Apollos, to bring home more forcibly to the Corinthians the great lesson that they must not think of any servant of the Lord above that which is written. The whole of Scripture demonstrates that God is everything and that the believer is but a willing channel and instrument in His service. But each and every one of the Corinthians were elevated with pride about some particular servant of their own liking.

A brother in Christ can find himself in a difficult position if, as a result of his own faithfulness towards God in service, others seek to elevate him to a status he would not desire. At least, a servant would not usually exalt himself in his own service. Paul had a thorn in the flesh "lest I should be exalted above measure", 2 Cor. 12. 7. If Paul would not exalt in his service, there was no room for others to seek to do so. The Lord Jesus described the proper attitude towards service: "He that humbleth himself shall be exalted", Luke 14. 11. Such exaltation comes only from the Lord and never by men. Indeed, every saint should learn "not to think of himself more highly than he ought to think", Rom. 12. 3, owning that it is God who deals to every man the measure of faith. Such an attitude exalts Christ.

7. Paul finally no longer addresses the Corinthians as "ye" as in the previous verse. He now uses "thou", implying a general observation to all. (A similar phenomenon may be found in Romans 2. 1, 3, 4, 17.) Every believer differs from the men of the world on account of the grace of

Christ making him different. Every spiritual blessing and every ability in service have been received from the divine hand through grace. Yet some would apparently take the attitude that it had not been received through grace after all. The fact that they gloried or boasted means that they looked to self or to men. They certainly did not look to the Lord, and thus they denied that He gave all things to His own. Such men ceased to abide in the vine, failing to realise that "without Me ye can do nothing", John 15. 5. Such an attitude would ultimately bring forth the works of the flesh, Gal. 5. 19, rather than the fruit of the Spirit. The Corinthians were certainly moving along that road.

Verses 8–13: Paul's Nothingness in the World

8 Now ye are full, now ye are rich, ye have reigned as kings without us: and I would to God ye did reign, that we also might reign with you.

9 For I think that God hath set forth us the apostles last, as it were appointed to death: for we are made a spectacle unto the world, and to angels, and to men.

10 We *are* fools for Christ's sake, but ye *are* wise in Christ; we *are* weak, but ye *are* strong; ye *are* honourable, but we *are* despised.

11 Even unto this present hour we both hunger, and thirst, and are naked, and are buffeted, and have no certain dwellingplace;

12 And labour, working with our own hands: being reviled, we bless; being persecuted, we suffer it:

13 Being defamed, we intreat: we are made as the filth of the world, *and are* the offscouring of all things unto this day.

8. Paul now uses his final argument to show how useless it is for any believer to take sides with him. He contrasts the state of the Corinthians with his own. They were "already" (not "now") full, already enriched, and reigning without Paul. In other words, they had reduced the blessed truth of 1. 5, "In every thing ye are enriched by Him", to a carnal level, as in Laodicea, Rev. 3. 17. The verb *reign* has reference to those who took open sides with others, having no time for the apostle Paul at all. It refers to those who were against his apostleship. It refers to the practice of many today who do not adhere to Paul's doctrine of the assembly. In Christendom, it will head up in the activity of the woman, mystery Babylon the great, "that great city, which reigneth over the kings of the earth", Rev. 17. 18.

This attitude is but a carnal imitation of the spiritual blessings of the millennial reign of Christ. Paul's desire that both they and he might reign looks forward to perfection in that day, when the scenes of weakness of the present day will be gone. In that day, the saints will legitimately reign with Christ. It is the truth of Luke 19. 17, where the Lord Jesus said, "Well, thou good servant: because thou hast been faithful in a very little, have thou authority over ten cities".

9. But until that day, Paul was far from being a king; rather he was as the filth of the world, as the offscouring of all things. In 12. 28, the apostles

were first in the matter of gifts; here, they were *last* and appointed to death—the end of that great line described in Hebrews 11. 33–38, men of faith who were the outcasts in this world. God had placed Paul in this position at his conversion, "I will shew him how great things he must suffer for My name's sake", Acts 9. 16. Paul's sufferings took place openly in the world; he was a "spectacle" or "theatre" unto many, namely

> *to the world*—that is, to the unsaved unregenerate man;
>
> *to angels*—that is, to the heavenly hosts watching the outworking of God's purpose in His servant;
>
> *to men*—that is, one feels, to the carnal Corinthians, as 3. 3.

But Paul always had that quiet confidence that "Christ shall be magnified in my body, whether it be by life, or by death", Phil. 1. 20.

10–13. This side of Paul's life was so different from the easy and satisfied life of the Corinthians. Readers will be able to fit fourteen phases of Paul's life of testimony to various passages from the Acts historically and from the Epistles and Gospels doctrinally. He followed in the footsteps of his Lord and Master, although one or two things in this list can hardly apply to the life of the Lord Jesus when upon earth. These fourteen phases are:

> we are fools for Christ's sake, but ye are wise in Christ;
>
> we are weak, but ye are strong;
>
> we are despised, but ye are honourable;
>
> we both hunger,
>
> and thirst,
>
> and are naked,
>
> and are buffeted,
>
> and have no certain dwellingplace, (see Matt. 8. 20);
>
> and labour, working with our own hands;
>
> being reviled, we bless;
>
> being persecuted, we suffer it;
>
> being defamed, we intreat;
>
> we are made as the filth of the world;
>
> the offscouring of all things unto this day.

Paul continued the list in 2 Corinthians 11. 23–33 in order to boast in his infirmities, "that the power of Christ may rest upon me", 12. 9. He took pleasure "in infirmities, in reproaches, in necessities, in persecutions, in distresses for Christ's sake: for when I am weak, then am I strong", v. 10.

Paul also dwelt upon this subject in 2 Corinthians 6. From experience and revelation, Paul provided a list of features that should be manifested in those whom he designated as "workers together", 6. 1. These twenty-eight features in 2 Cor. 6. 4–10 are subdivided by the words "in", "by" and "as". (In the original Greek the subdivisions afforded by these prepositions do not correspond exactly to their English equivalents.) The first ten (vv. 4–5 introduced by "in") represent the *outward circumstances in suffering* of the minister; the next eleven (vv. 6–8, introduced by "by") stress the *inward character* of the minister; the remaining seven (vv. 8–10, introduced by "as") deal with the *contrasts experienced* by the ministers of God.

Verses 14–20: The Relationship between Paul and his Converts

14 I write not these things to shame you, but as my beloved sons I warn *you*.
15 For though ye have ten thousand instructers in Christ, yet *have ye* not many fathers: for in Christ Jesus I have begotten you through the gospel.
16 Wherefore I beseech you, be ye followers of me.
17 For this cause have I sent unto you Timotheus, who is my beloved son, and faithful in the Lord, who shall bring you into remembrance of my ways which be in Christ, as I teach every where in every church.
18 Now some are puffed up, as though I would not come to you.
19 But I will come to you shortly, if the Lord will, and will know, not the speech of them which are puffed up, but the power.
20 For the kingdom of God *is* not in word, but in power.
21 What will ye? shall I come unto you with a rod, or in love, and *in* the spirit of meekness?

14. Having now embraced every possible argument, the apostle concludes this section by briefly showing the proper relationship that should exist between an evangelist and his converts. There is no unkindness in Paul's approach to the subject. Admittedly, the truth of the first four chapters may well humble a proud heart, but at the same time Paul is not writing to shame the saints (or to abash, or to chide as other translators give). He is not seeking from an apostolic position of strength to squash the saints. The apostle would be humble among them, 2 Cor. 12. 21. Rather, he writes to warn them, lest their testimony should cease to be for the glory of Christ, in which case God would come down in governmental correction. He would resist the proud, 1 Pet. 5. 5, who would be scattered in the imagination of their hearts, Luke 1. 51. It is therefore good to take heed to warnings in the Word of God. These are not given to provide doctrine, but are intended for immediate practical application.

15. The Corinthians had many "instructors" in Christ (or *tutors, child-guides*, as other translators give), even as many as ten thousand, to stress the point. These were the Lord's servants who had built upon the one foundation, 3. 10, the Lord Jesus Christ. But one can imagine the difficulty of even faithful servants coping with living stones who had rendered themselves carnal by reason of their natural whims. Paul goes back to the beginning. He had been used of God to bring about their conversion, "begotten you through the gospel", and in that sense was their evangelist-father. He does not call them his children or his sons, since they were not behaving like it—unlike verse 17 where he calls Timothy "my beloved son (child)".

16. The saints therefore should never forget their relationship with Paul. They should properly be "followers" of Paul, or rather, "imitators", see also 11. 1. Paul did not want them to *follow* him; that would merely lead to party-spirit. Rather he wanted them to *imitate* him, as a child would copy its parents in its early formative years. These four chapters have demonstrated Paul's conduct as a servant of God. He would have his converts grow likewise into such a spiritual outlook. All the errors Paul was seeking to correct would be eliminated if they imitated Paul who also imitated Christ Himself.

17. Paul sent Timothy to Corinth to make certain that this truth would be received by the Corinthians. Paul did not choose just anybody to go, but rather a brother in the same relation to him as the Corinthians were. For Timothy was also a "beloved son", or rather, a "beloved child". (The same translation also applies to the similar passages Phil. 2. 22; 1 Tim. 1. 2, 18; 2 Tim. 1. 2; 2. 1.) Timothy was faithful in the Lord (see 4. 2), and would place before the saints those ways of Paul that were in Christ and which should be imitated. In Corinth, Timothy would be a brother apart, not seeking to lead saints after him, but being an example amongst the believers, 1 Tim. 4. 12. Such men are very useful today. Paul's ways in Christ were taught in "every church", demonstrating the universal application of the apostolic authority. Timothy is an example to us, that we too should be able to teach others also; see 1 Cor. 16. 10.

18. But there was little love in Corinth. The fact that some were "puffed up" is the exact opposite of the manifestation of love, 13. 4. Paul loved the saints, 16. 24, even if there was little response. Some might not receive Timothy. They might think that Paul was not bold enough to appear again in Corinth if he could only send a "child" in the faith. Both this Epistle and the presence of Timothy might not be sufficient to bring about repentance in the heart of some.

19. So Paul proposed to visit Corinth personally—the apostolic authority would be the last method that God would use to bring the Corinthians to their knees. But the visit would be "if the Lord will", see also Rom. 1. 10, James 4. 15. This visit was accomplished in Acts 19. 21–22; 20. 1–3. And what would Paul do when he came in person?

20. He would know "not the speech of them which are puffed up, but the power. For the kingdom of God is not in word, but in power". In other words, the ultimate proof of the state of the heart lies not in words, however valuable this may be in testimony, but in its manifestation in character and in deed. This is power. Chapter 13 shows that love is a display of character rather than words. John the apostle exhorts his "little children" not to love "in word, neither in tongue; but in deed and in truth", 1 John 3. 18. The very gospel that Paul preached "came not unto you in word only, but also in power, and in the Holy Ghost", 1 Thess. 1. 5. Elsewhere, Paul had written that "the kingdom of God is not meat and drink; but righteousness, and peace, and joy in the Holy Ghost", Rom. 14. 17. All these verses tell the same story, that Christianity is very practical. The kingdom of God does not refer to the open manifestation of Christ in His kingdom in a day yet to come, although of course righteousness, peace and joy will be seen in that day. Rather it refers to the moral sphere of influence of God in a kingdom set up in the inner spiritual realm of the heart and life.

There Paul leaves this subject. Verse 21 should properly be taken with chapter 5.

1 CORINTHIANS 5

Section 3.   The Saints' Conduct
Subject 1.   Unsanctified Conduct

Background of this Subject

None can dispute the gravity of the particular sin of fornication that
Paul deals with in this chapter. Yet it is remarkable that this sin is placed
second in the Epistle and not first. The first error (the error of division
amongst the saints in chapters 1–4) was a *spiritual* weakness. The world
would not have sensed that anything was wrong even had they known of
the situation prevailing in the assembly. But this second sin is a *moral* one.
Even the world would have recognised that something was amiss. If the
second in this list is serious, how much more the former in the holy eyes
of God.

We must realise that Gentile converts were lamentably ignorant of the
first principles of Christian morality and decency. The apostles again and
again had to stress the very basic foundations of the system of Christian
morals to their depraved heathen converts. When the converted Gentiles
were freely admitted into assembly fellowship without the obligation of
obedience to the Mosaic law being imposed upon them, there was a
serious danger that the moral standards of the local assembly might fall
below that of the unconverted Jews around who were zealous of their law.

In Corinth, this sin existed in a particularly bad form, and Paul has to
deal with it. The situation demanded corrective action. The various forms
of corrective action available in the N.T. should be noted:

Reproof and rebuke. This is correction within the fellowship. Scripture
is available for reproof, 2 Tim. 3. 16, and those who sin should be
rebuked before all, 1 Tim. 5. 20. Fellowship, however, is maintained.

Withdrawal. This is established in 2 Thessalonians 3, but should not
be confused with practice common in certain circles today. There
were some brethren who walked "disorderly", that is, not after the
apostolic tradition. Such were not working at all, but were
busybodies, v. 11. The command is that the assembly should
"withdraw" from such, having "no company with him", vv. 6, 14.
Today, this might be interpreted in the sense, "We keep our hall, so
the brother goes out". This is materialistic confusion indeed, and is
equivalent to excommunication disguised under the Scriptural word
"withdrawal". Withdrawal means that the brother is admonished,
but not as an enemy, v. 15. There are thus *three spheres* in this case:
the assembly fellowship withdrawn, the lonely brother, and the
world outside. See also Romans 16. 17.

Excommunication. This is similar to the old synagogue practice: "lest

they should be put out of the synagogue", John 12. 42. The assembly
does not withdraw; they remain. Instead, the brother who has
sinned is put on the outside. This takes place for the list of sins
given in 1 Corinthians 5. 11. The brother is "put away", v. 13; he
has been delivered "unto Satan", v. 5. Here, there are only *two
spheres*: the assembly as the place where God dwells, and the world
outside, dominated by Satan. Hymenaeus had overthrown the faith
of some, by teaching that the resurrection was past already, 2 Tim.
2. 18. This was a profane and vain babbling, increasing unto more
ungodliness, v. 16, and the "great house" had to be purged from
"these", v. 21. Hence Paul had delivered him "unto Satan", so that
he may learn not to blaspheme, 1 Tim. 1. 20. This was no niggling
pretext for excommunication, but one ripe for correction. In some
of these cases, the sin would not be unto death (that is, falling
asleep under God's governmental hand), 1 John 5. 17, and as such
the man could be prayed for unto repentance, 2 Cor. 2. 5–11. The
Lord Jesus also spoke of this solemn act in Matthew 18. 15–18. The
last resource was assembly action, the man becoming "as an
heathen man and a publican" to the one trespassed against, v. 17.
That is, the man would be counted as unsaved, and hence on the
outside, being bound by the whole assembly, v. 18. Moreover, when
accomplished under these solemn divine principles, the Lord being
with the gathered assembly, the act would be recognised as binding
even by the occupants of heaven. Similarly, when restoration was
brought about in the soul of the man on the outside, the assembly
could loose its original decision with the Lord's authority, and this
again would be owned in heaven. Although the man would be on
the outside, untouched by the direct pastoral care of the assembly,
yet if the sin was not unto death, the assembly could pray for him,
and since the Lord would be there with the saints, this prayer would
be heard, v. 19–20. By this means, the saints could still interest
themselves in the need of the one on the outside, following the
example of the Lord who befriended such publicans and sinners to
call them to repentance, Mark 2. 15–17.

Chapter 4, verse 21, properly belongs to this present chapter. The sin is
so grave, that the apostolic rod would have to be used to excommunicate
the one who had sinned. Love and the spirit of meekness can still be
shown even when the rod is necessary: "For whom the Lord loveth He
chasteneth, and scourgeth every son whom He receiveth", Heb. 12. 6.

Exposition of 1 Cor. 5: Unsanctified Conduct

1 It is reported commonly *that there is* fornication among you, and such fornication, as is not so much as named among the Gentiles, that one should have his father's wife.

2 And ye are puffed up, and have not rather mourned, that he that hath done this deed might be taken away from among you.

3 For I verily, as absent in body, but present in spirit, have judged already, as though I were present, *concerning* him that hath so done this deed,

4 In the name of our Lord Jesus Christ, when ye are gathered together, and my spirit, with the power of our Lord Jesus Christ,

5 To deliver such an one unto Satan for the destruction of the flesh, that the spirit may be saved in the day of the Lord Jesus.

6 Your glorying *is* not good. Know ye not that a little leaven leaveneth the whole lump?

7 Purge out therefore the old leaven, that ye may be a new lump, as ye are unleavened. For even Christ our passover is sacrificed for us:

8 Therefore let us keep the feast, not with old leaven, neither with the leaven of malice and wickedness; but with the unleavened *bread* of sincerity and truth.

9 I wrote unto you in an epistle not to company with fornicators:

10 Yet not altogether with the fornicators of this world, or with the covetous, or extortioners, or with idolaters; for then must ye needs go out of the world.

11 But now I have written unto you not to keep company, if any man that is called a brother be a fornicator, or covetous, or an idolater, or a railer, or a drunkard, or an extortioner; with such an one no not to eat.

12 For what have I to do to judge them also that are without? do not ye judge them that are within?

13 But them that are without God judgeth. Therefore put away from among yourselves that wicked person.

1. The existence of this sin in Corinth was commonly (or universally) known, and it was reported to Paul as the previous weakness had been, 1.11. The facts had been declared through two or three witnesses, Matt. 18. 16; Deut. 17. 6, enabling Paul to act upon them.

We have here a sin of a brother in the assembly with his stepmother, as "his father's wife" must be interpreted. Evidently there was danger in a household when the things of God did not have first place; see Gen. 39. 7; 2 Sam. 11. 2. The law itself had been emphatic against this particular sin; see Lev. 18. 6, 8; Deut. 27. 20; 22. 22; Amos 2. 7. Regarding this sin, the Lord's mind was fixed for all time—under law and under grace, and hence the reference to it in the letter in Acts 15. 29. This sin is used in the O.T. as an illustration of the departure of Israel from her God. Jeremiah's prophecy is full of this departure; judgment into captivity resulted, but with final restoration in view, Jer. 33 . 10–18. See also Hebrews 3. 12.

2. The assembly was apparently unconcerned at such misconduct in their midst. They took no action to expel the brother involved, perhaps because he was too important, too wealthy, too influential, so that they did not want to bring him to book. Moreover, the effect of the sin was not only confined to the man; it was also seen in the morbid and frivolous self-conceit of the untroubled assembly conscience. This was no display of love, for love could not be "puffed up", 13. 4.

3. Paul realised that he could not do anything *personally* in this matter, since he was "absent in body". But he regarded himself as being present "in spirit". This was not day-dreaming, neither was he visualising what he would have done had he been present. Rather he considered that his apostolic *authority* was present in Corinth. Elsewhere, he had never met the Colossian church, Col. 2. 1, but he was with them "in the spirit, joying and beholding your order, and the stedfastness of your faith in Christ", 2.5. Here, the apostolic *satisfaction* was present in Colosse. See 1 Thessalonians 2. 17, where the apostolic *affection* was present.

Paul had already judged the situation. This is in no sense contrary to Matthew 7. 1–2, "Judge not that ye be not judged. For with what judgment ye judge, ye shall be judged". But Paul, in his judgment, followed the precepts of the Lord in John 7. 24, "judge righteous judgment". Such a principle of judgment would indeed reflect back upon himself, since he would appear before "the Lord, the righteous judge", 2 Tim. 4. 8.

4. Additionally, Paul would have the assembly take the necessary position of Matthew 18. 20, "*in the name of* our Lord Jesus Christ", when gathered together to deal with this matter. Gathering and acting in His name means that their actions were to be `as good as if He Himself had done them. See Col. 3. 17. "With the power of our Lord Jesus Christ" implies that it must be His outworking of discipline in the assembly that should be seen. If the assembly gathering merely produces a display of the flesh, then surely any decision is invalid. Again, Paul stresses the apostolic presence in spirit, in order to ensure that all should be done according to the divine intention.

5. The outcome would be excommunication. Paul knew this to start with. There could be no argument nor counter-argument. As already stated above, "unto Satan" means the sphere of his rule outside the sphere of assembly fellowship. "The destruction of the flesh" does not mean physical death, but rather that, since the body of sin has been destroyed, a believer should learn to reckon himself to be dead indeed unto sin, Rom. 6. 6, 11. This would imply true repentence on the outside of assembly fellowship, and this would be the first step towards restoration. In any case, the spirit would be saved in the day of the Lord Jesus, that is, before His judgment seat. This is grace abounding, but the prospect of grace in that day does not absolve saints who now fall, from submitting themselves to the practical discipline of an assembly.

6. The Corinthians were boasting in this open sin known in their midst, no doubt satisfied that everyone else was morally pure. But, given time, a little leaven could leaven the whole lump, and one sin could affect the whole company before long. In the O.T., many kings adopted an evil pathway, and most of the people rapidly followed them. Even "small" forms of sin are attractive to others, and, like germs, multiplication rapidly follows until all is leavened. Similarly, the inroads of false doctrine, Gal. 5. 9, and the rise of false and foreign methods in service, germinate and proceed in the same downward direction. How the saints should be watchful, seeking to strengthen the things that remain, lest Satan gain an advantage over us !

7. Hence the "old leaven" must go. In this case, it refers to the man in fornication and to the boasting of the Corinthians. The "old leaven" *may* consist of men, but more likely it would consist of boasting, pride, foreign methods, private interpretations and carnality, Matt. 15. 19. When such is eliminated, with all its expansive tendencies of growth and infiltration, nothing but a "new lump" remains, characterised by unleavened conditions. Such is the work of the Spirit in the heart. In the O.T., the porters at the gates of the house of the Lord kept out all that was unclean, 2 Chron. 23. 19. In many restorations, the house was purged of all uncleaness brought in by previous kings, 2 Chron. 29. 1–19; 2 Kings 23. 4–20.

8. Paul's reference to the typology of the passover goes far beyond the O.T. ceremony. Paul does not dwell on the ceremony; he names "Christ our passover" immediately. The sacrifice of Christ as the true Passover Lamb is visualised. The important point in Paul's argument is that the passover was followed by the days of the feast of unleavened bread; see Exod. 12. 1–20; Lev. 23. 5–8; Num. 28. 16–25; Deut. 16. 3–8. The application of the sacrifice of the Lord to our salvation forms a new beginning for the soul; "old things are passed away; behold, all things are become new". 2 Cor. 5. 17. Thus the Lord gave Himself "that He might deliver us from this present evil world", Gal. 1. 4. Similarly, in 1 Peter 1. 18–21, referring to the precious blood of Christ, as of a Lamb without blemish and without spot, we have been redeemed from our vain conversation (manner of life) that characterised us in times past. After faith rests in the Passover Lamb, life is different from that which preceded it. This life constitutes "the feast" of 1 Corinthians 5. 8; there is no *reference* to the Lord's supper here as a feast. The point is that nothing that had been prepared in Egypt before the passover was to be taken out with the children of Israel with their wilderness journey. Exodus 12. 39 shows that they had not been able to prepare any victual in Egypt, so *unleavened* cakes had to be baked in the wilderness. If they had baked leavened cakes, prior preparation would have been made in Egypt for the *leavening* process, and God would not allow this. Pre-conversion conduct is not suitable for the people of God. "Malice and wickedness" corresponds to this pre-conversion conduct, and if this is imported into the christian life and into the assembly, it can but bring forth further fruit of its own kind. Rather,

the new life in Christ is in "sincerity and truth".

9–11. Verse 9, "I wrote unto you in an epistle not to company with fornicators" suggests, in its English guise, that Paul had written a previous Epistle on the subject, and that in verse 11, "But now I have written unto you . . .", he adds to this previous epistle. But this is not the intended meaning at all. Other expositors interpret verse 9 to mean, "I have already written in this epistle", since "an epistle" should read "the epistle" according to the Greek text. But then these expositors run into difficulties, since no reference to this subject in the previous verses of this Epistle is to be found.

The point is that the Greek tense for "I wrote", v. 9, and for "I have written", v. 11, is one and the same, namely the aorist, *egrapsa*. There is no thought here of what he *had done*; both verbs refer to the same situation, namely to the letter he was actually writing. Such a verbal situation is called "the epistolary aorist". "The writer of a letter sometimes puts himself in the place of his readers, and describes as past an action which is present to himself, but which will be past to his readers when they receive the letter. The present is used in English."*

There are two exhortations:

    (a) *General*: not to keep company with fornicators—in the world. Saints are "in the world" but not "of the world", John 17. 14–16. And although we must rub shoulders with such sinners listed here (else we must needs go out of the world), yet we are exhorted to avoid fellowship with them. "Friendship of the world is enmity with God", James 4. 4.

    (b) *Special*: not to keep company with a brother in fellowship, who falls by embracing the sins characteristic of "a fornicator, or covetous, or an idolater, or a railer, or a drunkard, or an extortioner". One would judge that this list is not complete. But let brethren be very careful what they add to this list to meet present exigencies. A passing tiff between brethren, or a dispute on a subtle point of doctrine, or even the party-spirit manifested in chapters 1–4, provide no ground at all for adding such weaknesses to the list here demanding excommunication. "No not to eat" refers to common fellowship over a daily meal. Both assembly life and daily life are solemnly embraced. Unfortunately some have practised this solemn act, supposedly in the name of the Lord Jesus, for reasons outside those even imagined by the apostle here. Individual life, home life and assembly life have been broken up and ruined thereby. Hence, let brethren be very very careful when they exercise this prerogative of discipline.

12–13. The apostle cannot judge those who are *without* the assembly. God will judge them *then*, in that great day of judgment; "whoremongers and adulterers God will judge", Heb. 13. 4. Their part will be in the "lake

---

* A Short Syntax of New Testament Greek, H.P.V. Nunn; p. 70.

which burneth with fire and brimstone", Rev. 21. 8; such will be "without" the city, Rev. 22. 14–15.

But judgment of evil *within* must be accomplished by the assembly *now*, and the conclusion is, "put away from among yourselves that wicked person". Paul did not write harshly, but that he "might know the proof of you, whether ye be obedient in all things", 2 Cor. 2. 9. Moreover, he wrote "not for his cause that had done the wrong, nor for his cause that suffered wrong, but that our care for you in the sight of God might appear unto you", 7. 12. The assembly as a whole repented of their own puffed up attitude towards this sin, 7. 9–11. The man on the outside had repented, so the Corinthians could confirm their love toward him, 2. 8, with forgiveness, v. 10. Such forgiveness would be "in the person of Christ", v. 10. He forgives when there is repentance, and we cannot do less if we do all things in His name.

Various incidental matters arise from the subject matter of this chapter, and Paul deals with these in chapter 6.

1 CORINTHIANS 6

Section 3.   The Saints' Conduct
Subject 2.   Sanctified Conduct

Relationship of this Chapter to Section 3

The essential subject matter of the previous chapter was three-fold:
1.   the sin of fornication, 5. 1–6;
2.   the unleavened life after conversion, 5. 7–8;
3.   principles of judgment, 5. 9–13.

In chapter 6, Paul dwells further on these three subjects in the reverse order. The three paragraphs are:

Verses 1–8: principles of judgment—who judges, the saints or unbelievers?

Verses 9–13a: the unleavened life after conversion—practical conduct;

Verses 13b–20: flee fornication—the spiritual union.

The chapter proceeds largely by questions; compare 9. 4–13; 12. 29–30. Here, for example, "know ye not" occurs five times, vv. 2, 3, 9, 15, 19. The conscience is reached by such questions that demand an answer from the one questioned.

Exposition of 1 Cor. 6: Sanctified Conduct

Verses 1–8: Principles of Judgment

1 Dare any of you, having a matter against another, go to law before the unjust, and not before the saints?
2 Do ye not know that the saints shall judge the world? and if the world shall be judged by you, are ye unworthy to judge the smallest matters?
3 Know ye not that we shall judge angels? how much more things that pertain to this life?
4 If then ye have judgments of things pertaining to this life, set them to judge who are least esteemed in the church.
5 I speak to your shame. Is it so, that there is not a wise man among you? no, not one that shall be able to judge between his brethren?
6 But brother goeth to law with brother, and that before the unbelievers.
7 Now therefore there is utterly a fault among you, because ye go to law one with another. Why do ye not rather take wrong? why do ye not rather *suffer yourselves to* be defrauded?
8 Nay, ye do wrong, and defraud, and that *your* brethren.

1. At the end of the previous chapter, Paul had noted that believers could not judge evil *without* the assembly, but that they should judge evil *within* the assembly. But what judgment was within the scope of the unbelievers without, namely the unjust? Certainly they could judge those without. The Greek and Roman law permitted the settlement of disputes before the tribunals of heathen magistrates. The powers that be are declared to be ministers of God in this respect, executing wrath upon those that do evil, Rom. 13. 4; 1 Pet. 2. 11–15. But should such outsiders judge between brethren within?

Hence Paul exposes the situation in Corinth, where a dispute between brethren was taken for settlement before the tribunals of men. Paul's contention is that, in matters both of sin and of mutual dispute, brethren *within* are competent to judge.

2–3. In the day yet to come, saints will be competent to judge both the world and angels. Certainly, then, they should be mature enough to judge between brother and brother now. Even in the O.T., this had been so, Exod. 18. 21; such men were "able men, such as fear God, men of truth, hating covetousness". See, also, Deut. 16. 18–20. Solomon was particularly wise in his dealings with disputes amongst his people, 1 Kings 3. 16–28.

　　The saints shall judge the world. They will be associated with Christ in that day—He will have the supreme authority in judgment. Today, believers have no standing in the world; their Lord is rejected. But in that day, the Lord will be vindicated, His rule and authority will be universally owned, and saints will enjoy a "position", namely "with Christ". We may note the following Scriptures:

　　　　Psalm 49. 14, "The upright shall have dominion over them in the morning".

　　　　Daniel 7. 22, "Judgment was given to the saints of the most High; and the time came that the saints possessed the kingdom".

　　　　Malachi 4. 3, "Ye shall tread down the wicked; for they shall be ashes under the soles of your feet".

　　　　Matthew 19. 28, "Ye which have followed Me, in the regeneration when the Son of man shall sit in the throne of His glory, ye also shall sit upon twelve thrones, judging the twelve tribes of Israel". See Luke 22. 30.

　　　　Matthew 25. 21, "I will make thee ruler over many things".

　　　　2 Timothy 2. 12, "If we suffer, we shall also reign with Him".

　　　　Revelation 2. 26–27, "To him will I give power over the nations: and he shall rule them with a rod of iron". See Psalm 2. 9.

　　We shall judge angels. The angels that sinned are reserved unto judgment, 2 Pet. 2. 4; Jude 6. The association of the saints in their judgment is not hinted at in these two passages, but Paul asserts this fact here. We are in contact with such powers now, Eph. 6. 12, as we wrestle using the whole armour of God, and to these is made known by the church the manifold wisdom of God, Eph. 3. 10. If such powers are contrary to us now, it is the purpose of God that the tables will be turned in that day.

4. There are two ways of understanding this verse, namely, when disputes arise and have to be settled "set them to judge who are least esteemed in the church".

1. The verb may be taken as an ironical imperative, meaning that, since we shall be thoroughly competent in that day to judge these great matters, then the very *least amongst the saints* now should be able to deal with matters trivial in comparison.

2. The R.V. "Do ye set them to judge who are of no account in the church?" employs an interrogative rather than an imperative verb. The New English Bible also adopts this sense. That is, Paul asks in astonishment how possibly they can seek judgment from *outsiders*, these being implied by the description "of no account in the church".

The first interpretation is preferable, but one need not be dogmatic; the trend of the argument is clear without taking a decision as to the exact meaning of verse 4.

5. This verse supports the first interpretation of verse 4. The Corinthians lacked maturity; this was to their shame. It would seem that no wise brother (following after Exodus 18. 21 but with the mind of Christ) could be found, with respected authority and wise ability to judge between two brethren.

6. The reasons why brethren appeared before the heathen tribunals are two-fold:

1. *The lack of their own spirituality.* They had the strange feeling that better justice would be done by these outsiders than by those within. They would not desire to submit themselves to the judgment of one within.

2. *The lack of spirituality in the assembly.* Wise men had not emerged in the assembly, who would have the respect of any who might get involved in a dispute.

7. However, whatever reason there was for this situation in Corinth, it was wrong. If there was no remedy in the assembly, it would be better to "take wrong". If a brother thought he had been wronged financially by another, it would be better for him to suffer the loss if the only way for amends to be made was by seeking arbitration without. The latter course could not be for the advancement of the testimony of the assembly in Corinth. "For this is thankworthy, if a man for conscience toward God endure grief, suffering wrongfully", 1 Pet. 2. 19.

Two wrongs do not make a right—the brother A by his act of defrauding another brother B, and the act of brother B in bringing the matter before the heathen tribunal.

8. "Ye do wrong, and defraud" is a statement of the sin that brought about this apparent necessity for arbitration. The Lord Jesus had anticipated this in the sermon on the mount: "I say unto you, That ye resist not evil", Matt. 5. 39. Going to law before the unjust is resisting evil. But God will deal with those who perpetuate the evil in due time. A brother will not remain wronged for ever ! But, if a brother who has sinned does not make amends by his own repentance, then the only allowed method of arbitration is to be found amongst the saints. This, at least, is not resisting evil in the sense implied by the Lord Jesus.

Verses 9–13a: The Unleavened Life after Conversion

9 Know ye not that the unrighteous shall not inherit the kingdom of God? Be not deceived: neither fornicators, not idolaters, nor adulterers, nor effeminate, nor abusers of themselves with mankind,
10 Nor thieves, nor covetous, nor drunkards, nor revilers, not extortioners, shall inherit the kingdom of God.
11 And such were some of you: but ye are washed, but ye are sanctified, but ye are justified in the name of the Lord Jesus, and by the Spirit of our God.
12 All things are lawful unto me, but all things are not expedient: all things are lawful for me, but I will not be brought under the power of any.
13 Meats for the belly, and the belly for meats: but God shall destroy both it and them.

9–10. Paul now provides a list of unholy activities that characterise the lives of the unsaved. He writes to contrast the conduct of the believer with that of the unrighteous. The list embraces sins that were prevalent in his day; others could be added today. It is reminiscent of the apostle's more extensive treatment in Romans 1. 18–32, where he deals with "all ungodliness and unrighteousness of men", v. 18. Moral, natural and religious evils are described, and the apostle's contention is that such unbelievers cannot "inherit the kingdom of God". The kingdom of God would be the great moral realm under the rule of God, being far wider than the kingdom of the Lord Jesus yet to be established openly in this world. The kingdom of God is "righteousness, and peace, and joy in the Holy Ghost", Rom. 14. 17. Flesh and blood cannot inherit it, 1 Cor. 15. 50; those which do the works of the flesh shall not inherit the kingdom of God, Gal. 5. 21.

These two verses definitely refer to the unsaved. Believers are contrasted with them in the following verse. The state described resembles Egypt; nothing of Egypt should be taken over into the Christian life. Alas, that Paul had to write verse 5. 11: the very sins of the unrighteous could also be found in "any man that is called a brother". The leaven without had been working within.

11. This verse describes the change from Egyptian conditions to the atmosphere of the wilderness where God was found with His separated people. "And such were some of you" is no morbid recollection of the past. It is good to recall this occasionally, Eph. 2. 1–3, 11; 1 Tim. 1. 13, so that the work of God in the soul may stand out the more in pure unleavened conditions.

Their present state and standing are described as follows:

Ye are washed, or rather, "ye washed yourselves" or "ye had yourselves washed", since the Greek middle aorist is used. The English present tense "are" in all three verbs conveys the wrong meaning; this would have translated the Greek perfect tense had it been used. This verb *apolouo* appears on only one other occasion in the N.T., namely in Acts 22. 16, "Arise, and be baptized, and wash away thy sins, calling on the name of the Lord", the verb "wash away" being in the middle aorist imperative. The practical side of baptism, then, may be suggested, namely the stand taken by a believer in putting away the past in order henceforth to live for Christ. This is the practical side of entering upon an unleavened life, and our *state* is described by how far this truth has its expression in our conduct.

Ye are sanctified, or "ye were sanctified", R.V. This refers to the act of God, to the gracious power of God in Christ at conversion, when the believer is set apart to God once for all; see Hebrews 10. 10, 14. This work is absolute. The believer's *standing* rests upon this divine work in the soul. Practical holiness follows, 1 Pet. 1. 15–16, and should be seen throughout life, but this is relative. Certainly it was not being manifested in Corinth.

Ye are justified, or "ye were justified", R.V. Again, this is the work of God accomplished in unworthy souls that are not only born of God but stand acquitted before Him of all charge, through the work of Christ, Rom. 3. 24–31. The work of the Spirit makes these great truths real to the soul, 1 Cor. 2. 10–12, but it is the Lord Jesus Himself who made it possible for such blessings to be distributed. Faith in His name brings these blessings to the believer at conversion, Acts 3. 16.

12–13a Having been placed by grace in unleavened conditions, and having taken a stand in testimony at baptism to desire only unleavened things, what more can the believer do? Conduct is not to be assessed by what is *legitimate* but by what is *profitable.* "All things are lawful unto me" cannot refer to things not legitimate, such as verses 9–10. This question of all things being "lawful" is dealt with again in 9. 20–22; 10. 23. By itself the lawfulness of an action is no guiding light for conduct. That would be little better than the law itself. Leaven was lawful apart from the days of unleavened bread, but Paul would be more careful than that. Rather, is such lawful conduct "expedient" or "profitable", and that essentially for others? The Lord Jesus never did what was not profitable, so neither should the believer.

Paul would not have his life dominated by influences, customs, traditions, daily necessities. These can exercise a power over some, so that they can be entangled in circumstances, rather than abiding in the liberty of the love of Christ whereby we are made free. For example, daily food is a necessity that Paul would not deny, but its use was only temporal. Nevertheless, with a wrong outlook on life, its preparation can be a stumblingblock, Luke 10. 40, and partaking of it can likewise be a snare, if a person is marked by greed and over-indulgence.

Verses 13b–20: The Spiritual Union

13 Now the body *is* not for fornication, but for the Lord; and the Lord for the body.
14 And God hath both raised up the Lord, and will also raise up us by his own power.
15 Know ye not that your bodies are the members of Christ? shall I then take the members of Christ, and make *them* the members of an harlot? God forbid.
16 What? know ye not that he which is joined to an harlot is one body? for two, saith he, shall be one flesh.
17 But he that is joined unto the Lord is one spirit.
18 Flee fornication. Every sin that a man doeth is without the body; but he that committeth fornication sinneth against his own body.
19 What? know ye not that your body is the temple of the Holy Ghost *which is* in you, which ye have of God, and ye are not your own?
20 For ye are bought with a price: therefore glorify God in your body, and in your spirit, which are God's.

13b–14. Paul now discusses a momentous subject, namely the *present* position of the human body in the economy of God. The subject is the exact antithesis of fornication which the apostle still has before his mind. At the same time, it is an essentially personal subject. To read the assembly and the body of Christ into "The body is . . . for the Lord; and the Lord for the body" is to confuse the structure of the Epistle and the argument of the apostle. The corporate body is treated in chapter 12.

We usually tend to think that the physical body is the property of the inner self, which therefore has control both of its functions and activity. But this is a self-centered materialistic attitude indeed. All things— including our own bodies—were made by the Lord; for His pleasure they exist and were created, Rev. 4. 11. At the fall, death came in, and the body would return to dust, Gen. 3. 19. In spite of this, the sanctified mind in O.T. days could discern that the body was "fearfully and wonderfully made", Ps. 139. 14. But the value of the body was only seen in its true light when Christ came; His body was "that holy thing" Luke 1. 35, and in that holy body God could see a life divine here below for His glory. Thus God can now take fresh pleasure in His creation when bought by the blood of Christ and indwelt by the Holy Spirit. See Rom. 12. 1; 1 Thess. 4. 4; 5. 23.

How much greater will be His pleasure when He sees us changed into the likeness of His glory, Rom. 8. 11; Phil. 3. 21, when we share the triumph of His resurrection, 2 Cor. 4. 14. The body is for the Lord as His possession, and the Lord is for the body to achieve His future purposes. It is a great thought that the power of God wrought in Christ at His resurrection, Eph. 1. 20, is the same power still available for the resurrection of the saints. God will not suddenly take an interest in the body then; rather His interest then shows that He has an interest now.

15. Our bodies are declared to be the members of Christ. This truth is distinct from other similar passages:
> In chapter 12, we are members of His body, v. 27, in the sense that He is the Head, controlling the spiritual gifts of the saints who represent Him in this scene in *service*.
> In Ephesians 5. 30, "We are members of His body" refers to the saints as a distinct assembly, yet united to Christ, the marriage union being used as a type of what is involved. The assembly is seen as a *bride*.
> But in 1 Corinthians 6. 15, our actual bodies are seen as the members of Christ, and the context relates to *conduct* in the sense that "the life also of Jesus might be made manifest in our body", 2 Cor. 4. 10. See Gal. 2. 20.

16. It should be unthinkable for such a holy union to be marred by introducing a third party—the harlot. Could any brother engage in such an activity? Could he not realise that this is equivalent to putting Christ in contact with the harlot? Certainly the brother and the harlot would be one flesh; Genesis 2. 24 is quoted to prove this. "God forbid" or "May it not be" exclaims Paul, using in Greek the optative mood (expressing a wish) of the verb "to become" without an explicit subject. The A.V. translators have provided the suggested subject "God", though some have felt that this suggestion introduces His name where it does not occur explicitly in the Greek. This expression is used fourteen times in Paul's Epistles.

17. The union of the saints with the Lord is spiritual. In marriage, the union is regarded as "one flesh". But when we are united to the Lord, when His life is seen in our life, when He uses our bodies to display His virtues, this is regarded as "one spirit". Any other thought would be carnal, showing that one must be careful in one's thinking.

19–20. Finally two positive arguments are given as to why one should be very careful indeed about the inner functioning of one's own body .
> 1. *The body is the temple of the Holy Ghost.* In the N.T., the idea of the temple usually refers to the assembly, 1 Cor. 3. 10, 16, 17; Eph. 2. 21–22; 1 Tim. 3. 15. But here, one's individual body is seen as the dwelling place of the Holy Spirit, in keeping with the promised truth of John 14. 17. The Holy Spirit has been freely given us by God. Hence, every act of the body, of seeing, hearing, feeling, thinking, experiencing, tasting, must be regulated with this truth in mind. He knows all, not only because He is on high, but also because He dwells within.

2. *Ye are not your own.* Everything about a believer has been
    purchased, at the cost of the life laid down, the blood shed, of the
    Lord Jesus Christ. We are "a people for God's own possession", 1
    Pet. 2. 9 R.V. Hence, any thought of "self-possession" cannot be
    allowed. We do not belong to ourselves, since He has taken
    possession.

These two reasons should compel us to "glorify God in your body, and
in your spirit, which are God's". The "body" refers to the manifested
conduct, while the "spirit" refers to the motives behind the conduct. We
glorify Him when we walk according to the principles laid down in this
chapter. If we are submissive to Him, He will "Make you perfect in every
good work to do His will, working in you that which is well pleasing in His
sight, through Jesus Christ; to whom be glory for ever and ever", Heb. 13.
21.

1 CORINTHIANS 7

Section 4.   Christian Liberty
Subject 1.   Marriage and Service

Summary of Section 4

There now follows a section dealing with Christian liberty, and the four chapters in the section embrace the following topics:
    Chapter 7: marriage and service;
    Chapter 8: partaking of meats offered to idols (with believers);
    Chapter 9: living of the gospel;
    Chapter 10: partaking of meats offered to idols (with unbelievers).
Where there is liberty, there is no legislation, but there is a call for wise exercise before the Lord as to the attitude one should adopt in such circumstances.

Background of this Subject

In chapter 7, we find commands, principles and advice given to believers living in an age and a city with conditions very different from those of today in general outlook and state of morality. It may well be that a few of the verses do not apply directly to conditions that pertain to today's circumstances, but that does not mean that the chapter as a whole is irrelevant or not suitable for the careful study of the Lord's people presently.

We must indeed bear in mind the need for sanctified modesty in discussing things like these, but we must avoid giving the impression that they can properly be restricted to a corner. This is apparent when comparing what is said on these matters in ministry in local assemblies with what is openly promulgated at such length and frequency by the world outside.

The chapter is divided into three main sections:

1.   Verses 2–11 deal with apostolic *advice*, v. 6, and divine *commands*, v. 10, concerning marriage. The "commandments of the Lord" characterised most of Paul's writings—these commandments consisted not of repeating the verbal teaching of the Lord Jesus in second-hand form, but by special inspiration, as in 11. 23 and 1 Thessalonians 4. 15.
2.   Verses 12–24 deal with apostolic *instruction*, verses 12, 17, regarding mixed marriages.
3.   Verses 25–40 provide apostolic *advice*, v. 25, to those who were unmarried, regarding service.

It should be pointed out that Paul does not deal with the case of those who remain unmarried because a suitable partner in the Lord is not

available in their own circles. It is recognised that this prevails in some
assemblies today.

We should note that

(a)   to disregard the Lord's *command* is sin and spiritual failure;
(b)   to disregard apostolic *instruction* implies lack of wisdom and
        spiritual barrenness;
(c)   to disregard apostolic *advice* shows a lack of exercise towards
        service, but there is at least no question of sin in this latter case,
        v. 36.

In interpreting this chapter, faith knows that neither Scripture nor Paul
is contradictory on any subject. Hence positive teaching on Christian
marriage elsewhere in Scripture is not contradicted here by the apostle
Paul. We may therefore use other passages of Scripture to support our
interpretation here.

The difference in characteristics of the male and the female is
fundamental in God's creation of the wide range of life on earth. In
Genesis 1, we have the fruit of the earth, vv. 11–13, the animal kingdom,
vv. 20–25, and man, vv. 26–28. Such were to be fruitful, and to multiply
"after his kind". Such a process of reproduction of the original requires
male and female characteristics. Thus Paul observes in 1 Corinthians 12.
24 that "God hath tempered the body together, having given more
abundant honour to that part which lacked", namely to those
physiological processes concerned with the maintenance of life according
to His pattern. Let us seek to realise that we have our existence now not
only because of God's original creation but because of His continual
perpetuation of it. This applies both naturally and spiritually, as the Lord
said, "That which is born of the flesh is flesh; and that which is born of the
Spirit is spirit", John 3. 6; see also John 1. 13.

The Lord Jesus refers to this original creative act in Matthew 19. 4–6,
"Have ye not read, that He which made them at the beginning made them
male and female, . . . Wherefore they are no more twain, but one flesh.
What therefore God hath joined together, let not man put asunder".
Similarly in Ephesians 5. 31, Genesis 2. 24 is quoted with the comment,
"This is a great mystery: but I speak concerning Christ and the church".
The creatorial work of God is maintained in this scene as long as man has
existence here, and at the same time it is a fitting figure of the greater
spiritual and eternal purposes of God concerning Christ and the church.

In 1 Corinthians 7, Paul elevates the marriage union above the heathen
practices and customs of Corinth and the nations around. The chapter
must be understood in the light of this. We admit that some verses cause
difficulty at a casual reading. Moreover difficulties in exposition arise
because of the translation in various verses. It is to help the Lord's people
to rise above a casual reading that we write these lines.

It might appear that Paul is discouraging marriage altogether, and some
writers—usually those seeking to discredit Paul and the Scriptures
generally—emphatically assert that this is what Paul is doing. At the

outset, we would observe that Paul, by advice and *not* by command, discourages marriage for *one* reason only, at the end of the chapter. Through not observing what this one reason is, even believers often experience difficulty in fitting into this chapter the teaching of the rest of Scripture. The act of unbelievers in seeking to generalise, and extend Paul's remarks to include everybody, is a sign of the latter times, when "some shall depart from the faith, . . ., forbidding to marry", 1 Tim. 4. 1–3. Such insinuations are equivalent to giving heed to seducing spirits and doctrines of devils. Hence it is very necessary to "put the brethren in remembrance of these things", v. 6.

Those who misrepresent Paul in 1 Corinthians 7 also do so elsewhere. They would quote the blessedness of the hundred and forty four thousand on mount Sion in Revelation 14. 4 who were "not defiled with women, for they are virgins (males)", seeking thereby to deduce some impurity in the marriage relation. What lack of reading and understanding! It only means that they were not defiled with the fruit of the great whore, Babylon the great, Rev. 17. 1–6. The reference is entirely symbolic, in no way debasing the marriage union, as Hebrews 13. 4 shows, "Marriage is honourable in all, and the bed undefiled". Neither does 1 Corinthians 7. 34 "holy in body" (speaking of an unmarried woman) imply any unholiness in body if married. Rather Paul implies that she is set apart for special service in body and spirit. It is merely a special application of Romans 12. 1, "present your bodies a living sacrifice, holy, acceptable unto God". A married person may also demonstrate such a character.

Even the apostles had once thought "It is not good to marry", Matt. 19. 10. This remarkable observation was made before the Spirit was given, yet after following the Lord and being much instructed by Him. In the context, the apostles suggested this in order to avoid sin in *married life*. By contrast in 1 Corinthians 7. 2, Paul suggests marriage to avoid sin in the *unmarried life*.

The Lord's answer to the apostles' strange idea extends natural Jewish thoughts on this subject to a spiritual level. In His answer in Matthew 19. 11, 12, He lists three classes who cannot effectively marry.

1.   Eunuchs born thus naturally.
2.   Eunuchs made thus artificially. These two classes are marred physically in their functions, and hence were not allowed to enter into the congregation of the Lord, Deut. 23. 1. The actual word eunuch may also mean "court officer", as was Potiphar the master of Joseph in Egypt, Gen. 39. 1. In Acts 8. 27 both meanings are probably intended. He was returning through the desert frustrated with banishment from full worship in Jerusalem. He was then brought *in by grace* although kept *out by law*.
3.   The Lord extends these two Jewish concepts, by observing that there are some eunuchs, although normal physically, "which have made themselves eunuchs for the kingdom of heaven's sake". These obviously form a special class called apart for special

service, and it can refer only to them "to whom it is given", Matt. 19. 11. Peter was married, Luke 4. 38, so an apostle could be outside this class. Paul has this particular class in view in the last section of 1 Corinthians 7. Yet we shall see that there is a perfect balance between the call of God and one's own exercise in the whole matter.

Exposition of 1 Cor. 7: Marriage and Service

Verses 1–11: Regarding the Marriage Relation

1 Now concerning the things whereof ye wrote unto me: *It is* good for a man not to touch a woman.
2 Nevertheless, *to avoid* fornication, let every man have his own wife, and let every woman have her own husband.
3 Let the husband render unto the wife due benevolence: and likewise also the wife unto the husband.
4 The wife hath not power of her own body, but the husband: and likewise also the husband hath not power of his own body, but the wife.
5 Defraud ye not one the other, except *it be* with consent for a time, that ye may give yourselves to fasting and prayer: and come together again, that Satan tempt you not for your incontinency.
6 But I speak this by permission, *and* not of commandment.
7 For I would that all men were even as I myself. But every man hath his proper gift of God, one after this manner, and another after that.
8 I say therefore to the unmarried and widows, it is good for them if they abide even as I.
9 But if they cannot contain, let them marry: for it is better to marry than to burn.
10 And unto the married I command, *yet* not I, but the Lord, Let not the wife depart from *her* husband:
11 But and if she depart, let her remain unmarried, or be reconciled to *her* husband: and let not the husband put away *his* wife.

1. The introduction: Paul now deals with marriage in order to contrast the christian concept with the laxity amongst the population around, since such errors could be found in the assembly then. Similarly today, immediately after conversion, the common practices of the world may still exist in the life of young believers. Exhortation is needed today as well as in Paul's day, although the prevalent sin may be different. Nowadays, one might quote the dangerous appetite in some young converts for entertainment of all sorts provided by the ungodly in the world. In Ephesians 5. 3, Paul warns against dangers such as fornication even in those appreciating Christ as "a sweetsmelling savour". In those days in Corinth, conversion did not imply an immediate abandoning of the common worldly practices. The moral change was low even though they had been baptised. Constant instruction in the matter was needed.

Although we regard chapter 7 as starting a new section, there is a sense in which the actual subject follows on from the previous two chapters. Chapter 5 had dealt with a particular *internal* case of the sin of fornication in a brother, and verse 11 had concluded with a general principle regarding fellowship with a brother in such cases. Chapter 6 verse 9 had given a general statement regarding the position of *outsiders* with reference to such sin. To conclude, Paul had asserted in verses 13–20 the spiritual superiority of the body for the Lord and not for gross sin. The highest point is reached in the last two verses, that the body belongs to God and that it is the temple of the Holy Spirit. Paul now quotes the Corinthians' statement made in a letter, "It is good for a man not to touch a woman", similar to Matthew 19. 10. They could not discern the proper course for a Christian in a scene of abounding evil, so they confused complete abstention with a form of spirituality. Let us not confuse spirituality with abstention from legitimate things today. The black robes worn by certain religious orders suggest that abstention from colour is regarded as superior spirituality. However, God created "all things bright and beautiful", and that is so today in spite of sin. Similarly marriage is just as precious in spite of sin everywhere.

2. From verse 2 to verse 11 Paul deals with marriage in the Lord. The sin of fornication was one of the prevalent sins of nature. This term is used for immorality in general and would embrace among other things the common trend today of pre-marital relationships. It is wider than the term adultery, which is usually restricted to the breaking of the marriage bond, Luke 16. 18. The O.T often uses these concepts to describe the departure of the people from the true God to serve idols. Jeremiah particularly traces this departure in detail, and also shows the path of restoration.

Paul's argument is that, because of these, it is not best to abstain from marriage particularly if the grounds for abstention are that it is more spiritual. Some would say that this is a very low philosophical view of marriage, treating it as a mere safeguard against sin. But Paul is not dealing with a positive spiritual philosophy here; that may be found elsewhere, Eph. 5. 22–33. He is only dealing with certain practical implications.

In the christian profession, God's creatorial purposes in nature continue as in the beginning. The One "upholding all things by the word of His power", Heb. 1. 3, governs His universe uniformly until the end. The sacrifice of Christ did not put away the functioning of His own creation. It rather dealt with the sin surrounding much of it because of the sinfulness of man.

In this verse, Paul goes back to the beginning, namely to the uniqueness of the partners; he stresses "his own wife" and "her own husband". Whatever may have been the conduct of the patriarchs and of the kings in the O.T., whatever may be the doctrine of some cults today, and whatever may be the advice given by so-called experts regarding pre-marital experimentation, yet the purpose of God is clear to all who abide in His word, namely the uniqueness of the partners and the uniqueness of the relationship between them. Paul stresses this again in 1 Timothy 3 verses 2 and 12. Elders and deacons (that is, those who accomplish any service in the assembly) must be husbands "of one wife".

3, 4. The word "benevolence" does not enter into the various editors' texts, and it only appears in the Authorised Version through translation from the Received Text, which of course had no real textual authority. It should read "Render unto the wife her due". This reflects the truth of nourishing and cherishing, Eph. 5. 29. It embraces the mutual care that one partner should have for the other, as "heirs together of the grace of life", 1 Pet. 3. 7. The word "power" means "authority", and shows the selflessness of each partner towards his or her own interests. This mutuality in love, is quite distinct from the complementary truth that "the head of the woman is the man", 1 Cor. 11. 3, and "Wives, submit yourselves unto your own husbands, as it is fit in the Lord", Col. 3. 18. This latter is the permanent order in creation, reflecting on the spiritual constitution of the assembly. In 1 Corinthians 7, however, it is a question of mutual possession. This implies authority over each other, working both ways in the married state. In the spiritual sense chapter 6 verse 20 shows that the Lord's possession also implies His authority.

5. In verses 3 and 4, we have the truth of togetherness, but in verse 5, we find legitimate *untogetherness*. In the former verses, grace enhances the relationship, not weakens it. Yet grace allows mutual separation awhile for special service before the Lord. This is really the safeguard of the chapter. Paul is advocating an unmarried state for some, with a view to special service. But even then, if they marry they do not sin, v. 36. Under these circumstances, for the service to be accomplished, a period of separation by mutual consent before the Lord may be necessary.

The word "defraud" implies "do not deprive yourselves of the blessings of verses 3 and 4". The special service visualised here is one of "fasting and prayer", but the word "fasting" is omitted in the various editors' texts. These and similar exercises are of special importance, and are accomplished either alone or in company with those like-minded. For example,
  (a)   Anna, alone as a widow, "served God with fastings and prayers night and day", Luke 2. 37;
  (b)   the apostles, apart, gave themselves "continually to prayer, and to the ministry of the word", Acts 6. 4;
  (c)   the prophets and teachers at Antioch "ministered to the Lord, . . . and fasted and prayed", Acts 13. 2, 3.

This suggests special service apart even from married life, when one is called to it and when special circumstances demand it. For example, some missionaries, of necessity separated from home, wife and family for a time, know the experience behind this verse. As far as prayer is concerned, however, it is also a matter for home life: "dwell with them . . . that your prayers be not hindered", 1 Pet. 3. 7.

6. "But I speak this by permission, and not of commandment". In the previous four verses there is no commandment either for or against marriage, either for or against special service. Paul is writing by way of "permission", namely making "allowance for circumstances", the only time this word appears in the N.T. There is no legislation in Christian liberty. There must be a harmonious working of one's own exercises with the call of God to service.

7. This is the secret of Paul's whole argument; his desire was that others should be as he was. That is to say, not just to be saved, not just to be called, not just to be unmarried, but that these blessings and positions should be used in special devoted service—a service that could not be accomplished effectively if there were legitimate home and family ties. In this sense, Paul desired that others should be like himself. In Acts 26. 29, he had desired that king Agrippa should be "altogether such as I am" in the matter of salvation. In 1 Thessalonians 2. 8, he had desired to impart to these young saints "not the gospel of God only, but also our own souls", that they should be like him in service while waiting for His Son from heaven. Such desires would have led many into the fellowship of labouring "more abundantly than they all", 1 Cor. 15. 10.

But in spite of his own exercise in the matter, Paul realised that this could take place only in those, according to the Lord's words, "to whom it is given", Matt. 19. 11. He writes, "Every man hath his own proper gift of God, one after this manner, and another after that". "Gifts" are many and various, see chapter 12, and embrace the *ability to serve*. In the present context, however, one feels that it refers to a call to a particular service for every believer. Marriage must fit in to this call. For example, Aquila and Priscilla formed a perfect union in their calling to minister in their own home to the needs of the saints, Acts 18. 26; Rom. 16. 3–5.

Paul, however, desired to have the power to be undividedly for the Lord and His things in his own service and calling. He knew that such special service was blessed, and he wanted more of it in the saints. Nevertheless, our own will in this matter must dovetail with the calling of God. Such a dovetailing is a common feature of Scripture:

> 1 Chronicles 17. 2; David's exercise to build the house of God was in keeping with God's mind revealed later.
> 1 Corinthians 14. 1, 39; Particular spiritual gifts could be desired or coveted, in spite of the fact that it was the divine prerogative to distribute these gifts.
> 1 Timothy 3. 1; Overseership in the assembly could be desired by a qualified brother, although this was ultimately according to the Spirit's call, Acts 20. 28.

8, 9. Paul's conclusion demonstrates perfect liberty. On the one hand, we read of his desire that some should remain unmarried for service. On the other hand, those unmarried but desiring marriage should marry—

when circumstances permit—rather than live with unsatisfied desire. There is perfect liberty; there is no command either way—there is no sin either way. We all have our call to individual service. Some few must decide before the Lord whether marriage is compatible with their own particular calling. Some missionaries have to answer this very definitely before the Lord.

10, 11. We now have a *command* from the Lord regarding those believers who are married. No exercise or liberty is allowed in this matter. Paul is obviously referring to Christians who were subject to the conditions prevailing in Corinth. We should notice that he is not writing about mixed marriages between believer and unbeliever; that subject starts in verse 12.

Verses 3–5 demonstrate the *ideal* in marriage between believers. Verses 10 and 11 show *weaknesses* in marriage. In this latter case, the creatorial purpose of God remains for believers. If a wife had to depart because of trouble (but *not* having been put away by the husband), there were two possible courses of action.

1. She should remain unmarried, else the question of adultery would be raised, Luke 16. 18.
2. It would be better if reconciliation could take place, else the question of the altar would continually be raised, Matt. 5. 23.

We must realise that home life in those days was rather different from what it is today in christian families, hence these dangers and these exhortations. In those days, the young women had to be taught to be sober, to love their husbands and to love their children, Titus 2. 4. It would be strange if young married sisters in our days required such outspoken exhortations.

It should be noticed that Paul's teaching here is similar to that which he advocated for local assembly action. If a brother were "put away", 1 Cor. 5. 13, he could not join himself to another gathering in those days. He remained alone outside, until he repented. The assembly could also repent, 2 Cor. 7. 9, and the man could be forgiven and loved again, 2 Cor. 2. 8, 10.

Verses 12–24: Regarding Mixed Marriages

12 But to the rest speak I, not the Lord: If any brother hath a wife that believeth not, and she be pleased to dwell with him, let him not put her away.
13 And the woman which hath an husband that believeth not, and if he be pleased to dwell with her, let her not leave him.
14 For the unbelieving husband is sanctified by his wife, and the unbeliving wife is sanctified by the husband: else were your children unclean; but now are they holy.
15 But if the unbelieving depart, let him depart. A brother or a sister is not under bondage in such *cases*: but God hath called us to peace.
16 For what knowest thou, O wife, whether thou shalt save *thy* husband? or how knowest thou, O man, whether thou shalt save *thy* wife?
17 But as God hath distributed to every man, as the Lord hath called every one, so let him walk. And so ordain I in all churches.

18 Is any man called being circumcised? let him not become uncircumcised. Is any called in uncircumcision? let him not be circumcised.

19 Circumcision is nothing and uncircumcision is nothing, but the keeping of the commandments of God.

20 Let every man abide in the same calling wherein he was called.

21 Art thou called *being* a servant? care not for it: but if thou mayest be made free, use *it* rather.

22 For he that is called in the Lord, *being* a servant, is the Lord's freeman: likewise also he that is called, *being* free, is Christ's servant.

23 Ye are brought with a price; be not ye the servants of men.

24 Brethren, let every man, wherein he is called, therein abide with God.

There now follows apostolic *instruction* regarding mixed marriages. When Paul writes that *he* is speaking and "not *the Lord*", he implies that there is no direct divine *command*. This does not cancel the certainty of divine inspiration.

Mixed marriages cause grief to the Christian partner, but the apostle introduces into this section spiritual comfort by means of an "anticipated blessing". How do mixed marriages come about? Certainly believers should not get married in such a state, since marriage is to be "only in the Lord", v. 39. Likewise, the exhortation "Be ye not unequally yoked together with unbelievers", 2 Cor. 6. 14, in so far as it applies to marriage, refers to the original marriage. This was the ultimate cause of Solomon's downfall, 1 Kings 11. 1–3. Hence the mixed partnership of the present section can only come about either by the conversion of one partner after marriage, or else by an uninstructed Christian marrying an unbeliever without realising the seriousness of such an action. One would judge that Timothy's parents present an example of mixed marriage. His mother was a believer, Acts 16. 1 and 2 Timothy 1. 5. Her husband, one may fairly deduce, was an unbelieving Greek.

12, 13. Here we have instructions to the believing partner, either a man or a woman. Scripture here provides no directions for the unbelieving partner, the wife or the husband. The unbelieving partner could do as she or he pleased. There was to be no separation if this was not desired by the unbeliever. Such a one would either stay with or leave the christian influence of the other partner. This ease of staying or leaving must be understood in the light of the customs of the time. Such a thing could also be readily contemplated in the society of today. We must recognise that custom affects the actions of unbelievers. The apostolic injunctions are given wholly to the believing partner: to the husband, don't put his wife away; to the wife, don't leave her husband. These injunctions are independent of custom; they apply for all time. Paul states this as the *best* course rather than a divine command. One should observe that there is no reference at all to divorce.

14. "For the unbelieving husband is sanctified by the wife, and the unbelieving wife is sanctified by the husband: else were your children unclean; but now are they holy." This verse may only be understood in contrast to the law of the O.T. We quote several verses from Ezra and Nehemiah, relating to the period after the return from the captivity in Babylon and after the building of the temple and the walls around Jerusalem.

> Ezra 9. 1, 2: "The people of Israel, and the priests, and the Levites, have not separated themselves from the people of the lands, . . . For they have taken of their daughters for themselves, and for their sons: so that the holy seed have mingled themselves with the people of those lands".
>
> Ezra 9. 6: Ezra in prayer said, "O my God, I am ashamed and blush to lift up my face to Thee, my God: for our iniquities are increased over our head, and our trespass is grown up unto the heavens".
>
> Ezra 9. 12: The prophets had said, "Give not your daughters unto their sons, neither take their daughters unto your sons".
>
> Ezra 10. 3: "Now therefore let us make a covenant with our God to put away all the wives, and *such as are born of them*".
>
> Ezra 10. 11: The words of Ezra, "Separate yourselves from the people of the land, and from the strange wives".
>
> Ezra 10. 18, 24: The priests, singers and porters were all involved.
>
> Nehemiah 13. 23–31: "Jews that had married wives of Ashdod, of Ammon, and of Moab: and their children spake half in the speech of Ashdod, and could not speak in the Jews' language, ... Did not Solomon king of Israel sin by these things? ... nevertheless even him did outlandish women cause to sin ... They have defiled the priesthood, and the covenant of the priesthood, and of the Levites ... Thus cleansed I them from all strangers."

The reader can see that our verse 14 presents a complete contrast under grace. Far from being "put away" as in the O.T., the unbelieving partner and the children are now "sanctified" or "holy". The word "sanctified" here has no *spiritual sense*, unlike, for example, the description of believers given in chapter 1 verse 2 , "sanctified in Christ Jesus". The word implies being "set apart", unlike being "put away". The unbelieving partner and the children were set apart from the provision of the law as related in Ezra and Nehemiah.

Readers possessing Wigram's concordance should glance down the entries under *hagios*; this word does not always denote a *change* as in the believer's case. For example, the phrases "The temple that sanctifieth the gift", Matt. 23. 17, and "The altar that sanctifieth the gift", Matt. 23. 19, merely imply that the gift is set apart from ordinary circumstances.

Hence grace sets apart the unbelieving partner and the children from the demands of the law, their ultimate possible blessing in Christ being in view. We know that no "unclean person . . . hath any inheritance in the kingdom of Christ and of God", Eph. 5. 5. The conscience of the believing partner may regard with dismay their contact with such, so our verse represents God's sanction for a Christian's conscience in such a matter.

We should point out that there is no hint of infant baptism in this verse (see also on 1. 16; 10. 2). Some would use the verse to teach this, but this shows how desperate such teachers are if they are forced to cling to such a slender straw.

15. The ease by which the unbelieving partner could depart appears to be characteristic of the social customs in Corinth at that time. The believer had no part in the matter. A brother or sister not being "under bondage" might suggest that, when they were alone, there was to be no morbid anxiety to try and get the unbelieving partner back. They had been called "in peace" (not "to peace"); that is, the believing partner trusted in the will of the Lord and as such did not seek to cause strife. It should be noticed that in those days the believer had no licence to marry again, but is left to serve in this separation.

16. In spite of the believer's obvious dismay in accepting circumstances as they are, here is Paul's "anticipated blessing" to support the believer's testimony. The salvation of the unbelieving partner must be the objective, so no act or mode of conduct of the believer in the home must jeopardize this possibility of conversion. Moreover, this testimony is not so much one of speech as of conduct, as we read in 1 Peter 3. 1, "Ye wives, be in subjection to your own husbands; that, even if any obey not the word, they may without the word be gained by the behaviour of their wives", R.V. This is a marvellous provision; it is the powerful testimony of the living Christ in a soul.

17. The exhortation is to remain where God has placed you. The *distribution* of God appears to refer to *spiritual* circumstances, (the same word appears in Rom. 12. 3; 2 Cor. 10. 13); the *call* of God appears to refer in the context to one's *natural* circumstances. In our walk and conduct, we must desire to remain where we have been placed, knowing that "all things work together for good to them that love God", Rom. 8. 28.

"And so ordain I in all churches" shows a basis of unity. The apostolic instruction here (and in all matters) is universal in its applicability. Practical fellowship between local assemblies is a reality only when this is owned.

18–24. These verses emphasise the truth of remaining according to one's calling, yet not being legalistic about the matter. The question of circumcision or uncircumcision—physically distinguishing the Jew and the Gentile—were questions of fact that could not and should not be changed. Such distinctions in the flesh were irrelevant under grace. Even then, there was no law about this; see the cases of Timothy and Titus, Acts 16. 3; Gal. 2. 3, 4. The only real and lasting things were the keeping of the commandments of God in the new economy of grace—something far removed from the commandments governing O.T. ritual. Saints indeed are "elect . . . unto obedience", 1 Pet. 1. 2.

The idea behind verse 21 shows that Paul was not being legalistic here. W. Kelly translates it thus: "Wast thou called as a bondman? Let it not be a care to thee; but if also thou canst be free, use it rather" In other words, a change to liberty was not incompatible with one's original calling. In any case, one's natural position is changed spiritually for the Lord, "Ye are bought with a price; be not ye the servants of men". But nevertheless, the general principle is given by way of conclusion in verse 24, "let every man, wherein he is called, therein abide with God". This certainly applies to marriage, whatever other application it may have.

Verses 25–40: Regarding the Unmarried

25 Now concerning virgins I have no commandment of the Lord: yet I give my judgment, as one that hath obtained mercy of the Lord to be faithful.

26 I suppose therefore that this is good for the present distress, I *say* that *it is* good for a man so to be.

27 Art thou bound unto a wife? seek not to be loosed. Art thou loosed from a wife? seek not a wife.

28 But and if thou marry, thou hast not sinned; and if a virgin marry, she hath not sinned. Nevertheless such shall have trouble in the flesh: but I spare you.

29 But this I say, brethren, the time *is* short: it remaineth, that both they that have wives be as though they had none;

30 And they that weep, as though they wept not; and they that rejoice, as though they rejoiced not; and they that buy, as though they possessed not;

31 And they that use this world, as not abusing *it*: for the fashion of this world passeth away.

32 But I would have you without carefulness. He that is unmarried careth for the things that belong to the Lord, how he may please the Lord:

33 But he that is married careth for the things that are of the world, how he may please *his* wife.

34 There is difference *also* between a wife and a virgin. The unmarried woman careth for the things of the Lord, that she may be holy both in body and in spirit; but she that is married careth for the things of the world, how she may please *her* husband.

35 And this I speak for your own profit; not that I may cast a snare upon you, but for that which is comely, and that ye may attend upon the Lord without distraction.

36 But if any man think that he behaveth himself uncomely toward his virgin, if she pass the flower of *her* age, and need so require, let him do what he will, he sinneth not: let them marry.

37 Nevertheless he that standeth stedfast in his heart, having no necessity, but hath power over his own will, and hath so decreed in his heart that he will keep his virgin, doeth well.

38 So then he that giveth *her* in marriage doeth well; but he that giveth *her* not in marriage doeth better.

39 The wife is bound by the law as long as her husband liveth; but if her husband be dead, she is at liberty to be married to whom she will; only in the Lord.

40 But she is happier if she so abide, after my judgment: and I think also that I have the Spirit of God.

This last section provides apostolic advice to those who are unmarried (and to widows in the last two verses) with one specific object in view. In this section, there are difficulties in making sense of the usual translation, and readers should notice carefully suggestions adopted from other commentators.

25. "Concerning virgins I have no commandment of the Lord". The word "virgins" is to be understood as "unmarried people"—certainly not women only! There is no commandment here—only apostolic advice for a special type of service. "As one that hath obtained mercy of the Lord to be faithful" implies that Paul is looking back to verse 8. He considers his own special service and the grounds of his own faithfulness. As such, he gives his own judgment.

26–28. Paul's contention for the "present necessity" (rather than "present distress") is that it is good for a man not to marry if his exercise is to engage in Paul-like service, namely to labour more abundantly than all and to be occupied with the daily care of all the churches. The apostle is not talking about ordinary service—all saints engage in that. But whatever one's sphere of service, there is liberty to marry. No sin is attached to marrying even if one is called to special service, v. 28. Even Paul could have married, in spite of the character of his service, 9. 5.

But in verse 28 Paul gives a warning, "Such (masculine) shall have trouble in the flesh". It hardly makes good sense to read childbearing into this warning, 1 Tim. 2. 15, since the masculine is implied. Rather it may refer to the strain of overwork affecting the body, owing to the dual occupation of family life and spiritual service. It may refer to the trials and tribulations that overtake one partner to the grief of the other.

Paul's contention clearly does not refer to all and sundry, since it is impossible to contradict his exhortation in 1 Timothy 5. 14, "I will therefore that the younger women marry, bear children, guide the house".

29–31. Whatever one's state, Paul delineates faith's estimate of legitimate things. We hold with a loose hand all but Christ.

32–35. These verses must be carefully noticed, since a casual reading would suggest that married believers are more occupied with their families than with the things of the Lord. Verses 29 and 30 refer to brethren, and verse 31 to sisters. The ideal is to live without "carefulness", that is, "without worrying". The only other time this word appears in the N.T. is in Matthew 28. 14, "We will secure you"; that is, "so you need not worry about Pilate thinking you let the disciples steal away the body of the Lord".

Paul notes that if one is not married, one is usually *worried* only about service pleasing to the Lord, while if one is married, one is usually worried about pleasing one's wife. *Both attitudes are wrong.* Verse 35 provides the correct attitude, namely "that ye may attend upon the Lord *without distraction*". This false attitude was that of Martha, who was cumbered about much serving, Luke 10. 40. The Lord would have us free in mind and heart, like Mary, both in home life and in spiritual service. One must dispel the notion that in these verses Paul is seeking to demonstrate the superiority of unmarried life, and that it is only as unmarried that one can please the Lord.

36–38. Regarding the man and "his virgin", much nonsense in translation and exposition has appeared. The A.V. reads as if it were a question of
    (a)   a man and his fiancee;
    (b)   a father and his unmarried daughter.
Many commentators suggest that Paul had been asked about the duty of a father in connection with a daughter of age to marry. This makes verse 37 ridiculous, which obviously refers to the desire of the man to marry. But translators and expositors as J. N. Darby, W. Kelly, F. W. Grant, Bagster's interlinear, and so on, translate verse 36 as "If any man think that he behaveth himself uncomely toward his own virginity", that is, towards his own unmarried state. This has features that commend it to careful consideration, even though some may disagree. The same phrase occurs at the end of verse 37, namely the decree of the man to keep "his own virginity". Even in verse 38, the two words "her" are not really there, as the A.V. italics declare. It is not a question of an indefinitely long engagement, as the A.V. suggests.

The phrase "if she pass the flower of her age", v. 36, is a translation of a Greek word peculiar to the N.T., and hence of rather uncertain meaning, since it appears only once. The A.V. translators adopted this rendering to fit into their own interpretation of the passage. The expositors and translators mentioned above, however, usually employ "if he be beyond his prime", but this qualification appears unnecessary in Paul's argument. Souter's dictionary suggests the word means "of excessive vigour" referring to the man. This thought is consistent with our present exposition that:
    (a)   a special call to service for the Lord may best be fulfilled by a brother in an unmarried state, v. 37, but
    (b)   if such a brother feels constrained to marry, he should do just that, v. 36.
Paul concludes by stating that special service interrupted by the necessity of marriage is not sin, but really, such an one could have done better in the service of God by not marrying.

39, 40: *the liberty of widowhood.* "The wife is bound by the law as long as her husband liveth" is a statement of fact, bound up not only with the law but with God's creatorial purposes. Release from this and remarriage may only come if the husband dies. This is the truth of Romans 7. 2, 3, namely "she is loosed from the law of her husband" and "though she be married to another man". There is perfect liberty, with only one condition attached, namely, that it is "in the Lord".

Abiding unmarried depends on the calling of God. For example, the service of Anna in Luke 2. 36-38 demanded a single state.

By way of conclusion, we may note that in

      service together,

      service alone, though married,

      service alone as unmarried,

nothing is a trivial undertaking. All has to be accomplished in the light of divine commands, one's own exercises and spiritual advice.

1 CORINTHIANS 8

Section 4. Christian Liberty
Subject 2. Partaking of Meats

Relationships within this Section

Having considered the subject of christian liberty as related to marriage, Paul now turns his attention to another subject that was giving difficulty to the saints in Corinth. The four chapters dealing with christian liberty may be distinguished from each other as follows:

Chapter 7: liberty with regard to an individual partner;
Chapter 8: liberty with regard to a brother in the Lord;
Chapter 9: liberty with regard to the local assemblies;
Chapter 10: liberty with regard to unbelievers.

Background of this Subject

In Acts 2, the Holy Spirit suddenly came upon the gathered saints in order to form them into a new body in Christ, thereby placing them on new ground before God positionally, practically and in service. The Lord, who had died and now lives exalted at the right hand of God, had introduced heavenly assembly ground under grace. This had displaced the Jewish ground of law and ceremony. The shadows, Heb. 10. 1, and the patterns, Heb. 8. 5, had given place to reality; old things had passed away and all things had become new, 2 Cor. 5. 17. However, in the book of the Acts, we find that many Jewish converts moved only slowly to cast off in a practical way the tradition of their fathers, from which they had been redeemed with the precious blood of Christ, 1 Pet. 1. 18. Hence even at the end of Paul's third missionary journey, there were in Jerusalem thousands of Jewish converts who were "all zealous of the law", Acts 21. 20. They did not appreciate their own standing in grace, neither did they understand Paul's liberty in Christ. They were informed about Paul that he taught "all the Jews which are among the Gentiles to forsake Moses, saying that they ought not to circumcise their children, neither to walk after the customs", Acts 21. 21. Paul, the apostle to the Gentiles, had to contend with such an attitude throughout his missionary journeys. He dealt with the matter with constant understanding and grace, remaining faithful to the new assembly principles revealed to him by the Lord, yet not stumbling these weaker brethren who were still bound by troubled consciences to various phases of the law.

The matter came to a head in Acts 15 at the end of the first missionary journey. Certain of the sect of the Pharisees which believed rose up saying "that it was needful to circumcise them, and to command them to keep the law of Moses", Acts 15. 5. This referred, of course, to Gentile converts. False teachers from Judaea were preaching in Antioch that salvation

114   **First Corinthians**

depended upon the observance of these things, v. 1. It appears that, through ignorance and through difficulty of casting off practices that were engrained in their minds, these Jewish believers were stumbled by this new liberty offered to the Gentiles. It would be easy to squash such stumbled believers, but that would not help them to enter into their own liberty with greater understanding. The solution adopted was to meet these weaker believers on their own ground as far as possible, but *never compromising* at all the liberty of the assembly position under grace. Verse 22, "Then pleased it the apostles and elders, with the whole church" suggests that all were satisfied in their conscience, at least for the time being. Circumcision and the keeping of the law were *not* thrust on the Gentiles. This would have been compromise. The course adopted also "seemed good to the Holy Ghost", v. 28, implying that the understanding and grace shown by the assembly was approved by divine standards.

The four things mentioned in verse 29 are all negative in outlook; that is to say, Gentile saints were required to abstain from them. They appear to be things most offending to the Jewish conscience, and their application had to be interpreted in that light. Nothing positive was demanded; that is to say, no specific ceremony of the law was to burden the Gentiles. The four things were as follows:

1. "Meats offered to idols" — false peace offerings offered to the multitude of heathen gods, of which the offerer could partake and which was constantly available for sale afterwards in the market places.
2. "Things strangled" — victims for food from which the blood had not been shed. "Flesh with the life thereof, which is the blood thereof, shall ye not eat", Gen. 9. 4.
3. "Blood", Lev. 17. 10–14, — was most holy (that is, set apart from everything common), and to the enlightened soul spoke only of the precious blood of Christ.
4. "Fornication" — this was sin, no liberty could ever arise in connection with it. Paul had dealt with this in chapters 5–7.

Acts 15. 19 was not a law nor a command, but only a letter suggesting abstention from certain things, with a deep-seated motive in abiding by its terms. It is interesting that some Greek copies (though not the best editors' texts) insert a fifth requirement into the letter, namely "and do not do to others what you would not wish done to yourselves". This insertion has so little authority that it does not appear in the various translations possessed by the author, but he was very interested to note that this addition does appear in the common Russian translation. Compare Matthew 7. 12.

Abstention from fornication is the proper conduct of the people of God, not merely because it is sin (a negative reason), but also because of 1 Corinthians 6. 18–20 (a positive reason). Liberty looks to the glory of God when sin is in question. The fact that the body is the temple of the Holy Spirit should be final to all believers.

Acts 15 does not really show why one should abstain from meats offered to idols, or whether it is abstention only under certain circumstances. In this connection, we may note the following scriptures:

Revelation 2. 20: to encourage such a practice is Jezebelism, and is condemned by the Lord walking amongst His own.

1 Timothy 4. 2–5: everything is good, if it is received with thanksgiving, being sanctified by the word of God and prayer.

1 Corinthians 8 deals with a believer who does partake of such meat, yet this practice should never carry with it the risk of stumbling a weaker brother in the Lord.

1 Corinthians 10 deals with a believer who does partake of such meat, but this should never stumble an unbeliever.

Acts 21. 24–25 deals with Gentile believers not partaking of such meats so as not to stumble Jews that believe.

Hence, it appears that abstention is enjoined upon a believer (not as a command) only when it would give offence to the Jew, Gentile or to the church of God, 1 Cor. 10. 32. If the conscience of another is not involved then a believer strong in the faith has perfect liberty before the Lord in the matter. Chapter 8 deals with this subject in reference to the conscience of a weaker brother.

A summary of this chapter may be given as follows:

Verses 1–3: the principle of Paul's argument—knowledge and love;

Verses 4–6: the spiritual knowledge of the believer regarding the nature of idols;

Verse 7: the state of those who are weaker in the faith;

Verses 8–11: the liberty of the believer is not seen in relation to God but to the conscience of the weaker brother;

Verses 12–13: responsibility of the brother who claims liberty in the matter.

Exposition of 1 Cor. 8: Partaking of Meats

1 Now as touching things offered unto idols, we know that we all have knowledge. Knowledge puffeth up, but charity edifieth.

2 And if any man think that he knoweth anything, he knoweth nothing yet as he ought to know.

3 But if any man love God, the same is known of him.

4 As concerning therefore the eating of those things that are offered in sacrifice unto idols, we know that an idol *is* nothing in the world, and that *there is* none other God but one.

5 For though there be that are called gods, whether in heaven or in earth, (as there be gods many, and lords many)

6 But to us *there is but* one God, the Father, of whom *are* all things, and we in him; and one Lord Jesus Christ, by whom *are* all things, and we by him.

7 Howbeit *there is* not in every man that knowledge. for some with conscience of the idol unto this hour eat *it* as a thing offered unto an idol; and their conscience being weak is defiled.

8 But meat commendeth us not to God: for neither, if we eat, are we the better; neither, if we eat not are we the worse.

9 But take heed lest by any means this liberty of yours become a stumbling block to them that are weak.

10 For if any man see thee which hast knowledge sit at meat in the idol's temple, shall not the conscience of him which is weak be emboldened to eat those things which are offered to idols;

11 And through thy knowledge shall the weak brother perish, for whom Christ died?

12 But when ye sin so against the brethren, and wound their weak conscience, ye sin against Christ.

13 Wherefore, if meat make my brother to offend, I will eat no flesh while the world standeth, lest I make my brother to offend.

1. In those days, there were many gods among the peoples of Greece and Achaia in spite of the eminent philosophers who taught in Athens in olden times. The advancement of learning may remove such gods from the religious life of the people, but such advancement can never bring in "the way, the truth, and the life". In Athens, for example, the city was "wholly given to idolatry", Acts 17. 16, and to make sure that no gods had been overlooked in the multitude of idols, there was a special altar with the inscription "To the unknown god", v. 23. This did not mean that they worshipped the true God as unknown, as is sometimes suggested.

Much of the meat offered for sale in the public markets had first been offered in sacrifice to these idols. The believers in Corinth had to obtain their daily food from the usual public supply, and so they were concerned with the vital question as to how far the enlightened Christian conscience could partake with liberty of this meat, which after all was physically just the same as ordinary meat.

To deal with this question, Paul enunciates two principles:

1. *knowledge*—this can inflate one like a balloon, and can be burst;
2. *love*—this is like a well-planned edifice being built; it cannot be destroyed.

Though a believer may have all knowledge, if he does not possess love, that believer is nothing; that knowledge is of no profit to him, 1 Cor. 13. 2, 3. Knowledge by itself is academic; there was plenty of that in Corinth both inside and outside the assembly. Love, on the other hand, is spiritual. Love enables knowledge that glorifies God to work through the exercise of wisdom. The spirit of wisdom and revelation is necessary for true knowledge of Himself, Eph. 1. 17, but even then this knowledge is surpassed by the love of Christ, 3. 19, and it is in love that the body is edified, 4. 16. Knowledge in the mind is, of course, distinct from knowledge in the heart; the Corinthians possessed the former while the Ephesians possessed the latter.

2, 3. Paul now contrasts the cold barrenness of knowledge by itself with the warmth of love. There were those who thought that they had knowledge, that is, in an unspiritual, satisfied, elevated and proud way. Such are "proud, knowing nothing", 1 Tim. 6. 4. Christians, wholly taken up with doctrine, can get into this state. As such, they know nothing as they ought to; they are building upon a false basis altogether.

What Paul is driving at is that if one really loves God, then he will also love his brother. Loving God and loving one's brother or neighbour are linked together, Matt. 22. 37–39. The knowledge of God and the love of God bring us into a relationship of understanding our brethren and having compassion on them, 1 John 2. 5, 9–11; 3. 16–18. Certainly those who act according to this rule are acknowledged by God. Hence our relationships with our brethren and in the home, and our conduct generally, are all motivated by the stand we take regarding knowledge and love. Either it is *knowledge without love*, or else *love with knowledge*.

4. Paul now relates an absolute fact, appreciated by the stronger brethren but not necessarily by the weaker brethren. The physical idol is nothing in the world. Its essential nature is exactly the same as all other matter around. See Isaiah 44. 17–19, where the unalterable physical characteristics of the material before and after construction are the same. The evil exists in the hearts of the idolaters, not in the idol. The evil spirits which the Lord cast out existed within those ensnared by them; these were, however, not "gods". The devils to which the sacrifices were offered were no doubt real enough in many cases, 1 Cor. 10. 21, but these were external to the actual meat. In any case, God had created these things to be received with thanksgiving by those that believe and know the truth, 1 Tim. 4. 3, and this should be independent of any process to which unbelievers had submitted the meat in the meantime.

5. Paul admits that there may well be these many gods and lords both in heaven and in earth. For example, the gods of the nations were very prominent in the O.T., though often this was a cloak for immoral practices. We have but to recall the list given in 1 Kings 11. 4–7 relating to the gods of the nations that Solomon followed in his later years. 2 Kings 17 is full of the subject in relation to the reason for the captivity of the northern kingdom, while Jeremiah 2. 28 accuses the people of Judah: "for according to the number of thy cities are thy gods". Such men are deceived by their eyes, by their senses and by materialism. They "worshipped and served the creature more than the Creator, who is blessed for ever", Rom. 1. 25.

Even if the Corinthians did partake of such meats, there is no question of them engaging in actual idolatry. Even chapter 10 verse 14 "flee from idolatry" can only refer in the context to contact with the relics of idolatry. Certainly 1 John 5. 21, "keep yourselves from idols", does not refer to idolatry in this gross sense. There it refers to the love of the world rather than the love of the Father. As far as believers are concerned, idolatry may be an attitude of heart when it is sidetracked from the Lord. Such an attitude never deifies or gives any supernatural quality to the world or to idols.

6. Again Paul relates absolute fact regarding the Godhead. All believers

would acknowledge that there is but one God, but this would not necessarily dispel the uncertainty dwelling in the conscience of the weaker brother regarding idols.

Concerning the blessed truth of the one God, we may note the scriptures:

Genesis 1. 1; it was God and not another, who created all things.

Exodus 20. 3; in the commandments, God insisted that the people should have no other gods before Him.

Deuteronomy 4. 35; at the end of the wilderness-wanderings, Moses recalled the power of God that showed that "there is none else like Him".

Isaiah 45. 5; "I am the Lord, and there is none else, there is no God beside Me"; see verse 18 and 43. 10; 44. 6.

Ephesians 4. 6; the unity of the Spirit embraces the truth, "One God and Father of all, who is above all, and through all, and in you all".

Thus the God and Father of the Lord Jesus Christ is unique, and He has sent forth the Spirit of His Son into our hearts, crying "Abba, Father", Gal. 4. 6. We are thereby directed uniquely to this One. In relation to this uniqueness, Paul declares that we are *"for* Him". We realise that this unique One has created all things, and *for* His pleasure they exist and were created, Rev. 4. 11. We are for Himself, *"to* the praise of the glory of His grace", Eph. 1. 6.

Likewise the Son is unique, "one Lord Jesus Christ, by whom are all things, and we by Him". We may note the following scriptures:

John 3. 16; "the only begotten Son" implies He is unique. In French, this is translated "son Fils unique".

Hebrews 1. 6; this anticipates the time when the Firstbegotten will be brought again into the world (note this rendering which is rather distinct from the A.V. translation).

Ephesians 4. 5; assembly faith adheres to "One Lord".

2 Corinthians 11. 4; Paul fears the preaching of "another Jesus, whom we have not preached".

"By whom are all things" is illustrated by the great truth in John 1. 3, "All things were made *by* Him; and without Him was not any thing made that was made". "We *by* Him" implies that we, as sons of the new birth, own that all our blessings come by Him. *"By* Him" God has reconciled all things unto Himself, and we, though once alienated and enemies, are included in this grace, Col. 1. 20, 21.

7. Paul now makes mention of the weaker brother for the first time. Such a brother indeed knows the truth of the one God, but at the same time he senses the power of darkness behind an idol, and behind the meat offered to an idol, whereas in reality the actual material substance is the same as before. Paul is not criticising such a brother. It is as before the Lord that the brother has such a conscience, Rom. 14. 6. If there is to be criticism, it is against the stronger brother. By giving open display to his

liberty in the matter, he encourages the weaker brother to copy him, which is disastrous if his conscience is bound in the matter.

Paul writes that "his conscience being weak is defiled". This word appears only in two other places in the N.T.

1. "A few names even in Sardis which have not defiled their garments", Rev. 3. 4. That is, these names were not mixed up with things contrary to His walk.
2. "These are they which were not defiled with women", Rev. 14. 4. That is, they were not mixed up with the activity of the great whore, Babylon.

Hence the consciences of these weaker brethren are mixed up concerning the holy things of God and the things of darkness. The latter things, by no means adhered to, remain to instil fear into the conscience. This is equivalent to reaping what has previously been sown in the mind, Gal. 6. 7, and cannot be eradicated.

8. This verse refers to "us", that is, to the stronger brethren. Paul argues that the exercise of liberty and of knowledge gives one no special standing before God at all. As far as the eater is concerned, he is neither better nor worse. Such an act will not affect the eater, but it may affect another, namely the weaker brother. If such an act brings with it adverse consequences in another, then it is sin, v. 12. Romans 14. 17 should be read in this connection; the kingdom of God is not built upon such acts as eating or drinking, but upon conduct in righteousness and peace towards our fellow believers.

9. This verse is the central point of the apostle's argument. The abstention proposed in the letter in Acts 15 must be understood in the light of the inspired apostle's remarks here. The contents of that letter "seemed good to the Holy Ghost", Acts 15. 28, so consistency of thought must be retained throughout the inspired Epistles.

Actions performed under the pretext of christian liberty may be the means of stumbling another brother. There would appear to be only one legitimate stumblingstone in Scripture, but never to believers, however weak and failing they may be. This is "Christ crucified, unto the Jews a stumblingblock, and unto the Greeks foolishness", 1 Cor. 1. 23. For the Jews, "they stumbled at that stumblingstone", Rom. 9. 32, 33. This last verse is a remarkable mixture of the two O.T. verses Isaiah 8. 14 and 28. 16. Neither of these two verses contained the thought the inspired apostle required, so he had to make a mixture of them, quite altering the O.T. sense in so doing. Expositors today have no such liberty to mix verses to yield a different sense. See also 1 Peter 2. 6–8.

The exhortation to believers today is that "no man put a stumblingblock or an occasion to fall in his brother's way", Rom. 14. 13. This goes far beyond the application in verse 9, which may appear to be of little relevance in itself nowadays. The brother who seeks to go his own independent way, or who seeks to introduce new ideas and methods into service, thereby causing the rest of the assembly or perhaps just a few of the saints to grieve and to be bewildered, is in effect guilty of the sin dealt with in this chapter.

Men sought to put many stumblingblocks in the way of the Lord Jesus when here below, for example, questions seemingly impossible to answer, Matt. 22. 15–40. But the blessed Lord surmounted all this in keeping with Psalm 91. 11, 12: "For He shall give His angels charge over Thee, to keep Thee in all Thy ways. They shall bear Thee up in their hands, lest Thou dash Thy foot against a stone". Satan applied this verse quite wrongly in the temptation in the wilderness, Matt. 4. 6, applying it merely to a physical situation.

Hence Paul exhorts us to "take heed" that all we do is for the good of our fellow believers. We should indeed "take heed therefore that the light which is in thee be not darkness", Luke 11. 3 5. Paul uses a similar expression elsewhere in this Epistle; see 3. 10; 10. 12.

10. A weaker brother is bound to follow the example of the stronger brother, even against the convictions of his own conscience. This is the copying principle that is instinctive in us all. This is an example of bad copying, but elsewhere it may well be good, 1 Cor. 11. 1.

11. The weak brother, for whom Christ died, would therefore "perish", on account of the manifestation of knowledge without love by the stronger brother. Perish may mean "end of life", but it also means "no longer to be of use for its intended purpose". It may mean "lost" as in the case of the three parables in Luke 15. The weak brother would no longer be on a path of experiencing blessing, rather of confusion. He would be lost to the clear path of life lived in keeping with his conscience, and not be fit for effective service.

12. The testimony and mental state of this brother would be so impaired, with his weak conscience thus wounded, that Paul declares that this act is equivalent to sinning against Christ Himself. Offending one of the Lord's own people is seen as an act against Christ; see Matt. 25. 41–45; Acts 9. 4. From our point of view in this day of grace, we should note very carefully that the act of stumbling a brother is something that will be considered before the judgment seat of Christ, Rom. 14. 10–13. Our conduct before our brethren, and the consequences of our conduct in the lives of our brethren, will be manifested in that day.

13. *Paul's conclusion*. Paul would never use the liberty that knowledge gives him if his conduct did not manifest love at the same time. The contrary spirit is Jezebelism, Rev. 2. 20. Many brethren will not use their full liberty in Christ for this reason. They should not be judged by others who fail to appreciate their inner motives before the Lord; "let not him that eateth, despise him that eateth not; and let not him which eateth not, judge him that eateth", Rom. 14. 3. It really works both ways. The conclusion is that we should all be very careful in all things lest we make a brother to offend. Paul argued that, just in case, almost complete abstention was called for. He, at least, would not make full use of his liberty in Christ in this connection.

1 CORINTHIANS 9

Section 4.   Christian Liberty
Subject 3.   Living of the Gospel

Relationships within this Section

Paul now brings before the saints the third great manifestation of
christian liberty. Having dealt with
  (a)   the effect of marriage on service, and
  (b)   the effect of strength of outlook and knowledge upon the
         conscience of the weaker brother,
the apostle now deals with the question of full-time servants of the Lord
being maintained by the saints on account of their full-time service for the
Lord. In just the same way as Paul would not avail himself of the liberty he
possessed in chapters 7 and 8, so, here, Paul would not avail himself of the
liberty of living of the gospel, in case some among whom he laboured might
gain a wrong impression of the gift of God through the gospel message.

Background of this Subject

The apostle Paul had a divine call to full-time service in the Lord's
name. He thus joined the ranks of many others who had a like call. The
Lord provides for His own, both then and now. We shall see later in the
chapter the method God has instituted to accomplish this. Needless to say,
the means God uses are spiritual means—far removed from the methods
of man that have been invented in many circles. Paul had the liberty to
rest upon the means God would employ to provide His servant with the
necessities of daily life. Nevertheless Paul would not take up this liberty for
reasons given in the centre of the chapter. Rather, he would work with his
own hands—as a tentmaker in Corinth, Acts 18. 3—for the provision for
daily necessities, and would certainly not live of the gospel as a matter of
useage, though accepting gifts occasionally, Phil. 4. 16.

Because Paul took this position openly, some believers who should have
known better were calling into question the very apostolic position that
Paul occupied in the divine purpose. Could this be a sin similar to that of
Korah and his company who questioned the position of Moses, Num. 16.
3? Such a question as this, affecting the very apostolic authority of his
teaching, had to be dealt with first, before he dealt with the decline in
assembly service and prosperity in chapters 11–14.

Paul deals with the matter by showing
  (a)   that God has arranged that labourers may live as a result of their
         service, but
  (b)   that he, Paul, could accomplish apostolic service more effectively
         by not making use of this liberty.

The chapter divides into several sections:

Verses 1–6: general statements regarding Paul's ministry and service;

Verses 7–14: reasons (mainly from the O.T. and mainly in the form of questions) for full-time workers to have liberty to live as a direct result of their occupation in the Lord's service;

Verses 15–18: reasons why Paul would not take advantage of such liberty;

Verses 19–23: Paul's reward for taking this attitude, he would not work as a paid servant, but as a *free* servant;

Verses 24–27: the final spiritual reward for such an attitude, but this reward would not be for the body.

Exposition of 1 Cor. 9: Living of the Gospel

Verses 1–6: Paul's Ministry and Service

1 Am I not an apostle? am I not free? have I not seen Jesus Christ our Lord? are not ye my work in the Lord?

2 If I be not an apostle unto others, yet doubtless I am to you: for the seal of mine apostleship are ye in the Lord.

3 Mine answer to them that do examine me is this,

4 Have we not power to eat and to drink?

5 Have we not power to lead about a sister, a wife, as well as other apostles, and *as* the brethren of the Lord, and Cephas?

6 Or I only and Barnabas, have not we power to forbear working?

1. The opening phrases should be reversed in position, namely "Am I not free? am I not an apostle?" This transposition has the authority of the various editors of the Greek text. Paul asserts his liberty and then his apostleship. This, perhaps, is the only occasion on which he definitely asserts his position in the Lord. When he uses this title and position at the beginning of his epistles, it is really a statement of fact giving authority to his writing rather than a deliberate assertion of his position intended to quench argument. It is a serious thing not to abide by this apostolic authority, both then and now. In chapter 1 verse 1, his apostleship derives from a call through the will of God; here Paul bases it upon the sight that he had had of the risen Lord in glory. Five hundred brethren saw the Lord at once during one of His resurrection manifestations, 1 Cor. 15. 6, but only one hundred and twenty met together after His ascension, Acts 1. 15. We might ask, Where were the rest?, see Luke 17. 17. Only Paul, however, had the vision unto apostleship, as one born out of due time, 1 Cor. 15. 8.

Finally, his work in the Lord demonstrates his apostolic position. This was "a proof of Christ speaking in" him, 2 Cor. 13. 3. This context shows that he was approved by his work, and certainly not a reprobate (that is, not approved). His work in Corinth (and that of Peter in Acts 2–10) is characteristic of an apostle, and it cannot be repeated or attained today. Other verses we may cite are:

2 Corinthians 12. 12: "Truly the signs of an apostle were wrought among you in all patience, in signs, and wonders, and mighty deeds";

2 Corinthians 11. 5: "I was not a whit behind the very chiefest apostles . . . we have been throughly made manifest among you in all things";

1 Corinthians 12. 28: "God hath set some in the church, first apostles".

Yet Paul was always humble, knowing that it was all of grace that he had this position in the Lord's service. Having proved his apostleship here, later in the Epistle when occasion demands it he could appear humble before God, "I am the least of the apostles, that am not meet to be called an apostle, because I persecuted the church of God', 15. 9.

2. By writing "If I be *not* an apostle unto others, yet doubtless I am to you", Paul's argument appears to be "Don't look to other churches; just look to yourselves, and observe that you are what you are because of apostolic work". No one else without apostolic gift could have produced such results at Corinth had they gone there before Paul. For example, Priscilla and Aquila were in Corinth *first*, but they could accomplish nothing, Acts 18. 2. Again, Apollos went to Corinth afterwards, Acts 18. 27, but he would have been able to do little had he *preceded* Paul to Corinth. The vision and the purpose of God recorded in Acts 18. 9–10 were for the apostle only.

Amidst all the disorder in Corinth, the believers there were still "in the Lord". Disorder has to progress to a very great extent before a whole professing local assembly, such as Laodicea, is disowned by the Lord. In Revelation 2–3, where disorder was sought out by the Lord walking amongst His own, the exhortation is "strengthen the things that remain". Even when the saints connived at deadly immoral sin, 1 Cor. 5. 2, 6, the local company was not rejected. Governmental dealings by the brethren, 5. 3, and by the Lord, 11. 30–32, are intended to regain order out of disorder. This should be an encouragement to some believers today who grieve before the Lord on account of things coming to pass in their local assemblies.

3. Today, men hasten to justify themselves when awkward situations arise, but Paul was slow to engage in such a thing. The Lord remained silent rather than justify Himself, Matt. 26. 63; 27. 14; He was vindicated in resurrection with all authority given unto Him, and this will yet be manifested in this world when He reigns in triumph. But here, the Holy Spirit had to vindicate the apostle Paul, using Paul's own reasoning to do so. The apostolic authority had to be recognized both here and in chapters 11–14, where all readers have to acknowledge that the things written are "the commandments of the Lord", 14. 37. In verses 4–13 a series of questions is asked, designed to exercise the conscience regarding Paul's authority and the question at issue.

4–6. Here we find apostolic liberty and how Paul chose to deal with the basic necessities and circumstances of life. Verse 4 deals with his creatorial right to eat and to drink for the maintenance of life; verse 5 deals with his right or authority to have a sister in the Lord as his wife, even as the other apostles, the brethren of the Lord, and Peter, Luke 4. 38. This latter question had already been dealt with in chapter 7, where we have seen that Paul would not marry for the kingdom of heaven's sake, although others had liberty to do so. Verse 6 shows that Paul and Barnabas had the right or authority to forbear or to refrain from working for the daily necessities of life, but the chapter is devoted to Paul's reason for not using this liberty in Christ.

Throughout the years of grace, servants of the Lord have always been free in these matters, to work or to walk in the pathway laid down in this chapter, to marry or to walk in the light of chapter 7. It is a matter of experience nowadays that full-time workers usually marry and refrain from working. This is their exercise before the Lord making use of the liberty granted to them. Paul had reasons for doing exactly the opposite.

Verses 7–14: The Liberty of Gospel Preachers not to Work

7 Who goeth a warfare any time at his own charges? who planteth a vineyard, and eateth not of the fruit thereof? or who feedeth a flock, and eateth not of the milk of the flock?

8 Say I these things as a man? or saith not the law the same also?

9 For it is written in the law of Moses, Thou shalt not muzzle the mouth of the ox that treadeth out the corn. Doth God take care for oxen?

10 Or saith he *it* altogether for our sakes? For our sakes, no doubt, *this* is written: that he that ploweth should plow in hope; and that he that thresheth in hope should be partaker of his hope.

11 If we have sown unto you spiritual things, *is it* a great thing if we shall reap your carnal things?

12 If others be partakers of *this* power over you, *are* not we rather? Nevertheless, we have not used this power; but suffer all things, lest we should hinder the gospel of Christ.

13 Do ye not know that they which minister about holy things live *of the things* of the temple? and they which wait at the altar are partakers with the altar?

14 Even so hath the Lord ordained that they which preach the gospel should live of the gospel.

7. Paul now asks three questions about natural occupations, each implying a spiritual principle.

1. If one serves as a soldier, it is at someone else's expense. Soldiers are maintained by king and country, and they are not concerned directly about their support. In 1 Samuel 17. 17, Jesse asked David to take food to his three eldest sons and to the captain of their thousand in battle.

2. If a vine is planted, the worker is able to partake of the proceeds of such labour. In Isaiah 5. 1–7, the Wellbeloved planted a

vineyard (Israel), so that the Lord could satisfy Himself with fruit.
3. If a shepherd feeds a flock, he can be a partaker of the outcome of this work.

It is obvious that spiritual service proceeds along the same lines. There is spiritual warfare in service, 2 Cor. 10. 4; 2 Tim. 2. 3–4; there is spiritual husbandry, 1 Cor. 3. 8; there is spiritual feeding of the flock, Acts 20. 28; 1 Pet. 5. 2. Paul would imply that the servant may live as a direct result of his labours.

8. The Corinthians might have argued that these questions about natural occupations were irrelevant and proved nothing. They did not touch upon the spiritual question at issue. Hence Paul now quotes cases from the O.T., asking questions all the time to stimulate their consciences to answer appropriately. He deals with

(a) God's care for animals, v. 9;
(b) God's care for the labouring man, v. 10;
(c) God's care for those engaged in the ceremony of the Levitical service, v. 13.

The law, therefore, says the same thing. But the proof of the principle when applied to gospel-preachers is *not* drawn from the mere asking of questions, *neither* can it be drawn from any number of quotations from the O.T. The proof of the principle under grace is found in the only positive statement that Paul makes in the section, v. 14. The N.T. principle arises from the direct arrangements and intentions of God. It is very important to notice that in inspiration the Holy Spirit does not seek to prove things by illogical means from impossible premises.

The phrase "as a man" in this verse may be found elsewhere; see Rom. 3. 5; Gal. 3. 15. Sometimes it may mean as a natural sinful man arguing against Scripture; othertimes (as in the present context) it means using a natural argument to support Scripture.

9. "Thou shalt not muzzle the mouth of the ox that treadeth out the corn" is a quotation from Deuteronomy 25. The immediate context is about God's provision, as follows,

Verse 3: Punishment must not exceed forty stripes; this is the provision of God for safety. See 2 Cor. 11. 24.
Verse 4: This is God's provision for the working ox; access to the corn was not to be denied or prohibited. Food comes directly from the work being undertaken. This verse is also quoted in 1 Timothy 5. 18, which we shall consider when we arrive at verse 14 of this chapter.
Verse 5: If a man die and have no children, then his brother shall do the duty of a husband; this is God's provision for the birth of children to the wife and family. This is quoted in Matthew 22. 24.

Paul argues that this verse 4 was written not only for the oxen but *for us* as well; it is "altogether for our sakes". This is an example of one present-day value of the O.T. Scriptures; they are recorded to demonstrate principles of conduct and service. (1 Corinthians 10. 11 provides another present-day value, namely that of warning.)

10. "For our sakes, no doubt, this is written: that he that ploweth . . ." reads as though Paul is quoting another passage from the O.T. This is, however, not a quotation, and a comma rather than a colon should occur after the word "written". Paul is giving the reason why Deuteronomy 25. 4 is written for us. Other passages may be noted showing that the O.T. has a direct bearing upon the saints today:

> 1 Corinthians 10. 11: "they are written *for our* admonition".
> 2 Timothy 3. 15–17: "all scripture . . . is profitable . . . that *the man of God may be perfect* . . .".
> 1 Peter 1. 12: "unto whom it was revealed . . . *unto us* they did minister the things . . .".

Paul replaces the work of the ox by the work of the farmer engaged in ploughing. The order is: ploughing, sowing, watering, watching and waiting, reaping, threshing, partaking. Paul visualises a longer wait for the fruit; "the husbandman waiteth for the precious fruit of the earth, and hath long patience for it, until he receive the early and latter rain", James 5. 7. But at the end, the labourer partakes of his own labours. Of course, others also may partake of the results of his labours; for example, Ruth gleaned in fields where she had bestowed no labour, and the fowls of the air are fed although they neither sow nor reap, Matt. 6. 26.

11. Paul continues to ask questions. This was designed to cause the Corinthians much heart-searching to supply an answer. We repeat that verse 14 is the one only definite statement in this paragraph. Paul has sown spiritual things amongst the Corinthians, he had planted as a minister by whom they believed, 3. 5, 6. He had planted the truth of the gospel, of baptism, of assembly gathering, of breaking of bread, of practical conduct and of the Lord's return. Since Paul had sown such things of infinite and eternal value, then he would also reap in a coming day spiritual rewards for his faithfulness. How much smaller a matter, then, for a labourer in these spiritual things to reap a temporal harvest of "carnal things" provided by the saints. Being on such a lower level, it could be easily accomplished when the saints are suitably exercised about the matter.

12. The opening phrase "If others be partakers" suggests that other workers were being helped and maintained by the saints. Apollos may well have come within this category. But Paul would not use this power or authority, even if it meant suffering hunger and privation if necessary, 2 Cor. 11. 27. As is explained in more detail later in the chapter, Paul "would not hinder the gospel of Christ". His desire was that it should be "without charge", v. 18, and that it should be preached "freely", 2 Cor. 11. 7. Paul appreciated that the spiritual aspect of the gospel and the financial aspect of daily living would not mix satisfactorily in his hands. He speaks, however, only of himself; they may well mix satisfactorily in the hands of others. The Lord's servants have liberty in this matter. The Lord provides for His servants. Either outlook is legitimate, and there can be no legislation. Let none judge what another worker does in this matter.

Usually, then, workers are sustained by the saints among whom they work. God loves a "cheerful giver" in this matter, and blessing from the Lord returns to the one who gave initially; see 2 Cor. 9. 6–10.

13. We now come to Paul's last question, relating to the Levitical service in the O.T. Two distinct features arise:

1. To *"feed of the things of the temple"*, marg. Numbers 18. 20–24 should be read: "I have given the children of Levi all the tenth in Israel for an inheritance, for their service which they serve, even the service of the tabernacle of the congregation". The first tithe or tenth was God's special provision for His Levitical servants. The second tithe or tenth was intended for the people themselves to eat in "the place which the Lord your God shall choose", Deut. 12. 5. Verses 5–19 should be read carefully. The Levite was not to be forgotten, v. 19. Unfortunately, throughout O.T. history, the people often forgot the Levites. In Hezekiah's restoration, heaps of provisions were made of the newly brought tithes, to provide the "daily portion" of the Levites, 2 Chron. 31. 5–19. After the return from the captivity, in Nehemiah's day, the people promised not to "forsake the house of our God", Neh. 10. 35–39. The context implies that the provision for the Levites was in question. But this was a source of weakness with the people. The house was forsaken and the portions had not been given to the Levites, so they had fled to their fields to provide their own food, Neh. 13. 10–12.

2. *"Partakers with the altar"*. There were many O.T. instructions concerning what the priests, the offerers and the people could eat of the offerings made at the altar. For details, the reader may refer to our exposition of chapter 10 verse 18. The word "with" certainly implies intelligent fellowship with the altar and its offerings. Evidently the priests were abundantly provided for by the Lord.

We may, of course, spiritualise all this typically, and meditate upon the spiritual wealth in Christ that one saint provides for another, but here Paul uses the illustration entirely on a material level.

14. *The principle*: "Even so hath the Lord ordained that they which preach the gospel should live of the gospel". We now reach the N.T. ground of grace, and Paul makes his only positive assertion in the paragraph. Full-time workers should be provided for, both by the saints among whom they work and by other assemblies as acts of fellowship. There is no question of a regular salary. The faith of full-time workers enables them to live above the methods of the many others who are engaged in ordinary full-time employment. There is no question here of a man receiving a regular wage as a pastor or a "minister". One should note the various classes to which this principle applies:

Evangelists, as in the present verse. A similar principle is found in Matthew 10. 9–10 applied to the disciples sent forth during the life time of the Lord Jesus : "Provide neither gold, nor silver, nor brass in your purses, . . ., for the workman is worthy of his meat". Again in Luke 10. 7, "eating and drinking such things as they give: for the labourer is worthy of his hire". As such, the disciples lacked nothing, but at the end of His public ministry the Lord changed these instructions to "But now, he that hath a purse, let him take it, and likewise his scrip", Luke 22. 36. There was to be exercise in the liberty of faith.

Apostles. As an apostle, Paul received gifts from other assemblies from time to time: "When I departed from Macedonia, no church communicated with me as concerning giving and receiving, but ye only. For even in Thessalonica ye sent once and again unto my necessity", Phil. 4. 15–16. Even then Paul did not really desire it, but he knew that this was fruit added to the account of the Philippian assembly, so he graciously received the gift from their hands. This shows the proper pattern; there was no fixed salary, but an assembly "once and again" providing for a worker. There was no question of a minister receiving a salary from some headquarters. At the same time, we should point out that there is *nothing* here against a group of brethren as an act of fellowship and convenience acting as a channel to pass on gifts from individuals and assemblies to various full-time workers and missionaries.

Teachers. "Let him that is taught in the word communicate unto him that teacheth in all good things", Gal. 6. 6.

Elders. "Let the elders that rule well be counted worthy of double honour, especially they who labour in the word and doctrine", 1 Tim. 5. 17, and then Deut. 25. 4 and Deut. 24. 14–15 are quoted and referred to. In a sense, an elder may be fulltime, as was Peter for example, 1 Pet. 5. 1. This has nothing to do with an "ordained" minister or a resident pastor. Such elders would move about amongst the gatherings as Peter did.

Poor saints. "For it hath pleased them . . . to make a certain contribution for the poor saints which are at Jerusalem.... their duty is also to minister unto them in carnal things", Rom. 15. 26–27. See also Acts 11. 27–30; 1 Cor. 16. 3. Certainly such gifts are "to the glory of the same Lord", 2 Cor. 8. 19, and such acts can but feebly reflect His great act in becoming poor, that we through His poverty might be enriched, v. 9.

In 2 Timothy 2. 6, Paul lays down the general principle, "The husbandman that laboureth must be first partaker of the fruits". How gracious of the Lord to make this provision for His own, but alas, we often seem to act as if such matters were quite a secret transaction between an assembly treasurer and the labourer.

The whole principle is one of tremendous practical importance. To "pay the expenses" of a preacher has nothing in common with what we have in this chapter. It is only right to pay the expenses of a preacher, whether full-time in the work or whether in daily employment. But if a preacher is full-time, a gift should never be given under the cloak of expenses. Expenses are one thing, but the gift is for the brother and his family to live.*

Verses 15–18: Reasons for the Position that Paul took

15 But I have used none of these things: neither have I written these things, that it should be so done unto me: for *it were* better for me to die, than that any man should make my glorying void.
16 For though I preach the gospel, I have nothing to glory of: for necessity is laid upon me; yea, woe is unto me, if I preach not the gospel!
17 For if I do this thing willingly, I have a reward: but if against my will, a dispensation *of the gospel* is committed unto me.
18 What is my reward then? *Verily* that, when I preach the gospel, I may make the gospel of Christ without charge, that I abuse not my power in the gospel.

Paul now explains why he had liberty not to make use of the very provision that God had made for His servants. Certainly his remarks were not a subtle underhand request for gifts; some might even have accused him of such a thing.

15. Paul had "used none of these things". This had always been Paul's policy, as the following scriptures show:

Acts 18. 3: "He abode with them, and wrought: for by their occupation they were tentmakers".

1 Corinthians 4. 12: "And labour, working with our own hands".

2 Corinthians 11. 8–9: "I robbed other churches, taking wages of them, to do you service. And when I was present with you, and wanted, I was chargeable to no man: for that which was lacking to me the brethren which came from Macedonia supplied: and in all things I have kept myself from being burdensome unto you, and so will I keep myself". Robbing other churches implies that they gave gifts to Paul in Corinth, when there would have been no necessity to have done so had the Corinthians appreciated their own responsibility.

2 Corinthians 12. 14: "I will not be burdensome to you: for I seek not yours, but you: for the children ought not to lay up for the parents, but the parents for the children". Here, Paul regarded himself as their father, having begotten them in Christ Jesus through the

---

* The author feels he can write freely on these matters since he is not a full-time worker, and as such would only accept expenses which is not the subject of this chapter.

gospel, 1 Cor. 4. 15.

Acts 20. 34: "These hands have ministered unto my necessities, and to them that were with me". Paul thus put a very wide interpretation on the Lord's words, "It is more blessed to give than to receive".

1 Thessalonians 2. 9: "Our labour and travail: for labouring night and day, because we would not be chargeable unto any of you, we preached unto you the gospel of God". These verses show the consistency of Paul's policy in many places and among many young assemblies.

2 Thessalonians 3. 8: "Neither did we eat any man's bread for nought; but wrought with labour and travail night and day, that we might not be chargeable to any of you". Paul quotes his own conduct here in order to be an example, not to full-time labourers in the gospel, but to those who walked disorderly in Thessalonica by not working at all.

Why? This was one of Paul's boastings (see Gal. 6. 14 for another), namely, that the gospel should not only *be* free, but that in his hands it should also *appear to be* free.

16. Paul is not contradicting himself here. In the previous verse he boasts that the gospel is free, and he would rather die than have it otherwise. Here, he has nothing to boast about, in that his calling to preach and his ability to preach are not of himself but of God. "We have this treasure in earthen vessels, that the excellency of the power may be of God, and not of us", 2 Cor. 4. 7. Necessity was laid upon Paul to preach, since this was the call of God which demanded obedience to the heavenly vision in the ensuing service. We should all say, "Woe is unto me, if I accomplish not that service to which the Lord has called me".

17. The two parts of this verse may best be understood by an expanded paraphrase. *"Willingly"* implies: "If I had taken up the work of preaching, myself according to my own will, I might expect a reward". This is, alas, similar to ordained ministry today; it is usually a self-chosen vocation. *"Against my will"* implies: "If I am appointed by God's will and not of my own choosing, then in obedience I must dispense the gospel to others, seeking no glory since the choice and ability are of God". This is equivalent to "We are unprofitable servants: we have done that which was our duty to do", Luke 17. 10.

18. Paul's only boasting and reward is the satisfaction in knowing that the gospel is without charge, both in a spiritual and financial sense. A natural tendency, of course, would be to "abuse" one's authority in the gospel, that is, to dwell on any material gain rather than upon the aspect of spiritual giving. But Paul used his own liberty to make the gospel absolutely free, "Ho, every one that thirsteth, come ye to the waters, and he that hath no money; come ye, buy, and eat; yea, come, buy wine and milk without money and without price", Isa. 55. 1.

Paul's reward would be to gain less and to give more. Verses 19–23 explain how he accomplished this.

Verses 19–27: The Gain of Service

19 For though I be free from all *men*, yet have I made myself servant unto all, that I might gain the more.
20 And unto the Jews I became as a Jew, that I might gain the Jews: to them that are under the law, as under the law, that I might gain them that are under the law;
21 To them that are without law as without law, (being not without law to God, but under the law to Christ,) that I might gain them that are without law.
22 To the weak became I as weak, that I might gain the weak: I am made all things to all *men*, that I might by all means save some.
23 And this I do for the gospel's sake, that I might be partaker thereof with *you*.
24 Know ye not that they which run in a race run all but one receiveth the prize? So run, that ye may obtain.
25 And every man that striveth for the mastery is temperate in all things. Now they *do it* to obtain a corruptible crown; but we an incorruptible.
26 I therefore so run , not as uncertainly; so fight I, not as one that beateth the air:
27 But I keep under my body, and bring *it* into subjection: lest that by any means, when I have preached to others, I myself should be a castaway.

19. "For though I be free from all men, yet have I made myself servant unto all, that I might gain the more". Since Paul did not receive gifts from the Corinthians, he felt free to bring more energy and zeal into his service. He felt free from men; they had no control over his service even in an indirect way. Yet in this service for God he took the position of being the hardest working servant amongst men. Why? —in order to gain the more through the preaching of the gospel. He would very gladly "spend and be spent" for the Corinthians, 2 Cor. 12. 15, receiving nothing in return except to know that they were saved and being edified.

How perfectly was this manifested in the Lord's life here below. He was free from all men because he was the Servant of God. We may note the following verses:

Matthew 20. 28: "Even as the Son of man came not to be ministered unto, but to minister, and to give His life a ransom for many".
John 13. 4–17: He ministered by washing the disciples' feet.
In this respect, we must regard the Lord as the true example:
John 13; 17: "If ye know these things, happy are ye if ye do them".
Matthew 20. 26-27: "Whosoever will be great among you, let him be your minister; and whosoever will be chief among you, let him be your servant".
In his service, Paul was servant "unto all". This was because

of his original call, when God had chosen him to bear His name "before the Gentiles, and kings, and the children of Israel", Acts 9. 15. He became servant to *many folds*, in order to take out of them *one flock*. As servant, he took a lower position than they all; see 1 Cor. 4. 11–13; 2 Cor. 6. 4–10; 11. 23–33.

20–22. Verses 20–22 have often been interpreted in the sense of allowing evangelists to do almost anything they please in their zeal to reach souls. A careful reading of the Revised Version would, however, dispel such a notion. What Paul means is that he became servant in *every legitimate* way to many, so that by all means some would be saved.

As *a Jew*: Paul engaged in legitimate activities as a Jew. For example, he went into the synagogues at Antioch, Thessalonica and Corinth, Acts 13. 14; 17. 1; 18. 4. He addressed them as "men and brethren", Acts 13. 38, to show that their common origin pertaining to the flesh was not despised. At the same time, he always realised his own standing in grace. Things that were personal gain he counted loss for Christ, Phil. 3. 7. Such personal gain may, however, be occasionally useful in preaching the gospel.

As *under the law*: The Greek text, followed by the better English translations, inserts a safeguard here, "not being myself under the law". For example, in Acts 21. 23–26, Paul engaged in ceremonial purifying, in order to avoid giving any offence to Jews who were zealous of the law. The insertion just mentioned shows that Paul placed no value on this ceremony. He was not being double-faced in his activity.

As *without law*: He took his legitimate place with the Gentiles, (see Acts 11. 3, 17). Again Paul would never engage in sinful contact with the Gentiles without law. The safeguard is given here, namely "being not without law to God, but under the law to Christ". This would reflect not on the O.T. law as a covenant, but as something through Christ "fulfilled in one word, even in this: Thou shalt love thy neighbour as thyself", Gal. 5. 14.

As *weak*: Where weakness or simplicity existed among exercised unbelievers or young converts, Paul would not stumble them with a position of superior strength; see 1 Thess. 2. 5–12.

Thus Paul was "made all things to all men", in order to help them, to encourage them through to salvation, but never by using methods that would later stumble them in their christian pathway.

23. Paul regarded all this as his reward for service that did not attract financial gifts. He had no personal gain or interest in view; it was "for the gospel's sake". Today, instead of viewing these previous verses as a reward instead of gifts, some would use these verses to justify places and practices that are open to suspicion; Paul, however, would never run into sin. Paul would also be a "partaker thereof with you", or better translated, a "fellow partaker with it". He would be taken up with its service, its blessings, its results, its joy, its final reward and with other saints and assemblies engaged in a like work, Phil. 1. 5.

24–26. Paul concludes this subject by drawing attention to a metaphor of running a race in the games. In an ordinary race, everyone runs but only one is the winner. They all run legitimately, but one is distinct from all the others. In this chapter Paul regards himself in this category amongst other servants of God. All run legitimately, whether they receive gifts, or work with their hands. Paul believed that he was distinct from the others on account of the special point of view that he took. Spiritually, however, there were many first prizes. The fact that Paul regarded himself as a winner did not preclude others also from being first, even if they did accept gifts for maintenance; "So run, that ye may obtain" opens the door for all to win.

There are various characteristics of this outworking of service:

1. *Striving for the mastery*, or "to agonize": that is, every thing is being done with one end in view, and with no deviation. Similar roots are found in the nouns and verbs in the quotations: "Having the same *conflict* which ye saw in me", Phil. 1. 30; "*Striving* according to His working", Col. 1. 29; "What great *conflict* I have for you", Col. 2. 1; "*Labouring fervently* for you in prayers", Col. 4. 12; "*Fight the* good *fight* of faith", 1 Tim. 6. 12; "I have *fought* a good *fight*", 2 Tim. 4. 7.

2. *Temperate*: that is, the athlete shows self–control. He must recognise God-given liberty as to outlook and methods, but he must only use that which is most suited to his own particular service, and which is most suited to overcome his own particular weaknesses.

3. *An incorruptible crown*: this will be an eternal reward given at the judgment seat of Christ for faithfulness in one's own special sphere of service, and can be anticipated. It can never detract from the power of the gospel, as a corruptible financial gift might do. See 1 Thess. 2. 19; James 1. 12; 1 Pet. 5. 4; 2 Tim. 4. 8; Rev. 2. 10.

4. *Not as uncertainly*: that is, one is not to be doubtful as to the outcome, but to anticipate by faith the desired haven. Having put one's hand to the plough, there was no case for looking back, Luke 9. 62.

5. *Not as beating the air*: that is, doing something ridiculous in combat, and obviously making no impression at all. The Corinthians, alas, served in this fashion as chapter 14 demonstrates.

27. The last verse, suggests that Paul had a deep sense of his own weaknesses and of the dangers of the flesh. All workers should recognise these things within themelves. He had to keep his body in subjection. In the present context, it would appear that an abundance of gifts from the saints would have caused him to boast in the flesh. Hence he would rather work with his hands than allow these evil thoughts to mature and to burst forth. His Lord has said, "If thy right eye offend thee, pluck it out … If thy right hand offend thee, cut it off", Matt. 5. 29–30. He could, of course, preach the gospel even if such thoughts and boastings did manifest themselves within, but then he himself would be a "castaway". This word means "not approved" or "reprobate", 2 Cor. 13. 7. "Probate" in connection with a will means that it is approved: its mode of being drawn up, the signature and witness are all in order. Similarly with the believer before the judgment seat of Christ. Being approved for eternal reward results when service and faithfulness are in order. If disorder has reigned, then one cannot be approved for reward, one would be a "castaway", or "reprobate" or "not approved". Eternal life, of course, is not in question here.

1 CORINTHIANS 10

Section 4.   Christian Liberty
Subject 4.   Partaking of Tables

General Relationships of this Chapter

Chapter 10 is rather distinct from the other chapters in the Epistle, as the following list shows:

Chapters 1, 2: The unsaved and the saved in relation to preaching.
Chapters 3, 4: The saints' service in relation to assembly building.
Chapters 5, 6: The saints' conduct in relation to the assembly.
Chapter 7: The saints and marriage in relation to service.
Chapter 8: The saints' partaking of meats in relation to the assembly.
Chapter 9: The Lord's servants in relation to financial maintenance by local assemblies.
Chapter 11: The saints in relation to authority and the Lord's supper.
Chapters 12, 13, 14: The saints in relation to the outworking of spiritual gifts in the assembly.
Chapter 15: The saints in relation to correct doctrine.
Chapter 16: The saints in relation to the mutual care and interest shown by one to the other in the assembly.

These summaries show that essentially every one of these chapters deals with the saints in relation to spiritual and practical matters. But chapter 10 is distinct. Its summary is:

The saints' partaking of meats in relation to the *unsaved outside the assembly.*

Relationships within this Section

This chapter concludes the section dealing with christian liberty, namely chapters 7–10. In all, we observe the following principles:

Chapter 7: There is liberty for all to marry, but it would be better for some not to marry in order to engage in more effective service; Paul, at least, would not marry, v. 7.
Chapter 8: There is liberty for all to eat meats, but it would be better not to, in order not to stumble a weaker brother; Paul, at least, would not eat, v. 13.
Chapter 9: There is liberty for full-time workers to live of the gospel; Paul, however, would not, v. 15.
Chapter 10: Again in connection with the believer's liberty to eat meats, v. 23–25, this should not be engaged in whenever unbelievers would gain a wrong impression.

Background of this Subject

The concluding argument of the chapter illustrates the Lord's words:

"Then are the children free. Notwithstanding, lest we should offend them, . . .", Matt. 17. 26, 27. This was spoken in connection with the subject of paying the tribute money, and Peter's rash answer given without any prior consultation with his Lord. But the Lord would not use His divine liberty in these matters, so as not to offend the people—that is, not to provide them with even any *unreasonable cause* for complaint. The lesson is one of the *conduct of liberty* so as not to offend an outsider, with a view to the furtherance of the testimony, 1 Cor. 10. 33.

The overall picture is drawn in verse 32: "Give none offence, neither to the Jews, nor to the Gentiles, nor to the church of God". These three classes are all brought before us in connection with the subject of eating meats offered to idols.

Jews: Acts 15 refers to the Jews in relation to the subject matter of the letter sent by the apostles and elders. Verse 5, "the Pharisees which believed", shows that *believing* Jews had to be satisfied, while verse 21, "for Moses of old time hath in every city them that preach him, being read in the synagogues every sabbath day", shows that *unbelieving* Jews had to be considered. Absolutely, of course, Jewish believers cease to be Jews in the heavenly purpose of God (see Gal. 3. 28), but practically, national differences were not forgotten in day-by-day matters, see Acts 6. 1; 16. 1; 21. 20. Acts 21. 21–26 also deals with offence not being given to believing Jews.

Gentiles: This is the subject of 1 Corinthians 10, as seen in verse 27: "them that believe not".

Church of God: This has been treated in chapter 8, the chapter dealing with the danger of sinning "against the brethren", v. 12, and of offending "my brother", v. 13. Romans 14 likewise deals with this case, discussing the reception of brethren "weak in the faith", v. 1, yet not stumbling "thy brother", v. 21.

This chapter deals with the believer's contact with and participation in the relics of idolatry practised by the heathen around them. There is no question of believers *practising* idolatry, rather they only had circumstantial contact with it. Verse 19 shows that the same principles as recorded in chapter 8 apply, namely that the material idol and the sacrifices are not idolatrous in themselves (see 8. 4). However, the diabolical aspect is real as embracing the powers of darkness, 10. 20. The unbeliever is in contact with those powers of darkness in his practice of idolatry, but not the believer, even though he may be in contact with the relics for various reasons.

These two forms of idolatry must be distinguished, as indeed they are in chapters 5 and 6.

(a) In 1 Corinthians 5. 11 we read " have written unto you not to keep company, if any man that is called a brother be . . . an idolater". This is *internal*, and refers to a brother walking disorderly by being in contact with (but not worshipping!) idolatrous relics with no regard for the conscience of others. Paul implies a withdrawal of fellowship because of such disorder. Chapter 10 deals with the deeper implications of such ignorant or wilful practice, since this is opposed to the holy observance of the day-by-day fellowship of the Lord's table.

(b) 1 Corinthians 6. 9 "neither . . . idolaters . . . shall inherit the kingdom of God" refers to demon worship by the Gentiles, even by the Corinthians before their conversion, "and such were some of you: but ye are washed, . . .", v. 11. Such idolatry is *external*.

An overall summary of the argument of the apostle Paul in this chapter is as follows:

Verses 1–4: *Wilderness blessings*. Certain O.T. similarities to the N.T. blessings of baptism and partaking of the Lord's table are recorded.

Verses 5–10: *Partaking of incompatible things*. The Israelites engaged in idolatrous practices in the wilderness, and believers are exhorted not to engage in anything of similar character.

Verses 11–13: God's *present use of O.T. history* in times of temptation.

Verses 14–22: *The argument from the Lord's table*. Paul shows the incompatibility of fellowship at the Lord's table and contact with idolatrous relics, the nature of the contact being defined in verse 28.

Verses 23–30: *The practical subject itself*. Paul shows the necessity of liberty being restrained on account of the conscience of the unbeliever.

Verses 31–33: *Conclusions*. Conduct is to be regulated with a view to promoting and not marring the testimony of the gospel.

Exposition of 1 Cor. 10: Partaking of Tables

Verses 1–4: Wilderness Blessings

1 Moreover brethren, I would not that ye should be ignorant, how that all our fathers were under the cloud, and all passed through the sea;
2 And were all baptized unto Moses in the cloud and in the sea;
3 And did all eat the same spiritual meat;
4 And did all drink the same spiritual drink: for they drank of that spiritual Rock that followed them : and that Rock was Christ.

1. "I would not that ye should be ignorant" is the gracious way Paul writes to show that the Corinthians were really ignorant of things that they should know. He uses a similar expression in

Romans 1. 13, showing his purpose to visit Rome with the gospel;

2 Corinthians 1. 8, showing the trouble he had experienced in Asia, which some interpret as referring to a breakdown in health because of strenuous overwork;

1 Thessalonians 4. 13, concerning them "which are asleep" and the promise of the Lord's return.

Here, in verse 1, Paul shows the necessity of rightly interpreting the lessons of O.T. history. In his reference to "our fathers", Paul writes as a converted Jew, to which nation pertain "the covenants, and the giving of the law, and the service of God, and the promises", Rom. 9. 4. In Romans 9. 3, he refers to the nation as "my brethren, my kinsmen according to the flesh", while in Acts 13. 17 he commences his discourse in Antioch with the idea of God choosing "our fathers". Things gained to Paul in this connection were, of course, counted loss for Christ, Phil. 3. 5–7, but he rejoiced in the purposes of God in the nation, that led up to Christ.

Paul now singles out certain O.T. features that have similar characteristics to baptism and the Lord's table. They can hardly be regarded as direct types (types, or examples, start at verse 5), since many features are dissimilar. In any case, Paul does not press the analogy too far. The lesson drawn in verse 11 is the vital part of the argument.

"Under the cloud" has certain features similar to baptism, but we should note that the doctrine of baptism *cannot* be proved from O.T. features. We may observe the verses:

> Exodus 13. 21, "the Lord went before them by day in a pillar of cloud, to lead them the way";
>
> Deuteronomy 1. 33, " who went in the way before you, . . . to show you by what way ye should go, and in a cloud by day";
>
> Exodus 14. 19, "the pillar of the cloud went from before their face, and stood behind them".

The point is, they were underneath the cloud, and on account of this they were subject to the authority of the One in the cloud. Baptism today at the beginning of the believer's pathway includes the thought of subjection to authority, and certainly the ascended Lord is the true Guide of His people in the wilderness scene. Some seek to deduce infant baptism from this verse, using the word "all" to imply children. This is a thin straw to cling to (see also 1. 16; 7. 14), illegitimate since there is no N.T. teaching on this subject at all. The O.T. cannot be used to extract non-existent N.T. doctrine. In any case, verse 5 shows that the ground is one of adult responsibility.

2. The children of Israel were baptised "in the cloud and in the sea". The latter was really a position of death (for the Egyptians) and yet life for the people of God who passed through, Exod. 14. 27–30. We should note that the word "in" is one of position. The same applies to all references in the N.T. regarding baptism: baptism is *in* water not *with* water; it is *in* the Holy Spirit and not *with* the Holy Spirit, see Matt. 3. 11; Mark 1. 8; Luke 3. 16; John 1. 26, 31, 33; Acts 1. 5; 11. 16; 1 Cor. 12. 13. The word *in* occurs in the Revised Version margin and in Newberry's margin, although J.N.D. uses *with* in all cases with no alternative. We should therefore point out that the Greek word *en* usually means *in* positionally, but sometimes denotes an agent, *with*; hence the variations in different translations. The word *en* occurs in the four Gospels some one thousand times, and Wigram's concordance shows that it is used in the sense of *with* (agent) a very small number of times (see, for example, Luke 22. 49, "*with* the sword", where the context demands the translation *with*). But as far as baptism in water is concerned, the immediate context of Mark 1 shows clearly the thought of position, namely "did baptize *in* the wilderness", v. 4, "baptized *in* the river of Jordan", v. 5, and hence "baptized *in* water", v. 8. The common translation *"with* water" obviously originates from the traditional stress on the agent used in sprinkling, and a similar idea is then applied to Spirit baptism. The only occurrences of water as the agent used are in Acts 1. 5 and 11. 16, where the word *en* does not occur, but merely water in the dative case implying an agent. Even in these verses, "baptism *in* the Holy Spirit" is implied by the use of the word *en*.

The thought behind the cloud may suggest baptism in the Spirit.

The phrase "unto Moses" implies unto the authority of Moses. The Greek word *eis* is used, as in Matthew 28. 19 "in (*to*) the name of the Father", and in Galatians 3. 27 "As many of you as have been baptized *into* Christ have put on Christ". The old has passed away; all things are become new, as was the case at the Red Sea. Before this event, the children of Israel certainly had not been fully under the authority of Moses, (that is, of the Lord through Moses), see Exod. 14.11, 12.

3. After this baptism, they all partook of the special food and drink provided by the Lord. This is very similar to the aspect of the table brought out in this chapter: partaking of the Lord's provision and its associated fellowship rightly follow baptism. It would appear wrong, however, to be wholly legalistic about this usual order. With gracious understanding, circumstances sometimes transcend legalistic requirements. It should be noticed that the similarity to the table is confined to verses 16–24, and not to the Lord's supper treated in 11. 20–34.

In the phrase "*all* did eat the *same* spiritual meat", the words *all* and *same* denote mutual fellowship both by the participators and in the act itself. Two aspects of the manna given in Exodus 16. 15 should be noticed:

1. In Exodus 16. 33, a golden pot (Heb. 9. 4) containing manna was to be placed in the ark and laid up before the Lord. This is the *Godward* aspect within the veil. "That they may see the bread", v. 32, speaks of the effect of this provision on the heart of His people. It speaks of Christ as the substance of the worship of the Lord's people Godward—it corresponds to 1 Corinthians 11. 20–34. The fact that later the pot was no longer in the ark, 1 Kings 8. 9, suggests that worship Godward is something that can be lost amongst the saints. Aaron's rod that budded, speaking of resurrection life, was also missing, Heb. 9. 4. Others have suggested that the pot was retained as a reminder of their murmuring, and the rod of their rebellion. Their absence from the ark when it was taken into the temple would then correspond to the fact that painful memories will be removed in heaven after the judgment seat of Christ.

2. By way of contrast, we read in Exodus 16. 16–31 of the provision made for the people. This is the manward aspect appreciated by the people under wilderness conditions. This corresponds to

1 Corinthians 10. 16–21.

Note that Paul is *not* quoting an exact parallel, and so it would be wrong to associate Christ as the bread of life (in John 6. 48) with the Lord's supper. The differences appear to be as follows:

John 6. 51–57: The eating of His flesh and the drinking of His blood, v. 53, are the means of eternal life. They are spiritual concepts not symbolised today by bread and wine. Deuteronomy 8. 3 should be read in this connection. Manna is associated with feeding on "every word that proceedeth out of the mouth of God". This is the basis of life.

1 Corinthians 10. 16, 17: The partaking of the material symbols is the manward aspect of the Lord's table, demonstrating fellowship and the Lord's provision for His people. The practical expression of this lasts throughout the week.

1 Corinthians 11. 24–26: The partaking of the material symbols as an act of remembrance is associated with the Godward aspect of the Lord's supper. This is done only when the saints are "come together into one place", v. 20, or when they are "come together in the church", v. 18. This refers to the Lord's day.

4. This verse speaks of spiritual drink, following the spiritual food of verse 3 . The first miraculous provision occurred in Exodus 17. 6. The rock smitten at Horeb is suggestive of Christ, the strong yet smitten One, being the provision for His people. The last time occurs in Numbers 20. 8–11, the rock now being in the desert of Zin at the end of the wilderness wanderings, see v. 1. The Rock, *once* smitten, was regarded as following (going with) them, and always available to faith. Moses' smiting the rock on this last occasion did despite to the symbol, which "was Christ". God would not allow types to be spoilt when they spoke of His Son.

The two verses 3 and 4 are referred to in Psalms 78. 19, 20; the Lord furnished "a table in the wilderness". The idea of the Rock occurs often in the O.T. In the song of Moses, Deut. 32, it occurs several times, but the song ends in declension and judgment. In the song of David, 2 Sam. 22, the subject of the Rock ends in victory. The songs of the Psalms are likewise full of references to the Rock.

Verses 5–10: Partaking of Incompatible Things

5 But with many of them God was not well pleased: for they were overthrown in the wilderness.
6 Now these things were our examples, to the intent we should not lust after evil things, as they also lusted.
7 Neither be ye idolators, as *were* some of them; as it is written, The people sat down to eat and drink, and rose up to play.
8 Neither let us commit fornication, as some of them committed, and fell in one day three and twenty thousand.
9 Neither let us tempt Christ, as some of them also tempted, and were destroyed of serpents.
10 Neither murmur ye, as some of them also murmured and were destroyed of the destroyer.

5. Paul now shows that the people would engage in everything displeasing to God, in spite of His continual provision made in grace regardless of their conduct. Paul restricts himself to those evils most suited to his present purpose. The psalmists often spoke of those days: Asaph recalled them in Psalm 78. 17–53, while Psalm 106. 13–33 deals with similar evils in the wilderness, continuing the description into the land, in verses 34–43.

Those who are not well pleasing to God are always in contrast to those who are well pleasing to Him. Among other references, we may note:

Those not pleasing to God:

Romans 8. 8, "They that are in the flesh cannot please God".

1 Thessalonians 2. 15, "Who both killed the Lord Jesus, and their own prophets, and have persecuted us; and they please not God, and are contrary to all men". Paul is referring here to the Jews.

The Lord Jesus pleasing the Father:

John 8. 29, "For I do always those things that please Him".

Matthew 3. 17; 17. 5, "This is My beloved Son, in whom I am well pleased". As far as His earthly pathway is concerned, the former verse refers to His walk prior to His public ministry, while the latter refers to His walk during His public ministry.

Matthew 12. 18, "Behold My servant, whom I have chosen; My beloved, in whom My soul is well pleased", quoted from Isaiah 42. 1. The context deals with the Lord's servant character, not retaliating against the threats of the Pharisees, Matt. 12. 14.

The saints and their service pleasing to God:

Philippians 4. 18, "The things which were sent from you, an odour of a sweet smell, a sacrifice acceptable, wellpleasing to God". This refers to financial gifts sent to Paul from those who loved him, in contrast to 1 Corinthians 9. 15.

1 Thessalonians 2. 4, "As . . . put in trust with the gospel, even so we speak; not as pleasing men, but God, which trieth our hearts".

Hebrews 11.5, "Before his translation he (Enoch) had this testimony, that he pleased God. But without faith it is impossible to please Him".

Hebrews 13. 21, "Now the God of peace . . . make you perfect in every good work to do His will, working in you that which is well pleasing in His sight, through Jesus Christ".

"In the wilderness" refers to the period between the two Rocks discussed at verse 4. The people had obviously begun in the Spirit, but had ended in the flesh, Gal. 3 . 3 . The method of their overthrow is detailed in the following verses.

6. Paul is recording these things here to show a use of the darker sides of O.T. history. Some historical events are types of the Lord's sufferings (e.g., the story of Joseph), some events are prophetical in their implications (e.g., the flood, Matt. 24. 37–39), some show abounding grace (e.g., David's sin, 2 Sam. 12), some encourage by showing the guiding hand of God behind apparently coincidental circumstances (e.g., the book of Ruth), while others show the onward progress of God's purpose to bring in Christ and the kingdom in spite of the intrigues of men (e.g., the books of 1 and 2 Kings). Divine inspiration embraces not only an *exact record*, but also a *reason* for recording the events on the pages of Scripture.

Here, the word "examples" is the same word as "ensamples" in verse 11; the meaning of "types" is implied. (In Hebrews 8. 5 the word is translated "pattern". The word is often used to denote the living example of a believer, Phil. 3. 17; 1 Thess. 1. 7; 1 Tim. 4. 12; Tit. 2. 7; 1 Pet. 5.3). These happenings are here recorded to warn believers, not of judgment, but of the exceeding sinfulness of sin, Rom. 7. 13.

"Lust after these things": Psalm 106. 14 repeats this; they "lusted exceedingly in the wilderness, and tempted God in the desert". Such sin is recalled for a purpose, but in other fitting cases it is not recalled at all. For example, in the psalm of worship, suitable for the heavenly position of triumph of the ark on mount Zion, 1 Chron. 16, we note that verses 34–36 are quoted from Psalm 106, namely from the first verse and the last two verses. All the remaining verses about wilderness sin are omitted, not being suitable for praise on Zion.

The reference is, of course, to Numbers 11. 4–5. The people remembered "the fish, which we did eat in Egypt freely; the cucumbers, and the melons, and the leeks, and the onions, and the garlick". Lust is always after the things of the flesh, after activities of preconversion days, interests and things satisfying the natural man. Saints can be ensnared by unhealthy occupations which interested them before they were saved, returning in desire to the Egypt of their past lives. This is the idea behind the unleavened bread brought out of Egypt, Exod. 12. 39. Nothing prepared beforehand in Egypt could be brought out; victuals on the journey could not be influenced by Egyptian preparation. Hence, preconversion lusts should have no place in the desires of the child of God. For example:

   Titus 3. 3, "For we ourselves also *were* sometimes . . . serving divers lusts and pleasures . . .", but Paul stresses the good works of faith as the present manifestation of life in a believer.

   1 Peter 1. 14, "As obedient children, not fashioning yourselves according to the *former* lusts in your ignorance", and then Peter stresses the necessity for holiness in conduct.

   7. "The people sat down to eat and drink, and rose up to play", recalls the sin of making the golden calf in Exodus 32. Idolatry and immorality go together, as is witnessed by the phrase "rose up to play". This does not refer to harmless children's play, but is gross evil, Rom. 1. 23–32.

Aaron prepared "a feast to the Lord", Exod. 32. 5, and burnt offerings and peace offerings were offered. It is obvious that the things that the people ate were parts of the peace offerings, this being the only sacrifice of which the people could partake (as in 1 Cor. 10. 18). They were, in fact, partaking of the altar. The people turned the holy institutions into selfish and fleshly indulgences, such that the judgment of God had to fall. The priesthood and the service of God were vitally affected afterwards:

(a) Only the tribe of Levi was chosen for the service of God, since they were on the Lord's side, Exod. 32. 26; Num. 3. 45.

(b) Only Aaron's family was chosen for the priesthood instead of the whole nation being "a kingdom of priests", Exod. 19. 6. Grace took Aaron up from the deepest sin to the highest place attainable by mortal man, within the vail on the day of atonement. There appears a hint of national restoration in Isaiah 61. 6, "but ye shall be named the Priests of the Lord: men shall call you the Ministers of our God".

(c) The position of the (temporary) tabernacle was affected, Exod. 33. 7, since it was removed "without the camp, afar off from the camp".

Let no believer think that deliberate contact with and participation in unholy things, not according to the Lord's mind revealed in the N.T., will not have its dark repercussions on his own life or on the testimony of the local assembly.

One N.T. application appears to be in 1 Peter 2. After showing the blessed position of being a holy priesthood unto the Lord, v. 5, Peter exhorts his readers, as strangers and pilgrims, to "abstain from fleshly lusts, which war against the soul: having your conversation honest among the Gentiles", v. 11.

8. The evil of fornication, causing in one day twenty-three thousand to fall, is recorded in Numbers 25. There, in verses 1–5, whoredom with the daughters of Moab caused idolatry, sacrifice and eating. Verses 6–15 deal with the consequences of a Midianitish woman being brought into the camp. The result was that twenty-four thousand died during the plague, v. 9; that is, twenty-three thousand in one day, as 1 Cor. 10. 8, and one thousand on another day.

These events tested the priesthood:

(a) Eleazar the high priest and Ithamar his brother were found wanting; they did nothing.

(b) Phinehas, Eleazar's son, was zealous with the zeal of the Lord, v. 11 marg., and hence was awarded an "everlasting priesthood", that is, the high priesthood would pass through his family. How quickly men depart from the ways of the Lord, and how slow they are to make amends. Later Eli, the high priest in 1 Samuel 1, was in the wrong line of Ithamar and not of Eleazar and Phinehas. David partially restored the situation by having two high priests, one from each line, 1 Chron. 24. 1–5, but it was left to Solomon finally to rectify the matter by the disposal of Abiathar, 1 Kings 2. 27, and giving the unique position to Zadok, v. 35.

In 1 Corinthians 10, it should be noticed that verse 7 denotes the *internal manufacture* of false ideas, thereby displacing the authority of God. In verse 8, such false ideas are *imported internally* (Midian) or else *sought for externally* (Moab). We do well to examine our own movements in the light of such principles.

9. The specific reference here is to Numbers 21, but many forms of tempting occurred during the wilderness wanderings. We may note:

Exodus 17. 2, 7; the people tempted the Lord by murmuring against Moses for lack of water and by questioning whether the Lord was among them, or not. This was equivalent to rousing His anger by unbelief. The people doubted His word, His promises and His presence.

Numbers 14. 22; after the incident of the twelve spies, and after they had seen the Lord's glory and His miracles, they tempted Him "yet these ten times". The "ten" may have reference to the fact that ten spies returned in unbelief; other expositors seek out ten examples of murmuring from the previous history. Here, they tempted the Lord in the sense of provoking the Lord to destroy them. This actually took place, v. 29.

Numbers 21. 5; here they spoke against God, being discouraged because of the way as they encompassed the land of Edom, ready to go up the east side of the Dead Sea. 1 Corinthians 10. 9 indicates that they really tempted Christ on this occasion. This may be explained by the fact that the power behind the serpent of brass was actually the power of the One whom they had tempted. This serpent of brass speaks of Christ lifted up, John 3. 14.

Deuteronomy 6. 16; a general exhortation at the end of the jouney, "Ye shall not tempt the Lord your God".

Psalm 78. 17, 18; Asaph the psalmist understood that it was *in their heart* that they tempted God, provoking the most High. They continued this even in the land, v. 56, by tempting and provoking the most High to anger with their high places, until the ark was carried away from their midst.

It would appear that saints today can take a similar position, thereby calling down God's governmental dealings upon His people. Lack of blessing in spite of much service can be attributed to this cause. Revelation 2–3 demonstrate the governmental hand of God upon the local assemblies whose works were known to the One walking in their midst, and the command to repent was given to many of them.

10. The murmuring of the people refers in particular to Numbers 16. 41, when they complained that it was Moses and Aaron who had "killed the people of the Lord" in the judgment that followed the uprising of Korah. In verses 45 and 49, many were consumed, destroyed of the destroyer. See also Hebrews 3. 8–12.

We should note in verses 7 and 10 that Paul, by the use of the word "ye", does not include himself. He had already renounced in chapter 8 verse 13 the implications of contact with idolatry (verse 7). As an apostle he could not gainsay the governmental hand of God, else he could not have written such verses as chapter 11 verses 30–32.

Verses 11–13: God's present Use of O.T. History

11 Now all these things happened unto them for ensamples : and they are written for our admonition, upon whom the ends of the world are come.
12 Wherefore let him that thinketh he standeth take heed lest he fall.
13 There hath no temptation taken you but such as is common to man: but God *is* faithful, who will not suffer you to be tempted above that ye are able; but will with the temptation also make a way to escape, that ye may be able to bear *it*.

11. Why has Paul been recalling all these O.T. events? He now states that the blessings of verses 1–4 and the judgments upon the incompatible activity of verses 5–10 happened for "our ensamples", that is, types. In other words, one must look beyond the actual types and perceive through them principles applicable to N.T. times. Note that the sins themselves were not types. The types were brought in by God, and so can refer only to the blessings and the judgment.

Not only did these things *happen* as types, but they were *written* in the O.T. record. This is not to satisfy curiosity, nor to produce interesting reading, nor to provide a hunting-ground around which theologians could discuss their various source-theories, but "for our admonition", or "to put us in mind". This requires a humble and not an academic heart and approach.

Compare:

Romans 15. 4; "whatsoever things were written aforetime were written for our learning", to bring in patience and hope as we are likeminded according to Christ Jesus;

2 Timothy 3. 16; "all scripture is given . . . for reproof, for correction, for instruction in righteousness".

This shows how important it is not to neglect the study of the O.T. Scriptures. When the O.T. is quoted in the N.T., these quotations should be understood in detail.

"Upon whom the ends of the world are come". This phrase "ends of the ages" is variously translated in the N.T., and it is applied to a wide variety of situations. It may imply the eternal ages to come, or it may refer to the ages past. Here, it seems to mean "the end of O.T. history is come upon us since we are now in N.T. times, yet the O.T. record is still of value".

12. The fact that God realised that we need constantly to be warned about these things, shows that self-complacency and self satisfaction are dangerous both in an individual and in an assembly. The Laodicean assembly thought that they were standing, but the Lord showed that they had fallen, "Thou sayest, I am rich, and increased with goods, and have need of nothing: and knowest not that thou art wretched, and miserable, and poor, and blind, and naked", Rev. 3. 17. There is a need for constant watchfulness, but with no morbid introspection, in order constantly to "set in order the things that are wanting", Tit. 1. 5. This is similar to the porters in 2 Chronicles 23. 19 set at the gate of the house of the Lord to guard against the coming in of uncleanness.

13. In the list of O.T. sins in verses 6–10, the people were engaged in the practice of idolatry in spite of experiencing blessings in the wilderness. Paul did not imply that the Corinthians were *practising* idolatry; they were only in *contact* with relics of it. The motive leading to these unwise actions on the part of the saints is described by Paul as temptation. Moreover, in temptation, none is a special case all to himself; temptations are "common to man", or literally, "No *temptation* has taken you except what belongs to man". Saints today are far more privileged than those of the O.T., in that God in Christ has wrought wondrously to help His people, providing means for escaping the fruit of temptation, namely the ensuing sin (the order may be found in James 1. 14, 15). God is described as being faithful in this matter. In other matters also He has this character:

> 1 Corinthians 1. 8, 9: to confirm saints unto the end to be blameless in the day of the Lord Jesus Christ;
> 1 Thessalonians 5. 23: to preserve one's whole spirit and soul and body blameless unto the coming of the Lord Jesus Christ;
> 2 Thessalonians 3. 3: to stablish saints and to keep them from evil;
> 1 John 1. 9: to forgive us our sins if we confess them.

We should rejoice that we know that God is faithful, so that *we can trust Him.* Similarly, *He can trust us* in service if He counts us as faithful. There are six N.T. saints whom God could trust and who are designated as faithful:

> Paul, 1 Tim. 1. 12;
> Timothy, 1 Cor. 4. 17;
> Tychicus, Eph. 6. 21;
> Epaphras, Col. 1. 7;
> Onesimus, Col. 4. 9;
> Silvanus, 1 Pet. 5. 12.

Concerning temptation, we should notice the following Scriptures:

(a) Temptation originates *externally*, as 1 Thess. 3. 5, or *internally*, as James 1. 14. Not all the blame should be placed upon Satan, since the heart of man is also responsible. One should carefully notice that, in the Lord's case, *all* temptation was *external*, Matt. 4. 1–11.

(b) It is allowed as a trial of faith, James 1. 2, 3; 1 Pet. 1. 7.

(c) The Lord knows how to deliver the godly out of temptations, 2 Pet. 2. 9.

(d) The Lord intercedes for His people under temptation, Luke 22. 32. In this process of sifting, Satan wanted the chaff, but the Lord wanted the grain.

Verses 14–22: The Argument fom the Lord's Table

14 Wherefore, my dearly beloved, flee from idolatry.
15 I speak as to wise men; judge ye what I say.
16 The cup of blessing which we bless, is it not the communion of the blood of Christ? The bread which we break, is it not the communion of the body of Christ?
17 For we *being* many are one bread, *and* one body : for we are all partakers of that one bread.
18 Behold Israel after the flesh : are not they which eat of the sacrifices partakers of the altar?
19 What say I then? that the idol is any thing, or that which is offered in sacrifice to idols is any thing?
20 But *I say*, that the things which the Gentiles sacrifice they sacrifice to devils, and not to God : and I would not that ye should have fellowship with devils.
21 Ye cannot drink the cup of the Lord, and the cup of devils : ye cannot be partakers of the Lord's table, and of the table of devils.
22 Do we provoke the Lord to jealousy? are we stronger than he?

Paul now changes his tactics. Up to now, he has brought the O.T. to bear upon the conscience. Now he uses the privileged blessings of the Lord's table to support his argument. Some expositors deny any connection between the symbols of the cup and the bread here associated with the Lord's table and the similar symbols in chapter 11 verses 23–26 associated with the Lord's supper. We respect this view, but it is wiser sometimes not to be dogmatic.

W. Rodgers has written:*

"It is not easy to understand how anyone, with even a superficial knowledge of N.T. instructions regarding the supper, could hold that the two expressions in 1 Corinthians 10.16, 'The cup of blessing which we bless' and 'The bread which we break', have no reference to it. To what else could the Corinthian saints, accustomed as they were to the carrying out of these two things week by week when they came together, imagine the apostle's reference to be? . . . Paul is not here setting a theological puzzle for clever ones amongst them to solve; but is giving to the Corinthians plain and practical teaching and warning . . ."

In our exposition of the subject, we suggest that the symbols are the same, but as we have already remarked, the implications of the Lord's table and the Lord's supper are completely different. One is *saint-ward* while the other is *God-ward*. Only the saint-ward aspect is of relevance to Paul's argument here. In what is God-ward, the Lord sifts the preciousness of Christ out of our feeble utterances, but in what is saint-ward, we must do the sifting very carefully lest in practice contamination comes in.

14, 15. Paul now employs two deep appeals, through *love* in the first of these two verses, and through *spiritual wisdom* in the second. The first touches the *affections*, the second the *conscience* of the believer. "Dearly

---

* Bible Problems and Answers, by W. Hoste, W. Rodgers; page 324

beloved" is a term of uniting affection; Paul often used this phrase towards
the saints:

"Dearly beloved, avenge not yourselves", Rom. 12. 19;

"Dearly beloved, let us cleanse ourselves", 2 Cor. 7. 1;

"We do all things, dearly beloved, for your edifying",
2 Cor. 12. 19;

"My brethren dearly beloved . . . so stand fast in the Lord",
Phil. 4. 1;

"To Timothy, my dearly beloved son", 2 Tim. 1. 2;

"Unto Philemon our dearly beloved, and fellowlabourer", Philem. 1;

Also: "Dearly beloved, . . . abstain from fleshy lusts", 1 Pet. 2. 11.

Exhortation in love goes a long way, but the conscience must also be
reached. "As to wise men" implies christian wisdom, able to discern the
argument of the apostle, and far removed from the wisdom of the world,
1. 19; 3. 20. The conscience must examine the basis of all conduct,
particularly incompatible conduct, in the light of spiritual principles.

16. As previously in verses 1–4, Paul touches upon the positive side first
before dealing with incompatible action. So he deals with the communion
associated with the cup and the bread, being the fellowship of the blood
and body of Christ. The blood has only one implication, namely His life
given up *alone*. The bread has a greatly *extended sense* as the following verse
shows. The blood is the basis for the fellowship, so the cup is mentioned
first.

As far as the cup is concerned, it is that which "we bless", whilst the
bread is that which "we break". The word "we" implies that it is a common
act with common consequences. It is easy to lose sight of this in these days
of many counter-attractions to a full community spirit in a local assembly.
The word "bless" is a translation of the Greek word *eulogeo*, meanings "to
speak well of". The other word used much in this context is *eucharisteo*,
meaning "to give thanks". These two words, in the various contexts, are
used in connection with the bread and the cup in the following ways:

eulogeo, to speak well of:

Matt. 26. 26, the bread;

Mark 14. 22, the loaf;

(Luke 24. 30, the bread);

1 Cor. 10. 16, the cup;

eucharisteo, to give thanks:

Matt. 26. 27, the cup;

Mark 14. 23, the cup;

Luke 22. 17, the cup;

Luke 22. 19, the loaf;

1 Cor. 11. 24, the bread;

It can be seen that, totally, both words are used of both emblems. Needless
to say, in speaking well of both the bread and the cup, it is what the
symbols speak of, namely Christ Himself, rather than the symbols themselves.

The acts of blessing and giving thanks, of breaking, partaking and drinking, demonstrate a permanent fellowship. This is no act of temporary convenience or of a passing expedient, but a demonstration that we live in the light of the truth associated with His blood and body. The following Scriptures concerned with His blood show this:

Acts 20. 28, we submit to being fed by the overseers in the local company;

Romans 5. 8, 9, we live in the light of the love of God bringing in justification;

Ephesians 1. 7, we live in the light of redemption in the Beloved;

Ephesians 2. 13, Gentiles are made nigh, being built into an holy temple in the Lord;

Colossians 1. 20, with peace made, we own Him as Head of the body, the church, v. 18;

Hebrews 9. 14, it causes us to serve the living God;

Hebrews 10. 19, it allows us the liberty of access to draw near;

Hebrews 13. 20, 21, His will works out in us what is well pleasing to Him;

1 Peter 1. 2, it is connected with our sanctification and obedience;

Revelation 1. 4–6, it is associated with praise in connection with the seven churches.

This impressive list shows that the fellowship of His blood is a fulltime activity for the Lord's people who desire to live consistently after having partaken of the cup. "Occasional fellowship" does not seem to be a legitimate activity.

17. The teaching about the bread is enlarged upon, and it embraces
not only His body prepared, Heb. 10. 5;
His body in death, John 19. 40;
His body glorified, Phil. 3. 21;
but also "the church, which is His body", Eph. 1. 23, universally
"ye are the body of Christ", and 1 Cor. 12. 27, locally (this is only characteristic since no definite article appears in the Greek).

The fellowship of the body of Christ is seen in two ways.

1. *Absolutely*: the saints are one in Christ having been thus formed by God. Genesis 2. 24 in the natural creation, is typical of God's work in His new creation.

2. *Practically*: we partake of the one bread. If we do not live in the light of this fellowship, then we deny that there is any reality in the act of partaking. If the assembly is one in the corporate action of partaking of the symbols, then it should also be one in all other forms of service. If some brethren, including elders, feel that they can walk in independent service, to the grief of their fellow believers, then they should seriously question the ground on which they walk and serve.

18. Paul now quotes the O.T. ritual to show that sacrifice and fellowship go together. The verse is really in parenthesis, and deals essentially with the peace offering. The differences between the offerings should be noted:

Burnt offering: all was burnt on the altar, Lev. 1. 9, and the priest had only the skin, 7. 8.

Meal offering: part was burnt on the altar, 2. 9, while the priests partook of the rest, 2. 10; 7. 9–10.

Peace offering: part was burnt on the altar, 3. 5; the priests had special parts, 7. 15, 31, 32; the offerer had his portion, 7. 15–21, together with the people, 1 Chron. 16. 1–3.

Sin and trespass offerings: part was burnt on the altar, Lev. 4. 10, and part without the camp, 4. 12. The priests sometimes partook of the flesh, 6. 25–30; 1 Sam. 2. 13–17. The ritual of the trespass offering was similar to that of the sin offering, Lev. 7. 7.

Fellowship by priest, offerer and people occurs only in the peace offering, and so this is the offering refered to in 1 Corinthians 10. 18.

There are three classes of peace offering listed in Leviticus 7.

1. *Thanksgiving* for answered prayer, v. 12. See Psalm 50. 12. 14; 107. 22.
2. *For a vow*, v. 16; namely that if the Lord would grant a petition, then the offerer would do something in return, for example, offer a peace offering. See 1 Samuel 1. 11, 21, 24.
3. *As a freewill offering*, v. 16, because of what God was revealed to be, rather than for what He had done.

Under king David, the sweet psalmist of Israel, the peace offering merged into song, quite absent under the Mosaic ritual. For example, the song of 1 Chronicles 16. 8–36, associated with the ark being on mount Zion, follows the peace offering and contains thoughts akin to the peace offering.

Verses 8-22: This part starts with "Give thanks" for all His wondrous works. It is quoted from Psalm 105. 1–15, verses 16–45 being omitted. These refer to the peoples' *trials* in Egypt before redemption, and are unsuitable for worship.

Verses 23–33: This part starts with "sing", and deals with what God has revealed Himself to be. It represents the whole of Psalm 96, the ascension psalm.

Verses 34–36: This part starts with "Give thanks", and really represents a vow: "Save us, . . . *that* we may give thanks", v. 35. These verses are taken from Psalm 106. 1, 47, 48, the omitted verses referring to the peoples' failure in the wilderness, and are unsuitable for worship.

These three sections contain features that answer to the three classes of peace offering.

In the N.T., a general statement appears in 1 Peter 2. 5, that we as a holy priesthood should offer up spiritual sacrifices, acceptable to God by Jesus Christ. The various offerings are:

burnt offering: Philippians 2. 5–11; His devotion;

meal offering: Ephesians 5.11; His life of love ending in death;

peace offering: Hebrews 13. 15, "By Him therefore let us offer the sacrifice of praise to God continually, that is, the fruit of our lips giving thanks to His name". From verse 10, we conclude that this refers to the peace offering, since the question of eating arises. Certainly the aspect of the sin offering is excluded by verse 11, where the body is burnt without the camp.

1 Corinthians 10 verse 18 can only refer to the peace offering. The altar demonstrates the God-ward aspect; the partaking the manward aspect. Paul is showing that both sides are incorporated in the table. The food for God coming first, Lev. 3. 11, corresponds more properly to the Lord's supper and the fellowship of the Lord's people rightly comes next.

19. As in chapter 8 verses 4–6, Paul shows that materially neither sacrifice nor idol is anything. Physically, these things remain unchanged in spite of the use to which they have been put.

20. But Paul cannot now ignore, as he did in chapter 8, the facts behind the idolatrous sacrifices. Behind the physical manifestations of idolatry there were the powers of darkness. These things were sacrificed to "devils". The altars at Athens, Acts 17. 23, and the shrine of the goddess Diana of the Ephesians, Acts 19. 26, 35, were nothing in themselves, but the "god of this world" was there to influence the hearts of men.

If one does partake of these relics, to what extent is one having "fellowship with devils"? This is the crux of the chapter. The conclusion, based on Christian liberty, appears to be as follows:

If *a brother eats legitimately* of meats (that is, if he does not stumble either believers, 8. 9, or unbelievers, 10. 28), then this is not having "fellowship with devils".

If *he eats illegitimately* (that is, if he causes anyone to stumble), this corresponds to fellowship. It certainly has lasting effects on the ones who are offended.

21. We have here the incompatible conduct of partaking at two tables. (It should be noticed here that the word "table" seems to stand for the bread, in contrast to the cup.) If a brother pleases God in worship, and if he walks in the light of fellowship with the assembly, then these spiritual activities *do not* and *cannot mix* with the other offending activity of stumbling men by contact with idols. The wilderness blessings of verses 1–4 at the beginning of this chapter are incompatible with the evils of verses 5–10.

A reference to the cup of devils may be found in Deuteronomy 32.38.

The truth of the present verse may also be found elsewhere. For example, "What communion hath light with darkness? And what concord hath Christ with Belial? or what part hath he that believeth with an infidel? And what agreement hath the temple of God with idols?, 2 Cor. 6. 14–16.

22. Paul concludes this paragraph with two questions.

1. "Do we provoke the Lord to jealousy?" Are there brethren who think that they can conduct themselves independently in this matter, thereby giving Him cause to come in governmentally to protect His own holy things? See Psalm 79. 5; Luke 17. 2.

2. "Are we stronger than He?" Those who think they can partake obviously think that they themselves are strong, unlike their weaker brethren, Rom. 14. 1, 21;1 Cor. 8. 10–12. If they persist, they seek to be stronger than God, who denies them the right to persist in such activity. In fact, whatever their own thoughts, they know nothing correctly, 1 Cor. 8. 2.

A feeling of independence and of strength, in any matter relating to assembly conduct and testimony, is really damaging to spiritual prosperity. Brethren should learn when and how to climb down before God, taking a position of fellowship and weakness before their fellow saints.

Verses 23–33: The Resolution of the Question at Issue

23 All things are lawful for me, but all things are not expedient : all things are lawful for me, but all things edify not.

24 Let no man seek his own, but every man another's *wealth*.

25 Whatsoever is sold in the shambles, *that* eat, asking no questions for conscience sake:

26 For the earth *is* the Lord's and the fulness thereof.

27 If any of them that believe not bid you *to a feast*, and ye be disposed to go; whatsoever is set before you, eat, asking no question for conscience sake.

28 But if any man say unto you, This is offered in sacrifice unto idols, eat not for his sake that shewed it, and for conscience sake: for the earth *is* the Lord's, and the fulness thereof.

29 Conscience, I say, not thine own, but of the other: for why is my liberty judged of another *man's* conscience?

30 For if I by grace be a partaker, why am I evil spoken of for that for which I give thanks?

31 Whether therefore ye eat, or drink, or whatsoever ye do, do all to the glory of God:

32 Give none offence, neither to the Jews, nor to the Gentiles, nor to the church of God:

33 Even as I please all *men* in all *things*, not seeking mine own profit, but the *profit* of many, that they may be saved.

23, 24. Here we have three practical principles worked out in the remaining verses of the chapter. Readers should note in verse 23 that the various editors' texts omit the phrase "for me" which occurs twice. When Paul observes that "all things are lawful", he does not imply that *everything* is lawful *regardless* of the question of sin. A particular course of action is lawful only if it is not sinful, but that is no criterion for engaging in that course of action. How much grief to others in local assemblies would be avoided if brethren would measure their walk and service by this rule.

The three principles are:

1. Things must be expedient or *profitable*. (See John 16. 7; Acts 20.
    20; 1 Cor. 6. 12; 12. 7; Heb. 12. 10 for verses containing the same
    word). In other words, will positive good come out of my action?
    This principle is applied in verses 25–30.
2. Things must be for *edification*, namely, for building up so that
    unbelievers become believers, and believers develop to maturity.
    This is the good work of a good builder, and applies to verses 31
    and 32.
3. We must seek the *interests of others* and not of ourselves; this is
    applied in verse 33. Christianity looks outwards and not inwards.
    For example, "Look not every man on his own things, but every
    man also on the things of others", Phil. 2. 4, is illustrated in
    Philippians 2 by
    >   Christ Jesus, verses 5–11;
    >   Paul, verses 16–17;
    >   Timothy, verses 19–23;
    >   Epaphroditus, verses 25–30.

These three principles are also illustrated in Romans 15. 1–2:
1. The strong should bear the infirmities of the weak—this is
    profitable conduct.
2. One should please one's neighbour for his good to edification.
3. We should not please ourselves.

25–30. Paul discusses three possibilities of being in contact with
idolatrous relics. He deals with this in the light of whether or not it is
profitable to eat meats.
1. When one buys meat in the market, one would realise that it
    might have originated as an idolatrous relic. Don't however ask
    after its origin for *one's own conscience sake*. All physical things
    belong to the Lord, and on that ground one may freely eat with
    thanksgiving. If, however, a weaker brother knows the origin of
    the meat, then one should refrain from eating for the sake of the
    conscience of the weaker brother, 8. 10.
2. If one is invited to a meal by an unbeliever, acceptance of the
    invitation is not automatic. If one is "disposed to go", v. 27,
    implies an exercise about the matter. Again, one should ask no
    question concerning the origin of the meats for one's own
    conscience sake.
3. If, on the other hand, the origin of the meat is disclosed, then one
    should decline to eat for the sake of the *conscience of the
    unbeliever*. The believer has liberty to eat everything for which he
    gives thanks before the meal, 1 Tim. 4. 3–5, but since the
    unbeliever will now speak or think evil of the inconsistency of
    such action, the believer should refrain from eating. Unbelievers
    quickly sense when a Christian's conduct is inappropriate, and
    such a testimony is not profitable to the unbeliever. Today,
    believers may well have to refrain from partaking of certain foods

and beverages placed before them by unbelievers, and in all conduct, we should "abstain from all appearance of evil", 1 Thess. 5. 22. All this is, of course, quite distinct from doing good and yet being evil spoken of; see Matt. 5. 10–12; 9. 2–5.

31–32. These verses contain positive action towards others through the conduct of the Lord's people. When the results edify others, this is to the glory of God. It is the same as in the Lord's case described in John 17: "I have glorified Thee on the earth" v. 4. His service went out to others: He manifested His Father's name to His own, v. 6; He gave unto them the Father's words, v. 8; He kept them in the Father's name, v. 12; He sent them into the world with Himself as the sanctified object of service, v. 18; He gave them glory received from the Father, v. 22.

Similarly, this verse 32 deals with the believers' relation with men of all types (see the *subject background* of this chapter). All conduct is with a view to edifying, the opposite of offending.

33. Paul concludes with his own example in this last question of Christian liberty. He would not marry, 1 Cor. 7. 7; he would not eat meats, 8. 13; he would not live of the gospel, 9. 15; and now he would do nothing that would distract from the power of the gospel so that he could be spiritually powerful to the unsaved. His field was the world—all men. He did not think of himself in his service and toil, 2 Cor. 11. 21–33. "I will very gladly spend and be spent for you", 2 Cor. 12. 15, was his abiding motto. As for the unsaved, his whole conduct was for their salvation, 2 Cor. 4. 1–7.

Chapter 11 verse 1 really concludes this section. It is his final appeal for wise conduct, before dealing with a question where no liberty was allowed. The word translated "followers" really means "mimics, imitators". To be an *imitator* of Paul was the conclusion in chapter 4 verse 16 regarding the character of service. As young believers, the Thessalonians had become *followers* both of Paul and of the "churches of God which in Judea are in Christ Jesus", 1 Thess. 1. 6; 2. 14. They were likewise to be *imitators* of Paul in the orderly conduct of day-by-day living, 2 Thess. 3. 7, 9. By this means, saints really look beyond Paul, and see Christ Himself as the object and pattern set before them. Such a vision turns one's heart entirely from oneself.

1 CORINTHIANS 11. 2–16

Section 5. Assembly Service
Subject 1. Christ Manifested in Authority

Summary of Section 5

Having dealt with various phases of conduct where Christian liberty is allowed, Paul now turns his attention to assembly service. Various phases of assembly service were in disorder in Corinth, and thus needed apostolic correction. The Lordship of Christ and His authority is manifested at every stage in assembly service. There can be no liberty where divine principles are laid down for service, although of course there can be exercise in the outworking of one's service.

We have already noticed that verse 1, "Be ye followers of me", properly forms part of the previous chapter. Believers are called upon to imitate Paul, by making a most careful examination of all phases of their liberty in Christ. Paul would not use his liberty in various matters when it appeared that a use of liberty might hinder the work of the service of God. The Lord Jesus had infinite liberty in the world of His own creation, but He used it sparingly. He fed the multitude miraculously, but He would not provide food for Himself, Matt. 4. 4.

The section dealing with assembly service embraces chapters 11 to 14 as follows:

Chapter 11. 2–16: Christ manifested in authority;
Chapter 11. 17–34: the Lord's supper;
Chapter 12: the distribution of spiritual gifts maintaining the unity of the body;
Chapter 13: The necessity for the lubrication of love on the outworking of spiritual gifts;
Chapter 14: principles governing the use of spiritual gifts in assembly service.

The order of these subjects should be carefully noticed:
1.   The authority of Christ is established first, together with the outward means for demonstrating it practically.
2.   In the Lord's supper, assembly service Godward is presented first.
3.   Assembly service saint-ward is discussed next, spiritual principles receiving the first attention.
4.   Practical details of service amongst the saints are dealt with last.

This order is of vital importance. God receives His due first of all, wholesome doctrine follows, and then the practical outworking of this doctrine comes last. God's order cannot be reversed. Young believers should be taught to appreciate and to walk in the order given by God. Service can only then be blessed by Him.

A proper perspective should be maintained in studying this section. Chapters 1–10 deal essentially (but not exclusively) with *individual* conduct, while chapters 11. 17 to 14. 40 deal with *collective assembly* conduct. The verses dealing with the present subject separates them, showing individual action deeply connected with collective testimony.

Background of this Subject

Verse 2 is an example of Paul's spiritual psychology. "Praise" in this verse comes before "praise not" in verses 17 and 22, although there seems to be little that Paul could praise the Corinthians for. Similarly, there was spiritual commendation in chapter 1 verses 1–9 before a full discussion of weaknesses. The word "praise" applied to individuals may also be found in Luke 16. 8, "the lord commended the unjust steward", and in 2 Corinthians 8. 18, "the brother, whose praise is in the gospel". It is a different word from that used in such verses as Luke 2. 13; 24. 53 where "praising God" is in question.

Remembering Paul in all things is obviously different from *imitating* Paul. One can remember the things Paul introduced without owning the authority Paul had from the Lord. Today, many may think about Paul's teaching, but practising what he wrote is a different matter altogether.

Ordinances or traditions may vary greatly in character:

Bad traditions: "tradition of the elders", Matt. 15. 2, 3, 6; "tradition of men", Mark 7. 3, 5, 8, 9, 13,

Self-righteous traditions: "zealous of the traditions of my fathers", Gal. 1. 14,

Philosophical tradition: "through philosophy and vain deceit, after the tradition of men", Col. 2. 8,

Paul's teaching: "hold the traditions which ye have been taught, whether by word, or our epistle", 2 Thess. 2. 15; "the tradition which he received of us", 2 Thess. 3. 6.

In the verse before us, it would appear that the traditions referred to are those most intimately connected with assembly practice, namely baptism and the Lord's supper. The word tradition is, of course, not used here in any derogatory or religious sense.

These traditions were being kept, but whether the actual mode of keeping them was satisfactory is another matter. Verses 20–22 show otherwise. Although Paul could see nothing perfect in practice, he valued any little sign of life, commending it whenever possible. For example, on one occasion he wrote, "Notwithstanding every way, whether in pretence, or in truth, Christ is preached; and I therein do rejoice, and will rejoice", Phil. 1. 18.

The uncovering of the brethren's heads and the covering of the sisters' heads in service was not being observed at Corinth, therefore this observance cannot be called a tradition. Rather it was to be a seemly act of intelligent spiritual conduct—the outward display of the acknowledgement of certain divine principles. The recognition of the Lordship of Christ is in question, and this had to be acknowledged by all *before* the various assembly matters could be rectified in the following chapters.

None would dispute the positive teaching of this section, but there is a difference of opinion as to the actual error manifested in Corinth. The fact that able teachers differ, suggests that the Holy Spirit deliberately left open the description of the error, so that the passage should have its widest possible application in these later days.

Some say: In the synagogues both men and women were covered; hence in assembly gatherings the uncovering of the man's head was an innovation. Sisters would consequently still be covered in assembly gatherings, and this needed no correction. The fact that prayer and prophesying are mentioned in verse 5 suggests that assembly gatherings are not in question nor in dispute, and that Paul is dealing with correction outside assembly gatherings rather than inside, which were automatically in order.

Others say: The reference to prayer and prophesying by women in verse 5 was something actually carried on in assembly gatherings in Corinth. Paul corrects one thing at a time, firstly the covering of the sister's head, and then the silence of sisters, 14. 34.

The difference between these two points of view lies, not in what should be observed in assembly gatherings, but in what was actual error that Paul was correcting. If the former point of view is expounded, it is difficult to apply the teaching to weaknesses in gatherings today. To say that sisters today should merely follow synagogue tradition is no help to those who are perplexed about the matter. All in all, the passage should be expounded for maximum usefulness as the Spirit intended, even if the exposition needed today is not quite the same as that needed to correct the particular disorder in Corinth.

A summary of this subject is:

Verse 3: principle of headship;

Verses 4–5: the *spiritual* reason, the manifestation of Christ as Head and not man as head;

Verses 6–10: the *creatorial* reason, the manifestation of the glory and authority of Christ and not the glory of man;

Verses 11–12: the safeguard-parenthesis, the common mutuality between men and women;

Verses 13–15: the *natural* reason, the comeliness of conduct;

Verse 16: no custom for the woman to be uncovered.

Exposition of 1 Cor. 11. 3–16: Christ Manifested in Authority

1 Be ye followers of me, even as I also *am* of christ.

2 Now I praise you, brethren, that ye remember me in all things, and keep the ordinances, as I delivered *them* to you.

3 But I would have you know, that the head of every man is Christ; and the head of the woman *is* the man; and the head of Christ *is* God.

4 Every man praying or prophesying, having *his* head covered, dishonoureth his head.

5 But every woman that prayeth or prophesieth with *her* head uncovered dishonoureth her head: for that is even all one as if she were shaven.

6 For if the woman be not covered, let her also be shorn: but if it be a shame for a woman to be shorn or shaven, let her be covered.

7 For a man indeed ought not to cover *his* head, forasmuch as he is the image and glory of God: but the woman is the glory of the man.

8 For the man is not of the woman; but the woman of the man.

9 Neither was the man created for the woman; but the woman for the man.

10 For this cause ought the woman to have power on *her* head because of the angels.

11 Nevertheless neither is the man without the woman, neither the woman without the man, in the Lord.

12 For as the woman *is* of the man, even so *is* the man also by the woman; but all things of God.

13 Judge in yourselves: is it comely that a woman pray unto God uncovered?

14 Doth not even nature itself teach you, that, if a man have long hair, it is a shame unto him?

15 But if a woman have long hair, it is a glory to her: for *her* hair is given her for a covering.

16 But if any man seem to be contentious, we have no such custom, neither the churches of God.

3. The word *head* is used here, not in a physical sense, but in a metaphorical sense. It denotes one to whom subjection is yielded. Three cases are brought before us in this verse.

1. "*The head of every man is Christ*". Man has two heads—his own physical head and Christ Himself. His spiritual position as being saved by grace demands his subjection to Christ and to His will. Right from the time of his conversion, Paul asked "Lord, what wilt Thou have me to do?", Acts 9. 6. This authority and position of Christ is reflected by His Headship over the assembly.

2. "*The head of the woman is the man*". This is the order of God in creation and in family life. The usual policy-maker is the husband, although such authority must be in the Lord. Such verses as Ephesians 5. 21, 22; Colossians 3. 18; Titus 2. 5; 1 Peter 3. 1, 5, should be noted in this conection, the wife taking the position as "unto the Lord" and as "fit in the Lord". Nevertheless, Scripture provides its own safeguard in this matter. Married life is not wholly one of authority and subjection shown by the partners. Mutuality of love, interest, and concern, is independent of both authority and subjection, and 1 Corinthians 7. 3–4; 11. 11–12 provides for this, since "there is neither male or female: for ye are all one in Christ Jesus", Gal. 3. 28.

3. "*The head of Christ is God*". This cannot imply any unequal partnership in the Godhead, no distinguishing of various personalities with varying authority, nor does it refer particularly to the order given in Matthew 28. 19 and 2 Corinthians 13. 14. It can refer only to such thoughts as "Lo, I come to do Thy will, O God", Heb. 10. 9; "I seek not mine own will, but the will of the Father which hath sent Me", John 5. 30; "Nevertheless not as I will, but as Thou wilt", Matt. 26. 39.

4. Paul now brings before us the spiritual functioning of the man. Prayer is directed God-ward, and is indited by the Spirit, Rom. 8. 26. (Prayer in the flesh is merely to oneself, Luke 18. 11.) Prophecy is directed man-ward, yet is indited by the Spirit, 1 Cor. 12. 11; 2 Pet. 1. 21. In such service, the uncovering of one's natural head demonstrates one's spiritual Head, namely Christ. It is a deliberate testimony on the part of brethren, and reflects the subjection of the whole assembly to its living Head. The idea of men uncovering their head in service was a new concept in the early days of the church. This act was essentially novel, and needed deliberate attention on the part of the men-folk to abide by it. This act glorifies Christ, and should be undertaken with this in view. Today, alas, it has become a mere custom, particularly if brethren wear no hat out-of-doors. But we should regard the act in a sense just as positive as that of sisters. If a brother's head remains covered, this is equivalent to dishonouring his Head, namely Christ. This word means to "disgrace" or "put to shame". (The same word is used in 1 Corinthians 1. 27 "to confound the wise", and in 11. 22 "and shame them that have not".) The implication is that a public disgrace is placed upon Christ as Lord and Head, because He is not being displayed in His superior position of Lordship.

5. Exactly the opposite holds for women. Their head displays subjection to the authority of man. This is correct in its right place, and is certainly appropriate in the home and even in many assembly activities. But in service there can be no rivalry for headship. The Lord has the ultimate authority, and thus the woman's head must be covered to show that the Lord is all in all. Otherwise her head (man) is dishonoured and disgraced. It makes an outward show of man, when he should rightly be hidden so Christ can be preeminent.

Both these displays of uncovering by brethren and covering by sisters are necessary to show the principles involved. Neither of these should be done as an act of blind custom, but with an understanding of the deep meaning involved, thereby to glorify the Lord. These principles do not imply, of course, that men and women are on the same footing as regards service. The subjective side of the women's sphere is not eliminated by these principles. Verses such as 1 Timothy 5. 17; 1 Peter 5. 5 show that there is subjection to the elder brethren. If this is so, then there is also subjection to the Lord. Natural relationships foster spiritual relationships.

Paul concludes these remarks by observing that if a woman does pray or prophesy with her head uncovered, this is the same thing as if she were shaven. That is to say, there would be a demonstration that something is missing. If her hair were shaven, this would be observed to be *missing*, and her natural head would be disgraced. Similarly, if her covering were missing, this would be observed by brethren and sisters alike, and brethren would thereby be disgraced. Thoughtless action by a few sisters ignorant of these principles can cause grief to brethren and sisters who desire assembly order to be preserved.

Regarding women praying or prophesying, this prayer will be silent in an assembly gathering, but would, of course, be audible in other circumstances, for example, in the home perhaps, in a Sunday school class, or with a group of sisters, or with an unsaved lady being led to the Lord. Women can never prophesy in an assembly gathering, 1 Cor. 14. 34, although it may have taken place in the disorder prevalent in the assembly at Corinth. In the circumstances of today, the spiritual gift of prophecy has ceased since the New Testament Scriptures are complete, but in those early days, some women possessed the gift of prophecy outside assembly gatherings, Acts 21. 9.

6. Paul now changes his argument. He is no longer writing about authority and headship (based on spiritual concepts), but about authority and glory (based on creatorial concepts). The conclusions are the same— a man's head should be uncovered but a woman's should be covered.

Paul now argues that a woman should either have two coverings or *none* at all. The first covering of her head is her hair, and this is her natural creatorial glory, v. 15. The second covering during service, is an artificial covering, a hat, over her hair. Paul's argument is that, although such creatorial glory is for the pleasure of God in its rightful place, Rev. 4. 11, yet in spiritual service even the best and most legitimate things of the flesh (and we do not use this term in any derogatory sense) are out of place. The hair, then, must either by covered or removed. Now God is never unreasonable in His holy demands, so He insists upon the covering of the hair and not its removal. This would avoid natural shame and embarrassment, and would of course permit the woman's glory to be manifested in its proper sphere.

For the word shave, see Acts 21. 24, while for the word shear (or cut) see Acts 18. 18; 8. 32. This latter verse, referring to the shearing of a lamb's wool, can refer only to a complete cutting not merely a trim. The argument here implies that Paul means the complete removal of all hair.

Note in Deuteronomy 21. 12, the glory (hair) of a captive maid is removed in order to test the affection of the man for her after a month.

7–9. God's order in creation declares the manifestation of glory. Man was created "in our image, after our likeness", Gen. 1. 26. He is supposed to reflect some of the attributes of God. This is impossible for the unregenerate man, but a man saved by grace may in, conduct, reflect something of the Lord, even if the flesh is still subject to death by reason of the fall. He thus uncovers his head to demonstrate figuratively the glory of the Lord. Psalm 8. 5 shows man crowned with "glory and honour", having dominion over the works of God's hands. This refers firstly to the position that man occupied before the fall, and secondly to "the world to come", Heb. 2. 5, when all will be subject to Christ. In the meanwhile, saints are still able to demonstrate this creatorial glory which was placed upon man. The uncovering of the man's head demonstrates the Lord's position and glory. Man's own headship and dominion in creation reflects the Lord's headship in deeper eternal things.

Conversely, the apostle writes, "The woman is the glory of man" (the word *the* should not appear before the word *man*, as in the A.V.). She was created *from* and *for* the man, and Paul concludes that these reasons give her glory creatorially. She is of the man in the sense of Genesis 2. 22, and she is *for* the man in the sense of verse 18. This glory is reflected in her outward glory, namely her hair, so this is covered in circumstances where the spiritual glory of Christ transcends the natural glory, even though given by God.

10. The creatorial glory derived from man has no standing in spiritual functioning. Hence, again, Paul concludes that the woman must have "power on her head", that is, the "sign of authority", thereby covering creatorial glory and natural authority. It is left to the men to show forth the glory and authority of Christ. In one sense, then, the act of sisters is negative, while the act of brethren is positive. The whole assembly is needed to set forth the whole truth.

"Because of the angels" has caused much difficulty to expositors. Even if we fail to grasp the implied sense of this phrase, the argument of the apostle is in no way diminished. Certainly the angels watch the activity of believers with interest, 1 Cor. 4. 9; (see also Eph. 3. 10; 1 Tim. 5. 21). These angels are in subjection to the Lord in resurrection and ascension, 1 Pet. 3. 22; those not in subjection had long since been cast into hell, 2 Pet. 2. 4; Jude 6. Angels are subject to His authority, knowing that judgment is still reserved for those that sinned. As they watch they expect that believers, having passed out of judgment, should acknowledge the same principles of subjection to the Lord. They watch the profession of it in the covering and uncovering of the head. They also watch the accomplishment of it in the outworking of christian conduct and assembly service. In any case, the saints will judge angels, 1 Cor. 6. 3. The saints should be more subject than those whom they will judge. The angels, therefore, are very much interested in what sisters demonstrate.

11–12. These are safeguard-verses. Even though the woman is in subjection, both in the assembly and at home, after the creatorial order, yet both sexes are necessary for each other (see chapter 7 verses 3–4). Neither can live effectively without the other in God's order for marriage "in the Lord". The phrase "as the woman is of the man" refers to the original creatorial *of* in Genesis 2. 22. The phrase "the man also *by* the woman" implies "*on account* of the woman". A similar preposition occurs in John 1. 3 and Acts 3. 18, for example, and it denotes "agency, instrumentality, by means of". The phrase refers to natural birth, as distinct from creatorial processes. Cain and Abel were "*by* Eve", while Eve was "*of* Adam". However one views this process, ultimately we recognise the truth: "all things of God". Whether in creation or in multiplication, He accomplishes all things, and works all things after the counsel of His own will. The Lord Himself upholds all such processes by the word of His power, Heb. 1. 3. This shows the necessity of recognising with esteem each born again individual, the argument of the previous verses in no sense relegating the woman to an inferior position.

13–15. Paul's third argument is of a *natural* character (not using this word in any derogatory sense). He deals with the natural sensitivities of Christians, based on what they had got used to in the synagogue service prior to their conversion. Over the years, they had come to sense that it was a shame for a man to have long hair. This applied to the time in which they lived; it is not a spiritual argument which would have had previous application. Indeed long hair was no shame to Absalom in O.T. days, 2 Sam. 14. 25–26, nor to Samson nor to the Nazarite, Num. 6. 5. In Ezekiel's day, the command is given for the priests to have neither shaved hair nor long hair, Ezek. 44. 20.

But for the woman, her long hair is naturally her glory. Her hair is given her for "*a covering*". In Greek, this is a different word from that occurring in verses 4, 5, 6, . . ., 13. Failure to notice this and failure to appreciate Paul's argument throughout the paragraph has caused some to believe that a sister's hair is an adequate covering already, not requiring a second artificial covering. Such a belief is absolutely invalid, and shows either the inability to follow an argument or else a refusal to own the authority of Christ. The word *covering* in this verse means *something cast around*, a veil. It occurs in Hebrews 1. 12, "as a vesture shalt thou fold them up". The hair is a "veil of glory and beauty". Even the natural senses of a believer would cause him or her to own that such natural glory has no place in spiritual service or in the presence of God. A second covering is therefore called for.

16. This is Paul's concluding remark on this subject. It is Paul's fourth and final argument for believers who still feel that sisters can serve uncovered, in spite of the spiritual, creatorial and natural reasons advocated above. Paul bluntly observes that "we" (that is, the apostles and Sosthenes) and all the other "churches of God" have no such custom whereby sisters can serve uncovered. Saints must follow Paul (11. 1) and other churches (1 Thess. 2. 14), so a particular assembly has no legitimate right to introduce any other contrary custom. The value of copying something that is spiritual along with a spiritual motive is fully demonstrated here.

1 CORINTHIANS 11. 17–34

Section 5.   Assembly Service
Subject 2.   The Lord's Supper

Background of this Subject

The first ten chapters of this Epistle have been occupied with the *external* activities of the assembly, the activities of the saints not viewed as gathered together "in assembly". These activities include preaching, some types of service, conduct, marriage, meats and daily maintenance. Chapters 11–14 are occupied with the *internal* activity of the assembly, when the saints are viewed as gathered together "in assembly".

First of all, the apostle establishes the Lordship of Christ. The understanding of this is essential for proper spiritual activity internally. Not only is a profession of His Lordship required, but also subjection to His authority is expected practically. The covering or uncovering of the head is a sign that this authority is accepted and also acted upon. The first ten chapters must also be seen as a necessary preparation for effective assembly service. One can make a mockery and a farce of spiritual service when gathered "in assembly", if one's life at other times is not governed by the great principles brought out previously in the Epistle. A believer is justified by faith and not by works, Rom. 4. 1–5; yet after a believer has been justified by faith, works are a proper expression of faith within, James 2. 21–26.

Again, God's order is that service among the saints cannot be effectual if things are amiss with their service God-ward (let alone the saint's service in the gospel among the unsaved—which is not the subject in chapters 12–14). The first call upon the service of God's people is His portion in Christ, and blessed are the saints who appreciate the divine order in these things. Hence Paul deals with the Lord's supper before the question of spiritual gifts.

The Lord had introduced the supper at the beginning, in the night in which He was betrayed. Then had taken place the last passover that God could recognise. That most holy type of redemption through the blood of the slain lamb had given place to the reality of redemption accomplished through the blood of the Lamb of God. The account of the institution of the supper may be found in Matthew 26. 17–30. They had gathered to partake of the passover, but they left with the supper newly instituted. The ground of the gathering had been described in verse 20, "Now when the even was come, he sat down *with the twelve*". This should be contrasted with the account given in Luke. See Luke 22. 7–23. In particular, verse 14 shows the ground of the gathering, "And when the hour was come, He sat down, and the twelve apostles *with Him*". In the latter passage, they sat down with Him—that is characteristic of the passover. In the former passage, He sat down with them—that is characteristic of the supper. The Lord comes now where His people are gathered in His name; see John 20. 19, 26.

Since the Lord introduced the supper, He has the sole right to maintain the perpetuation of it according to His will. That is why the Lordship of Christ is established immediately prior to the apostolic correction of the Corinthians' observance of the supper. When the ideas of men are allowed to come in, God-ward things are bound to be the first to suffer. The Lord could foresee the ceremony, ritual and tradition that men would build around this holy observance. So He took adequate steps in His Word to preserve all necessary details of the supper for those who look to Him and not to man for instruction on these matters. In this connection, we may quote Luke 6. 46, "Why call ye me, Lord, Lord, and do not the things which I say?". One is built either on a rock or on the sand. It is so possible to be built on the latter without realising it.

After the ascension of the Lord Jesus, and after the descent of the Spirit to form the assembly and to indwell believers, continuance in the breaking of bread was a characteristic feature of the early converts, Acts 2. 42. This act was for them only; the world outside had no part in such holy priestly functioning. The young converts were rapidly introduced to baptism and the breaking of bread, and it would be a good thing today if young converts were more rapidly grounded in these fundamental things. When such converts are saved, they realise that their salvation rests so intimately upon His death. Why, then, should these other things that speak of His death remain behind a cloak of silence? Can it be because there is some fear that young converts would go away backwards if the actual requirements of the Lord were enjoined upon them? If such were so, surely such folk *still* require to be saved.

Paul deals with the situation in Corinth by pointing out the error, the truth, and the means of correction. There are three paragraphs:

1. Verses 17–22: things as they were in Corinth;
2. Verses 23–26: things as instituted by the Lord;
3. Verses 27–34: God's government, the saints' examination, Paul's correction.

Exposition of 1 Cor. 11. 17–34: The Lord's Supper

Verses 17–22: Things as they were in Corinth

17 Now in this that I declare *unto you* I praise *you* not, that ye come together not for the better, but for the worse.
18 For first of all, when ye come together in the church, I hear that there be divisions among you; and I partly believe it.
19 For there must be also heresies among you, that they which are approved may be made manifest among you.
20 When ye come together therefore into one place, *this* is not to eat the Lord's supper.
21 For in eating every one taketh before *other* his own supper: and one is hungry, and another is drunken.

22 What? have ye not houses to eat and to drink in? or despise ye the church
of God, and shame them that have not? What shall I say to you? shall I
praise you in this? I praise *you* not.

17. Paul now has before him the assembly gathering; he sees the
Corinthians coming together "in assembly", not in a spiritual manner, but
merely in a physical manner after the fashion in which worldly people
would congregate. Paul praises them not, in spite of the little praise
forthcoming in verse 2. Similarly in Revelation chapters 2 and 3, the Lord
praises the little to be praised in the various assemblies' testimony and
conduct before He praises them not. The fact that the Corinthians were
coming together "for the worse" means that there was a manifestation of
carnal appetite rather than a holy appreciation of the Lord's supper. It was,
in fact, man's supper and not the Lord's supper.

18. The gathering together is described by the technical (yet spiritual)
phrase "in assembly", the definite article *the* being omitted. We must not
think that this phrase has any similarity with such common phrases of our
language as "in school", "in church", "in bed", and so on. Such common
phrases mean that "school", "church", "bed" are regarded as physical
places, and that people are inside these places. But "in assembly" is a
spiritual concept, having nothing to do with a building or a hall. It refers
to the ground by which the saints gather together in (or to) the name of
the Lord Jesus, see 1 Cor. 5. 4; Matt. 18. 20. It is to own the presence of
the living Head and to manifest the various characteristics of the body. No
dogma should be attached to this phrase "in assembly", since Scripture
does not exactly define the phrase. People may be gathered for many
purposes, both socially and religiously, but it is only "in assembly" when
the gathering is for the specific purpose for believers to exercise their
priestly calling, or to exercise their spiritual gifts. This is in keeping with
chapters 11–14, and avoids taking sectarian ground.

But there was no unity when the Corinthians thus came together.
There were "divisions" and "heresies" amongst them.

   Divisions mean *schisms*, as 1. 10. The word means "rent into parties",
   and it comes from a verb meaning "to split". For example, "There
   was a *division* among the people because of Him", John 7. 43. In our
   chapter, the divisions centred around various leaders caused by a
   party spirit amongst the Corinthians, 1. 12.

   Heresies mean *sects*. It implies a *choice* or *option*, from a verb meaning
   "to choose". Here, it refers to the strange carnal outlook that the
   Corinthians had regarding the Lord's supper. See Matthew 12. 18
   for an example of this verb "to choose" being used in a good sense,
   namely of God Himself.

19. When such dishonouring activity is found in a local gathering, the
faithful remnant amongst them will be "approved" by the attitude that
they take. They will be "approved" by God, Mal. 3. 16. The root is the

same as that occurring in the words "proof", "prove" and "reprobate" in 2 Corinthians 13. 3–7. The proof that Christ was working through and in Paul was his actual work in Corinth, even though they may judge him as "reprobate" or "not approved". A faithful saint is approved by results; "by their fruits ye shall know them", Matt. 7. 20.

20. "This is not to eat the Lord's supper" shows that Paul knew that they were not doing the thing that they professed they had come for. A mere outward act certainly does not mean that anything spiritual is achieved.

We must distinguish carefully the meaning of the word "Lord's". In the Greek, the possessive or genitive form of the noun "Lord" is not used here, even though the English version may use the possessive form. Rather, the Greek adjective *kuriakos* corresponding to the noun *kurios* is used. This adjective is used only on one other occasion in the N.T., namely, "the Lord's day", Rev. 1. 10. Again, this possessive form should be rendered by an adjective. The Lord's day, being the first day of the week, is distinct from "the day of the Lord", referring to the times of judgment after the rapture of the saints. In French, a language not endowed with a possessive form, "the day of the Lord" and "the Lord's day" are both translated usually by "le jour du Seigneur", which is bound to cause confusion. J. N. Darby, in his French version, gets over the difficulty by translating Revelation 1. 10 "le jour dominical", namely, he uses an adjective corresponding to the noun "Lord" as in the Greek. Similarly, 1 Corinthians 11. 20 is translated "la cene dominicale". In his English version, however, he follows the A.V., using "the Lord's supper" and "the Lord's day". Some believers use the English word "lordly", and speak of "the lordly day", but this is hardly correct. Fortunately English, like French, does have an adjective corresponding to "lord", but unfortunately it uses a different root, a Latin one. So we may speak of "the dominical supper" and "the dominical day", thereby avoiding a genitive or possessive implication. The word "dominical" means that the day or the supper takes character from the Lord, that it pertains to the Lord. It is remarkable that "the Lord's day" and "the Lord's supper" observed on the first day of the week are two of the most spiritual characteristics of the present assembly age; they are uniquely singled out in the N.T. to share the designation "dominical". It should be mentioned that "the Lord's table", 1 Cor. 10. 21, means "the table of the Lord" and not "the dominical table".

This word is perhaps unfamiliar to most English-speaking people. The difference between it and the possessive form "Lord's" can perhaps be best pointed out by drawing attention to other similar forms. The noun "Spirit" has the corresponding adjective "spiritual"; the noun "body" has the corresponding adjective "corporal". One talks about "spiritual gifts" but not "the Spirit's gifts"; the former refers to character while the latter to origin or possession. Similarly, "a bodily shape", Luke 3. 22, is quite different from "a body's shape".

The remembrance of the Lord Jesus is called a "supper" because the saints partake of the emblems, although these are not primarily spiritual food for them. The primary portion is for God Himself through the worship and adoration of His people. One feels, however, that God does not partake of the supper as such; it is not a meal for God. The replacement of "Lord's" by "dominical" removes that thought altogether, although some teachers would assert that the Lord's portion in the saints' worship is equivalent to His supper. To the present author, (and this suggestion is made for enquiry and thought), the word "supper" characterises the *moral time* in which the emblems are partaken. The word "breakfast" is not used. In the Gospels, "it was night", John 13. 30, a feature now translated into moral conditions. "The night is far spent, the day is at hand", Rom. 13. 12, describes the conditions outside, when the saints gather "in assembly" "till He come". He is the only true Light that lightens this scene.

Some suggest that this last reference to "the Lord's supper" in the N.T. provides the only name by which it is to be known during this dispensation. The original name, the "breaking of bread", Acts 2. 42, has been superseded, they suggest. But one questions whether this is really correct. In Troas the disciples came together on the first day of the week "to break bread", Acts 20. 7. This, however, took place one year *after* 1 Corinthians was written from Ephesus (1 Cor. 16. 8 and Acts 19). Hence Luke used the idea of breaking bread *some time after* Paul wrote about "the Lord's supper". It would appear to be an unfair use of scriptural words to adhere only to the latter form and to avoid the former. One refers to the act itself, the other to conditions behind the act.

21. This is the sin: "Having come together professedly to eat the Lord's supper, first of all everyone partakes of his own supper". The Corinthians' first thought was of themselves. The holy things of God were completely eclipsed. Satisfied appetitites and intoxication were the order of the day, and we may fairly judge that the very emblems were being used to produce these effects. But Paul had already written that drunkards within were not suitable company for fellowship, 5.11, and that drunkards without could have no part in the kingdom of God, 6. 10. It is remarkable that elsewhere Paul had to warn against drunkenness in the very context of hymns and spiritual songs, Eph. 5. 18–19. Such manifestations in the flesh are the exact opposite to manifestations of worship, see Lev. 10. 1, 2, 9. Excess of strong drink is one thing, but even to partake of it seems contrary to the cross of Christ: "I was the song of the drinkers of strong drink", Ps. 69. 12 marg.

22. All legitimate acts of eating and drinking should be accomplished in the home prior to a gathering. This should be distinguished from Acts 2. 46, where it appears that the early saints had constant fellowship with actual meals, since many had sold their houses. Hence, the Corinthians disparaged the assembly gathering by lowering its holiest activities to a natural level. They also shamed the poor saints who did not have a real home of their own, and thus who enjoyed fellowship over ordinary meals in the homes where the assembly met; see 1 Cor. 16. 19; Rom. 16. 5.

Verses 23–26: Things as Instituted by the Lord

23 For I have received of the Lord that which also I delivered unto you, That the Lord Jesus the *same* night in which he was betrayed took bread:
24 And when he had given thanks, he brake *it*, and said, Take, eat: this is my body, which is broken for you: this do in remembrance of me.
25 After the same manner also *he took* the cup, when he had supped, saying, This cup is the new testament in my blood: this do ye, as oft as ye drink *it*, in remembrance of me.
26 For as often as ye eat this bread, and drink this cup, ye do shew the Lord's death till he come.

23. This holy remembrance appears to be so different from all that men would build around it. The Lord's people today observe this remembrance because
(a)   it was instituted by the Lord in the Gospels;
(b)   it was practised by the assembly in the Acts;
(c)   the details were repeated by apostolic inspiration.
Paul received the truth from the Lord. No doubt he had also learnt of it from the other apostles and early assemblies before he embarked on his missionary journeys, but his authority had the special stamp that he had received it from the Lord. He "conferred not with flesh and blood", Gal. 1. 16, but was a chosen vessel to receive the divine revelation. Paul delivered this truth to his converts. In Corinth, this would have taken place during the one and a half years that he had laboured there. We should note the speed at which the young assemblies grew at that time.

The Lord Jesus took bread "the same night in which He was betrayed". The night would indicate the conditions of darkness in the world around, out of which believers gather in His name until He come. The reference to the betrayal would cause one to think of Judas, and his avaricious character, John 12. 6; Luke 22. 5. There was a certain similarity between the conduct of Judas and that of the Corinthians. Their state was one of greed in the matter of the supper. Judas had been guilty of the body and blood of the Lord, and as such was the son of perdition, John 17. 12. The Corinthians were likewise guilty, though in a different sense; they at least could not be lost. Rather through grace they were destined for glory, 1 Cor. 1. 8, but subject to the governmental judgment of God while in this scene.

In the O.T., the bread and the cup were a sign of mourning: "Neither shall men tare themselves for them (or, break bread for them, marg.) in mourning, to comfort them for the dead; neither shall men give them the cup of consolation to drink for their father or for their mother", Jer. 16. 7.

At first sight, there might appear to be a connection—that the Lord took up a custom amongst the Jews and used it to replace the passover feast. It is suggested that too much attention should not be given to this. The reference in Jeremiah refers to *mourning* for one *dead*, but the Lord's supper refers to the *remembrance* of One who now lives for ever. There is no mourning now even at the thought of His death, although the heart may be deeply moved at the thought of His sufferings. The mourning of death, John 20. 11, had given place to the joy of resurrection, Matt. 28. 8.

24. When He instituted the supper, the acts of the Lord Jesus are recorded to be those of giving thanks, breaking the bread and giving to the disciples. There seems to be little to commend speculation as to whether the Lord also partook of the emblems. Personally, the author would suggest that He did not, since the emblems were for the disciples and their remembrance of Himself; He needed nothing to symbolise His sufferings of the next day—they were divinely real to Him. The word "broken" in the text has no real authority, and is best omitted. The resulting translation "which is for you" sounds as if a verb is necessary to complete the sense; Luke supplies the word "given", Luke 22. 19. This contains the sweet thought that He gave Himself for us, Gal. 2. 20, but the idea of a body broken through crucifixion is rather outside the teaching of Scripture. Any sense of breaking refers to the bread and to fellowship, 1 Cor. 10. 16, not to His body.

This simple act perpetuates in worship the remembrance of Himself. The ceremony of the law was designed to remember again sins every year, Heb. 10. 3. But now the one true Sacrifice has been offered. He is the great displacer of the remembrance of sins, substituting the blessed remembrance of Himself

The thought behind His body is not only His body crucified; rather Himself in all His fulness is embraced. We should remark, however, that the thought of His body in the extended sense, 1 Cor. 10. 17, is not the basic thought here. The Spirit would bring before us several of the features connected with His body:

Hebrews 10. 5: "a body hast thou prepared Me";

John 2. 21: "the temple of His body";

Matthew 26. 12: "in that she hath poured this ointment on My body, she did it for My burial";

I Peter 2. 24: "who His own self bare our sins in His own body on the tree";

Hebrews 10. 10: "the offering of the body of Jesus Christ once for all";

Matthew 27. 58: "and begged the body of Jesus";

Philippians 3. 21: "His glorious body".

Some would ask if the bread should be unleavened, as in the original supper at the passover. If some feel, before the Lord, that unleavened bread should be used, then let them not sow discord and uncertainty amongst the majority who feel otherwise. The idea of leaven was an O.T.

ceremonial symbol, and nothing of that is imported into assembly service. The Lord interprets it in Matthew 16. 12, and therewith may we be content. The fact that unleavened bread had to be used when the people came out of Egypt, Exod. 12. 39, means that nothing that had been pre-prepared in the world (as leavened bread would have been) was suitable for the position that the people now took as delivered from Egypt. The implications are obvious; prior works of the flesh have no place at the Lord's supper. In any case, to insist upon unleavened bread would be mere occupation with the symbol, which is nothing *in itself.* Occupation with the symbol means that occupation with Christ is not complete. The Lord took the bread that was most conveniently to hand, and the saints today should do the same without question.

Some would notice that all scriptural references to the breaking of bread contain no direct thought of worship. They would point out that gatherings today for remembrance are occupied with worship, the act of breaking of bread occurring at some suitable time during the meeting. Are such gatherings therefore scriptural?

We would point out that Scripture does not provide a definite list of meetings. Meetings are convened for the convenience of the saints; there is no legislation on the matter. The Scriptures provide spiritual principles to govern meetings that are arranged. We are enjoined to break bread, and we are enjoined to exercise the functions of a holy priesthood, Heb. 13. 15; 1 Pet. 2. 5–9. The latter would be inappropriate when teaching, or evangelisation, or prayer are in view. The Lord merits His portion in worship apart from these other activities, so a gathering convened for worship is also highly appropriate for breaking bread. These also dovetail the two most holy activities of the believer's service.

25. Whereas the bread speaks of all that led up to His death on the cross, the cup speaks of the yielding up of His life temporarily into death. It is a cup of blessing when viewed saint-ward, 1 Cor. 10. 16, but that is not the immediate thought here. In the purpose of God the Lord's cup of suffering is found in Gethsemane, Matt. 26. 39; it had been given to Him by the Father, John 18. 11. This cup was real; it was for the Lord to drink. But the cup at the supper is a symbol of remembrance; the saints partake of it, and thus remember Him.

The connection between the blood and the covenant (or new testament) should be noticed. It is found typically in Exodus 24. 8, "Behold the blood of the covenant", and this is expounded in Hebrews 9. 18–28. In Exodus 24. 5 it is connected with the burnt and peace offerings, not with the sin offering. In other passages in Hebrews 9 and 10 the sin offering is connected with the day of atonement, not with Exodus 24. What is suitable for worship can clearly be seen! Practically, the blood of the everlasting covenant makes us perfect in every good work to do His will, Heb. 13. 20–21, and what can be a higher and better work than worship before Him?

A covenant is a mutual agreement between two parties. Under law, the agreement was one of obedience, Exod. 19. 8. The new covenant was made essentially with the Jews, Jer. 31. 31–34; Heb. 8. 8–13; Rom. 11. 27. Saints today are now found on the ground of grace; no covenant was made with the assembly—it has been called in the eternal purpose of God. Of course, saints enter upon their blessings through the blood of Christ in just the same way as the restored Jewish nation will enter upon their blessings under the new covenant. The fact that we are not under a covenant does not minimise at all the great truth of 1 Corinthians 11. 25. Today, we enjoy freedom and promise, not bondage and conditions to be kept, Gal. 4. 24–31.

26. The act of eating and drinking is to show the Lord's death. The word "show" means "to announce", and is usually translated "preach", as in 2. 1 and 9. 14 where the words "declare" and "preach" are used. Such an announcing of these holy things is essentially to God Himself, since He is receiving His portion from His saints. The act is done, as it were, in the secret of the upper room; it is not done for the public eye. Again, the act is done "till He come", which is another secret event, not for the public eye. Sometimes we sing "No gospel like this feast". Certainly it shows forth the basis of the Gospel, namely His death. Unsaved people, who may be present though separated from the partakers, may perceive something of the Gospel as Christ Himself and His death are made much of. But this surely, should not be directly before the hearts of the saints. Cannot we watch with God for one hour a week, without having other motives in our minds at the same time? For a brother to rise and discourse on the Gospel knowing an unbeliever to be present in the hall seems particularly out of place.

The act is intended for the saints only in this scene; it is "till He come". His coming touches many phases of our lives and service, such as:

worship, 1 Cor. 11. 26;
conduct, 1 John 3. 3;
service, Matt. 24. 44–45 (principle only);
love abounding, 1 Thess. 3. 12–13;
mutual sympathy, 1 Thess. 4. 18.

Verses 27–34: Practical Considerations

27 Wherefore whosoever shall eat this bread, and drink *this* cup of the Lord, unworthily shall be guilty of the body and blood of the Lord.
28 But let a man examine himself, and so let him eat of *that* bread, and drink of *that* cup.
29 For he that eateth and drinketh unworthily, eateth and drinketh damnation to himself, not discerning the Lord's body.
30 For this cause many *are* weak and sickly among you, and many sleep.
31 For if we would judge ourselves, we should not be judged.

32 But when we are judged, we are chastened of the Lord, that we should
not be condemned with the world.
33 Wherefore, my brethren, when ye come together to eat, tarry one for
another.
34 And if any man hunger, let him eat at home; that ye come not together
unto condemnation. And the rest will I set in order when I come.

27. To eat and drink "unworthily" means, in this context, the turning
of most holy things into that which satisfies one's own lusts. This can, of
course, be done in other ways; for example, in Acts 5. 1–11 a couple saw
fit to remain secretly rich at the expense of the poor. In the present
Epistle, saints were gathering for the holy remembrance with the sins and
weaknesses recorded in chapters 1–10 unconfessed and uncorrected. The
actual word "unworthily" occurs only in 1 Cor. 6. 2; 11. 27, 29, but its
opposite, as a verb or an adverb, occurs dozens of times in the N.T. For
example, "He that loveth . . . more than Me is not worthy of Me", Matt.
10. 37. Worthy means deserving, comparable to, suitable for, in a
becoming manner. One's life, conduct and motives must bear some
resemblance to His.

Otherwise, one is "guilty of the body and blood of the Lord". The same
word is used as in the condemnation "He is guilty of death", Matt. 26. 66,
and "he is guilty of all", James 2. 10. The expression Paul uses is one of
extreme solemnity, since it looks beyond the symbols to the Lord Himself.
The Corinthians would have been ignorant of the fact that they were
offending against the Lord personally. It can hardly be supposed that
believers could engage in such activity if they realised the true nature of
their acts. But it is God's own verdict upon the acts that really matters in
the long run, and it is God's judgment that Paul expresses here.

28. Any believer with a self-satisfied approach to the Lord's supper may
be guilty of something that he is ignorant of, for the time being. Hence the
call to "examine himself". This word "examine" is translated "try" in 3. 13
and "approve" in 16. 3. Their motives had to be proved, and then they
could eat of the bread and drink of the cup. If their motives were found
wanting, and if they would not repent, they merely opened the way for
God's corrective hand to be upon them.

29. Different consequences follow upon eating either worthily or
unworthily:
If a saint eats *worthily*, it turns into his own blessing, since the supper
God-ward also contains implications of the table saint-ward. This is
not, of course, the object of the gathering; the motive is His glory,
that His body may be discerned.
If a saint eats *unworthily*, it turns into his own judgment, vv. 30–32.
This is not, of course, the expectancy of such saints; their motives
are such that His body cannot be discerned. They are merely
thinking of their own bodies.

In this latter connection, Numbers 11. 33 and Psalm 78. 30 should be read; judgment fell even when the flesh was between the teeth of the people.

30. Three physical categories of correction are given here, namely "many are weak and sickly . . . and many sleep". This cannot refer to the soul. God never visits such things upon the souls of saints. This would defeat the very object of restoration. Rather the body is affected, so that the recipients in the first two cases should learn and repent, while in the last case their removal from this scene was the best thing to prevent further failure. Commentators do not seem to be able to decide which is the stronger of the two descriptions, "weak" or "sickly". Some suggest the latter from its useage in 2 Chronicles 32. 24 (in the Greek translation of the O.T.). The former word, weak, occurs in many places in the N.T.; for example, Luke 10. 9; Acts 4. 9. Some suggest it refers to weaklings, persons whose powers have failed spontaneously. The latter word, sickly, also occurs many times; for example, Matt. 14. 14. They suggest that it refers to persons whose powers are enfeebled through sickness.

The word "sleep" often refers to physical sleep, Luke 22. 45; Acts 12. 6. But the context must decide when it means physical death in the christian sense, as in Matthew 27. 52, 1 Corinthians 15. 6, 1 Thessalonians 4. 13. Here, it must mean physical death, since physical sleep would not make proper sense in the context.

We should point out, to avoid confusion and difficulty, that sickness and death are *not always* associated with God's correction on account of sin. See John 9. 3; 11 . 4, where the works and glory of God are in view.

31. To avoid God's hand upon the saints, we are exhorted to "scrutinise" ourselves. We must judge our own motives and service, to know whether we are being faithful, that we are in keeping with His will, that we are putting the Lord and His glory first, and that all greed and self-satisfaction have no place at all in our hearts.

32. But if we fail in that, God in grace comes out to "discipline" us, with the object that we should always be distinct from the world. Unbelievers are already condemned, John 3. 18, and will be finally judged before the great white throne, Rev. 20. 13. Believers are spared from all that, and will be spared, but this does not mean that they can do as they like; God intervenes to preserve His holy things here in this world.

33–34. *Paul's conclusion.* He still calls them "brethren" in spite of the darkness of the subject. When they come together to partake of the Lord's supper (and with that sole object before them) they should wait until everyone had accomplished the natural necessities of eating at home. Then the glory of God and not the judgment of the saints would be the outcome of the gathering. In our day, a regular hour of gathering half-way through the Lord's day morning allows these necessities to be accomplished, but we may fail in other directions.

"And the rest will I set in order when I come" refers to things entirely peculiar to Corinth. Such things would be of no relevance to believers elsewhere, so the Spirit did not record them for us.

1 CORINTHIANS 12

Section 5.   Assembly Service
Subject 3.   Variety and Unity in the Purpose of God

Relationships within this Section

We have already called attention to the structure of chapters 11–14. In all assembly matters, the Lord has divine control through His position as Head. Each member of the assembly, under the control of the Head, owns Him as Lord. *Headship* implies control from the divine side; *Lordship* implies obedience from individual saints. Chapter 11. 2–16 establishes, not His Headship, but His Lordship—that is, the saints are seen in responsibility to their Lord, rather than the Head in grace to His members. This responsibility is no lip-service. Subjection to the Lord is demonstrated openly by brethren and sisters alike, by the uncovering or covering respectively of their heads.

The first thing that is due to the Lord from redeemed hearts is something quite independent of service among the saints. We refer to sanctuary service, the holy priesthood taking up the exercises of worship and the Lord's supper, described in chapter 11. After that, in chapter 12, Paul deals with the doctrine behind the outworking of spiritual gifts. A young convert must grasp this before he can take up any service that uses these gifts. Moreover, gifts are exercised by love, and it is quite wrong to read chapter 13 out of context as if it had no bearing on chapters 12 and 14. Chapter 14 provides practical details as to how the gifts may be exercised among the saints. Work among the unsaved, namely the truth of the Gospel, comes in at the beginning of chapter 15. This would require the spiritual gift of the evangelist, Eph. 4. 11. The fact that this is missing in chapters 12–14 means that Paul had only the internal working of the assembly in view.

Hence we may summarize these chapters:
Chapter 11. 17–34: service towards God;
Chapters 12–14: service towards saints;
Chapter 15 (opening verses): service towards sinners.

Background of this Subject

We must notice first of all how spiritual gifts and the use of them fit into the totality of the activity of a local assembly, and how some of these activities must dovetail with others. We also need to observe who is concerned with any particular activity, and whether some brethren are expected to have more than one function.

There are four main spiritual activities amongst the saints:
1. *Local administration of a mundane kind.* We refer to the necessary temporal organisation which requires constant attention, such as finance, upkeep of the property of the local assembly, etc. Acts

chapter 6 deals with this subject. The whole multitude "chose Stephen . . . and Philip . . .", v. 5. That is, the brethren chose men having the confidence of the assembly. The choice was made by the *saints*, not by the *Holy Spirit*. The choice was based not on mere business ability, though this is valuable if used according to Scriptural principles, but it was based on spirituality. These men were full of faith, of the Holy Spirit and of power, vv. 5, 8. The mundane matters would be handled in a spiritual way. Such work, of course, is the work of the *few* in an assembly, but it *does not represent the only work* of a brother thus chosen by the assembly. The exercise of spiritual gifts is also obligatory upon such a brother: Stephen manifested miracles, wonders, wisdom and teaching, vv. 8, 10; Philip was an evangelist, Acts 8. 5–40; 21. 8. A brother engaged in local administration but showing no sign of spiritual gift is acting contrary to the truth of 1 Corinthians 12.

2. *Local spiritual charge.* We refer briefly to the elders in a local assembly. Again, this is the work of a *few*, but by way of contrast, such are not chosen by the *saints* but by the *Holy Spirit*, Acts 20. 28. Elders originate by this choice of the Spirit, by the exercise and desire of qualified men, 1 Tim. 3. 1, and by the recognition by the saints of this calling, 1 Thess. 5. 12. At the same time, elders are expected to exercise spiritual gift as well as engaging in their work of overseership. For example, some may feed the flock, 1 Pet. 5. 2, some may use sound doctrine in exhortation, Tit. 1. 9, some may labour in the word, being apt to teach, 1 Tim. 3. 2; 5–17.

3. *Sanctuary service God-ward.* This is the function of all the holy priesthood; none is exempt. It is independent of gift or local spiritual charge. The hearts of all are concerned, although only brethren may openly lead the praises of the assembly.

4. *Spiritual gifts.* This is the subject from verse 4 onwards of 1 Corinthians 12. Again, it refers to all believers, and is independent of the previous three cases.

We should point out that the service of deacons (servants), 1 Tim. 3. 8–13, is not restricted to category 1; all assembly service is embraced including category 4. Sisters are also included, as Romans 16. 1 shows: "Phebe our sister, which is a servant of the church".

There are four major lists of spiritual gifts in the N.T., each demonstrating a different aspect of the subject, but consistently stressing that *all* believers are included.

1. Romans 12. 3–21. Romans is not a church epistle, but the truth of the responsibility of the members of the body follows the truth of justification by faith. The list, gradually merging from actual spiritual gifts to manifestations of motive and conduct, demonstrates the sacrificial giving of one's whole self for the

outworking of gift, v. 1. The verse that embraces all believers is verse 3, "as God hath dealt to *every* man the measure of faith".

2.   1 Corinthians 12. This chapter demonstrates the divine control of the body through the Spirit. Verses that embrace every believer are: ". . . is given to *every* man to profit withal", v. 7; "dividing to *every* man severally as He will", v. 11; "even as the Lord gave to *every* man", 3. 5.

3.   Ephesians 4. 7–16. This section, showing the Lord as ascended, demonstrates the manifestation of the Head by His members, and shows the heavenly purpose of God for the edification of the assembly. The verse embracing every believer is verse 7: "unto *every* one of us is given grace".

4.   1 Peter 4. 8–11. This paragraph demonstrates that God is glorified through Jesus Christ by the practical outworking of spiritual gifts. The verse embracing every believer is verse 10: "as *every* man hath received the gift".

Chapter 12 of 1 Corinthians deals with the doctrine of variety of gift, yet unity in this variety is made absolute by God. This unity must also be preserved and maintained practically by the saints. Chapter 13 deals with the *inward* means while chapter 14 with the *outward* means. Love maintains the unity of variety. Ephesians 5. 28–29, notes the love for one's own body—the nourishing and cherishing of the members. Similarly each member of a local assembly should show love for the body, consisting of an organism of united yet differing functions.

The summary of the chapter is as follows:

Verses 2–3: contrast between the old and the new; who leads?

Verses 4–6: the Trinity engaged in spiritual work in the saints;

Verses 7–11: variety-list of the Spirit's manifestations—the names of the gifts and not the recipients are given, contrast Eph. 4. 11;

Verses 12–26: reasons for unity in spite of variety;

12: argument of "the Christ":

13: argument of Spirit baptism:

14–20: members are the arrangement of God:

21–26: mutual care and interest display unity:

Verses 27–31: preliminary application to the Corinthians.

Exposition of 1 Cor. 12: Variety and Unity in the Purpose of God

Verses 1–11: Variety

1 Now concerning spiritual *gifts*, brethren, I would not have you ignorant.

2 Ye know that ye were Gentiles, carried away unto these dumb idols, even as ye were led.

3 Wherefore I give you to understand, that no man speaking by the Spirit of God calleth Jesus accursed: and *that* no man can say that Jesus is the Lord, but by the Holy Ghost.

4 Now there are diversities of gifts, but the same Spirit.

5 And there are differences of administrations, but the same Lord.

6 And there are diversities of operations, but it is the same God which worketh all in all.

7 But the manifestation of the Spirit is given to every man to profit withal.

8 For to one is given by the Spirit the word of wisdom; to another the word of knowledge by the same Spirit;

9 To another faith by the same Spirit; to another the gifts of healing by the same Spirit;

10 To another the working of miracles; to another prophecy; to another discerning of spirits; to another discerning of spirits; to another *divers* kinds of tongues; to another the interpretation of tongues:

11 But all these worketh that one and the selfsame Spirit, dividing to every man severally as he will.

1. Paul now changes the subject to "spiritual gifts". It should be pointed out that there is no noun "gifts" here in the Greek, only a plural adjective. Even using the translation "spiritual manifestations" is not quite correct, since an additional thought is thereby added. "Spiritual things" appears to be the best that English can provide, though the plain word "spirituals" would be better if the mind could entertain such a word. Gifts proper start at verse 4, since verses 2–3 deal with another aspect of "spirituals" namely that of confessing the Lord Jesus. Paul implies that it is absolutely essential for every saint to know all about this subject; none can prefer to remain ignorant about the topic. They are poor metaphors, but we suggest that this ignorance is similar to an electrician knowing nothing about electricity, or to learning a language without bothering about the grammar.

2. Paul recalls their past—they were Gentiles, but not now. Our citizenship is now in heaven, Phil. 3. 20 R.V.; we are but strangers and pilgrims here, 1 Pet. 2. 1. As Gentiles, they had been occupied with "dumb idols", so characteristic of the O.T. for example:

Isaiah 44. 9–20: general observations regarding the formation of a god, or graven image that is profitable for nothing;

1 Kings 18. 26, 29: Elijah on Carmel, "there was no voice";

Psalm 115. 4–8: "they have mouths but they speak not", v. 5;

Jeremiah 10; 3–5 "they are upright as the palm tree, but speak not, v. 5.

Habakkuk 2. 19: "the dumb stone".

The Corinthians had been led away to these things by the spirit of the evil one, by the prince of the power of the air, Eph. 2. 2–3. There is a leading unto evil as there is a leading unto spiritual good. Sinners and saints are the object of the leading of the powers of bad and good respectively. See Gal. 5. 16–18.

3. The Greek word *en* in the last phrase "but by the Holy Ghost" is best translated by "in" and not "by". Thus believers speak "in the Holy Spirit"; similar thoughts occur in

Revelation 1. 10: "I was *in* the Spirit";

John 4. 23: ". . . worship the Father *in* spirit and in truth";

1 Corinthians 12. 9: both words "by" should be "in", (but not in verse

8 where the prepositions are actually "by" and "according to").
The thought behind the phrase "in the Spirit" is not one directly of agent, but rather of the element in which the speaker speaks, the power that pervades the speaker and that characterises him. In Matthew 22. 43, the Lord Jesus asserts that David "*in* spirit" uttered Psalm 110. It is also true that the Spirit spoke by David, 2 Sam. 23. 2, but "*in* spirit" implies a conscious subjection to the pervading Spirit. See also Hebrews 1. 1–2, where "by" should twice be "in".

Only in the Holy Spirit can a believer confess "Lord Jesus" (this is a translation preferable to "Jesus is the Lord"). Similarly, the Spirit of His Son in our hearts enables us to cry "Abba, Father", Gal. 4. 6; Rom. 8. 15. By this means, the Spirit does not speak of Himself, John 16. 13, but directs to the Father and to the Son. Prayer and worship are thus not directed to the Spirit; rather the Spirit directs our hearts to the Father and the Son.

Paul is dealing with this subject to show that confession is a "spiritual", that the Holy Spirit is deeply concerned with such a thing. Saints must be able to discern this. In just the same way, later, they must be able to discern whether gifts are being used properly or else abused. There is a spirit of truth and a spirit of error; these must be discerned, 1 John 4. 1–6. Our spirits in the Holy Spirit confess "Lord Jesus" and that Jesus Christ is come in the flesh. This divine enabling is necessary to own the Lordship of the Man.

The world may say every derogatory thing about the Lord Jesus. This is but the spirit of man, 2. 11, and certainly not the Spirit in the inner man, Eph. 3. 16. The difference between cursing and confession is one of discerning of spirits. It is the difference between the pre- and post-conversion appreciation of Christ.

4–6. The three persons of the trinity of God are occupied in assembly service. What humility, what responsibility, yet what dignity, this thought brings! The three persons are concerned at the baptism of believers, Matt. 28. 19; their abiding presence in grace, love and fellowship are the portion of believers, 2 Cor. 13. 14; the promise is given that they abide with us for ever, John 14. 16, 23.

The diversities of gifts, administrations and of operations fall, respectively, within the interests of the Spirit, the Lord, and God the Father. The word "differences" is the same as "diversities". The "same" Spirit, the "same" Lord and the "same" God imply that there is one central heavenly control over all the wide variety of gifts, service and results. May man not seek to take control where none is offered him! The three ideas behind these three verses may be summarised as follows:

Gifts: this word reflects upon the *ability* freely bestowed according to the distribution of the Spirit. The root of the word is that of grace.

Administrations: this word reflects upon the *action*, the service, what is done. The Lord deals with the channels through whom the gifts are manifested, and the types of service in which the gifts are used. See a similar idea in Matthew 8. 9.

Operations: this word reflects upon the *achievement*, both in its mode of working and in the effects of the service. (This word is found on only one other occasion in the N.T., namely in verse 10, "the working of miracles".) The root of the word is the same as the word *working*, "it is the same God which *worketh* all things in all men".

For example, the Spirit gives the enabling, Acts 13. 1–4; the Lord deals with the channel and the service, Acts 9. 1–18; 18. 9–10; and God with the results, 1 Cor. 3. 7. These distinctions should not be stretched too far, since other Scriptures can be selected with different suggestions. But it is noteworthy that this list in 1 Corinthians 12 deals with the distribution of gifts by the Spirit, that Ephesians 4 deals with the Lord and service, and that Romans 12 presents God and the outworking of gift.

7. We have already stressed in connection with the four N.T. lists that "every man" is included in this manifestation of the Spirit; none is excluded. Every part of a physical body is a chemical and physiological miracle of God's own construction; similarly every member of a local assembly is a miracle with a part to play. We must realise that these gifts are *over and above* any natural endowment that we may possess. They are a result of the Spirit dwelling within, and so this applies only to believers. Admittedly, natural endowment has its place when this is sanctified in the Lord's service, but there *must* also be spiritual endowment for such to be effective. It is sometimes thought that because a person is a school teacher, he has the making of a teacher among the Lord's people. It would be more appropriate if this were reversed, namely, because a brother has the beginnings of the gift of teaching in an assembly, he may also make a good school teacher.

The author likes to illustrate this from some of the principles occurring in the parable of the talents, Matt. 25. 14–30, stressing that these remarks are for illustration only. The third man with the one talent possessed but natural ability, indeed given by the Lord, but incapable of producing gain in the Lord's service by itself. The first man with the five talents possessed one natural talent but four spiritual talents; all were used in the Lord's service. Each talent duplicated itself in gain. Similarly the second man with two talents would possess one natural talent but one spiritual talent also. He also was a good and faithful servant, using both in the Lord's service. And even if the parable does not refer directly to the assembly, yet these principles are of general applicability. More specifically, the order is that gift is given according to ability, then grace is given according to gift, Eph. 4. 7, that is ability (natural) is followed by gift (spiritual) and by grace.

Still discussing the idea of "every man", we suggest that the reader turns to 1 Chronicles 25–26, where the Levitical service for the temple—the singers, porters and treasurers—is distributed amongst every family and to every individual. See also Numbers 4.

All gifts are given for "profit". Their usefulness, effectiveness and results must be seen and appreciated; for example, they must lead to edification, exhortation, comfort, 14. 3. Any manifestation not having such ends in view must be treated as suspect. This is the burden of chapter 14. This is a *test*, not of whether the source is the Spirit or not, but whether the gifts are being used rightly. The usefulness of the consequences are weighed; the expediency of the acts can then be measured, John 16. 7; 1 Cor. 10. 23.

8–10. *List of abilities*. This list dealing with abilities should be contrasted with Ephesians 4. 11 where workers are listed, and 1 Corinthians 12. 28 where a mixture occurs. Believers are endowed with gifts from the time that the Holy Spirit indwells them. In just the same way as a child develops natural latent abilities, so the believer develops from the time of his second birth. He is not an imitator of any other gifted believer (11.1 does not refer to gifts but to Paul's use of liberty), but develops as a distinct individual before God. The young believer does not rush into service, in just the same way as a young child does not rush into employment. School days come first. The Levites were numbered to service from the age of one month, Num. 3. 15, but could engage in their service only from the age of thirty, Num. 4. 3, 23, 30. Five years of probationary service in the complicated ceremonial duties placed upon them, preceded the age of thirty, Num. 8. 24. David lowered the age to twenty, 1 Chron. 23. 24, 27. Even the blessed Lord Himself started His public ministry at the age of thirty, Luke 3. 23. Paul's immediate testimony in Damascus, Acts 9. 20, merely demonstrated the joy of the Lord at conversion. His actual service started later in Antioch, Acts 11. 26; 13. 1–4. Timothy's constant preparation for service, thereby not to neglect the gift within, was one of reading, doctrine, meditation, 1 Tim. 4. 13–16.

This list of gifts is divided naturally into three parts. The A.V. translation fails to bring out the fact that two different Greek words are used for "another", namely *allos* "another of the same kind", and *heteros* "another of a different kind". We may paraphrase verses 8–10 as follows:

> "To one is given by the Spirit the word of wisdom; to another of the
> same kind the word of knowledge according to the same Spirit;
> To another of a *different* kind faith in the same Spirit; to another of
> the same kind the gifts of healing in the same Spirit; to another of
> the same kind the working of miracles; to another of the same kind
> prophecy; to another of the same kind discerning of spirits;
> To another of a *different* kind divers kinds of tongues; to another of the
> same kind the interpretation of tongues".

We may well be surprised that Alford, in his "Greek Testament", observes that this distinction is "imaginary"! Theology can sometimes be blind ! This distinction is vital in Galatians 1. 6–7, if sense is to be preserved: ". . . so soon removed . . . to another gospel of a *different* kind, which is not another of the *same* kind". What else could be implied? Alford quotes Matthew 16. 14 and Hebrews 11. 35–36, both Greek words coming in both passages, and states that there is no difference between them. Let the reader decide for himself. In the following quotations we render in italics the Greek word heteros, and we assert that "another of a *different* kind" is implied:

> Matthew 16. 14: "And they said, Some say that thou art John the Baptist: some (others), Elias; and *others*, Jeremias, or one of the prophets".

> Hebrews 11. 35–36: "Women received their dead raised to life again: and others were tortured, not accepting deliverance; that they might obtain a better resurrection: and *others* had trial of cruel mockings and scourgings, yea, moreover of bonds and imprisonment".

The implied difference in each case is obvious. Those who adhered to John the Baptist and Elias (often linked together, see Matt. 17. 11–13; Luke. 1. 17) were different from those who adhered to Jeremiah or the prophets. The latter referred to the books of the prophets; the former did not. Again, in Hebrews 11. 35–36, resurrection is the thought behind those mentioned before the word *others*, while afterwards this thought is absent. A special difference is thereby marked out by the use of the word *others*, *heteros*. On the other hand, the word *allos* (the word "others" not in italics) distinguishes between those of the same category. This distinction in meaning is real, and is vital to a proper understanding of 1 Corinthians 12.

It follows that we must distinguish three groups of gifts in these verses, the first ones named in each group being basic to the others. Hence the word of knowledge is possessed only by some already possessing the word of wisdom. The gifts of healing, miracles, prophecy and discerning of spirits are possessed only by some already possessing faith. The gift of the interpretation of tongues is possessed only by some already possessing the gift of tongues.

We may consider briefly the various gifts. A comprehensive account of these gifts has been given, for example, by Gaston Racine, in "Servir en L'attendant" from October 1958 to December 1959.

The first group. It has been suggested that the word of wisdom is associated with the pastor, and the word of knowledge with the teacher. These two types of servant are found in Ephesians 4. 11, the evangelist not being included here since external service is not the subject of these chapters. Without questioning the necessity of a pastor possessing wisdom, we do question whether this is really implied in the first group, on account of our previous observation that the word of knowledge demands the prior possession of the word of wisdom. It could not be correct to say that to be a teacher one must first be a pastor.

All saints, of course, possess wisdom and knowledge in their measure. Here, however, it is the *word* of wisdom and of knowledge, namely the faculty to communicate and to use wisdom and knowledge. If a brother has knowledge, but not the faculty to communicate it, let him remain silent. The particular order—wisdom and knowledge—appears to characterise many Scriptures:

Romans 11. 33: "O the depth of the riches both of the wisdom and knowledge of God".

Colossians 2. 3: "In whom are hid all the treasures of wisdom and knowledge".

Exodus 31. 3: "I have filled him (Bezaleel) with the spirit of God, in wisdom, and in understanding, and in knowledge".

Luke 2. 40, 52: The Lord was "filled with wisdom" and "increased in wisdom", and later taught in their synagogues, 4. 15.

See also Isaiah 11. 2; 33. 6.

Wisdom is difficult to define. It refers to a moral discernment and to a practical judgment according to God, to an insight into the ways and purposes of God, to the application of divine principles to life. Wisdom is fundamental. Christ is the wisdom of God, and He is made unto us wisdom, 1 Cor. 1. 24, 30. Solomon was possessed of this wisdom, 1 Kings 3. 9, 12; 4. 29–34. The book of Proverbs demonstrates wisdom but hardly knowledge.

Knowledge, on the other hand, is quite different. This refers to the understanding of revealed truth, to the possession of truth. Those to whom Peter wrote in his second Epistle benefited from the wisdom of Paul in declaring the practical implications of the things of the end times, but to consolidate and to perpetuate this wisdom they had to grow in the knowledge of the Lord Jesus Christ, 2 Pet. 3. 15, 18.

It appears that wisdom has precedence over knowledge. Knowledge without wisdom is impossible in the economy of God, and the same is observed in the gifts. Knowledge by itself is cold, formal, barren and theological. Wisdom is the warmth and life of knowledge; "cold chunks of doctrine" are unknown in Scripture, but doctrine has the warmth of Christ pervading it. "As the body without the spirit is dead", James 2. 26, so we may say that knowledge without wisdom is dead.

The second group. The basis of this second group is faith. This is quite distinct from *saving faith* and *living faith* possessed by every saint. We are all "justified by faith", Rom. 5.1; we all possess "faith which worketh by love", Gal. 5. 6; all our lives are regulated by "whatsoever is not of faith is sin", Rom. 14. 23; and we know that "without faith it is impossible to please Him", Heb. 11. 6. But faith, as a spiritual gift, refers to the basis of supernatural acts for His glory, something that was essentially characteristic of the early church. It is the faith that could remove mountains, 1 Cor. 13. 2; Matt. 21. 21, the faith that could pluck up a sycamine tree (black mulberry) to replant it in the sea, Luke 17. 6. This faith is specially manifested in the testimony in the Acts of the Apostles. We may note the examples given in this second group:

Healing: This continued one of the remarkable features of the Lord's ministry according to His own promise, Mark 16. 18. We recall the lame man healed by Peter and John, Acts 3. 7; the healing of every one brought to Jerusalem out of the cities round about, 5. 16; the healing accomplished by Philip, 8. 6–7; the case of Aeneas, 9. 33–35; the case of Paul and the father of Publius, 28. 8. Cases are recorded today of healing granted through various missionary servants of the Lord. Other cases attract newspaper headlines. In any alleged case of healing, one should obviously be careful to enquire, what was the status of the one supposed to have accomplished the healing. Was he a brother in Christ? one who loved the Lord and His assembly? one who adhered to the truth of the Word, and who walked in the light of truth regarding the assembly? Was he, like Stephen, full of the Holy Spirit, of faith and of power? Else such may be deceitful workers, with an ability "after the working of Satan with all power and signs and lying wonders", 2 Thess. 2. 9. We are not prepared to discuss whether the explanation of alleged cases that attract attention is according to the powers of darkness, or merely according to physical or psychological means, but we are assured that gifts of healing can only be a *gift of God* if the life, testimony and assembly outlook of such persons are completely for God according to His word. In any case, the will of God is of first importance in such matters. Paul's thorn in the flesh could not be removed, 2 Cor. 12. 7; Timothy was subject to stomach trouble and "often infirmities", 1 Tim. 5. 23; Epaphroditus had been sick for some time even nigh unto death, Phil. 2. 30, while Trophimus had been left sick at Miletum with no recorded prospect of being healed, 2 Tim. 4. 20.

Miracles: Again these perpetuated the work of the Lord Jesus. This word, meaning "works of power", occurs many times in the Gospels by Matthew, Mark and Luke, being variously translated as "mighty works", "power" or "virtue". It must be distinguished from "miracles" in John's Gospel, where "signs" is the correct rendering. In the Acts, we read of the miracles of Stephen, 6. 8; of the raising of Tabitha, 9. 36–41; of the case of Paul and Eutychus, 20. 9–10; of Paul and the viper, 28. 3; see Mark 16. 18. Again, Scripture gives examples where miracles are accomplished under the control of the powers of darkness, Exod. 7. 11, 22; 8. 7; Matt. 24. 24.

Prophecy: This is a special gift often linked closely to that of apostleship, Eph. 2. 20; 4. 11; Paul places it "secondarily", immediately after the apostles, 1 Cor. 12. 28. Both O.T. and N.T. prophets were granted the miraculous knowledge of the mind of God, prior to the completion of the written Word of God; see Rom. 16. 26. It must be distinguished from the gift of teaching. Prophesying was the direct exposition of the revelation of God to the prophet's soul. This was necessary since the N.T. was not then available, only a few Epistles having been written and not in general circulation. Teaching, on the other hand, implies the exposition of that which is received through another channel, namely that of a prophet or of the written Word. In the Acts, we find Agabus used of God to foretell future events, 11. 28; 21. 10; we find prophets at Antioch, 13. 1; we read of the four virgin daughters of Philip who did prophesy, 21. 9.

Discerning of spirits: This involved a deeper discernment than that concerned in testimony, 1 Cor. 12. 3; 1 John 4. 1–6. Peter discerned the state of Simon, Acts 8. 21; Paul discerned the state of heart of Elymas, and used words that one not so gifted should never use, 13. 10; he later discerned the state of the damsel possessed with a spirit of divination, 16. 16–18; and he was able to deal with evil spirits in men at Ephesus, 19. 12. Conversely, Barnabas discerned the spirit of salvation in Saul, Acts 9. 27.

All these miraculous workings were the result of "the Lord working with them", Mark 16. 20, the continuation of the things that "Jesus began both to do and teach", Acts 1. 1. God allows the right gifts at the appropriate times. He showed signs and wonders when the children of Israel came out of Egypt, but later they settled down to life without such signs. It was the same with the early church. These particular gifts demonstrated a spiritual intervention into the physical realm. Nowadays faith within is shown by good works, Matt. 5.16, "Let your light so shine before men, that they may see your good works, and glorify your Father which is in heaven". The good life of a Christian has won many for the Saviour.

We find many other gifts in the other lists, gifts that are no doubt more relevant today. For example, gifts of teaching, exhortation, ruling (that is, a leader in a group engaged in a particular service), Rom. 12. 7–8; helps, governments, 1 Cor. 12. 28; the gift of a pastor, Eph. 4. 11; and the gift of hospitality, 1 Pet. 4. 9. These contrast with the Lord's promise of signs in Mark 16. 17–18, which can only refer to the outwardly miraculous gifts occurring in our second and third groups. They were evidently manifested in the book of Acts, but gave way to the more enduring ministrations of the Spirit found in these other lists. The complementary verse, Matthew 28. 20, also refers to these lasting gifts.

The third group. We must now consider the gift of tongues and the interpretation of tongues in detail, since many believers read these Scriptures and remain confused. The interpretation of these passages often rests upon tradition or upon confused ideas about what is known to be practised in certain circles. Those who have read widely what commentators have to say on the subject of tongues will agree that many extravagant claims are made. Many arguments are put forward, most of which are without basis when examined in detail, merely representing the ideas (usually borrowed from earlier commentaries) of other writers.

There are three main lines of thought:

1.   Whenever tongues are mentioned in the N.T. (including Acts 2), the reference is to ecstatic utterances originating from an elevated spiritual feeling, having no bearing upon any natural

languages on earth.

2. The reference in Acts 2 concerns natural languages on earth, but the references in 1 Corinthians 12–14 are to ecstatic utterances in the assembly.

3. All references are to natural languages on earth.

It must be admitted that few adopt the third possibility. Nevertheless, without appearing unkind to writers who have given thought to the matter and arrived at other conclusions, the present writer does adopt the third possibility as providing a perfectly consistent and satisfactory explanation of the subject. Readers may treat the following exposition as suggestive.

We must observe that service God-ward has been treated in chapter 11, and that spiritual gifts are given for service amongst the saints. Ecstatic languages (whether or not understood by the speakers but not usually by the hearers) would be supposed to be praise and prayer to God, but this is *not* the object of spiritual gifts. All the lists of spiritual gifts should be examined in order to see the validity of this statement.

A language other than one's mother-tongue is learnt either from childhood as a bilingual, as a study at school or through acquisition through removal to another land; or as an immediate gift from God, a miraculous brain process granted in the early days of the church, by no means an intermittent but rather a permanent ability of the speaker.

We may note the various references in the Acts to this subject.

Acts 2. 4–14: The immediate manifestation of the filling with the Holy Spirit was that they began to speak with other tongues. The word "other" is *heteros*, of a kind distinct from their own language. Verse 6 stresses the understanding of the people; here were no ecstatic utterances, but the language of every man. We may note the plural verb "heard" with the singular "every man". There is a distinction between the general and the particular. All men heard everything, but only those understood what was spoken in their own tongue. In verse 13, some mocked, "These men are full of new wine". That is, if they did not understand a particular speaker they claimed he was drunk. They would not mock with this accusation if they did understand. They knew the simplicity of the apostles beforehand in not being thus multi-lingual, 4. 13. From verse 14 onwards, Peter controlled his speech, and with no further mention of Peter speaking in tongues it would seem that his first great sermon was spoken in his own Galilean dialect to the men of Judaea and Jerusalem only. To Peter had been granted the ability to speak in foreign tongues, and it was a deliberate act on his part to choose suitable subject matter to express in those tongues. This is similar to the case of Moses in Exodus 4. 10–12. The Lord would be with his mouth—the physical capacity to speak; what he had to speak was taught by the Lord.

Acts 9. 17: There appears to be no record of Paul having such a gift of tongues through the reception of the Holy Spirit. He was not powerful in speech, which was contemptible, 1 Cor. 2. 3–4; 2 Cor. 10. 9–10. "I thank my God, I speak with tongues more than ye all", 1 Cor. 14. 18, should read "I speak in a tongue" in the singular; see J.N D., who follows many editors of the Greek text. That is, he employed a tongue in his journeys and in his teaching more frequently than the misguided Corinthians. He merely used Greek more often than Hebrew, Acts 21. 37; 22. 2.

Acts 10. 45–46: The gift of the Spirit was now poured out on Cornelius, a Roman centurion, speaking Latin and no doubt Greek as well. He was now able to speak with tongues, but this was no arbitrary ecstatic speech. Rather it was praise to God such that Peter understood that it was magnifying God.

Acts 19. 6: The speaking with tongues and the prophesying of these twelve men of Ephesus was something continuous. The prophecy would be the subject-matter of their speaking. Language, combined with revelation of truth impressed upon their hearts, would be immediately useful at Ephesus. Scripture is silent as to whether this gift was ever used in Ephesus afterwards; certainly it has no place in Ephesians 4. 7–16.

Hence the interpretation placed upon "divers kinds of tongues", 1 Cor. 12. 10, is that these refer to the miraculous ability to speak in various languages necessary in the vast city of Corinth. Whereas Acts 2 refers to preaching to the unsaved in Jerusalem, 1 Corinthians 12–14 refers to speech in the assembly at Corinth.

The interpretation of tongues is an additional gift given to some. If A preaches to B in a language B does not understand (because A cannot speak B's language), there is the necessity of a translator, namely one knowing both the language of A and B; see 14. 27. Similarly, if A preaches to B and C (when B understands but C does not), then A may do his own interpreting if possible so that C can understand, 14. 5. It is obviously the province of a man to interpret *only* if he knows the languages in question; this is implied in the phrase "to another of the *same* kind the interpretation of tongues". This may be contrary to certain practice today, but we cannot gainsay Scripture. Someone has written of the gift of tongues: They are "not just foreign languages, for a person gifted naturally would be his own interpreter". We must observe that this is just not true; interpretation is an ability over and above the ability to speak. Else what would be the necessity of an organisation like the United Nations School of Interpreters in Geneva? There are immense mental difficulties associated with languages which have little grammatical and vocabulary connection. A miraculous language suddenly implanted upon the mind would have little connection with the mother-tongue. The ability to interpret would be gained only over the months in a natural way. One has written of a certain case, "A woman had learned Romanian and Hungarian in childhood, but who was unable to translate a sentence from one language into the other. In her mind the two languages formed systems separated by a staunch wall".* Hence God granted to some the miraculous gift of interpretation—to those already possessing the languages granted by divine imparting, thereby to undo in measure Genesis 11. 7. Paul returns to this subject in chapter 14.

11. Having provided this list of gifts, Paul stresses that it is the selfsame Spirit that works and divides. The working—the ability to use the gifts—is of the Spirit. Any methods used in the service of God must be treated as suspect if they cannot honestly be ascribed to Him. The dividing likewise is His work. This word *dividing* (having the same root as *diversities* in verses 5–7) occurs only here and in Luke 15. 12, the parable of the prodigal son, "He divided unto them his living". In the parable, the living after the division was entirely in the hands of the sons. Gifts, however, are still under the Spirit's control after they are divided.

In the background to this chapter we have already commented upon the phrase "every man". The stress that Scripture places upon this shows up the convictions of the apostles on the matter. Gifts may change to suit local conditions over the years, but the distribution to every man does not change.

The distribution is "as He *will*". This is remarkable, and few Scriptures use this particular Greek word for *will* in connection with the persons of the Godhead. Here, the word is used in connection with the Spirit; in Matthew 11. 27, "to whomsoever the Son will reveal Him" refers to the Son; in Hebrews 6. 17, "Wherein God, willing more abundantly to shew unto the heirs of promise the immutability of His counsel" refers to God the Father. We need hardly remark that this apparent *independence* is also characterised by *subjection*. The Godhead works as one in this matter of gift. Here, we are concerned with the distribution by the Spirit. In Ephesians 4. 8, it is the risen Lord who gives the gifts, "He . . . gave gifts unto men", (quoted from Psalm 68. 18 with slight changes, referring to the time when the ark ascended up mount Zion, 1 Chron. 16. 1). "In Romans 12. 3, "as God hath dealt to every man", God the Father is concerned. Hence, no believer can plead inability, ignorance or lack of power. The trinity of God is involved in the giving, the working, the service and the results.

Verses 12–31: Unity

12 For as the body is one, and hath many members, and all the members of that one body, being many, are one body: so also *is* Christ.
13 For by one Spirit are we all baptized into one body, whether *we be* Jews or Gentiles, whether *we be* bond or free; and have been all made to drink into one Spirit.
14 For the body is not one member, but many.
15 If the foot shall say, Because I am not the hand, I am not of the body; is it therefore not of the body?

Languages in Contact, by Uriel Weinreich, 1953, p. 74. Publications of the Linguistic Circle of New York, I. *See also* "To Translate is Impossible", p. 146 vol. 9, 1963, ASLIB Technical Translation Bulletin.

16 And if the ear shall say. Because I am not the eye, I am not of the body;
   is it therefore not of the body?
17 If the whole body *were* an eye, where *were* the hearing? If the whole *were*
   hearing. where *were* the smelling?
18 But now hath God set the members every one of them in the body, as it
   hath pleased him.
19 And if they were all one member, where *were* the body?
20 But now *are they* many members, yet but one body.
21 And the eye cannot say unto the hand, I have no need of thee: nor again
   the head to the feet, I have no need of you.
22 Nay, much more those members of the body, which seem to be more
   feeble, are necessary:
23 And those *members* of the body, which we think to be less honourable,
   upon these we bestow more abundant honour; and our uncomely *parts*
   have more abundant comeliness.
24 For our comely *parts* have no need: but God hath tempered the body
   together, having given more abundant honour to that *part* which lacked:
25 That there should be no schism in the body; but *that* the members should
   have the same care one for another.
26 And whether one member suffer, all the members suffer with it; or one
   member be honoured, all the members rejoice with it.
27 Now ye are the body of Christ, and members in particular.
28 And God hath set some in the church, first apostles, secondarily prophets,
   thirdly teachers, after that miracles, then gifts of healings, helps,
   governments, diversities of tongues.
29 *Are* all apostles? *are* all prophets? *are* all teachers? *are* all workers of
   miracles?
30 Have all the gifts of healing? do all speak with tongues? do all interpret?
31 But covet earnestly the best gifts: and yet shew I unto you a more
   excellent way.

12. Paul now provides four reasons why this variety given by God is, at
the same time, constituted a unity by God. These are
   verse 12: the argument of "the Christ";
   verse 13: the argument of Spirit baptism;
   verses 14–20: the argument of God's own arrangement;
   verses 21–26: the argument of mutual care and interest shown by the
   members.
The first two arguments, being of a more general nature, appear to go
far beyond the confines of local considerations. The body in question is
the great universal church, Eph. 1. 22–23. The second pair of reasons
brings in more local considerations, namely the specific gifts granted to
local assemblies, this being the essential subject of the chapter.
   In the present verse, Paul uses the picture of the human body, which is
a structure planned and formed by God, Psa. 139. 14–16. In just the same
way the assembly in all its eternal detail has been planned and formed by
God. Paul has a dual idea before him—one body has many members and
many members are one body. Unity demands diversity and diversity
demands unity—both are essential. All recognise that this is true of the
natural body; so, too, must the saints recognise that it is true of "the
Christ". The last phrase "so also is Christ" possesses the definite artide in

Greek, namely "so also is *the* Christ". Usually, of course, the article does not occur; for example, Galatians 3. 16 "And to Thy seed, which is Christ" refers solely to the man Christ Jesus. But the idea "the Christ" refers to the living Head as the Lord in glory *plus* the body of Christ consisting of His people throughout the whole of the church dispensation. His life flows through us as we are "partakers of the divine nature", 2 Pet. 1. 4. This extension of His name embraces His own. Even now we can appreciate what it means to have His name and that of His God written upon us, Rev. 3. 12. We bear His name inwardly and also outwardly by way of testimony, Acts 9. 15. We are one in Him as He is also in us, John 17. 21–23.

This blessed position that we occupy through grace is absolute, but the practical side of growing into the unity of the "perfect man" is dealt with in Ephesians 4. 13–16. Gifts achieve this as they work out in service. Readers should notice that it is the name "the Christ" that is extended to embrace His own people. The titles "Lord" or "Saviour" could not be thus extended. In Acts 9. 5, "Jesus" is linked with the church—that is, as a Man not as a Saviour; in this sense He is seen *by the world*. But in the verse before us, "Christ" is extended to His church; in this sense He is known by *the saints*.

13. "*In* one Spirit are we all baptised into one body" was promised by John the Baptist in Matthew 3. 11 prior to the Lord's ministry. John looked beyond the confines of traditional Judaism to the heavenly purposes of God. Again, the risen Lord promised a like baptism, Acts 1. 5. This took place in Acts 2, and now all believers partake of the blessed Spirit at conversion. We should note three points:

1. This baptism was independent of their prior state— whether Jews or Gentiles, whether bond or free; see Galatians 3 . 28. In the early beginnings of the assembly, we should note that baptism in water preceded the Holy Spirit, in the case of those who had crucified the Lord of glory, Acts 2. 38. Similarly in the case of the Samaritans, Acts 8. 16. They had first to own the apostolic authority (amongst the Jews with whom they had no dealings). But in the case of the Gentiles—forming the essential picture for today—the Holy Spirit was received before water baptism, Acts 10. 47. This does not provide legitimate grounds for lengthy delay between conversion and water baptism, as is sometimes the case today.
2. The baptism in this verse 13 cannot, by any stretch of the imagination, be made to refer to water baptism. Water baptism today is usually regarded as a means of entering into fellowship with a local assembly, but this verse refers to the universal church. Water baptism connects us with Christ's death and resurrection practically, Rom. 6. 1–11, but Spirit baptism connects us with His ascension, Acts 2. 33.

3. In the phrase "to drink into one Spirit", some reliable expositors see something of water baptism and the Lord's supper. One cannot quite agree with this suggestion. If one is immersed *in* the Spirit by baptism, then one partakes by being made to drink (not in the sense of 10. 4) so that the Spirit is immediately within (as 6. 19).

By this act, the Spirit unites all believers into one body, regardless of variety that afterwards may be manifested. Faith in the soul of an individual is unto salvation. Faith does not unite, but the Spirit does.

14–20. *Members are the arrangement of God.* There are two points of view mixed in this paragraph:

1. A member A is part of the body although A is quite distinct from a member B.
2. A body cannot consist of members all of type A.

Case 1 is *false humility.* Verses 15–16 form the metaphor; verse 18 gives God's side, and verse 20 is the conclusion, "many members, yet but one body".

Case 2 is *false pride.* Verse 17 forms the metaphor; verse 19 continues God's side, and verse 14 is the (prior) conclusion, "the body is not one member, but many". The reader should carefully check these verses to see that this is so.

Verses 15–17 form a metaphor designed to stimulate the conscience of the readers, so we suggest that the various members of the natural body should not be interpreted in detail *too far.* The *foot* would speak of one who leads in a particular service; the *hand* of one who engages in a particular service. Paul would be the foot, but Luke and the others would be hands, Acts 16. 9–10. The *eye* may refer to one who discerns in an outward and open way, Acts 13. 9–10, but *ears* and *smelling* would refer to those who can discern a spiritual atmosphere in a more indirect way, as Paul in his discernment of the errors in Corinth.

It suffices to say that the arrangement is according to the pleasure of God, v. 18. None can rightly say, "Why hast Thou made me thus?", if Romans 9. 20 may be quoted out of context. The mouth, ears and eyes are under the control of God, as He said to Moses, Exod. 4. 11. Moses disagreed with God, and the anger of the Lord was kindled against him. Paul was a chosen vessel, and as such the Lord "enabled me, for that He counted me faithful, putting me into the ministry", 1 Tim. 1. 12. To realise the arrangement of the Lord, and to abide therein with faithfulness, is the beginning of blessing in service. In just the same way as qualified men can "desire the office of a bishop", 1 Tim. 3. 1, according to the distribution of the Spirit of God, so, too, in the matter of gifts, one may covet earnestly the best gifts, and desire to prophesy, 12. 31; 14. 1.

21–26. *Mutual care and interest shown by the members.* The burden of verse 21 is that all are needful; the arrangement of God is such that the eye cannot dispense with the hand, nor the head with the feet. When Paul wrote "the head", he did not have the living Head in mind. The verse is suggestive of weakness on the part of the saints; the Lord on high values every one of His members here below. All are needful, so the teacher cannot dispense with the evangelist (as may be the case in an assembly not zealous in the gospel), nor can the evangelist dispense with the teacher (as may be the case in an assembly where evangelism displaces all other forms of service amongst the saints). A spiritual balance in service is difficult to find and to maintain. In this connection, we may note the case of Philip:

(a)   As an evangelist in Samaria, Philip needed the apostles Peter and John, Acts 8. 14. He showed no resentment when other men with other gifts came in to help.

(b)   Later, as evangelist in Caesarea, 8. 40, he was not used for the conversion of Cornelius, although he was living in that town. Rather the Spirit of God brought in the apostle Peter with further gifts. Peter was necessary to give apostolic authority to Gentile conversion. Also he was gifted to build up the converts afterwards as he tarried with them, 10. 48, a thing Philip evidently could not do. Again, Philip was not grieved. He continued his evangelistic work according to the call of God, appreciating other gifts when sent of God, Acts 21. 8–9.

Similarly, in Antioch, Barnabas realised that Saul would be necessary for the work, Acts 11. 25. The other teachers there did not resent only Paul and Barnabas being sent forth on the first missionary journey, 13. 1–4. Their fellowship was displayed by the laying on of their hands.

Similarly, the feeble members—the limbs of a child for example— are necessary. Spiritually, these are the lambs of the flock, capable of development into useful members of the community.

The reference to "less honourable" members, v. 23, looks back to Genesis 2. 25; 3. 7. Some expositors mention feet in this connection, but that suggestion seems to lack any reason. Verse 23 refers to what man does to obviate the effects of sin in the beginning. But verse 24 refers to God's work, arising from the creatorial structure of His own design. In verse 23, we "bestow", but in verse 24, God "hath tempered the body together". The word "bestow" means "to put about" and may refer to clothes. For example, the word is used in Matthew 27. 28 where they "put on him a scarlet robe". The verb "temper" only appears one other time in the N.T., in Hebrews 4. 2, dealing with the mixing of the Word and faith. The thought is one of mingling, combining. We provide "abundant honour" for these parts merely by the act of clothing, but God has provided "abundant honour" by the complicated physiological functions accorded to these parts, for example, in excretion and reproduction. The honour God provides involves life itself. Organic unity is therefore provided in a marvellous way.

Spiritually, some men and women are gifted as personal workers, to deal with the dark side of society in our large cities. Yet as evangelists in these places they are enabled to bring forth life. How necessary is such work. Reading reports of work in such conditions makes one feel sometimes that ability in teaching is as nothing in comparison.

The dove-tailing of such functions and interests leads Paul to dwell on mutual care, suffering and rejoicing. It is this that shows whether an assembly is living on doctrine alone or on love.

The same care: We may mention various cases:

Acts 2. 45: the provision for all, as every man had need;

Acts 9. 34: the sympathy of Peter for Aeneas;

Acts 24. 23: the acquaintances of Paul ministered to him;

Acts 28. 15: the encouragement given to Paul at Appii forum;

Romans 16. 2: Phebe a succourer of many (The whole of Romans 16 should be read in this connection);

2 Timothy 4. 11: "only Luke is with me".

Suffering: Mutual sympathy and practical kindness associated with it, shows the reality of fellowship. The Lord Jesus demonstrated this, particularly in John 11, for example. In Acts 12. 12, such sympathy drove the saints to prayer on behalf of the imprisoned Peter.

Rejoicing: When spiritual work is successfully accomplished, the saints should rejoice in God who directed such work. For example:

Acts 11. 23: Barnabas was "glad" when he saw the work in Antioch;

Acts 11. 18: the apostles "glorified God" as a result of Peter's work in Caesarea;

Acts 21. 20: the brethren in Jerusalem "glorified the Lord" on account of Paul's work amongst the Gentiles.

Eulogization of the workers is quite out of place. Report meetings—for missionary work or for local assembly endeavour—would be transformed if these Scriptures were kept to the fore.

27–31. Paul concludes that he has laboured the spiritual principles behind diversity and unity long enough; he now provides a preliminary application to the Corinthians. The word "ye" in "Now *ye* are (the) body of Christ" demonstrates that he now has specifically before him the local assembly at Corinth. At the same time, the principles and their outworking are of general application.

In verse 27, the "body of Christ" comes before "members"; the Lord comes first. Saints have a responsibility to show that the unity among them has prior claims over individual service.

Verse 28 provides a restatement of the gifts at Corinth. The apostolic authority comes first in the list, even though the apostles were not resident in Corinth. One at least had worked there and laid the foundation of all truth in Jesus Christ, 3.10.

We need not comment again on some of these gifts, see verses 8-10. But the following points should be observed.

Prophets: These had a miraculous acquisition of truth from the Lord, with ability to pass it on to others. Teachers could pass on what they had received from the Word or from the apostles and prophets. Prophets were not to be despised, 1 Thess. 5. 20, else the Spirit would be quenched.

Helps: This noun comes only once in the N.T. It implies assistance. The corresponding verb is found three times:

Luke 1. 54 "He hath *holpen* His servant Israel";

Acts 20. 35: "ye ought to *support* the weak";

1 Tim. 6. 2: "*partakers* of the benefit".

This is a very practical gift. One is able to assist the needy saints, and the scope is tremendous. Those without the gift would rush in and make themselves a nuisance. See 2 Cor. 1. 4–7; Gal. 6. 10; 1 Tim. 5–10 for examples.

Governments: Again, this noun appears only once in the N.T. It refers to the office of one who directs. A similar noun with the same root is "pilot", Acts 27. 11; Rev. 18. 17. These are brethren able to perceive the paths of God in service and to lead in them; see Acts 16. 6–10.

The questions occurring in verses 29-30, "Are all apostles? are all prophets? . . .", are designed to stimulate the conscience. Paul used this method in chapter 9 verses 4–13. The intended answer is "no", and so this should be reflected in practice. It would appear that most of the Corinthians thought that they had the gift of tongues, 14. 23. This was the cause of all the trouble and confusion in Corinth which these chapters were designed to meet.

In verse 31, all are enjoined to *covet* the most profitable gifts. The verb covet is associated with *zeal* in a good sense (see 2 Cor. 11. 2), and with *envy* in a bad sense (see Acts 7. 9). Although the Spirit of God allows such a desire, the state of heart that practises the gifts is more important than the practice itself. Paul deals with this question of love in chapter 13.

1 CORINTHIANS 13

Section 5.   Assembly Service
Subject 4.   The Influence of Love

Relationships within this Section

We have already seen that chapters 12, 13 and 14 form a connected whole, in which Paul is dealing with spiritual gifts.

> Chapter 12 deals with *doctrine*—God's side, in variety and unity known by the saints.
>
> Chapter 13 deals with the *inner man of the heart*—the manifestation of christian character.
>
> Chapter 14 deals with the *practical side*—how gifts should be used for the edification of the assembly.

The main error which Paul seeks to correct, is that most or all of the Corinthians thought that they possessed the gift of tongues, and they used this gift indiscriminately, regardless of whether it brought barrenness or edification. The conduct of an assembly gathering was thus marked by a two-fold error:

1. *"Not holding the Head"*, Col. 2. 19. Paul dealt with this in chapter 12, where he showed that the Lord is in control of the gifts. This would correct those believers who used their gifts without any particular thought being given to the Head.

2. *Confusion and not order was manfested*, 14. 23–26. Paul deals with this in chapter 13, where he shows that love must motivate the gifts. This would correct those believers who used their gifts without giving thought for one another.

Chapter 13 divides itself into three paragraphs:

> Verses 1–3: Gifts and good works by *themselves* are of no profit. God wants more than activity. He wants the inner man of the heart.
>
> Verses 4–7: Love is recognised by its manifestations. It is not defined (for God is love, 1 John 4. 8, 16). Two positive, eight negative and another five positive manifestations are given.
>
> Verses 8–13: Paul describes the transitory character of gifts in this world contrasted with the abiding character of spiritual virtues. God expects a balance to be preserved in every believer.

Love is not a slack easy-going state of sitting back, indifferent to weakness, false doctrine, practice and conduct. Love with meekness is not *weakness*. Moses was the meekest man, Num. 12. 3, but he used the rod in correction many times. The Lord Jesus loved all, but He used a scourge of small cords to preserve holiness, John 2. 15. And as for Paul, would he come to Corinth either with a rod or else with love and a spirit of meekness?, 1 Cor. 4. 21. Certainly not with love and a spirit of meekness, but with a rod of correction. Whereas *love with the rod* is not mentioned, nevertheless during this corrective process love existed in his heart towards the Corinthians. The last verse of the Epistle, 16. 24, extends his love to them, and later he exposed the state of his heart in writing this first Epistle, "For out of much affliction and anguish of heart I wrote unto you with many tears; not that ye should be grieved, but that ye might know the love which I have more abundantly unto you", 2 Cor. 2. 4.

Chapter 13 is a very difficult chapter to expound. It is perhaps easy to make casual remarks about the various features of love, but do these remarks really apply to Paul's observations? To make sure, a concordance and even a dictionary are necessities for spiritual study. Young people should aim at a diligent and intelligent use of these helps to Bible study.

Exposition of 1 Cor. 13: The Influence of Love

Verses 1–3: Gifts and Good Works of no Profit by Themselves

> 1 Though I speak with the tongues of men and of angels, and have not charity, I am become *as* sounding brass, or a tinkling cymbal.
> 2 And though I have *the gift of* prophecy, and understand all mysteries, and all knowledge; and though I have all faith, so that I could remove mountains, and I have not charity, I am nothing.
> 3 And though I bestow all my goods to feed *the poor*, and though I give my body to be burned, and have not charity, it profiteth me nothing.

1. The "I" occurring in these first three verses does not refer particularly to the apostle Paul. It is the general "I" of proposition and may refer to any believer. Paul mentions the question of tongues or languages first because this has a direct bearing upon the state of the assembly in Corinth. We must distinguish between tongues of men and of angels:

Tongues of men: This refers to the natural ability to speak one's mother tongue or another acquired language. For example, Paul could speak in Hebrew, Acts 21. 40, and in Greek, v. 37. Again, Rabshakeh of Assyria could speak in the Jews' language, 2 Kings 18. 28.

Tongues of angels: This does not refer to ecstatic languages uttered in a state of emotion as some suppose and practice. Such a notion must be rejected, since gifts are given for service among men. Rather it should be noticed that angels always spoke in the language of the people whom they visited. Gabriel spoke to Zacharias and to Mary in a language immediately understood, Luke 1. 19, 28. The blessed Lord spoke to Paul from heaven in the Hebrew tongue, Acts 26. 14, even though the inspired historian may give the Greek translation of His words. In other words, the angels were equipped of God to speak to men in their own human languages, as indeed was the dumb ass to Balaam, Num. 22. 28. Hence, the reference is to a miraculous divine enabling, to the spiritual gift of tongues given to some of the Lord's people.

But Paul visualises the case when such gifts are in operation without the exercise of love, or "charity". All readers will know that "charity" in its

modern meaning is not implied here. We owe this word to Wycliffe
(1330–1384), and the A.V. has perpetuated it ever since, though the R.V.
uses the word "love". If love were absent when such languages were used,
then the men would be as "sounding brass, or a tinkling cymbal".

Such instruments possess the features:

(a)   there is no manifestation of life;
(b)   they are entirely automatic, as is God's control over the physical
        creation;
(c)   they make a great variety of noise, but there is nothing of lasting
        value in such a noise; languages without love is akin to words
        without power.

2. Paul now mentions various forms of appreciation of truth. It is not
quite the same as a spiritual gift now, since the words in italics "the gift of"
do not occur in the original. Neither does Paul particularly mean "the
word of" as the faculty to communicate, 12. 8.

Prophecy: The mind of God made known by prior revelation to an
    individual.

All mysteries: These are divine secrets until they are made known by
    the Spirit of God. The saints are the stewards of these mysteries, 4.
    1. Amongst others, we may mention:

    1 Corinthians 2. 7, the purpose of God in Christ and the cross;
    Matthew 13. 11, the mysteries of the kingdom of heaven;
    1 Corinthians 15. 51, the mystery of change at the resurrection;
    Ephesians 3. 3, the union of Jew and Gentile in one body;
    2 Thessalonians 2. 7, the mystery of iniquity both now and in the
        coming day;
    Revelation 10. 7, the mystery of God to be finished,
        namely all opposition to be subdued and Christ shown to be all
        in all.

One's mind would be full if all this was understood, but what about
    the heart?

All knowledge: This can be cold and formal if the mind and not the
    heart is active. It refers to the particular mind possessed by the
    teacher and those taught, when facts are marshalled in a way
    suitable for this world only. Romans 15. 14 declares that we are all
    "filled with all knowledge", but the context (verse 13) shows that
    other virtues are possessed as well, namely the fruit of the Spirit.

The reference to the possession of "all faith" goes back to 12. 9. Not a
saving, living faith is implied, but a faith (as a gift) able to bring about
miraculous events. The Lord Jesus had spoken of this in Matthew 17. 20
and Luke 17. 6, where faith could remove both the mountain and the
sycamine tree.

If love is absent although these great things are in operation, such a
person is nothing, being a machine of the Spirit in the same way as the
creation is. God desires something more than this; He desires our hearts.

But if our hearts are empty and quiet, the very stones of the physical creation would cry out, Luke 19. 40. What is needed is the "work of faith, and labour of love", 1 Thess. 1. 3, and "faith that worketh by love", Gal. 5. 6.

3. Finally Paul touches upon good works and testimony even of the extreme kind. The bestowal of goods to feed the poor often occurs in the N.T., with and without love:

Matthew 15. 32: The Lord provided for the four thousand, because He had compassion on them; this is love.

Acts 4. 34–35: All sold their lands and houses, so that distribution could be made to those in need; this was love manifested in power. But Ananias and Sapphira kept back part of the price, 5. 1–2, showing what can happen when there is no love.

John 12. 5–6: Judas wanted to know why the ointment could not be sold for three hundred pence, which would be given to the poor. But here was no love; he wanted what was placed in the bag. If he could not obtain three hundred pence, then he would shortly obtain the thirty pieces of silver.

In other words, "charity" in the modern sense is useless unless motivated from a heart where love dwells. See also James 2. 14–17.

Similarly, to give one's body to be burned has no value if love is absent. This refers essentially to the giving up of one's life by way of self-sacrifice in the cause of Christ. It might also refer to the Roman method of cruel torture, accomplished in spite of the loving motives of the one so evilly abused. There were those who had been "stoned . . . sawn asunder . . . slain with the sword", Heb. 11. 37, but faith was working there by love. Again, there might be in believers an anticipation of these things about to happen. Paul was ready "not to be bound only, but also to die at Jerusalem for the name of the Lord Jesus", Acts 21. 13. But Paul's heart of love was fixed; his friends could not "break his heart", v. 13.

Verses 4–7: Love Recognised by its Manifestations

4 Charity suffereth long, *and* is kind; charity envieth not; charity vaunteth not iself, is not puffed up.
5 Doth not behave itself unseemly, seeketh not her own, is not easily provoked, thinketh no evil;
6 Rejoiceth not in iniquity, but rejoiceth in the truth;
7 Beareth all things, believeth all things, hopeth all things, endureth all things.

4–7. Whereas spiritual gifts are concerned with activity, affecting each *differently*, yet the fruit of the Spirit is concerned with the heart, and all should be affected identically. Love is the first of the nine-fold fruit of the Spirit in Galatians 5. 22–23, and it is the last of the seven-fold list of diligent endeavour in 2 Peter 1. 5–8, leading to the blessed position where we are "neither barren nor unfruitful in the knowledge of our Lord Jesus

Christ".

As we have already remarked, love is not defined. Its nature is too deep, and its manifestations too vast to permit definition. Absence of definition need not disturb either the spiritual mind or the natural intellect, for ultimately nothing admits of a verbal definition. Yet love is known by its fruits. We are exhorted by love to serve one another, Gal. 5. 13, to seek edification in love, Eph. 4. 16, and to abound in love one toward another, and toward all men, 1 Thess. 3. 12.

There can be nothing more humbling than to examine the details of the manifestation of love given here. In John 21. 15–16, Peter twice used a weaker word for love than that used in this chapter. He evidently felt that 1 Corinthians 13 was too high for him. The third time, the Lord Himself used the weaker form, "Lovest thou Me?". This grieved Peter that the Lord should lower the tone of His question to meet the need of His servant, but at least Peter's answer now fitted the question.

Each of these fifteen virtues can be traced in Christ Himself. In fact, it is a sweet meditation to substitute the word "Christ" in place of "charity" in verses 4–7; the Master is thereby revealed. Yet at the same time, this substitution can be dangerous, for we would tend to forget that this truth has a direct bearing upon our own conduct. But if Christ is thus formed in us, we shall be blessed.

There are firstly two positive virtues, love suffereth long, and is kind.

1. *Suffereth long*: or, love has patience. This is the same word as that used by the servant who owed a certain king ten thousand talents, "Lord, have *patience* with me, and I will pay thee all", Matt. 18. 26. The word is used of the Lord Himself, "The Lord . . . is *longsuffering* to us-ward, not willing that any should perish, but that all should come to repentance", 2 Pet. 3. 9. It may be legitimate to take corrective measures as a result of sin and weakness in others, but love does not rush into action, expecting that the very delay would correct the weakness or bring about repentance. The Corinthians displayed no patience in their exercise of gift. They should wait one upon another, but it appears that they merely wrought confusion by many taking part at one and the same time.

2. *Kind*: This verb only appears once in the N.T., but its root appears in an adjective and in a noun implying *goodness, gentleness*. For example, "For My yoke is easy, and My burden is light", Matt. 11. 30; "the *goodness* of God leadeth thee to repentance", Rom. 2. 4; "after that the *kindness* and love (pity) of God our Saviour toward man appeared", Tit. 3. 4. This suggests that love displays kindness and goodness in action even if circumstances are undeserving. Certainly Paul was displaying this feature of love in his dealings with the Corinthian errors.

Now follows a list of eight negative features of love. The positive sides are implied though not explicitly mentioned.

1. *Envieth not*: In the good sense, this word implies zeal, as "covet earnestly", 12. 31. But in the bad sense, envy, jealousy and rivalry are implied. In Corinth, there were "*envying, and strife, and divisions*", 3. 3, and when Paul would visit them again, there was the danger that there would be "debates, *envyings*, wraths, strifes", 2 Cor. 12. 20. Elsewhere, James wrote that some "*desire to have*, and cannot obtain", James 4. 2. But if love is present, no such foreign sentiments would be seen in the outworking of gift.

2. *Vaunteth not itself*: Such a verb would imply showing off, bragging, a manifestation of vain-glory. Simon in Samaria engaged in such activity, "giving out that himself was some great one", Acts 8. 9. The humility of Paul should rather be emulated, "As unknown, and yet well known; as dying, and, behold, we live; as chastened, and not killed", 2 Cor. 6. 9.

   J.N. Darby, in 1832, at the beginning of a long life of service teaching and expounding the Scriptures, wrote a spiritual song, "The Call", containing the twenty-second verse:

   > Lord, let me wait for Thee alone;
   >   My life be only this—
   > To serve Thee here on earth, unknown;
   >   Then share Thy heavenly bliss.

   At the end of his life in 1882, this same verse was inscribed on the memorial stone standing over his grave in Bournemouth cemetery.

3. *Not puffed up*: That is, love is never inflated with conceit nor satisfied with success. Such conceit could be either about another, 1 Cor. 4. 6, or about oneself, "Vainly puffed up by his fleshly mind", Col. 2. 18, or about an immoral act, 1 Cor. 5. 2. But love demonstrates a spirit of humility both in service and in conduct.

4. *Doth not behave itself unseemly*: That is, love never walks with something to be hidden. The same word, or the same root, may be found in 12. 23 and in Revelation 16. 15. Had David really loved Bathsheba in 2 Samuel 11? Nathan had to say "Thou didst it secretly", 12. 12. Rather, all service should be open and frank so that all may approve of it. Nothing in service should be hidden or partially hidden with shame. The Lord's words are very much to the point here, "I spake openly to the world; I ever taught in the synagogue, and in the temple, whither theJews always resort; and in secret have I said nothing", John 18. 20

5. *Seeketh not her own*: That is, a servant manifesting love does not indulge in his own self-interests. Many verses in the N.T. contrast with this beautiful feature of love. For example, "All seek their own, not the things which are Jesus Christ's", Phil. 2. 21; "Demas hath forsaken me, having loved this present world", 2 Tim. 4. 10, meaning that he loved liberty in service rather than being bound

to Paul in prison; Ananias and Sapphira showed no love when they sold a possession and kept back part of the price for their selfish use, Acts 5. 2. Rather the lack of self-interest is shown in such verses as "First gave their own selves to the Lord, and unto us by the will of God", 2 Cor. 8. 5.

6. *Not easily provoked*: That is, sharp contention is not manifested. In Acts 15. 39, "the contention was so sharp" between Paul and Barnabas, that they parted company. This is the final mention of the work of Barnabas, but if there was weakness of love there, love does not forget, and Paul recalls him later, 1 Cor. 9. 6. In Acts 17. 16, Paul's spirit was stirred or provoked in Athens because of the idolatry on every hand. Hence he tended to dispute rather than preach Christ more clearly. On the other hand, this word "provoke" can be used in a good sense: "Let us consider one another to provoke unto love and to good works", Heb. 10. 24.

7. *Thinketh no evil*: This verb means to *reckon* or to *impute*. It occurs eleven times in Romans 4, that great chapter on the imputation of righteousness. Love does not imagine a grievance against another brother in Christ, neither does it harbour up evil thoughts against a fellow-believer. Quite generally in our mutual relations to one another, we are exhorted to "Recompense to no man evil for evil", Rom. 12. 17, to "See that none render evil for evil unto any man", 1 Thess. 5. 15, with the general observation "Love worketh no ill to his neighbour", Rom. 13. 10. The proper way would seem hard to the flesh, namely "Whosoever shall smite thee on thy right cheek, turn to him the other also", Matt. 5. 39.

8. *Rejoiceth not in iniquity*: that is, in *unrighteousness*. The opposite dominates the behaviour of the ungodly. As we know, many newspapers and other means of entertainment reaching the minds of people are got up solely to stimulate the base natural desire to rejoice in iniquity. Balaam "loved the wages of unrighteousness", 2 Pet. 2. 15 and the unregenerate "have pleasure in them that do them", Rom. 1. 32, that is, in those who commit the unrighteous acts listed before. But love is "of purer eyes than to behold evil" and cannot look on iniquity, Hab. 1. 13. That is, love will not *dwell* on such, although it can *discern* it.

Finally, another list, of five positive features of love, follows.

1. *Rejoiceth in the truth*: This contrasts with the previous statement, and shows the proper atmosphere for the display of love. The shepherd and the woman said "Rejoice with me", Luke 15. 6, 9. Here was something love could dwell upon, the finding of the sheep and the piece of silver. Love has the greatest interest in everything according to truth, according to the Lord and His Word. Elsewhere, Paul had written, "Whatsoever things are true,

honest, just, pure, lovely, of good report, . . . think on these things", Phil. 4. 8. The absence of this betrays the absence of love.

2. *Beareth all things*: Strictly, this verb means to *cover*, having the same root as *roof* see Matt. 8. 8. Love "covers all things", not in the sense of being blind, but in the sense of not retaliating, and showing patient endurance. Love would not bring down the twelve legions of angels, but endured at the hands of men, Matt. 26. 53. If a legion consists of six thousand, and if one angel could smite a hundred and eighty five thousand, 2 Kings 19. 35, then twelve legions could deal with over thirteen thousand million. But love beareth all things, until the purposes of God in judgment are abroad, and "who shall be able to stand" in that day?, Rev. 6. 17. Love must sometimes bear with others who introduce things that grieve the conscience. Not all have the responsibility or the ability to correct under such circumstances. Conversely, this verb "beareth all things" can be used in the opposite sense with a good meaning. For example, in 1 Thessalonians 3. 1, 5, Paul could "no longer forbear"; that is, he could no longer endure not knowing how the Thessalonians were getting on in times of affliction.

3. *Believeth all things*: The love of God and the faith of saints go together, John 3. 16. All things are ours, 1 Cor. 3. 21–22, and love cannot call into question the promises and blessings of God. Love cannot dissect the Word of God, taking up that which satisfies the intellect and rejecting other passages critically. Else one would be like those "that are unlearned and unstable", who distort the Scriptures to their own destruction, 2 Pet. 3. 16.

4. *Hopeth all things*: The scope is vast in these features; "all things" goes beyond the possibility of enumeration. Love looks to the future in the purposes of God. One's hope or expectation does not waver. See Romans 8. 24; Titus 1. 2; 2. 13; 3. 7. The Corinthians needed to be reminded of this, since their hope in the resurrection had almost disappeared as chapter 15 will show.

5. *Endureth all things*: This may mean that love sustains various purifying circumstances from the Lord given with a view to repentance. In another sense, the Lord endured the cross, Heb. 12. 2; but the Hebrews had to endure chastening in order that they might profit unto the production of the peaceable fruit of righteousness, 12. 7, 11.

A saint who displays these features of love in his walk and service possesses the very character of Christ upon him. Every minister of the Word should therefore know something of the exercise of Paul, when he desired to travail in birth again until Christ be formed in the saints, Gal. 4. 19. But it is essentially practical. John insists that the love of God is perfected in those who keep His word, 1 John 2. 5. And again, the apostle exhorts us to love not "in word, neither in tongue; but in deed and in truth", 3. 18. It is dangerously possible to deceive ourselves in this matter.

"Unfeigned love", with no show of pretence or artificiality, is called for, both from young believers, 1 Pet. 1. 22, and from the ministers of God, 2 Cor. 6. 6. Otherwise, one may be like the people in Ezekiel's day, "They sit before thee as My people, and they hear My words, but they will not do them: for with their mouth they shew much love, but their heart goeth after their covetousness", Ezek. 33. 31.

Verses 8–13: Things Transitory and Abiding

8 Charity never faileth: but whether *there be* prophecies, they shall fail; whether *there be* tongues, they shall cease; whether *there be* knowledge, it shall vanish away.
9 For we know in part, and we prophesy in part.
10 But when that which is perfect is come, then that which is in part shall be done away.
11 When I was a child, I spake as a child, I understood as a child, I thought as a child: but when I became a man, I put away childish things.
12 For now we see through a glass, darkly; but then face to face: now I know in part; but then shall I know even as also I am known.
13 And now abideth faith, hope, charity, these three; but the greatest of these *is* charity.

8. What can be eternal in a scene of change, decay and death? Brethren and their gifts come and go over the years. Where can stability be found? Paul answers, "Love never faileth" or "falleth". The flower of the grass may fall, James 1. 11; 1 Pet. 1. 24, but love is a permanent feature of spiritual life. It is like an eternal flower by which the Spirit can ever bring forth blessed fruit. The "more excellent way" consists of recognising and practising the consequences of eternal character. Thereby the transitory nature of spiritual gifts are moulded by eternal virtues. All gifts, given for edification here below, would ultimately pass away. Even in Paul's day, some were almost ready to vanish away, such as prophecy and tongues. But he does not stress the fact that they were ready to vanish away there and then; in chapter 14, he still encourages the proper use of both.

Prophecies: The ability to speak forth the mind of God, known by direct communication from the Spirit, would fail in due time. This verb *katargeo*, to be done away, occurs some twenty-seven times in the N.T., and its usage is sometimes remarkable, as a glance down a concordance will show. It occurs four times in verses 8–11. Prophecy would be no longer useful after the written Word had been completed, and then God would arrange for the gift no longer to be available.

Tongues: As a gift, these would cease as soon as God decreed that they were no longer required. Tongues were not only a *gift*, but a *sign*, 14. 22. Many signs were promised by the Lord, but the five named in Mark 16. 17–18 would fail after the initiatory period of the church. The Lord's signs (the "miracles" of John's Gospel), valuable though they were, ceased when He was taken up. Only signs with spiritual significance remained, Matt. 12. 39; 16. 4. The word "cease" is distinct from *katargeo* used with prophecy and knowledge; the word is stronger and suggests a more immediate cessation. See Luke 8. 24.

Knowledge: The verb "shall vanish away" is the same as "fail" previously used, and as "done away", v. 10, and "put away", v. 11. This knowledge cannot refer, of course, to the blessed knowledge of Christ which is eternal. Rather, we take it to refer to the mind of the teacher, 12. 8, 28, who has doctrinal facts marshalled in the special way required for passing on the doctrine to others. This will ultimately fail when there is no more need of teachers in the assembly at the coming of the Lord.

9. The gifts of the teacher with knowledge, and of prophecy, are "in part". They only partly fulfil the purpose of God in a soul; they use creatorial means—speaking, hearing, reading—to accomplish spiritual ends. Even the first and best gifts, the apostles and prophets, 12. 28, were partial. That is, they were suitable for the saints in wilderness conditions. If these would pass away, how much more other gifts of lesser import, some sooner some later.

10. Such partial conditions terminate "when that which is perfect is come". Some expositors suggest that this refers to the completed written Word of God, the completion of the N.T. Scriptures. They observe that prophecy is no longer required when the written Word is available. But it is not possible to use this argument in connection with knowledge, which also vanishes away. It still exists, long after the canon of Scripture has been completed by God. Paul observes that things which are "in part shall be done away" when "that which is perfect is come". Now, many gifts remain, including knowledge, so we cannot see how the N.T. in written form is alluded to here. "That which is perfect" is yet to come.   *I agree.*

We suggest that what Paul has in mind is the accomplishment of the full purpose of God in the soul, that which can only take place when creatorial features are replaced by eternal features, when that which is spiritual ceases to be dimmed by that which is material.

However spiritual and godly a brother may be, none would admit that he is as appreciative of Christ now as he will be in the day yet to come. Paul's work was to accomplish the ideal; his labours were directed to the end "that we may present every man perfect in Christ Jesus", Col. 1. 28–29. But this can only be fully accomplished in that future day when God's own gracious work is complete in the soul.

The difference between the work of God in a soul now through gifts unto edification and the completed work on high in that day is similar to circumstances surrounding the ark of the covenant of the Lord. The staves were in the rings of the ark during its wilderness journey, Exod. 25. 15, corresponding to conditions "in part". But when established in the temple in the land, the staves were withdrawn, 1 Kings 8. 8, corresponding to "perfect" conditions.

11–12. Paul now gives two metaphors to stress this change.

1. A *child*. Speaking, understanding and reasoning as a child correspond to the use of gifts. Thus speaking has in mind the gift of tongues; understanding—the gift of prophecy; and reasoning—the gift of knowledge. The thought is one of growth in this scene below. Becoming a man, thereby putting away childish things, refers to that future day when God's work is complete in the mature spiritual man. Those who interpret the coming of the perfect thing as the complete N.T. would interpret these "childish things" in terms of those particular gifts that would *quickly* pass away, such as prophecy and tongues. Whereas this is of course true, we do not feel that this is what Paul has in mind in this particular passage.

2. A *glass*. The only other time this word occurs in the N.T. is in James 1. 23, "beholding his natural face in a glass". The reference is to metal mirrors Exod. 38. 8, giving imperfect reflection, though even a tarnished mirror is perfect underneath! The word "darkly" means "obscurely" in the context of a mirror; others translate it as "in a riddle". Paul means that all truth is obscurely appreciated now compared with that day when all will be known directly—"face to face". (This is the only time in the N.T. that this expression occurs. In 2 John 12 and 3 John 14 it really means "mouth to mouth".) The coming of the complete N.T. in written form did not remove this obscurity of appreciation. Peter speaks of "things hard to be understood" in Paul's written epistles, 2 Pet. 3. 16. Obscurity will only be removed when we cease to be in the flesh, when the spirit is liberated in a glorified body to enjoy the truth as it is in Christ Jesus.

The change to perfection that Paul visualises is similar to the thought, "then shall I know even as also I am known". Men knew Paul clearly, not vaguely, but the Lord knows His own perfectly now. He knows His sheep, John 10. 14, and "The Lord knoweth them that are His", 2 Tim. 2. 19. Can any say today that their appreciation of truth now, even possessing the written Word, is similar to that great divine knowledge? But in that coming day, all barriers will be broken down and removed. The great lesson seems to be that we must hold all gifts now in proper perspective, using them for edification, but recognising that God may withdraw some as and when He will. Gifts can only partially render "perfect" the soul; but God will finalise the work in that day.

13. Paul finally stresses that character transcends gift even now. Gifts are not the goal of activity. Rather, God would have us occupied with and displaying spiritual virtues. Faith, hope and love abide throughout this present dispensation. They cannot be withdrawn until that day. But when that day dawns and the shadows flee away, faith and hope will have given place to the glories of spiritual reality, but love will remain eternally. To recognise this is to appreciate the "more excellent way".

It is only right to point out that other expositors hold different views regarding the explanation of verses 8–13, and the author would suggest that readers form their own judgment. These expositors claim that the three gifts in verse 8, namely prophecy, tongues and knowledge, all vanished when the canon of the N.T. Scriptures was available. Such a group of three gifts contrasts therefore with the group of three characters of soul in verse 13, namely faith, hope and love. The first two of these remain until the rapture, whilst the last abides eternally. In verses 9 and 10, both knowledge and prophecy, being but "in part", are said to vanish away at the same time when the written Word is come. Childhood, in verse 11, is taken to refer to these particular gifts that vanished away when the N.T. was complete, and, "becoming a man", is understood to refer to the believer's experience after the N.T. became available. Hence, in verse 12, the "glass, darkly" refers to the state in Corinth when these spiritual gifts alone were available, and "face to face" for the more blessed state later when the N.T. had been completed.

If the Corinthians were to understand what Paul meant, it is implied that both they and he knew that the N.T. canon was to be produced by the Holy Spirit through His servants in just the same way as the O.T. had been written and collected together. Can this assumption be justified? In any case, the reader will notice that both lines of exposition are valid in christian experience. The expositions differ in as far as the various symbols are taken to refer to different features.

1 CORINTHIANS 14

Section 5.   Assembly Service
Subject 5.   Principles of Edification

Relationships within this Section

Chapters 12–14 form an integrated whole, the central subject of love forming a necessary part of the apostle's argument. To use a very poor metaphor, we may observe that a motor engine requires petrol, oil and a driver. The proper use of spiritual gifts similarly requires the Spirit of God, love in the hearts of the saints, and the divine Head in control. Then the engine should go, if it has been made according to the original design. Hence, chapter 14 shows how an assembly should function internally. Admittedly, the inspired mechanic is dealing with a fault, seeking to correct, following the original pattern. But if correction is heeded, the assembly should thereafter function unto edification.

The stress is on one particular spiritual gift throughout, namely that of "tongues". But the same principles unto edification apply today, so whereas this particular gift may not now be of relevance, yet the principles outlined in the chapter are of permanent value to the people of God seeking to walk according to the divine pattern.

The chapter may be divided into paragraphs as follows:

Verses 1–5: relative profitability of prophecy and tongues;
Verses 6–11: all must understand;
Verses 12–20: all must be useful;
Verses 21–25: tongues essentially affect the unbeliever;
Verses 26–35: conduct of a meeting;
Verses 36–40: conclusion.

Exposition of 1 Cor. 14: Principles of Edification

Verses 1–5: Relative Profitability of Prophecy and Tongues

1 Follow after charity, and desire spiritual *gifts*, but rather that ye may phophesy.
2 For he that speaketh in an *unknown* tongue speaketh not unto men, but unto God: for no man understandeth *him*; howbeit in the spirit he speaketh mysteries.
3 But he that prophesieth speaketh unto men *to* edification, and exhortation, and comfort.
4 He that speaketh in an *unknown* tongue edifieth himself; but he that prophesieth edifieth the church.
5 I would that ye all spake with tongues, but rather that ye prophesied: for greater *is* he that prophesieth than he that speaketh with tongues, except he interpret, that the church may receive edifying.

1. Love is to be pursued *first; then* one may have a zeal for gifts, or "spirituals" as the word really is. For sake of contrast, Paul deals with only two outstanding miraculous gifts, namely those of prophecy and tongues. Other gifts, such as teaching, helps, and so on, may not be so outstanding, but are equally necessary. The two that Paul deals with are the first two listed in 13. 8. At the same time, Paul shows that the saints may desire those gifts that are the most profitable. Such a sanctified desire is in no way contrary to the divine prerogative to distribute gifts as He will.

2. Paul now tackles the subject of "unknown tongues", and we should observe that this word "unknown", which occurs six times in italics in this chapter, is a translator's fancy—a word that has caused difficulty and confusion in so many minds. The word is not there in the Greek, and should be omitted in the English version, as in J. N. Darby's translation. This word "unknown" causes the mind to think in terms of ecstatic tongues, but we have already stated in detail (see 12. 10) that these tongues merely refer to other languages distinct from the mother tongues of the speakers. A brother speaking in a tongue, refers to a man not using the general language of the assembly. Rather, he is using either
— his own mother tongue (if this should be different from that used in the assembly), or
— an acquired language distinct from his mother tongue (again if this language should be different from that used in the assembly), or
— a language given him as a gift, but not understood by the majority of the assembly members.
Such a speaker would be taking part just for show, with perhaps many brethren actually taking part at the same time. Hence no one would "understand", or "hear" according to the Greek text. The brother may well be speaking the truth, but as a mystery—that is, something needing explanation for understanding. In this case, explanation would be interpretation. Compare the proper use of speaking mysteries, 4. 1, where a divine explanation is necessary.

3. Such an application of gift contrasts with the activity of one who prophesies, since prophecy in the general language of the assembly yields immediate results. Prophecy may be directed into various channels. Here, Paul mentions three:
1. *Edification:* This would refer essentially to doctrine, the word of His grace, which is able to build us up, Acts 20. 32.
2. *Exhortation:* By this means, one is encouraged to walk in the light of doctrine already received. In Romans 12. 8, it is a gift in its own right. Some brethren are particularly able to encourage the saints to walk according to the truth. For example, Barnabas (meaning son of consolation or exhortation, Acts 4. 36) exhorted the saints in Antioch "that with purpose of heart they would cleave unto the Lord", Acts 11. 23.
3. *Comfort:* This can be both individual and collective, meeting many open and hidden needs. Paul exhorted and comforted the

Thessalonians to "walk worthy of God", 1 Thess. 2. 12, explaining later that they should "comfort the feebleminded, support the weak", 5. 14.

4. This verse summarises verses 2 and 3. If truth is spoken in a tongue, the speaker only is edified. He understands, and by expounding the truth gains one a better understanding of its principles —this is edification of self. However, prophecy, on the other hand, is valuable for the edification of the whole local assembly, since all understand.

5. Paul has nothing against the gift of tongues as compared with prophecy (see verse 39). However, prophecy is better on the grounds of its maximum usefulness, since many are edified. The prophets, who speak to all, are greater than those speaking in a language only to themselves (or at the most to just a few). But a prophet ceases to be "greater" than the one speaking in a tongue if the latter "interpret, that the church may receive edifying". In verses 27, 28, another brother may do the interpreting. Of course there would be no point in speaking only to oneself if one could also speak in the language of the assembly. The truth could and should have been expressed in that language to start with! But it was here that the Corinthians were going astray in their zeal to use their gifts, even if no mutual profit was forthcoming.

Verses 6–11: All must Understand

6 Now, brethren, if I come unto you speaking with tongues, what shall I profit you, except I shall speak to you either by revelation, or by knowledge, or by prophesying, or by doctrine?

7 And even things without life giving sound, whether pipe or harp, except they give a distinction in the sounds, how shall it be known what is piped or harped?

8 For if the trumpet give an uncertain sound, who shall prepare himself to the battle?

9 So likewise ye, except ye utter by the tongue words easy to be understood, how shall it be known what is spoken? for ye shall speak into the air.

10 There are, it may be, so many kinds of voices in the world, and none of them *is* without signification.

11 Therefore if I know not the meaning of the voice, I shall be unto him that speaketh a barbarian, and he that speaketh *shall be* a barbarian unto me.

6. In this verse, Paul uses the "I" of argument. Clearly he does not refer to himself, since Paul would not do what is contemplated here. The word "if" in the supposition "*if* I come unto you speaking with tongues" is the Greek *ean*, expressive of real doubt. It must be understood however that the word "if" in the N.T. does not always have this meaning. For example, Matthew 4. 3 is quite distinct; "If thou be the Son of God" does not employ this word *ean* expressing doubt. A different word is used, the "if" of argument, "seeing that". Some preachers say that Satan was placing doubts before the Lord, but this was impossible. Both the Lord Jesus and Satan knew the facts.

But others, apart from Paul, may come to Corinth and speak with tongues. This would be of no profit. Edification would result only if these preachers spoke to the Corinthians in one or another of the various forms of instruction listed here:

Revelation: The mind of God would be made known to the speaker there and then.

Knowledge: A speaker speaks from a store of truth organised in his mind. Ultimately, it would have originated from God, but came indirectly, Luke 1. 77.

Prophesying. The mind of God made known directly by prior communication.

Doctrine: Here one speaks as a teacher, making known the mind of God previously learnt from others or from the Word.

7. Paul draws a parallel from the inanimate world of musical sounds. An ear which appreciates music would find instruments profitless if all sounded alike, or if all gave the same note. A distinction or difference is necessary for the ear to understand. There would be no point in using the instruments or in listening to them if understanding were impossible. The word "distinction" used here is the same as the word "difference" in Romans 3. 22 and 10. 12.

8. Similarly with the trumpet; its sound must be recognised if its message is to be heeded. In Numbers 10.1–10, two silver trumpets were used for signals in the camp. Their different uses had to be interpreted with understanding. Sometimes it was for marching orders, sometimes for war, sometimes for their solemn days. Again in the N.T., sometimes it is a trump of fear, Heb. 12. 19, sometimes of anticipation, 1 Cor. 15. 52, and sometimes of gathering, Matt. 24. 31.

9. Similarly with speakers in the assembly. They must use words "easy to be understood", their speech must be intelligible. Otherwise, they would appear to be speaking "into the air". The hearers would sense that their words were being lost in the air around rather than entering into their ears with understanding. Speaking "into the air" would be useless, as would be the service of one "that beateth the air", 9. 26.

Quite apart from the question of tongues, preachers today should adjust and adapt their style of vocabulary and exposition to meet the needs of the hearers. These might be young, aged, not able to follow anything complicated, tired, and so on. If one speaks beyond the ability of the hearers, the message is quite lost. Similarly, a complicated O.T. type, expounded as a gospel message, may be quite incomprehensible to an unsaved hearer.

10. Paul now discusses variety. In the world, there are many "kinds of voices" or "sounds"; none is "without signification", or "dumb, without distinct sound". Verse 11 shows that he is referring to the great variety of human languages. Every one has meaning to the appropriate hearer, none being ecstatic. The variety is the result of Genesis 11. 7, when God confounded "their language, that they may not understand one another's speech".

11. If there is no mutual contact of mind, then the relationship of "barbarian" or "foreigner" comes in. Literally, a barbarian is one who is not a proper Greek, Rom. 1. 14; Acts 28. 4. Less specifically, it may refer to a foreigner speaking a strange language. But Paul would not have such a relationship in the assembly. "There is neither Jew nor Greek, . . ., for ye are all one in Christ Jesus", Gal. 3. 28; "There is neither Greek nor Jew, . . ., Barbarian, Scythian, bond nor free: but Christ is all, and in all", Col. 3. 11. Christ had dissipated the antagonism between races, and Paul would not have the barrier erected again in an artificial way, thereby introducing a division of understanding in the assembly.

Verses 12–20: All must be Useful

12 Even so ye, forasmuch as ye are zealous of spiritual *gifts*, seek that ye may excel to the edifying of the church.
13 Wherefore let him that speaketh in an *unknown* tongue pray that he may interpert.
14 For if I pray in an *unknown* tongue, my spirit prayeth, but my understanding is unfruitful.
15 What is it then? I will pray with the spirit, and I will pray with the understanding also: I will sing with the spirit, and I will sing with the understanding also.
16 Else when thou shalt bless with the spirit, how shall he that occupieth the room of the unlearned say Amen at thy giving of thanks, seeing he understandeth not what thou sayest?
17 For thou verily givest thanks well, but the other is not edified.
18 I thank my God, I speak with tongues more than ye all:
19 Yet in the church I had rather speak five words with my understanding, that *by my voice* I might teach others also, than ten thousand words in an *unknown* tongue.
20 Brethren, be not children in understanding: howbeit in malice be ye children, but in understanding be men.

12. Paul first enunciates a general principle: how the saints should put their zeal into practice, since such zeal may be misplaced. The Corinthians were "zealous of spiritual gifts", or rather, "zealous of spirits", according to the Greek text. This is rather a difficult concept, unlike the word "spirituals" in 12. 1; 14. 1. Perhaps the sense would be that the believers were zealous for the wellbeing of the spirits of the saints, as in Rom. 1. 9; 1 Cor. 6. 20; 16. 18. The outworking of such zeal was strangely misplaced, although they evidently could not discern this. True zeal excels "to the edifying of the church". The thought behind the word "excel" may be gleaned from other passages that use the same word.

> Luke 15. 17: "How many hired servants of my father's have bread *enough and to spare*".
>
> John 6. 13: ". . . the fragments of the five barley loaves, which *remained over and above* unto them that had eaten".

Such superabundance leaves no room for any lesser activity of no comparable profit. Yet some preachers think that sermons full of mundane matters are a useful substitute for the wholesome exposition of God's Word.

13. If a brother speaks in a language (now obviously legitimately, for the sake of two or three others—not for himself), let there be an interpretation of his message that the whole assembly may profit. The preacher, realising that few can understand, should pray for the ability to interpret (see our remarks on 12. 10), or for some other brother to interpret, 14. 27.

14. When Paul writes "If I pray in a tongue, my spirit prayeth, but my understanding is unfruitful", he continues the thought of the previous verse. Paul means that he is listening in an attitude of prayer to another brother praying in a language that he cannot understand. This can easily be the experience of any one who has been in a foreign country. Such a brother praying in a language others could not understand would cast a spirit of prayer over the meeting. Thus the "spirit" of the hearer would be in prayer because of the atmosphere, but there would be no understanding.

15. Paul would have all to pray and sing with the spirit (namely the spiritual atmosphere would be captured) and with the understanding (the subject matter of the prayer or song would be captured). The verb "sing" is the Greek word *psallo*. Originally, this verb meant to strike chords on an instrument. But the N.T. usage of the verb implies that only the heart and voice were active. In this verse, for example, mental understanding is envisaged. In Ephesians 5. 19, "singing and making melody in your heart to the Lord" implies an act of the heart, while James 5. 13, "Is any among you afflicted? let him pray. Is any merry? let him sing psalms" places prayer and song on the same footing.

16. Otherwise, if a brother thus prayed openly in a tongue (not boastfully, but actually in the spirit), anyone else in the gathering (that is, the unlearned, the uninstructed in this particular language, Paul included) could not say "Amen". *Amen* implies that one acquiesces spiritually in all that has been said before the Lord, but mental understanding is a prior necessity for this.

17. The speaker, if praying spiritually in the Lord's name and according to His will, with no display of boasting or of self achievement, is quite in order. He gives thanks "well". What is at fault is the fact that his hearers are not edified. We normally associate edification with ministry, but Paul extends its meaning here. We can be edified by listening to another brother in prayer, since by this means our hearts are being led out to the Lord. Any progress in spiritual exercise amounts to edification.

18. Paul brings the matter down to himself, so as to apply his teaching forcefully. He spoke "in a tongue", J.N.D., more than the others. He referred to his constant use of Greek on his missionary journeys rather than his mother tongue Hebrew. But would he use Greek in a Jewish assembly consisting solely of Hebrew-speaking believers? Would he think of himself rather than the other saints?

19. Paul's conclusion is that there needs to be understanding all round. As a preacher, Paul would desire to restrict his utterances to "five words" if that was all he could understand. Of course, he understood the language. The understanding of the preacher must concern *the doctrine under exposition*. After the resurrection of the Lord, the apostles could have spoken a lot, but without understanding. They could have occupied themselves with the strange ideas expressed by the two on the Emmaus road, Luke 24. 19–24. But it were best for them to remain silent until the Lord opened "their understanding", v. 45. Then they could preach with intelligence as witnesses of His resurrection. Today, for a preacher to try to speak on a subject about which he is ignorant, is folly indeed.

The exact opposite to this, would be extreme verbosity in a language that no one understood. Such a multiplicity of words spoken into the air would cover up the speaker's lack of understanding of his own subject. Paul shunned this.

The reader who followed our remarks on the two different Greek words for "another" in 12. 8–10 may be interested to observe the same ideas here. "That I might teach others also" means "others of the same kind" — in understanding what is spoken. But in verse 21, "With men of other tongues", the meaning is "others of a different kind", namely foreign languages not understood.

20. The word "understanding" in the phrase "be not children in understanding" was an unfortunate choice on the part of the A.V. translators. The R.V. gives "be not children in mind" in keeping with the Greek text. That is, they were not to be like children who often speak of things they are not certain about, and often have to listen to things they do not fully appreciate. Rather, they were to be like men in their minds (not understanding), being of ripe age and fully grown, avoiding weaknesses prevalent in Corinth. On the other hand, they were to be babes in malice, having no evil intent regarding gifts not used to edification.

Verses 21–25: Tongues essentially affect the Unbeliever

21 In the law it is written, With *men* of other tongues and other lips will I speak unto this people; and yet for all that will they not hear me, saith the Lord.

22 Wherefore tongues are for a sign, not to them that believe, but to them that believe not: but prophesying *serveth* not for them that believe not, but for them which believe.

23 If therefore the whole church be come together into one place, and all speak with tongues, and there come in *those that are* unlearned, or unbelievers, will they not say that ye are mad?

24 But if all prophesy, and there come in one that believeth not, or *one* unlearned, he is convinced of all, he is judged of all:

25 And thus are the secrets of his heart made manifest; and so falling down on *his* face he will worship God, and report that God is in you of a truth.

21. Paul does something here that we cannot do today. With apostolic authority he built a practice on an O.T. quotation. "With men of other tongues and other lips will I speak unto this people; and yet for all that will they not hear Me, saith the Lord" is quoted from Isaiah 28. Verse 7 shows that drunken priests were trying to teach drunken people, and that the Lord could only teach knowledge to babes, v. 9. Even the simplest teaching from the Lord would result in many being broken, snared and taken, v. 13. Hence the Lord would ultimately speak to this people in another language—a real language we should note, that of their captors— but even then they would not hear. But the point of the quotation is to stress that a language, other than the mother tongue is a sign to the disobedient and sinful.

22. From this, Paul concludes that the real object of the gift of tongues when properly used is that it should be a sign to unbelievers, as in Acts 2. Admittedly in Isaiah 28. 12, they would not hear, but we cannot conclude that this will be so in the present passage. No doubt many of the strangers and proselytes in Acts 2 repented when they heard the message of the gospel in their own languages. It would seem, however, that Peter's great sermon was not preached in a tongue, but in the common language of Jerusalem. The apostle spoke, not to the great variety of visitors to Jerusalem, but to the men of Judaea and those that dwelt at Jerusalem, v. 14. These had mocked, but later many repented, v. 38.

On the other hand, the gift of prophesy was given solely for the blessing of the saints. Paul goes on to observe, however, that crumbs of blessing may fall from this table to affect the unsaved.

23. Here, Paul visualises a gathering of the assembly, and their weakness is shown by the fact that the gift of tongues is being improperly used. All sought to speak with tongues, the suggestion being that all took part at once, thereby introducing double confusion. The unlearned no doubt refers to believers, present but remaining in ignorance as to what was actually taking place, v. 16. But Paul also contemplates an unbeliever present, as so often happens today. They do not have fellowship, of course, and elder brethren should see that such strangers are somewhat apart from the circle engaged in holy activity before the Lord. But Paul rightly observes that if unbelievers heard such confusion, they would judge the assembly to be mad. The great point is that unbelievers must gain the impression that something useful is being done, even if they fail to understand the spiritual character of it. This would apply to many forms of service. If unbelievers raise their eyebrows in horror at some activity that appears to them to be unseemly, then something is wrong with the activity. The sanctified priestly functioning of believers, and their proper use of spiritual gift, would never induce such feelings into the minds of unbelievers.

24. Prophecy is not for these unbelievers, although they can be affected by it when they can understand what is being spoken. However, a meeting convened for the edification of the saints, or for the holy act of worship, is not to be turned into a gospel meeting for these souls. The truth itself will convince and judge an unbeliever. To convince means "convict, reprove, rebuke", as in Titus 1. 9; John 16. 8; Titus 1. 13; "of all" refers to all who prophesy, not to all his sinful deeds. Similarly, the word *judge*, used ten times in this Epistle means "to examine", again accomplished by all who prophesy. Today, we are often afraid of the power of the Word of God, or perhaps we do not believe that the Word is really living and powerful to affect a soul. Saints may use all sorts of methods in their service, but nothing can take the place of the Word of God.

25. "The secrets of his heart made manifest" does not mean that they are openly expressed. Rather they are made known to the man himself by the spiritual power of the preaching that was not directed to him at all—except by the gracious Spirit. Compare John 8. 9, where hardly a word was spoken, yet the men were convicted. These unbelievers would realise that there was an unseen power present to convict the conscience. There is nothing emotional about this at all, no artificially worked-up atmosphere.

The result is that he will fall down on his face. Again, this is not emotional; it is the humble position that a convicted soul must take before God. Such a concept occurs several times in the Gospels. Moreover, the man will "worship God". This is quite distinct from the holy exercise of the saints, John 4. 23; 9. 38. The word means "render homage", in a traditional religious sense if the conviction does not lead to repentance, but otherwise it is the first stirrings of the heart if repentance has taken place. Elsewhere, we read of the Greeks, John 12. 20, of the leper, Matt. 8. 2 and of the ruler, Matt. 9. 18; these likewise rendered homage to the Lord.

At the same time, they would recognise that God was among the believers gathered together. This would be because of the compelling power for good, manifested in them by the Spirit taking up the preacher's message. The presence of a divine Person is a most precious blessing, an earnest of eternal days. It is even more precious when His presence amongst the saints coincides with them having to live in a place "where Satan dwelleth", Rev. 2. 13. The true Light can dispel the darkness, and the believer's outlook is transformed.

Verses 26–35: Conduct of a Meeting

26 How is it then, brethren? when ye come together, every one of you hath a psalm, hath a doctrine, hath a tongue, hath a revelation, hath an interpretation. Let all things be done unto edifying.
27 If any man speak in an *unknown* tongue, *let it be* by two, or at the most *by* three, and *that* by course; and let one interpret.
28 But if there be no interpreter, let him keep silence in the church; and let him speak to himself, and to God.
29 Let the prophets speak two or three, and let the other judge.
30 If *any thing* be revealed to another that sitteth by, let the first hold his peace.
31 For ye may all prophesy one by one, that all may learn, and all may be comforted.
32 And the spirits of the prophets are subject to the prophets.
33 For God is not *the author* of confusion, but of peace, as in all churches of the saints.
34 Let your women keep silence in the churches: for it is not permitted unto them to speak; but *they are commanded* to be under obedience, as also saith the law.
35 And if they will learn anything, let them ask their husbands at home: for it is a shame for women to speak in the church.

26. Having outlined the previous principles, Paul now goes into further details regarding the conduct of a gathering of the Lord's people. There is no legislation as to what kind of activity should be carried on during a meeting. The list provided here shows that many different functions were permitted in one meeting, but this does not set the style for every gathering. In Acts 4. 31; 12. 12, the meeting was essentially for prayer; in Acts 20. 9, preaching was the chief occupation of the meeting, although they had come together to break bread, v. 7. Here, in 1 Corinthians 11. 20 and 14. 26 Paul seems to distinguish between the Lord's supper and other spiritual activities.

A unique pattern is not laid down. Circumstances locally, the time available, the particular needs of the saints, and so on, must determine when a meeting is held and the primary reason for holding it. One assembly cannot legislate for another in this matter. No local assembly should think that this liberty gives grounds for neglect of the principles underlying all gatherings. Today, the saints have enough time available, free from daily employment, to devote a whole session to worship and the Lord's supper. It is good that the Lord should be given a session devoted entirely to Him and not to the needs of the saints. The prayer meeting, the ministry meeting, the Bible Reading, and the Gospel meeting provide enough opportunities to meet the needs of saints and sinners. Let a balance be preserved, and when meetings are convened for a specific purpose let all the saints respect that purpose. On the other hand, if a change is needed, let not the elders be slack in arranging it, lest it be tradition and not spirituality that motivates the assembly in its weekly exercises.

In spite of all the error, Paul still calls the Corinthians "brethren". This is grace, and the manifestation of love. Such a description appears in this Epistle twenty times; in this section on "Assembly Service" it may be found in 11. 2, 33; 12. 1; 14. 6, 20, 26, 39.

Paul now lists various features of the gatherings in Corinth:

Psalm: This is an exercise of praise, perhaps using an O.T. Psalm or the outward expression of melody in the heart, Eph. 5. 19.

Doctrine: This refers to a teacher expounding Scripture.

Tongue: This refers to the desire to exercise this gift, perhaps for the benefit of just a few, or merely for oneself. Paul does not commend its use under the wrong circumstances.

Revelation: This refers to something received directly from God during the gathering; it formed part of the Spirit's communication before the N.T. was complete.

Interpretation: This was the ability to repeat in the common tongue of the assembly what other speakers may have said in other languages.

As far as the saint-ward exercise was concerned, there was but one criterion, namely that of edification. This would be glorifying to the living Head who had ultimate control of all activity in the gathering. Edification is the Lord's desire. This criterion should test all that we do and arrange; for example, it should test our hymnsinging. The questions should be raised: In a meeting arranged for ministry of the Word, are the traditional four hymns necessary for edification? Are they for filling in time, to allow saints time to arrive late, or because the speaker cannot engage in ministry for more than half an hour? Let every brother who gives out a hymn, in whatever meeting it may be, question himself beforehand as to whether the hymn is really necessary.

27. As far as exercising the gift of tongues is concerned, the remarks of Paul only apply to occasions when it is legitimate that other languages should be spoken. Paul notes that no more than three such gifted brethren should take part in one meeting. This limitation is in keeping with the Spirit's control of what takes place. Moreover, such speakers were not to speak at once, as apparently had been the case in Corinth, but they were to speak in succession, that is, "by course". But whatever was done, the assembly was never to be left in the dark as to what was being said. Interpretation is essential for the wellbeing of all the saints and for their edification.

28. Nothing could be plainer than this verse. If no brother in the meeting was able to interpret, the intending speaker must remain silent, engaging in quiet meditation in his own heart before the Lord. God, at least, knows the hearts, Rom. 8. 27. The point is that the assembly as a whole deserves the chief consideration. Nothing should be allowed which did not have the edification of all the saints at heart. In spite of this clear statement, confusion is practised today in some circles, firstly through a false explanation of "tongues", and secondly through turning a blind eye to a verse like this.

29–33. The prophets, being more useful in a meeting, are likewise under divine control. Paul's observations are of relevance today, although we have teachers and not prophets. Both seek to exercise in the meeting that which they have received from the Lord. Their reception of truth is different, but their ability to impart it is the same. Hence the same principles apply. Moreover, Paul's remarks disallow "one-man" ministry and "every-man" ministry. There is no such thing as one man in a church having the sole prerogative to preach. If this ever comes about in religious circles, it is the result of man's arrangement . Similarly, the "everyman" type of activity is equally absent from Scripture. Paul here refers to prophets but to no other exercise of gift. Those who do not possess the gift of teaching should remain silent, by not seeking to expound in a public Bible Reading, and by not accepting invitations to preach even if they can "talk" easily. The ability to *talk* does not imply the ability to *preach*.

The special features of the prophets' ministry are as follows:

1. The Scriptures visualise that only two or three prophets should take part in any one meeting. By this means, a lot of little "tit-bits" would be avoided, with something more solid and lasting being provided for the saints. For example, in Antioch, Acts 13. 1, there were many prophets and teachers gathered together, but in the light of this verse not all could take part in any one meeting. It would appear that the Bible Reading of today, where many take part, is not really seen in these verses.

2. When one brother was speaking, the others were to judge or discern ("others" is in the plural, denoting "of the same kind"—the other prophets are referred to). These other prophets would be those most capable of recognising the mind of the Spirit, even to the extent of stopping ministry if it was not profitable. Without this constant discernment, false doctrine may creep in, regarding which Paul exhorted Timothy, "be thou ware", 2 Tim. 4. 15, "watch thou", 4–5, "shun", 2. 16.

3. Further truth could be revealed to another ("of the same kind", that is, to other prophets) during the meeting. In the context, this refers to the mind of God being made known there and then, so teachers are not really in question. When this gracious divine intervention takes place, the brother speaking must know when

to step down. There can be no rivalry in ministry of this character. For example, in Acts 11. 25–26, Barnabas readily gave place to Saul.

4. All may prophesy, subject of course to the possession of this gift, and to the requirement that not more than three should take part. A meeting thus convened is characterised by the exhortation: "Quench not the Spirit. Despise not prophesyings", 1 Thess. 5. 19–20.

5. By this means, all the saints in the gathering may learn, bringing with it the responsibility of continuing in these things learned, 2 Tim. 3. 14. Likewise, all may be comforted, or rather "exhorted", as in v. 3.

6. "The spirits of the prophets are subject to the prophets" means that love is demonstrated. Mutual understanding amongst the prophets, together with forbearance and toleration, enable one to give place to the other in assembly service.

If the saints thus abide, then they abide in the will of God. Such holy conduct demonstrates that "God is not the author of confusion". This word "confusion, tumult, disorder" occurs five times in the N.T.; "commotions", Luke 21. 9, "tumults", 2 Cor. 6. 5; 12. 20, "confusion", James 3. 16. Any manifestation of this, whether inside the assembly, outside on the part of believers, or outside on the part of the unsaved, savours of the flesh. The contrast is "peace", the reverent deportment of the saints in their holy functioning. Only such is of God, so this is a test as to what is of God and what is not. All saints have the opportunity of applying this test calmly before the Lord. (One may note a similar test in 1 John 4. 1–3, the test of spirits). Moreover this great principle applies in "all churches of the saints", in space and in time. The applicability is general, to believers in every place, 1. 2.

34–35. Paul concludes this paragraph with a special exhortation to sisters. Some expositors feel that the correction was needed in the light of 11. 5. Most editors of the Greek text omit "your" in the opening phrase "Let your women". Thus Paul refers to the general, and not to the particular in Corinth. They were to "keep silence" in the churches, as in verse 28 (referring to speaking with tongues) and as in verse 30 (referring to prophets). In the light of this continuity of thought, Paul refers to the necessity of resisting the urge to speak in service, not to common chattering as some would suggest. The fact that speaking was "not permitted" means that there can be no liberty for exercise in the matter. Sisters must be "under obedience", or "in subjection", taking the same position as ascribed to them in 11. 3. Their position of silence would be a sign of obedience and subjection in the same way as the wearing of a hat. Paul dwells on the same subject in 1 Timothy 2. 11–15. Sisters were to learn in silence, not seeking to teach "nor to usurp authority over the man". This order in creation is to be reflected in the assembly, thereby showing forth the subjection of the assembly to the Lord. The law itself had expressed general principles on the same matter in Genesis 2–3; see also 1 Peter 3. 5–6.

"It is a shame" for women to speak in the church, means that such activity is completely out of place in the mixed company of a gathering. Paul's remarks apply to occasions "when ye come together", v. 26. Some may try and raise questions as to when a meeting is an assembly meeting and when it is not. The better principle would be that if there is any doubt as to whether a particular convened meeting is an assembly gathering, no sister should speak, else others will be grieved and offended. The principles of chapter 8 apply.

But there is plenty of scope for sisters to exercise a gift of teaching in other places apart from an assembly gathering. They are exhorted by Paul to teach the young women, Titus 2. 3–5. In the home, Priscilla expounded the word to Apollos, Acts 18. 26. See also Acts 21. 9, but in a meeting, a man, Agabus, prophesied, Acts 11. 28.

Verses 36–40: Conclusion

36 What? Came the word of God out from you? or came it unto you only?
37 If any man think himself to be a prophet, or spiritual, let him acknowledge that the things that I write unto you are the commandments of the Lord.
38 But if any man be ignorant, let him be ignorant.
39 Wherefore, brethren, covet to prophesy, and forbid not to speak with tongues.
40 Let all things be done decently and in order.

36. Can the Corinthians do as they like? Firstly, did the Word *originate from them* and their prophets, so that they could lead the way and set the style? Secondly did the Word *come to them* only, so their differences from all other churches need not cause concern? Although in other places it was good when the Thessalonians became followers of the churches of God in Judaea, 1 Thess. 2. 14, none could rightly follow the Corinthian method of service.

37. The *origin* of assembly conduct is the commandments of the Lord. These are *given* to "any man", implying generality, and not to the Corinthians only. Here, Paul mentions a man who is a prophet because he is chiefly concerned with this particular gift. But he also mentions a man who is "spiritual", that is, any brother using a spiritual gift in a spiritual way. We must all test ourselves, not according to our feelings, but according to the written Word, apostolic authority and the commandments of the Lord.

38. But there would always be a few men who would remain ignorant of the divine origin of assembly conduct. "Let him be ignorant" means that a servant of the Lord need not work indefinitely to correct such men. At the same time, discipline can be used to safeguard the well-being of the assembly, if men insist upon remaining ignorant. See 2 Thess. 3. 14; Titus 3. 10–11; Rev. 22. 11.

39. All should desire to prophesy, or to engage in whatever else lends itself to edification. But the gift of tongues is nowhere condemned. It is the gift of God, and may be used in its right place. Any gift used in the wrong place is distasteful, as was the manna in the wilderness, Exod. 16. 24.

40. We have Paul's great concluding principle for this section, "Let all things be done decently and in order".

> *Decently* means "becomingly". It is the same word as in Romans 13. 13, "Let us walk honestly". Its root occurs in 1 Cor. 12. 23, 24. All must be done so as to be suitable for the public approval of the assembly as a whole.

> *In order* has a spiritual meaning. In Luke 1. 8, Zacharias executed the priest's office before God "in the order of his course", 1 Chron. 24. 1–19. This was a legal rigid order. But here, the order is according to the spiritual principles dealt with in this chapter. Elsewhere, Paul had been "joying and beholding your order", Col. 2. 5. But the Lord, too, can rejoice when He sees His people walking after the due order, "walking in truth, as we have received a commandment from the Father", 2 John 4.

1 CORINTHIANS 15

Section 6.   Pay Attention to Doctrine
Subject: The Resurrection

Background of this Subject

We have already stressed the spiritual order described in chapters 11–15. Chapter 11 deals with the *authority of the Lord and His portion*. Chapters 12–14 deal with the *exercise of spiritual gift* among the saints for their edification, both from God's side and from the believer's side. Now Paul brings in the *testimony of the Gospel*. It would appear that this is God's order for service; all things should be done decently and in order.

We may note a similar ordering in Exodus 25, the commencement of the instructions given to Moses for the building of the tabernacle. First things come first, in the following order:

Verses 10–22: the *ark*, relating to God's portion in Christ within the vail, corresponding to worship;

Verses 23–30: the *table of shewbread*, corresponding to provision for the Lord's people;

Verses 31–40: the *candlestick*, corresponding in part to testimony.

Error in doctrine is always a serious thing; hence the need for constant Bible study. We should always "take heed . . ., and unto the doctrine", 1 Tim. 4. 16. Otherwise, we are liable to be carried about "with every wind of doctrine, by the sleight of men, and cunning craftiness, whereby they lie in wait to deceive", Eph. 4. 14. The consequences of an initial error stretch far beyond the original deviation, as seen in this chapter before us.

There were some in Corinth who doubted the resurrection of the body; see verses 12, 35. Agrippa previously had thought this "incredible", Acts 26. 8. This arose because the believers were earthbound, failing to see that the miraculous power of God transcends the experiences of everyday life. At least, this error seems to have been one of *honest difficulty*, although it could have been overcome had faith been operative. The Corinthians were *not* denying the resurrection of Christ as part of their system of doctrine, but Paul shows, nevertheless, that they were unwittingly taking this ground. There was death in the pot and they knew it not, 2 Kings 4. 39. Moreover, they were not like Hymenaeus and Philetus who expounded an organised body of false doctrine, "saying that the resurrection is past already; and overthrow the faith of some", 2 Tim. 2. 18. This was a "canker", and as such Paul in 1 Timothy 1. 20 states that he had delivered Hymenaeus and Alexander "unto Satan". This amounted to their rejection from the fellowship. This man Alexander likewise had caused trouble by resisting the doctrine of Paul, 2 Tim. 4. 15. But the error in Corinth was not such as to demand excommunication; that is why this error is the last one the apostle deals with in the Epistle. In 1 Corinthians 15, it is a *correction within the fellowship*, contrasted with 1 Timothy 1 where it is *rejection from the fellowship*.

A summary of the chapter is as follows, Paul starting his argument at quite a different point from that wherein their error lay.

Verses 1–11: proof of Christ's resurrection;
Verses 12–19: consequences if Christ is not raised;
Verses 20–28: consequences since Christ is raised;
Verses 29–34: consequences if believers are not raised;
Verses 35–58: consequences since believers will be raised;
Verses 35–50: the body in resurrection;
Verses 51–58: the scene and victory of resurrection.

Exposition of 1 Cor. 15: The Resurrection

Verses 1–11: Proof of Christ's Resurrection

1 Moreover, brethren, I declare unto you the gospel which I preached unto you, which also ye have received, and wherein ye stand;

2 By which also ye are saved, if ye keep in memory what I preached unto you, unless ye have believed in vain.

3 For I delivered unto you first of all that which I also received, how that Christ died for our sins according to the scriptures;

4 And that he was buried and that he rose again the third day according to the scriptures:

5 And that he was seen of Cephas, then of the twelve:

6 After that, he was seen of above five hundred brethren at once; of whom the greater part remain unto this present, but some are fallen asleep.

7 After that, he was seen of James; then of all the apostles.

8 And last of all he was seen of me also, as of one born out of due time.

9 For I am the least of the apostles, that am not meet to be called an apostle, because I persecuted the church of God.

10 But by the grace of God I am what I am: and his grace which *was bestowed* upon me was not in vain; but I laboured more abundantly than they all: yet not I, but the grace of God which was with me.

11 Therefore whether *it were* I or they, so we preach, and so ye believed.

1. Paul reiterates the Gospel which embraces both Christ and His resurrection. The word "gospel" means "glad tidings". The root of this word occurs in a verb in Luke 2. 10, where it is translated "good tidings". There, the angel spoke of His birth, but the name "Saviour" also embraces His death and resurrection. Elsewhere, Paul amplifies the word "gospel". In Romans 1. 1, it is the "gospel of God" carrying the ideas of promise, purpose and origin. In Romans 1. 9, it is the "gospel of His Son", relating to the ground of service. In Romans 1. 16; 15. 29, it is the "gospel of Christ", relating to salvation and blessing. These three amplifications refer to the divine side, to the preacher's side and to the hearer's side respectively.

There is a progression of the tenses in Paul's remarks here:

"Which also ye have received". This is the Greek *aorist*, and relates to a single act in the past when the Corinthians first believed, Acts 18. 8.

"Wherein ye stand", as Romans 5. 2. This is the Greek *perfect* tense, implying that the saints have been built on a foundation in the past, but also that the blessed effects remain up to the present. We find here the security of their salvation, even though this doctrinal error had entered their thinking.

"By which also ye are saved", v. 2. This is the Greek *present* tense, "ye are being saved", unlike other references as Ephesians 2. 5, 8 where the perfect tense is used. There is a past, present and future sense of salvation. The same ideas occur in 2 Corinthians 1. 10, where we read of the past, present, and future aspects of deliverance. It has often been said that we have been saved in the past from the penalty of sin, in the *present* from the *power* of sin, and in the *future* from the *presence* of sin. In spite of the error in Corinth, the Corinthians had this present and blessed aspect of salvation .

2. The word "if" does not imply a doubt as to their salvation. It is the "if" of argument, and gives the idea of "since". The A.V. translation "if ye keep in memory what I preached unto you" appears to have omitted a word; the literal rendering would be "if ye hold fast with what *discourse* I announced to you". Holding fast to the apostle's doctrine would demonstrate the reality of faith, even if mental reasonings disturbed the quiet serenity of faith.

The other possibility that Paul visualises is "unless ye have believed in vain". There is no salvation here. A mere mental assent to the preaching is contemplated, an assent taken lightly and rashly to no purpose without plan or course. Such an effect is dangerously possible in gospel efforts which rely upon a mixture of the Spirit's power and techniques which appeal to the emotions.

3. There is a contrast here as to how the message is known. The Corinthians possessed only second-hand knowledge by preaching. Paul had delivered the truth to them, and this was made real by the Spirit of God, 2. 12. On the other hand, Paul had first-hand knowledge of the message, as indeed he had of all truth for the new dispensation. His apostleship was direct from God, Gal. 1. 1; his commission to serve was from Christ, Acts 26. 16; the revelation about the Lord's supper was from the Lord, 1 Cor. 11. 23; the Gospel was received from Jesus Christ by revelation, Gal. 1. 12; his knowledge of the rapture was by the word of the Lord, 1 Thess. 4. 15. Such first-hand information becomes multi-hand by the time it reaches us, but this is God's method, 2 Tim. 2. 2. But the Spirit's working is the same, making the truth real to many hearts.

The basis of the Gospel is "Christ died for our sins according to the Scriptures". This firstly assumes that we recognise our guilt and that we are sinners before God. Self-righteousness can see no sacrificial meaning in the death of Christ. Secondly, we can perceive the love of God toward us, "in that, while we were yet sinners, Christ died for us", Rom. 5. 6–8. His death was no after-thought on the part of God. He had been the Lamb "foreordained before the foundation of the world", 1 Pet. 11. 20. It is the realisation of this fact that gives spiritual meaning to all the types, promises and prophecies of the O.T. This central fact of history had been prominently before God throughout O.T. days. The prophet had declared, "He was wounded for our transgressions, . . . He shall bear their iniquities.... He bare the sin of many", Isa. 53. 5, 11, 12. See Matthew 26. 54; John 19. 36–37.

4. The fact that He was buried in a sealed tomb demonstrates that His death had been a fact. The Spirit would anticipate, as it were, the strange doctrines of the present day which seek to eliminate the miraculous in the death and resurrection of the Lord Jesus. Had He not entered into death, believers could have no confidence that He tasted death for every man, Heb. 2. 9. The fact that the Lord was buried fulfilled the sign of the prophet Jonas, "For as Jonas was three days and three nights in the whale's belly; so shall the Son of man be three days and three nights in the heart of the earth", Matt. 12. 40. See also Psalm 88. 6.

Some seek to read these three days in the experience of the Lord into 1 Peter 3. 19, "By which also He went and preached unto the spirits in prison", but we believe this can hardly be the meaning. Rather Peter means the *same* Spirit operates at all times. In this particular verse, we feel Peter meant that the Lord by this one Spirit went and preached *in Noah's day* to the spirits of men who are *now* in prison. Noah also had been warned of God on that occasion, Heb. 11. 7. He had listened to the divine voice while others had not. He had been saved by this faith, and then he had been saved by this figure of baptism, according to Peter, which is the outward working of present salvation.

Far from going to the place of the "spirits in prison", the Lord went to paradise, Luke 23. 43, and the repentant malefactor would accompany Him there. This would correspond to "Abraham's bosom", Luke 16. 22, but the rich man lifted up his eyes in hell. The former was a place that existed as a consequence of *death passing upon men of faith*; the latter existed (and still does) as a consequence of *death passing upon men of sin*. The Lord Jesus suffered this when He hung upon the cross in darkness, He actually tasted death so that saints now might pass directly into His presence, Phil. 1. 23. The Lord's resurrection took place from paradise, the place of the righteous, not from hell, the place of the unbelievers.

The fact that the Lord "rose again the *third* day" causes mental difficulties to many. Much has been written regarding the chronology of those crucial days, both regarding the number of days in question and also the actual days of the week on which the Lord Jesus was crucified and on which He rose again. The facts certain to faith are these:

1.   the Lord's own words about rising again on the third day, Matt. 12. 40; 16. 21; 17. 23; Luke 18. 33; John 2. 19;
2.   He was manifested as risen on the first day of the week, namely, on the Lord's day (or the common Sunday, a name tainted by mythology), Matt. 28. 1; John 20. 1. 19.

Based on the complicated internal data of the Bible, some have calculated that His death took place on Wednesday 14 Nisan, and that His resurrection took place on Saturday 17 Nisan, A.D. 30, in spite of a verse such as Luke 24. 21. Certainly the traditional Friday has little Scriptural evidence to support it. It is but a religious relic that gives the truth a bad name to unbelievers. There is no Scripture that states that the Lord was raised on the first day of the week; all we read is that He was *manifested in resurrection* to His own on that day.

There are other difficulties surrounding these dates. Matthew 26. 18 suggests that the feast of the passover took place the day before the Lord was crucified, while John 18. 28 suggests that the feast took place on the day He was crucified. It is a sweet thought that the true passover Lamb was sacrificed at the same hour as the passover lambs were slain in the temple. Taken all in all, we may care to think that the Holy Spirit has withheld information that would only satisfy the mind and not the heart. Some devout scholars have attempted to explain matters on Scriptural evidence alone.

Paul insists that the Lord's resurrection was according to the Scriptures. In the beginning of the Acts, it could be substantiated by eye-witnesses, but today faith rests on the Scriptures alone. We delight to know that even the O.T. "testified beforehand the sufferings of Christ, and the glory that should follow," 1 Pet. 1. 11. For example,

> Psalm 2. 2, 6 declares His death (see Acts 4. 25), but shows the Lord alive as King on mount Zion;
>
> Psalm 8. 5 shows Him as a little lower than the angels, but now crowned with glory and honour;
>
> Psalm 16. 10–11, "Thou wilt not leave my soul in hell" is used by Peter in Acts 2. 25–31; see Acts 13. 35;
>
> Isaiah 53.10 passes from "an offering for sin" to "He shall prolong His days, and the pleasure of the Lord shall prosper in His hand;
>
> Hebrews 11. 19 presents a type of Christ in resurrection, namely Isaac received from the dead in a figure.
>
> See Luke 24. 46; Acts 17. 2–3.

5–8. Paul now presents an impressive list of eye-witnesses of the resurrection of Christ. Even if faith were lacking on the part of the Corinthians, they could not honestly choose to remain ignorant of facts of sight. Such facts are not to be despised; these constituted the "many infallible proofs" of Acts 1. 3. Similarly, the apostle Matthias was chosen on the basis that he had been a witness of the resurrection of Christ, Acts 1. 22.

Paul's list is as follows:

1. *Cephas.* Paul implies that Peter was the first apostle to have seen the risen Lord. This event is not recorded in the Gospels, but in the Corinthians' day Peter was still present to testify of the fact. The first words of the apostles to the two on the Emmaus road

who had returned to Jerusalem were "The Lord is risen indeed, and hath appeared to Simon", Luke 24. 34. (Prior to this, in John 20. 11–18, He had appeared to Mary in the garden, while in Matthew 28. 9 two women are implied.) Peter had seen the empty tomb, Luke 24. 12, but a special vision of the risen Lord was also granted to one who needed special help after his denial of his Lord, and who would bear the brunt of the initial testimony concerning the resurrection of Christ.

2   *Then of the twelve.* This would apply to the upper room of John 20. 19. From Luke 24. 33–34, we see that the two on the Emmaus road were there also, and additionally, "them that were with them". The word "twelve" may refer only to the name of the apostolic group. Certainly only ten apostles were present. Judas had hanged himself, Matt. 27. 5, Acts 1. 18, and Thomas was absent, John 20. 24. Perhaps the two on the Emmaus road could be counted with the ten to make twelve—they had been privileged to see the risen Lord before the apostles except Peter!

3.   *Five hundred brethren at once.* This, no doubt, was the resurrection appearance to the largest group at once, all of whom were "witnesses chosen before of God", Acts 10. 41. With such an inspiration to continue in fellowship, we might have expected to find these five hundred after His ascension, but in Acts 1. 15 the number of the disciples was about a hundred and twenty. Hence it is difficult to discern who constituted the "all" on the day of Pentecost, Acts 2. 1.

4.   *James.* This cannot refer to James the brother of John, who had been killed by Herod years before, Acts 12. 2. Rather it would refer to the James of Acts 15. 13; 21. 18, and to the author of the Epistle bearing his name.

5.   *All the apostles.* This happened on several occasions. In Matthew 28. 16 it was in a mountain in Galilee, in Acts 1. 3–12 it was on the mount of Olives, while in John 21 it was by the sea of Tiberias (though only to seven disciples, not all apostles). The first reference gives the commission to make disciples, the second to wait for the promise of the Spirit, and the third to work amongst the flock of the Lord.

6.   *Paul.* Certainly *last it time*, but in humility he also places himself *last in worth*. In fact, he regarded himself as an abortion, "born out of due time". The idea of an abortion relating to the second birth is remarkable, and in fact is impossible to those who are "born . . . of God", John 1. 13. But Paul really visualises himself in disgrace, on the Damascus road, when he saw the Lord in glory. This true spiritual birth was all of grace, and he had no merit at all. In Acts 9. 3, he saw the light from heaven, and realised that the man Christ Jesus was identical with Jehovah of the O.T. (manifested so often in light and glory, Exod. 40. 34; 1

Kings 8. 11). In verse 7, the others heard a voice (but did not discerning the words) but saw no man. On the other hand, in Acts 22. 9 the others saw the light (without discerning the Man) but heard no voice (they heard a sound, but did not discern the words). It was Paul only who perceived the Man in the light, and heard Him speaking in the Hebrew tongue, Acts 26. 14. The purpose of the vision was to make him a minister and a witness of the things he had seen and would see, 26. 16. Hence, in his preaching and in his writings, Paul made known what he had seen and heard.

It is interesting to note that Paul does not name any women explicitly in these verses, although one would not doubt that the term "brethren" in verse 6 implies sisters as well (see verse 1, where "brethren" refers to the whole assembly). It may be that Paul has in mind the possibility of public witness in the assembly, so in the light of 11. 3 and 14. 34 sisters are not named. However, their testimony, faith and service is appropriate in the proper place; see Matthew 28. 10 where the women were the first witnesses to testify to the disciples of His resurrection; Acts 18. 26 where Priscilla was active in her own home; Hebrews 11. 11, 31, 35 where women rich in faith are listed with the men.

9. Paul regards himself as "least" and "not meet" because of his pre-conversion activity. Others had been fishermen and taxgatherers, but he had persecuted the church of God, which the Lord Jesus had taken as Himself, Acts 9. 5. In grace the Lord remembers sins and iniquities no more, Heb. 10. 17, but Paul would remember throughout his service here below, his sinful state before his conversion. Certainly he loved much for much had been forgiven, Luke 7. 47, and as the chief of sinners he could be a pattern to all who would afterwards believe, 1 Tim. 1. 15–16.

Regarding this persecution, we may quote the verses:

Philippians 3. 6: "concerning zeal (Jewish), persecuting the church";

1 Timothy 1. 13: "who was before . . . a persecutor";

Galatians 1. 13: "how that beyond measure I persecuted the church of God, and wasted it";

Acts 8. 3: "Saul, he made havock of the church, entering into every house, and haling men and women committed them to prison".

See Acts 22. 4–5; 26. 9–11.

The church was precious to Paul's heart during his years of service. He also realised it had been precious to Christ during the time when he had been persecuting it.

10. The change in Paul had been all of grace, both for salvation and for service. This grace "was exceeding abundant with faith and love which is in Christ Jesus", 1 Tim. 1. 14. This purpose and grace was not according to works, but had been given to the saints "in Christ Jesus before the world began", 2 Tim. 1. 9. Because of this there could be no boasting in man; all that other believers could do was to glorify God in Paul, Gal. 1. 24.

Moreover, this grace was not bestowed in vain upon Paul. That is, the grace was not empty and void, but productive unto service. This word "vain" should be distinguished from the same word in verse 2, where it means "without plan, rashly to no purpose", and from verse 17, where it means "useless, unprofitable". The same word meaning "empty, void" occurs again in verse 14. (The A.V translators unfortunately repeated the English word "vain" for three different Greek words).

God had found a vessel willing to be devoted to His will. Paul laboured more abundantly than the other apostles. They had laboured in Jerusalem and Judaea, with the "gospel of the circumcision", Gal. 2. 7, but Paul laboured to the uttermost parts of the earth in his work amongst the Gentiles. "In labours more abundant", 2 Cor. 11. 23, characterised his service. Yet in spite of this, it was God who was working and not the apostle. God gave the increase, 1 Cor. 3. 6, "the same God which worketh all in all", 12. 6. It is a hard thing for an able servant to work, believing that all his service is really being accomplished by the grace of God.

11. "Whether it were I or they, so we preach, and so ye believed" means that, no matter which servant it is through whom one believes, all have a common basis of testimony, namely Christ crucified and raised again.

Verses 12–19: Consequences if Christ is not Raised

12 Now if Christ be preached that he rose from the dead, how say some among you that there is no resurrection of the dead?
13 But if there be no resurrection of the dead, then is Christ not risen:
14 And if Christ be not risen, then *is* our preaching vain, and your faith *is* also vain.
15 Yea, and we are found false witnesses of God: because we have testified of God that he raised up Christ: whom he raised not up, if so be that the dead rise not.
16 For if the dead rise not, then is not Christ raised:
17 And if Christ be not raised, your faith *is* vain; ye are yet in your sins.
18 Then they also which are fallen asleep in Christ are perished.
19 If in this life only we have hope in Christ, we are of all men most miserable.

12–13. We must recall that the Corinthians did not dispute the fact that Christ had been raised—they merely reasoned about the resurrection of the bodies of the saints. How they would have interpreted Matthew 27. 52–53 had that Gospel been then in their hands, we cannot conjecture. But Paul carries their argument to its conclusion. The saints are so blessed by being one with Christ, that if they are not raised, then neither is He! Philippians 3. 21 shows this same oneness in the fashioning of our bodies like unto His glorious body. In the light of the previous paragraph, namely of the testimony of the Scriptures and of all the eyewitnesses, the Corinthians were on illogical ground. We should note that faith is very logical. Logic is not abandoned upon conversion—it is not the product only of the natural mind. It is the basis that counts. The most spiritual truth can be logically developed. Indeed, throughout this Epistle, we have seen the apostle reasoning concerning the truth to combat their errors.

The same deduction that Christ is not risen if the saints are not raised, appears also in verses 15 and 16.

14–19. Paul now lists seven further consequences if Christ is not raised. These would be further implications of the Corinthian position, but to none of these would the saints subscribe. Paul is really using the *reductio ad absurdum* type of argument.

1. *Preaching vain.* Preaching without resurrection (so characteristic of many today) is described as vain *(kenos)*, meaning empty, fruitless, void of effect. For example, "the rich he hath sent *empty away*", Luke 1. 53; "why did . . . the people imagine *vain* things", Acts 4. 25, showing the emptiness of crucifying the Lord of glory; "let no man deceive you with *vain* words", Eph. 5. 6, meaning words that carry no spiritual value for the soul.

2. *Faith vain.* Faith partakes of the same character as the preaching that gives rise to it. If the preaching is light and lacking depth, then faith will also be light and lacking depth. In verse 14, faith is empty if the preaching is empty. Paul uses the verbal form of this word in Romans 4. 14, "For if they which are of the law be heirs, *faith is made void*".

3. *False witnesses.* Paul's whole preaching had concerned the living Christ as risen. Hence if Christ had not risen, the testimony would have been a lie. This is a solemn observation in the light of the fact that "all liars" would have their part in the lake burning with fire and brimstone, Rev. 21. 8. All who preach any other gospel or any other way of salvation are false witnesses, and are accursed, Gal. 1. 8. Such false witness is contrary to the mind of God revealed in the commandment, Exod. 20. 16. It displayed the character of those who crucified the Lord, Matt. 26. 60, and marks the unregenerate heart, Matt. 15. 19.

4. *Faith vain*, verse 17. The word for "vain", *mataios*, is different from that used in verse 14. It occurs, for example, in 1 Cor. 3. 20. "The Lord knoweth the thoughts of the wise, that they are *vain*", and in James 1. 26, "this man's religion is *vain*". The word means unprofitable, useless. In verse 14, the man had *nothing* at all, his faith was empty; here, he has *something*, but it is useless.

5. *Yet in sins.* Liberation from sins comes through the preaching of the Gospel, and this preaching is possible because Christ is raised. The disciples did not preach between the day of His death and His resurrection. Moreover, by His resurrection, the Lord has entered into heaven itself, Heb. 9. 24, with the efficacious value of His sacrifice to put away sins. Again, in Romans 4. 25 we read that He "was raised again for our

justification".

6. *Those fallen asleep in Christ are perished.* This word "perish" occurs many times in connection with physical death, as Matthew 26. 52, "they . . . shall perish with the sword". It often refers to spiritual death, as the familiar verse John 3. 16, "should not perish". In the present context, the word perish seems to refer both to spiritual and physical death with no hope of any resurrection. This word *apollumi* appears some ninety times in the N.T., but rarely with this full implication. Matthew 10. 28 being one of these, "able to *destroy* both body and soul in hell". What Paul means is that after death, the believer's expectation would be a portion with sinners if Christ were not raised.

7. *Most miserable.* Such teaching pushed to the bitter end would imply that we can know Christ here and now only. Only judgment for sin or annihilation would be the logical outcome. Indeed that would make us "more miserable than all men". The only other occasion this word "miserable" occurs in the N.T. is in Revelation 3. 17, where the Lord describes the Laodicean church as "wretched, miserable". The word comes from a verb meaning "to have mercy, to pity". Paul implies that such believers would be in a pitiable condition—worse than that of the unsaved—as discerned by a teacher who knew the truth. Their state would be the opposite to that of the Thessalonians, who were exhorted to hope, joy and comfort, 1 Thess. 4. 13–18.

Verses 20–28: Consequences since Christ is Raised

20 But now is Christ risen from the dead, *and* become the firstfruits of them that slept.
21 For since by man *came* death, by man *came* also the resurrection of the dead.
22 For as in Adam all die, even so in Christ shall all be made alive.
23 But every man in his own order: Christ the firstfruits; afterward they that are Christ's at his coming.
24 Then *cometh* the end, when he shall have delivered up the kingdom to God, even the Father; when he shall have put down all rule and all authority and power.
25 For he must reign, till he hath put all enemies under his feet.
26 The last enemy *that* shall be destroyed *is* death.
27 For he hath put all things under his feet. But when he saith all things are put under *him, it is* manifest that he is excepted, which did put all things under him.
28 And when all things shall be subdued unto him, then shall the Son also himself be subject unto him that put all things under him, that God may be all in all.

20. Paul immediately states the certainty, "But now is Christ risen from the dead". He employs the Greek perfect tense for "is risen", referring to a past act but with blessed present consequences. The Lord Himself had authority to take His life again, John 10. 18, but the use of the passive implies that another was working. Elsewhere Paul writes of the power "which He wrought in Christ, when He raised Him from the dead, and set Him at His own right hand in the heavenly places", Eph. 1. 20.

Moreover, Paul refers to "them that slept", or "them that sleep" according to the R.V. Again, the Greek perfect tense is used, the past act of falling asleep in Christ being maintained, as far as the body is concerned, until the resurrection day.

Christ has become the firstfruits through resurrection. In testimony, Paul had stated that "He should be the first that should rise from the dead", Acts 26. 23. That is, Christ was the first in time and *importance* compared with the saints who would be raised at His coming, v. 23. This comparison leaves no room for argument as to where Moses, Matt. 17. 3; Jude 9; Lazarus, John 11. 44; 12. 1; the widow of Nain's son, Luke 7. 15, fit in and, also the general statement of Matthew 11. 5. These are just not visualised in the comparison. In any case, they died again, but Christ is "alive for evermore", Rev. 1. 18.

The word "firstfruits" occurs several times in the N.T., and believers should know what position is theirs through grace:

Romans 8. 23: Saints now have the firstfruits of the activities of the Spirit within.

Romans 11. 16: Gentile converts are the firstfruits of the promises of the Gospel to the Jews in the O.T. Note that assembly blessings were not promised in the O.T.

Epaenetus, Rom. 16. 5 and Stephanus, 1 Cor. 16. 15, were the original converts of Paul in Achaia. Better texts substitute "Asia" for "Achaia" in Romans 16. 5.

James 1. 18: Those born with the Word of truth are the first-fruits to God from all creation.

The idea of the firstfruits finds a prominent place in the O.T. The feast of unleavened bread at the passover would correspond to the firstfruits of barley harvest, while the feast of weeks (or Pentecost) would correspond to the firstfruits of wheat harvest.

Regarding the passover, we may notice the following scriptures:

Exodus 12. 1–28 stresses the passover lamb, deliverance from Egypt, and the feast of unleavened bread for seven days.

Leviticus 23. 9–14 stresses the sheaf of the firstfruits of the barley harvest waved before the Lord. This would speak of Christ, the firstfruits of resurrection, manifested before God; He is "the firstborn from the dead", Col. 1. 18.

Numbers 28. 16–25 stresses the offerings to be brought during the seven days of the feast of unleavened bread. This feast would correspond to the conduct of the believers in the light of His death, see 1 Cor. 5. 8.

Deuteronomy 16. 1–8 stresses the place where the Lord would choose to place His name. There the passover lamb would be roasted and eaten.

Regarding Pentecost, or the feast of weeks, we note:

Exodus 34. 22 stresses that it is "the firstfruits of wheat harvest", showing that it came several weeks *after* the previous first-fruits of the barley harvest.

Leviticus 23. 17 stresses that the presentation was to be in the form of two wave loaves baked with leaven. This refers to the establishment of the assembly at Pentecost—the first fruits of the death of Christ seen in His people. The fact that the leaven was baked means that it was no longer capable of working. It refers to the end of the reign of sin in believers' lives. See also Numbers 28. 26–31 and Deuteronomy 16. 9–12.

There is a difference between Christ as "the *firstfruits* of them that slept" and as "the *firstborn* from the dead", Col. 1. 18. The "firstfruits" is indicative of the beginning with the promise of more to come. The resurrection of Christ is thus the *pledge* that believers will later have their portion in resurrection. The "firstborn" denotes an accomplished pattern. Believers will likewise share in that pattern. The resurrection of Christ was in keeping with the plan of God for His Son, and thus Christ in resurrection became, as it were, the *prototype* of those who would follow. Men value prototypes in this age of machinery. They are made before bulk production starts, in order to test the machine and to modify it where necessary. How unlike the Lord ! This first One in resurrection needed no testing or modification—the work of God was perfectly accomplished in Him. This makes the resurrection of the saints certain—no mistakes can possibly be made.

21. Resurrection through Christ contrasts with the end of the natural man, apart from redemption. "In Adam all die" links together under one head all those ever born by natural processes (Enoch and Elijah excepted, Gen. 5. 24; 2 Kings 2. 11). The Lord Jesus of course was not born entirely under natural processes, Matt. 1. 18–20; by this means God kept His Son distinct from the sinful scene into which He came. Paul elaborated this theme elsewhere: "As by one man sin entered into the world, and death by sin; and so death passed upon all men, for that all have sinned", Rom. 5. 12. It had not been God's purpose that man should die; rather His governmental prerogative decreed this when sin entered.

On the other hand, "by man came also the resurrection of the dead". One man in each case laid the basis for others to follow. By man, by the second Man, Christ Himself, resurrection came. The contrast between Adam and Christ is complete; Romans 5 deals with this in detail. We may note the contrasts there:

verse 15: *many be dead*—the gift abounded unto *many*;
verses 16, 18: *condemnation—justification*;
verse 17: *death* reigned—they shall reign in *life*;

verse 19: one man's *disobedience*—the *obedience* of One.

The mind of the flesh may delight in the activity of the first man, but those who have the mind of Christ delight in the activity of the Second Man.

22. From whom do we now take our nature? "In Adam all die, . . . in Christ shall all be made alive". *All in Adam* would apply to all who have his nature in the flesh—both created and fallen. The only exceptions to death will be those who are alive and remain unto the coming of the Lord, 1 Thess. 4. 15. There can be no exception to the fallen state apart from redemption: all are dead in trespasses and in sins, Eph. 2. 1. Similarly, *all in Christ* would apply to all who have the blessings of redemption, those who are born again. They possess the divine Company within, and await the resurrection.

Some understand *all in Christ* to refer to saint and sinner, each awaiting their respective resurrection. Certainly there are two distinct resurrections, as the following verses show:

> John 5. 29: ". . . they that have done good, unto the resurrection of life; and they that have done evil, unto the resurrection of damnation".
> Daniel 12. 2: "Many of them that sleep in the dust of the earth shall awake, some to everlasting life, and some to shame and everlasting contempt".

There is at least a thousand years between these two resurrections, as Revelation 20. 6 and 13 show. The fact that Daniel said "many" and not "all" suggests that in that passage, the Spirit was not contemplating the saints of the present dispensation. They will be raised before the first resurrection of Revelation 20. 6. The first is a resurrection unto life, and that eternally, but the second is unto death, even the second death. However, this resurrection unto death seems rather out of context in verse 22 under discussion. Paul is discussing only the resurrection of believers, and the effect of the resurrection upon them. Saints are made alive because they are "in Christ". Unbelievers are not in that position. They are raised only because they hear His voice, John 5. 28.

23. God has His own order—His own timetable—in resurrection. This order preserves the pre-eminence of His Son.

1. Christ is first raised as the firstfruits, having been sown as the precious seed in death, John 12. 24.

> Thou wast alone, till like the precious grain,
> In death Thou layest, but didst rise again;
> And in Thy risen life, a countless host
> Are "all of one" with Thee, Thy joy and boast.

2. Then the Lord's people are raised at His coming for His own. This would embrace those who had already died, 1 Thess. 4. 15.

Those believers living on the earth at that time will not "prevent"—go before—those rising from the tombs to meet the Lord in the air.

3.   Immediately prior to the thousand years' reign those are raised who would be killed towards the end of the tribulation period, Rev. 20. 4–6. This properly is the first resurrection.

4.   The resurrection of damnation follows after this period of one thousand years, Rev. 20. 12. The lake of fire is the portion of those not written in the book of life. Would certain O.T. Gentiles also appear before this Throne, yet not be subject to the second death? Does Matthew 12. 41–42 suggest that the men of Nineveh and the queen of the south, through previous repentance and confession of His name, will attain *at this time* ultimate blessing, their names being written in the book of life?

The time of the general resurrection of the O.T. saints is not explicitly given. It would occur either at the same time as the rapture of the N.T. saints, or between that time and the first resurrection in Revelation 20. 4–6. The usual interpretation placed upon the wedding guests called to the marriage supper of the Lamb, Rev. 19. 9, is that these guests, obviously distinct from the church forming the bride, are the O.T. saints who have been raised. John the Baptist, the last of the prophets, called himself "the friend of the bridegroom", John 3. 29. This would correspond to "the spirits of just men made perfect", Heb. 12. 23, namely the O.T. saints recorded as men of faith in Hebrews 11. One cannot be wholly dogmatic where Scripture is silent explicitly; inferences and suggestions may be made which are not completely certain. Neither can many words cover up uncertainty, though they may gloss over it in a measure.*

24–26. With the first resurrection, the kingdom comes in glory and display. Paul deals here with one object of the kingdom and its final outcome.

The *end* here does not refer to the end of the age, as Matt. 24. 3; 28. 20. In Matthew, it is not the end of the universe that is in view, but the end of the dispensation (age) prior to the Lord's advent to take the kingdom. By contrast, Paul here refers to the absolute end of the universe, immediately prior to the eternal state. This is the time when ". . . the earth and the heavens . . . shall perish", Heb. 1. 10–11; when "the first heaven and the first earth were passed away", Rev. 21. 1.

Now, the Lord is at Jehovah's right hand, until He makes His enemies His footstool, Ps. 110. 1; Heb. 1.13. But the display of glory in the coming day will show that the kingdom is God's ("Thy kingdom come", Matt. 6. 10) and that the selected King is Christ. It will be God's King who is placed in authority over the nations, Ps. 2. 6, 8, 9. In that day, God will ensure that all things are subjected to the Son of man, although now, at the present time, "we see not yet all things put under Him", Ps. 8. 4–9; Heb. 2. 8. Now He is crowned with glory and honour, waiting for that day.

---

* See, for example, pages 393-398, Lectures on the Book of the Revelation, by W. Kelly.

One objective of the kingdom will be to put down all independent rule and authority (so loved by men today), and to vindicate the One who was crucified, in the very scene where later His triumph would be revealed. In Revelation 20. 2, the binding of Satan will assist in this objective, but the evil heart of men will remain untamed. Indeed, nature will be subdued, Isa. 11. 6-8, but the nations under His authority will be ready at the end to take advantage of any opportunity to display the true darkened state of their heart, Rev. 20. 8. Hence the Lord's last work in His first creation will be to eliminate all that offends, death itself being the last enemy. This last work will involve the preparation for the judgment of the great white throne, Rev. 20. 11. This will end His reign as man upon the first earth, where everything, after all, was not for God. The Lord's final victory will be when death and hell are cast into the lake of fire, v. 14. How this contrasts to the Lord's victory in the saints, when at their resurrection it is written that "death is swallowed up in victory", 1 Cor. 15. 54.

27. To put "all things under His feet" is the prerogative of the Godhead. The Son, as Man, will be manifested in all authority over the universe, the Godhead excepted. Such a position is the aspiration of man, whether in politics or in science. Any little success of men today will be relegated to a state of nothingness then, whether it be to bend the will of their fellows into subjection, or to harness the secrets of the atom, the recesses of space, or life itself (which secrets are ultimately in the hands of God alone).

28. When all is accomplished in this scene, then "shall the Son also Himself be subject unto Him that put all things under Him, that God may be all in all". The Son will withdraw His display on earth (which is to vanish away), thereby subjecting Himself to the divine will to end the "first earth". The eternal state then is instituted, as apart from all these first things. God—the Father, Son and Holy Spirit—will be all in all. This is the scene of Revelation 21. 1–7, involving a remarkable change in divine names compared with the rest of that book. Here it is "God" only, referring to the Godhead possessing the kingdom in the eternal state.

Verses 29–34: Consequences if Believers are not Raised

29 Else what shall they do which are baptized for the dead, if the dead rise not at all? why are they then baptized for the dead?
30 And why stand we in jeopardy every hour?
31 I protest by your rejoicing which I have in Christ Jesus our Lord, I die daily.
32 If after the manner of men I have fought with beasts at Ephesus, what advantageth it me, if the dead rise not? let us eat and drink; for to morrow we die.
33 Be not deceived: evil communications corrupt good manners.
34 Awake to righteousness, and sin not; for some have not the knowledge of God: I speak *this* to your shame.

29. It must be admitted that this is a difficult verse, that has given rise to heresy and false practice, as well as to many strange and curious explanations. It is, in fact, easier to say what it *does not mean* than what it *does mean*. On the face of it, the *actual words* "baptized for the dead" appear to refer to a believer still alive being baptized on behalf of one who has died not having been baptized. A general principle of scriptural exegesis is to take words at their face value unless by so doing one would find serious conflict with other passages. In the present case, if we do accept the face value of the verse Paul would be contradicting himself regarding the doctrine of baptism. It is impossible for a believer, to be baptized on behalf of another, and it is not possible to change the state of one departed. Moreover, the actual meaning of baptism is for the present life; it relates to *present* salvation. Hence it is irrelevant to suppose that a substitute baptism could avail for those now departed. Some expositors suggest that the Corinthians had actually adopted this false practice, and that Paul merely argues about the resurrection from their point of view. But we believe that such a flagrant violation of Scripture would have received apostolic rebuke immediately, particularly in this Epistle of correction.

Others suggest that the word "for" means "with a view to joining the dead", in the sense of taking one's place with them as crucified with Christ in baptism, Rom. 6. 5. However, this would be useless without also taking part in His resurrection by coming out of the waters of baptism. But this view relates to death metaphorically, rather than physically, which is the subject of the chapter.

We suggest that the idea behind the verse concerns the perpetuation of practical testimony. Those who had passed on had left a gap in the testimony on earth. This would be filled by new converts taking their place by being baptized. It would be useless to seek to perpetuate a testimony if the one now dead were not to rise again. For example, Stephen was killed, Acts 7. 60, but Saul was converted and baptized to fill the gap, 9.15,18.

Other examples may be quoted, where a fallen testimony is replaced by a spiritual testimony. Judas was replaced by Matthias; his bishoprick (overseership) was to be taken by another, Acts 1. 20. Similarly, through the fall of the Jews, salvation is come to the Gentiles, Rom. 11. 11.

30. Moreover, Paul was always in jeopardy or danger: "in deaths oft", 2 Cor. 11. 23, 25–27. Elsewhere he had said that he counted not his life dear unto himself, Acts 20. 24. This must be viewed in the light of the instinct of self-preservation that God has placed in us all. Peter rightly called "Lord, save me", Matt. 14. 30. The instinct was there as he started to sink, but his faith looked to the Master. Hence Paul was going beyond this God-given instinct by submitting himself willingly to the danger of death. But it would all be useless and to no avail if there were no resurrection.

The attitude he took before the Lord was in the light of being "clothed upon", 2 Cor. 5. 2, in the coming day. For examples of his willingness to die in service, we may note the towns and cities:

Damascus, Acts 9. 24;
Lystra, Acts 14. 19;
Philippi, Acts 16. 23;
Jerusalem, Acts 21. 31;
Rome, 2 Tim. 4. 6.

See also 2 Corinthians 4. 9–18.

31. The verb "protest" does not appear explicitly in the Greek text; only a small particle *nee* enters the text, being an adverb of affirmation used in oaths. It occurs nowhere else in the Greek N.T. Moreover, many Greek editors insert the word "brethren" into the verse.

The A.V. translation is difficult; "I protest by your rejoicing which I have in Christ Jesus our Lord, I die daily"; it represents a fair literal translation of the Greek. Other translations seek to interpret the meaning:

Weymouth: "I protest, brethren, as surely as I glory over you— which I may justly do in Christ Jesus our Lord—that I die day by day".

New English Bible: "Every day I die: I swear it by my pride in you, my brothers—for in Christ Jesus our Lord I am proud of you".

The fact that Paul died daily (that is, he was ready to die under the persecutions and afflictions of the Gospel) was just as certain as the fact that Paul gloried in his converts. After all, both these facts looked forward to the coming day of resurrection, 1 Thess. 2. 19. We should note that Paul's readiness to die was physical; in a moral sense, he was dead already since he had been crucified with Christ, Gal. 2. 19–20.

32. Paul discusses further afflictions nearly unto death. Regarding fighting with beasts at Ephesus, some have observed that Paul, as a Roman citizen, could not have been thrown to actual beasts; the reference must be metaphorical. In this connection, we should also note 2 Timothy 4. 17, "delivered out of the mouth of the lion". Paul must refer to some extraordinary event that took place in Ephesus, but not recorded in Acts 19. It cannot really refer to the case of Demetrius, since this happened just before Paul left Ephesus. 1 Corinthians was written before that, while he was engaged in service among the Ephesian saints. There may be a reference to it in Acts 20. 19, "temptations, which befell me by the lying in wait of the Jews". See also 1 Corinthians 16. 8–9; 2 Corinthians 1. 8. Whatever the explanation, the implication is: Why sustain all that if the promise of the resurrection is not true? If there is no resurrection, the logical thing to do would be to eat and drink at ease *today*, leaving death until *tomorrow*. Eating and drinking was always the occupation of those who had no thought of death or resurrection before them, Matt. 24. 38.

33–34. Paul concludes this paragraph with two exhortations.

1. *Be not deceived, or led astray.* "Evil communications corrupt good manners" is regarded as a quotation from a profane author,

though it may have been in common use. The word *communications* (appearing only once in the Greek N.T.) arises from a verb meaning "to associate with, to converse with". Again, the word *manners* (also appearing only once in the N.T.) means "a settled habit of mind and manners". Hence the saints must not be led astray by insidious undermining suggestions, not by open preaching but by subtle private conversation, to overthrow the firm faith of some. See Proverbs 6. 19.

2.   *Awake to righteousness, and sin not.* The originators of the supposed difficulty about the resurrection obviously had not the true knowledge of God; literally, "some have ignorance of God". This leads to sin and not righteousness. It lulls the unsuspecting into false complacency, causing them to rely upon natural reasoning. The basis of their life is changed from the certainty of faith to the uncertainty of the wisdom of the world. Hence saints must awake. This word *awake* is not the usual word "to rise from sleep". Rather it means "to awake sober after intoxication, to shake off mental bewilderment". It means to return to the certain ground of faith—to build upon a rock and not on the sand, Matt. 7. 24–27.

Verses 35–58: Consequences since Believers will be Raised

35 But some *man* will say, How are the dead raised up? and with what body do they come?

36 *Thou* fool, that which thou sowest is not quickened, except it die:

37 And that which thou sowest, thou sowest not that body that shall be, but bare grain, it may chance of wheat, or of some other *grain:*

38 But God giveth it a body as it hath pleased him, and to every seed his own body.

39 All flesh *is* not the same flesh: but *there is* one *kind of* flesh of men, another flesh of beats, another of fishes, *and* another of birds.

40 *There are* also celestial bodies, and bodies terrestrial: but the glory of the celestial *is* one, and the *glory* of the terrestrial *is* another.

41 *There is* one glory of the sun, and another glory of the moon, and another glory of the stars: for *one* star differeth from *another* star in glory.

42 So also *is* the resurrection of the dead. It is sown in corruption; it is rasied in incorruption:

43 It is sown in dishonour; it is raised in glory: it is sown in weakness; it is raised in power:

44 It is sown a natural body; it is raised a spiritual body. There is a natural body, and there is a spiritual body.

45 And so it is written, The first man Adam was made a living soul; the last Adam *was made* a quickening spirit.

46 Howbeit that *was* not first which is spiritual, but that which is natural; and afterward that which is spiritual.

47 The first man *is* of the earth, earthy: the second man *is* the Lord from heaven.

48 As *is* the earthy, such *are* they also that are earthy: and as *is* the heavenly, such *are* they also that are heavenly.

49 And as we have borne the image of the earthy, we shall also bear the

image of the heavenly.

50 Now this I say, brethren, that flesh and blood cannot inherit the kingdom of God; neither doth corruption inherit incorruption.

51 Behold, I shew you a mystery; We shall not all sleep, but we shall all be changed,

52 In a moment, in the twinkling of an eye, at the last trump: for the trumpet shall sound, and the dead shall be raised incorruptible, and we shall be changed.

53 For this corruptible must put on incorruption, and this mortal *must* put on immortality.

54 So when this corruptible shall have put on incorruption, and this mortal shall have put on immortality, then shall be brought to pass the saying that is written, Death is swallowed up in victory.

55 O death, where *is* thy sting? O grave, where *is* thy victory?

56 The sting of death *is* sin; and the strength of sin *is* the law.

57 But thanks *be* to God, which giveth us the victory through our Lord Jesus Christ.

58 Therefore, my beloved brethren, be ye stedfast, unmoveable, always abounding in the work of the Lord, forasmuch as ye know that your labour is not in vain in the Lord.

This paragraph is subdivided into various parts:
Verse 35: the difficulty of the resurrection;
Verses 36–41: the similitudes of the resurrection;
Verses 42–49: the transformation of the resurrection;
Verses 50–53: the moment of the resurrection;
Verses 54–58: the victory of the resurrection.

35. Some of the Corinthians were raising the question—and seeking to instil it into the minds of the others—"How are the dead raised up? and with what body do they come?" Such a question was based upon a mere natural level of understanding, more in keeping with the rationalism and wisdom of the world. One may wonder why the ministry of the prophets and teachers in Corinth had not dispelled the doubt. Clearly those who were taken in by these questions failed to see the activity and power of God in resurrection. Faith failed to perceive His power to raise and His power to re-form the body. Certainly believers have experienced this *spiritually* already—they have been raised and also transformed, Rom 6. 5–8; 12. 2, but this provides no ground for asserting that the resurrection is past already. On the other hand, the idea of a *physical* resurrection and transformation is beyond the range of natural experience. But we can view this power of God in Christ. His body in resurrection, Luke 24. 39, taken together with the display of glory at His transfiguration, Luke 9. 29, gives faith the view of His glorious body now.

36–41. Paul now deals with certain similitudes of resurrection in order to accustom the Corinthians to a new way of thinking. Not all the same features of resurrection are stressed in these four similitudes. If this is borne in mind the argument of the apostle will not be lost in these verses.

Botanical similitudes. God's creatorial method regarding the germination of seeds reflects His method in resurrection. The seed is not the final plant, rather it is derived from the seed. The seed decays as life rises from it—as can be observed when potatoes are dug up, the mother potato merely being a mass of decay. "God giveth it a body" reflects upon variety in God's handiwork. What we see around us in the present cannot exhaust the variety of God either in the past or in the future. "How manifold are Thy works" the psalmist cried, Ps. 104. 24, as he looked around on different structures, while any one particular structure—the body for example— itself displays the variety of many parts or members, 1 Cor. 12. 14–26. In verse 38 of our chapter, Paul stresses that the variety of seeds gives rise to distinct forms of life. Even naturally, men do not know how this takes place (neither in Paul's day and certainly not in ours), Mark 4. 27. How then can one logically deny the resurrection of the dead on the grounds that the process cannot be understood? Moreover, this variety comes by the *will* of God. "As it hath *pleased* Him" is not quite correct; Paul is speaking of His *will* not His *pleasure*. It is the same word as in 12. 18, referring to the members of the body. The Greek word *thelo* enters the N.T. some one hundred and fifty times, but it is rarely translated "please". Paul refers to the divine prerogative rather than the divine pleasure.

Zoological similitudes, verse 39. The same arguments apply to animal and bird life. It merely repeats the phrase "after his kind" of Genesis 1. 21, 25. Moreover, these verses are not wasted as far as spiritual exposition is concerned; Paul is stressing the natural creation as the work of God to show up also the resurrection as the work of God. Both are miracles— His handiwork.

Geological similitudes. By "bodies terrestrial" Paul refers to geological structure, for example, mountains, volcanoes, glaciers, cliffs, rivers, deserts, islands. All display beauty, but not radiant glory. Moreover, these various forms are in the process of constant change— mountains yield valleys and rivers, which in turn give rise to plains, which in turn become seas or are raised again into mountains. Change and variety are manifested everywhere.

Astronomical similitudes, verses 40–41. Paul refers to the heavenly bodies, either seen by the naked eye, through telescopes, or by other methods such as photography and radio telescopes. The planets, moons, comets, suns, stars of various sizes and types, star clusters, and the island universes known as nebulae, are radiant examples of the variety of God in creation. Changes take place in their features, some changing into others. The theories of the origin, development and decay of these astronomical structures are still often at variance one with the other. It is important to notice that each radiant body is distinct in itself. God is not a God of repetition. Orion differs from the Pleiades, Job 9. 9. How unlike the work of men! The mass production of an article or a book or a machine, is man's method for making repetitively in abundance. But how different is God's work naturally, or spiritually in resurrection. One would assume if we could find two identical structures in God's creation then we would have liberty to deny the resurrection. Certainly this fact of variety provides a strong argument for asserting that the saints will recognise each other in heaven.

42. "So also is the resurrection of the dead"—that is, the various features of death, change, order, glory, seen in the natural creation, are features likewise seen in resurrection. To describe these features of the resurrection, Paul introduces several contrasts:

verse 42: corruption—incorruption;
verse 43: dishonour—glory;
verse 43: weakness—power;
verses 44–46: natural—spiritual;
verses 47–49: earthy—heavenly.

Four times Paul uses the idea "it is sown". The seed corresponds to our present life; the plant produced by the seed corresponds to the life after resurrection. The idea of corruption refers to the decaying nature of the body in the grave, such as John 11. 39. Nevertheless, from this rises life after resurrection, a life that can know no decay. The substance and the home of that life can admit no corruption, Matt. 6. 20. This will correspond to an eternal summer, the decay and death of autumn being entirely absent.

Some readers may be interested to note that the word used for "corruption" is slightly different from that used in Acts 2. 27; 13. 35, where Psalm 16. 10 is quoted. The special testimony in these passages is that the Lord's body did not see decay in the tomb.

43. Dishonour giving place to glory is the testimony of many scriptures. The Lord "shall change our vile body, that it may be fashioned like unto His glorious body", Phil. 3. 21. Dishonour relating to blemish, thought, deeds, habits, weakness, illness, old age—all will have disappeared, when God "shall wipe away all tears from their eyes; and there shall be no more death, neither sorrow, nor crying, neither shall there be any more pain", Rev. 21. 4. Rather, "we shall be like Him; for we shall see Him as He is", 1 John 3. 2.

Similarly, weakness gives place to power. This word "weakness" is usually translated "infirmities". Paul refers to the infirmities of the body and of the mind. In that day, there will be power, with nothing hindering the heavenly service of Revelation 5. Even now, we can live in the light of victory, though this will be perfected on high in the coming day. We may note the scriptures:

Romans 8. 26: "the Spirit also helpeth our infirmities";

Hebrews 4. 15: "we have not an high priest which cannot be touched with the feeling of our infirmities";

2 Corinthians 12. 9: "My strength is made perfect in weakness";

Hebrews 11. 34: "out of weakness were made strong".

44–46. The natural gives place to the spiritual. The meaning of the word "natural" must be properly understood in the context. The same Greek word has occurred in 2. 14; there it had a *moral* meaning and did not apply to believers. Here, however, the meaning is *physical*, and applies to believers. In Greek, the root of this word "natural" is the same as that in "soul". The connection may be brought out by observing that as the adjective *spiritual* is to the noun *spirit*, so the adjective *natural* is to the noun *soul*. The "natural body" refers to the life within the physical body. It is certainly higher than animal life, since man was created on distinct ground in Genesis 1 apart from the animal creation.

The last sentence of verse 44 should more properly read, "If there is a natural body, there is *also* a spiritual body". Paul stresses, not only God's order, but the necessity of considering the spiritual body immediately one recognises the existence of the natural body. In verse 46, Paul rightly observes the order that the natural precedes the spiritual. And if some would doubt this, Paul draws this conclusion from the fact that Adam preceded Christ. The fact that Adam preceded Christ (the last being better, John 2. 10) is but a clear picture that the spiritual follows the natural. This order is also reflected in the resurrection of believers.

"The first man Adam was made a living soul" is quoted from Genesis 2. 7. This was an act of creation. The dust yielded a body, but the breath of life from God produced a living body. This was then passed on to all the human race. Physically, the transfer of physical form has always been by the complicated physiological process of cell subdivision. The ultimate structure of the cell, the mechanism of its power to subdivide, and the mechanism by which a body is produced by this process are still unknown. Men may seek for a rational explanation of all phenomena, but believers know that the Lord upholds all things by the word of His power, Heb. 1. 3. But this process is now marred by sin, bringing in sinful acts, illness and death.

By contrast to the federal headship of the first man, we find the "last man" made a quickening spirit. This refers only to Christ Himself. In resurrection, He possesses that spiritual body characterised by that spirit *which makes alive*. In other words, He transfers resurrection life, in just the same way as Adam transferred physical life; "because I live, ye shall live also", John 14. 19.

We should draw a distinction between Christ as "the last Adam" and "the second man".

The last Adam, in the context, is connected with the *transference of life*. In this sense, He followed Adam from whom physical life was transferred. But the designation *last* implies that throughout eternity no other can come in to displace both Adam and Christ. Christ as the last Adam has dispaced the first Adam, and similarly the spiritual body will displace the physical body. But that is all; there can be no third type of body. The last is absolute in this context. Christ is described as being "the first and the last", Rev. 1. 11.

The second Man, in the context, is connected with the *origin of life*. The word *second* stresses the fact that there had been a necessity of *one* more after Adam—not several, but One, which is Christ. There are thus only two types of life; one is now fallen and the other eternal in Christ. The ideas of origin and of transference are both found in John 6. 57: "As the living Father hath sent Me, and I live by the Father: so he that eateth Me, even he shall live by Me".

47–49. The earthy gives place to the heavenly. The first man is "out of earth, made of dust" the reference being to Genesis 2. 7, where the Lord God formed man of the dust of the ground. After sin had come in, Adam had not only been taken from the dust, he would return to it, Gen. 3. 19. This dissolution of the body is general; it is a fact of nature. God would insist upon this complete dissolution of the body before manifesting the miracle of resurrection, *except* of course in Christ who saw no corruption. Moses' body had been buried, Deut. 34. 6, but in spite of dissolution his body was available, Jude 9, when required, no doubt for the transfiguration scene.

The second Man came in by contrast, originating "out of heaven". The sentence "the second man is the Lord from heaven" is often quoted in worship and ministry upon the Lord's person, but we must point out that the name "the Lord" is omitted in many Greek texts, and translators such as the R.V. and J.N.D. omit this name. Jesus Himself had testified of this great fact, "I came forth from the Father, and am come into the world: again, I leave the world, and go to the Father", John 16. 8. His body had been specially prepared by God, Heb. 10. 5. This holy thing had not been the result of mere creatorial processes, in order that He might be distinguished immediately from the first man. It was only love and grace that caused this distinct second Man to pass from this life by means of the death due to the first man. The second Man tasted death to deliver from its grip believers who were characterised by the nature of the first man.

The continuity of nature is stressed in verse 48, the twice-repeated word "as" giving the meaning of the verse. Adam was earthy—of the dust; then, like son, like father. All others who partake of the first birth are "as" Adam, fallen. But "the heavenly" refers to Christ. "The heavenly ones" (in the plural), sons of the new birth, will be "as" He is in that day. No verbs occur in the Greek text for this verse; the two words "is" and the two words "are" are in italics in the A.V. to show this. Verse 49 shows that the past and future tenses respectively are required to complete the sense. In other words, believers pass from the one to the other. Physically, we are earthy now, and morally we are now raised with Christ, Col. 2. 12; but in that coming day we shall be raised to appear with Christ in glory, Col. 3. 4.

50. Paul now deals with the moment of the resurrection, by providing a few details as to how God will carry through this promised programme. The combination "flesh and blood" is important; such cannot inherit the kingdom of God. In its physical form as laid in death, this combination is corruption and cannot inherit incorruption. Certainly such a combination will inherit the earth in the coming kingdom glory, Matt. 5. 5, but it can never enter "an inheritance incorruptible, and undefiled, and that fadeth not away, reserved in heaven", 1 Pet. 1. 4. The corruption of the body in death cannot *in that form* enter a sphere where incorruption dwells.

Scripture testifies that the life of the flesh is in the blood, Lev. 17. 11. The blood absorbs food, and then this food is conveyed through circulation to every part of the body for growth and nourishment. Moreover, the blood then carries away the unwanted parts of the growth process, after which it is then purified from these defiling elements. In this verse, Paul deals only with the physical side of the body; the verse cannot be spiritualised.

On the other hand, in resurrection the Lord had said to His disciples "a spirit hath not flesh and bones, as ye see Me have", Luke 24. 39. This does not contradict Paul's remarks, rather the two ideas are complementary. The blood of the Lord had been shed. The testimony of an eye-witness remains to declare the truth of this fact, John 19. 35. The Lord took His life again, but not His blood. The absence of blood speaks of redemption accomplished; the possession again of His life speaks of redemption distributed freely. Hence even the body of the Lord was changed in resurrection, and this will testify throughout eternal days that He once gave Himself. The fact that the Lord had a glorious body in resurrection was hidden from the disciples. Their eyes could not have beheld His own intrinsic glory, 1 Tim. 6. 16, since this would have been even more overpowering than His kingdom glory seen on the mount, 2 Pet. 1. 17. Paul had seen this light, but had been blinded by it, Acts 9. 8. This intrinsic glory was essentially associated with His ascension back into the Father's presence, Luke 24. 26; Acts 3. 13; 1 Pet. 1. 11.

Hence, for the saints in resurrection, their flesh and bones—lying mostly in corruption—will be changed into an incorruptible nature and, at the same time, they will be glorified. But the blood— typical of the original life in Adam—will not be represented. Is there any difficulty with this concept? Certainly there was to the Corinthians, while the rationalistic Sadducees denied the resurrection altogether, Matt. 22. 23; Acts 23. 8. Unbelievers of all ages mock at the thought of the miraculous in the future day, 2 Pet. 3. 3. But let rationalism look to itself before mocking at that which is precious to Christians. Rationalists may exploit the fact that believers cannot actually explain the change that will take place in that day. However, this digs away the ground from under their own feet. For they can not explain the ultimate physical, chemical and physiological structure and functioning of the body. Research may delve more deeply into these things, but God has His methods for keeping His own ultimate secrets concerning the body, both in this creation and in resurrection.

51. Paul declares a mystery—see chapter 2 verse 7 for a list of mysteries. The mystery described here is not the *fact* of resurrection; rather it is the fact that not all believers will die. Long before this, even Job had had the hope of actual resurrection before him, Job 19. 25–27. Two words demand attention in this verse:

> *We shall not all sleep*. This word *sleep* appears eighteen times in the N.T. Four times it refers to ordinary sleep, John 11. 12; Acts 12. 6; fourteen times to physical death, as Stephen, Acts 7. 60, for example. These references are almost exclusively to the death of believers, the one exception being 2 Peter 3. 4. The idea is, of course, that sleep implies *an awakening later*, although the additional idea of *relief from pain and suffering* is often present in our minds. Unbelievers speak of the latter but not of the former. But not every believer will enter into this sleep. The same word occurs in 1 Thessalonians 4. 13, 14, 15. The exceptions are those "which are alive and remain unto the coming of the Lord", v. 15.

> *We shall all be changed*. This word *change* occurs six times in the N.T. Here it is from physical to spiritual. The heathen, however, reverse this process, changing "the glory of the uncorruptible God into an image made like to corruptible man", Rom. 1. 23. The change that Paul describes embraces the variety of verses 37–41. Individuals will be recognisable in glory through variety. For example, Paul was not allowed to return to the Thessalonians before the resurrection, but he would meet them with the Lord after the resurrection, 1 Thess. 2. 19; he would know them there.

52. This change will be instantaneous. This verse contains the only occurrence of the word "twinkling, wink, rapid jerk," in the N.T. As a verb, the word means *to cast*, used, for example, in Matthew 27. 5 (the twelve pieces of silver) and in Acts 27. 29 (the anchors). God's miracle of change is instantaneous, as is the new birth upon the response of faith in the heart. How unlike God's physical creation, in which a period of gestation of nine months may be necessary. When the Lord returns there will be no time for putting one's house in order, nor for repentance.

The "last trump" denotes the *call of God*; for example, in Revelation 1. 10 and 4. 1 the *voice* is likened to a trumpet. See John 11. 43. Some expositors assert that Paul's last trump (1 Cor. 15. 52; 1 Thess. 4. 16) is identical with John's (Rev. 11. 15) and that mentioned by the Lord (Matt. 24. 31). This assumption brings with it complete confusion as to God's prophetic programme. We believe that Paul's last trump comes before the trumps mentioned by the Lord and by John. Some scorn the idea that the "last" will not actually be the ultimate last. One has written *

> "When the Last Trump sounds, in England a Royal Commission will be set up to decide whether it is really the Last Trump or the Last Trump but one."

The point is that the word "last" is relative to a particular sequence, and is not absolute. A railway announcement may call out "last train", but it usually means the last train of the day. Rarely would it mean that the line would be closed!

The two sequences are:

> *First sequence*: the voice of Christ, Rev. 1. 10, speaking to the seven churches, 2. 1, 8, 12, 18; 3. 1, 7, 14. His voice provides a summary of church history, the last trump concluding the testimony of the church on earth.

> *Second sequence*: the trumpets given to the seven angels in Revelation 8. 2; they are sounded in 8. 7, 8, 10, 12; 9. 1, 13; 11. 15. Matthew 24. 31 concludes this period; see also Isaiah 27. 13.

53. The voice of God in Genesis 1 brought about the creation. Similarly at the rapture, the power of God will ensure that "this corruptible" will put on "incorruption", and "this mortal" will put on "immortality". Paul states that this "must" take place. It is certain because it is part of the determinate counsel of God, in just the same way as was the death of Christ, Acts 2. 23. Some expositors feel that the words "corruptible" and "mortal" *both* refer to those who are alive at the coming of the Lord. We feel, however, that verse 51 must be taken into consideration, where two classes of saints are visualised, namely those who will have died before this event and those who have not. Looked at from this point of view, "this corruptible" would refer to believers already in death, with bodies not only susceptible to corruption but actually dissolved in death. "This mortal" would refer to those still physically alive. But the final result is the same; the saints will be rendered incorruptible and immortal. Then mortality will be "swallowed up of life", 2 Cor. 5. 4.

54–56. Paul concludes with the victory of the resurrection. He repeats the truth of verse 53, but with a difference. In verse 53, he views the resurrection from the stand-point of those *yet to be raised*; in verse 54, he views the resurrection from the stand-point of those *raised*. Two O.T. quotations are given:

> 1. "Death is swallowed up in victory" is taken from Isaiah 25. 8. The context, shows that the kingdom is viewed as established on Zion, 24. 23. The first resurrection would then cause death to disappear so that the kingdom-victory may be seen. Paul transfers this idea (but not the actual context) to the rapture, which of course was not prophetically referred to in the O.T. It should be noted that the concept of death being swallowed up has no

---

* See page 194, The Revelation of Jesus Christ, by G.H. Lang.

connection with death being cast into the lake of fire, Rev. 20. 14.

2. Verse 55 is taken from Hosea 13. 14, "O death, I will be thy plagues; O grave, I will be thy destruction". Obviously Paul has given another rendering, or has quoted from a different translation, or has even quoted from memory. Whatever the reason for the difference, Paul's statement has the authority of divine inspiration behind it. Moreover, the various Greek manuscripts give different renderings of this quotation. The form most favoured by the textual editors is "Where death is thy victory? where death is thy sting?". The reader will see that the word "grave" (properly "hades") is changed to "death", and the words "sting" and "victory" are transposed. In Hosea, the context deals with the millennial restoration for Israel. The nation had destroyed itself, v. 9, but there was no Saviour save the Lord, v. 4.

In resurrection, death has neither victory nor sting. Apart from resurrection, death is inevitable. It must claim its own and thus *appears* to have the victory. Medical skill may lengthen life somewhat, and even a miracle may add fifteen years to Hezekiah's life, Isa. 38. 5, but death is inevitable. There could be no possibility of living for ever in this scene, Gen. 3. 22–24; God had decreed it.

Moreover, death has its sting. There is that poisonous sting that gains its prey, Rev. 9. 10. This sting is sin, and it is enforced upon every soul born after Adam. The thick hide of an elephant may be impervious to the sting of a wasp, but the sting of sin has strength and power; none can resist it naturally. Its strength is seen in the law. In itself, this was holy, just and good, "but sin, that it might appear sin, working death in me by that which is good; that sin, by the commandment might become exceeding sinful", Rom. 7. 13. Such was the natural man apart from Christ. But in resurrection all these influences and effects will be annulled.

57. A statement of doctrine precious to the heart can only bring forth praise and thanksgiving. The anticipation of resurrection in that day causes Paul to give thanks to God, who gives us the victory through our Lord Jesus Christ. Contrast this with Romans 7. 24–25, where Paul thanks God through Jesus Christ for present deliverance from the body of this death. Whether moral or physical, present or eternal, the victory comes through Christ.

> "His be the Victor's name,
>   Who fought the fight alone;
> Triumphant saints no honour claim,
>   His conquest was their own."

58. This great truth is not only a matter for praise, anticipation, and doctrine. It is of great import regarding practical conduct and service. Paul addresses the Corinthians as "my beloved brethren". In spite of their weakness and failures, there is nothing between them and the apostle Paul who so desired them to be strengthened and built up in their faith. The saints were to be

    Steadfast: as Colossians 1. 23, "grounded and settled": *where* faith is fixed;

    Unmoveable: the opposite occurs in Colossians 1. 23 as a verb,"not be moved away from the hope of the gospel": *how* faith is fixed;

    Abounding: a word often used in the N.T., for example, ". . . in the faith . . . abounding therein with thanksgiving", Col. 2. 7: *why* faith is fixed.

Thus the saints may "abound in every good work", 2 Cor. 9. 8. Paul uses two words here: *work and labour*. Work refers to the service of the Lord; labour refers to toil involving weariness and fatigue. (Both words may be found in 1 Thess. 1. 3; Heb. 6. 10; Rev. 2. 2.) Such work and labour are not void when accomplished in the light of the resurrection. This is the true purpose of life, a purpose that prevents us from drifting aimlessly, and gives spiritual character to the service we take up in the Lord's name.

The anticipation of the Lord's return characterises the service and conduct of the Lord's people, in keeping with the scriptures:

    1 John 3. 3: holiness,
    Col. 3. 4–5: mortification,
    Titus 2. 12–13: godliness,
    1 Thess. 5. 6: watchfulness,
    1 Pet. 1 . 13: readiness,
    1 Pet. 1. 8: joyfulness,
    James 5. 8: patience.

1 CORINTHIANS 16

Section 7.   Concluding Remarks
Subject: Brotherly Love

Background of this Subject

Paul now reaches the conclusion of his letter. The doctrine, reproof, correction, and instruction in righteousness are complete, 2 Tim. 3. 16. The saints could now take heed to cleanse their ways according to the Word of God, Ps. 119. 9. Others had had the word preached, but when this was not mixed with faith, such preaching could not profit them, Heb. 4. 2.

At the end, Paul is not estranged from his converts on account of the stand he has taken for the Lord's glory among His own. The last chapter is therefore one of brotherly love, providing details of practical fellowship among the Lord's people.

It may be subdivided as follows:
Verses 1–4: collection for the poor saints in Jerusalem;
Verses 5–9: Paul's movements from Ephesus;
Verses 10–12: movements of Timothy and Apollos;
Verses 13–16: recognition of the work of Stephanas;
Verses 17–18: fellowship of three brethren from Corinth;
Verses 19–24: greetings from Ephesus to Corinth.

Exposition of 1 Cor. 16: Brotherly Love

1 Now concerning the collection for the saints, as I have given order to the churches of Galatia, even so do ye.
2 Upon the first *day* of the week let every one of you lay by him in store, as *God* hath prospered him, that there be no gatherings when I come.
3 And when I come, whomsoever ye shall approve by *your* letters, them will I send to bring your liberality unto Jerusalem.
4 And if it be meet that I go also, they shall go with me.
5 Now I will come unto you, when I shall pass through Macedonia: for I do pass through Macedonia.
6 And it may be that I will abide, yea, and winter with you, that ye may bring me on my journey whithersoever I go.
7 For I will not see you now by the way; but I trust to tarry a while with you, if the Lord permit.
8 But I will tarry at Ephesus until Pentecost.
9 For a great door and effectual is opened unto me, and *there are* many adversaries.
10 Now if Timotheus come, see that he may be with you without fear: for he worketh the work of the Lord, as I also *do*.
11 Let no man therefore despise him: but conduct him forth in peace, that he may come unto me: for I look for him with the brethren.
12 As touching *our* brother Apollos, I greatly desired him to come unto you with the brethren: but his will was not at all to come at this time; but he will come when he shall have convenient time.
13 Watch ye, stand fast in the faith, quit you like men, be strong.

14 Let all your things be done with charity.

15 I beseech you, brethren, (ye know the house of Stephanas, that it is the firstfruits of Achaia, and *that* they have addicted themselves to the ministry of the saints,)

16 That ye submit yourselves unto such, and to every one that helpeth with *us*, and laboureth.

17 I am glad of the coming of Stephanas and Fortunatus and Achaicus: for that which was lacking on your part they have supplied.

18 For they have refreshed my spirit and your's: therefore acknowledge ye them that are such.

19 The churches of Asia salute you. Aquila and Priscilla salute you much in the Lord, with the church that is in their house.

20 All the brethren greet you. Greet ye one another with an holy kiss.

21 The salutation of *me* Paul with mine own hand.

22 If any man love not the Lord Jesus Christ, let him be Anathema Maranatha.

23 The grace of our Lord Jesus Christ *be* with you.

24 My love *be* with you all in Christ Jesus. Amen.

1–4. Paul firstly deals with "the collection for the saints". This word "collection" is the same as the word "gathering" in verse 2, and it occurs nowhere else in the N.T. The apostolic direction embraces both Corinth and the churches of Galatia. The errors abounding in Galatia (the demands of the law essential for salvation) differed widely from those in Corinth, yet there is this common apostolic instruction regarding the collection. A feature such as this demonstrates the universal application of this Epistle.

Paul associated the collection with the first day of the week, the Lord's day. Hence this is the day for giving in worship, in service, and in the collection. These are linked in Hebrews 13. 15–16, where the offerings of the sacrifice of praise and of doing good are embraced. This does not justify the usual custom of taking the collection immediately after the breaking of the bread and the drinking of the cup. The Lord's day is long enough for the Lord to have His portion without this being in too close juxtaposition to the portion of the saints. Some assemblies have collection boxes at the door, and these can be used either before or after the gathering, without interrupting, the more spiritual things. Tradition and custom weigh heavily in this matter. Believers who have tasted both methods of procedure can best judge which is preferable. Verse 2 may of course only imply that the believers put money on one side in their own homes on the Lord's day, collections being made at other times.

The collection that Paul is dealing with is *by* the saints *for* the saints. It has nothing to do with the collection necessary for the running of a hall where meetings take place. Money provided for heating, lighting, etc. is really given mutually among the assembly members, and can hardly be said to be given to the Lord. Moreover, Paul does not require a tithe here, but rather "as God hath prospered". Some brethren believe in tithing. Usually they tend to be somewhat forceful in their emphasis upon it, but often overlook that there were at least two tithes in the O.T., Deut. 12. 5–28.

Paul deals with the whole subject at much greater length in 2 Corinthians chapters 8–9. There he stresses that giving needs a willing mind, 8. 12, and that the donor must not give grudgingly or of necessity, but "as he purposeth in his heart", 9. 7.

Moreover, Paul stresses that "there be no gatherings when I come". In this Epistle, there is apostolic direction, but Paul seeks to avoid the appearance of apostolic pressure and compulsion. Giving must be done willingly. Needless to say, the apostle is not present today, so this phrase is now rather irrelevant. Moreover, 2 Corinthians 9. 4–5 suggests that Paul wanted to avoid his Macedonian fellow-travellers thinking that his boasting in the Corinthian zeal of giving, needed a last minute boost.

The method by which the gift was distributed should be noticed. Evidently the collection had been made with a specific object in view, for the poor saints in Jerusalem. In their initial zeal they had sold all, Acts 2. 45; 4. 34. Others had then provided for their need in time of famine, Acts 11. 29, and afterwards, constant financial gifts had been made, Acts 24. 17; Rom. 15. 26; 1 Cor. 16. 3; 2 Cor. 9. 12; Gal. 2. 10.

Verse 3 should more properly be translated, "Whomsoever ye shall approve, them will I send with letters to carry your gift unto Jerusalem". The assembly had no authority to choose elders, servants with spiritual gifts, or brethren to lead in priestly worship, but they *did* choose brethren to be responsible for mundane matters. (See our introduction to chapter 12.) The assembly at Corinth chose brethren to take their gift to Jerusalem. Moreover, in 2 Corinthians 8. 19 Paul writes of a brother "who was also chosen of the churches to travel with us with this grace". In Acts 6. 5–8, brethren with spiritual character were chosen, and we have a principle laid down for all to follow. This brother chosen by the churches was no exception, since his "praise is in the gospel throughout all the churches", 2 Cor. 8. 18. Similarly, in verse 4 we read that the Macedonians had chosen Paul to distribute their gift.

The "letters" that Paul mentions were written by him to the saints whom he knew in Jerusalem (not by the Corinthians, as the A.V. suggests). This would be a true letter of commendation to introduce strangers, written by one who knew both parties. Perhaps Paul would be able to go himself to Jerusalem if that were the Lord's will. But there would be a considerable delay before the collection was ready. In the meanwhile, Paul had to send Titus to Corinth to expedite matters, 2 Cor. 8. 16–24. He was Paul's "partner and fellow-helper", v. 23, and could be relied on to deal with matters in the same way as Paul would have done.

Even though financial matters are in question, the spiritual side shines through. This gift to the saints at Jerusalem was by way of reciprocation, since "if the Gentiles have been made partakers of their spiritual things, their duty is also to minister unto them in carnal things", Rom. 15. 27. But there is more than this. When Epaphroditus brought to Paul in Rome a gift from Philippi, Paul described this gift as "an odour of a sweet smell, a sacrifice acceptable, wellpleasing to God", Phil. 4. 18. The heart behind the gift transforms it from earthly to spiritual values—from temporal to eternal ones. Moreover, a gift yields abundant thanksgivings unto God, 2 Cor. 9. 12, reaching far beyond the financial side, and leading the heart in thanks "unto God for His unspeakable gift", v. 15. The sacrifice of Christ can never be far from the hearts of those who give sacrifically.

5–9. Paul now describes his proposals for his future movements in the service of God. These are not provided to satisfy curiosity but to lay the foundation for fellowship. These verses must be read in the light of the fuller contexts of Acts 19. 21; Romans 15. 25–28 and 2 Corinthians 1. 16. The apostle hoped to leave Ephesus (where he was writing), travelling through Achaia (in which province Corinth was situated), into Macedonia to the north. Then he would return through Corinth passing over to Jerusalem, from whence he hoped to visit Rome and Spain.

In actual fact, Paul sent Titus to Corinth from Ephesus. Later he left Ephesus and preached in Troas, 2 Cor. 2. 12, 13. Here, he had expected the return of Titus bringing news of the reaction of the Corinthians to his first letter. It is at this point that Paul's plans changed. Since Titus had not returned, Paul crossed directly into Macedonia, Acts 20. 2, where he wrote the second Epistle to the Corinthians (deduced from 2 Cor. 7. 5–7), upon the return of Titus. He visited Corinth shortly afterwards as in Acts 20. 2, returning via Macedonia and Troas to Jerusalem, Acts 20. 3, 16.

Paul's original intentions were different from what actually transpired, so "if the Lord permit", 1 Cor. 16. 7, is always an essential proviso when proposals are made. In some service, the saints make arrangements, though subject to the will of God. In other service, the Spirit leads without prior preparation. See Acts 16. 6–10, where the Lord had called His servants to preach in Macedonia, although they were originally travelling through Galatia and Asia. This is the truth of James 4. 13–15: some said "To day or to morrow we will go into such a city, and continue there a year, and buy and sell, and get gain", whereas believers ought to say "If the Lord will, we shall live, and do this, or that". See also Proverbs 27. 1.

Paul's trust that the Corinthians would "bring me on my journey whithersoever I go", v. 6, is very practical. He looks for a home, for lodgings, and for daily succour. After all the correction given in the previous chapters, hospitality and fellowship remain. Other scriptures likewise demonstrate this practical side of love:

Acts 15. 3: (from Antioch to Jerusalem), "being brought on their way by the church".

Romans 15. 24: (from Jerusalem to Spain), "I trust to see you in my journey, and to be brought on my way thitherward by you".

Acts 28. 14–15: (at Puteoli and Appii forum), "We found brethren, and were desired to tarry with them seven days: . . . he thanked God, and took courage".

Hebrews 13. 1–3: "Let brotherly love continue. Be not forgetful to entertain strangers".

Luke 19. 5: the words of the Lord Jesus, "To day I must abide at thy house".

John 12. 1–2: "Then Jesus . . . came to Bethany, . . . there they made Him a supper".

See also Titus 3. 13; 3 John 5–8.

Meanwhile Paul would tarry at Ephesus till Pentecost. His movements were not hurried, and he would remain in a fruitful field for three years if necessary, Acts 20. 31. Although there were many adversaries in Ephesus "a great door and effectual" was opened. (See Acts 19. 9, where "divers were hardened, and believed not, but spake evil of that way before the multitude".) Paul recognised these signs of blessing. In Athens there had been no open door, so he had quickly departed, Acts 17. 33, but in Ephesus "mightily grew the word of God and prevailed", 19. 20. Paul recalled this fruitful field of service to the Ephesian elders in Acts 20. 18–31 .

Other open doors are found in the apostle's experience:

Acts 14. 27: (at the end of the first missionary journey) "they rehearsed all that God had done with them, and how He had opened the *door of faith* unto the Gentiles".

2 Corinthians 2. 12: "when I came to Troas to preach Christ's gospel, and a *door* was opened unto me of the Lord".

Colossians 4. 3: "praying for us, that God would open unto us a *door of utterance*, to speak the mystery of Christ, for which I am also in bonds".

Having finally left Ephesus, the apostle spent some time in Macedonia, giving them "much exhortation", Acts 20. 2. Then he came into Greece, spending three months there, during which time we presume he was able to "winter with" the Corinthians. The chapter continues to show that he returned again through Macedonia, Philippi, and Troas, hastening to be in Jerusalem on the day of Pentecost, 20. 16 (compare Acts18. 21). Evidently Paul was laden with the offerings collected by the Gentiles for the Jewish believers in Jerusalem, Acts 24. 17.

This description suggests that Paul visited Corinth twice. For arguments that tend to show that there were more than two visits, works of a more theological character should be consulted.*

10–12. Since Paul could not go immediately to Corinth, his concern and interest for the saints would be shown by other visitors being sent from him. We have here the case of Timothy and Apollos; one would go and the other would not.

Timothy: Here was a man whom Paul could trust. Previously, on his second missionary journey, Paul had sent Timothy from Athens to Thessalonica to see how the young church there fared under persecution. 1 Thessalonians 3. 1, 2, 6 records this, and his return. Paul declares of Timothy that "he worketh the work of the Lord, as

---

* For example, see the article "Corinthians, Epistles to the" on page 252 in *The New Bible Dictionary*, I.V.F., for a detailed summary.

I also do", 1 Cor. 16. 10; elsewhere, 4. 17, he had written that
Timothy would "bring you into remembrance of my ways which be
in Christ, as I teach every where in every church". Thus Timothy
was a reflection of the apostle, as Paul was of Christ. But in spite of
his faithfulness, the Corinthians might take advantage of his youth;
hence they were not to despise him nor give him fear, 1 Tim. 4. 12.
By this means, Timothy would bring instruction to the Corinthians,
and then take back news to the apostle. Later, he was probably with
Paul on his next visit to Corinth, Acts 20. 3–4, and he was able to
join with Paul in writing the second Epistle to the Corinthians, to
those whom he had got to know.

Apollos: In Acts 18. 27, Apollos had been originally commended from
Ephesus to Corinth, where he "helped them much which had
believed through grace". It was then that he had "watered", 1 Cor.
3. 6. At the same time, Paul came to Ephesus to start his three years'
stay with them. Meanwhile, in Corinth, the party-spirit "I am of
Paul; and I of Apollos", 1.12, had grown up. Therefore Apollos
would not accompany Timothy's party to Corinth. No doubt he felt
that this state of affairs required direct apostolic intervention in
person in order to eliminate this party-spirit. Only then would he
come later. Our verse, 12 suggests that the *will* of Apollos was
contrary to the *desire* of Paul, but in no sense was there a
contention, as in Acts 15. 39. Indeed, a brother's consciousness of
the will of God cannot be gainsaid, although it might be clarified by
the exercise of another.

Titus also went, 2 Cor. 2. 13; 7. 5–7, 15; 8.17–18; 12. 17–18.

13–16. We have here certain exhortations to meet weaknesses, which
are not, however, explicitly mentioned. In 3. 1, Paul had described the
Corinthians as babes, lacking any maturity on account of the party-spirit
they demonstrated. The exhortations are to attain characteristics the
exact opposite to those shown by babes.

Quit you like men: This is really one word in the Greek text, being the
middle (reflexive) imperative of *andrizo*: to render manly, act in
manly fashion, display manly qualities. The condition of babyhood
is left behind, thereby displaying the spirituality of faith. This is
equivalent to being a "man of God , 1 Tim. 6. 11; 2 Tim. 3 . 17.

Watch ye: That is, taking special care to avoid weaknesses; see Matt.
24. 42; Acts 20. 31; Rev. 3. 2 for other occasions when this word is
used.

Standfast in the faith: This word "stand fast" occurs eight times in the
N.T. It implies that the saints must be stedfast concerning error both
within and without. We should stand fast in liberty, Gal. 5. 1; in one
spirit, Phil. 1. 27, and in the Lord, Phil. 4. 1.

Strong: Occurring four times in the N.T., this word implies spiritual
strength. It is used of John the Baptist, Luke 1. 80, of the Lord Jesus,

Luke 2. 40, and of the inner man of believers, Eph. 3. 16.

All things done with love: This may look back to 8. 1 and 14. 1, where relationships with one another and the use of spiritual gifts are to be governed by intelligent love.

Submit yourselves: This follows chapter 4; believers must recognise, appreciate, and have fellowship with all those who serve the saints. This would avoid certain carnal believers placing some servants on a pedestal and debasing others. The verb "helpeth with" means "worketh with". See 15. 58 for the combination "work and labour". Here, the word "work" has the prefix *sun* attached, meaning "together with", and mutuality in the Lord's service is implied. See Mark 16. 20; Rom. 8. 28; 2 Cor. 6. 1, for other examples.

In verse 15, Paul calls Stephanas the first convert in Achaia. In Romans 16. 5, Epaenetus appears to be the first convert there, but the best Greek texts read "a firstfruit of *Asia* for Christ".

17–18. These three brethren mentioned here evidently had special fellowship with the apostle. This peculiar service of Stephanas might have brought objections from those not in the "Paul party"; hence the special exhortation in verse 16. The other two names, Fortunatus and Achaicus occur nowhere else in the N.T. Evidently these three brethren came from Corinth, and although the assembly there had not assisted Paul with gifts (see 2 Cor. 11. 8; Phil. 4. 15), yet these three brethren had done so as individuals. Certainly individual believers can show fellowship even if an assembly lacks in this respect.

Paul was refreshed by this demonstration of love and concern, the word *refresh* being also translated by "to give rest"; see Matt. 11. 28; 2 Cor. 7. 13; Philem. 7, 20. From Paul's statement it appears that the Corinthians were refreshed by this act as well, no doubt by the incentive of these three brethren, which others lacked. Such practical love was to be recognised by the church. This act was somehow openly known in the assembly, but the motive of the donors was exactly the opposite to that described by the Lord Jesus in Matthew 6. 1–4, "that they may have glory of men". Rather, their light was shining before men, Matt. 5. 16.

19. The word "salute" (or *greet*) was a favourite word used by Paul at the end of many Epistles—it is used twenty-one times in Romans 16. The greetings conveyed by Paul are wide, starting with the churches of Asia. These would be the local assemblies around Ephesus where Paul was working, formed since all in Asia had heard the Word, Acts 19. 10. The seven churches in Revelation 2–3 would also be included.

Aquila and Priscilla had originally come from Rome, Acts 18. 2. Then they had moved to Corinth, 18. 2–18, and later to Ephesus, 18. 26. They may still have been there when Paul wrote 1 Corinthians, and appear later to have returned to Rome, Rom. 16. 3. Paul remembered these faithful labourers at the end of his life, 2 Tim. 4. 19. "The church that is in their house" implies that it was used as a gathering point (see also Rom. 16. 5, 23; Col. 4. 15; Philem. 2). Today, believers usually possess or rent a hall for this purpose, though the use of a brother's house is still necessary in some places. But this would mean that everything in the home would be done in the light of the fact that an assembly gathered there regularly. We may compare this with the ark in the house of Abinadab, 1 Sam. 7. 1, and later in the house of Obed-edom, 2 Sam. 6. 11, who was therefore blessed of the Lord.

20. The fact that "all the brethren" sent their greetings implies that they all knew that Paul was writing. This is true fellowship, owning and following intelligently the service of others. See also 2 Cor. 13. 13; Phil. 4. 22.

An "holy kiss" also occurs in Romans 16. 16; 2 Cor. 13. 12; 1 Thess. 5. 26. It is always described as "holy". This suggests that the reference to a "kiss" was a custom then, rather than being a lasting pattern. The custom was sanctified by the motives and attitude adopted by the saints using it. Today, any form of greeting used among believers should be elevated above similar customs used in the world.

21 Paul's own hand finally takes over, and dictation ceases; see also Gal. 6. 11; Col. 4. 18; Philem. 19. This was a token in every epistle, 2 Thess. 3. 17, and referred to the benediction at the end of every epistle. Here, it refers to verses 22–24. It is the most personal touch that Paul could give in his absence.

22. But what solemn words Paul writes! He gives a warning to any who would follow a form of godliness but deny the power thereof, to those not saved who had been allowed into fellowship, on account of the weak state of the Corinthians.

Anathema means a curse. Paul would insist on excommunication if one was not truly the Lord's. If they took part publicly, they would but preach "another gospel", Gal. 1. 8, 9, and were declared to be accursed.

Maranatha is the Aramaic word for "Our Lord cometh, or is at hand". The holiness of the gathering was to be preserved in the light of His return, and in the light of Jude 14–15 showing judgment on outsiders who use the assembly for their own ends.

23. At the commencement of his epistles, Paul wrote "grace *from* the Lord Jesus"; here it is "*grace of* our Lord Jesus Christ". This thought terminates every epistle of Paul. (Some suggest that the three such occurrences in Romans 15. 33; 16. 20, 24 terminate three different closing paragraphs sent to distinct groups in Rome.) In 2 Corinthians, the blessing of the triune God occurs, 13. 14. The *grace* of the Lord Jesus refers to 8. 9; the *love* of God to 13. 11; the *communion* of the Holy Ghost to "be of one mind, live in peace", 13. 11. These reflect divine help to overcome the weaknesses dealt with in the first Epistle.

24. This is the only time (apart from the general doxology in Romans 16. 25–27) that anything else is added at the end of an epistle. Paul's love in Christ Jesus is added to dispel any lingering hard feelings that the Corinthians may still have about Paul, on account of his numerous corrections; see 2 Corinthians 2. 4. It was the last and best that Paul could do.

The A.V. statement "The first epistle to the Corinthians was written from Philippi by Stephanas, and Fortunatus, and Achaicus, and Timotheus" is obviously not true. It does not appear in the best Greek texts and should therefore be omitted.

Conclusion. Only those who have been grieved concerning a church's departure from the Word can sense in any small measure the burden of the apostle's heart as he sent this epistle to Corinth. It had been written with much affliction, anguish of heart and many tears, 2 Cor. 2. 4. Who took the letter to Corinth is not stated, but Timothy was going to Corinth shortly afterwards to instruct them in the apostle's ways, 1 Cor. 4. 17. Titus also was going to deal with the collection, 2 Cor. 8. 16, and to bring back to Paul the news of the Corinthian's reaction to the letter. Paul would be instant in prayer on their behalf.

We have seen that Paul's intention was to visit Macedonia, passing through Corinth on the way. With this in view, he left Ephesus and came to Troas, 2 Cor. 2. 12, expecting to find Titus there with news from Corinth. But Titus had not returned. Paul had no rest in spirit, v. 13, fearing that the Corinthians were being slow in rectifying their conduct and service, thereby delaying the return of Titus. Hence Paul would not visit Corinth at that juncture, 1. 23, so he passed over into Macedonia directly. Again, still with no news of Titus, Paul could describe his state of heart, "our flesh had no rest, but we were troubled on every side; without were fightings, within were fears", 7. 5. Then at last Titus arrived with good news. Paul was comforted not only by the coming of Titus, but also by the favourable reaction of the Corinthians to his first letter, v. 6. Titus told him of "your earnest desire, your mourning, your fervent mind toward me", v. 7. The whole of chapter 7 is taken up with this theme. They had sorrowed to repentance, v. 9; they had cleared themselves, v. 11; they had refreshed Titus, v. 13; they had been obedient, enabling Paul once again to have confidence in them, vv. 15, 16. He was able to boast to the Macedonians, even with apostolic exaggeration, concerning the zeal of the Corinthians in their collection, 9. 2.

With this rejoicing, Paul wrote the second Epistle from Macedonia, and it preceded him into Achaia and Corinth. In this second letter Paul prepared the ground for his arrival. He dealt with the situation in which some would note the power of his writing, but the apparent weakness of his presence, 10. 10–11. He likewise warned those who had not as yet repented, 12. 19–21 .

At the same time, Paul, in all his labours, would be "unto God a sweet savour of Christ", 2. 15. The Corinthians likewise would be an "epistle of Christ", 3. 3, known and read of all men. Paul's letters radiate Christ, and the lives of all who profess His holy name should similarly radiate His glory and His praise.

SECOND
CORINTHIANS

2 CORINTHIANS 1

Section 1. Historical: Paul's Grief
Subject 1. Apostolic Sufferings

Background of this Subject

In chapters 1–7, the apostle provides grounds for the approval of his own *teaching*, while in chapters 10–13 he gives grounds for the approval of his own *conduct*. The approval of his teaching is developed *historically* in chapters 1, 2, and 7, and *doctrinally* in chapters 3–6.

The first Epistle had been a letter of *correction*, while the second Epistle develops the subject of the *ministry of restoring grace*. In this first section, Paul recalls his deep grief after writing the first Epistle. Some theologians assert that another letter was sent to Corinth by Paul, written between first and second Corinthians. In fact, they declare that chapters 10–13 of the second Epistle constitute this other letter, on account of this portion's more personal and dogmatic style. Such assertions neglect the inspiration of Holy Scripture, in many cases denying it altogether. The Holy Spirit would have been well able to preserve three distinct epistles had they been written separately, as He has done in the case of the three Epistles of John.

The Corinthians had to learn the grace of restoration by experiencing the grief of their own repentance. Paul, on the other hand, had to learn this grace of restoration by a deeper exercise outlined in this chapter. This influenced the Epistle throughout its length, and certainly removed any confidence in the flesh.

Having written First Corinthians, he would write *no more*. He did not keep on and on with endless words and debate. His closing words had been a declaration of love, 1 Cor. 16. 24, and he would write no more until the Corinthians repented. But the grief of the apostle remained. A true servant of God must feel grief as he views departure, morally and ecclesiastically. This grief was particularly marked during his last months in Ephesus, 2 Cor. 1. 8, in Troas, 2. 13, and in Macedonia, 7. 5. In Ephesus he endured physical suffering, Acts 19. 24–41, but his grief for the saints in Corinth affected his heart, mind and health, 2 Cor. 1. 8, 9. It was expedient to recall this to the Corinthians. The sufferings of the minister demonstrate the lowly position he was taking, prior to taking an authoritative position. In other words, he brings the Corinthians into his burden in a gracious way.

The chapter unfolds wheels within wheels. He was comforted by God in his affliction so that he could later comfort the Corinthians in their sorrow to repentance. The Lord before him had been touched with the feelings of our infirmities, so that He could have compassion on us through His own experiences, Heb. 4. 15; 5. 2.

The chapter divides into several paragraphs:

Verses 1–7: *Paul comforted of God in Macedonia*. He appreciated the special comfort of God in his trouble, so as to be able to pass it on to the Corinthians in trouble because of the apostolic correction. Job's comforters failed here; they had had no experience of comfort in sorrow. There was no one to comfort the Lord on the cross, since none could share His sufferings, thereby to understand the type of comfort needed; "I looked for some to take pity, but there was none; and for comforters, but I found none", Ps. 69. 20.

Verses 8–11: *Paul's trouble in Asia.* His anxiety had many causes but he overcame through the Lord, v. 10, and through the prayers of the saints, v. 11.

Verses 12–14: *Paul's rejoicing in the Corinthians.* Briefly mentioned here, the subject is elaborated in chapter 7.

Verses 15–24: *Paul's purpose in his movements.* He dwells on his apparent change of plan whereby he bypassed Corinth for a season, and for which he was criticised by the believers in Corinth.

Exposition of 2 Cor. 1: Apostolic Sufferings.

Verses 1–7: Paul Comforted of God in Macedonia

1 Paul, an apostle of Jesus Christ by the will of God, and Timothy *our* brother, unto the church of God which is at Corinth, with all the saints which are in all Achaia:

2 Grace *be* to you and peace from God our Father, and *from* the Lord Jesus Christ.

3 Blessed *be* God, even the Father of our Lord Jesus Christ, the Father of mercies, and the God of all comfort;

4 Who comforteth us in all our tribulation, that we may be able to comfort them which are in any trouble, by the comfort wherewith we ourselves are comforted of God.

5 For as the sufferings of Christ abound in us, so our consolation also aboundeth by Christ.

6 And whether we be afflicted, *it is* for your consolation and salvation, which is effectual in the enduring of the same sufferings which we also suffer: or whether we be comforted, *it is* for your consolation and salvation.

7 And our hope of you *is* stedfast, knowing, that as ye are partakers of the sufferings, so *shall ye be* also of the consolation.

1. Paul announces himself as an apostle of Christ Jesus, a fact known by the Corinthians, though it could do with considerable repetition, both then and now. He had previously dwelt upon his calling as an apostle, and also the grace of God that enabled him to labour more abundantly than all the other apostles, 1 Cor. 15. 9, 10. He used this title in all his letters, except in Philippians where he describes himself as a *bondservant*, Phil. 1. 1; in Thessalonians where he is a *nurse*, 1 Thess. 2. 7; and in Philemon where he is a *prisoner*, Philem.1.

Timothy is now included in the authorship, since he had returned to Paul in Macedonia just after Titus had come. Timothy—Paul's brother and son in the faith—had been sent to Corinth with the first Epistle, 1

Cor. 4. 17; 16. 10, 11 so he was known to the Corinthians. The grace of God would enable an apostle to write a letter with a joint author who was not an apostle. Similarly in 1 Corinthians 1. 1, Sosthenes was the joint author, a man also known to the assembly, if he is identical with the man of the same name in Corinth previously, Acts 18. 17. Joint authorship is in no way detrimental to divine inspiration; the Spirit takes up whom He will. But it makes nonsense of certain modern literary investigations which declare that Paul did not write some of his Epistles, on the grounds that the word frequency is not consistent throughout his writings. Rationalists really are at enmity with God in making such declarations. Believers would hesitate to assert that Paul himself chose every phrase in an Epistle with a joint authorship, but they would believe that Paul gave his concurrence to everything, and that the Holy Spirit of God is the ultimate authority behind what was written.

The Epistle was written to "the church of God" at (in) Corinth, namely a local assembly, far removed from a state church and the vast ramifications of ecclesiastical development. This was a local spiritual unit, manifesting life because its Head controlled its conduct and service. Even in the first Epistle, it is still called the "church of God", 1. 2, in spite of the departure from the truth. This is grace, but if departure is not remedied, there comes a time, when the church is disowned by the Head, as Laodicea, Rev. 3. 14–16.

The first Epistle was also sent to "all . . . *in every place*", 1 Cor 1. 2; the corrective effect of the Word had wide horizons, 2 Tim 3. 16. The second Epistle was more localised, in that it was addressed to "all saints which are in all *Achaia*", 2 Cor. 1. 1. Other assemblies, having a knowledge of departure in a neighbouring assembly, rejoice in the grace that brings restoration to saints nearby: if "one member suffer, all the members suffer with it; or one member be honoured, all the members rejoice with it", 1 Cor. 12. 26.

2. "Grace . . . and peace" forms no vain repetition of words at the beginning of each Epistle; such was not of apostolic origin but divine. Relationship with the Father and with the Son is achieved because *grace* came by Jesus Christ, John 1. 17, and He leaves His *peace* with us, 14. 27. In that verse, the Lord raises His offer far above the formal greeting of the world, so Paul, too, would reiterate the offer on spiritual ground.

3. In 1 Corinthians 1. 4, he thanked God for the *riches granted* to the *Corinthians*. Here, he blessed God, the Father of our Lord Jesus Christ, for the *comfort* granted to *himself*. This is the blessed fruit from tribulation. He expresses such thanks for one reason or another near the beginning of every Epistle, with the exception of Galatians, a fact that need not surprise us. Other great outbursts of praise in the present Epistle are found (a) in chapter 2 where Paul is led in triumph as he manifests a sweet saviour of Christ in all his service, v. 14, and (b) in chapter 9 where the apostle

thanks God for His "unspeakable gift" that surpasses all human gifts, v. 15.

Paul uses the touching title "Father of mercies". The other three similar titles occurring in the N.T. should be noticed:

Father of glory, Eph. 1.17;
Father of spirits, Heb. 12. 9;
Father of lights, James 1. 17.

Mercy and comfort are much before Paul throughout the Epistle, otherwise rendered *compassion* and *consolation*. Both words again appear together in Philippians 2. 1, "If . . . any consolation in Christ if . . . mercies". The Father and the thought of mercy (or compassion) go together, "Be ye therefore merciful, as your *Father* also is *merciful*", Luke 6. 36; "his father saw him, and had compassion, and ran and fell on his neck, and kissed him", Luke 15. 20 (though this is a different Greek word). Similarly, the thought of God and comfort (or consolation) go together, "the *God* of patience and *consolation*", Rom. 15. 5.

4. The word "tribulation" in the phrase "in all our tribulation", and the word "trouble" in the phrase "them which are in any trouble", are one and the same word, often translated "affliction", 2 Cor. 2. 4; 4. 17. More often than not, the word refers to persecution at the hands of men, Acts 14. 22. Through the strength of Christ, Paul was able to rise above this kind of tribulation; "we glory in tribulations" he wrote, Rom. 5. 3; he was "patient in tribulation", 12. 12; he knew that tribulation could not separate a believer from the love of Christ, 8. 35; and he exhorted the Thessalonians that they should not be "moved by these afflictions", 1 Thess. 3. 3.

The comfort that Paul received from God was manifested in Macedonia, by the coming of Titus, 2 Cor. 7. 6. It appears that Paul could not be comforted while in Ephesus and Troas; he was like Rachel before him who would not be comforted, Matt. 2. 18. The reason is that the tribulation suffered was *not physical*. This would not have moved him. Rather his soul was in distress as he beheld the departure of his children in the faith. Many are too complacent today to be thus afflicted in soul when assemblies go astray. The modern form of love smiles and condones such departure. But true love is pained deeply at heart, and cannot be comforted until the cause is removed through restoration.

Comfort is circular in its movements. It comes from God, but is not selfishly received. It can be passed on in the sense of "Go, and do thou likewise", Luke 10. 37. Paul knew very well the hidden needs of many saints who needed comfort. Not all believers have the warm ability to comfort others. Tychicus was "a beloved brother and faithful minister in the Lord", and able to comfort both the Ephesians and the Colossians, Eph. 6. 21, 22; Col. 4. 7, 8. Paul's "fellow workers unto the kingdom of God" could be a comfort to the apostle, Col. 4. 11.

If 2 Corinthians is the great book of comfort in the N.T., then the outstanding O.T. book of comfort is Isaiah. Comfort comes from Jehovah, who will become the nation's salvation, strength and song, Isa. 12. 1, 2; the

Lord will comfort Zion and all her waste places, making it like the garden of Eden, possessing joy, gladness, thanksgiving and melody, 51. 3; the Lord's people are comforted by Himself since He redeems Jerusalem, 52. 9; "so will I comfort you; and ye shall be comforted in Jerusalem", 66. 13.

Need believers today be downcast without divine aid? The Comforter has been given to all, and His work is described in John 15. 26; 16. 13, in the contexts of tribulation, 15. 18–25; 16. 1–4.

5. Paul now dwells on the level of his sufferings: "the sufferings of Christ abound in us". Up to verse 14, Paul uses the word "us", while from 1. 15 to 2. 13 he refers to himself only. Here he associates Timothy with his own suffering.

Paul does not refer to the sufferings that Christ endured here on earth as Man. Rather he refers to sufferings sustained by a servant for the cause of Christ. The Lord suffered first; the servant follows in the footsteps of the Master, John 15. 20. The common religion of the day would preserve anyone from these sufferings, but Paul would count as loss such confidence in the flesh, that he might know "the fellowship of His sufferings", Phil. 3. 10. Elsewhere, Paul rejoiced in "the afflictions of Christ in my flesh", Col. 1. 24. It is through the risen Christ that consolation comes. Sorrow cannot turn into rejoicing apart from Christ risen, John 16. 19–22. Hence in Philippians 3, Paul would also know "the power of His resurrection", v. 10, and in Colossians 1, his sufferings were discounted through the resurrection work of Christ in making Paul a minister able to labour according to His working, vv. 25, 29. In the case of the Lord, the suffering of death has given place to glory and honour, the Captain of our salvation made perfect through sufferings, Heb. 2. 9, 10.

This was not just a doctrine to Paul; these things abounded in him. The superabundance of grace is characteristic of this Epistle, shown as follows:

Devoted channel. 1 Corinthians 15. 10 shows that the *grace* of God bestowed on Paul was not in vain; it enabled him to labour "more *abundantly*" than they all.

Direction of service. 2 Corinthians 1. 12 shows that the *grace* of God (and not fleshly wisdom) enabled Paul to work "more *abundantly*" among the Corinthians than in the world.

Character of one's life. 2 Corinthians 6. 1 shows that the *grace* of God is not received in vain, but it enables a servant to be "*enlarged*" and not straightened, vv. 11–13.

Selflessness in giving. The *grace* of God bestowed on the churches of Macedonia yielded an "*abundance* of joy" that "*abounded* unto the riches of their liberality", 2 Cor. 8. 1, 2. Such grace is described as "*exceeding*", 9. 14.

Keeping power. The *grace* of God is promised to be "*sufficient*" for the servant of God, 12. 9.

6. Only after the apostle was comforted in Macedonia, he realised the object of God in his tribulation. There is always a divine objective in suffering, even though the most spiritual man may not be able to discern it at the time. It may, indeed, be difficult to realise this. Only faith can rise to the unknown will of God. Only the Lord knew the object of His sufferings: He went through them to glory, accomplishing the will of His God.

At the *beginning* of this verse, Paul states that his *sufferings*, and at the *end* of the verse his own *comfort*, were *both* for the "consolation and salvation" of the Corinthians. Paul would endure all things for their sakes, since he had written that love "endureth all things", 1 Cor. 13. 7. The end of his *sufferings* was their blessing. The hymn "God moves in a mysterious way" contains the verse:

> "His purposes will ripen fast,
>   Unfolding every hour;
> The bud may have a bitter taste,
>   But sweet will be the flower."

The apostle writes that the Corinthians were now able to endure the "same sufferings" which he also suffered. Only grace could take this point of view. Strictly, their suffering was one of grief on account of *their own sin*. Paul's was grief on account of the *sins of others*. Yet, with their repentance, Paul brings them into his own heart, both regarding sufferings and regarding consolation.

Paul was not only concerned with their consolation, but with their salvation. Consolation is only *temporary*, lasting while the sense of sorrow is deep; salvation, on the other hand, is *lasting*. Usually in the N.T., salvation refers to the future. Occasionally it refers to a lasting deliverance from sin in the present life. The Corinthian grief yielded repentance and salvation, that could not be regretted, 2 Cor. 7. 10. Present salvation must be worked out, Phil. 2. 12, but the Corinthians were in no state to do this had they not repented. Their future salvation was secure. Paul was not concerned with this since they had believed the Gospel and their security was based on the work of Christ. But their present salvation was upon his heart, and he would "gladly spend and be spent", 2 Cor. 12. 15, (spent in grief and spend his comfort) to assist to that end.

7. In some Greek manuscripts, the phrase "and our hope of you is stedfast" is slightly altered in position, coming in the previous verse between the words "suffer" and "or". The R.V., some editors of the Greek text, including Tischendorf and Nestle's version for the British and Foreign Bible Society, as well as the New English Bible and Panin's text (if any attach importance to it), all follow the A.V. arrangement. But translations by J.N.D. and W. Kelly follow the other Greek manuscripts of repute, placing the phrase in the middle of the previous verse. Only those who do not know the problems involved in taking a decision will be dogmatic here; others will tread with care where one cannot be certain.

On the other hand, the meaning is clear. The apostle had regained confidence in the saints; see 2 Cor. 2. 3; 7. 16; 8. 22; 9. 4. Regained confidence is not only a talking point; it is something to be acted upon. Reservation is not confidence at all. Knowing that they had repented, Paul was quite certain that their fellowship in his sufferings would lead them into fellowship with the comfort he had available for them.

Verses 8–11: Paul's Trouble in Asia

8 For we would not, brethren, have you ignorant of our trouble which came to us in Asia, that we were pressed out of measure, above strength, insomuch that we despaired even of life:

9 But we had the sentence of death in ourselves, that we should not trust in ourselves, but in God which raiseth the dead:

10 Who delivered us from so great a death, and doth deliver: in whom we trust that he will yet deliver *us*;

11 Ye also helping together by prayer for us, that for the gift *bestowed* upon us by the means of many persons thanks may be given by many on our behalf.

8. Having shown the relationship between his sufferings and their comfort, the apostle would now say a little more about his own trouble (or tribulation). Although speaking of himself, Paul's object is to show that it is God who delivers. His tribulation came to a head in Asia (that is, in Ephesus), when he wrote the first Epistle.

"*We were pressed out of measure, above strength*", or literally, "excessively burdened beyond our power". The word "press" as a noun appears six times in the N.T., meaning "burden", either physically, mentally or spiritually, Matt. 20. 12; Gal. 6. 2. The verbal form also occurs six times. Three times it has a physical meaning, men being *heavy* with sleep, Matt. 26. 43; Luke 9. 32. Here Paul seems to refer to an overworked mind, through labour, writing, sorrow and prayer. The human frame is made to withstand only so much, and even a strong constitution cannot go beyond these bounds. Some suggest that Paul suffered a temporary nervous breakdown. If this was for the good of the Corinthians, we cannot say that Paul should have taken more care of his health. Today, it is not unknown for servants of the Lord to be similarly afflicted, but for different reasons. The burden of overwork without relaxation can be an enemy to good health. Usually there is no good reason why this should be allowed.

"*We despaired even of life*". Paul thought that the end of his life of service was near. How truly he was "burdened" in his tabernacle, 2 Cor. 5. 4. Of course, he could not be sure, as he was later, "I am now ready to be offered, and the time of my departure is at hand", 2 Tim. 4. 6. It was only the Lord who knew exactly when His hour was come, John 17. 1. He had been "sorrowful, even unto death", Matt. 26. 38. The work of Christ had also brought Epaphroditus "nigh unto death", Phil. 2. 30.

9. Paul could see the hand of God through the gloom. The phrase "the sentence of death in ourselves" contains the word "sentence" occurring only here in the N.T. It is derived from the very common word "to answer", and means a "judicial sentence". It would appear that God Himself brought His servant to the end of himself, so that he could continue his service in a new way.

If there were life within the natural man which would satisfy the heart of God, then no doubt He would use that life in His service. But there is nothing of spiritual value in the flesh—a thing of dismay to those who have not judged themselves before God. Our verse suggests that even Paul needed the lesson not to "trust in ourselves". Perhaps he had thought that *he* could do something in Corinth, whereas the correction and service were from God alone. The realisation of the nothingness of our own position, and that the position of Christ is all in all, would colour all our service in His Name. It is God who raises the dead, so it is only He who introduces the life of Christ within us, leaving the old man as dead; this man, at least, cannot be raised.

Such nothingness pervades Scripture, as the following examples show:

Moses. "Who am I", he asks in weakness, Exod. 3. 11 and is sustained by the revelation that God is "I AM THAT I AM", v. 14. In the flesh, he was not eloquent, but of a slow speech and tongue. Yet if there were faith, God would be with his mouth to teach him what to say , 4. 10–17.

David. "Who am I", he asks in weakness, 1 Chron. 29. 14, as he beholds the greatness of the preparations for the building of the temple. He was sustained of God, from whom all things come, vv. 10–16.

Solomon. "I am but a little child: I know not how to go out or to come in", 1 Kings 3. 7, he said in weakness, as he contemplates the work of his throne. In the vision, he was enabled by God to take up the task given him, vv. 10–14.

The woman with the issue of blood. She had spent all her living on physicians, and yet remained in death, Luke 8. 43. Only the Lord could heal her, giving her life through her faith, v. 48.

Peter. In himself he had nothing with which to heal the lame man, having no silver and gold, Acts 3. 6. His ability was only in the Name of Jesus Christ of Nazareth.

Paul. He had written that "no flesh should glory in His presence", 1 Cor. 1. 29; and "let no man glory in men, 3. 21. In his flesh dwelt no good thing, Rom. 7. 18, but he was delivered by "God through Jesus Christ our Lord", v. 25. He could have had confidence in the flesh, Phil. 3. 4, but counted "all things but loss for the excellency of the knowledge of Christ Jesus my Lord", v. 8. He acknowledged that only Christ lived in him, Gal. 2. 20.

When a servant reckons himself to be incompetent and in death, the Lord may often use material means to sustain him in service. The great point is, where is his faith centred? In what does he trust?

10. We have here a past, present and future deliverance. All three aspects come from God alone. Writing from Macedonia, he had just experienced the past deliverance from his tribulation, by the good news brought by Titus. Such a deliverance lasted because Paul had confidence that the repentance of the Corinthians was genuine and enduring. He also trusted for the future, knowing that God could repeat such a work of deliverance in his soul and body when necessary.

But the mind of the apostle in his rejoicing appears to refer to something beyond his own "sentence of death". He refers to "*so great* a death". This word "*so great*" occurs only four times in the N.T. Here it stands in contrast with "*so great* salvation", Heb. 2. 3. (The other references are to *so great* ships, James 3. 4, and "*so mighty an earthquake*", Rev. 16. 18.) Paul seems to refer to the ultimate death, the final consequence of sin upon unbelievers. Salvation from this has its past, present and future aspects for the believer:

Past. He "hath saved us", 2 Tim. 1. 9, from the *penalty* of sin.

Present. We work out our own salvation, but it is God who works in us to show us His will and to do of His good pleasure, Phil. 2. 12–13. As His will is done in us, we are saved from the *power* of sin.

Future. Our salvation is now nearer than when we believed, Rom. 13. 11. It is "ready to be revealed in the last time", 1 Pet. 1. 5. We will then be delivered from the *presence* of sin.

11. Paul continues to write graciously, bringing out the good in the Corinthian church. The Lord saw the good in the churches in Revelation 2–3, as well as seeking to correct their faults.

The "gift" obviously refers to the deliverance just wrought by God in the health of His servant. "Many persons" had been praying for him, as well as the Corinthians who were now "helping together" (or labouring together) by prayer. The word "together" (really a prefix in the Greek text) suggests that the assembly as a whole in Corinth was engaged in this intercession. The needs of the apostle formed a subject in their prayer meetings. The Ephesians would have been included in the "many people" praying when Paul was among them. We can assume that the Corinthians only started praying after they had repented.

Answered prayer brings forth thanks. Paul desired that "many" should now give thanks on his behalf. The Corinthians, too, could engage in this. An assembly should surely not be like the ten lepers; only one returned to give glory and thanks to God, Luke 17. 18.

This exercise of prayer is one of the privileges of the saints. Paul's exhortation to the Ephesians was "Praying always with all prayer and supplication in the Spirit, and watching thereunto with all perseverance and supplication for all saints: *and for me*, . . ." Eph. 6. 18–19. See also Col. 4. 3; 2 Thess. 3. 1; Philem. 22.

Verses 12–14: Paul's Rejoicing in the Corinthians

12 For our rejoicing is this, the testimony of our conscience, that in simplicity and godly sincerity, not with fleshly wisdom, but by the grace of God, we have had our conversation in the world, and more abundantly to you-ward.

13 For we write none other things unto you, than what ye read or acknowledge; and I trust ye shall acknowledge even to the end;

14 As also ye have acknowledged us in part, that we are your rejoicing, even as ye also *are* our's in the day of the Lord Jesus.

12. "For our rejoicing is this" contains a key-word which dominates this Epistle, the thought of *rejoicing* or *boasting*. In its two noun forms in the Greek, it occurs ten times in the Epistle, whereas it occurs only thirteen more times in the rest of the N.T. The corresponding verb form appears in the Epistle twenty-one times, against seventeen times elsewhere.

Paul's boasting in this verse is not exactly of the Corinthians themselves. This occurs later, 2 Cor. 7. 4, 14. Here, he boasts in the manner of his conduct (conversation). Moreover, this rejoicing was not something nebulous. It was based on the fact that the substance of his rejoicing was according to "the testimony of our conscience". There was a conviction within him that his conduct and service were in keeping with the will of God. It was Christ Jesus who had put Paul into the ministry, 1 Tim. 1. 12, appointing him to be a preacher, and an apostle, and a teacher of the Gentiles, 2 Tim. 1. 11 . Paul knew this, and the conduct of his service was in keeping with the high dignity of his calling in Christ.

The apostle rejoiced in two great contrasts between his own conduct of service, and that of a carnal believer or a man in the world.

1. "*in simplicity and godly sincerity*". Some Greek texts replace "simplicity" by "holiness". "Simplicity" occurs in Ephesians 6. 5 and Colossians 3. 22, where it is translated "*singleness* of heart". Paul's life was simple, in the sense that it had one direction, namely the accomplishment of the will of God. The word "sincerity" is derived from the thought of being found clear and pure when viewed in sunlight. Paul's handling of the Word of God is thus described in 2 Corinthians 2. 17. Such sincerity is determined by the Lord whose countenance is "as the sun shineth in his strength", Rev. 1. 16. Elsewhere, such sincerity is contrasted with "the leaven of malice and wickedness", 1 Cor. 5. 8. In other words, we have here the transparency of the inner motives.

2. "*by the grace of God*". This contrasts "with fleshly wisdom". The apostle always shunned "the wisdom of men", 1 Cor. 2. 5 while James declared that the wisdom of the unsanctified mind is "earthly, sensual, devilish", James 3. 15. Only the grace of God keeps a servant from using these unholy things in His service

In this verse, Paul is referring to his conduct rather than to his preaching. Before his conversion, he had this "conversation" among the children of disobedience, Eph. 2. 2, 3. After his conversion, his "conversation" was changed to suit the new birth, when it was manifested before the world and before the Corinthians. Such conduct *before the unsaved* is important, so that one's testimony for Christ is not marred; see 1 Thess. 2. 3. Conduct *before the saints* is seen in one's behaviour in the house of God, 1 Tim. 3. 15.

13. Paul was writing nothing new regarding his conduct, his mode of testimony or his doctrine. He was perfectly consistent before God. Even the Corinthians would acknowledge this. (This word "acknowledge" means *recognise*, and is usually translated *know*).

The Corinthians had accepted his teaching when he had originally been with them, Acts 18. 8, 1 Cor. 2. They had also received his teaching given in the first Epistle. His hope that they would accept this is contained in 14. 37, "let him acknowledge that the things that I write unto you are the commandments of the Lord".

Paul's trust was that they would acknowledge these things "even to the end". He knew that he was consistent. He desired that all his children should likewise be consistent. God would have all His people to be consistent in their faith. A faith that wavers shows up an unstable man, James 1. 6–8. When lack of consistency is seen in an elder or in a teacher, untold harm can be done to the flock. In any case, we are responsible to be consistent in our faith, "*If* ye continue in the faith grounded and settled, and be not moved away from the hope of the gospel", Col. 1. 23. Paul's *trust* (or hope) in the Corinthians was replaced by his *confidence* in the Thessalonians, as he wrote, "And we have confidence in the Lord touching you, that ye both do and will do the things which we command you", 2 Thess. 3. 4.

14. In the previous verse, the acknowledgement was *present* and *future*. Here it is *past*; "ye have acknowledged us *in part*". This was their state before their correction and repentance, while Paul was writing the first Epistle. Some would *not fully* recognise his teaching, a weakness so characteristic of the religious world today. Even some believers will go only part of the way in practice with apostolic teaching about the assembly. The Word plus their own taste can only equal the Word acknowledged *in part*.

But the rejoicing is mutual. The Corinthians could rejoice in Paul before God (in their thanksgivings, 2 Cor. 1. 11), and they could also boast in him before others who were not so certain, 5. 12. Such boasting, however, is restricted to the *present*.

Paul's boasting of them is both in the *present* and in the *future*. In the present, he could boast of them to the Macedonians, 9. 2; see 2 Thess. 1. 4. But in the future, the fulness of his rejoicing in them would be manifested "in the day of the Lord Jesus". What Paul has in mind is seen in 1 Corinthians 1. 7–8. The revelation of Christ will not only be to the world, but will be a display of Himself with His saints. During the display of that day, the apostle's rejoicing will be in his converts, that they are blameless before their Lord for His glory, in the Corinthians, in the Philippians, Phil 2. 16, and in the Thessalonians, 1 Thess. 2. 19. This should be the outlook of all the people of God who work for the edification of others.

Verses 15–24: Paul's Purpose in his Movements

15 And in this confidence I was minded to come unto you before, that ye might have a second benefit;

16 And to pass by you into Macedonia, and to come again out of Macedonia unto you, and of you to be brought on my way toward Judaea.

17 When I therefore was thus minded, did I use lightness? or the things that I purpose, do I purpose according to the flesh, that with me there should be yea yea, and nay nay?

18 But *as* God *is* true, our word toward you was not yea and nay.

19 For the Son of God, Jesus Christ, who was preached among you by us, *even* by me and Silvanus and Timotheus, was not yea and nay, but in him was yea.

20 For all the promises of God in him *are* yea, and in him Amen, unto the glory of God by us.

21 Now he which stablisheth us with you in Christ, and hath anointed us, *is* God;

22 Who hath also sealed us, and given the earnest of the Spirit in our hearts.

23 Moreover I call God for a record upon my soul, that to spare you I came not as yet unto Corinth.

24 Not for that we have dominion over your faith, but are helpers of your joy: for by faith ye stand.

15. Paul writes, "And in this confidence I was minded to come unto you before, that ye might have a second benefit (grace, or favour)". This is grace indeed, for Paul had this confidence of rejoicing when he wrote the first Epistle, before their correction. This grace is shown at the *beginning* of the first Epistle, 1 Cor. 1. 1–9, and at the *end*, ch. 16. Neither the prelude nor the conclusion deals openly with the faults and errors in Corinth. At the beginning, he rejoiced at the grace given them, since they were enriched with a confirmed testimony, coming behind in no gift, vv. 5–7. At the end, he showed that he intended to come to Corinth, 16. 5.

And why would he come? No longer with a rod, 1 Cor. 4. 21, but that they may have a second grace. That is to say, he wanted to give them further help, over and above what he had given them during his first stay. He had done this at the end of his first missionary journey, Acts 14. 22, when the souls of the disciples were confirmed. He wished to visit Rome too, so that he could impart some spiritual gift, Rom. 1. 11, as he came to them in "the fulness of the blessing of the gospel of Christ", 15. 29. An evangelist who is also a teacher has a certain responsibility towards his converts even after a period of time. Moreover, every believer has need of a second, even a third, grace. There can be no complacency in one's present spiritual attainment as if further help were not needed.

16. Paul now states what he "was minded" to do after having sent the first Epistle. His immediate intention had been "to pass by you into Macedonia, and to come again out of Macedonia unto you, and of you to be brought on my way towards Judaea". Such plans were made with the inner conviction "if the Lord permit", 1 Cor. 16. 7. We have already outlined these events on pages 17 to 19, in the paragraphs entitled "The results of the the first Epistle" and "Paul accused of vacillation", so we need not repeat details here.

What was the reaction of the Corinthians when they realised that Paul had passed into Macedonia directly, without *first* passing through Achaia and Corinth? They would think that he was like the man in the parable who said, "I go, sir: and went not", Matt. 21. 30. There were those in Corinth who accused Paul of vacillating in his intentions, carnal men who would not recognise that the hand of the Lord was behind changed plans. The apostle would not pass over the charge unnoticed and unanswered. Spiritual principles were at stake, so he provides reasons from verse 17 onwards.

Even when he wrote the first Epistle, the bonds of fellowship were still in his heart. The apostle wanted "to be brought on my way toward Judaea" by the Corinthians, he desired hospitality on his journey. He had said the same thing in the first Epistle, in spite of all his criticism and correction: "I will abide, yea, and winter with you, that ye may bring me on my journey whithersoever I go", 1 Cor. 16. 6. How characteristic this is of practical Christianity, fellowship shown to the Lord's servants by those with more settled homes. The theme pervades the N.T.:

> Luke 19. 15: The Lord said to Zacchaeus, "To-day I must abide at thy house".
>
> Luke 21. 37: "At night He went out, and abode in the mount that is called the mount of Olives". In other words, fellowship in their home was shown by Mary, Martha and Lazarus in Bethany, Matt. 21. 17; John 12. 2.
>
> Acts 15. 3: Paul and the others were "brought on their way by the church" from Antioch to Jerusalem.
>
> Acts 21. 8: Paul abode with Philip the evangelist, who had a settled abode in Caesarea.
>
> Acts 21. 16: They were to lodge with Mnason, an old disciple.
>
> Acts 28. 14: As they went to Rome, they tarried seven days with brethren in Puteoli.
>
> Romans 15. 24: In his proposed journey to Spain, Paul desired "to be brought on my way thitherward" by the saints in Rome.
>
> Philemon 22: Paul wrote, "prepare me also a lodging".
>
> Hebrews 13. 1–3: "Be not forgetful to entertain strangers".

17. Paul asks questions which deal with the Corinthian objections. The strange expression "yea yea, and nay nay" must be understood in the light of these questions. The expression implies motives of uncertainty, a haphazard execution of plans, a vacillation in movement, with the mind and will of God being left out altogether. Hence Paul asks the questions:

Did I use lightness? That is, lightness of mind, thoughtlessness, a word occurring only once in the N.T. It suggests weighing neither one's actions nor their consequences. It is like the man who started to build a tower without first counting the cost, or like the king who went to war with only a few men, Luke 14. 28–32.

Do I purpose according to the flesh? Were his intentions merely fleshly, reflecting his own whims? In service, motivation by the flesh is dangerous, and if this had been so, the Corinthians would have had grounds for complaint.

18. Editors of the Greek text change the past form "was" to the present: "But as God is true (faithful), our word toward you *is* not yea and nay". By "word", Paul refers to all his preaching and to the first Epistle, as well as to the declaration of his plans. Verse 19 makes this clear. Paul was so certain of the faithfulness of God, that he knew that He would not allow His servant to be led in pathways described as "yea and nay".

This was a permanent feature of Paul's *ministry*; it did not apply only to his *movements* at this particular time. There was never self-assent(yea) or self-refusal (nay) in his service. There was only one way—God's way. His faithfulness always leads along this pathway. If we ever feel uncertain in our service, oscillating between one thing and another, this is not following Paul's example. In Acts 6. 2, the apostles did not hesitate in service between serving tables and ministering the Word; they knew what the Lord would have them to do. Paul, too, would not meddle in another man's line of things, 2 Cor. 10. 16.

19. The example of "the Son of God, Jesus Christ" raises the heart to heavenly things. The pathway of Christ must have been a holy topic of preaching when Paul first went to Corinth, since he mentions the combined labours of Silvanus and Timothy, Acts 18. 5. "The Son of God … was not yea and nay, but in Him was yea" writes Paul. Here was no vacillation of purpose and pathway, but only a life lived according to the mind of God. His will was subject with a "yea" to the will of His God and Father, John 5. 30; 6. 38; Matt. 26. 39; Heb. 10. 7. In Luke's Gospel the progress of the Lord as He journeyed to Jerusalem illustrates this truth in a very touching way. Physically, the Lord's pathway went in circles, but the final object before Him was Jerusalem, the place of sacrifice. Luke continually returns to the theme of the Lord on this pathway.

Luke 9. 31: On the mount, they spoke of His decease that He would accomplish at Jerusalem.

Luke 9. 51: "When the time was come that He should be received up, He stedfastly set His face to go to Jerusalem" through the land of the Samaritans, where He was not received.

Luke 13. 22: "He went through the cities and villages, teaching, and journeying toward Jersalem". It was impossible for a prophet to perish "out of Jerusalem", v. 33.

Luke 17. 11: "as He went to Jerusalem, . . . He passed through the midst of Samaria and Galilee".

Luke 18. 31: The Lord said to the twelve, "Behold, we go up to Jerusalem, and all things that are written by the prophets concerning the Son of man shall be accomplished". From this point onwards, the actual pathway of the Lord led straight to the city.

Luke 19. 11: "He added and spake a parable, because He was nigh to Jerusalem".

Luke 19. 28: "And when He had thus spoken, He went before, ascending up to Jerusalem".

Luke 19. 41: "when He was come near, He beheld the city, and wept over it".

Only after His sufferings and His resurrection did He lead His own "out" of the city to the place of ascension, Luke 24. 50.

20. Paul seems to have two distinct ideas in mind when he writes, "For all the promises of God in Him are yea, and *through* (not *in*) Him Amen, unto the glory of God by us". Firstly, all the promises and purposes of God in Christ's life were accomplished with full certainty. This was brought out in the previous verse. But secondly, the purposes of God in Christ were accomplished in Paul's service, as he writes, "to the glory of God *by us*". If Paul were faithful, he was an instrument of service *by* whom God could accomplish His promises of the Gospel to men around. Paul's change of plans merely constituted the outworking of God's purpose, since He was working *by* Paul. The apostle had previously written, "do all to the glory of God", 1 Cor. 10. 31. He, at least, would abide by this, and no man could criticise him for the way in which God worked out His own purposes through His servant.

21–22. This great guiding principle of service was not for the apostle Paul only. All may share in it, as he writes, "He which stablisheth *us with you* in Christ". If the Corinthians realised this, they could not criticise Paul. If we realise it today, what possibilities are latent in our service which our God can use according to His will. The common portion of the saints is described under the phrases:

He which stablisheth us. This means to confirm, to make one stronger in the faith: "Rooted and built up in Him, and *stablished* in the faith, as ye have been taught", Col. 2. 7.

He which hath anointed us. This refers to the giving of the Spirit. The context suggests that it is not so much the giving of the Spirit as the Comforter, but as the One who prepares and directs for service. The Lord Himself was anointed to preach the gospel to the poor, Luke 4. 18.

He which hath sealed us. This refers to the stamp of divine authority and certainty, and the security of the servant. It is used in Matthew

27. 66: the stone of the sepulchre of the Lord was *sealed* by men to make it sure.

He which hath given the earnest of the Spirit in our hearts. When a prospective buyer of a house pays a deposit on it, it is a pledge of sincerity of further payment. Here, the earnest of the Spirit is a pledge of the certainty of the guidance of God in all service. In 5. 5, the pledge concerns the certainty of being clothed upon in resurrection. In Ephesians 1. 14 it refers to the certainty of our future inheritance when the purchased possession will be finally redeemed.

23. Paul now returns to his own movements, and he invites the witness of God upon his motives. Men today may do this in blasphemy, but Paul was transparent before God and men. "God is my witness", he wrote in Romans 1. 9, and "God is my record," in Philippians 1. 8. See Deuteronomy 30. 19 for Moses' words.

One reason why Paul did not go directly to Corinth was because he wanted "to spare" them. That is, at Troas he decided to avoid Corinth until he knew their response. Otherwise he knew that he would have to arrive in Corinth with the rod, 1 Cor. 4. 21. This decision could only have been taken after deep exercise in prayer before God. He would wait until the grace of repentance was manifested in the Corinthians. If he spared them the *first* time, he would not spare them the *second* time, for he knew that there were some who still had not repented, 2 Cor. 13. 2.

24. A contrast occurs in this verse. On the one hand, Paul would not desire "dominion over your faith", that is, with a rod ruling over their faith. This would have been apostolic compulsion. This would have bent their minds to him, but would hardly have gained them for Christ. Rehoboam thus ruled after his father Solomon was dead, 1 Kings 12. 14. It is tragic that some elders in an assembly can seek to rule in this fashion, 1 Pet. 5. 3.

On the other hand, the apostle desired to be a helper of the Corinthians' joy, for it was by faith and not by compulsion that they stood. The word *helper* really means "fellow-worker", Paul being one of them rather than one ruling over them. Their rejoicing had a mutual origin: they themselves repented, thus inducing joy; Paul also was able to comfort them, thereby inducing further joy. Paul sought to be amongst his converts, thereby removing the pedestal effect which some had erected in 1 Corinthians 1–4. The Lord had said, "I am among you as He that serveth", Luke 22. 27.

2 CORINTHIANS 2

Section 1. Historical: Paul's Grief
Subject 2. Apostolic Exercises

Background of this Subject

In this chapter, the apostle continues to explain why he did not go to Corinth after writing the first Epistle. Paul was under no obligation to the Corinthians to explain his motives and exercises. These were known to the Lord, and Paul believed that the will of the Lord was being accomplished in the outworking of his plans. However, he devotes the introductory sixth of the Epistle to the subject, in order to gain the ear of the Corinthian assembly. If they were satisfied on this point, they would be more willingly listen to the rest of Paul's message in the Epistle.

The apostle is really expanding verse 23 of the previous chapter, "to spare you I came not as yet unto Corinth". This was such an important feature of his exercises that he counted God as a witness of his written statement. He gives three reasons why he wrote the first Epistle:

1. to avoid the necessity of using the rod upon them, 2. 3;
2. so that they may know his love to them, 2. 4;
3. so that he may know of their obedience, 2. 9.

How could he visit them if news concerning their repentance and obedience were delayed? His further exercise to visit Macedonia had to be fitted in to the time allowed by the delay. The return of Titus with the required news is not given in this chapter, although Paul makes much of his knowledge of the repentance of the *one man* in Corinth. Later in chapter 7, he describes the return of Titus with the news of the repentance of the *many*.

Exposition of 2 Cor. 2: Apostolic Exercises

1 But I determined this with myself, that I would not come again to you in heaviness.
2 For if I make you sorry, who is he then that maketh me glad, but the same which is made sorry by me?
3 And I wrote this same unto you, lest, when I came, I should have sorrow from them of whom I ought to rejoice; having confidence in you all, that my joy is *the joy* of you all.
4 For out of much affliction and anguish of heart I wrote unto you with many tears; not that ye should be grieved, but that ye might know the love which I have more abundantly unto you.
5 But if any have caused grief, he hath not grieved me, but in part: that I may not overcharge you all.
6 Sufficient to such a man *is* this punishment, which *was inflicted* of many.
7 So that contrariwise ye *ought* rather to forgive *him*, and comfort *him*, lest perhaps such a one should be swallowed up with overmuch sorrow.
8 Wherefore I beseech you that ye would confirm *your* love toward him.
9 For to this end also did I write, that I might know the proof of you, whether ye be obedient in all things.

10 To whom ye forgive any thing, I *forgive* also: for if I forgave any thing, to whom I forgave *it,* for your sakes *forgave I it* in the person of Christ;

11 Lest Satan should get an advantage of us: for we are not ignorant of his devices.

12 Furthermore, when I came to Troas to *preach* Christ's gospel, and a door was opened unto me of the Lord,

13 I had no rest in my spirit, because I found not Titus my brother: but taking my leave of them, I went from thence into Macedonia.

14 Now thanks *be* unto God, which always causeth us to triumph in Christ, and maketh manifest the savour of his knowledge by us in every place.

15 For we are unto God a sweet savour of Christ, in them that are saved, and in them that perish:

16 To the one *we are* the savour of death unto death; and to the other the savour of life unto life. And who *is* sufficent for these things?

17 For we are not as many, which corrupt the word of God: but as of sincerity, but as of God, in the sight of God speak we in Christ.

1. It is good for a servant of God to have determination. Lack of it may cause a servant to turn from the pathway chosen by the Lord. If a man puts his hand to the plough and then looks back, that man, says the Lord, is not "fit for the kingdom of God", Luke 9. 62. "Determined" is merely the usual word for "judge"; literally, he writes, "I judged with myself". Such judgment is no hasty decision, but the fruit of long experience in the ways of God. In the N.T., the word usually has its common meaning of judicial judgment, but there are a few cases relating to Paul where determination is implied. For example, in Acts 20. 16 he "*determined* to sail by Ephesus"; in 1 Corinthians 2. 2 he "*determined* not to know any thing among you, save Jesus Christ, and Him crucified"; in Titus 3. 12 he "*determined* there (in Nicopolis) to winter". In all cases, Paul judged the expediency of the proposed course of action.

Paul was intent upon not going to Corinth "in heaviness". This word (as a verb or a noun) comes in this Epistle many more times than in any other book of the N.T. It is characteristic of many sections of the letter, expressing a distressed and troubled state of heart. It is translated in various ways throughout the Epistle. Note that the various renderings represent but one word in the Greek text. Elsewhere, we find "to make sorry", 2. 2; 7. 8; etc.; "to grieve", 2. 5; "grudgingly", 9. 7. Paul would sustain his grief for the Corinthians in Ephesus, Troas and Macedonia, but not in Corinth itself. He would rather wait for his grief to be relieved.

2. There is an order in the grief and rejoicing mentioned so often in this Epistle, and Paul was very conscious of it. The gracious manner in which Paul dwells on this order is designed to commend the Corinthians and to help them. There were four phases:

1. Paul had grief because of the original state of the Corinthians. This in turn led to

2. the Corinthians being sorrowful as a result of reading the first Epistle sent to them. This led to

3. Paul rejoicing because they had repented, 7. 6, 7, 13. This

comfort was then transferred to
4. the Corinthians, who were comforted by Paul in this second Epistle, 1. 4, 6.

The apostle was sorrowful, and then the Corinthians were also; Paul was comforted, and then the Corinthians were likewise. He regarded himself as comforted of God so that he could comfort them through his own experiences.

In these first two verses, Paul makes mention of these phases: "in heaviness" refers to (1); "if I make you sorry", refers to (2); "he then that maketh me glad" refers to (3); "the same which is made sorry by me" refers to (2). Phase (4) is referred to specifically in chapter 1 verses 5–7, where he shows that God was behind the order. If an assembly is wayward in practice, service, or doctrine, another more godly brother may be suffering acutely at the hand of God, as His means for bringing the assembly back to the mind of Christ.

3. Paul would not have the order given above reversed or altered in any way. Phase (1) had to lead to phase (2). The first Epistle was written for that purpose, to avoid the apostle having sorrow from the Corinthians in whom he ought to rejoice. In other words, he did not want his sorrow to be multiplied by coming to an unrepentant assembly. In spite of their state, Paul had confidence that they would repent. Then his joy would be transferred so as to become the joy of the Corinthians. Had the apostle done anything else, he would have interrupted the means God was using to bring the Corinthians to their spiritual senses.

4. Paul outlines the burdened heart which caused him to write the first Epistle. It is interesting to note that his "much affliction and anguish of heart" is not alluded to in the first Epistle, where the authoritative doctrine of the apostle was developed in an open way . Had Paul mingled with this a description of his own feelings, the Corinthians might have accused him of merely being sentimental. The apostle would open no door for false accusations; he was wise in anticipating danger before it happened. (See 1 Corinthians 1. 15, where he states that he anticipated the danger of a party-spirit arising had he done a lot of personal baptising in Corinth.) Doors are opened which are hard to shut, if one is not watchful in one's dealings with fellow believers.

Tears also can be the portion of a servant who sees his converts departing from the truth. The Lord had wept at the sorrow of Mary and Martha, John 11. 35; He wept over Jerusalem as He anticipated its anguish and suffering at its judgment and destruction at "the time of thy visitation", Luke 19. 41–44. They would indeed crucify the Lord of glory, but shortly afterwards they would suffer at the hands of the Roman conquerors. The minute details of the events at which the Lord wept in anticipation, have been recorded in many long chapters by the Jewish historian Josephus, though this historian passes over the sufferings of

Christ in one line*. Weeping is therefore no make-believe in a hard heart, rather it shows the deep-seated sensitivities of the soul. It stands in contrast with rejoicing. If tears are related to *departure*, rejoicing is related to *faithfulness*, "I rejoiced greatly, when the brethren came and testified of the truth that is in thee, even as thou walkest in the truth", 3 John 3.

The first Epistle caused sorrow in Corinth, but it appears that Paul did not particularly want that to happen, "not that ye should be grieved". His primary object was their repentance. On the other hand, he would not regret if they were made sorry, because their sorrow was unto repentance, 2 Cor. 7. 8, 9. To remove any lingering suspicion that he was trading in their sorrow, he states that his primary motive in writing the first Epistle was to show them the love that he had the more abundantly unto them. How could he hate them if God loved them? He had previously written that service without love is of no profit, 1 Cor. 13. 3. The apostle would not be so inconsistent as to try and serve the Corinthians without loving them. It was quite plain in the first Epistle that he loved them. Apart from Romans, the termination of that Epistle is unique in Paul's writings. All his other Epistles terminate with a doxology. But in 1 Corinthians 16. 24 he adds a thought *after* the closing doxology, "My love be with you all in Christ Jesus"; this was his motive towards the assembly.

When love has to correct and reprove, it is often strangely received. The Lord also said, "As many as I love, I rebuke and chasten", Rev. 3. 19, but the next verse suggests that some in Laodicea would not hear His voice. In Paul's case, he had to own that "the more abundantly I love you, the less I be loved", 2 Cor. 12. 15. Love that is not received is criticised violently, the action of such love often branded as barren, formal and bitter. But love wanted the best for the Corinthians, even if achieving it were painful . Paul's love for the Galatians necessitated a "travail in birth again until Christ be formed in you", Gal. 4. 19. Travail in birth is bound to be painful although it is a direct consequence of love.

5. The previous verse displays Paul minimizing phase (2) outlined above. The present verse shows him minimizing phase (1), the one referring to his own grief caused by the Corinthian state. The grace of relief causes him to do this. Note that he does not minimize the gravity of the sin which caused this grief. Grace does not overlook sin, rather it provides a righteous basis under which it can be put away. Repentance takes hold of this basis so that the grief is minimized.

Paul considers here "any", a word in the singular referring to one man, and it is likely that the man in 1 Corinthians 5 is referred to. Some expositors disagree with this suggestion, in which case we must ask, Who is this man? We feel that the Holy Spirit does not leave us conundrums to solve! That sin of fornication had not only concerned the man in question, but the whole assembly had been "puffed up", and had not mourned, 1 Cor. 5. 2. The A.V. continues, "he hath not grieved me, but in part: that I may not overcharge you all". The R.V. translates this rather differently, "he

---

* *The Jewish War, by Josephus.*

hath caused sorrow, not to me, but in part (that I press not too heavily) to you all". The A.V. suggests that Paul was only partially grieved, adopting this attitude so as not to burden the Corinthians too much. The R.V. suggests that Paul was now able to cut out his own sorrow completely, the grief of the Corinthians being now only "in part" since they were rejoicing through repentance. The latter fits the context better, since Paul wants the sorrow to be forgotten in the light of present rejoicing: "A woman when she is in travail hath sorrow, because her hour is come: but as soon as she is delivered of the child, she remembereth no more the anguish, for joy that a man is born into the world", John 16. 21.

6. The man in question had been dealt with by the assembly as a whole. When the discipline had brought forth its fruit the matter was to be closed: "Sufficient to such a man is this punishment, which was inflicted of many". The word "punishment" means *censure, rebuke*. As a noun, it occurs only once in the N.T., but as a verb it occurs many times in the first three Gospels, usually being translated "rebuke". This rebuke was usually administered by the Lord. The whole principle is brought out in the Lord's own words, "Take heed to yourselves: If thy brother trespass against thee, *rebuke* him; and if he repent, *forgive* him", Luke 17. 3. Such repentance and forgiveness could take place seven times, v. 3, and even seventy times seven, Matt. 18. 22. In 1 Corinthians 5, there is a list of sins given in verse 11 demanding excommunication. (One should add to this list only with great hesitation and exercise before the Lord.) Such a man would be delivered "unto Satan for the destruction of the flesh, that the spirit may be saved in the day of the Lord Jesus", v. 5. But if repentance takes place *on the outside* of the assembly fellowship, this, says Paul, is sufficient. The reception back again of such a one demands care. Forgiveness cannot cure a damaged testimony, and a restored brother should not expect to take up service that was laid down at his excommunication. The expediency of such a course must be weighed up carefully by the elders of the assembly, and their decision must be acted on by all concerned. A servant must first be "proved", 1 Tim. 3. 10. Excommunication, repentance, forgiveness, and being received again certainly do not prove the character and ability of a servant.

7. When Paul wrote 1 Corinthians 5 concerning this man, he did not trace the process of judgment and restoration in its entirety. The hand of God against believers is intended for their ultimate welfare, not for their abandonment. In 1 Corinthians 5, Paul commanded the excommunication of the man firstly, v. 13. His future salvation was still secure, since this did not depend on his works, but verse 5 shows that the intended outcome was "the destruction of the flesh". The man should come to judge as evil all the motives and works of the flesh, that "the body of sin might be destroyed" practically, Rom. 6. 6.

This present verse 7 looks beyond this "destruction of the flesh". As

Paul had previously instructed them in the necessity of excommunication, so here he instructs them in three features regarding their attitude to the restoration of the man.

Forgiveness: The apostle states that this new attitude is to be "contrariwise", namely the opposite to their rebuke. The grounds for forgiveness are (a) that we have previously been forgiven by God for Christ's sake, Eph. 4. 32; Col. 3. 13, and (b) that the man to be forgiven shows genuine signs of repentance and a desire to be restored, at the same time bringing forth "works meet for repentance", Acts 26. 20. In the case of the Corinthians, their own attitude of heart to the sin in question had first to be changed, since originally they had condoned the sin.

Comfort: This particular Greek word (and its corresponding noun) is found in Corinthians more times than in any other book of the N.T. In the Acts, it is usually translated "exhort". In 2 Corinthians, in which the thought of *comfort* after sorrow dominates, this is the most appropriate rendering. The manifestation of this grace was for the good of the man who had repented. If the Corinthians were to adopt a superior attitude of indifference, the man may be "*swallowed up with overmuch sorrow*". Already on the outside of the pastoral care of the assembly, he would be drowned by greater grief, in the domain of the world where Satan conducts his activity, finding no rescue and no relief. Satan seeks those whom "he *may devour*", 1 Pet. 5. 8, (this is the same word). No assembly should let a repentant backslider remain engulfed in darkness because they will not let him in again into a city of light.

Love: Love was to be confirmed to the man v. 8. This does not mean a cold, barren, formal declaration of love, declared only by word and tongue. It must be "in deed and in truth", 1 John 3 . 18; contrast Ezek. 33 . 31. God's love was not only declared, but it was worked out in the giving of His Son, John 3. 16. Faith, too, is not only declared, but is manifested by works, James 2. 14–16. If Peter loved the Lord, he had to show this love by feeding the Lord's sheep, John 21. 16. The Corinthian love was to know no end in its effort to gain the brother lost from the fellowship.

9. In verses 6–8, Paul relates why he was writing the *present section* regarding the Corinthian attitude to the man. But in verse 9, he explains why he wrote the *first Epistle*: it was a test of their obedience. Not that he appeared to take this point of view in the first Epistle; there it had been a direct command to "put away . . . that wicked person", 1 Cor. 5. 13. He had written to them "the commandments of the Lord," 14. 37. But as the obedience of the Romans came abroad to all men, Rom. 16. 19, so too was the obedience of the Corinthians manifested before Paul. In the case of Philemon, Paul had confidence in his obedience *before* he wrote to him, Philem. 21. Here, however, Paul's confidence in their obedience was

proved only *after* the return of Titus with news, for he remembered their
obedience with abundant inward affection, 2 Cor. 7. 15. Adherence to the
commands of the Lord would enable them to bring "into captivity every
thought to the obedience of Christ", 10. 5.

Today likewise, the written Word is a test for obedience in a soul. Saints
must examine their own hearts in this respect; then they are exhorted to
note any other man who fails to obey the Word, and admonish him as a
brother, but not as an enemy, 2 Thess. 3. 14, 15.

10. Paul's gracious attitude in this matter would touch the hearts of the
believers. He would forgive any whom they also had forgiven. It really was
a matter of fully knowing the circumstances, which he could not know
fully, even though he had received news from Titus. But he now relied
upon the Corinthians' assessment of the man's repentance. If their opinion
gained in the fear of the Lord was such as to warrant their forgiveness,
then Paul was satisfied that this could provide adequate grounds for the
exercise of his forgiveness. We have here the principle by which our
confidence in a person's judgment enables us to endorse what he has done,
even though we are not able to examine independently the grounds by
which he came to that judgment. This contrasts with chapter 5 of 1
Corinthians. There Paul was also absent from Corinth, but he had judged
as "present in spirit", and he required the assembly to copy what he, Paul,
would have done.

11. Christ and Satan stand in contrast in these two passages. In 1
Corinthians 5, Paul's judgment was "in the name of our Lord Jesus Christ".
Also "the power of our Lord Jesus Christ" would enable the saints to carry
out the judgment decreed, v. 4. In 2 Corinthians 2, forgiveness is proffered
in "the person of Christ", v. 10. Discipline and restoration are not arbitrary
whims based on individual taste, but decisions taken with the fear of the
Lord upon the soul. The Lord had said, "Whatsoever ye shall bind on
earth shall be bound in heaven: and whatsoever ye shall loose on earth
shall be loosed in heaven", Matt. 18. 18. Such solemn acts which heaven
itself recognises, can only be accomplished by those gathered in the Lord's
name, where He is in the midst of His own, v. 20. If those who administer
discipline are torn by differences, strife, and anger, any decision reached
can hardly have the stamp of heavenly authority on it.

In 1 Corinthians 5, the man is delivered unto Satan, v. 5, to a sphere
outside of the fellowship of the assembly where the Lord is found amongst
His own. In 2 Corinthians 2, Paul would copy the Corinthians "lest Satan
should get an advantage of us". Paul anticipates a danger of division
brought about by differing attitudes. If they forgave the man but he, Paul,
did not, the situation would be ripe for Satan to use to his own ends. The
apostle knew a lot about the "devices" (or, mind, thoughts) of Satan, and
had learnt to put on the whole armour of God so as to be able to stand
"against the wiles of the devil", Eph. 6. 11. Sometimes a series of addresses

is given, or a series of Bible Readings conducted, on the subject of Satan. These may appear novel and interesting, but let the hearts of those listening rise above this level. The purpose of the series should be to forewarn the believer, so as to be forearmed against all the devices and wiles of the evil one.

12. The A.V. rendering "furthermore" is perhaps rather extravagant; the Greek word is a common little particle meaning "now". But it is clear that Paul changes the subject here, opening a new paragraph. Up to verse 11, the apostle is rehearsing his exercises *after* Titus had returned to him in Macedonia. Now he recalls his movements *before* Titus had returned. Chapter 1 had been occupied with his intentions *while in* Ephesus (see verses 8, 16). The present verses are concerned with his movements *after he had left* Ephesus. It looks as if Paul came to Troas still intending to visit Corinth before entering Macedonia, although Acts 20. 1 suggests that Paul planned to go into Macedonia straight away from Ephesus. Taken together, it appears that the apostle was still uncertain of the will of the Lord. The Spirit of the Lord had guided him to Troas before, Acts 16. 6–8, and He could do so again. It seems certain that Paul was acting on his policy not to visit Corinth until he had news from them through Titus.

In Troas, he came "to preach Christ's gospel", but this A.V. rendering inserts the verb "to preach" where it is missing in the Greek. A more literal rendering is "having come to Troas for the gospel of Christ". There must have been an assembly at Troas by this time, so Paul's intentions could have been both ministerial and evangelical. The word "gospel" embraces both kinds of service. The gospel not only brings us to the faith, but keeps us on its pathway. Paul was ready to preach the gospel at Rome, but this included imparting to the Roman believers "some spiritual gift" for their establishment, Rom. 1. 11, 15. In Troas, however, there was the open door, and this would refer more specifically to the evangelical side of testimony; see Acts 14. 27; 1 Cor. 16. 9; Col. 4. 3. In this latter reference, prayer opens doors, seeking that God would give His servants the ability to speak.

13. Even an open door cannot be grasped if the soul of the evangelist is not exercised towards it by reason of pressure of other circumstances. Such a situation is in no way contrary to the will of God. Even in the Lord's case, there was an open door in His own country, but persistent unbelief meant that He "did not many mighty works there", Matt. 13. 58. The explanation is that Paul's heart was on the saints in Corinth. His anxiety for the assembly there caused him to decide to forsake temporarily the promising harvest field of Troas. His anxiety was manifested *inwardly* by possessing "no rest in my spirit", and *outwardly* by his leaving Troas. Titus had not returned, so he passed over to Macedonia, though with little prospect of relief or of ability in evangelical testimony, until God's good time. Note that he took his "leave of *them*". This does not seem to refer to the men in Troas embraced in the open door, rather to the assembly in Troas. He found fellowship there even if Corinth was weighing upon his soul. His delight in the saints in Troas is reflected by the fact that he visited them again for a week on his return journey from Corinth and Macedonia, Acts 20. 6.

14. The historical portion of this chapter is continued from verse 5 of chapter 7, where he relates that he still had no rest in his soul until Titus returned to Macedonia. Why does Paul suddenly break off here by writing, "Now thanks be unto God . . ."? Paul wanted to show the Corinthians that his comfort did not come from even the choicest of circumstances of earth, even though granted by God. Rather the apostle was going to triumph in Christ. No doubt the return of Titus with good news was the occasion of this outburst of praise, but Paul would record it as something distinct, so that the work of God may be seen as all important.

The triumph was God's, not Paul's or the Corinthians'. The A.V. rendering "causeth us to triumph" should more properly read "leads us in triumph". Paul knew it was an honour to be led in triumph by such a Victor as Christ, being able to diffuse the savour of His knowledge in every place. This is really a metaphor, taken from a victorious general's triumphal procession. The spiritual thought goes far beyond the natural, since here the willing captives as led by God join in the triumph of Christ. "The savour of His knowledge" is an allusion to the fragrance of the incense scattered by the bearers. Paul regards himself as such a bearer. In all his movements, there was made known the savour of the knowledge of God as revealed in Christ. Moreover, this savour was distributed "in every place," these verses showing that the distribution was towards God, the saints and sinners.

15. The God-ward aspect is presented in this verse. In everyday life, the fragrance of a flower, of a cooked meal, or of an ointment can be appreciated because our nostrils are developed to catch the fragrance over a distance. Spiritually, the fragrance of Christ flows to God from His people. Their testimony, ministering to those being saved and evangelically to the perishing, is one means by which fragrance rises to God. God appreciates Christ when He is transferred in this way. We must not think, therefore, that a specific act of worship is the only means by which believers can bring Christ before their God.

The idea of a "sweet savour" pervades the O.T., where sacrifices described by this name were thus acceptable before God. How much more is the offering up of Christ "an offering and a sacrifice to God for a sweetsmelling savour," Eph. 5. 2. On a different level, the gifts of the believers in Philippi were "an odour of a sweet smell, a sacrifice acceptable, wellpleasing to God," Phil. 4. 18.

16. Towards sinners, Paul and his fellow labourers were "the savour of death unto death," that is, an odour of death, ending in death. Paul was this to the unbelievers in Antioch; Christ was presented, but they judged themselves unworthy of everlasting life, Acts 13. 46. Also to the men in Athens, he had preached Jesus and the resurrection, but by this Man God would judge the world in righteousness, 17. 18, 31.

Towards the saints, Paul was "the savour of life unto life," that is, an odour of life, ending in life. Such was Paul in his Epistles, where the Spirit enabled him to unfold all the glories of Christ that could be expressed in words.

But how could a man, albeit an apostle, cause such fragrance to be diffused in every place? "Who is sufficient for these things?", asks Paul, anticipating that some in Corinth may accuse him of being too boastful in his abilities. He answers, "Our sufficiency is of God", 3. 5. To this end, he disassociates himself from the "many", thereby implying that only a few have this holy motive of service before them; see Phil. 3. 17, 18. The "little flock" is precious to Christ, since only a "few" are found on the narrow way, Matt. 7.14.

17. Paul finally shows something of the few who handle the word acceptably, thereby enabling them to diffuse this fragrance of Christ. This is not behaviour, but qualifications for ministry, for deacon service, 1 Tim. 3. 8.

> *Which corrupt the word of God:* No servant can make merchandise of the Word for his own gain. He cannot water it down to suit his hearers, or present it to please men. Its subject matter is too holy and serious for a servant to take sides with "deceitful workers", 2 Cor. 11. 13.

> *As of sincerity:* The searching gaze of God will seek out the reality of all motives and service. Our conduct should be like that of the apostle when he could recall, "that in holiness and sincerity of God . . . we behaved ourselves in the world and more abundantly to you-ward", 2 Cor. 1. 12 R.V.

> *As of God:* The servant hears and speaks the Word of God; nothing else is of value; John 8. 47.

> *In the sight of God:* Service may be "unknown" before men, but "well known" before God, 2 Cor. 6. 9. It is accomplished before His all seeing eye, and He tries our hearts, 1 Thess. 2. 4.

> *Speak we in Christ:* Service must be of such a character that Christ Himself could do the same things if He were present. His interests and not the interests of self will then be in the mind of the servant.

When such faithfulness is manifested, we shall be like the house at Bethany, that was filled with the odour of the ointment with which Mary anointed the feet of the Lord Jesus, John 12. 3.

2 CORINTHIANS 3

Section 2. The Service of the True Minister
Subject 1. The Ministry of the Minister

Relationships of this Section

Paul now opens a new section of his Epistle, although it should be pointed out that some regard chapter 2 verse 14 as the appropriate starting point of this new section.

The Corinthian assembly was not one hundred per cent on Paul's side. The majority accepted him as a result of the corrective influence of the first Epistle, while the minority still regarded him and his apostolic authority as suspect. When reading this second Epistle, the reader must decide which part is written for which class of men. The same spiritual discernment is necessary when reading, say, Matthew's Gospel. Was the Lord's teaching directed to all men of all time, or was some of it directed only to His disciples *there and then?* Many who say that the "Lord's prayer", Matt. 6. 8–13, is intended for all because of the word "ye" in verses 8 and 9, ignorantly pass over other verses such as 10. 5–6 where the command is given not to preach to the Gentiles. It is obvious that discrimination is necessary. But how many are willing to allow themselves to be liberated from the bondage of religious tradition? Tradition is a most unsound basis on which to make spiritual discrimination.

Chapters 1–2, and 7–9 are historical chapters in this Epistle, and are written to all. Chapters 3–6 describe true ministry, and are written to those who would receive Paul, in order to confirm them in their faith and service. Chapters 10–13 describe the true minister, the Holy Spirit describing the apostle Paul with his own pen; these chapters are written to all who do not receive Paul and his apostleship.

We note:

Chapters 1–2: Paul's *grief*—historical matters.
Chapters 3–6: Paul's *rejoicing*—doctrinal matters.
Chapters 7–9: Paul's *rejoicing*—historical matters
Chapters 10–13: Paul's *grief*—personal matters.

In the Epistle we have two large letters of commendation, written about Paul by himself because there was no one else to write them. Ultimately they must be understood as character studies written by the Holy Spirit— relating to his service and conduct—and no doubt the sort of thing that will come out before the judgment seat of Christ. In the first letter of commendation, chapters 3–6, Paul uses the description "we" consistently; it may refer to all true ministers of the Gospel. In the second letter, chapters 10–13, Paul uses "I" consistently; his apostleship was the essential theme, a subject so necessary today for those who deny the authoritative character of his writings.

It should be noticed that the present section does not deal essentially with matters in Corinth. Elsewhere in the Epistle, we read of the man who repented, 2. 6–8; of the many who repented, 7. 7–10; and of some who were still unrepentant, 13. 2. But this section presents a wholesome account of service for all those who would seek to serve the Lord Christ.

Background of this Subject

In this section, Paul gives details both of the *vessel* that God chooses for ministry, chapter 4, and of the minister's *character*, chapter 6. The *object* before the minister—both God-ward, saint-ward and sinner-ward—is presented in chapter 5, while the transcendency of the *message* carried by the minister has the first place in chapter 3.

Paul is writing about a deeply spiritual subject, so the subject opens with a spiritual letter:

Verses 1–5: *The spiritual letter of commendation*. Paul has already gained their ears, and these verses put the finishing touch to this.

Verses 6–18: *The glories of the new testament contrasted with the old*.

From the time of their conversion some believers are fully emancipated from the dark religious tradition which is engrained in many a soul. Some never seem to enter into the glorious liberty of the children of God. For others, it may be a long and painful process, full of debate and dispute, of encouragement and discouragement, of waxing and waning, until the liberty of the Spirit is enjoyed. The *contrasts* given in the present chapter should help such souls struggling to find the way of God more perfectly. We may note:

written not with ink, but with the Spirit, v. 3;
not in tables of stone, but in the heart, v. 3;
the letter—the Spirit, v. 6;
the ministration of death—of the spirit, vv. 7–8;
condemnation—righteousness, v. 9;
no glory—glory that excelleth, v. 10;
done away—remaineth, v. 11;
vail—plainness of speech, vv. 12–13;
past, v. 13; present, vv. 14–15; future, v. 16;
liberty (instead of bondage), v. 17;
from glory to glory, v. 18.

Exposition of 2 Cor. 3: The Ministry of the Minister

Verses 1–5: The Spiritual Letter of Commendation

1 Do we begin again to commend ourselves? or need we, as some *others*, epistles of commendation to you, or *letters* of commendation from you?
2 Ye are our epistle written in our hearts, known and read of all men:
3 *Forasmuch as ye are* manifestly declared to be the epistle of Christ ministered by us, written not with ink, but with the Spirit of the living God; not in tables of stone, but in fleshy tables of the heart.

> 4 And such trust have we through Christ to God-ward:
> 5 Not that we are sufficient of ourselves to think any thing as of ourselves;
> but our sufficiency *is* of God;

1. "Do we begin again to commend ourselves?" writes Paul, touching upon a very delicate subject. He was about to write his own letter of commendation—indeed by the Holy Spirit—but distasteful in as far as self appears to exalt self. There was a need for such a letter about Paul to be read to the assembly in Corinth, but there was no one else to write it. Before starting the letter (in verse 6, say), he shows that he *already* has a letter—not a description in words, but a manifestation of living souls. With such a manifestation before the Corinthians, Paul can afford to set out these matters in a more developed way in writing. The Corinthian assembly was his letter. He adopted the same tactics in this second letter to the few who would not receive him; he pointed to his work in them, 13. 3–5.

Others visiting Corinth would need a letter of introduction to the assembly, and believers in fellowship in Corinth would need a letter if they journeyed elsewhere. A letter written for a believer would be about his faith and service, written by those who know him well, to others who do not know him. Ultimately the proof of the believer's faith is known by his consistent testimony and walk. Strangers could not detect such consistency immediately, so a letter is needed as an immediate introduction.

In Paul's case, he had laboured among them for so long; he had even founded the assembly in Corinth. Were they now so suspicious of him that they needed verification of his faith and service?

A letter of commendation is a recommendation to others likeminded in the faith, to receive the one commended to them. The letter is written about the character, service and needs of the one commended. Romans 16. 1–2 are verses written to commend Phebe from Cenchrea to Rome. The spiritual nature of the letter requires that it is not reduced to a formality, and that it is not demanded and accepted mechanically. If a brother asks for a letter, and is given a pre-printed document, what value is this? Other circumstances may prevent a brother from presenting a letter at the required moment; do the elders mechanically turn him away? The lessons of second Corinthians are needed by those who sign such letters and those who receive them. Make sure that the letter is an adequate description of the brother or sister in question, and let the receiving assembly receive them warmly in the light of the information given.

2–3. Paul was a good writer of letters, a fact witnessed to by his many Epistles, but the letter referred to here was not written by himself. The writer was, in fact, divine. In Genesis 9. 13, after the flood, the rainbow was written in the heavens; God set His bow in the clouds as a token of His own remembrance. In Exodus 32. 16, we read of the "writing of God"

upon the tables; see Exod. 34. 1; Deut. 10. 2. Then there was the writing
on the wall of king Belshazzar's palace, Dan. 5. 5, and the Lord Jesus
Himself "wrote on the ground", John 8. 6. In a less physical sense, God
would write His law "in their inward parts, and write it in their hearts", Jer.
31. 33 .

The features of this letter should be carefully noted, for it should be
possible to write a similar letter concerning every saint who serves.

> *Author:* It is declared to be "the epistle of Christ". The author is
> divine. He perceives the details of all that He writes.

> *Subject of the letter:* In verse 2, Paul states that "ye" are the subject,
> whilst in verse 3 he uses the expression "ministered by us". Hence
> the letter concerns Paul's own service, to the salvation of souls and
> the edification of the saints. Lasting service is recorded by the
> divine Author, and that in unexpected places.

> *Readers:* Men may not see the recording itself, but they can perceive
> the subject matter—the Corinthians saved and blessed as an
> assembly. "All men" is embracive; believers see a spiritual work,
> unbelievers see outward signs and changes in conduct and practice.

> *Ink:* Christ uses "the Spirit of the living God" to effect the record.

> *Paper:* not physical, but in "fleshy tables of the heart", that is, in *Paul's*
> heart, v. 2. Paul carried his own letter, a permanent record of
> acceptable service.

All believers today have a similar record engraved upon their hearts by
the divine Writer. Others may wrongly comprehend our character, motives
and service, but God makes no mistake in the divine writing. The letter
fits the individual perfectly, and is quite capable of being unfolded before
the judgment seat of Christ. God's assessment will then be displayed, so
that the believer can be rewarded.

Some of the things recorded in Paul's heart are found in this Epistle:

> a sweet savour of Christ, 2. 15;
> changed into the same image from glory to glory, 3. 18;
> God had shined in his heart, 4. 6;
> the life of Jesus was manifested, 4. 10;
> he was a new creature, with old things passed away, 5. 17;
> Christ dwelled in his heart by faith, Eph. 3. 17;
> he sanctified the Lord God in his heart, 1 Pet. 3. 15.

Such a precious epistle can, alas, be hidden in a distasteful envelope;
the old nature without can restrict the manifestation of Christ within.
After all, which is more valuable, the envelope or the letter? Years ago, the
author had the odd habit of preserving all the letters he received together
with their envelopes! Wisdom eventually dawned, and the envelopes were
thrown away, but not the letters. Again, when letters arrive through the
post, the envelopes may be dirty and torn. They are franked, covered with
bad handwriting, and sometimes readdressed. When it arrives, the proper
course is to extract the letter and discard the envelope. Christ can only be
fully appreciated in a believer as the works of the flesh are discarded.

To change the figure slightly, sometimes an envelope is sufficiently thin for the contents to be dimly discernible, or there may be a transparent pane in the envelope, and some of the contents can be seen. A postcard is a letter without an envelope. The spiritual implications are obvious. Our bodies—their deeds and conduct—are like these envelopes; how transparent are they to the life of Christ within?

4–5. Through the Lord Jesus, Paul could trust God that an exact record would be engraved upon his heart, and that He would enable Paul to continue in service in a way which was consistent with the letter written. Pride might cause a man to try and dictate to God what He should write. This would not be trusting Him. Again, success or popularity in service may give rise to motives and methods that are inconsistent with previous service. A trust in the Lord can remove such dangers.

In any case, Paul had no confidence in the flesh; all his sufficiency came from God. Service resulting from confidence in the flesh could hardly be recorded by God in the letter. Only service engendered by Himself would be worth recording. Paul had to make this point, since he was now going to write about his own ministry. If God had previously recorded it, there would be no harm in repeating it in a humble way if it were needed for edification. This repetition was expedient, but Paul did not want to be misunderstood.

After all, the apostle could do nothing for himself, and neither can we. Salvation is of grace through faith; it is not "of yourselves: it is the gift of God", Eph. 2. 8. The apostle writes that we have been saved "not according to our works, but according to his own purpose and grace", 2 Tim. 1. 9. In all Paul's service, it was the grace of God that worked rather than he himself, 1 Cor. 15. 10. Everything he did was "through Christ which strengtheneth me", Phil. 4. 13. Dross in service is caused by not realising—or not caring to realise—this fundamental fact that "our sufficiency is of God".

Verses 6–18: The Glories of the New Testament Contrasted with the Old

6 Who also hath made us able ministers of the new testament; not of the letter, but of the spirit: for the letter killeth, but the spirit giveth life.

7 But if the ministration of death, written *and* engraven in stones, was glorious, so that the children of Israel could not stedfastly behold the face of Moses for the glory of his countenance; which *glory* was to be done away:

8 How shall not the ministration of the spirit be rather glorious?

9 For if the ministration of condemnation *be* glory, much more doth the ministration of righteousness exceed in glory.

10 For even that which was made glorious had no glory in this respect, by reason of the glory that excelleth.

11 For if that which is done away *was* glorious, much more that which remaineth *is* glorious.

12 Seeing then that we have such hope, we use great plainness of speech:

13 And not as Moses, *which* put a vail over his face, that the children of
   Israel could not stedfastly look to the end of that which is abolished:
14 But their minds were blinded: for until this day remaineth the same vail
   untaken away in the reading of the old testament; which *vail* is done away
   in Christ.
15 But even unto this day, when Moses is read, the vail is upon their heart.
16 Nevertheless when it shall turn to the Lord, the vail shall be taken away.
17 Now the Lord is that Spirit: and where the Spirit of the Lord *is*, there *is*
   liberty.
18 But we all, with open face beholding as in a glass the glory of the Lord,
   are changed into the same image from glory to glory, *even* as by the Spirit
   of the Lord.

6. It was God who had made Paul an "able minister of a new covenant",
R.V. This word "able" means *competent*, the same root as the word
"sufficiency" in verse 5. The word "minister" means *deacon*; Paul refers to
those who render spiritual service to others. Such a calling is not a result
of a decision made by self nor through a process known as ordination in
ecclesiastical circles; rather it is solely the prerogative of God to put a man
"into the ministry", 1 Tim. 1. 12. A preacher is not made "able", or
competent, through training and education. God can accomplish this in
those whom He calls to this service. This does not mean that a speaker
should remain slovenly in his manner of preaching. He may well profit
from advice given by more experienced preachers in the local assembly. A
servant, therefore, possesses nothing of his own, and can do nothing by
himself; he is exactly the opposite to Pharaoh, king of Egypt, who said "My
river is my own, and I have made it for myself", Ezek. 29. 3, 9.

Paul contrasts this one new covenant with one covenant of old,
although we find reference to several covenants during O.T. times. We
briefly mention them in passing, without entering into explanations.

Covenant *in Eden*, Gen.1. 26–28, regulating the life of man and
   woman in innocency.
Covenant *to Adam*, Gen. 3. 15–19, deals with the life of man in his
   fallen state, but with the promise of a Redeemer.
Covenant *to Noah*, Gen. 9. 1–17, introduces human government upon
   the earth.
Covenant *to Abraham*, Gen. 15. 18; 17. 1–14, introduces the nation of
   Israel.
Covenant *to Moses*, Exod. 19. 25, . . ., really brings in condemnation.
   It is this covenant that Paul has in mind in our present chapter.
Covenant *relating to Palestine*, Deut. 28. 1; 29. 1, deals with conduct in
   the land, with judgment and restoration, 30. 3.
Covenant *to David*, 2 Sam. 7. 8–16, establishes the family of David, in
   which Christ would be born.
New Covenant, Jer. 31. 31–34, promised to Israel (not to the church),
   but entered into by believers now, allowing for dispensational
   differences. Ezekiel 37. 26 refers only to Israel in the future.
The old covenant, of which Paul writes, was a contract made by God for

the blessing of the people. It was based on formal obedience and works, together with ceremonial sacrifice. The foolishness of the people, in thinking that they could attain blessing by their own efforts, is shown by their words, "All that the Lord hath spoken we will do", Exod. 19. 8. The basis of the covenant was an epistle, written "in tables of stone", which were either broken on the hillside, 32. 19, or else hidden in the ark, Deut. 10. 5. They were so holy, since they were written with the finger of God, that they could not be seen by sinful eyes. Hence they had to be broken or hidden.

Such a covenant leads to death, for if a law could have been given that would have brought forth life then it would have been given, Gal. 3. 21. Such a state of affairs is called by Paul "the letter," and "the letter killeth". Elsewhere he uses the expression "the handwriting of ordinances that was against us", Col. 2. 14. Disobedience is the natural response of any heart to the law. Its holy requirements are contrary to the trend of natural desires, originating from a desperately wicked heart that nothing can cure. "When the commandment came, sin revived, and I died", wrote Paul, Rom. 7. 9. It is through the law that "all the world may become guilty before God", 3. 19, and "by the deeds of the law there shall no flesh be justified in his sight: for by the law is the knowledge of sin", v. 20. Moreover, "as many as are of the works of the law are under the curse", Gal. 3. 10; the law cannot lead to justification in the sight of God, v. 11.

What a change was brought in by the coming of Christ ! "The law was given by Moses, but grace and truth came by Jesus Christ", John 1. 17. Even in the O.T., better things were promised, as of course had been foreseen by God long before the law was given. The choicest promise was given through Jeremiah as the children of Israel went into captivity, "Behold, the days come, saith the Lord, that I will make a new covenant with the house of Israel, and with the house of Judah: not according to the covenant that I made with their fathers in the day that I took them by the hand to bring them out of the land of Egypt; which My covenant they brake, . . . After those days, saith the Lord, I will put My law in their inward parts and will write it in their hearts, and will be their God, and they shall be My people", Jer. 31. 31–34. It is important to observe that this new covenant was *made* with the house of Israel and the house of Judah. They shall *enter* into its blessings in a day yet to come. God found fault with the first covenant, Heb. 8. 7, and thus promised the new. Jeremiah 31 is quoted at length in Hebrews 8. 8–12 to show that the very existence of a promise of a new covenant means that the old covenant is already prepared to vanish away. The point is that it has even *now* vanished away, even if Israel and Judah have not yet entered into their blessing.

The Lord Jesus is "the mediator of the new covenant", Heb. 9. 15, His blood being the "blood of the new testament, which is shed for many for the remission of sins", Matt. 26. 28. Although the new covenant was *made* prophetically only to Israel and Judah, yet its scope is wider than for this nation only. Others *enter* into the blessings of the efficacious power of His blood, not because the covenant was made with them, but because the blessings are for "whosoever will". It must carefully be borne in mind that nowhere does Scripture speak of a covenant being made with the church.

Paul observes that he was a "minister" of this new covenant. He was used by God to serve these accomplished promises to men around. Yet how could a mere man, although an apostle, transfer such blessings to a sinful heart? To answer this, Paul introduces the Spirit of God. The A.V. uses "spirit" with a small initial letter in our verse 6; some expositors interpret it as referring only to the mind of God. Other translators use the name "Spirit" twice in the verse, and we are more happy with this. Hence, the new testament is "of the Spirit", for "the Spirit giveth life". The new birth is "of the Spirit", says the Lord in John 3. 6; the Spirit of God quickens, the flesh profiting nothing, 6. 63.

7. Paul now contrasts the two covenants, not in detail, but pertaining to one feature only, namely glory . In verse 7, the apostle deals with the introduction of the old covenant. The A.V. uses the translation "was glorious", being a continuous description of the covenant. But the Greek verb employed is not merely "was". The R.V. gives "came with glory", another literal translation reads "was produced in glory". Paul refers to the *introduction* of the old covenant. The book of Exodus—the book dealing with the introduction of the covenant—is full of references to the glory. In many cases it is recorded that the people could not sustain the sight of this glory; the state of their hearts necessitated hiding their eyes from the sight. We note the references:

> Thunders and lightnings on mount Sinai, with a thick cloud; the Lord descended upon it in fire, Exod. 19. 16, 18.
>
> The people were not to break through and gaze, v. 21.
>
> The people stood afar off, 20. 21.
>
> The glory of the Lord abode on mount Sinai, and the sight of it was like devouring fire on the top of the mount in the eyes of the people, 24. 16, 17.
>
> The tables of stone could not be introduced into the moral darkness of the camp, so they were broken, 32. 19.
>
> In the temporary tabernacle outside the camp, with the pillar of cloud at the door, 33. 10, Moses asked to see the glory of God, v. 18.
>
> On the mount again, the skin of Moses' face shone as he spoke with the Lord, 34. 29; the same thing happened on the mount of transfiguration, Luke 9. 31.
>
> Aaron and the people were afraid to come near to Moses, Exod. 34. 30.
>
> Hence Moses put a vail on his face while he talked to the people, but took it off when he went in before the Lord to speak with Him, vv. 33–35. In other words, Moses was charged with the glory of the Lord; he was in contact with the source. In a similar manner, an electric battery is charged through contact with a source, after

which it becomes in itself a source of electricity.

Afterwards, when the tabernacle was first set up, the glory of the Lord filled the tabernacle, and even Moses could not enter in because of the overpowering nature of the glory of the Lord, 40. 34, 35

Because of the satisfaction of God with all that the priests did in connection with their initial consecration, the glory of God appeared to all, Lev. 9. 23.

Yet immediately afterwards, fire came forth from the Lord in judgment, 10. 2.

How truly Paul wrote of the Israelites, "to whom pertaineth the adoption, and the glory, and the covenants, and the giving of the law, and the service of God, and the promises", Rom. 9. 4. Yet this display of glory touched the chords of fear and not love in their heart. The people could "not endure", and so terrible was the sight that even Moses had to say, "I exceedingly fear and tremble", Heb. 12. 20, 21. Moreover, this law brought in nothing but bondage, Gal. 4. 24.

Paul describes the glory by which the old covenant was introduced as that which "was to be done away", the reason being given in the following verses.

8. "How shall not the ministration of the Spirit be rather glorious?" asks Paul, where we employ the word "Spirit" with a capital initial letter. It is a well known fact of daily experience that during the hours of sunshine, the stars are not seen. During the day, the stars are still in the heavens, shining exactly as they do during the night. But their light becomes insignificant when the light of the sun dominates. The glory of the old covenant was very real, but God has brought in a Light that dominates the scene. Moreover, the stars are still there in their appointed places when the sun shines, but the glory of the old covenant has disappeared. God would have no rivalry with the glory of His Son. Many men—both Jews adhering to their ancient religion, and Gentiles adhering to traditional theology—seek to maintain the principles of the old covenant, but the glory has gone, 1 Sam. 4. 22.

If the law abounded with light, how much more the service of the Spirit relating to Christ Himself? Where Christ is, the glory is better and eternal. The phrase "shall be glorious" in our verse should read "shall be in glory". Paul does not refer only to the *introduction* of the new covenant, but to the *settled state* of grace in which the glory of Christ is now known. We do not see His glory openly now; it is on high where He has entered, 1 Pet. 1. 11. His miracles and His works showed forth His glory, John 2. 11; 11. 40. But now believers essentially know by faith the moral glory of His Person, John 1. 14; 17. 24, "that they may behold My glory".

9. Verses 9, 10 and 11 all start with the word "for". Reasons are being given for the implied answer to the question asked in verse 8. In fact, three contrasts are given:

Verse 9:   condemnation—righteousness;
Verse 10:   contrast in magnitude;
Verse 11:   contrast in duration.

Condemnation was associated with the glory of God seen physically under the law. This refers to the fact that a person is declared guilty by God, "the Lord will not hold him guiltless", Exod. 20. 7. It also refers to the consequences of guilt, namely punishment. The law regularised the position that had existed since Adam, since "sin is not imputed when there is no law", Rom. 5. 13. But condemnation arose on account of the sin of Adam, "by the offence of one, judgment came upon all men to condemnation", v. 18. Today, those who believe not are "condemned already", John 3. 18, while those who believe rejoice in their standing that "there is therefore now no condemnation to them which are in Christ Jesus", Rom. 8. 1.

By contrast, the service of righteousness exceeds in glory, because Christ stands in such contrast to Adam: "by the righteousness of one: the free gift came upon all men unto justification of life", Rom. 5. 18. Through Christ, God imputes (reckons) righteousness to believers without works, Rom. 4. 6. Not only are we made righteous because sins are pardoned and we ourselves are accepted to glory, but we are not counted as guilty although in ourselves we should be. In Christ, God counts us as not having sinned, and hence there is no judgment to follow. We indeed had sinned, but judgment had been expended upon Another. Hence the glory of Christ exceeds the glory of God seen physically under the law, on account of what has been accomplished.

10. Here we have a contrast in magnitude. The glory of the old covenant must be interpreted in the light of the fact that it *was made* glorious. In other words, it had a *beginning*, and does not reflect an eternal characteristic of the past. Certainly this cannot rival "the glory that excelleth", seen in Christ the mediator of the new covenant. His glory had *no* beginning in the past, and hence surpasses anything that is finite and connected with temporal conditions. He had glory with the Father before the world was, John 17. 5, and this is to be manifested again in the presence of the Father, v. 24. Such a blessed meditation would provide comfort to the One who was about to pass into darkness for a season.

11. The contrast is now not with the *past* but with the *future*. If something temporal was glorious, how much more glorious is that which now subsists to eternal ages? But has the old covenant been annulled? Does the law remain today? It might appear so; are not these things "read every sabbath day" in the synagogues, Acts 13. 27? The formal services of the established church might also suggest that the old covenant remains. But in the sight of God it has gone as a covenant, although still left on record for our profit. We must therefore be convinced whether salvation comes through grace alone, or whether, as some would declare, salvation

through Christ is compatible with living under the law. The Epistle to the Galatians shows the incompatibility of such a belief. The law was given "*till the seed should come to whom the promise was made*", Gal. 3. 19; it was only a "schoolmaster (child-instructor) to bring us unto Christ . . . But *after* that faith is come, we are *no longer* under a schoolmaster", vv. 24, 25. Paul would never put himself under law again, for if he built again the things destroyed, he would make himself a transgressor, 2. 18.

12–13. Here we have a contrast between that which is open and that which is closed. The reality of the blessed hope in Christ enabled Paul to use "great plainness (or boldness) of speech". There was boldness in his ministry to make Christ known. This was no ministry hidden in an upper room for fear of the Jews, but something for worldwide dissemination. Even in Corinth, the saints would remember that he had "testified to the Jews that Jesus was Christ", Acts 18. 5. The declaration of the new covenant was not something "done in a corner", 26. 26; rather Paul preached "Jesus Christ, and Him crucified", 1 Cor. 2. 2. In other words, Paul radiated Christ continuously. Having seen His glory on the day of his conversion, the apostle was charged with the glory of Christ, so that through Paul faith could be attracted to the Man above.

How this contrasts with the minister of the old covenant, Moses. As he came down from the mount with the two tables of testimony, the skin of his face shone, Exod. 34. 29. We read that the people were afraid, but the Spirit of God through Paul adds another explanation. The vail was necessary so that "the children of Israel could not steadfastly look to the end of that which is abolished". There were two things which could not be seen, the tables and the glory of Moses' face. God would not allow Israel to look on something that was only temporary, else it might have become an object of veneration, displacing from their eyes the glory that excels in Christ. Note that Moses' face was not vailed to the three apostles on the mount of transfiguration, since this was related to N.T. grace and not O.T. law. The mountain top became a sanctuary since the Lord was there.

14–16. These verses present the whole history of the Jews. The past, present and future history of the nation is dealt with.

Past. "Their minds were blinded" means that the people could not see the reason why the Lord gave the law. Minds are blinded by Satan, 2 Cor. 4. 4. But if men reject the opportunity to receive sight, showing no desire to know the mind of God concerning what He introduces, then God further blinds their eyes, John 12. 40. The prophet had to shut their eyes, Isa. 6. 10, and the people themselves shut their own eyes, Matt. 13. 15; Acts 28. 27. To such folk the mysteries of the kingdom were spoken in parables so that they could not understand. But the eyes of the apostles were blessed, for they saw, Matt. 13. 16. How true it is that the rest of Israel "were blinded, according as it is written, God hath given them the spirit of slumber,

eyes that they should not see, and ears that they should not hear",
Rom. 11. 7, 8. This is quoted from Isaiah 29. 10–12, where the
reference is to a "book that is sealed". See also, Deut. 29. 4; Ps. 69.
23; Jer. 5. 21; Ezek. 12. 2. Thus Moses and the three major prophets
all take up the same subject.

Present. For the Jews, the same vail remains when the O.T. is read,
although to faith this vail has been done away in Christ. The vail
exists between the unbelieving mind of the Jew and the O.T. itself.
Such a mind of unbelief will not see that Christ pervades the O.T.,
that He is found in "all the scriptures", Luke 24. 27. The N.T. makes
Him known more fully, but there is sufficient in the O.T. to
enlighten any earnest seeker, for the Lord said, "had ye believed
Moses, ye would have believed Me: for he wrote of Me", John 5. 46.
The Lord knew that there was a vail upon the heart of his hearers
when Moses was read, but more than that, He Himself was the
stumbling block to the Jewish mind.

Future. In spite of all the past, the certainty remains, "when it (that is,
their heart) shall turn to the Lord, the vail shall be taken away".
This is God's order, and it works by grace. It is not first, take the vail
away, and then the ground is more easily prepared so that the heart
can turn to the Lord. Seeking and the initial formation of faith
come *before* a fuller knowledge of divine things. In Luke 24, there
was a little faith, so the Lord "opened their understanding, that they
might understand the scriptures", v. 45. But it is hard for men to ask
expecting to be given, for men to knock expecting the door to be
opened, Matt. 7. 7. Yet even for the Jew, those who seek shall find.
Turn to Him, and the vail is taken away, showing the glories of the
ministry of Christ apart from the lesser light of the law. This is the
crux of the Gospel. But men want certainty before they say they can
believe. God insists that things work the other way round! But as for
the Jews, in a coming day, faith will enable them to say of the One
then unvailed in their minds, "we hid as it were our faces from Him;
He was despised, and we esteemed Him not", Isa. 53. 3.

17. Yet how can such a transformation of opinion, outlook and faith
take place in a soul? How can a heart turn to the Lord, abandoning the old
and appreciating the new for the first time? It is all very well saying "turn
to the Lord" when certainty is previously lacking. There is no room for
manoeuvre under the old covenant, where bondage rather than liberty
grips the soul. In fact, a soul may well find itself in an impossible position,
but God is the God of the impossible, Matt. 19. 26.

Galatians 4. 22–31 deals with the distinction between bondage and
liberty, between "the liberty wherewith Christ hath made us free" and "the
yoke of bondage", 5. 1. The flesh and the Spirit are associated respectively
with Abraham's two sons, Ishmael and Isaac, 4. 29. The former is of
bondage—the son of the bondwoman Hagar. The latter is of promise—the

son of the freewoman, v. 30. The former relates to Sinai, "to Jerusalem which now is", the latter to "Jerusalem which is above". The only method of changing from one to the other is by the Spirit of God. The Spirit alone liberates through promise, and by faith unto life. Modern techniques cannot effect such a change. Only the Spirit enables one to be a minister of the new covenant, giving a hearer the power and liberty to receive the message.

18. "We all" embraces all believers who have tasted this liberty. "With open face" suggests that we take sides with Moses, not with the people who feared greatly. Believers are now unvailed, as was Moses in the presence of God. Initially we behold as in à glass the glory of the Lord. This does not refer to a modern mirror, where the reflection is clear and exact. Rather Paul implies a dim imperfect sight of the glory of the Lord, at the moment of changing from darkness to light, from the bondage of the old to the liberty of the new, when the heart turns to the Lord, in all its weakness and impotence. That is our side. The Spirit of God is then enabled to work, changing the seeking soul "into the same image from glory to glory". We are changed by the divine power, and transformed into that which we gaze upon, even Christ Himself

"From glory to glory" would indicate progress in the soul, initiated by the Spirit. More specifically in the context it would indicate a change from adhering to the glory of the old covenant to the surpassing glory of the new. Even Moses himself changed from one glory to the other, when he came down mount Sinai and appeared on the top of the mount of transfiguration. Finally, Paul stresses that it is by "the Spirit of the Lord", or, more properly, "the Lord the Spirit". The change is a miracle of accomplishment.

In chapter 4, Paul is going to deal with the vessel containing such glory. The apostle shows how a believer should radiate out this glory in spite of himself and the weakness of the vessel.

2 CORINTHIANS 4

Section 2. The Service of the True Minister
Subject 2. The Vessel of the Minister

Background of this Subject

The secret of Paul's service was two-fold. *God-ward,* he was "unto God a sweet savour of Christ", 2 Cor. 2. 15, while *saint-ward,* he did all things for the edifying of those whom he called "dearly beloved", 12. 19. The Spirit of God continues this great letter of commendation (chapters 3–6) for the benefit of those who have sensitive hearts to appreciate these secrets of service.

This letter brings before us every aspect of Paul's ministry. The message itself is described as the "ministration of the spirit . . . of righteousness . . . of the new testament", 3. 6, 8, 9, and the "ministry of reconciliation", 5. 18. But such ministry requires a minister, and a letter of commendation should describe the servant as well as the service, showing the consistency of the life of the servant engaged in such holy service. Hence chapter 4 deals with the motives of the minister *man-ward,* showing the frail vessel that God takes up for service. Chapter 5 deals with motives *God-ward,* in the light of the resurrection body and the judgment seat of Christ. Chapter 6 deals with the character of the minister, as well as with the position of separation that he must take for divine approval.

A summary of the chapter is as follows:

> Verses 1–2: *Transformation of the vessel.* The servant is open before all, with nothing done of an underhand nature.
>
> Verses 3–6: *Testimony of the vessel.* Christ is preached as from a vessel filled with light.
>
> Verse 7: *Treasure of the vessel.* This demands the manifestation of the power of God, the only thing which is of value when contrasted with the flesh.
>
> Verses 8–13: *Trouble of the vessel.* The life of Christ is manifest through persecution.
>
> Verses 14–18: *Trust of the vessel.* The inner man is renewed, while the outward man is to be raised.

Exposition of 2 Cor. 4: The Vessel of the Minister

Verses 1–2: Transformation of the Vessel

> 1 Therefore seeing we have this ministry, as we have received mercy, we faint not;
> 2 But have renounced the hidden things of dishonesty, not walking in craftiness, nor handling the word of God deceitfully; but by manifestation of the truth commending ourselves to every man's conscience in the sight of God.

1. In the previous chapter, Paul had contrasted the ministra-ion of Moses and the ministration of righteousness. Even for Moses the task had been too great, so others were chosen to assist him. Moses retained the highest functions, "Be thou for the people to God-ward, that thou mayest bring the causes unto God: and thou shalt teach them ordinances and laws, and shalt shew them the way wherein they must walk, and the work that they must do", Exod. 18. 19, 20. The other men, who had to judge "every small matter", v. 22, were men of spiritual character, "able men, such as fear God, men of truth, hating covetousness", v. 21. The strength of God was with Moses, so that at the end his natural force was not abated, Deut. 34. 7.

How much more would the ministration of the Spirit be a task greater than the vessel of the apostle could sustain. Yet he had the confidence that his sufficiency was of God, 2 Cor. 3. 5. He had received the ministry in the purpose of God, and God would provide, to see His servant through. Hence he writes "seeing we have this ministry, as we have *received mercy*, we faint not". Referring to his conversion, he wrote elsewhere that he had "*obtained mercy*", thus being put "into the ministry", 1 Tim. 1. 12, 13. He also *obtained mercy* to be a pattern of longsuffering to all who would believe, v. 16. Moreover, he had *obtained mercy* so as to offer apostolic advice when a direct commandment of the Lord was lacking, 1 Cor. 7. 25. But here in our verse, he *obtained mercy* so as not to *faint* in his task of proclaiming the Gospel. The Lord has shown that prayer is a safeguard to *fainting*, Luke 18. 1. Later Paul observed that he did not *faint* because his inward man was renewed day by day, 2 Cor. 4. 16, enabling him not to "*be weary* in well doing", Gal. 6. 9; 2 Thess. 3. 13. Hence Paul was transformed in strength, but verse 2 shows that he was also transformed morally.

2. Transformation involves the renewing of one's mind, Rom. 12. 2. Here, Paul lists three features of the old man which could not possibly live side-by-side with a renewed mind, in a minister of the Gospel.

Renounced the hidden things of dishonesty (or shame).These hidden things of shame are fit only for judgment, both in the unsaved, Rom. 2. 16; Jude 13, and in the saved, 1 Cor. 4. 5; Rev. 3. 18. Even in the Lord's case, the shame of the cross, Heb. 12. 2, was hidden from the eyes of men by the darkness, He sustained the judgment of God against sins not His own. A servant must renounce or disclaim all such things fit for judgment. (The Greek word for *renounce* occurs only once in the N.T.)

Nor walking in craftiness. By this means, a soul in darkness seeks to appear in the light, so as to drag a believer down to his own level. The chief priests sent spies to the Lord to tempt Him in this fashion, Luke 20. 23; the Ephesians were warned against such men and practices, Eph. 4. 14, while Satan himself takes this attitude when direct methods of darkness fail, 2 Cor. 11. 3.

Nor handling the Word of God deceitfully, or "not falsifying the Word of God". Many seek to turn the Word to their own advantage, by changing "the truth of God into a lie", Rom. 1. 25. But the devoted servant will say, "How sweet are Thy words unto my taste! yea, sweeter than honey to my mouth!" Ps. 119. 103

Paul would have dealings with the truth only. As such, he commended himself before God to all who loved the truth. He would not *preach* himself, 2 Cor. 4. 5, but he would *commend* himself by manifestation of the truth. As an apostle, he knew that he had to gain a hearing from the Lord's people, if the truth of God was to be spread abroad. This is why he commended himself in these valid ways. He commended himself in this first letter of commendation to those who would receive him. He adopts different tactics in the second letter of commendation, written to those who would not receive him, chapters 10–13. There, he would not commend himself, realising that it was the Lord's prerogative to commend, 10. 18.

Verses 3–6: Testimony of the Vessel

> 3 But if our gospel be hid, it is hid to them that are lost:
> 4 In whom the god of this world hath blinded the minds of them which believe not, lest the light of the glorious gospel of Christ, who is the image of God, should shine unto them.
> 5 For we preach not ourselves, but Christ Jesus the Lord; and ourselves your servants for Jesus' sake.
> 6 For God, who commanded the light to shine out of darkness, hath shined in our hearts, to *give* the light of the knowledge of the glory of God in the face of Jesus Christ.

3. "But if our gospel be hid, it is hid to them that are lost" must be understood in the light of the following verse. Paul is not referring to an evangelist who, through weakness or lack of zeal, fails to preach the gospel. There is no connection either with the word spoken to Ezekiel, "if the watchman see the sword come, and blow not the trumpet, and the people be not warned", Ezek. 33. 6. The evangelist may be as faithful as Paul, saying "woe is unto me, if I preach not the gospel", 1 Cor. 9. 16, and yet his gospel may be hid (or, veiled). The Lord Jesus was "the faithful and true witness", Rev. 3. 14, yet His holy teaching was often hidden through the interference of the powers of darkness. On other occasions, He deliberately caused the truth to be hidden, as in the case of the parables in Matthew 13; see Matt. 13. 11–16.

4. In this verse, it should be pointed out that "the god of this world" should read "the god of this age", and "the glorious gospel" of Christ should read "the gospel of the glory of (the) Christ", (see the R.V. and its margin).

Early expositors denied that Satan was implied by the phrase "the god of this world", and suggested that God Himself was preventing unbelievers from believing. This is objectionable, since the paragraph under discussion shows God providing preachers of Christ Jesus the Lord, so that men may come to a knowledge of the truth. Conversely, it is true that *first* Satan acts, and *then* God acts in the hearts of hardened unbelievers.

The "god of this world" is often called "the prince of this world" or "the prince of the power of the air", John 12. 31; 14. 30; Eph. 2.2. This personality—whether as an angel of light or of darkness—has power over the minds of men, but men are responsible for what they allow Satan to do. Moreover, he acts both on unbelievers and on believers.

> *The case of unbelievers*. When men have allowed Satan to influence them, when they "became vain in their imaginations, and their foolish heart was darkened", Rom. 1. 21, God steps in, and it is written that He "gave them up", vv. 24, 26. In Isaiah's day, Satan had already wrought in the hearts of men to such an extent that God steps in, "see ye indeed, but perceive not.... shut their eyes; lest they see with their eyes ... and convert, and be healed", Isa. 6. 9, 10. Similarly in the Lord's day. Satan had induced in the peoples' minds accusations of blasphemy against the Lord . Hence the Lord stepped in, and to such folk the mysteries of the kingdom of heaven were not given, Matt. 13. 11. Isaiah 6. 10 is quoted again, showing that the Lord will not tolerate blasphemous unbelief for long, vv. 13–15. See Hos. 4. 6; Acts 7. 42.

> *The case of believers*. Here we have a great contrast. Satan still seeks to influence their hearts by blinding them to the truth, but the Lord now works through His Spirit to counteract this. When the Lord Jesus told His disciples that He had to be crucified, using words that appear to us to be so plain, Luke 9. 45 and 18. 34 show that this saying was "hid from them" By whom? Certainly not by the Lord who desired them to know of these solemn things. But by the "god of this world", who had worked in Peter's heart on a similar occasion, Matt. 16. 21–23. The Lord graciously waited for the Holy Spirit to be sent to enlighten His own, and then blindness of heart gave way to a deep understanding of the death of Christ. This can be so today. Believers may fail to understand divine truth, but the Spirit is ever ready to guide us into all truth, John 16. 13.

It does not take much to blot out a great light. Our own eyelids are sufficient to shut out the most blinding light on earth. But what of "the light of the gospel of the glory of Christ, who is the image of God"? Men could not resist this, if there was not a power which blinded their eyes.

The word *image* in its physical sense means "a material image, likeness, effigy". The coin given to the Lord had the *image* of Caesar upon it, Matt. 22. 20. The book of Revelation contains ten references to "the *image* of the beast" ; Rev. 13. 14. Physically, man was created in the *image* of God, Gen. 1. 26–27; 1 Cor. 11. 7. Spiritually, believers are "conformed to the *image* of His Son", Rom. 8. 29; Col. 3. 10. But in all these examples, the image is distinct from the original substance. Optical images produced by a mirror or a lens are real or virtual, and they also are distinct from the original body from which the light comes. These ideas fail when applied to the Godhead, although the same words must be used. Christ is "the *image* of the invisible God", Col. 1. 15. The Father and the Son are *one*, yet no man has seen God at any time, but the only begotten Son has declared Him, John 1. 18. Those who have seen the Son have seen the Father, 14. 9; see Matthew 11. 27. This One is the brightness of His Father's glory, Heb. 1 . 3, "dwelling in the light which no man can approach unto", 1 Tim. 6. 16. In other words, all that can be seen and known of God must be seen and known in Christ. The reference to "His glory" in John 12. 41 suggests that all the manifestation of the glory of God in the O.T. was really the glory of Christ Himself before He became Man, since this glory was mutual, John 17. 5.

5. Even if the Gospel were hid (or, veiled), Paul would not use any other means to gain the ears of the unsaved. Under the guise of providing other means for reaching the hearts of blinded men today, entertainment provides many outlets for the flesh and for the misplacement of zeal. Paul had one subject of testimony, "we preach ... Christ Jesus the Lord". Elsewhere he declared that he would know nothing among the Corinthians "save Jesus Christ, and Him crucified", 1 Cor. 2. 2. Certainly nothing of Paul—nothing of the servant—would be proclaimed, except in taking the lowly position of a servant. Servants must not push themselves forward as objects of interest or of veneration. It is wrong for something to stand out in such a way that the emotions of the hearers are gained. If a preacher does not know that his manner displays himself rather than the Lord, he should be quietly warned that this is so. Paul writes adopted this lowly position "for Jesus' sake". In other words, the Lord relied on men like Paul to continue the testimony that He had started on earth.

> "Not I, but Christ," in lowly, silent labour;
>   "Not I, but Christ," in humble, earnest toil;
> Christ, only Christ! no show, no ostentation;
>   Christ, none but Christ, the gatherer of the spoil.

6. In verse 4 we have Satan's side, in verse 5 the servant's side, and in verse 6 God's side. Physically, God commanded (or merely, spoke) "the light to shine out of darkness". This is in keeping with Genesis 1. 3, "And God said, Let there be light", since darkness was upon the face of the deep. Light has no ultimate explanation although it is so fundamental. Men have produced their theories, and indeed are still doing so. Theories attempt to explain light in terms of something that is not light, namely in words or symbols. The ideas of waves and particles may help to explain the properties of light, but what light is in *itself* is a mystery known only to the Creator. The order of creation in the physical realm reflects the mind of God in the moral realm. Darkened hearts are enlightened before anything else can take place; He "hath shined in our hearts". But physically, light is often reflected or transmitted. (Only a black surface absorbs it completely with no effect produced outwardly.) The same with an enlightened soul; he becomes a source of testimony. A bell, when struck, is a source of sound. A heart, when enlightened, is intended "to give the light of the knowledge of the glory of God in the face of Jesus Christ".

The word "to give" is the Greek preposition *pros*, indicating the direction of intention. The word "light" is not the usual word; here it means "radiancy, illumination, shining forth". This implies the character of being able to give light rather than the light itself. Many editors of the Greek text omit "Jesus" at the end of the verse. Through preaching, the heart gives out the testimony of what it knows. What believers know is the "glory of God in the face of Christ". The works of Christ showed His glory, John 2. 11, but here Paul refers to something greater than His works. He refers to His Person. "His face did shine as the sun", Matt. 17. 2, is the ultimate of vision. The vessel of the servant is equipped by God to make this known and the dignity and solemnity of all preaching and service cannot be denied.

In their testimony the Lord's people are the light of the world, even as He was the Light of the world. As the Light, He shone "in darkness; and the darkness comprehended it not", John 1. 5. The world that God loves is also condemned (and that by themselves), "this is the condemnation, that light is come into the world, and men loved darkness rather than light, because their deeds were evil", 3. 19. Today, the gospel testimony of believers radiates outwards into the darkness. Apart from Christ, nothing else can pierce that darkness whatever may be the efforts of the evangelists concerned. Believers too, have to walk in the darkness of the world, though not of it. Their portion also is to receive the light, "We have a more sure word of prophecy; whereunto ye do well that ye take heed, as unto a light that shineth in a dark place, until the day dawn, and the day star arise in your hearts", 2 Pet. 1. 19.

Verse 7: Treasure of the Vessel

> 7 But we have this treasure in earthen vessels, that the excellency of the power may be of God, and not of us.

7. The purpose of God is that such treasures of extreme spiritual excellency should be contained, though temporarily, in "earthen vessels". The only other occasion where this word is used in the N.T. is in 2 Timothy 2. 20 where its use is uncomplimentary. This reference is to a vessel of the first creation, physically weak and persecuted, holding the blessed contents of the new creation. Illness, natural inability, ageing, and a sense of death all contribute to this weakness. In Paul's own experience, he had been blinded and cast down, Acts 9. 8; he had written, "the first man is of the earth, earthy.... we have borne the image of the earthy", 1 Cor. 15. 47, 49; he had "the sentence of death in ourselves" in Ephesus, where he had "despaired even of life", 2 Cor. 1. 8, 9; he regarded his body as "our earthly house of this tabernacle", 5.1; he had "a thorn in the flesh . . . to buffet" him, to avoid self-exaltation, 12. 7; and finally he described himself as "Paul the aged" Philem. 9. A vessel in this state is empty of everything which would prevent it from containing the treasure.

A work of art, placed in a museum which itself is an interesting historic building, will not get the attention it rightly deserves; there will be a conflict of interests. Similarly in the spiritual realm: this treasure is placed in earthen vessels so that attention may be directed to the treasure and not to the vessel. The excellency of the power of testimony must be seen to come from God and not from man. This word *excellency* means "surpassing, excelling character", and is used several times in this Epistle; for example, "the *abundance* of the revelations", 12. 7. The body was kept weak, so that "the power of Christ may rest upon me", 12. 9. By this means, Paul learned that "we should not trust in ourselves, but in God which raiseth the dead", 1. 9. Paul was always consistent in his exercises regarding this matter. In his first Epistle, he recalled his original manner when in Corinth, "I was with you in weakness . . . and in much trembling. And my speech and my preaching was not with enticing words of (man's) wisdom, but in demonstration of the Spirit and of power", 1 Cor. 2. 3, 4.

Outward display, fleshly ambition, financial gain, and desire to be known, characterise a vessel that God cannot use. Such would form a closed opaque vessel, completely hiding any treasure that might be contained therein. The Lord Jesus warned His followers about these dangers: "The light of the body is the eye: if therefore thine eye be single, thy whole body shall be full of light. But if thine eye be evil, thy whole body shall be full of darkness. If therefore the light that is in thee be darkness, how great is that darkness!" Matt. 6. 22–23. The vessel is full of what the eye takes in. A believer should therefore be full of heavenly treasure without distraction.

But light may be darkness, contrary to usual expectations. A convex lens pressed against a flat glass surface produces a black spot at the point of contact. Our everyday experience would make us wonder how a black spot could be produced where we would expect to find nothing but light. This black spot consists of a series of black concentric rings, known as Newton's rings, seen when magnified. They are formed due to a hidden property of light, its wave motion. Two distinct waves, if exactly superimposed, can cancel each other out and this happens between the lens and the glass surface. Spiritually, the singleness of the eye answers to one object before the heart. There can be no conflict and no cancellation. The treasure will be guarded. But if there are dual interests they will cancel each other out, and the treasure will become dim. The light within will be darkness. Such interests could be God and mammon, the desire for the power of God and the power of man, a double mindedness seeking on the one hand to testify for Christ and on the other to display oneself.

In the context, the treasure that Paul has in mind is the glory of the new covenant. He is referring to the light of the gospel of the glory of Christ, v. 4, and to the glory of God in the face of Christ, v. 6. The tabernacle in the wilderness was covered with badger skins on the outside, Exod. 26. 14. But priestly eyes could see the symbolic beauty of Christ inside, lit up by the light of the golden candlestick.

Verses 8–13: Trouble of the Vessel

8 *We are* troubled on every side, yet not distressed; *we are* perplexed, but not in despair;

9 Persecuted, but not forsaken; cast down, but not destroyed;

10 Always bearing about in the body the dying of the Lord Jesus, that the life also of Jesus might be made manifest in our body.

11 For we which live are alway delivered unto death for Jesus' sake, that the life also of Jesus might be made manifest in our mortal flesh.

12 So then death worketh in us, but life in you.

13 We having the same spirit of faith, according as it is written, I believed, and therefore have I spoken; we also believe, and therefore speak;

8–9. Paul continues to show that the vessel is kept low by the world's hatred for the testimony. The Lord uses the trouble, trial, and tribulation sustained by the vessel, so that He Himself may be manifested in it. In these two verses, Paul gives four troubles, with their effects. The effects are the exact opposite to what the world would have expected under such circumstances. The Lord promised this; *in Him* there would be peace, although *in the world* there would be tribulation, John 16. 33. The Lord Himself experienced this joy and peace even though the world was arrayed against Him, Matt. 11. 25; Luke 10. 21. We may consider these four contrasts as experienced by the Lord Jesus.

1. *Troubled on every side, yet not distressed.* This more properly means that Paul (or the Lord) was oppressed in every way, yet not straitened. In John 8. 12–59 we read of the verbal oppression placed upon the Lord by the Pharisees, yet His teaching was as full as ever. He maintained supreme calm, authority, and dignity.

2. *Perplexed, but not in despair.* In Matthew 11. 16–24 we find the Lord, speaking as man to men, apparently perplexed at the unrepentant cities. Yet He was never in despair, since He knew that the truth was revealed unto babes, v. 25.

3. *Persecuted, but not forsaken.* Men had persecuted Him during His life, John 15. 20, but He was never alone for the Father was with Him, 16. 32. Strange mystery of the cross! There, "they persecute Him whom Thou hast smitten", Ps. 69. 26, yet there He was forsaken of His God, Ps. 22. 1.

4. *Cast down, but not destroyed*. Men would seek to cast Him down from the brow of the hill on which the city of Nazareth was built, but He quietly went His way. Elsewhere angels would bear Him up in their hands when in a more moral sense men would seek to cast a stumbling stone before Him, Ps. 91. 12. The word *destroy* means perish, as the bottles in Matthew 9. 17 were rendered useless. But Paul would still be useful even though cast down mentally and spiritually for a season.

10–11. Paul realised that he was a fool for Christ's sake, 1 Cor. 4. 10. The circumstances that he sought, and his reactions to them, were exactly the opposite to the expectations of the world. He would always bear "about in the body the dying of the Lord Jesus". No doubt he primarily refers to the persecutions he endured as he was "delivered unto death for Jesus' sake"; indeed, he was "in deaths oft", 2 Cor. 11. 23. The immediate reference is to what he was suffering in Ephesus, 2 Cor. 1. 8–10, at the hands of many adversaries. The "sentence of death" would also embrace his mental anxiety caused by his grief for the Corinthians. In his *pre-conversion days*, he had persecuted the church of God, and the Lord Jesus counted this as sin committed against Himself, Acts 9. 4. *Now* such persecution fell upon the apostle, and he similarly counted this as relating to "the dying of the Lord Jesus". The Lord would feel for His servant suffering for His sake.

Morally, too, Paul counted himself as dead. He was "dead to the law", Gal. 2. 19, and "crucified with Christ". Having been baptised, he would daily recognise that he had been "buried with Him by baptism into death", Rom. 6. 4. He had become "dead to the law", Rom. 7. 4, describing the natural man as "the body of this death", v. 24. If all were dead, 2 Cor. 5. 14, then so was Paul, being in times past "dead in trespasses and sins", Eph. 2. 1.

All these passages make much of the glorious contrast referred to in verses 8-9. It was not a mere matter of words when the apostle writes "that the life also of Jesus might be made manifest in our body . . . in our mortal flesh". He lived, since Christ lived in him, Gal. 2. 20. His baptism demanded that he should walk in newness of life, in the likeness of His resurrection, Rom. 6. 5. We now serve in newness of spirit, 7. 6, since God has delivered us through Jesus Christ our Lord, v. 25. Those who were dead, but now believe, live unto Him, 2 Cor. 5. 15. We are quickened with Christ and raised up together, Eph. 2. 5–6. All these contrasts serve to show what life "more abundantly" really is, John 10. 10. The sheep are sustained by the same Life that passed the way of death before them, by the Good Shepherd who gave His life for the sheep. This is the life of Jesus within, when His life overcomes our weakness by the power of God, 2 Cor. 13. 4.

12. In this verse, "So then death worketh in us, but life in you", Paul refers to himself as in the previous verses. But what of Paul's reference to the Corinthians; is this a contrast? What life was in them?

On the surface, it looks as if Paul experienced "deaths oft" while the Corinthians enjoyed the best of life naturally. In this life, they were rich, 1 Cor. 4. 8, emulating Smyrna and Laodicea after them, Rev. 2. 9; 3. 17. They would eat, drink, and be merry, Luke 12. 19. But we must remember that Paul is writing to believers who had repented. The later phrase, "For all things are for your sakes", 2 Cor. 4. 15, suggests that Paul means his experience of death enabled the Corinthians to experience revival in their hearts, the life of Christ appreciated anew. A burdened servant will accomplish more for his converts than one who merely talks of numbers.

13. Paul finally quotes a passage from the Psalms, to show that his attitude towards a suffering vessel displaying light, is not something characteristic only of servants of the new covenant. Such servants have "the *same* spirit of faith" as men of God in the O.T. The quotation "I believed, and therefore have I spoken" is taken from Psalm 116. 10, and is intended to show that Paul endured the same things as the Psalmist.

As far as the Greek text is concerned, Paul has quoted from the Septuagint, the Greek version of the O.T. The English A.V. rendering of Psalm 116. 10 is similar, "I believed, therefore have I spoken", implying that a living faith in the heart will express its convictions with the mouth, Rom. 10. 10. Expositors of the Hebrew text, however, inform us that the Hebrew will not admit of such a rendering, and suggest the alternatives "I believe when I speak", or "I believe; for I must speak". Whatever the possible interpretation of the verse in Hebrew, it is certain that the Spirit of inspiration through Paul, had the liberty to alter slightly the meaning to suit His immediate purpose, by quoting the Greek version. Certainly Paul's readers would be able to understand the Greek version rather than the Hebrew text. Inspiration *then* may change a phrase when importing it into the N.T., but expositiors *now* have no liberty at all to alter the Word as written.

The bearing of Psalm 116 on Paul's subject is obvious. Faith leads to testimony even in a vessel marked by death. In verse 3, the Psalmist is compassed by the sorrows of death, and held by the pains of hell; he was brought low, v. 6; his soul was in death, v. 8; he was greatly afflicted, v. 10; the death of the saints of the Lord was precious in His sight, v. 15. No doubt this does not refer to physical death, but to a life surrendered to God but surrounded by men. In the midst of death he had deliverance and life, vv. 6, 8, 9, 16; he would walk before the Lord "in the land of the living". This recognition of the miracle of life in the place of death, appropriated by faith, brings forth testimony. It also brings forth public praise—the sacrifice of thanksgiving—in the courts of the Lord's house, vv. 17–19.

Verses 14–18: Trust of the Minister

14 Knowing that he which raised up the Lord Jesus shall raise up us also by Jesus, and shall present *us* with you.

15 For all things *are* for your sakes, that the abundant grace might through the thanksgiving of many redound to the glory of God.

16 For which cause we faint not; but though our outward man perish, yet the inward *man* is renewed day by day.

17 For our light affliction, which is but for a moment, worketh for us a far more exceeding *and* eternal weight of glory;

18 While we look not at the things which are seen, but at the things which are not seen: for the things which are seen *are* temporal; but the things which are not seen *are* eternal.

14. Paul possessed this life of Jesus during his sojourn here on earth. He would have been most miserable had he possessed this life *only* while here below, 1 Cor. 15. 19. Rather he had implicit trust in God who raises the dead. "Knowing" the reality of resurrection is no make-believe, but an anchor to the soul. Paul thus suffered many things, knowing "whom I have believed, and am persuaded that He is able to keep that which I have committed unto Him against that day", 2 Tim. 1. 12.

Paul's trust was in the resurrection power of God. This had been manifested in Christ, and this same "exceeding greatness of His power", Eph. 1. 19, will also be wrought in His people. This applies not only in the future but also now, so it shows the folly of trusting in our own power and methods in service. Our expectation is that God "shall raise up us also by Jesus". The A.V. translation should be corrected here, as in the R.V., to read "shall raise up us also *with* Jesus". This change occurs because the editors of the Greek text change the preposition *dia* to *sun*. It is true, of course, that we shall be raised "*by* Jesus"; see John 6. 39, 40, 44, 54, but that is not Paul's thought here. Rather Paul is thinking of the unity "with Jesus"; he refers to "Jesus, us, you". The Lord is supreme, then come the servants of the Lord who are in "death" now, and finally the many believers, not suffering as Paul did, who are in "life" now.

There will be no difference in that day; He shall present "us with you". In this verse the presentation is by God; elsewhere, it is by

the Lord: "Behold I and the children which God hath given Me", Heb. 2. 13;

Paul: "that we may present every man perfect in Christ Jesus", Col. 1. 28;

the believer: "present your bodies a living sacrifice, holy, acceptable unto God", Rom. 12. 1.

15. "For all things are for your sakes" refers to the things that Paul suffered on their behalf. Paul wanted not only grace to be received, but also to provoke a response. Believers receive their blessings through grace, so as to produce a response of thanksgiving to His glory. Blessings lead, not to self-occupation, but to thanksgiving and glory. Paul teaches the same thing in chapter 9 verses 11–15; the reception of material gifts leads to thanksgiving, vv. 11, 12, and to glorifying God, v. 13. The attitude of the heathen is exactly the opposite. When they received the knowledge of God in creation they *"glorified* Him not as God, neither were *thankful"*, Rom. 1. 21 .

16. Because of this trust in the resurrection and the presentation, "we faint not". Fainting may be caused by lack of food, or by the reduction of blood pressure as supplied to the brain. It may be prevented or rectified by arranging circumstances to provide that which is lacking. Similarly the Lord provides for His own now. He expects us to take what He provides to prevent spiritual fainting—becoming tired or disinterested in the service of God, or even giving up that to which we had originally committed ourselves. In Matthew 15. 32, the Lord would not send the people away in the wilderness, "lest they faint in the way"; rather He provided for their physical needs. In Hebrews 12. 3, we feed upon Himself by considering Him, lest we "be wearied and faint" in our minds. By this means, He enables us to continue in our labour of love in His Name, in spite of opposition or persecution, taking heed to the exhortation, "let us not be weary in well doing: for in due season we shall reap, if we faint not", Gal. 6. 9.

The outward man may more than faint, it may "perish". The apostle refers back to verse 11, "alway delivered unto death". This was his experience, "I die daily", 1 Cor. 15. 31; "For Thy sake we are killed all the day long", Rom. 8. 36. He describes this under different metaphors in the opening verses of the next chapter.

But Paul's trust was not only in the future, it was there in his present experience also, "the inward man is renewed day by day". Circumstances without required a constant renewing within. This renewing of the Holy Spirit had been experienced at conversion, Titus 3. 5; we can be "renewed in knowledge", Col. 3. 10, and "in the spirit of your mind", Eph. 4. 23. Such renewing of strength and conduct produces a transformation which is the exact opposite to all that the world would expect to see in an unconverted man, Rom. 12. 2.

17–18. Paul finally looks beyond the temporary stage of life. The present little-while yields "a far more exceeding and eternal weight of glory". Does glory have weight? It is calculated that fifty-eight thousand tons of light fall from the sun on to the earth every year. The sun radiates into space two hundred and fifty million tons of light a minute. The theory of relativity teaches us that mass can be changed into such radiated energy. No wonder then that affliction now works "a far more exceeding and eternal weight" of glory. The sufferings of Christ led to glory, Luke 24. 26; 1 Pet. 1. 11. Endurance now leads to glory, 2 Tim. 2. 10; 1 Pet. 4. 13; 5. 1.

Paul thrives on superlative descriptions; see Ephesians 3. 20 for another example. He also provides a series of contrasts in the two verses here:

    a moment—eternal;

    light—weight;

    affliction—glory;

    things seen—things not seen;

    temporal—eternal.

This Epistle and that to the Romans were written at about the same time. The same pressing thoughts and truths are found in both Epistles. The apostle wrote, "I reckon that the sufferings of this present time are not worthy to be compared with the glory which shall be revealed in us", Rom. 8. 18. His heart was upon the eternal things far off. The flesh may cherish things that can be seen and handled, but faith has its trust in better realities. Paul observed, "hope that is seen is not hope: for what a man seeth, why doth he yet hope for?" v. 24. A life at ease is not inclined to be interested in eternal things. When God speaks through suffering, pain and death in a home, man needs to think of deeper things. Theology may discard the eternal hope, but has nothing to comfort a soul in need. We need to remember that the former things shall pass away, Rev. 21. 4, and only that which is of Christ shall pass into the new creation.

2 CORINTHIANS 5

Section 2. The Service of the True Minister
Subject 3. The Object of the Minister

Background of this Subject

To those whose hearts he had gained in Corinth, Paul continues to show the whole panorama of the minister approved by God. Having dealt with the ministry of the servant occupied with the new covenant and not with the old, and having shown the features of the vessel that God chooses to herald this ministry to saint and sinner, the apostle now declares the object and aim of such a minister. Those who have this object before them have not received "the grace of God in vain", 2 Cor. 6. 1.

A summary of the chapter is as follows.

Verses 1–11. The future of the body and soul according to God. In the affliction of his vessel for the Corinthians, Paul is sustained by faith in eternal things.

Verses 12–17. The motivation of the minister in his service. The constraining love of Christ, v. 14, is basic in the exercises of the apostle.

Verses 18–21. The ministry of reconciliation. Here is Paul's object in his testimony as an ambassador for Christ in the world, v. 20.

Exposition of 2 Cor. 5: The Object of the Minister

Verses 1–11: The Future of the Body and Soul

1 For we know that if our earthly house of *this* tabernacle were dissolved, we have a building of God, an house not made with hands, eternal in the heavens.

2 For in this we groan, earnestly desiring to be clothed upon with our house which is from heaven:

3 If so be that being clothed we shall not be found naked.

4 For we that are in *this* tabernacle do groan, being burdened: not for that we would be unclothed, but clothed upon, that mortality might be swallowed up of life.

5 Now he that hath wrought us for the selfsame thing *is* God, who also hath given unto us the earnest of the Spirit.

6 Therefore *we are* always confident, knowing that, whilst we are at home in the body, we are absent from the Lord:

7 (For we walk by faith, not by sight:)

8 We are confident, *I say,* and willing rather to be absent from the body, and to be present with the Lord.

9 Wherefore we labour, that, whether present or absent, we may be accepted of him.

10 For we must all appear before the judgment seat of Christ; that every one may receive the things *done* in *his* body, according to that he hath done, whether *it be* good or bad.

11 Knowing therefore the terror of the Lord, we persuade men; but we are made manifest unto God; and I trust also are made manifest in your consciences.

In these verses, Paul distinguishes three distinct kinds of existences which the *majority* of believers will experience. The *minority* namely those "which are alive and remain unto the coming of the Lord", 1 Thess. 4. 15, will not experience the second of these. They will pass from the first to the third in "the twinkling of an eye", 1 Cor. 15. 52. Paul uses various metaphors to describe these three kinds of existences.

1. *The state of being physically in the body.* Paul continues the thought of the previous chapter, "our mortal flesh", 4. 11, "our outward man", v. 16. Here, the metaphors Paul uses to describe this existence are, "earthly house of this tabernacle", v. 1; "at home in the body", v. 6; "things done in his body", v. 10. The apostle thus refers to a vessel of affliction and groaning.

2. *The state when the physical body is in the grave*, between death and the resurrection at the return of the Lord. Paul describes this by the phrases, "found naked", v. 3; "unclothed", v. 4; "absent from the body", v. 8.

3. *The resurrection state*, when the conscious and spiritual inner man will be reunited to the body which has been raised. This is described by the words, "building of God", v. 1; "our house which is from heaven", v. 2; "clothed", v. 3; "mortality . . . swallowed up of life", v. 4.

The relationship of this subject to other references should be noticed. Prior to the resurrection of the Lord, *hades* (that is, hell) was the place of departed spirits while the bodies were in the grave. The A.V. often translates this word by "grave", but this introduces considerable confusion. A concordance or a more exact translation is needed to get round this error of the A.V. Hades consisted of two parts, the first containing those awaiting the resurrection of life, and the second those awaiting the resurrection of judgment, John 5. 29. Thus Lazarus was found in the first part known as "Abraham's bosom", Luke 16. 22, while the rich man was found in the second part, also described as "hell", v. 23. A great gulf prevented passage between the two parts, v. 26. During the days between the death of the Lord and His resurrection He was in hades, namely the first part, in keeping with Psalm 16. 10, quoted by Peter in Acts 2. 27, "Thou wilt not leave my soul in hell". The Lord's body was in the grave, as the quotation goes on to imply, "neither wilt Thou suffer Thine Holy One to see corruption". The Lord referred to this on the cross, when He said to the repentant malefactor, "Today shalt thou be with Me in paradise", Luke 23. 43, and Paul refers to it in Ephesians 4. 9, "He also descended first into the lower parts of the earth".

After Christ's resurrection, when believers die and are thus out of the body, they go to be with Christ, Phil. 1. 23. Until the return of Christ when the graves shall be opened, these believers will be "unclothed" and "absent from the body", although in the presence of Christ, no doubt in what is later called "the third heaven", 2 Cor. 12. 2. Hades has no room for believers now. Indeed we believe that the first part of hades, known as

Abraham's bosom, was emptied of its occupants as the Lord left it and ascended to heaven, in keeping with the scripture, "He led captivity captive", Eph. 4. 8.

At the Lord's coming, the soul and body of believers, who in this dispensation form His church, will be reunited in resurrection, as Paul writes elsewhere, "this corruptible must put on incorruption", 1 Cor. 15. 53. But those who die for the witness of Jesus in the period after the rapture of the church will remain "unclothed" for a season. This is clearly shown by what John saw, "I saw under the altar the *souls* of them that were slain for the word of God", Rev. 6. 9. These will be waiting for the "first resurrection", 20. 5, prior to the millennium. These events illustrate the principle of resurrection, "every man in his own order", 1 Cor. 15. 23. By way of contrast, the wicked dead will await resurrection at the end of the world.

1. The certainty of faith embraces a doubt, which is rather a remarkable concept. "We know that if" is distinct from "we know that when", since the "if" implies doubt. Faith does take this ground, because even in Paul's day the death of a believer was by no means certain. To an unbeliever, with no knowledge of the promised return of Christ, the death of any man is certain. But believers know that there is the certainty that one day Christians living on the earth will not taste of death. Hence Paul rightly talks about "*if* our earthly house of this tabernacle were dissolved".

The word "earthly" in the phrase "our earthly house" refers to its position. The present body is terrestrial in its sphere. For example, elsewhere Paul speaks of "bodies *terrestrial*", 1 Cor. 15. 40. The Lord used the word in John 3. 12, "If I have told you earthly things", namely things pertaining to the physical creation and understood by a rational mind. The word must be distinguished from a similar word in English, "the first man is of the earth, *earthy*", 1 Cor. 15. 47. This latter word refers to the composition of the body, *made of dust*. God originally formed man "of the dust of the ground", Gen. 2. 7.

The idea of a "house" means that the body is a dwelling place for the inner self. It is difficult for us to imagine the inner man detached from the body, so intimately are they connected in our present experience. But the future, anticipated by faith, is not guided by present experience, but by the Word of God. In the Lord's case, His holy body was the "temple" of His inner self, John 2. 21, truly God manifest in the flesh. In another sense, our bodies are the temple of the Holy Spirit, 1 Cor. 6. 19, "which is in you".

Paul adds that this is a "tabernacle", containing the thought of temporary conditions of pilgrimage. The tabernacle built by Moses was for wilderness conditions of pilgrimage, until a permanent structure should be built in the land. Peter uses the same word when he wrote, "shortly I must put off this my *tabernacle*", 2 Pet. 1. 14. The putting off reveals the inner man within. Paul uses the word "dissolved" to describe the end of the tabernacle. This word means destroyed, a word used by the Lord when referring to the temple in Jerusalem, "There shall not be left here one stone upon another, that shall not *be thrown down*", Matt. 24. 2. The disintegration of the temple, stone by stone, is similar to the dissolution of the body, since God had said that the body would return "unto dust" Gen. 3. 19. This in no sense negates the truth of resurrection, when the power of God will gather all things together again.

Paul's expectation was to have "a building of God", namely a new dwelling place for the soul. There will be a new heaven and a new earth, Rev. 21. 1, so it is not surprising that God will create all things new. Moreover, this building is a house "not made with hands", that is, it will be a miraculous construction. This is the same as our second birth, which was "not of blood, nor of the will of the flesh, nor of the will of man, *but of God*", John 1. 13. Of course our physical birth was not actually accomplished "with hands", since God Himself had initiated and maintained the complicated physiological and biochemical processes involved over the centuries. The phrase "with hands" means a physical rather than a spiritual act of God.

But the things "not made with hands" should form the chief interest of the people of God, since the character of such things is "eternal in the heavens". The "circumcision made without hands in putting off the body of the sins of the flesh", Col. 2. 11, lasts beyond the confines of time. Similarly in the Lord's case; in John 2. 19, all He said was "Destroy this temple, and in three days I will raise it up". The people would do the destroying, but the divine power would do the raising. The false witnesses in Mark 14. 58 changed the Lord's words to avoid the inconvenient reference to His charge that men would destroy Him, "We heard Him say, I will destroy this temple that is made with hands, and within three days I will build another made without hands". The folly of man is made to speak the truth during this attempt at false witness; their added words in reference to "made with hands" and "made without hands" appear to be in order. But when every tongue will confess that Jesus Christ is Lord, Phil. 2. 11, truth only will be wrung from their lips with no possibility of a mixture of truth and error.

2. Meanwhile, awaiting that day, believers express their inward sighs of deep aspiration for these better things (that is, they "groan"). If spiritual intelligence is lacking as to what God has prepared for the future, the afflictions of the present life will lead only to *moaning*. This is a natural sentiment, contrasted with the spiritual sentiment of *groaning*. These aspirations are that one should be clothed upon with one's "house which is from heaven". This suggests something to *surround* the present body when it is changed in resurrection. Believers put on immortality or incorruption as the case may be, 1 Cor. 15. 53. This surrounding by something put on occurs in present experience. Examples are:

> Romans 6. 17, "ye have obeyed from the heart that form of doctrine which was delivered you". This is like a mould surrounding a jelly. From the mould it takes its exact shape.

Galatians 3. 27, we have "put on Christ".

1 Kings 8. 4 suggests that the tabernacle was brought up to Jerusalem at the dedication of the temple in order to be placed inside it. Then only the new order would be seen in its permanence, with the temporary old order kept out of sight.

The phrase "which is *from* heaven" implies that something definite comes from heaven with the Lord, in addition to the change at the resurrection. We rise to meet the Lord, and He has the resurrection clothing with Him. The clothing will have a character derived from heaven. Christ-likeness will then be as complete as is consistent with the purposes of God. The apostle's desire goes beyond what he expressed later in Philippians 1. 21–24, namely to be with Christ, but not clothed upon. The reason for the difference may lie in the fact that in Philippians, the thought of still abiding in the flesh for service was in the apostle's mind, whilst in 2 Corinthians 5, such service as an ambassador for Christ is in a different paragraph (verses 18–21).

3. Paul now contrasts the desired state of "being clothed" with the state of being "naked", referring to the temporary period when the body is in the grave, but the soul with Christ.

4. Again Paul stresses the ultimate desire in resurrection, for the complete glorified body, Phil. 3. 21. Then mortality "will be swallowed up of life". In resurrection, the human form will still exist but will be embraced into the interior so that the clothing of the life in Christ alone may be seen. The same thought appears in 1 Corinthians 15. 54. "Death is swallowed up in victory". This does not refer to the second death which has power over the unbeliever. It refers to the change wrought in the corruptible or in the mortal, now that physical death is at an end (the body either being susceptible to it or having passed through it).

Paul states that believers are "burdened". This does not contain any element of fear. Prior to Christ and His death, men had been in bondage through fear of death, Heb. 2. 15. But Paul's burden was the affliction of the vessel described at the end of 2 Corinthians 4. The perishing of the outward man, 4. 16, induced the burden, but faith induced the groaning.

5. Paul now shows that these great facts are not something only for the future. He indicates that present-day believers possess two things now in relation to the future.

1. *Capacity for change.* God has "wrought us" for this self same thing, that is our bodies are already prepared for this future change. In the realm of nature our bodies have a certain capacity for healing a wound to restore its original condition. A caterpillar has the inherent mechanism within itself for its future metamorphosis into a butterfly. In the spiritual and miraculous realm, our bodies have the essential mechanism for a glorious change, so that the

body may, either before or long after death, react with its house
and clothing from heaven, to form its new body "fashioned like
unto His glorious body". The power that God wrought in Christ
when He raised Him from the dead, Eph. 1. 20, is latent in His
people, awaiting the day when it shall be released.

2. *Capacity for certainty*. Believers are not expected vainly to try and
    convince themselves of the reality of this hope. Faith is not an
    effort of self-deception against rational reasoning based solely on
    present experiences. Rather the Holy Spirit has been given as the
    "earnest", or pledge, or deposit. According to the Oxford
    Dictionary, the word "earnest" means "Money paid as an
    instalment to confirm a contract". One reason for the possession
    of the Spirit, is that He might be a confirmation to faith of the
    reality to come and of the certainty of God's declared purposes.
    In 2 Corinthians 1. 22, the apostle again mentions the "earnest of
    the Spirit in our hearts", relating to the certainty of the
    accomplishment of the will of God in one's daily life. Finally, in
    Ephesians 1. 14, the earnest is stated as being the pledge of our
    future inheritance, this pledge being possessed *until* the
    "redemption of the purchased possession".

6–8. In the light of these *two* grounds for certainty, the apostle states
that he is also confident in *two* distinct things. The particular form of
Greek word used for "confident" (or bold) occurs only six times in the
N.T., five of them in this Epistle. We have therefore a man confident in
many ways in this letter, both in the future experience of the body and in
the restoration of his converts, 7. 16. The certainty granted by the
indwelling Spirit is not attained by natural means; "we walk by faith, not
by sight". The religion of nature around may lead the contemplative mind
to the appreciation of a Creator God, but that is "sight". The things that
God has prepared for those who love Him are known by the Spirit dwelling
within; these are known only by "faith". Anyone claiming to have the
former knowledge, yet showing no interest or belief in the Word of God,
can hardly be described as a child of God and born again.

Paul's confidence relates to two states of existence, namely the first two
described on page 316; in God's good time the third final and most blessed
state will follow.

1. Verse 6 refers to the believer's life here and now, "at home in the
    body, . . . absent from the Lord". This is the vessel of groaning,
    but with the pledge of eternal things to come. Being absent from
    the Lord does not negate such promises as "I am with you alway",
    Matt. 28. 20; "the Lord stood by him", Acts 23. 11; "the Lord
    stood with me", 2 Tim. 4. 17. Paul refers to being absent from the
    Lord *on high*, not to the Lord's presence *here below*.
2. Verse 8 refers to the intermediate state between death and the
    resurrection day at His coming again. The believer would be

absent from the body (in the grave) and present with the Lord (on high). Hades does not come into the picture at all. Paul was willing to end his years of affliction to enter into this second state, knowing that the third and final state of being clothed awaited him.

9. Paul finally brings his hopes down to the level of responsibility, by writing "Wherefore we labour, that, whether present or absent, we may be accepted of Him". A casual reading of this may suggest that the glorious future just described rests after all on our present responsibility and labour. Such a notion must be dispelled. The word "labour" does not mean "work in service". The word only appears three times in the Greek N.T. (see Romans 15. 20, "so have I *strived*"; 1 Thess. 4. 11, "that ye *study* to be quiet"). The word properly means "to be ambitious for honour", or "to be ambitious", or even "zealous" as some translators give. It refers to the motives of a believer possessing diligence towards the object in view.

"Whether present or absent" appears to refer to being present in the body or absent from the body (namely in the order of verses 6 and 8), rather than present with the Lord or absent from the Lord. But whichever way is understood, the implication is the same. Paul refers to both states described in verses 6 and 8. Paul does *not* say that he wants to be ambitious when in the second state. He is ambitious *in the present life*, so that *both now* and in *the future* he may be "well pleasing" unto God. The translation "may be accepted" presents quite a wrong picture. The word used has nothing to do with the blessed fact that believers are accepted in Christ on the grounds of grace alone, Eph. 1. 6. The word means "well-pleasing" (see Hebrews 13. 21, "working in you that which is *wellpleasing* in His sight, through Jesus Christ"). As those who have been accepted in Christ, are we ambitious that everything about us and in our service should provide our God with pleasure both now and in the future? We must confess that there is much chaff with the wheat in our conduct and service. The wheat will be well-pleasing unto God, but the chaff must be discarded, as it will be at the judgment seat of Christ.

10. The certainty of the judgment seat of Christ shows that we have a responsibility now towards the future resurrection body. A very careful distinction must be drawn between this judgment seat and the judgment of the great white throne, Rev. 20. 11–15. Every feature of the latter is distinct from that of the former. If believers ever confuse the two, or even identify them, it shows that they are not living in the light of the truth of imputed righteousness. The great white throne relates to *judicial* judgment, whilst the judgment seat of Christ pertains to *governmental* judgment. In the present life, believers are saved from judicial judgment since Christ "bare our sins in His own body on the tree", 1 Pet. 2. 24. Grace removes condemnation due to guilt. But during our present lives, God *still* sees the bad even though we are forgiven. His governmental judgment is always abroad upon His people in one way or another. For example, in Corinth many were "weak and sickly . . . and many sleep", 1 Cor. 11. 30, because of their attitude to most holy things, namely the Lord's supper. Are we to suppose that their physical removal from this scene through death also implied an end of God's governmental judgment? Not at all; their lives—"whether ... good or bad"—will be reviewed at the judgment seat. This is not as a judicial judgment with punishment in store, but to finalise once and for all the corrective process of separating the wheat from the chaff. The result will be that the bride will have made herself ready, with the fine linen being "the *righteousnesses* of the saints", Rev. 19. 8, J.N.D., or "the righteous *acts* of the saints". R.V. The word is in the plural, not in the singular as in the A.V. The state of righteousness is imputed through the work of Christ, but righteous acts manifested in that day come from one's present life and service.

Paul says that "every one may receive the things done in his body, according to that he hath done, whether it be good or bad". The word for *receive* in this verse is not the word usually employed to designate this meaning. It is a word with a special connotation, meaning to get by earning. Hence Peter writes about the elders who, through their labours, "shall *receive* a crown of glory that fadeth not away", 1 Pet. 5. 4. By contrast (and not at the judgment seat of Christ), the unjust "shall *receive* the reward of unrighteousness", 2 Pet. 2. 13. Again, if a servant has accomplished good service, "the same shall he *receive* of the Lord", Eph. 6. 8. By contrast,* a servant "that doeth wrong shall *receive* for the wrong which he hath done", Col. 3. 25. The same idea occurs in our verse 10. The review is for payment, but God has only good things as a reward for good service and conduct, 1 Cor. 3. 14. The chaff will be burned, in which case the man would "suffer loss" although saved, v. 15. He suffers the loss of the reward that would otherwise have been his.

When Paul writes that we "must all appear", the word "appear" means more than merely standing before the judgment seat. The word means "to be manifested". In Luke 12, the Lord warned His own of this manifestation, "there is nothing covered, that shall not be revealed; neither hid, that shall not be known. Therefore whatsoever ye have spoken in darkness shall be heard in the light; and that which ye have spoken in the ear in closets shall be proclaimed upon the housetops", vv. 2, 3. Believers may be saved from the exposure of that day by exposing themselves to the light now, so that any hypocrisy may be unmasked and put away. The Lord was warning His own against leaven, and we may notice:

> leaven of the Herodians, Mark 8. 15 – this is worldliness;
> leaven of the Sadducees, Matt. 16. 6, 12 – this refers to rationalism, wisdom and superstition;
> leaven of the Pharisees, Luke 12. 1 – this refers to formalism, ritualism and hypocrisy.

Elsewhere we find the leaven of impurity, 1 Cor. 5. 7; the leaven of

---

*This same Greek word is used in the Greek version of the O.T. in Leviticus 20. 17, "He shall *bear* his iniquity".

doctrinal unsoundness, Gal. 5. 9; the leaven of evil teaching, Matt. 13. 33.

The reader should not fail to notice the other primary passages dealing with the judgment seat, and the point of view that each passage presents. These are:

Romans 14. 10–12: assessment of *motives for conduct.*

2 Corinthians 5. 10: assessment of *conduct.*

1 Corinthians 4. 5: assessment of *motives for service.*

1 Corinthians 3. 13–15: assessment of *service.*

11. Paul concludes with practical lessons. We must distinguish the persons involved in these verses. When Paul writes "we" in verses 10 and 11, he refers to believers. But when he writes "we persuade *men*", he clearly refers to another class, namely the *unsaved*. The terror of the Lord is not related to the judgment seat of Christ but to the final judicial judgment of the ungodly. This was Paul's motive in preaching the Gospel, to deliver men from the terror of that day. By means of this service, "we are made manifest unto God". The previous verse links with this manifestation, *not* with the terror. Moreover, the Greek perfect tense is used here. Paul has *already* been manifested unto God, and the results of it are still continuing both to the time when Paul was writing and to the future judgment seat. All service should be accomplished in the light of that day. A manifestation of faithfulness both now and then ensures that the believer is well-pleasing unto God, "whether present or absent", v. 9.

Paul adds a phrase for the particular benefit of the Corinthians: "I trust also (we) are made manifest in your consciences". If God recognises the zeal and labour of the apostle, so should the Corinthians. This recognition was one of the apostle's burdens as he wrote the letter. Moreover today, all believers should learn to recognise the manifestation of Paul's service, so that it may be directly applied to them, without the gainsaying of an invented or a developed religious tradition.

Verses 12–17: The Motivation of the Minister

12 For we commend not ourselves again unto you, but give you occasion to glory on our behalf, that ye may have somewhat to *answer* them which glory in appearance, and not in heart.

13 For whether we be beside ourselves, *it is* to God: or whether we be sober, *it is* for your cause.

14 For the love of Christ constraineth us; because we thus judge, that if one died for all, then were all dead:

15 And *that* he died for all, that they which live should not henceforth live unto themselves, but unto him which died for them, and rose again.

16 Wherefore henceforth know we no man after the flesh: yea, though we have known Christ after the flesh, yet now henceforth know we *him* no more.

17 Therefore if any man be in Christ, *he is* a new creature: old things are passed away; behold, all things are become new.

12. Paul recognised various reasons which motivated and prompted his inner man, so that he might be given over to the service of God. In the previous verse 11, he thinks of the unsaved before the terror of the Lord, and he considers himself manifested unto God as well-pleasing. Later, he dwells on the constraining love of Christ, v. 14.

In verse 12, Paul distinguishes between outward show and inward loyalty. The majority in Corinth now appreciated Paul as the sent one of God, manifesting inward loyalty to Christ rather than outward show to gain the glory of man. But the minority in Corinth, who were causing division and unhappiness in the assembly by their attitude, would rather be satisfied with a man who gloried "in appearance, and not in heart". In other words, this minority wanted outward show only. It is always difficult for a faithful assembly to deal with a minority group intent upon going their own way, regardless of the effect being produced upon the assembly as a whole. But Paul placed the manifestation of his own service into the hands of the faithful, so that they could use this as a confirmation of their own position, as a lever to influence the minority to repentance. Such a manifestation of self would, of course, be distasteful to a spiritual man, although accomplished with good motives. How quickly Paul brings Christ into the situation, v. 14.

The desire for outward show is very subtle, showing itself in many ways. Carnality in service, or taking a prominent position in a local assembly by "being lords over God's heritage", 1 Pet. 5. 3, are ways in which outward show may rear its ugly head. Examples in the N.T. are many and various:

> Luke 22. 24: After the institution of the supper, there was strife amongst the disciples, "which of them should be accounted the greatest". Greatness is the gain of lowly service not the pomp of outward display.
>
> Matthew 20. 21: The desire of an unwarranted position, uniquely, seated at the right hand and the left hand of the Lord, with all other saints displaced to make room for the two.
>
> Acts 8. 9: Simon bewitched the people of Samaria, displaying himself as a great one.

13. Paul had no ulterior motive in displaying somewhat of himself, namely that which Christ had wrought in him, Rom. 15 . 18. Yet the apostle takes great care in what he writes. Was he right or wrong in displaying himself, even if the end of his exercise was right? In this present verse, we suggest that Paul makes allowance for either situation.

> *If he were wrong*, he excuses himself with the words, "For whether we be beside ourselves, it is to God". In its middle form, this verb means "to put oneself out of place", and is usually translated "to be astonished, amazed". One's usual calm approach to events is

displaced by something unusual. Only twice is the word translated "to be beside oneself"; see Mark 3. 21, referring to the Lord Jesus. Paul suggests that he may have placed himself outside his usual calm approach, no doubt unwittingly. If this were so, even if men did not understand, God would. He knew the motive of His servant. Other expositors feel that Paul's ecstacy was deliberately before God and not before men.

But if Paul were right, he writes, "whether we be sober, it is for your cause". This word "sober" and its derivatives contain the idea of being in one's senses, in one's right mind. It is the opposite of the previous word "to be beside oneself". The man who was "possessed with the devil, and had the legion" was "in his right mind" after being cured by the Lord, Mark 5. 15. This is an example of the use of the word in the Gospels. Such a manner of thinking is not centred on self, but "according as God hath dealt to every man the measure of faith", Rom. 12. 3. Paul's thinking could be described like this, and the results of such sober thought should be seen in the Corinthians. Paul thought clearly about divine things, and he desired all believers to do so, "Young men likewise exhort *to be sober minded*", Titus. 2. 6.

14. The motives of Paul originated from deeper considerations than his desire to help the Corinthians deal with a few rebels in their midst. The love of Christ constrained him.

> "Because Thou dost accept me,
>   I love Thee and adore!
> Because *Thy* love constraineth,
>   I'll praise Thee evermore!"

This verb *constrain* means literally "to hold together", and is used in many different contexts in the N.T. Examples occur in Matthew 4. 24, where sick people "*were taken with*" many diseases; Luke 8. 45, where multitudes *thronged* the Master; Luke 12. 50, where the Lord said He *was straitened* till His baptism should be accomplished. The reader will note the common implication of the word—a body held in or a mind held down. In Paul's case, he *was pressed* in the spirit on one occasion, Acts 18. 5, while later he wrote that he *was in a strait* between two desires, to depart or to remain, Phil. 1. 23.

The mind of Paul was wholly governed by the love of Christ. There was no law, no forceful vertical walls of rock, Num. 22. 24–26, to keep him on the straight and narrow way of devotion, conduct and service. The love of Christ was a superior spiritual force to keep the apostle in all his ways. Moreover, he explains how he came to be under this constraint. The reason is that the sacrifice of Christ requires believers not to live for themselves, but "unto Him that died for them, and rose again", 2 Cor. 5.15.

"Were the whole realm of nature mine,
    That were an offering far too small;
Love so amazing, so divine,
    Demands my soul, my life, my all".

15. The apostle's exercise was based on his judgment "that if one died for all, then were all dead: and that He died for all, that they which live should not henceforth live unto themselves, but unto Him which died for them, and rose again". The stamp of death is upon all men, being shown very clearly by the fact that the Lord died "for all". None was excluded, no one was exempt from sin and its consequences. But "death passed upon *all* men, for that *all* have sinned", Rom. 5. 12; "*all* the world . . . guilty before God", 3. 19; "*all* have sinned, and come short of the glory of God", 3. 23; "God hath concluded them *all* in unbelief, that he might have mercy upon all", 11. 32.

Although Christ truly died for all, and although the death of the Man necessitated the death of all men, yet salvation accomplished on the cross is not received by all. As Paul says, He died for all, but *only* "they which live" are blessed. In Romans 3. 22, the apostle makes the distinction very clear; the faith of Jesus Christ is "unto all", but it is *only* "upon all them *that believe*". God loved the world, *but* not all the world will be saved. The Lord gave Himself a "ransom for all", 1 Tim. 2. 6, but *only* Christians know that He gave Himself for them, Titus 2. 14, and for the Church, Eph. 5. 25. In Matthew 13. 44, *all* the field was bought, but *only* the treasure was gained for Himself.

Believers, then, by the very fact that Christ died for them, were dead already prior to their conversion. Any life that we possess now originates from His resurrection life. The Lord said, "I . . . was dead; and, behold, I am alive for evermore", Rev. 1. 18, and believers must pass the same way if they are to be of service to Him. We must reckon ourselves "to be dead indeed unto sin, but alive unto God through Jesus Christ our Lord", Rom. 6. 11. We must now yield ourselves to God, "as those that are alive from the dead", v. 13. Thus believers cannot please God if they seek to gain the "best of both worlds". The natural man and the new spiritual man in Christ cannot dwell together. His death means our death, and certainly His resurrection life will not raise again "our old man" and his deeds. Only His life in us now avails before God. Paul appreciated this when he wrote, "I live; yet not I, but Christ liveth in me: and the life which I now live in the flesh I live by the faith of the Son of God, who loved me, and gave Himself for me", Gal. 2. 20.

16. Paul's judgment had been that he wanted to know men on resurrection ground only. There was no value in knowing men who were dead. It should be noticed that Paul is taking spiritual ground here, not physical ground. Of course in his day-by-day relations with men around he knew them after the flesh physically. But that is not the point of the passage at all. Spiritually he had no contact, no common ground, no common point of view, no fellowship with men in the world. He could only have contact and fellowship with those in whom the life of Christ was dwelling. "Wherefore henceforth know we no man after the flesh" shows that the constraining love of Christ keeps His people from such unsavoury contacts.

It follows that the following sentence, "yea, though we have known Christ after the flesh, yet now henceforth know we Him no more" must also refer to moral and spiritual issues. Expositors differ as to what this means. We cannot agree with the suggestion that Paul had known Christ in His lifetime as a Man amongst men, having been in the multitudes that had seen His miracles and heard His teaching, but that now this was forgotten in favour of knowing Him only as raised on high. John the apostle rejoiced in the recollection of his contact with that holy life even in his later ageing years, 1 John 1. 1. Believers must seek an answer to the question: the life that we live now, is it based on His life before His death, or on His life as raised after His death? The difference is vital. Before His death, He came to minister to Israel; after His death He now ministers to the Church. Before His death, the apostles were forbidden to preach to the Gentiles, Matt. 10. 5–6, but after His death this was cancelled in Matthew 28. 19, the testimony going to the uttermost parts of the earth, Acts 1. 8. After His death, He introduced our relation to His Father and His God, John 20. 17, absent from John's Gospel prior to this resurrection scene. Mary could not touch Him in this context; the previous relationship had been broken, but the new one was not yet completely forged until the Lord ascended on high. This, of course, in no way contradicts the Lord's invitation in Luke 24. 39 to touch Him; the context is different, being one of proving the resurrection of the *body*.

17. As we have said before, the life of Christ now raised does not resurrect the natural man of the flesh. Those who are born of God are "a new creature", or "a new creation" as it should be translated. The passing of the old, and the bringing in of the new are works of God. This newness is an accomplished act. The Greek perfect tense is used to describe its introduction, the verb "are become" not only implying an act in the past, but also the continuation of its blessed results up to the present. The work of changing the old for the new is characteristic of God's method for introducing things pleasing to Himself. Israel would have a "new heart and a new spirit", Ezek. 18. 31, while in the end times there will be "a new heaven and a new earth" to replace the former things, Rev. 21. 1. Such a work of God in the soul demands the corresponding response from us in responsibility. We are to "put off" and to "put on", Eph. 4. 22, 24; Col. 3. 8, 12. By these means we then "walk in newness of life", Rom. 6. 4.

The incompatibility of the new with the old is shown by the Lord in Matthew 9. 16–17; the old garment could not sustain the new cloth, while the new wine could not be put into old bottles. Here, there is a *religious* rather than a *moral* element in view. The old garment and the old bottles represent Judaism, either as men had made it "in meat, or in drink, or in respect of an holyday, or of the new moon, or of the sabbath days", Col. 2. 16, or as God had instituted the righteousness and ceremony of the law. Christianity is not Judaism added to, but it is a new beginning via the new birth. Men were slow to learn this in the Acts; the believing Jews resisted Paul's efforts, while today religious systems are often still based on O.T. ritual, with priests, altars and choirs.

Verses 18–21: The Ministry of Reconciliation

18 And all things *are* of God, who hath reconciled us to himself by Jesus Christ, and hath given to us the ministry of reconciliation;
19 To wit, that God was in Christ, reconciling the world unto himself, not imputing their trespasses unto them; and hath committed unto us the word of reconciliation.
20 Now then we are ambassadors for Christ, as though God did beseech *you* by us: we pray *you* in Christ's stead, be ye reconciled to God.
21 For he hath made him *to be* sin for us, who knew no sin; that we might be made the righteousness of God in him.

18. The thought of this verse follows on from the previous one, but Paul now introduces another object of his life. Previously in this chapter, we have had his object as *the judgment seat* of Christ, v. 10, and then his object towards the *Corinthians*, vv. 12–13. Now we have his object *to the world* as an ambassador for Christ, v. 20.

In the putting away of the old and the creation of the new, the essential personality remains. This is dealt with by the process of reconciliation unto God by Christ (the word "Jesus" is omitted by the best texts). This refers to the removal of the barrier created by enmity between man and his God. Such enmity was *on the part of man*, as Romans 5. 10 and Colossians 1. 20 amply show. We are reconciled to God, not *vice versa*. Ephesians 2. 11–18 is the great passage dealing with reconciliation. The work is *entirely the work of God*: "made nigh by the blood of Christ", v. 13; "He is our peace", v. 14; "having abolished the enmity", v. 15; "to make in Himself of twain one new man, so making peace", v. 15; "that He might reconcile both unto God . . . by the cross", v. 16; "came and preached peace", v. 17; "through Him we both have access by one Spirit unto the Father", v. 18. These quotations show that reconciliation (of the Jews who were nigh, and of the Gentiles who were far off) is no mere doctrine. It affects our whole being and relationship with God, introducing us into the fellowship of others similarly reconciled, namely into the assembly. Appreciating such nearness to God, believers have a corresponding ministry, namely the service of reconciliation, or the "word of reconciliation" as verse 19 gives. This word "ministry" is really "deacon service", showing how far the work of deacons transcends the level of mundane things to which some believers would reduce it.

19. This appears to refer to the *ministry* of Christ rather than to His *work* to accomplish reconciliation *through death*; verse 21 refers to this latter side of the truth. Here, rather, we have the ministry of the Man in whom God was, "for God was with Him", Acts 10. 38. This One brought peace, v. 36, to sin-stricken hearts, and their sin was not brought up again by the Lord when it had been dealt with. In Luke 7. 48, the woman was reconciled to Him with her sins forgiven; in John 4, the woman found peace after the exposure of her sin and the confession of her heart; in John 8, the woman found peace with no condemnation from the Lord. Sin was not imputed or reckoned to these souls again, after they had had dealings with Christ.

20. This One who preached peace is no longer in the world to accomplish such a gracious ministry. Believers are now His "ambassadors" to continue His work (see Ephesians 6. 20 for the only other occurrence of this word in the N.T.). Moreover, as God was in Christ, so too God beseeches today through His people.

Note that the word "you", occurring twice in italics in the A.V., is not in the Greek. Paul is *not* beseeching the Corinthians to be reconciled to God; they already were, even though they now lived in spiritual weakness. Rather, Paul quotes his general object *towards the world*. Paul knew that he spoke "in Christ's stead", namely replacing the testimony of the Man in verse 19. "Be ye reconciled to God" is the general plea to a world whose thoughts and whose ways are as far off from God as the heavens are higher than the earth, Isa. 55. 8.

21. By the cross alone can reconciliation be effected, and righteousness imputed. This was the goal of the Lord's life, as "He steadfastly set His face to go to Jerusalem", Luke 9. 51. The barrier of sin could only be removed by ensuring that it was displaced "as far as the east is from the west", Ps. 103. 12.

The sacrifice was perfect; He was One "who knew no sin". The testimony of others was that "in Him is no sin", 1 John 3 . 5, and that He "did no sin", 1 Pet. 2. 22. Mystery supreme that this One should be made sin, but God had no other way. The Saviour was made a curse as He hung in death, Gal. 3. 13; He had borne "our sins in His own body on the tree", 1 Pet. 2. 24; indeed the Lord had "laid on Him the iniquity of us all", Isa. 53. 6. The sufferings of Christ had been foretold long beforehand by ceremony and by the prophets. God's heart was full as He awaited the event when His hour was come. Although made sin, this blessed One still maintained in Himself the intrinsic perfection of His Godhead. He was at the same time both the sin offering and the burnt offering. The former brought shame to Himself, the latter glory to His God and Father.

Through this work, believers are now made righteous, and in this grace they carry the message of reconciliation through the blood of His cross, to all who will listen to their proclamation.

2 CORINTHIANS 6

Section 2. The Service of the True Minister
Subject 4. The Character of the Minister

Background of this Subject

This chapter concludes the section dealing with the service of any sincere minister of Christ. Attention is directed to the character of the servant. In the first three verses, Paul beseeches all servants of Christ that they should possess their salvation keeping a purpose in view. To assist in his exhortation, the apostle uses the example of Christ. This appears in verse two in rather a hidden style, but the examination of this O.T. quotation will make the matter clear. From verse 4 to verse 10, Paul enumerates twenty-eight features of the character of those whom he calls "workers together". In the English translation, these features are obviously divided into three groups:

1. ten features in verses 4–5, introduced by "in", referring to the outward circumstances of the minister;
2. eleven features in verses 6–8, introduced by the word "by", referring to the inward character of the minister;
3. seven features in verses 8–10, introduced by "as", providing various contrasts experienced by the minister.

Such was Paul, so in verses 11–13 he desires that the Corinthians should also be enlarged to embrace these blessed features of Christ. Yet enlargement has its dangers, so in verses 14–18 (including verse 1 of the following chapter 7) he shows that one cannot go beyond the divinely appointed bounds of sanctification in one's enlargement. This latter paragraph has caused much difficulty because readers fail to see its relevance to and connection with its own context.

God has standards to maintain in a local assembly, and these are much more exacting than standards in earth-bound institutions such as schools, hospitals and clubs. These standards are maintained by the practical outworking of holiness, under which we are set apart, not to man's will, but to God's will and boundaries, as it is written, "Upon the top of the mountain the whole limit thereof round about shall be most holy", Ezek. 43. 12. There were bounds under law in the O.T., but in the N.T. the bounds are under grace. In the O.T., the bounds had to be kept for blessing to be received; in the N.T. we are blessed *first* by faith, and *then* we seek to appreciate the bounds of His will. The bounds of the O.T. brought bondage but the bounds of the N.T. bring liberty, for "where the Spirit of the Lord is, there is liberty", 2 Cor. 3. 17. Yet liberty is not a licence to abandon our calling within the bounds of holy standards. Liberty is the "yoke and burden" of Christ, Matt. 11. 30. Liberty is not the pretext to go where we please nor to do what we please. It does not give anyone the right to call "legal" or "in bondage" those who place themselves humbly under the bounds of the yoke and burden of Christ as His bondservants.

The bounds of liberty surround the place where Christ is. How careful believers should be not to break through the hedge that God has placed around them. In another Epistle, Paul had to write, "Stand fast therefore in the liberty wherewith Christ hath made us free, and be not entangled again with the yoke of bondage", Gal. 5. 1. The Galatians were called to liberty, but they were not to use their "liberty for an occasion to the flesh", v. 13. Peter too had to write, "As free, and not using your liberty for a cloke of maliciousness, but as the servants of God", 1 Pet. 2. 16. The Lord Jesus fully manifested this truth, as man being subject to the divine bounds; He was "holy, harmless, undefiled, separate from sinners", Heb. 7. 26.

Holiness within divine bounds is not only a matter for the individual, but it has its implications for the whole assembly. If one or more believers in a local company break these bounds, then the whole gathering can be affected. A sheet of ice is homogeneous and perfectly safe as long as it is not cracked. But a few cracks affect the safety of the whole sheet, and more cracks rapidly appear. Weeds spread rapidly in a cultivated plot if not dealt with immediately, while germs and viruses abundantly multiply under suitable conditions. In the language of Scripture "a little leaven leaveneth the whole lump", 1 Cor. 5. 6; see Haggai 2. 12–13. A river may be confined between its banks, but if flood waters cause a breach, then this is rapidly widened. Paul's first Epistle to the Corinthians attempted to close such a breach in the Corinthian defences. The last paragraph of our present chapter provides his exhortation to keep the defences permanently closed in future.

Exposition of 2 Cor. 6: The Character of the Minister
Verses 1–10: The Character of the Minister

1 We then, *as* workers together *with him*, beseech *you* also that ye receive not the grace of God in vain.

2 (For he saith, I have heard thee in a time accepted, and in the day of salvation have I succoured thee: behold, now *is* the accepted time; behold, now *is* the day of salvation).

3 Giving no offence in any thing, that the ministry be not blamed:

4 But in all *things* approving ourselves as the ministers of God, in much patience, in afflictions, in necessities, in distresses,

5 In stripes, in imprisonments, in tumults, in labours, in watchings, in fastings;

6 By pureness, by knowledge, by longsuffering, by kindness, by the Holy Ghost, by love unfeigned,

7 By the word of truth, by the power of God, by the armour of righteousness on the right hand and on the left,

8 By honour and dishonour, by evil report and good report: as deceivers, and *yet* true;

9 As unknown, and *yet* well known; as dying, and, behold, we live; as chastened, and not killed;

10 As sorrowful, yet alway rejoicing; as poor, yet making many rich; as having nothing, and *yet* possessing all things.

1. In chapter 5 verse 20, Paul (as a channel for God) beseeches *the world* to be reconciled to God; enmity on their part would be removed by the grace of God. Now in verse 1, Paul beseeches *believers*. In this, he associates himself with those whom he designates "workers together with him", obviously not including the Corinthians, since he is writing to them. Timothy, Titus, and others intimately associated with the apostle would be embraced by the term.

The thought behind the expression "workers together with Him" touches the heart, but true service cannot be motivated by emotions not based on the solid rock of Scripture. In point of fact, the expression in italics "with him" is lacking in the Greek text. Moreover, the expression is part of a verb, "working together", referring to the fellowship of those like-minded in the work. It is true that the Lord works with us; see Mark 16. 20 referring to the ascended Lord, and 1 Corinthians 15. 10 referring to the grace of God. But the opposite view-point, of the saints working together with God, is a familiarity not really found in Scripture. Admittedly, we read elsewhere that "we are labourers together with God", 1 Cor. 3. 9. This really means "we are God's fellow-workers", that is, believers who work together are God's possession. Forbid the thought that God is only "one of us" in our service, or that we are assisting God in His own work.

Paul desires that grace should be received with a *purpose* in view: it must not be received "in vain". The particular purpose Paul has in mind is that of enlargement. His character and conduct in the world were enlarged through grace, and he wanted the Corinthians likewise to abound in this purpose. Many examples of abounding through grace occur in these two Epistles: labouring abundantly through grace, 1 Cor. 15. 10; a more abundant conduct towards the saints through grace, 2 Cor. 1. 12; the grace of abounding in financial care, 8. 6–7; the all sufficiency of the strength of God manifest through grace, 12. 9. In chapter 6, there is emphasis on both *quality* and *quantity*. Quality arises because the list of twenty-eight features, when found in a believer, is honouring to God. Quantity arises on account of the great number of features listed which show deliberate purpose when they are sustained through grace.

2. This verse appears as a parenthesis. It would be rash to observe that it seems to have little connection with Paul's subject.

The first half of the verse is quoted from Isaiah 49. 8, "Thus saith the Lord, In an acceptable time have I heard thee, and in a day of salvation have I helped thee". Whatever may be the prophetic import of this verse, Paul adds that the time *there and then present* was both the accepted time and the day of salvation.

The twelve verses, Isaiah 49. 1–12, are spoken by one who claims to be the Servant of Jehovah. The reader should study these verses carefully. In some verses, the words are those of the Servant, while in others the Servant quotes the words of Jehovah:

verses 1–2: the words of the Servant;

verse 3: the Servant quotes Jehovah's words to Him;

verse 4: the Servant's reply.

verses 5–12: the Servant quotes the words of Jehovah, concerning Himself as despised of men, v. 7, and concerning His work in gathering together the outcasts of Israel, vv. 9–12.

The prophecy clearly refers to the Lord Jesus Christ, for in verse 6 the Servant is described as the "light of the Gentiles" and as being God's "salvation unto the end of the earth". None but the Lord Jesus was the true Light and the bringer of salvation. The Gentiles saw a great light when He walked among them, Isa. 9. 1–2; Simeon testified, saying that this was "Thy salvation, which Thou hast prepared before the face of all people; a light to lighten the Gentiles, and the glory of Thy people Israel", Luke 2. 30–32.

Hence the passage refers to restoration and blessing brought by the Lord both to Gentiles and to Israel. But during His life below, how did this work out? A few responded to His call, but apart from this, "the kings of the earth stood up, and the rulers were gathered together, . . . with the Gentiles, and the people of Israel" against the Lord, against His Christ, against the holy child Jesus, Acts 4. 26–27. The band of soldiers gathered against the Lord to mock Him, was a "cohort" consisting of six hundred men, Matt. 27. 27. The Jews formed a "multitude", easily led by the chief priests and elders, 27. 20. Had the Lord's mission been a success in gathering men to Himself? We hear Him say prophetically, "I have laboured in vain, I have spent my strength for nought, and in vain", Isa. 49. 4. See Matthew 11. 20; 23. 37 for further examples.

This phrase "in vain" immediately links Isaiah 49 with 2 Corinthians 6, where the thought of not receiving grace "in vain" is under discussion. Although the outward *results* of His *life* (we are not here referring to the *fruit* of His *death*) may appear to have been "in vain", yet what did Jehovah think about the labours of His Servant? He knew that restoration would come later as a result of sacrifice. He knew that His Servant's purpose throughout life was to go to Jerusalem, there to be crucified. Hence in the hour of His greatest need, in the time when He gave Himself, in the day of accomplishment of divine purpose, Jehovah said of His Servant, "In an acceptable time have I heard Thee, and in a day of salvation have I helped Thee: and I will preserve Thee". His death was acceptable to His God, and through it He wrought salvation.

In Paul's application, he states that "now" is the accepted time, "now" is the day of salvation. Far from believers living their lives "in vain", they are to realise that the help and strength of God is ever available—even "now"—in their service taken up through grace, and that God has a purpose for them in placing them in His service. In Paul's own case, Acts 26. 17, deliverance was promised and a purpose declared, as he was sent to the Jews and Gentiles "to open their eyes, and to turn them from darkness to light".

3. The Lord gave "no offence in any thing, that the ministry be not blamed". Servants of the Lord should place no obstacle in the way of the ungodly which might cause them to become hostile towards the Gospel generally; see Acts 24. 16 for Paul's testimony in this direction. A believer may act unworthy of his calling in Christ Jesus, and an unbeliever, seeing this may turn against Christianity completely. How careful must the Lord's people be, lest their conduct stumbles others.

It is a different matter if unbelievers take offence at the righteous acts and teaching of a believer. In the Lord's case, the Pharisees were offended by His teaching on defilement, Matt. 15. 12, but this would not cause the Lord to cease. Truth cannot be softened to pacify a contender. Ultimately, welldoing will put to silence the ignorance of foolish men, 1 Pet. 2. 15, although this may not happen until "the day of visitation", v. 12.

4. Rather, the walk, conduct and character of the believer must be approved (or, commended). One's life must be consistent with one's teaching if the "ministers of God" are to be commended. This word "ministers" means "deacons". In the Epistles, a deacon is any believer who serves both in spiritual and everyday matters. 1 Timothy 3. 8–13 presents some of their qualifications, but this passage should always be read in conjunction with 2 Corinthians 6. 4–10. It should be stressed that the seven men chosen in Acts 6. 5 were *not* deacons because they were selected for the financial work of serving tables; they were deacons *already*.

At the beginning of this chapter, we have already pointed out that these twenty-eight features are divided into three groups, in English introduced respectively by the prepositions "in", "by" and "as". These three groups deal with the outward circumstances of the minister, his inward character, and the various contrasts experienced by the minister. In the original Greek, however, the prepositions are slightly different, although this does not alter the English meaning. The first group of ten features in verses 4–5 are introduced by *en*, meaning in. Of the second group of eleven features in verses 6–8, the first eight are *still* introduced by *en*, although the English rendering "by" is not out of place. The last three in this second group are introduced by *dia*, meaning through. The last group is introduced by *hos*, correctly rendered by the preposition "as".

4–5. Here we have ten features governing the outward circumstances of a servant who will be commended.

Patience. Service being accomplished with a purpose and not in vain, requires patience to wait for the resulting fruit of service in a scene of corruption and danger. James could quote the case of the husbandman who "waiteth for the precious fruit of the earth, and hath long patience for it", 5. 7. James goes on to write that the prophets are an example of patience, v. 10. Peter observes that if patience is added to faith, then we shall not be barren or unfruitful in the knowledge of the Lord Jesus Christ, 2 Pet. 1. 6, 8. The zeal for immediate results may cause the energy of the flesh to displace the power of God, but how can a convert stand under these circumstances?

Afflictions. Tribulations at the hands of men were forecast by the Lord. The mind of the unconverted can be so warped as to think that such persecutions can do God service, John 16. 2. Paul endured such afflictions on all his missionary journeys, a chosen vessel to suffer for the sake of the name of the Lord Jesus, Acts 9. 16. His first journey was a baptism in such sufferings, when he was even stoned until they supposed him to be dead, 14. 19, and this in spite of the signs and wonders done by their hands, v. 3.

Necessities. This refers to the privations experienced by the apostle. He had previously written to them that "we both hunger, and thirst, and are naked", 1 Cor. 4. 11, having "no certain dwellingplace", thereby following in the footsteps of his Master. By drawing attention to such things, Paul writes his own letter of personal commendation to those who would receive him, just as he did later to those who would not receive him, 2 Cor. 12. 10, 11.

Distresses. Properly, this word means "straits", a narrow place, having the same root as "straitened" in verse 12. Paul refers to his own anxious interest in prayer, intercession, correction, and teaching of wayward assemblies, such as Corinth and later Colosse and those in Galatia. To have no concern for the weak can hardly commend a worker zealous for the truth.

Stripes. These were bodily afflictions of a severe kind, and only endured because the sufferer had an intimate knowledge of Christ. Paul had been beaten in Philippi, Acts 16. 22, while later he testifies that he had received stripes from the Jews on five distinct occasions, 2 Cor. 11. 23, 24.

Imprisonments. The other apostles had suffered this in the early days of the testimony, and Paul had followed in due course, Acts 16. 23. By such means the priests and magistrates hoped to silence the testimony for Christ, but on many occasions God intervened miraculously. The Lord had come "to proclaim liberty to the captives, and the opening of the prison to them that are bound", Isa. 61. 1.

Tumults, or commotions. These are common in political and racial strifes, being triggered off by a few extremists who know that human nature in the masses will then take over. On Paul's first journey, an "assault" was made at Iconium by the multitude, Acts 14. 5; on the second journey there was public trouble in Thessalonica and Berea, 17. 5, 8, 13; on the third journey the whole city of Ephesus was "filled with confusion", 19. 29, while later the whole city of Jerusalem "was moved", 21. 30. Such methods of public and emotional violence are used by the few to cover up their own underhand activities.

Labours. Paul seldom seemed to relax in the service of God. In daily employment, he laboured, working with his own hands, 1 Cor. 4. 12. In spiritual things, he laboured more abundantly than all the other apostles, 15. 10. He knew what it was to work for three years "night and day with tears", Acts 20. 31. Here was no half-hearted application to service, no crowding out of spiritual things by mundane occupations or worldly interests. Modern methods of entertainment in the home, so unworthy of the name of Christ, distract from spiritual labour in the assembly.

Watchings. In 11. 27, Paul adds that these watchings were "often". He was constantly in prayer and intercession before the throne of grace, on behalf of the churches and individual believers. The word suggests seasons of night-time exercise, as it is said of David who would not go up into his bed, or give sleep to his eyes, or slumber to his eyelids, Ps. 132. 3, 4. During conditions of night before the Lord comes, He exhorts us to "watch and pray", Mark 13. 33.

Fastings. Later in 11. 27, the apostle says that these fastings were "often". He had apparently fasted immediately upon his conversion, Acts 9. 19. This characterised the prophets and teachers in Antioch, giving them that right attitude of soul whereby they could recognise the voice of the Holy Spirit, 13. 2. Fasting with prayer was the method employed when elders were chosen, and when the assembly at Iconium was commended to the Lord, 14. 23. Indulgencies of the day were abandoned, in order to leave full room for the things of God.

Paul did not imply that the Corinthians were to display all these outward circumstances during their service. Some are enjoined upon all believers, but others only come the way of the servant in the permissive will of God. For example, one must not go out of one's way to invite public trouble if such is not forthcoming. But zeal in these various phases of service can be manifested by all.

6–8. Paul now lists eleven features relating to the inward character of the minister. These can be the portion of all the people of God.

Pureness. This allows no mixture or compromise in the home or in the assembly. Believers must cleanse themselves "from all filthiness of the flesh and spirit", 2 Cor. 7. 1, else the flesh is made worse and the spirit is not improved. The furniture of the tabernacle was overlaid with pure gold. No mixture of ceremony or service was consistent with the holiness of God, and the offering of "strange fire" was ripe for judgment, Lev. 10. 1. The Lord promised that the "pure in heart" are blessed so as to "see God", Matt. 5. 8, so how important it is that we should think upon "whatsoever things are pure", Phil. 4. 8. As far as the Corinthian repentance was concerned, they had proved themselves to be "clear", that is, pure, 2 Cor. 7. 11.

Knowledge. Not merely by itself, nor acquired naturally by the means

that the world uses, else knowledge can "puff up" where love is
absent, 1 Cor. 8. 1. Rather knowledge comes via the Holy Spirit, 1
Cor 2. 13, by the teacher, 12. 8, and by the Word, 2 Tim. 3. 16.

Longsuffering. When our love "suffereth long", 1 Cor. 13. 4, it reflects
one of the great divine features of mercy. In the Lord's case, He said,
"how *often* would I have gathered thy children together, . . . and ye
would not!" Matt. 23. 37. In God's case, we read that the
longsuffering and goodness of God lead men to repentance, Rom. 2.
4, and that His promise is not slack since He is longsuffering
towards men, not willing that any should perish, 2 Pet. 3. 9.

Kindness. This is one of the features that is "put on" since the new
man has been put on, Col. 3. 10, 12. The new man is to be dressed
with the spiritual dress suitable for Christ Himself. Thereby we
"adorn the doctrine of God our Saviour in all things", Titus 2. 10.
God manifests this kindness, since the word "goodness" in Romans
2. 4 just quoted is really this same word "kindness".

Holy Ghost. When men are moved by the Holy Spirit, it is obvious to
others that the control is from heaven, Acts 13. 2. At the same
time, unbelievers may mock, and even accuse the apostles of being
drunk, 2. 13. Natural abilities and the powers of darkness may
intrude to confuse the issue, so the recognised work of the Holy
Spirit in a believer must be consistent with the declared testimony
of Scripture.

Love unfeigned. That is, love must not be hypocritical, but be genuine
for the good and edification of others, and must not be self-seeking.
Such love is formed of God; it is no mere emotion and natural
sentiment. Love is to be without dissimulation (that is, unfeigned),
Rom. 12. 9. Our souls have been purified in obeying the truth
through the Spirit "unto unfeigned love of the brethren", 1 Pet. 1.
22.

Word of truth. The true minister of God will resist evil by taking up the
Word of God. We are warned in many places that there would be
false teachers among the saints, 2 Pet. 2. 1, so it is not surprising
that believers have to take a stand on many important points of
doctrine and practice. Some will say that love is absent when error
is resisted, but Paul had to withstand Peter to his face because of
fundamental error, Gal. 2. 11. Even leaders sometimes fail to
manifest the truth, and others may easily follow, John 21. 3.

Power of God. The arm of the flesh cannot touch the conscience,
although it can feed the emotions. The leaders in the popular
entertainment industry know how to exploit this principle to the
full. But the power of God touches the conscience and the heart,
although it does not feed the natural inclinations and appetites of
men. Happy is the evangelist who knows how to be a channel for
the right kind of power affecting the right part of a sinner. Happy is
the teacher who allows the right power for edification to feed the

new man in a believer.

Armour of righteousness. Later, Paul writes that believers do not war after the flesh, since the weapons are spiritual, 2 Cor. 10. 3, 4. These are mighty through God, since we may put on "the whole armour of God", Eph. 6. 11. Many defensive items are granted, but only one offensive weapon, namely "the sword of the Spirit, which is the word of God", v. 17. The armour of righteousness is defensive; it protects all round, leaving no loop-hole for the enemy to access. When thus protected, we may take up "the sword of the Spirit", that our testimony may be "I have fought a good fight", 2 Tim. 4. 7.

Honour and dishonour, or, glory and dishonour. The former comes from the Lord who owns the character and labours of His servants; the latter comes from man who disowns everything spiritual.

Evil report and good report. A faithful servant may be deliberately misrepresented by those *without,* as the Lord was by the false witnesses at His trial, Matt. 26. 61, and as Paul was by the masters of the "damsel possessed with a spirit of divination", Acts 16. 16, 21. But by those *within,* a servant should be well represented. For example, Paul was well reported of by Timothy, 1 Cor. 4. 17, while Timothy had a good report from the brethren in Lystra and Iconium, Acts 16. 2. To be misrepresented by those *within* the fellowship is disheartening indeed, but Paul had to suffer that at the hands of the Corinthians before they repented.

9–10. We now have seven contrasts introduced by the word "as". Totally, in verses 8–10, we have nine contrasts, the first six (verses 8, 9) at the hands of man, and the last three (verse 10) referring to trials in the wilderness.

Every approved servant of God can know something of these contrasts in his experience, but the implications can best be brought out by discussing these contrasts in the experience of the Lord Jesus.

By honour and dishonour. The Pharisees dishonoured the Lord by accusing Him of having a devil, John 8. 49. By contrast He received from God the Father honour and glory, 2 Pet. 1. 17.

By evil report and good report. We have already mentioned the false witnesses who gave evil report about the Lord; likewise He was accused of the chief priests and elders, Matt. 27. 12. By contrast, He received adequate testimony from heaven, as the Father declared His report concerning the Son, 3. 17; 17. 5.

As deceivers, and yet true. Many people accused Him of being a deceiver on account of His words, John 7. 12. By contrast, grace and truth came by Jesus Christ, John 1. 17. He declared that He was the "truth".

As unknown, and yet well known. The Lord was unknown to the masses, as they speculated on His holy person, suggesting that He was but John the Baptist, Elias or Jeremias, Matt. 16. 14. By contrast, the Lord said that "no man knoweth the Son, but the

Father", 11. 27. Elsewhere He testified "As the Father knoweth Me", John 10. 15. He was indeed well known by the Father, and by the hosts of heaven.

As dying, and, behold, we live. This is the great secret of the Lord's work. Paul testified of this great contrast in the synagogue in Antioch, Acts 13. 28–30. The Lord recalled the same great basic fact to His servant John on the isle of Patmos, a literal translation of Revelation 1. 18 being, "(I am) the living One, and I became dead, and behold I am living to the ages of the ages".

As chastened, and not killed. Chastening at the hands of man is, of course, different from that at the hand of God. A servant may endure both kinds, but the Lord sustained it only from men. In the Lord's case, cruel chastising (the same word) led to His death afterwards, Luke 23. 16. In other cases when men sought to kill Him, He escaped from their hands since His time had not yet come, 4. 30, John 8. 59.

As sorrowful, yet alway rejoicing. The Lord was a Man of sorrows. As He entered the garden, He "began to be sorrowful and very heavy", Matt. 26. 37. Yet in spite of all the hardness of the hearts of men, He "rejoiced in spirit" as He gave thanks to His Father, Luke 10. 21.

As poor, yet making many rich. As man, He had no possessions with which to feed the four thousand, Matt. 15. 32; He had no place to lay His head, 8. 20; He had no funds with which to pay taxes, 17. 27, and no coin upon Him with which to illustrate His answer to the wickedness of the hypocrites, 22. 19. Yet "He hath given to the poor", 2 Cor. 9. 9. Through His poverty we have been enriched, 8. 9.

As having nothing, and yet possessing all things. Amazing contrast of grace, that the lowly man should at the same time be the "possessor of heaven and earth", Gen. 14. 19. The psalmist confessed, "The heavens are Thine, the earth also is Thine", Ps. 89. 11, while David blessed the Lord saying, "all that is in the heaven and in the earth is Thine: Thine is the kingdom, O Lord, and Thou art exalted as head above all", 1 Chron. 29. 11.

These great principles apply to God's servants now. We can illustrate one of them, "as unknown, and yet well known". In the last century, one servant of God wrote, "This is true greatness, to serve unnoticed, to work unseen". In 1832, at the beginning of a long life of service in teaching and expounding divine truth among the Lord's people, he burst into spiritual song with the hymn* containing the twenty-second verse:

> Lord, let me wait for Thee alone;
>   My life be only this—
> To serve Thee here on earth, unknown;
>   Then share Thy heavenly bliss.

At the end of his life in 1882, this same verse was inscribed on the memorial stone standing over his grave in Bournemouth cemetery, and it

---

* The Call, in *Spiritual Songs*, by J.N. Darby

may still be read today. Admittedly he became well known outwardly among brethren, but this verse captures his desire to stand in service before the Lord alone.

It is fitting that servants of God should meditate upon this principle of true service. Reward and greatness come from God and not from man. They are not even sought after by the labourer who rather seeks the Lord's glory. As such, he can afford to serve unnoticed and to work unseen. As far as the world is concerned, the servant serves without the camp, bearing His reproach. Within the assembly, Paul took the position of being the "least of the apostles", 1 Cor. 15. 9. After his conversion and preparation by the Lord in Arabia, his service started in Syria, Cilicia and Antioch, although he "was unknown by face unto the churches of Judaea which were in Christ", Gal. 1. 22. These churches only heard reports of Paul's labours, and as such glorified God, v. 24, because of the service of one unknown.

The blessedness of true service comes from the quiet realisation that all—both servant and service—is known to the Lord. He knows His own sheep, John 10. 14, and calls them by name as He leads them out. The foundation of God is sure and has the seal that the"the Lord knoweth them that are His", 2 Tim. 2. 19. In Hebrews 2. 11–13, He owns those who are His children and who are the sons and daughters of the Father, 2 Cor. 6. 18. Indeed it is true that the servant is "well known" in his service, and here we can rest. We may, of course, also be known by our brethren, by the few or by the many, but this is really a matter of fellowship in service, and can be approved of only when the principle just outlined is before the heart.

Verses 11–18: Spiritual Enlargement and its Bounds

11 O ye Corinthians, our mouth is open unto you, our heart is enlarged.
12 Ye are not straitened in us, but ye are straitened in your own bowels.
13 Now for a recompence in the same, (I speak as unto my children,) be ye also enlarged.
14 Be ye not unequally yoked together with unbelievers: for what fellowship hath righteousness with unrighteousness? and what communion hath light with darkness?
15 And what concord hath Christ with Belial? or what part hath he that believeth with an infidel?
16 And what agreement hath the temple of God with idols? for ye are the temple of the living God; as God hath said, I will dwell in them, and walk in them; and I will be their God, and they shall be my people.
17 Wherefore come out from among them, and be ye separate, saith the Lord, and touch not the unclean thing; and I will receive you,
18 And will be a Father unto you, and ye shall be my sons and daughters, saith the Lord Almighty.

11–13. These previous twenty-eight spiritual features of the approved minister of God show progress and maturity in the Christian life. Paul recognised that these features characterised himself, but he also knew that this pathway was God's will for everyone. Hence he desired that the Corinthians should experience a similar enlargement. His inner man yearned for them, his mouth was open in exhortation, and his heart enlarged in desire. Such intense desire was nothing new to the apostle. Previously he had been willing to have imparted to the Thessalonians his own soul, 1 Thess. 2. 8.

The word "straitened" occurring in verse 12 is the opposite of "enlarged"; it means to be crowded together in a narrow place, to be cooped up and cramped from action. Very few of these blessed features were manifest in the Corinthians. "Ye are not straitened in us" signifies that there were no cramped desires, no restriction of activity, on Paul's part for his children in the faith. He had great things for them. He had the wide outlook of a father desiring the widest possible blessings for his converts. How wise is the evangelist who is perfectly balanced in what is wide and in what is narrow, for this paragraph teaches both sides of the truth. The evangelist is not authorised to make his own definitions regarding the wide blessings on the narrow way, and the necessary bounds that keep out the activity of the broad way.

But Paul adds, "ye are straitened in your own bowels", that is, their deepest spiritual sentiments were restricted and inhibited through weakness. He speaks to them as to his children, desiring their spiritual expansion. Expansion has its "recompence"; this is the positive side of these twenty-eight features. These are the true riches. Gold that perishes fades alongside of the formation of character that lasts to eternal days. Moreover, such character formation affects every phase of christian activity, in the sanctuary for worship, in the assembly for service among the saints, and in the world for testimony before the unsaved.

But what a contrast between the closing phrase of verse 13 and the opening phrase of verse 14, "be ye . . . be ye not". Enlargement must have its bounds, else the world may also be embraced. Believers are sanctified and sent into the world, but there "they are not of the world", John 17. 15–18. How necessary it is for enlargement to be sanctified, else sanctuary service, assembly service and gospel testimony will be affected adversely. Hence, in verses 6. 14 to 7. 1, Paul describes the bounds set by God. See Deut. 33. 20, where the enlargement of Gad is according to God.

14. Paul gives one exhortation and then asks five questions. This style of ministry often occurs in Paul's writings (see 1 Cor. 6. 1–9; 9. 1–13; 12. 29–30). Questions are asked which demand an answer from the reader. Answers are supplied by the conscience, so the reader is stirred to consider the applications of these answers to his own life. Paul assumes, of course, that his readers know the answers beforehand. There is no room for attempting to give false answers that would negate the practical truth being brought out.

It should be noticed very carefully that the *five* questions illustrate the *one* exhortation, "Be not unequally yoked together with unbelievers". This is shown by the word "for" which commences the questions. Paul is not providing a *series* of situations in which believers should remain separate, rather it is *one* situation which can be manifest in various ways. Paul is not, in the context, writing about believers separating from other believers because of some moral or ecclesiastical weakness that would dishonour the Lord. Admittedly, "unrighteousness" and "darkness" may also affect believers, but principles from other scriptures would have to be examined in order to ascertain the appropriate conduct of a believer who seeks to be loyal to his Lord. Here, Paul is writing about "unbelievers" and features governing them.

The participle "unequally yoked together" is a verbal form of the two words *other* and *yoke* (that is, a cross bar for joining together) . The particular word *other* used here means different, diverse, of a different kind. It must be distinguished from a second word for *other* meaning of the same kind. Believer and unbeliever often have to work together in a common occupation—the *same kind* of occupation which does not break divinely given principles of contact. But here Paul visualises a situation in which believer and unbeliever are rigidly fixed together in a common commitment, when this comitment is of a *different kind* from what God allows. Two may work together by necessity without being bonded together. This would be no yoke. But a yoke is formed by a definite agreement to share a life together, to share the organisational and financial running of a business together, to share interests together, to share religious experiences together. Then a rigid yoke would mean a believer being irresistibly under the control of the other partner.

A yoke is different from being "conformed to this world", Rom. 12. 1. Copying the world is one thing, but joining with it is worse, for a yoke is a very powerful influence. Human nature being what it is, one can be certain that the controlling influence of the unbeliever will control the believer. There can be no independent action when two are yoked together. In Acts 15. 10, there were those who wanted "to put a yoke upon the neck of the disciples", by demanding circumcision for salvation. Such false teaching was succeeding in its object, else there would not have been such a stir to rectify the error introduced. A yoke can be "a yoke of bondage", Gal. 5. 1, and being entangled with it can mean that Christ is of no profit to such a man, v. 2. More generally, two cannot walk together, except they are agreed, Amos 3. 3. Lack of agreement on spiritual things will make it impossible for them to walk together in the affairs of life, even if a yoke is formed. Success may appear for a season, but eventually death and the two distinct forms of judgment upon believer and unbeliever will separate eternally those once yoked. Even in ceremony and in its routine regulations, God marked this principle. Divers seeds were not to be sown, else the vineyard would be defiled; an ox and an ass should not plough together; a garment of mixed materials was not to be worn. Deut. 22. 9–11. The yoke between King Jehoshaphat and Ahab was criticised by Jehu, 2 Chron. 19. 2; "Shouldest thou . . . love them that hate the Lord?"

The strength of a yoke has blessed results in proper circumstances. The yoke of the Lord Jesus is easy, Matt. 11. 29–30. His yoke was His obedience to the Father, and this should be easy but binding to believers, although for Him it meant a sacrificial death on the cross. In service, the status of the "true yokefellow", Phil. 4. 3, is something to be sought after. This unnamed saint had the great privilege of being yoked to the apostle Paul. Marriage also is a yoke, although this is not the dominant and only thought in Paul's mind in the context. Elsewhere, he had stated that it was to be "in the Lord", 1 Cor. 7. 39, this being a permanent yoking together of kindred minds in holy things. The O.T. had demonstrated this principle: there was to be no marriage between the Jews and the surrounding nations, Gen. 24. 3; Exod. 34. 16.

14–16. The five words *fellowship, communion, concord, part* and *agreement* should be carefully noticed.

Fellowship. The word used here is not the usual word employed for fellowship. Here, it means *participation*. For example, the idea occurs in Luke 5. 7, where those in one ship "beckoned unto their *partners*, which were in the other ship". The yoke of participation in a venture is inconsistent with the Christian calling, when one partner is characterised by righteousness and the other by lawlessness (as the word unrighteousness should read).

Commmunion. This word properly means *fellowship*. If the former yoke of participation refers to the activity of partners, then this word refers to their common state of mind. Light and darkness are complete opposites. They were thus arranged physically by God in the beginning, to demonstrate the moral opposites that God knew would shortly enter His creation. The state of unbelievers is described in Romans 1. 21 as "their foolish heart was darkened", but believers are exhorted to "walk in the light, as He is in the light", 1 John 1. 7. Thereby proper fellowship between believer and believer is possible. The incompatibility of these features is seen by the fact that "the light shineth in the darkness; and the darkness comprehended it not", John 1. 5. See Ephesians 5. 11.

Concord. This word means a *sounding together*. The contrast is thus like a beautiful hymn and an ugly piece of jazz. Such discord is immediately apparent, for example, when a spiritually minded man visits unconverted relatives in a home governed by worldly entertainment and talk. Such a visit would not constitute a yoke. The believer would have "vexed his righteous soul from day to day with their unlawful deeds", 2 Pet. 2. 8. A yoke would be formed only if the believer tried to serve both God and mammon, seeking to turn discord into concord.

To whom are we loyal? "To whom ye yield yourselves servants to obey, his servants ye are to whom ye obey", Rom. 6. 16. Either we serve Christ or Satan, as the name Belial must be construed. The

derivation of this latter word is in doubt. Depending upon the
vowels used in the Hebrew word, it can mean *worthlessness*, or
engulfing sin. For example, the two sons of Eli are described as "sons
of Belial" not knowing the Lord, 1 Sam. 2. 12. Their sin in seeking
to satisfy their own carnal appetites according to their own tastes,
concocting to roast the sin offering instead of boiling it, merely
shows how far from the Lord they really were, 1 Sam. 2. 15–17.
Their sin was thus very great before the Lord, and no true follower
of divine ceremony could have dealings with them. This is of
relevance today when unconverted men engage in religious
practices according to human traditions and modern doctrines. A
believer can have no concord with such men and practices. Even if
weaker believers adhere to these men and practices, owing to
ignorance, this still gives no licence to other believers better taught
in the Word to have fellowship or serve there.

Part. This word means a share or a portion. A believer cannot be
yoked to an unbeliever so as to have a share in his interests and
business. In Nehemiah's day, Eliashib the priest had a part in the
interests of Tobiah the Ammonite. Such men were not to be
allowed in the congregation of the Lord for ever, but this priest had
prepared for Tobiah a chamber in the courts of the Lord's house
where he kept his "household stuff", Neh. 13. 1–9. This common
policy rapidly led to the temporary disintegration of the Levitical
service so that many were adversely affected by the policy of the few.

Agreement. This word occurs only once in the N.T., and the
corresponding verb also occurs only once, "Joseph . . . a good man,
and a just . . . had not *consented* to the counsel and deed of them",
Luke 23. 50–51. There can be no alliance between a believer, and
any man or group of men who practise evil and ungodly ways. The
temple of God is absolutely distinct from idols. In the O.T., idolatry
in the temple brought on the ruin of Israel, the Lord's glory having
forsaken its abode among His people. In Samuel's early days, their
high places caused God to forsake the tabernacle of Shiloh, Ps. 78.
58–61. This was recalled in the days of the prophet Jeremiah, when
every form of idolatry was practised in the house, Jer. 7. 8–12. But
the people took no warning, and Ezekiel finally saw the last of the
idolatrous acts in the temple, Ezek. 8. 3–16, prior to the Lord's glory
forsaking His house and city, to take up an abode on the mount of
Olives, 11 . 22–23. It is no use feeling that such practices cannot be
found in assemblies today. That would be a sort of perfectionism
quite out of keeping with what the Lord saw in some of the churches
in Revelation 2. The doctrine of Balaam, v. 14, the doctrine of the
Nicolaitans hated by the Lord, v. 15, and the teaching of Jezebel, v.
20, were found there. But those who are faithful can repent, and
remain apart from corresponding practices today, thereby not
consenting or agreeing with the counsel of the ungodly.

16. No unequally-yoked practices can be allowed among the Lord's people because they are "the temple of the living God". In 1 Corinthians 3. 16–17, we find the same truth: "ye are the temple of God", and as such the Spirit of God dwells there. This renders the temple holy—separated from all that lies outside the bounds of collective assembly functioning. In 1 Corinthians 6. 19–20, the individual body of a believer is seen as a temple of the Holy Spirit, and thus is separated from all that lies outside the bounds of divinely-given bodily functioning.

As the temple of God, believers function as a holy priesthood, 1 Pet. 2. 5, in relation to the One who dwells among them. The quotation given by Paul comes from Leviticus 26. 11–12, "And I will set My tabernacle among you . . . and I will walk among you, and will be your God, and ye shall be My people". Today, this is more precious and vital, since the temple of God for us is not with a house made with hands, but a living organism of born-again souls, rendered fit for God to dwell among His own by the work of Christ.

17. Yet the bounds are not kept today by cherubim and a flaming sword turning every way, Gen. 3. 24. They are not kept by compulsion or by law. Rather they are kept by the obedience of the exercised heart. Hence an exhortation is necessary, "Wherefore come out from among them, and be ye separate, . . . and touch not the unclean thing". See Isaiah 52: with Zion now clothed, v. 1, and that freely, v. 3, with the Gospel published, v. 7, leading to salvation and singing, vv. 9–10, no wonder there is this call to depart from the unclean, v. 11, in order to have holy eyes and hands to contemplate the Man of sorrows introduced in chapter 53.

18. Paul closes with a promised blessing, and with words of responsibility in verse 1 of the next chapter. It must be realised that the blessedness of being the sons and daughters of the Father does not rest upon our faithfulness in this matter of bounds. We are such by grace because we have been born of God, John 1. 13. The Father of the Lord Jesus Christ is also our Father, John 20. 17. The point that Paul seems to be making is that we cannot *appreciate* this position if we are "out of bounds". Spiritual relationships are not sensed if the heart is clouded by the affairs of the world. But if believers rest within the bounds of the atmosphere of heaven, then all the delightful relationships with the Father and with the Son can be entered into without restraint. Here is reception into the Father's house in keeping with the promise "I will receive you".

We are not only to "come out", but we are to "cleanse ourselves". "Coming out" refers to the movement of heart and practice from the outside to the inside. "Cleansing ourselves" refers to the movement of practices from the inside to the outside. We deal with this in the next chapter.

2 CORINTHIANS 7

Section 3.　Historical: Paul's Rejoicing
Subject 1.　Encouragement after Discouragement

Background of this Subject

For a more comprehensive account of how this chapter fits into the Epistle as a whole, the reader should refer to the introductory account to chapter 8. Notice that verse 1 properly belongs to chapter 6, the subject of the present chapter 7 starting with verse 2.

Even a casual reading of this Epistle shows that the subject matter of chapter 7 follows immediately after that at the end of chapter 2. Chapters 1–2 form the *first* historical section, in which Paul describes his *grief*. Chapters 7–9 form the *second* historical section, outlining the apostle's *rejoicing*. In chapter 7, he rejoices at the *repentance* of the assembly at Corinth, while in chapters 8–9 he rejoices in the *collection* gathered both by the Macedonians and the Corinthians.

There appears to be no superficial reason why chapters 3–6 should form a kind of parenthesis between these two historical sections. The reading of chapters 1, 2, 7, 8, 9 in that order would make perfect sense; nothing would appear to be omitted. The reason for the parenthesis comes in two verses:

1. the first verse of the parenthesis, "Do we begin again to commend ourselves? or need we, as some others, epistles of commendation to you . . . ?" 3. 1;
2. the first verse of the second historical section, "Receive us; we have wronged no man . . .", 7. 2.

In other words, the question of Paul's *reception* by the Corinthians is the common thought. Paul had been outspoken in his denunciations and corrections in the first Epistle. To what extent would they receive him now? Paul knew from Titus that the majority would willingly receive him, so he approaches the subject in two ways.

1. In chapters 3–6 he deals with the *intrinsic character* of a true minister, producing a valid letter of commendation, namely themselves, as his work in the Lord. But he dwells at great length on various great features that characterise any servant of God worthy of being received by an assembly.
2. In chapter 7 he deals with the *practical side* of his work that warrants reception by the repentant Corinthians.

It is interesting to note that the *doctrinal side* precedes the *practical side*. To have one's mind taken up with God's point of view is a great asset before considering things practically. Some believers think that doctrine is of secondary importance. "Let's do something," they cry. This is not God's way. For forty years Moses *learned* before *serving* in the wilderness for forty years. Even in Paul's style of exposition, the doctrine behind spiritual gifts,

1 Cor. 12, precedes their practical outworking, 1 Cor. 14. The doctrine of the heavenlies, Eph. 1.1 to 4. 16, precedes the practical responsibilities, Eph. 4. 17 to 6. 24. The doctrine of justification by faith, Rom. 1–8, precedes its application to life and practice, Rom. 12–16. We cannot afford to reverse God's methods. God's ways are discarded if believers act as if they have no need for the assembly ministry meeting or the Bible reading or other means convened by the elders for their instruction. These meetings precede service and properly prepare for it.

To complete the picture, we may note that chapters 10–13 also refer to commendation. There, Paul addresses himself personally to those men in Corinth who would receive neither him nor his apostolic qualifications. He had to glory to write his own letter of commendation. He should have been commended by the Corinthians, but this was not forthcoming, 12. 11. In the last chapter, he concludes with a very trenchant reason why they should approve of him, again pointing to themselves as his very letter of commendation.

Chapter 7 relates Paul's trouble and anxiety in Macedonia as he awaited news of the Corinthians. Paul recalls the return of Titus with the good news, and of the relief he had before the Lord upon learning of their repentance. His whole outlook and confidence in them suddenly changed for the good; indeed this was

> "Light after darkness, gain after loss,
>   Strength after weakness, crown after cross;
> Sweet after bitter, hope after fears,
>   Home after wandering, praise after tears.
>
> Near after distant, gleam after gloom,
>   Love after loneliness, life after tomb;
> After long agony, rapture of bliss,
>   Right was the pathway leading to this."*

A summary of the chapter is as follows:
> Verses 1–4: apostolic jubilation;
> Verses 5–7: the coming of Titus to Macedonia;
> Verses 8–11: the Corinthians' reactions to the first Epistle;
> Verses 12–16: the reaction of Paul and Titus to this repentance.

Exposition of 2 Cor. 7: Encouragement after Discouragement

Verses 1–4: Apostolic Jubilation

1 Having therefore these promises, dearly beloved, let us cleanse ourselves from all filthiness of the flesh and spirit, perfecting holiness in the fear of God.

2 Receive us; we have wronged no man, we have corrupted no man, we have defrauded no man.

---

* Sacred Songs and Solos, Hymn 830, by Frances R. Havergal.

> 3 I speak not *this* to condemn *you:* for I have said before, that ye are in our hearts to die and live with *you.*
>
> 4 Great *is* my boldness of speech toward you, great *is* my glorying of you: I am filled with comfort, I am exceeding joyful in all our tribulation.

1. As we have intimated, this verse properly concludes the previous chapter. There, Paul had firstly outlined the character expected of the "ministers of God" (that is, servants, deacons, engaged in all kinds of service); then he had desired the Corinthians to be similarly enlarged in such ministry, yet not beyond the bounds of spiritual propriety. Enlargement without proper bounds would cause the believer to be yoked to many suspicious men and practices. If these are shunned, special promises are made to those who are "the temple of the living God", v. 16. The thought in verse 16 of God dwelling with His people is taken from Leviticus 26. 11–12, while in verse 17 that of departing and touching not the unclean thing is taken from Isaiah 52. 11. These special promises relate to God dwelling and walking among His people, and to our relationship to Him as sons and daughters to their Father. These blessings are, of course, absolute, and in a sense independent of responsibility. But here Paul would be talking about the believer's recognition and appreciation of these blessings. They cannot be known when unholy practices are allowed in the precincts of his own testimony.

It is on this ground that chapter 7 opens. The promises are made first, and then *from our side* we enter into them by *cleansing ourselves* from unholiness. This is quite distinct from the absolute cleansing that comes freely through the blood of Christ.

The O.T. shows up the great principle that holiness precedes the entrance of the glory of the Lord. As far as the tabernacle is concerned, in Exodus 40. 17–33 we find it reared up for the first time. Seven times in this passage the phrase "as the Lord commanded Moses" shows that Moses' mind was sanctified to God's will. This suitable prelude enabled the glory of God to fill the tabernacle, v. 34. Again in Leviticus 7–8, the commands of God for the anointing of the priesthood were carried out to His satisfaction, so He appeared in glory to all the people, 9. 23. But later, Psalm 78 shows how unsanctified conditions came in among the people; the Lord would no longer dwell there. He abhorred Israel, forsaking the tabernacle of Shiloh and delivering the ark into the enemy's hand, vv. 59–61.

As far as the temple was concerned, many things had to be cleansed before the glory of God could appear once more. Solomon eliminated four unwanted men from the kingdom:

Adonijah, 1 Kings 2. 14–25, the man who aspired after leadership;

Abiathar, 1 Kings 2. 27, the man who aspired after the priesthood;

Joab, 1 Kings 2. 34, the man who aspired after warfare according to the flesh;

Shimei, 1 Kings 2. 46, the man who rebelled against David.

These characteristics marked some men in Corinth, a subject brought out in chapters 10–13 of this Epistle. With this restoration, blessing could fall upon this nation, and the glory of God filled the house of the Lord, 1 Kings 8. 11.

The glory of God did not appear again, except to Isaiah and Ezekiel, but the cleansing of the temple by Hezekiah, 2 Chron. 29. 16–19, and later by Josiah, 2 Kings 23. 1–20, led to temporary spiritual prosperity during the great passover feasts in the reigns of these kings.

Later, the abominations of idolatry committed in the house would cause the Lord to "go far off from My sanctuary", Ezek. 8. 6, and this took place when the glory of the Lord went up from the city and stood on the mount of Olives, Ezek. 11 . 23. This mountain had been previously cleansed from the relics of idolatry to make it a suitable resting place for the glory, 2 Kings 23. 13. But in Ezekiel's vision of future restoration, when the law of the house would be that "the whole limit thereof round about shall be most holy", Ezek. 43. 12, the glory of God would once again enter from the east from the mount of Olives, vv. 4–5. God maintains this great principle of holiness prior to the recognition of His presence, firm to the end.

The presence of the Lord Jesus is no make-believe in unholy conditions, so all believers should be exercised about their own state and activity in the local assembly, so that it may be suitable for the Lord. We must cleanse ourselves from all "filthiness of the flesh and spirit", the former relating to that which is external and the latter to that which is internal. We are to perfect holiness, that is, to bring it to its end, to complete it, by His grace to abandon every aspect of unholiness, since "holiness becometh Thine house, O Lord, for ever", Ps. 93. 5.

2. Paul commences this subject by writing "Receive us". It should be noticed that the ordinary word for receive is not used here. Elsewhere, Paul uses the ordinary word in connection with Phebe, Rom. 16. 2, and Epaphroditus, Phil. 2. 29, showing in each case their work and character. But in our verse, a special word is employed, occurring only nine times in the N.T. The basic meaning is "to make room", an echo of the opposite idea contained in the previous chapter, "ye are straitened in your own bowels", 6. 12. That is, the Corinthians were cramped or cooped up, and Paul wanted them to make room for him. In more physical terms, the word occurs in Mark 2. 2, where "there was no *room to receive* them" because of the press, and in John 21. 25 where even the world "could not *contain*" the books that should be written about the Son of God. A local assembly is a large place, and spiritual hedges cannot be erected against the true work of God. One makes room for a qualified newcomer, not only by sharing fellowship at the Lord's supper, but making room for him in service for which he may be equipped of the Lord.

Some in Corinth may have been holding wrong ideas about the apostle, so he provides them with three negative qualities to assist them in their reception.

    1. *We have wronged no man*: this verb means to act unjustly towards. In all of Paul's service towards saints and sinners, none could

justly complain of any unrighteous acts on his part. Elsewhere, Paul had said to Festus, "to the Jews have *I done no wrong*, as thou very well knowest", Acts 25.10.

2. *We have corrupted no man*: literally this means to destroy or waste, but when referring to men it means to corrupt morally. Paul was dealing with the church of God, and previously he had condemned those who *defiled* (or destroyed) the temple of God, 1 Cor. 3. 17 (the same word is used).

3. *We have defrauded no man*: this verb means to have more than another, to overreach or to make a gain of. In other words, Paul sought no personal gain from the Corinthians as a result of his service among them. This verb appears in the N.T. only five times, four of them being in this Epistle. See 2. 11 referring to Satan, 12. 17 referring to Paul and 12. 18 referring to Titus.

Throughout, Paul was working not for himself but for the good and edification of the Corinthians, even if they chose to misinterpret his service and some of his necessary corrections.

3. Although he had to mention these things, he was not trying to condemn them, to show them up or to criticise. He had made his position clear before—perhaps in writing or in oral ministry—that "ye are in our hearts to die and live with you". That is, his heart was sufficiently enlarged to embrace them into his very character, 2 Cor. 6. 11, one feature of which was "as dying, and, behold, we live", v. 9. But he proceeds to dwell on what is good and commendable in the Corinthian assembly, even if it does not match up to his own character.

4. Paul now comes to the great change of attitude in his heart towards the Corinthians, a change not described in chapter 2. It was brought about by the return of Titus. The apostle gives four stages in his jubilation.

1. *Boldness of speech*, that is, freedom in speaking. In Mark 8. 32, the Lord spoke the word of the cross *openly*; in John 11. 54, He walked no more *openly* because the people sought His death; in Acts 2. 29, Peter said, "let me speak *freely* unto you". Paul used the same word in 2 Corinthians 3. 12, "we use great *plainness* of speech", namely he spoke of the new covenant freely, unlike Moses who had to cover his face. In his jubilation Paul could now say things that were denied him previously in 1 Corinthians. Inability to speak with such freedom is no reflection upon a speaker as if he were in bondage; more often than not it reflects upon circumstances around caused by *other men*. The most spiritual man may sometimes be silenced by opposing conditions, and it is sad if any seek to take advantage of such a situation to gain their own ends, as if the brother's silence were his condonement. Of course, if purely personal

interests are involved, a spiritual man can afford to be silent.

2. *Great is my glorying of you.* Paul would boast in others when this glorified Christ, but he would not desire to boast of himself, 2 Cor. 12. 5, 11. Hence he boasted of the Corinthians to Titus, 7. 14, and to the Macedonians, 9. 1–4. Elsewhere, he provided them with legitimate grounds for boasting in him, 5. 12. Where such glorying is concerned, look outwards and upwards, but not inwards.

3. *Filled with comfort,* or rather, "I have been filled with encouragement". He implies that this newly found encouragement in them had not waned between the arrival of Titus and the writing of the Epistle. It was not a "here today, gone tomorrow" effect; spiritual realities are not fleeting like that.

4. *Exceeding joyful in all our tribulation,* or "I overabounded with joy". In other words, Paul's previous anguish on their behalf gave place to excessive joy. This was no sullen acceptance of a repentance only half desired; rather it reflects the father's joy at the return of the repentant prodigal son, Luke 15. 22–24, 32. Relationships are immediately restored when this kind of joy is manifested. If there is no joy at repentance the atmosphere will remain cold and pained. The fault would then not lie at the door of the one who repents, but of the other. In Paul's case, however, the sufferings described in chapter 1. 8 are completely reversed. It is interesting that the only other occasion in the N.T. where this particular word "overabound" occurs is in Romans 5. 20, "where sin abounded, grace did *much more abound*".

Verses 5–7: The Coming of Titus to Macedonia

5 For, when we were come into Macedonia,our flesh had no rest, but we were troubled on every side; without *were* fightings, within *were* fears.
6 Nevertheless God, that comforteth those that are cast down, comforted us by the coming of Titus;
7 And not by his coming only, but by the consolation wherewith he was comforted in you, when he told us your earnest desire, your mourning, your fervent mind toward me; so that I rejoiced the more.

5. Paul repeats some of his anxieties, upon which he had dwelt at such length in chapters 1–2. We have pointed out several times what is implied by the phrase "when we were come into Macedonia". The route was not according to his original intention, under which he would go from Ephesus directly into Corinth and thence into Macedonia, 2 Cor. 1. 16. Rather he went directly through Troas into Macedonia, 2. 12–13, since Titus had not returned with any news. From there, he would pass into Corinth, Acts 20. 2. Notice the stages in the apostolic anxiety as he waited for news from Corinth:

In Ephesus (Asia), 1. 8, "pressed out of measure, above strength, insomuch that we despaired even of life"; this refers to his *soul*.

In Troas, 2. 13, "I had no rest (ease) in my spirit", clearly referring to his *spirit*.

In Macedonia, 7. 5. "our flesh had no rest (ease)", referring to his *body*. Spirit, soul and body can thus be affected in a devoted servant of God. Moreover, "without were fightings (contentions)", referring to the contentions and strifes in Corinth about which he had written the first Epistle. Also "within were fears", referring to his inward uncertainty about their testimony. The apostle was almost in the state described in Psalm 143. 4, "Therefore is my spirit overwhelmed within me; my heart within me is desolate".

Yet how quickly can the relaxation of constraint bring with it immediate spiritual liberty. His inability to preach in Troas, even though there was an open door of the Lord, was changed immediately into the ability of giving the believers in Macedonia "much exhortation", Acts 20. 2.

6. But relief comes from God in the form of comfort—an echo of 1. 4, "the God of all comfort; who comforteth us". In other words, God arranged for Titus to return at the right moment. He will not allow us to be tried above what we are able to bear, and God recognized the need in His servant. The verb "comfort" in this verse properly means to "encourage,

The phrase "cast down" means "brought low", usually translated "lowly, humble" when the individual acts thus upon himself. For example, the Lord was "lowly in heart", Matt. 11. 29. As a verb, the Lord "humbled himself", Phil. 2. 8, and believers are to "humble yourselves", 1 Pet. 5. 6. But in Paul's case the cause was an *external agency*, so the thought is properly "brought low". John the Baptist had quoted Isaiah 40. 4 giving an external cause, "every mountain and hill shall be *brought low*", Luke 3. 5. Similarly in this Epistle, Paul later writes that "my God *will humble* me among you", 12. 21, implying that he would be brought low in tears and sorrow because of the few in Corinth who would not repent. The thought is quite distinct from Paul being "cast down", 4. 9, where he means he is thrown down by unbelieving persecutors.

This verse is very reminiscent of Psalms 42, 43 . There the psalmist was "cast down", 42. 5, 6, 11; 43. 5. Yet he knew that he must hope in God, 42. 5, and that "the Lord will command his lovingkindness in the daytime", v. 8. At one stage, he had been mocked with the question, "Where is thy God?" and he had gone with this multitude that kept holyday to the house of God, 42. 3, 4. There was, however, no release through crowds, even though they formally went to the house of God. The One who brought relief was God Himself; "O send out Thy light and Thy truth: let them lead me; let them bring me unto Thy holy hill, and to Thy tabernacles. Then will I go unto the altar of God, unto God my exceeding joy", 43. 3, 4. The soul that thirsts for God, for the living God, 42. 2, because of the perplexities of the way, and because of tears day and night, will find comfort only when He leads in His own good time, and not when the multitudes take control.

7. "And not by his coming only" suggests that Titus came alone. Timothy, who also went to Corinth, must have remained, although he had returned to Paul by the time this second Epistle was written, 2 Cor. 1. 1. Moreover, it was not only the physical event of the return of Titus, nor the renewed fellowship, that comforted Paul. Note that the word for "coming" is the Greek word *parousia*, often used in reference to the coming of the Lord Jesus for His own. Paul was encouraged "by the consolation (encouragement) wherewith he (Titus) was comforted (encouraged) in you". Encouragement is contagious when based on a good report that can be relied on. Titus' encouragement turned into Paul's, who "rejoiced" the more. It is interesting to note the first reasons that Paul gives for his encouragement. It was not their repentance, but their willingness to accept him as an apostle again. Believers today are likewise encouraged when they see converts accepting the authority of Paul in matters pertaining to church fellowship.

Paul gives three reasons:
1. *Your earnest desire*: the same Greek word is translated "vehement desire" in verse 11 . As a verb it is rendered "desiring greatly", 1 Thess 3. 6. This described the heart of the Corinthian assembly to see Paul again.
2. *Your mourning*: the only other occasion this word appears in the N.T. is Matthew 2. 18 quoted from Jeremiah 31. 15, "In Rama . . . great *mourning*, Rachel weeping for her children". The scene depicted is the mourning for the children of Israel as they went into captivity under Nebuchadnezzar, but a word of comfort from the Lord follows in verse 16. The Corinthians were similarly mourning as they considered their past in being dragged down into bondage. They too were granted words of comfort from the Lord in this second Epistle. This word "mourning" is much stronger than that used elsewhere, as "mourn" in Matthew 5. 4 and "bewail" in 2 Corinthians 12. 21.
3. *Your fervent mind*: this whole expression merely means "zeal", as in verse 11, "yea, what zeal", and in 11. 2, "I am jealous over you with godly jealousy". The Corinthian mind went out with ardent affection for Paul.

Verses 8–11: The Corinthians' Reaction to the First Epistle

8 For though I made you sorry with a letter, I do not repent, though I did repent: for I perceive that the same epistle hath made you sorry, though *it were* but for a season.
9 Now I rejoice, not that ye were made sorry, but that ye sorrowed to repentance: for ye were made sorry after a godly manner, that ye might

receive damage by us in nothing.

10 For godly sorrow worketh repentance to salvation not to be repented of:
but the sorrow of the world worketh death.

11 For behold this selfsame thing, that ye sorrowed after a godly sort, what
carefulness it wrought in you, yea, *what* clearing of yourselves, yea, *what*
indignation, yea, *what* fear, yea, *what* vehement desire, yea, *what* zeal, yea,
what revenge! In all *things* ye have approved yourselves to be clear in this
matter.

8. Various points relating to the translation of these verses must be
noticed. The word "to be sorry" means to grieve, distress or pain, as
Ephesians 4. 30, "grieve not the holy Spirit of God". The word "repent" in
these verses consists of two different Greek words, namely "regret" (twice
in verse 8 and the second "repent" in verse 10) and the ordinary word for
repentance (as in verse 9 and the first word "repentance" in verse 10).
Lastly the expression "after a godly manner" in verse 9 and "godly" in verse
10 both mean "according to God". The divine name is actually used, and
the grief thus described would be the type that He values with no make-
believe; His point of view would be appreciated. We now repeat these
verses from the A.V., the preferred renderings being given in brackets.

"For though I made you sorry (grieved you) with a letter, I do not
repent (regret it), though I did repent (if even I did regret): for I
perceive that the same epistle hath made you sorry (grieved you),
though it were but for a season (if even for an hour). Now I
rejoice, not that ye were made sorry (were grieved), but that ye
sorrowed (were grieved) to repentance: for ye were made sorry
(were grieved) after a godly manner (according to God), that ye
might receive damage (suffer loss) by us in nothing. For godly
sorrow (grief according to God) worketh repentance to salvation
not to be repented of (regretted): but the sorrow (grief) of the
world worketh death. For behold this selfsame thing, that ye
sorrowed (grieved) after a godly sort (according to God), what
carefulness (diligence) it wrought in you, yea, what clearing of
yourselves (defence), yea, what indignation, yea, what fear, yea,
what vehement desire, yea, what zeal, yea, what revenge. In all
things ye have approved yourselves to be clear (pure) in this
matter."

These alterations in translation help to clarify the argument of the apostle,
since the English words used in the A.V. are confusing.

In verse 8, Paul makes two opposite statements. Firstly he writes "I do
not repent (regret)", since he now sees the fruit of his first letter unto
repentance. Their *grief* for an hour gave place to *relief*. There can be no
present joy in chastening, since such is grievous, Heb. 12. 11; yet
afterwards "it yieldeth the peaceable fruit of righteousness unto them
which are exercised thereby".

Secondly, he writes "though I did repent (regret)". Upon hearing of
their grief through Titus, he had thought that he had written the first

letter too strongly; his letters tended to be "weighty and powerful", 2 Cor. 10. 10. Instead, he wanted them to know that he loved them too abundantly to cause grief, 2. 4.

However, their grief was short-lived; it was "but for a season", or, "for an hour". God would not have a repentant soul remain in the dust. Grace raises such a soul to the blessings of His presence. For example, in 2 Samuel 12. 13–20, David fasted all night on the earth because of his sin and because of God's hand upon him. Afterwards, when he perceived the will of God, he "arose from the earth, and washed, and anointed himself, and changed his apparel, and came into the house of the Lord, and worshipped: then he came to his own house". Concerning this same event, David said first of all, "my sin is ever before me", Ps. 51. 3, but after restoration he would sing songs of praise and offer burnt offerings, vv. 15–19, and engage in open service and testimony that others may be converted to the Lord, v. 13.

9. Paul rejoiced because the grief had led to repentance. It must be realised that grief does not always end in repentance in saint and sinner. Conviction through grief does not always have the desired end. In Matthew 14. 9, King Herod "was sorry", but he would not change his course of conduct, so John was beheaded. Later, in Matthew 19. 22, the young man "went away sorrowful", but this did not lead to following the Lord and abandoning the stumbling block of his great possessions. The reason why the grief of the Corinthians had such a happy result was because their grief was "according to God". They saw His point of view in the matter and were happy to abide by His will, unlike the rich young man who would not see the point of view of the Lord Jesus. If the "courage of one's convictions" is lacking, then the desired end may also be lacking.

When they perceived Paul's corrections to be the mind of God, it was not possible for them to "receive damage", or to "suffer loss". The same word appears in the first Epistle, "he shall suffer loss", 3. 15. The Word of God is given "for doctrine, for reproof, for correction, for instruction in righteousness", 2 Tim. 3. 16, which can only lead to gain, the gain of being "throughly furnished unto all good works", v. 17. On the other hand, if the Word is not received from God's point of view, then men would suffer loss, for the word spoken by the Lord would "judge him in that day", John 12. 48.

10. Paul does not dwell here on the past sins of the Corinthians; rather he views the matter from the point of view of "salvation", that is, present salvation. In the same way as there is a past, present and future deliverance, 2 Cor. 1.10, so too in the matter of salvation. In the *past*, it is absolute through the efficacy of the blood of Christ; in the *present*, we are exhorted to work out our own salvation, Phil. 2. 12; in the *future*, salvation is "ready to be revealed in the last time", 1 Pet. 1. 5. We have been saved from the *penalty* of sin; we are being saved from the *power* of sin; we shall be saved from the *presence* of sin.

Paul also dwells on the two kinds of "sorrow", namely that "according to God" and that "of the world". The former refers to a believer taking the point of view of God to be his own; the blessed results unto repentance can never be regretted. If a believer appears to regret possessing spiritual blessings, being disposed to favour the old man and not the new, then it should be questioned whether he is a true believer in the Lord Jesus. A true believer does not practice sin nor does the new man delight in unrighteousness. But the grief of the world leads to nothing spiritual; no repentance follows. In men of the world, this leads to death, both present and future. In a believer, when he just copies the trends and style of the world, death means that he is ineffective in his life here and now.

11. Paul lists eight features proving that the Corinthian grief was according to God. Such minute detail of their repentance shows how observant Titus was, how accurate and factual was the report brought back to Paul, and how truthfully he comunicated this to Paul without exaggeration. Plain gossip merely seeks out the bad as interesting news items. This is typified by the raven, Gen. 8. 7, which was content with the flotsam and jetsam of the products of death caused by the flood. Truth, however, is the only thing that should be favoured by the Christian bearer and hearer of news. If there was none of that character, then the dove would return empty and bring nothing unfavourable into the holy precincts of the ark, Gen. 8.9.

> *Carefulness*, namely diligence. This is necessary in order to be able to add to faith the list of virtues given in 2 Peter 1. 5–7. The Corinthians showed such earnest application in the outworking of their own repentance and the fruit thereof.
>
> *Clearing of yourselves*, or defence, answer or apology. This was no argument to seek to justify their previous waywardness; rather their repentance now enabled them to use Scripture and the authority of Paul to "*give an answer* to every man that asketh you a reason for the hope that is in you with meekness and fear", 1 Pet. 3. 15.
>
> *Indignation*, or displeasure at their previous conduct. As a verb, Jesus was "much displeased" as the disciples rebuked those that brought young children to Him, Mark 10. 14.
>
> *Fear*, no doubt of again departing from the revealed ways of God. In Acts 5. 11, "great fear" came upon all the church as they saw the hand of God upon Ananias and Sapphira; this is salutary in times of weakness and declension.
>
> *Vehement desire*, or "earnest desire" as in verse 7. The soul was under great pressure to walk henceforth in paths of righteousness, and also to accept the apostle's authority.
>
> *Zeal*, or "fervent mind" as in verse 7. Again, the Corinthian motive was compelled to take a stand on Paul's teaching, seeking better things.
>
> *Revenge*, or vengeance: they did not spare themselves in self-judgment, 1 Cor. 11. 31.

Clear in this matter, that is, pure, chaste. The demonstration of their repentance was not artificial and feigned; it was transparent in its validity. It was not words but deeds; their motives and spiritual sensitivities were seen to be transformed.

Verses 12–16: The Reaction of Paul and Titus to this Repentance

12 Wherefore, though I wrote unto you, *I did it* not for his cause that had done the wrong, nor for his cause that suffered wrong, but that our care for you in the sight of God might appear unto you.
13 Therefore we were comforted in your comfort: yea, and exceedingly the more joyed we for the joy of Titus, because his spirit was refreshed by you all.
14 For if I have boasted any thing to him of you, I am not ashamed; but as we spake all things to you in truth, even so our boasting, which *I made* before Titus, is found a truth.
15 And his inward affection is more abundant toward you, whilst he remembereth the obedience of you all, how with fear and trembling ye received him.
16 I rejoice therefore that I have confidence in you in all *things.*

12. Paul first of all refers to his practical motives for writing previously; we take this to refer to his first Epistle. Three classes of men appear in the verse:

1. the one who had done the wrong;
2. the one who had suffered wrong;
3. the whole assembly.

The first two classes form a pair, of which several occur in the first Epistle. The man who had committed fornication had wronged another, and the whole assembly was puffed up with a sense of pride, 1 Cor. 5. 1–2. Again, "brother goeth to law with brother", the former suffering wrong and the latter doing wrong, 6. 6. Again, there was the man with liberty to eat meats offered to idols, stumbling the brother who was weak; the former did wrong and the latter suffered wrong, 8. 9–12.

Paul was of course concerned about such individuals, but he was also concerned about the effects on the assembly as a whole. Hence he wrote more particularly that "our *care* for you in the sight of God might appear unto you". The word used here is *diligence* (as "carefulness" in the previous verse). He had diligent interest in the wellbeing of the saints. Later, he wrote that he had the "*care* of all the churches" at heart, 11. 28. Here the word means "anxious interest". A third Greek word translated "*care*" occurs in 1 Timothy 3. 5, referring to the elders taking "*care* of the church of God"; this time the word actually means to meet the needs of the church; see also Luke 10. 34, 35. Both the first and third meanings occur in Proverbs 27. 23, "Be thou diligent to know the state of thy flocks, and look well to thy herds". The work of elders and teachers in a local assembly should be one of persistent effort to establish the flock. In practical matters too, the "same earnest *care*", 2 Cor. 8. 16, (that is, *diligence*) can be found in the hearts of those thus exercised.

It should be pointed out that the R.V. offers a different rendering, "but that your (not our) earnest care for us (not you) might be manifest unto you in the sight of God". J.N.D. follows the A.V., but Kelly in his translation allows both renderings. The New English Bible follows the R.V. The reason for the difference is that the principal Greek manuscripts vary amongst themselves, and opinion favours the R.V. rendering. If any value can be attached to the Greek text established "by means of Bible Numerics" by Ivan Panin, it is worthwhile pointing out that his text agrees with the R.V. rendering. Here is a phrase where the rendering by J.N.D. is now not wholly substantiated. We mention this since some adhere rather slavishly to this version, in spite of recent advances on the Greek text. J.N.D. did his best with the versions of the various editors *that existed in his day*. The whole basis of his translation was to adhere to the best available knowledge of his day. Had he been still alive no doubt he would have revised his own translation in deference to further light on the manuscripts. Faith is not blind to matters of Bible translation, but is susceptible to education.

Hence, referring to this preferred rendering, it seems that Paul wanted the Corinthians to know that he recognised that their interest in him (as a result of their repentance) now blossomed forth again.

13. Paul describes the feelings of his soul upon receiving the good news from Titus: he was comforted (encouraged), he joyed and he was refreshed. Some translators punctuate the first part of the verse differently: "Therefore we were encouraged. In our (not your) encouragement the more abundantly we rejoiced at the joy of Titus". When the apostle writes that he was comforted or encouraged, the perfect tense is used, meaning that the encouragement and its effects lasted up to the time when he was writing. It was not encouragement on the spur of the moment; it was not a spiritual emotion characterised by a "come today, gone tomorrow" attitude. Encouragement on account of a work "according to God" cannot evaporate from the heart of someone able to discern when God is truly working. Paul's whole changed testimony was one of rejoicing; he caught the atmosphere of the joy of Titus. Moreover, if Titus was refreshed by the Corinthians, it is not out of place to believe that Paul was also refreshed by the news, although absent from them.

Refreshment describes the state of a soul released from previous distress. The Lord Himself gives such relief to His own: to those who are heavy laden, He says, "I will give you *rest*", Matt. 11. 28; elsewhere, He took His disciples apart into a desert place, there to "*rest* a while", Mark 6. 31. Again in the context Paul uses the perfect tense to describe the refreshment of Titus. He was refreshed when in Corinth, and this was maintained on his return to Paul with goodly results.

14. Paul recalls the fact that he had boasted to Titus of the Corinthians before he sent him to Corinth with the first Epistle. Perhaps it had been difficult thus to boast, knowing of all the weaknesses dealt with in the letter. But Paul would boast of the holy features of the Corinthian assembly during his original stay with them on his second missionary journey. In fact, 1 Corinthians 1. 4–9, mentions some of these holy features, without reference to any departure from them. It is blessed to talk about the good things in a believer, even if that believer is temporarily not living up to that standard. To talk about the bad may rapidly degenerate into idle gossip and fleshly exaggeration.

Did Titus fully believe such a glowing report? The truth of the apostolic testimony rested upon the fact that Paul always spoke all things "in truth". Such reports were "found a truth" (or, *became* truth) to Titus when he observed the Corinthian repentance. Later, in a similar manner, the Macedonians, to whom Paul had boasted of the Corinthians, would learn the veracity of Paul's boasting, by observing these things firsthand, 2 Cor. 9. 1–5.

15. The inner affections of Titus remained centred upon the Corinthian saints, because he remembered their obedience. They had received him "with fear and trembling", as if the apostle himself had come among them. After all, Titus was Paul's "partner and fellow-helper concerning you", 2 Cor. 8. 23. It is good when apostolic authority is reflected in the example, conduct, and teaching of others, causing the same fear and trembling in believers. It is proper to tremble at the Word of God. The love of Christ casts out fear in those who are suitably exercised thereby. But even if fear is removed, it always behoves the saints to maintain awe and reverence, humility and respect, for the greatness and wonder of the Word of God. This is the basis of lasting repentance and of walking in the light.

16. Paul concludes by referring to himself, "I rejoice therefore that I have confidence in you in all things". This particular word for "confidence" occurs only six times in the N.T., five of them being in this Epistle. Paul had *confidence* in the truth of being at home with the Lord, 2 Cor. 5. 6, 8; later he wrote that he was *bold* (or confident) before the gainsayers in Corinth, 10. 1–2; finally in Hebrews 13. 6, believers have *confidence* in the Lord as their helper. But here in our verse, Paul's confidence, which had almost disappeared in the first Epistle, had been reawakened. Confidence is always a difficult thing to regain in one who has gone astray. Genuine repentance followed by works meet for repentance is the first step. But regained confidence is nothing forced or suspicious. It follows encouragement, rejoicing, refreshment, and the perception of obedience to a revelation of the truth.

2 CORINTHIANS 8–9

Section 3.   Historical: Paul's Rejoicing
Subject 2.   The Corinthian Collection

General Relationships

When studying any book of Holy Scripture, and a point in that book is discovered at which the subject matter seems to change abruptly, it is important to relate this change to the overall trend of teaching in that book as a whole. Failure to follow this simple rule may result in a complete lack of understanding of the mind of God being taught in that particular book.

To illustrate this, we may cite the well-known examples of Isaiah, Matthew, and Revelation.

Isaiah. Even a superficial reading shows a major break in the prophecy at the end of chapter 39. Some theologians even postulate a second author, deuteroIsaiah, taking over from chapter 40 onwards. A common authorship, however, is maintained by John 12. 38–40, where both parts of Isaiah are quoted, namely 6. 9 and 53. 1. Believers who value the Word of God need not be puzzled nor dismayed at the various source-theories propounded by those who do not believe in divine inspiration. Rather they take their stand on the fact that the three persons of the trinity of God had their part in the production of the sacred record; see 1 Peter 1. 11 where the Spirit of Christ (that is, before He became Man) testified of His sufferings through the prophets; 2 Timothy 3. 16 where God is stated as inspiring the Scriptures; 2 Peter 1. 21 where the Holy Spirit moved holy men to utter prophecy.

The break in Isaiah is by divine intent. Chapters 1–35 describe events of darkness and of judgment, both for Judah and the nations, broken here and there by scenes restoration. Chapters 36–39 present a historical interlude, showing the deliverance of Jerusalem from the Assyrian invasion, and king Hezekiah's recovery from a sickness that had been almost unto death. Such historical events delineate the deliverance of Israel from the great tribulation, and their ultimate recovery from their present spiritual sickness whose end would otherwise be death. From chapter 40 onwards, we read of the means that God will use to effect this restoration. The growing crescendo of the restoration of Zion takes the cross as its basis (chapter 53). Chapters 54–62 deal with the ultimate scope of millennial blessing, the pinnacle being found in chapter 62. Such a development of spiritual order is satisfying and sweet to a spiritual mind.

Matthew. The end of chapter 12 of this Gospel forms a natural break in the narrative. Prior to this, the Lord taught and preached directly without the use of parables, but from chapter 13 onwards the Lord made much use of parables. The reason for this change is clear. The Lord was presented to Israel to be received, and His teaching and works were *attractive*. Hostility gradually developed until the crisis of the Pharisees speaking blasphemy, Matt. 12. 24. From then on, the Lord spoke in parables, not to simplify the truth, but *to hide it* from those who would not receive it, 13. 10–17. At the same time, deeper truths are introduced–the kingdom, ch. 13, His person, 16. 16, the church, 16. 18, His death and resurrection, 16. 21, and His kingdom glory, 17. 1–9, .

Revelation. The end of chapter 3 presents an obvious break and change of subject. Prior to this, John had recorded the "things which are", Rev. 1. 19, namely letters to the local assemblies established on earth, representing conditions up to the time when He shall come for His own. But from chapter 4 onwards, namely "After this", John saw "things which must be hereafter", 4. 1, presenting conditions in heaven and on earth with the assembly no longer present.

At the expense of repetition, we must notice the position of this eighth chapter in this Epistle. Chapters 1, 2, 7, 8 and 9 are what may be termed historical chapters, containing also doctrinal and practical instruction and encouragement. The first two of these chapters give a deep insight into the apostle's exercises of *grief* (before he received news from Corinth), while the last three lay bare the apostle's *joy* (after he received news from Corinth). More specifically:

chapter 1 tells of Paul's exercise in *Ephesus*—verse 8 shows his trouble, and verse 16 his plans to leave for Corinth;

chapter 2 gives the apostle's exercise in *Troas*, vv. 12–13: having left Ephesus and come to this city, he could not preach the gospel even though there was an open door, since Titus had not returned;

chapter 7 follows, showing Paul's state of heart in *Macedonia*, grief giving place to joy at the coming of Titus, vv. 5–6, reminiscent of Psalm 30. 5, "Weeping may endure for a night, but joy cometh in the morning".

In chapter 2, Paul expressed his joy at the repentance of one man, vv. 5–8, but in chapter 7 he expressed his joy at the repentance of many, vv. 9–10. Spiritual joy is contagious, as Paul wrote elsewhere, "Rejoice in the Lord alway: and again I say, Rejoice", Phil. 4. 4. Hence at the end of chapter 7, Paul continues the theme of his joy and rejoicing into chapters 8 and 9, before embarking on the final subject of the Epistle concerning which there could be no joy. Moreover, chapter 7 deals with the work and movements of Titus, so in the following two chapters Paul continues to outline the character and work of this servant of God. At the same time, he dwells further on the *confidence* he has in them 7. 16.

Finally, to note the overall structure of the Epistle, we may repeat that

Paul, on his proposed visit to Corinth, feared that, while some in the assembly (the majority) would accept him, others (the minority) would not. Notice the following contrasts:

Chapters 3–6 are written to those who *would receive* him. They consist of the *exposition* of the service of the true minister, written to *encourage* those in Corinth who *had repented* as a result of reading the first Epistle. The style employs "we" throughout.

Chapters 10–13 are written to those who *would not receive* him. They consist of the *example* of the life of the true minister, written to *correct* those in Corinth who *had not repented* as a result of reading the first Epistle. The style employs "I" throughout.

Background of this Subject

In spite of Paul's constant movements in service among the Gentile nations, he was not ignorant of the work of God in Jerusalem from whence the gospel had originally spread, Acts 1. 8, nor of the needs of the believers there. We may note the following references to Paul in Jerusalem prior to his writing this second Epistle:

1. Acts 9. 26–29; after his conversion, "he was with them coming in and going out at Jerusalem", Barnabas having brought him and introduced him to the apostles. While in the temple at Jerusalem at about this time, he had the vision of the Lord telling him to "get thee quickly out of Jerusalem", Acts 22. 17–21.

2. Acts 11. 27–30; 12. 25. A famine had caused great need among believers at Jerusalem, and the disciples at Antioch decided "to send relief unto the brethren which dwelt in Judaea". This was sent to the elders through the instrumentality of Paul and Barnabas. Thus even before his first missionary journey, Paul had experience of this kind of fellowship and practical love.

3. Acts 15. 2–4, 22. Between Paul's first and second missionary journeys, he visited Jerusalem with Barnabas to deal with the question of circumcision which certain false teachers from Judaea had sought to introduce amongst Gentile converts.

4. Acts 18. 21. At the end of his second missionary journey he sought "by all means" to keep "this feast that cometh in Jerusalem". It was on this visit that Paul would learn of the pressing needs among the saints in this city. Unable to do anything about it while there personally, he would encourage help to be sent, as soon as he had departed to other districts where such need was not so prevalent.

At the beginning of his third missionary journey, Paul passed through the country of Galatia, Acts 18. 23, on his way to Ephesus. He evidently gave "order to the churches of Galatia", 1 Cor. 16. 1, regarding a collection. The churches of Macedonia, were commended for their zeal in the collection, 2 Cor. 8. 1–5. They were formed during Paul's second missionary journey and embraced, no doubt, the assemblies at Philippi and Thessalonica. Romans 15. 26 also refers to the activity of these assemblies. This latter verse also refers to believers in Achaia, the province in which Corinth was situated. Paul had exhorted the assembly in Corinth regarding this collection in his first Epistle, 1 Cor. 16. 1. It is not obvious whether this is the first time the apostle mentioned the collection to this assembly, or whether he had previously contacted them from Ephesus, using the first Epistle to encourage and direct them further in this good work. There seems to be no reference to Ephesus, a church founded on his third journey, gathering a collection. Is there a possibility that the Ephesians were backward in these practical acts of fellowship, having grown into heavenly truth as the Epistle to the Ephesians so emphatically witnesses? Is there a reference to this backwardness in the apostle's final words as he took his leave of the elders at Ephesus *en route* for Jerusalem taking the collection with him, "I have shewed you all things, how that so labouring ye ought to support the weak, and to remember the words of the Lord Jesus, how He said, It is more blessed to give than to receive", Acts 20. 35?

The object of the collection should be specially noticed. It was *not* for local need, as in Acts 6. 1–4. Moreover, it was *not* for labourers in the service of God, as in 1 Corinthians 9. 14; Philippians 4. 15–19. Rather, it was *for* "the poor saints which are at Jerusalem", Rom. 15. 26. To Paul's heart, the duty of the Gentiles in this direction was obvious. They were the debtors of the saints in Jerusalem, since "if the Gentiles have been made partakers of their spiritual things, their duty is also to minister unto them in carnal things", Rom. 15. 27. Salvation had radiated out from Jerusalem, both by the Old Testament scriptures bringing in the Gentiles through promise, Rom. 15. 8–12, by the original testimony starting in Jerusalem, Acts 1–2, and by Jews being converted and called to service amongst the Gentiles, Rom. 15. 16; Gal. 2. 8. The reception of a free gift spiritually from God should call forth practically good works to others. The "cup of cold water", Matt. 10. 42, and the things done "unto one of the least of these My brethren", 25. 40, are really reciprocations to Christ from hearts filled with His blessings and goodness. The reader should notice that there is nothing distasteful about the word "carnal" in Romans 15. 27, as there is, for example, in 1 Corinthians 3. 1–4.

It appears that the saints in Jerusalem were always in need, depending upon God to exercise the hearts of other believers not thus afflicted. They had sold all their possessions and goods, Acts 2. 45; 4. 34–37, perhaps thinking that the Lord's coming was nigh, and that His words in Matthew 24. 17–18 were relevant regarding the uselessness of personal possessions in that period. After this, money was distributed where there was need, Acts 6. 1, and a famine was serious for them, 11. 29. When all was expended, there was nothing of a material nature to fall back upon. Faith would look to God, who therefore opened the hearts of converts further afield, who had goods and money to spare.

The collection gathered in Corinth, as recorded in 1 Corinthians 16. 1–4, was perhaps distinct from current practice today. Usually, an offering is taken today in connection with an assembly gathering on the Lord's day. But Paul does not seem to hint at a common assembly collection in his remarks. All that can fairly be deduced is that each brother put aside in his own home on the Lord's days, a certain amount according as God prospered him. It was not a general assembly collection, but with a distinct purpose in view. These individual collections would form a whole when the apostle came to arrange for its transport to Jerusalem. Not that there is anything against a common collection when the saints are come gether. The method of taking a collection is not laid down; varying circumstances demand differing means. Each assembly must decide before the Lord, basing its practice, not on tradition, but on spiritual common sense according to present need. Certainly, at least, Hebrews 13. 15–16 links praise God-ward with giving, doing good and communicating to others.

When Paul wrote the first Epistle to the Corinthians, he sent it to Corinth with several brethren; this has a bearing upon the subject of the Corinthian collection. These visitors to Corinth were:

Timothy. He was sent from Ephesus, according to 1 Corinthians 4. 17: "For this cause have I sent unto you Timotheus, who is my beloved son, and faithful in the Lord, who shall bring you into remembrance of my ways which be in Christ, as I teach every where in every church". Paul humbly realised that his ways and his teaching were according to the mind of God; as such they could be displayed to others to follow. Paul's ways and teaching are evidently of universal appeal, as is seen in the phrase "every where in every church". Moreover, not anybody could convey the apostolic conduct to others; only one "faithful in the Lord" was competent to do this. Timothy was also one who "worketh the work of the Lord", 1 Cor. 16. 10, which would give added weight to his words. Note that Timothy conveyed in *spoken form* the ways and teaching of the apostle. The second Epistle conveyed in *written form* the same features, his *ways* in chapters 10–13 and his *teaching* in chapters 3–6.

Apollos. This man of God had visited Corinth after Paul's original work there, Acts 18. 27. It would seem that the faction built around him by some in Corinth, 1 Cor. 1. 12; 3. 4, was sufficient to keep him away, 16. 12, although it was the apostle's desire for him to visit the assembly.

Titus. 2 Corinthians 8. 16–17 shows that Titus was forward enough in his zeal and exercise to go on his own accord, and in particular to deal with the collection. Paul also expected him to return with news of the Corinthian reaction to the first Epistle; see 2 Cor. 2. 13; 7. 6, 7, 13.

The brother. In 2 Corinthians 8. 18, Paul sent with Titus "the brother, whose praise is in the gospel throughout all the churches", one who was "chosen of the churches" to travel in connection with the collection. As we shall see later, this may be an oblique reference to Timothy.

Our brethren. Finally, it would seem that there was a group of brethren accompanying these specifically named servants of God: "our brethren . . . they are the messengers of the churches, and the glory of Christ", 2 Cor. 8. 23. Oftentimes, brethren moved in company, Acts 20. 4 (representing churches formed on the first, second and third missionary journeys), or in ones and twos, 18. 27; 13. 2.

Under Titus, the Corinthian collection was to be continued and stimulated. Paul wrote so that even further efforts could be made, this being the essential subject matter of chapters 8 and 9. When finally Paul would visit Corinth, he would take possession of this collection, and take it with him to Jerusalem at the end of his third journey, 1 Cor. 16. 3–4; Rom. 15. 25–26.

Chapters 8 and 9 are subdivided into five well-defined paragraphs:

Chapter 8. 1–5: *Paul's boasting of the Macedonian collection to the Corinthians.* He had just found out the details of this collection upon his arrival in Macedonia, 2. 13; 7. 5; Acts 19. 21; 20. 1–2, causing him so great joy that he burst forth on this subject in this Epistle to the Corinthians.

Chapter 8. 6–15: *The fruits of giving—the recipients blessed.*

Chapter 8. 16–24: *The administration of finance* dignified and beyond suspicion. Paul outlines the work and character of the various messengers sent to Corinth.

Chapter 9. 1–5. *Paul's boasting of the Corinthian collection to the Macedonians.* He had just heard this news from Titus, and as the fruit of his joy he burst forth on the topic to the Macedonians. But in case he was too enthusiastic, he declared this boasting to the Corinthians, lest he should have boasted in vain.

Chapter 9. 6–15. *The fruits of giving—the donors blessed.*

There is a trend of thought through these two chapters, not consisting merely of wandering thoughts. Notice that these subdivisions provide two paragraphs concerning Paul's boastings, two paragraphs on the fruits of giving, and one central paragraph on divinely ordered administration.

Exposition of 2 Cor. 8: The Corinthian Collection

Verses 1–5: Paul's Boasting of the Macedonian Collection

1 Moreover, brethren, we do you to wit of the grace of God bestowed on the churches of Macedonia;

2 How that in a great trial of affliction the abundance of their joy and their deep poverty abounded unto the riches of their liberality.

3 For to *their* power, I bear record, yea, and beyond *their* power *they were* willing of themselves;

4 Praying us with much intreaty that we would receive the gift, and *take upon us* the fellowship of the ministering to the saints.

5 And *this they did*, not as we hoped, but first gave their own selves to the Lord, and unto us by the will of God.

1. The A.V. translation "we do you to wit" is given an alternative rendering in the margin "we must inform you". This particular Greek word *gnorizo*, merely meaning *to make known*, provided the A.V. translators with scope for using many and various strange expressions. In Galatians 1. 11, this word is translated "I *certify* you", while in Philippians 1. 22, we find "yet what I shall choose I *wot* not". Elsewhere in Corinthians, a more simple rendering is adopted, as "I give you to understand", 1 Cor. 12. 3, and "I declare unto you the gospel", 15. 1.

In this particular section comprising chapters 7–9, Paul uses various designations to describe the Lord's people in Corinth.

Brethren, 8. 1. This denotes practical fellowship in a family, God being owned as the Father of His people, John 20. 17. He uses the same description in 8. 22; 9. 3, 5.

Dearly beloved, 7. 1. This refers to Paul's sensitivity of soul, being endeared to those in whom he perceives the grace of God working unto correction.

Saints, 8. 4; 9. 1. This represents the exercise of Paul and the assemblies, to others similarly set apart in like circumstances. The collection was not to be handed over to some general fund being raised by the national or local civic authorities. It was for the people of God set apart for Himself. It would be unseemly for God's method of distribution to be overthrown, by placing the work under the discretion of unbelievers.

In this opening verse, Paul is drawing the attention of the Corinthians to "the grace of God bestowed on the churches of Macedonia". This was to be an example to them. Apart from the knowledge of need around them, there are various reasons for giving. For example, *grace* is the prompting of God, representing a favour from a superior to an inferior; and *love* in the prompting of the heart of a believer to give. The desire, and even the ability to give, come from the Lord as "the grace of God". David recognised this when gathering together the materials for the building of the temple, when he said "for all things come of Thee, and of Thine own have we given Thee", 1 Chron. 29. 14. Moreover, believers give according to the "*grace* of God" and not according to the *law* of God. In the O.T. Israel was under law to give to the Lord for the purpose of maintaining the priesthood and Levitical service. Tithing was introduced for this under law. For example, "And all the tithe of the land, . . . is the Lord's: it is holy unto the Lord", Lev. 27. 30; "the tithes of the children of Israel, which they offer as an heave offering unto the Lord, I have given to the Levites to inherit", Num. 18. 24; "unto the place which the Lord your God shall choose out of all your tribes to put His name there, . . . thither ye shall bring your . . . tithes", Deut. 12. 5–6 (verses 17–18 refer to the "second tithe" which the people themselves were to eat before the Lord; verse 19 refers to the tithe for the Levites); Nehemiah 10. 38 refers to "the tithe of the tithes", namely the tenth of what was given to the Levites had to be given to the priests. All this was accomplished under law; how much more now do the Macedonians abound unto every good work when God intervenes with grace.

The idea of *grace bestowed abundantly* for various purposes is prominent in these two Epistles. For example:

"His grace which was bestowed upon me was not in vain; but I laboured *more abundantly* than they all: yet not I, but the grace of God which was with me", 1 Cor. 15. 10.

"By the grace of God, we have had our conversation in the world, and *more abundantly* to you-ward", 2 Cor. 1. 12.

"We . . . beseech you that ye receive not the grace of God in vain", 2 Cor. 6. 1, after which up to verse 10, the apostle shows the *super-abundance* of the fruit of such grace in endurance and character.

Various times in these two chapters the idea of grace occurs: 2 Cor. 8. 1, 6, 7, 9, 19; 9. 8, 14. The supreme example of the Lord Jesus Christ occurs in 8. 9, while the subject closes with the words "the *exceeding* grace of God in you", 9. 14.

It can be seen that the effect of grace is nothing small or meagre. Rather the effects abound according to the purpose of God in bestowing that grace.

2. The churches of Macedonia were unlike Corinth in one respect. These churches would embrace Philippi and Thessalonica, places where Paul, in Acts 16–17, suffered persecution and imprisonment. This did not happen in Corinth; see Acts 18. 9–11. This persecution was passed on to the newly formed assemblies when Paul left them; "For ye, brethren, became followers of the churches of God which in Judaea are in Christ Jesus: for ye also have suffered like things of your own countrymen, even as they have of the Jews", 1 Thess. 2. 14. See also 1 Thess. 3. 3, 4. Under these conditions, there was no complacency amongst the believers in Macedonia. They were alive to their Christian duty both in witness and in good works. The Corinthians, on the other hand, apparently without such trials of affliction, tended to be more self-satisfied. Practical Christianity abounded in the face of great opposition, a reflection of the greater work of Christ on the cross, accomplished when the hatred of man reached its climax. Hence, for the Macedonians, "in a great trial of affliction the abundance of their joy and their deep poverty abounded unto the riches of their liberality".

It was a joy to give, even though the saints were found in "deep poverty", unlike the Corinthians who appeared to be rich, 1 Cor. 4. 8. The giving of the two mites left the widow in need herself, Mark 12. 44. In Philippians 4, Paul was in need; he knew how to be abased, to be hungry and to suffer need, v. 12. The Philippians, communicating with Paul in his affliction, sacrificed to such an extent that they left themselves in need.

Such a sacrifice was acceptable and well pleasing to God, who therefore supplied the need of the saints "according to His riches in glory by Christ Jesus", v. 19. Again, the poor saints in Jerusalem had a need, and the Macedonians were prepared to sink into greater need in order to meet it. This amounted to the "riches of their liberality", a word often meaning simplicity, that is, frankness, sincerity, willingness. But as in Philippians 4. 19, so here also; the donors are blessed by God, as Paul brings out at length, later in the last paragraph of chapter 9.

3. Paul now describes how the Macedonians went about this business. He bears record (or witnesses) that according to their power and even beyond it they were willing themselves. That is to say, they went beyond what could reasonably be expected of them. After all, the saints in Jerusalem had originally done the same. It could hardly have been called reasonable to have sold all their possessions, goods, lands, and houses, Acts 2. 45; 4. 34. But whatever their motive, it was done in the first glow of Pentecostal days. Everything was sold so that none lacked then, but as time passed, funds would run out and need became dominant. The remarkable thing is that no command appears to have been given to these early believers to sell their possessions. It had been a spontaneous exercise, yet one that could bring in sin and deception on the part of Ananias and Sapphira, Acts 5. 1–11. Similarly in Macedonia: they had been willing to follow the churches in Judaea regarding persecution, 1 Thess. 2. 14; now they are "willing of themselves" to embark upon this collection without a command from the apostle Paul. Paul had commanded the believers in Galatia and Corinth, 1 Cor. 16. 1, but it was the pleasure of the Macedonians thus to do without command, Rom. 15. 26. They had merely heard of the need from Paul, and then had been "willing of themselves". This word appears only twice in the Greek N.T., the other occasion being in verse 17 of this same chapter, where Titus is described as "being the more forward, of *his own accord* he went unto you". Hence the Macedonians needed no prompting as the Corinthians did.

This is, of course, the basis of true charity. This motive from the heart is altogether absent from many door-to-door collections. These are merely subtle forms of prompting which certainly the apostle Paul would not engage in, although he had verbally to prompt the Corinthians. This basis is seen in the Lord's devotion, when He said, "Lo, I come . . . to do Thy will, O God", Heb. 10. 7. This was also the basis of the non-obligatory offerings and sacrifices of the O.T. The devotional bringing of burnt offerings in Leviticus 1 must therefore be distinguished from the statutory burnt offerings in Leviticus 6. 9–13; Exodus 29. 38–42.

4. The A.V. translation here is far from exact. First, the phrase "that we would receive" represents one Greek word which competent editors of the Greek text affirm is not in the original. Second, the phrase in italics "take upon us" is inserted by the translators to make some sort of sense. The

A.V. reads as if the desire of the Macedonians was that Paul should take possession of the completed collection, in order to convey it to the saints in Jerusalem. This may have been true in the background, but it forms a poor conclusion to the demonstration of sacrificial zeal in verse 3. Is this all they could be zealous about, that Paul should take upon himself administrative and travelling responsibility? The verse literally means that the Macedonians beseeched Paul with much entreaty, the grace and fellowship of ministering to the saints. They wanted to have a share in it. It almost appears that Paul, realising the poverty of the Macedonians, did not even expect them to make any contribution. He may even have spoken against it, thus provoking their beseeching and begging. The motive was altogether on the Macedonian's side, and the verse continues the thought of verse 3, by showing the independent spiritual initiative on the part of the Macedonians. No wonder Paul was using this as an example to the Corinthians, and indeed to all believers of every generation!

5. "Not as we hoped" suggests that Paul originally had had no expectation at all that the Macedonians would be able to collect a sum together. In spite of this, they did things in the proper order.

> *Firstly*, they "gave their own selves to the Lord". This is always the first essential for the accomplishment of any exercise. It implies that the saints are viewing things from God's point of view; that spirituality and not worldliness is dominating. Hannah had this outlook in the O.T. when she said after the birth of Samuel, "Therefore also I have lent (or returned) him to the Lord; as long as he liveth he shall be lent to the Lord. And he worshipped the Lord there", 1 Sam. 1. 28. This contrasts with Eli, the high priest after the family of Ithamar and not Eleazar, who kicked at the sacrifices and offerings of God, 2. 29. Believers today, knowing the great truths of justification by faith, are exhorted right at the beginning of the practical section in Romans 12–15, to "present your bodies a living sacrifice, holy, acceptable unto God", Rom. 12. 1. Such an attitude of body, soul and spirit leads to God-ward things being held in proper perspective, things saint-ward following afterwards. Praise to God precedes doing good and communicating to others, Heb. 13. 15–16.

> *Secondly*, the apostle goes on to say, they gave themselves "unto us by the will of God". The giving of oneself over to the spiritual jurisdiction of a man—even if he be an apostle—is hardly a wise course, unless it be according to the will of God, as it was in this case. The Macedonians had no first-hand knowledge of the need in Jerusalem, but they recognised that Paul's testimony of the facts was sufficient for them to act upon it. Today, we also can give ourselves to the apostle in the sense that we yield ourselves to the apostolic writings and principles. We are in fact giving ourselves to the Lord by owning the authority of these writings, which are stated to be "the commandments of the Lord", 1 Cor. 14. 37.

Verses 6–15: The Fruits of Giving—the Recipients Blessed

6 Insomuch that we desired Titus, that as he had begun, so he would also finish in you the same grace also.

7 Therefore, as ye abound in every *thing, in* faith, and utterance, and knowledge, and *in* all diligence, and *in* your love to us, *see* that ye abound in this grace also.

8 I speak not by commandment, but by occasion of the forwardness of others, and to prove the sincerity of your love.

9 For ye know the grace of our Lord Jesus Christ, that, though he was rich, yet for your sakes he became poor, that ye through his proverty might be rich.

10 And herein I give *my* advice: for this is expedient for you, who have begun before, not only to do, but also to be forward a year ago.

11 Now therefore perform the doing *of it;* that as *there was* a readiness to will, so *there may be* a performance also out of that which ye have.

12 For if there be first a willing mind, *it is* accepted according to that a man hath, *and* not according to that he hath not.

13 For *I mean* not that other men be eased, and ye burdened:

14 But by an equality, *that* now at this time your abundance *may be a supply* for their want, that their abundance also may be *a supply* for your want: that there may be equality:

15 As it is written, He that *had gathered* much had nothing over; and he that *had gathered* little had no lack.

6. Paul now starts to apply the Macedonian example to the more backward Corinthians. He reiterates one reason why Titus had been sent to Corinth. It was not only to ascertain their reaction to the first Epistle, but also to deal with the collection. Paul had "desired", or rather *exhorted,* Titus to accomplish this task. The movements of Titus are not all recorded in Scripture. Certainly he was with Paul when he went up to Jerusalem between the first and second missionary journeys, Gal. 2.1. But then there is silence until this visit to Corinth during the third journey. Certainly the faithfulness, zeal, and trustworthiness of Titus had not waned during the intervening period. Indeed, his fellowship with the apostle was maintained to the end, 2 Tim. 4. 10.

In our verse, the expression "as he had begun" may suggest that Titus had been Paul's messenger to Macedonia. He had thus begun a good work there, and Paul wanted him to finish it in Corinth. The lesson is that a believer should continue in a faithful and fruitful work among the Lord's people when there is apostolic exhortation to do so. On the other hand, the willingness of Titus should be contrasted with the attitude of Apollos in 1 Corinthians 16. 12. Here, Paul "greatly desired" (or rather, exhorted) Apollos to go to Corinth, but his will was not to go at that time. There is no conflict here; ultimately one is responsible to the Lord as to one's movements.

The work of Titus among the Corinthians was to finish the collection, or at least to move upon the hearts of the saints there so that they were prepared to conclude the collection satisfactorily themselves. Paul refers to it as "the same grace also", implying a copying of the Macedonian example, the desire and ability to give freely to those who cannot give in return. A few months later, Paul would be quoting the words of the Lord Jesus to the Ephesian elders at Miletus, "It is more blessed to give than to receive", Acts 20. 35. Elsewhere the Lord had said, "freely ye have received, freely give", Matt. 10. 8. See also Luke 6. 33, 34.

7. Paul sees so many favourable abounding characteristics of the Corinthians that he desires that they should also abound in this good work. Paul observes that "ye abound in every thing", a remarkable echo of the first Epistle. In the introduction to the first Epistle, the apostle had remarked upon the grace given them by Christ Jesus, "That in every thing ye are enriched by Him, in all utterance, and in all knowledge, . . . So that ye come behind in no gift", 1 Cor. 1. 5–7. After dwelling upon the *grace* of God, Paul dealt at greater length with the *failure* of the Corinthians to use these gifts of grace according to the divine mind, 1 Cor. 14. But here, in the second Epistle, Paul again provides a list of gifts and spiritual virtues, without the necessity of a paragraph dealing with failure. It would appear that the Corinthians had repented and rectified their ways as a result of the reading of the first Epistle. This should always be the effect of the Word of God, which is profitable for "doctrine, for reproof, for correction, for instruction in righteousness", 2 Tim. 3. 16. As the author has seen hanging in a certain hall:

> *Doctrine* – what is right.
> *Reproof* – what is not right.
> *Correction* – how to get right.
> *Instruction* – how to keep right.

We may now note Paul's list:

Faith. In 1 Corinthians 12. 9, this is regarded as a spiritual gift, a prerequisite for the other gifts mentioned afterwards. Here, Paul may still have in mind faith as a gift, or it may have a wider implication as in 2 Peter 1. 5 where all believers have their portion.

Utterance. This refers to the various spiritual gifts for communication.

Knowledge. This appears as a gift in 1 Corinthians 12. 8; 13. 8, and we have suggested that it refers to the special ability possessed by some, to marshal doctrinal facts ready for dissemination. Elsewhere, Paul had observed that knowledge without love could puff up, thereby stumbling a weaker brother, 1 Cor. 8. 1.

Diligence. Or haste, care, endeavour; "that our *care* for you in the sight of God might appear", 2 Cor. 7. 12. See Proverbs 27. 23.

Love to us. To make such an observation shows Paul's ready joy in accepting the repentance of the Corinthians. He had always loved them, 1 Cor. 16. 24; 2 Cor. 2. 4. Nevertheless he knew that there would still be a few who did not love him: "the more abundantly I love you, the less I be loved", 12. 15. This has always been the experience of the people of God who, through love of the truth, have loved their fellow believers though not the various things that they have introduced from time to time.

These characteristics, gifts and virtues just listed are to be evenly distributed and displayed. The fine flour of the meal offering, Lev. 2. 1, speaks of the evenness displayed in the Lord's life, as seen through the microscope of the divine mind declared in the Scriptures. No one feature of the divine Person outshone another; there was harmony and balance in His teaching, walk, and works. God would have His people maintain the same evenness in their conduct, worship, witness, and service. The grace of gift is seen in such verses as:

"having then gifts differing according to the *grace* that is given to us", Rom. 12. 6;

"but unto every one of us is given *grace* according to the measure of the gift of Christ", Eph. 4. 7;

"as every man hath received the gift, . . . as good stewards of the manifold *grace* of God", 1 Pet. 4. 10;

This grace of gift must be equally mingled with practical grace, the grace of giving, "see that ye abound in this grace also". Moreover, as God is the author of *spiritual gifts*, so too is He the divine originator of this practical *grace of giving*: "God is able to make all grace abound toward you; that ye . . . may abound to every good work", 2 Cor. 9. 8; "Being enriched in every thing to all bountifulness", v. 11. We may finally notice the third grace received from God, that of *salvation*, which is of course the first in the experience of believers: "much more the grace of God, and the gift by grace, which is by one man, Jesus Christ, hath abounded unto many", Rom. 5. 15.

8. Paul here explains why he is thus exhorting the Corinthians. Although he is emphatic in his exhortation, it is not the commandment of a principle of God. (Compare 1 Cor. 14. 37, where it is a question of the commandments of the Lord, with 1 Cor. 7. 25, where a commandment of the Lord is stated *not* to be in question.) Commandments would deal with unchangeable principles for service, but elsewhere apostolic judgment, using divinely given wisdom, is given for the most appropriate course of action under particular circumstances. Believers today may exercise such judgment as to what course of action is most befitting under given circumstances.

The apostle gives two reasons:

1.   "*by occasion of the forwardness of others*". The example of the Macedonians should inspire the Corinthians. Very appropriately, the word for "others" used here means "others of a different kind". To be honest, Paul must draw a sharp distinction between the attitude of the Macedonians and that of the Corinthians. Even if men fail to see a difference between attitudes and motives in different assemblies, the Lord can see and rewards accordingly. The word "forwardness" applied to the Macedonians is not the same word as used of the Corinthians in verse 2 of chapter 9. In

the present verse, the word means "diligence, with haste". The Macedonians, having an exercise, were swift to fulfil it. But in 9. 2, the word means "readiness"; the Corinthians were ready to take a collection, but apparently were slack in the fulfilment of it. A doer and not a hearer only is required, James 1 . 22.

2. "*to prove the sincerity of your love*". The words of love are one thing, but the deeds of love are another; "let us not love in word, neither in tongue; but in deed and in truth", 1 John 3. 18. The proof of the pudding is in the eating, and Paul writes to test the genuineness of their love.

9. The example of the Macedonians was useful to demonstrate what can be done by believers. But it fades into insignificance when the example of Christ is contemplated. In the context, the "grace of our Lord Jesus Christ" is that of freely giving to others from the divine store of riches. From His personal store, He gave to us. The Macedonians may abound to deep poverty, v. 2, but the Lord became poor, not only by becoming flesh, but by going into death itself. In His life here, virtue went out of Him when miracles were performed, Luke 8. 46, but in His death, He was a worm and no man; trouble was near with none to help; He was compassed by bulls and dogs (Jews and Gentiles); His strength was dried up, and His garments were parted, Ps. 22. 6–18.

In the case of believers, we have the principle quoted in chapter 9 verse 6, "he which soweth bountifully shall reap also bountifully". How much more would this apply to the Lord. His loss gave rise to His gain, "I am poor and sorrowful: let Thy salvation, O God, set me up on high", Ps. 69. 29. It was through sufferings that He entered into His glory, Luke 24. 26; 1 Pet. 1. 11. He laid down His life that He might take it again, John 10. 17. See John 12. 24.

Yet His poverty not only led to *His* resurrection glory; He became poor for our sakes, that *we* might be enriched. (The A.V. reads "might be rich", a static implication. The proper translation is "might be enriched", in an active sense.) We are enriched in many ways. In John 10, four times the thought occurs that He laid down His life for the sheep. In Paul's writings, the thought that He gave Himself occurs five times, with various blessings of enrichment in view:

1. Galatians 1. 4, He "*gave Himself* for our sins, that He might deliver us from this present evil world".
2. Galatians 2. 20, "the Son of God, who loved me, and *gave Himself* for me". The object was that Christ should live in the believer, who lives his life in the flesh by the faith of the Son of God.
3. Ephesians 5. 25, "Christ also loved the church, and *gave Himself* for it". The enrichment of the church is that of sanctification and cleansing, ready to be presented unto Him "a glorious church, not having spot, or wrinkle, or any such thing; but that it should be holy and without blemish", v. 27. See also verse 2.

4. 1 Timothy 2. 5–6, "For there is one God, and one mediator between God and men, the man Christ Jesus; who *gave Himself* a ransom for all, to be testified in due time". Here the blessing is the spreading of the Gospel message concerning Himself as the Ransom and Mediator.
5. Titus 2. 14, "Who *gave Himself* for us, that He might redeem us from all iniquity, and purify unto Himself a peculiar people, zealous of good works". The object here is the change of nature and interests in the child of God.

10. The ability to give advice is the fruit of years of experience of practical, yet spiritual, wisdom. Paul must give advice, since he sees the Corinthians in such a different state from the willingness exhibited by the Lord. He deals with what is "expedient for you" namely what is profitable for *them*, and that for their *own* blessing as God would turn things out. It appears that the Corinthians had been slow in this matter for a whole year. Originally, they had been active in gathering the sum together, and they had been "forward". This word is distinct from the two similar words occurring in 8. 8. and 9. 2. Here, it means "willing". Willingness and accomplishment are two great features of a believer's life; as Paul writes elsewhere, "it is God which worketh in you both to *will* and to *do* of His good pleasure", Phil. 2. 13, since such good works "God hath before ordained that we should walk in them", Eph. 2. 10.

The Lord's willingness and accomplishment are seen, for example, in His recognition of *His hour*. He moved towards it willingly knowing "the determinate counsel and foreknowledge of God", Acts 2. 23. In John 2. 4, He knew His hour *had not yet come*, but in John 13. 1; 17. 1, He knew it *had come*, and He went forth willingly to accomplish the work of the cross.

Evidently Paul feels that the Corinthian collection had only just begun. The results of his exhortation in the first Epistle to put away funds on each first day of the week, 1 Cor. 16. 1–2, and the efforts of Titus in Corinth, are regarded by Paul as a beginning only. Obviously a work of this magnitude demanded continuous exercise and encouragement. There is no thought of only one small collection being made on one Lord's Day. The work in Jerusalem was so vital and precious to him that it demanded months of in-gathering for a worthy and worth-while gift to be sent.

11. Paul exhorts that *doing* should not lag behind *willing*. Again, to mention the Lord's example, His willingness in such a verse as "Lo, I come . . . to do Thy will, O God", Heb. 10. 7, found its proper conclusion in His words "I have finished the work which Thou gavest Me to do", John 17. 4. Willingness without doing is reflected in the parable of the two men who had to work in their father's vineyard, since one man "answered and said, I go, sir: and went not", Matt. 21. 30.

12. The expression "willing mind" is the translation of one Greek word, namely *readiness* (the same word occurs in the previous verse). Moreover, editors of the Greek text omit the word "man" in this verse (a word meaning anyone), so we may read the verse as "he is accepted according to that he hath". Note that it is *"he* is accepted", not *"it* is accepted"; see Genesis 4. 7, "shalt *thou* not be accepted?".

The idea of this verse continues the thought at the end of verse 11, namely "out of that which ye have". God treats each believer personally in this matter; it is not a question of what any brother *might* have. There must be accord between *readiness* and what is actually *possessed.* God accepts the man in whom these two features are dove-tailed. Mere mechanical giving, or giving under law of compulsion, is excluded. He can discern if the gift attains the standard of being "an odour of a sweet smell, a sacrifice acceptable, wellpleasing to God", Phil. 4. 18.

13. Paul concludes this paragraph by dealing with the question, how far should a believer go in giving? One principle at least, emerges, namely, "I mean not that other men be eased, and ye burdened"; the last word bears the thought of *pressure.* The exact balance between being eased and being burdened must remain an individual exercise before God. Certainly Scripture must not be interpreted so as to contradict Scripture. To the author it seems that Paul is showing that the "widow's mite" is an exceptional case and not a general example.

Mark 12. 41–44 should be read in this connection. There the rich cast in much, out of their abundance. There was no spiritual motive, no readiness, no exercise; they merely wanted to be seen of men, that self-satisfaction might be their reward, see Matt. 6. 1–4. But the Lord saw them too, He "beheld how the people cast money into the treasury". He saw, not merely the outward display, but "the thoughts and intents of the heart". Contrast the attitude of the rich, with the zeal and faithfulness demonstrated by the people in Hezekiah's day, when they brought willingly to the house of the Lord to form the "heaps", 2 Chron. 31. 5–12.

But the widow was also seen by the Lord; she had put in "all that she had, even all her living". Yet the Lord does not exhort His disciples to do likewise. Where riches are a stumbling block to discipleship, indeed the Lord would have the rich young ruler dispose of his possessions, Mark 10. 21–22, but elsewhere He exhorted His servants to take their purses, Luke 22. 36. Obviously the widow was burdened by her giving; the Lord does not commend this, and Paul does not support it either. Rather, the Lord uses the incident to contrast her action with that of the rich. He does not support the expediency of her action although devotion was there, particularly as the mites were given for the maintenance of Herod's temple which would be completely thrown down, Mark 13. 2 (two verses later).

14. Far from some being eased and some burdened, here Paul argues for a two-way traffic "that there may be equality". This cannot mean that Paul had in mind a grey uniformity for all believers, or, to think of a greater

extreme, that he advocated communism. This would make nonsense of
the recognized relationship of master to servant found elsewhere in the
Epistles, Eph. 6. 5–9; Col. 3. 22 to 4. 1. Moreover, in this verse, Paul is not
writing *only* about material things. "*Your* abundance" certainly refers to the
financial state of the Corinthians, but "*their* abundance" refers to the
spiritual abundance of the church at Jerusalem. Faithfulness in this latter
place could meet the "want" in the assembly at Corinth.

Equality in material things appears to refer to no believer having need
of the basic necessities of life. There is a supply from both sides as and
when they can. Want is eliminated, not by any being made rich by those
who are richer, but by a supply of the necessities of life. Luke 16. 9–12
should be read. A literal translation of verse 9 is "Make to yourselves
friends *by means* of the mammon of unrighteousness, that when *it* shall fail,
they may receive you into the eternal dwellings". Here there is fellowship
and reciprocation "in that which is least".

15. Finally, Paul quotes from Exodus 16. 18, to demonstrate the true
idea of equality, "He that had gathered much had nothing over; and he
that had gathered little had no lack". The command of the Lord had been
"Gather of it every man according to his eating, an omer for every man",
v. 16, showing that the idea of *what is necessary* is involved. That which
was *beyond their need*, and left over to the next day, merely "bred worms,
and stank", v. 20. As for those who inadvertently had not gathered
enough, miraculously the Lord made sure it was sufficient; they had "no
lack". Similarly in the financial realm; the Lord intervenes to provide for
His own, by exercising the hearts of others. Moreover, an omer of this
manna was laid up in the ark as a memorial, showing that the exercise of
meeting the need of others is a sweet savour of Christ in the conduct of
the Lord's people.

Verses 16–24: The Administration of Finance

16 But thanks *be* to God, which put the same earnest care into the heart of
   Titus for you.
17 For indeed he accepted the exhortation; but being more forward, of his
   own accord he went unto you.
18 And we have sent with him the brother, whose praise *is* in the gospel
   throughout all the churches;
19 And not *that* only, but who was also chosen of the churches to travel with
   us with this grace, which is administered by us to the glory of the same
   Lord, and *declaration of* your ready mind:
20 Avoiding this, that no man should blame us in this abundance which is
   administered by us:
21 Providing for honest things, not only in the sight of the Lord, but also in
   the sight of men.
22 And we have sent with them our brother, whom we have oftentimes
   proved diligent in many things, but now much more diligent, upon the
   great confidence which I *have* in you.
23 Whether *any do enquire* of Titus, he is my partner and fellowhelper

concerning you: or our brethren *be enquired of, they are* the messengers of the churches, *and* the glory of Christ.

24 Wherefore shew ye to them, and before the churches, the proof of your love, and of our boasting on your behalf.

The administration of finance in a local assembly must be clothed with dignity to raise it from a mere carnal level, and the means adopted must have the confidence of the saints. Moreover, as we shall see, the responsibility for financial matters must fall upon those who have laboured spiritually among the flock. It must not be a cloak of outward activity to cover up a carnal disposition, or barrenness, or lack of interest in spiritual things. A brother engaged in financial matters in his daily business is not *thereby* qualified to handle assembly funds. But if he has shown himself diligent in the spiritual service of the assembly, then his outside qualifications may then commend themselves to the confidence of the saints. The paragraph now before us mainly deals with the qualifications of brethren engaging in such matters.

16. God is the origin of all true service of whatever kind it is. Paul is praising God (not man) for exercise manifested in another, namely Titus. The "same earnest care" in the heart of Titus refers to diligence. The Corinthians themselves had abounded in this, v. 7, though perhaps not so much in financial matters. The word "same" no doubt refers to a repetition of Titus' exercise. Titus had originally showed such care when he was among the Macedonians. Paul now realises that this is to be repeated towards the Corinthians. Such repetition of exercise and service is not just a mechanical activity, rather it is bringing forth fruit *after its kind* unto God. Timothy also had this same capacity for fruit-bearing. Knowing this already, Paul intended to send him to Philippi, "For I have no man likeminded, who will naturally care for your state", Phil. 2. 19–20.

17. It was Paul's desire that Titus should go to Corinth, but in the event, Titus went on his own initiative; he was "more forward", namely diligent. This may be the reason why Titus is not mentioned in the first Epistle; Paul wanted Timothy to go, and wrote this even in chapter 4. But no doubt the Epistle was complete before the exercise of Titus was known to Paul. The point to observe is that there was fellowship in this service—a plurality of interest and exercise on the parts of both Paul and Titus. Such mutuality of thought is invaluable in a local assembly, avoiding the necessity of one or two brethren having to jog along the remainder in their exercises. Independent judgment, which nevertheless blends with that of other brethren, is something to be diligently sought after. No wonder in verse 23 Paul can refer to Titus as "my partner and fellowhelper concerning you". This was the qualification of Titus to engage in such a mission.

We may notice various examples in all fields of service where a divinely given exercise and call, corresponds with the spiritual intentions of the servant.

Financial care. The exercise for this service came both from God and
from the promptings of the inner heart of Titus, vv. 16, 17

Eldership in a local assembly is of divine origin, "over which the Holy
Ghost hath made you overseers", Acts 20. 28, and also of individual
personal exercise, "If a man desire the office of a bishop, he desireth
a good work", 1 Tim. 3. 1.

Spiritual gifts. These are distributed by the Spirit to whom He will, 1
Cor. 12. 11, yet individual saints can "desire spiritual gifts, but
rather that ye may prophesy", and "covet to prophesy", 1 Cor. 14. 1,
39. This reflects similar situations in the O.T.

Moses had the personal exercise to build a tabernacle, Exod. 15. 2, (as
recorded in chapter 33. 7–11), but God gave the details in His own
time, 25. 9

David had the idea of building the house, 2 Sam. 7.1–7, but it was God
who gave the details, 1 Chron. 28. 12, 19.

In our own application of this truth, how careful we must be lest we merely
interpret our own whims to be the will of God for us.

18. "The brother" was also sent. Can this be an oblique reference to
Timothy, who was also writing the Epistle as 1. 1 shows? Certainly his
name would not be mentioned openly under such circumstances, in the
light of such a glowing account of the spiritual ability of "the brother".
Some have suggested that the reference is to Luke, Mark, Barnabas, Silas,
Aristarchus, Gaius, but these are mere guesses. The fact that his name is
not given makes his qualifications even more pertinent for believers today,
since his "praise is in the gospel throughout all the churches". Some will
ask, what has an evangelist to do with financial matters? The whole point
is that spiritual qualifications come first, as with the seven chosen in Acts
6 for serving tables.

To say that financial work is what is appropriate to deacons, is taking a
very low point of view regarding deacons. A deacon is *any brother who
serves in any way.* In Acts 6, the apostles did deacon work by giving
themselves "to the *ministry* of the word", v. 4, the root of the word ministry
being service or deacon's work. Similarly, the word "serve" in "*serve* tables"
contains the same root. Spiritual things and mundane things are alike
embraced by men called "deacons". We find these men in Acts 6, full of
faith and of the Holy Spirit, full of faith and power, doing great wonders
and miracles among the people; men full of the Holy Spirit and wisdom,
vv. 3, 5, 8.

Hence it should not be counted as unusual, that financial
administration should be undertaken by a brother "whose praise is in the
gospel throughout all the churches". Other churches recognised this zeal
and ability, which evidently was not only practised locally, but was
manifest in a large number of surrounding assemblies. Provided one's heart
goes out to the Lord, it is appropriate to recognise special gifts and zeal in
another. Other cases occur in the N.T.

Timothy, Acts 16. 2, "which was well reported of by the brethren that were at Lystra and Iconium".

James, Cephas, John, Gal. 2. 9, "who seemed to be pillars".

Onesiphorus, 2 Tim. 1. 18, "in how many things he ministered unto me at Ephesus, thou knowest very well".

19. Here we have the principle of selection for this kind of administrative work. It was "not that only", namely not only Paul's decision to send this brother. He "was also chosen of the churches to travel with us with this grace". The idea of the local assembly choosing, appears in other passages: "whomsoever *ye shall approve*", 1 Cor. 16. 3; "*look ye out* among you seven men . . . whom we may appoint over this business", "*they chose* Stephen, . . . whom they set before the apostles", Acts 6. 3, 5, 6. In other words, the local assembly selects, chooses, and approves those responsible in financial matters. No doubt this would be accomplished by mutual consultation, but ultimately the assembly as a whole must approve the arrangements. It is wrong for a small group of men to seek to gain control of such matters by their own unbecoming forwardness. This method of selection would also be suitable for other matters, such as the choice of brethren responsible for the maintenance of assembly property. But this should be contrasted with selection for spiritual work such as eldership and the use of spiritual gift, which takes place by the risen Lord. For existing elders to select others to join them, and to present this as a *fait accompli* to the assembly, is hardly in keeping with the Scriptures. Rather elders discern a man fitted by God for this charge. There is a desire for fellowship in the work both in their hearts and in his. They then inform the assembly of their exercise, in order to ascertain if there are valid objections from those who must know the elders who will lead them.

This brother was also chosen to travel with Paul in this work. "To travel with us" means *our fellow-traveller*, one going the same way with the same intentions. The only other time this word occurs is in Acts 19. 29, where at Ephesus, Gaius and Aristarchus, men of Macedonia, were Paul's "companions in travel".

The gift that was administered by Paul and the others was raised above the level of mere earthly charity. Two reasons are given:

1. To the *glory* of the same Lord". The object of the Lord's own work was that "the Father may be *glorified* in the Son", John 14. 13. The same exhortation comes to the Lord's people, "whatsoever ye do, do all to the *glory* of God", 1 Cor. 10. 31; "filled with the fruits of righteousness, which are by Jesus Christ, unto the *glory* and praise of God", Phil. 1. 11.

2. The "declaration of *your* ready mind" should read, according to the editors of the Greek text, "of *our* ready mind". The work showed up their character in being willing to spend and be spent in the service of God.

20. Paul now explains why it is necessary to have "the brother" engaged in this work. He would avoid blame falling on anyone. Joint action would prevent suspicion falling on an individual by a false (or even a well-intentioned) accuser. Today, financial responsibility in a local assembly should not rest in the hands of one man. This removes the risk of an unspiritual man pointing an accusing finger at an individual.

Scripture gives abundant witness to this procedure.

John 8. 17, "the testimony of *two men* is true", taken from the O.T., Deut. 17. 6.

Acts 6. 3, "look ye out among you *seven men* of honest report", though shortly afterwards this was reduced to six by the death of Stephen, and to five by the removal of Philip to Caesarea, Acts 8. 40; 21. 8.

1 Corinthians 16. 3, "*them* will I send to bring your liberality to Jerusalem". In this verse note that Paul wrote the letters to the saints in Jerusalem commending to them the messengers chosen by the Corinthians.

Acts 11. 30, "they . . . sent it to the *elders* by the hands of *Paul and Barnabas*". This shows that the elders were not disassociated from the financial work, although theirs was a spiritual work. Brethren who deal with money matters are servants of the assembly, and the elders may therefore exercise a wise influence over these matters.

2 Kings 12. 10–11, dealing with the temple restoration in the days of Jehoiada the high priest, "when they saw that there was much money in the chest, that the *king's scribe and the high priest* came up, and *they* put up in bags, . . . and *they* gave the money . . . into the hands of *them* that did the work, that had the oversight of the house of the Lord".

21. "Providing for honest things, not only in the sight of the Lord, but also in the sight of men" is the reason for several brethren to be occupied with financial affairs. The Lord knows whether an individual is honest, but this character must also be known by believers as well. The Lord sees the heart, but men can only see the outward display. The greater the number occupied in the work, the greater will be confidence of the assembly in what is done. It is not sufficient for an individual brother to hide behind the Lord's knowledge of him that shall be manifested at the judgment seat of Christ. All must be open before the brethren as well. As far as David's sin was concerned, Nathan said to him, "thou didst it secretly", 2 Sam. 12. 12, by which we understand that David felt that the people had no knowledge of the underhand way in which he had ordered circumstances. But the Lord knew, "the thing that David had done displeased the Lord", 11. 27. Again, in the case of Judas, the disciples failed to understand the implication of the Lord's words, "That thou doest, do quickly", John 13. 27. The Lord knew, but the disciples thought that everything was in order "because Judas had the bag". If financial matters are not kept in order, no amount of spiritual work will cover up error and incompetence. "He that is unjust in the least is unjust also in much", Luke 16. 10.

22. "We have sent with them our brother" suggests that a third messenger was sent by Paul to Corinth, in addition to Titus and "the brother". The *identity* of such a brother is irrelevant. The Spirit of inspiration would bring his *character* before us, for it is this that fits him for the administrative work of this mission. Paul had often times proved him "diligent in many things", showing that he was not a novice but a man of considerable experience. Newcomers to the church of God through salvation, must not expect an opening in service until progress has been made through a period of growth in grace. Moreover, this diligence superabounded when confidence had been regained in the Corinthians.

23. The qualification of Titus was that he was Paul's "partner and fellowhelper" for the Corinthians. Paul was an apostle; Titus was not. Yet the apostle never thought that he did not need companionship and helpers in the gospel of Christ.

> *Partner.* This refers to one who is a partaker of the same circumstances, having the same unity of outlook in zeal, trials, and faith.
> *Fellowhelper,* or fellow worker, those whom Paul valued to work together with him. Thus named in Paul's letters are Priscilla and Aquila, Rom. 16. 3, Urbane, v. 9, Timothy, v. 21, Epaphroditus, Phil. 2. 25, Tychicus, Onesimus, Aristarchus, Mark, Justus, Col. 4. 7–11, Philemon, Demas and Luke, Philem. 1, 24. Those who follow on in the apostle's ways may be styled similarly, with the promised blessing that the names of such fellow labourers "are in the book of life", Phil. 4. 3.

Paul again refers to the other messengers, namely "the brother" of verse 18 and "our brother" of verse 22. The word translated "messengers" is really "apostles"; yet not in the *specific* sense of referring to the twelve and Paul, but in the *general* sense referring to the fact that they were sent. Epaphroditus is also called an apostle or "messenger" in this general sense of having been sent, Phil. 2. 25. Some would pervert the Word of God today, by saying that apostles are still present in the church. In the *specific* sense of apostolic gift and calling, that which was "first" certainly no longer pertains, as in 1 Corinthians 12. 28, such being called and chosen *by the Lord*, Eph. 4. 11. In the *general* sense, a messenger sent *by men* is an apostle, as in the verse before us. Clearly such men may exist today, but such men on a mission must not be confused with the original apostles who were sent forth by the Lord.

Note that these men were chosen by the churches and sent forth, not for their own self-importance, but for "the glory of Christ"; see also verse 19. It is heartening to know that faithful work in these mundane matters is just as glorifying of Christ as work of a more spiritual nature and calling.

24. Paul finally touches upon the responsibility of the Corinthians, and this subject continues into chapter 9. The fact that they had to show the proof of their love to the messengers shows that only Titus had returned to Paul and that the other two brethren were still in Corinth.

The progress of the collection had to be made known to these messengers and also to the churches. The light of the Corinthians had to "shine before men", Matt. 5. 16. Here, it cannot be what individuals give, since alms are to be "in secret", 6. 4. But the collective assembly bounty was to be made known to the messengers, and from them to their home assemblies in Macedonia. At the same time, the knowledge of the progress of the collection was not for carnal boasting or curious inquisitiveness but that the following might be achieved.

1. "The proof of your love". The inner heart can only be laid bare by outward actions. The heart going out to the poor saints in Jerusalem is manifested by deeds. Note that deeds by themselves do not show that love is present, as Paul wrote elsewhere, "though I bestow all my goods to feed the poor, . . . and have not charity, it profiteth me nothing", 1 Cor. 13. 3. God would have His people avoid mere mechanical action.

2. "Our boasting on your behalf". Paul had already boasted of the Corinthian collection to the Macedonians, as he elaborates in the next chapter. Even the apostle realised that his enthusiasm was based upon the report by Titus. Several months may elapse before he arrived in Corinth, and in that time the zeal of the Corinthians may have diminished again. Paul is writing to avoid this.

Exposition of 2 Cor. 9: The Corinthian Collection (continued)

Verses 1–5: Paul's Boasting of the Corinthian Collection

1 For as touching the ministering to the saints, it is superfluous for me to write to you:

2 For I know the forwardness of your mind, for which I boast of you to them of Macedonia, that Achaia was ready a year ago; and your zeal hath provoked very many.

3 Yet have I sent the brethren, lest our boasting of you should be in vain in this behalf; that, as I said, ye may be ready;

4 Lest haply if they of Macedonia come with me, and find you unprepared, we (that we say not, ye) should be ashamed in this same confident boasting.

5 Therefore I thought it necessary to exhort the brethren, that they would go before unto you, and make up beforehand your bounty, whereof ye had notice before, that the same might be ready, as *a matter of* bounty, and not as *of* covetousness.

1. This verse is another demonstration of Paul's wise way of dealing with believers. In 1 Corinthians 11. 2, he praised the Corinthians for keeping the ordinances he had delivered to them. This praise precedes the rest of the chapter occupied with correction of fundamental error. Similarly in this verse 1. A note of praise concerning service for the saints in the words "it is superfluous for me to write to you", precedes exhortation on the same matter. Paul combines *commendation* with *carefulness*. Commendation may cause pride, unless suitably toned down with caution about responsibility. Today, commendation of an assembly and its service, by a speaker from the platform, is far from wise. It may easily lead to pride and self-esteem, instead of the attitude of the true servant who said "We are unprofitable servants: we have done that which was our duty to do", Luke 17. 10.

2. Paul recalls the subjects of which he was boasting to the Macedonians. A year had elapsed since their original exercise, in which they were
(a) *forward in mind*, indicating that they were *willing*, showing as in chapter 8 verses 11, 12, "readiness" and "a willing mind;
(b) *ready*, that is, *prepared*, as in Acts 10. 10, 1 Cor. 14. 8. The former refers to motive; the latter refers to plans to put the exercise into execution.

Paul wanted the matter brought to fruition, but the Corinthians over the year had shown slackness in putting the plans into effect. Delay in practical matters seldom has a beneficial effect. In 2 Kings 12. 4–7, the king Jehoash was willing and ready to repair the house of the Lord, but there was long delay on the part of the priests to repair the breaches of the house.

As a result of Paul's first visit to Corinth in Acts 18. 1–18, he had known their original spiritual stature and strength. He had therefore been able to boast to Titus about their standard in *spiritual* things, 2 Cor. 7. 14, a standard recorded in 1 Corinthians 1. 5–7. Similarly in our verse 2, Paul now boasts to the Macedonians of their *practical* forwardness. The spreading abroad of such features, which reflect the grace of Christ and not the work of men, has as its basis the *usefulnesss of example*. The zeal of the Corinthians in this work had "provoked" others to follow, no doubt referring to other assemblies in the province of Achaia. It is a good thing to follow the godly example of others, such as the witness of local assemblies where men have their heads uncovered and women their heads covered, 1 Cor. 11. 16, or the example of the churches in Judaea who suffered for their own faith in Christ, 1 Thess. 2. 14, or the pattern of Paul's own conversion, 1 Tim.1. 16.

3. Speaking now to the Corinthians more specifically and bluntly, Paul states in verses 3–5 his reasons for sending Titus, "the brother", and "our brother", namely the messengers. Certainly he would not seek to exert apostolic pressure on the believers as if they were under law. Rather he sought to ensure by exhortation
(a) the continuity and the volume of the practical outworking of the exercise of the Corinthians;

(b)   the validity of his own boasting to others, which otherwise might
       have disastrous consequences. (He felt that his boasting might
       have been "in vain in this behalf", that is, void, empty, of no
       reality);

(c)   that he, Paul, should have no cause for being ashamed as a result
       of this boasting, v. 4.

4. Some of the Macedonians would accompany Paul to Corinth (see
Acts 20. 4, where a list is given of those accompanying Paul, from
churches formed on each of his three missionary journeys). They would be
able to witness firsthand whether the state of the Corinthians
corresponded to the confidence which Paul had expressed to them. Note
that "in this same confident boasting" should read "in this confidence'"
according to editors of repute. To understand Paul's point of view, we have
only to imagine the effect on the queen of Sheba as she visited Solomon,
if everything had been exaggerated, instead of "the half" not having been
told her, 1 Kings 10. 7. The lesson to learn is that, when giving a report of
blessing or endeavour elsewhere, one must be factual. Saints are prone to
exaggerate just as men of the world do.

5. Paul thought it necessary to send the messengers to Corinth so that
the collection should be completed before he arrived, namely "that there
be no gatherings when I come", 1 Cor. 16. 2. This would ensure that his
Macedonian fellow-travellers would have no cause to think that his
boasting needed a last minute boost!

The funds were to be seen as a matter of "bounty", or *blessing*, and not
as a matter of "covetousness", or *extortion*. It must not appear that Paul was
extracting the gift by force. Paul was *exhorting*, not *extorting*; it was a matter
of *grace*, not *law*.

The "bounty" was a *blessing* from believers to believers, a thought
prominent in Scripture. We may note the examples:

Genesis 33. 11, Jacob to Esau, "Take, I pray thee, my *blessing* that is
   brought to thee; because God hath dealt graciously with me, and
   because I have enough".
Joshua 15. 19, Achsah to Caleb, "Give me a *blessing*; for thou hast
   given me a south land; give me also springs of water". See also
   Judges 1. 15.
1 Samuel 25. 27, Abigail to David, "And now this *blessing* which thine
   handmaid hath brought unto my lord, let it even be given unto the
   young men that follow my lord".
2 Kings 5. 15, Naaman to Elisha, "Now therefore, I pray thee, take a
   blessing of thy servant", which was, of course, refused.

Verses 6–15: The Fruits of Giving—the Donors Blessed

6 But this *I say*, He which soweth sparingly shall reap also sparingly; and he
   which soweth bountifully shall reap also bountifully.

7 Every man according as he purposeth in his heart, *so let him give*; not grudgingly, or of necessity: for God loveth a cheerful giver.

8 And God *is* able to make all grace abound toward you; that ye, always having all sufficiency in all *things*, may abound to every good work:

9 (As it is written, He hath dispersed abroad; he hath given to the poor: his righteousness remaineth for ever.

10 Now he that ministereth seed to the sower both minister bread for *your* food, and multiply your seed sown, and increase the fruits of your righteousness;)

11 Being enriched in every thing to all bountifulness, which causeth through us thanksgiving to God.

12 For the administration of this service not only supplieth the want of the saints, but is abundant also by many thanksgivings unto God;

13 Whiles by the experiment of this ministration they glorify God for your professed subjection unto the gospel of Christ, and for *your* liberal distribution unto them, and unto all *men*;

14 And by their prayer for you, which long after you for the exceeding grace of God in you.

15 Thanks *be* unto God for his unspeakable gift.

6. This appears to be the first hint given by Paul in the development of the subject, that blessing will return to the donors, that there will be a reciprocal reward from the Lord. "He which soweth sparingly shall also reap sparingly; and he which soweth bountifully shall reap also bountifully" is a clear example from the harvest field. Assuming good soil, Matt. 13. 8, the amount of the return depends upon the amount of seed sown. Such a truth as this needs to be stated plainly, and the Corinthians needed to be encouraged in it. Moreover, financial sowing is not the only possibility; time devoted to the service of God and the preparation for it is also richly rewarded by God. The Scriptures are full of examples of this principle:

John 12. 24, "Except a corn of wheat fall into the ground and die, it abideth alone: but if it die, it bringeth forth much fruit". In the Lord's case, there was but one corn of wheat— all He possessed, namely Himself. Yet all was given, and this was sufficient to bring forth much fruit. He reaped the many sons He will bring to glory.

Luke 12. 16–21 provides a contrast. Here is a man who sowed much practically and naturally, but nothing spiritually. His ground "brought forth plentifully"; he had "much goods laid up for many years", but he was "not rich toward God". There could be no reward, since he had merely laid up "treasure for himself"; his soul was required when he least expected it.

Matthew 19. 22 shows the rich young ruler going away "sorrowful: for he had great possessions". His worldly adherence to possessions clearly prevented any return.

Luke 16. 19–31 shows the rich man with no thought of Lazarus laid at his gate and full of sores. This man sowed much for himself in that he "fared sumptuously every day", but he reaped nothing but judgment in the flame.

Luke 6. 38 provides the Lord's own enunciation of this principle,

"Give, and it shall be given unto you; good measure, pressed down, and shaken together, and running over, shall men give into your bosom. For with the same measure that ye mete withal it shall be measured to you again".

Galatians 6. 7–8 shows that this principle may also be taken in a spiritual sense; sowing in spiritual things will also result in spiritual return: "God is not mocked: for whatsoever a man soweth, that shall he also reap. For he that soweth to his flesh shall of the flesh reap corruption; but he that soweth to the Spirit shall of the Spirit reap life everlasting". The practical side of doing good to all men, and reaping in consequence, follows in verses 9,10. See also Malachi 3.10–12.

7. Bountiful sowing is accomplished by right motives; in this connection, we have only to think of the heart of God in giving His own Son. Paul stresses what the donor "purposeth *in his heart*". It is not a question of copying anyone else, even though a faithful example of another may be stimulating. It is not a question of adhering to the law or to tithing which would involve no true purpose. The Lord had gone so far as to say, "let not thy left hand know what thy right hand doeth", Matt. 6. 3. Moreover, it does not seem to be a question of giving what cost the donor nothing, 2 Sam. 24. 24. The following features should be noticed:

"*not grudgingly*": that is, with a heart that would like to retain what is being given. The fact that Ananias and Sapphira in Acts 5. 1–4 kept back a part shows that their desire was not to have given at all.

"*or of necessity*" that is, not under external compulsion or statutory requirements.

"*a cheerful giver*": This adjective "cheerful" appears only once in the N.T., and the corresponding noun also occurs only once, "he that sheweth mercy, with *cheerfulness*", Rom. 12. 8. Being cheerful is the opposite of being sorrowful, Matt. 19. 22. We should be careful to note anything that God loves in a believer. This seems to be the only N.T. reference where God loves something in a believer.

8. In this verse we find what we may term *circulation*. Having given according to the previous verse, grace returns in abundance— this is God's work. And why? So that the donors may still have sufficient, and be able still to continue the good work. This is the principle of constant circulation. Left to itself, circulation comes to a stop, as with water in a basin, for example. But with a hand stirring the water, the circulation can be maintained as long as is desired. In the present verse, it is God who maintains the circulation, yet depending upon the exercise and purpose of His people. It would be difficult to stir a bowl of syrup for long, owing to its resistance. Even so, God would not continue His process through channels that prove to be resistive. In His natural creation, God has introduced circulation. Trees and plants absorb certain chemicals from the soil through their roots. These chemicals are used in leaf formation, which in turn fall to the ground and decay into basic chemicals, so that the whole cycle may be reconstituted. Such circulation was envisaged by the Preacher in chapter 1 of Ecclesiastes; the rising and setting of the sun in verse 5, the whirling of the wind in verse 6, the cycle of the waters in verse 7, from the rivers to the sea, from the sea through evaporation and condensation into the clouds, and from the clouds through rain into the rivers again. David rejoiced that all that is in heaven and in the earth belongs to God, that riches are from Him, that it is in God's hand to make great and to give strength to all. All personal possessions come from God, and David could offer the things of God back to God, in preparing abundantly for the building of the temple, 1 Chron. 29. 11–16.

9. Paul quotes from the O.T. namely from Psalm 112. 9. The word "he" occurring in the verse refers, of course, to the man who distributes. The Psalm deals with a man that fears the Lord and who delights greatly in His commandments, v. 1. The subject of the psalm is *practical righteousness in action*, shown by three different features associated with money matters, each *leading* to righteousness. This should not be confused with the basic truth of the Gospel, namely justification by faith with imputed righteousness. *Practical* righteousness follows *imputed* righteousness; the latter leads to eternal life, the former to rewards. The three features are:
1. *Possessing*: "Wealth and riches shall be in his house: and his righteousness endureth for ever", v. 3.
2. *Lending*: "A good man sheweth favour, and lendeth: . . . the righteous shall be in everlasting remembrance", vv. 5, 6.
3. *Giving*: "He hath dispersed, he hath given to the poor; his righteousness endureth for ever", v. 9.

This is the same truth re-echoed in Proverbs 19. 4, "Wealth maketh many friends; but the poor is separated from his neighbour"; see also Luke 16. 9. Wider implications are found in Isaiah 3. 10: "Say ye to the righteous, that it shall be well with him: for they shall eat the fruit of their doings".

10. This verse is a little parable based on these ideas; its meaning may be considered phrase-by-phrase:

Parable	Meaning
He that ministereth	It is God who gives.
seed	All the believer's possessions, in the context, financially.
to the sower	To individual saints to give.
both	Two results are in view.
minister bread for your food,	There is a return for the believer himself to use.
and multiply your seed sown,	More possessions are granted in order to give.
and increase the fruits of your righteousness.	To circulate again.

11. Finally, Paul turns his attention away from the blessing received by the recipients, and from the reciprocal blessing received by the donors, and he considers the results God-ward.

"Being enriched in every thing" embraces many features:

Spiritual blessings, implied in 8. 9. These would include all our possessions in the heavenlies, Eph. 1. 4, enabling us as a holy priesthood to render to God His portion in worship.

Spiritual gifts, implied in 1 Corinthians 1. 5 enabling us through service saint-ward, to lay the foundation for spiritual growth, in character, and in the knowledge of the Lord Jesus.

Material gifts, as in the two chapters before us, leading us to "all bountifulness" or liberality.

It is obvious that all these possessions are not merely for self to enjoy; they are to be shared in their appropriate spheres. The lasting result is that this "causeth through us thanksgiving to God". Firstly the recipients thank God for mercies received. Their thanks to the donors are merely subsidiary, and should not be overdone as if they were the ultimate source of the mercies. Secondly, Paul himself would thank God for the fulfilment of the Corinthian exercise, having "no greater joy than to hear that my children walk in truth", 3 John 4. Thirdly, the Macedonians and others would hear *through* Paul of this work of grace, and they likewise would appear in thanksgiving before God.

The word "causeth" in this verse means to *work out*.

12–13. The meaning of these two verses can be found by reading them through slowly several times, but a "modern translation", usually unnecessary in Bible study, throws more immediate light on them. For example, the New English Bible translates the verses thus:

"For as a piece of willing service this is not only a contribution towards the needs of God's people; more than that, it overflows in a flood of thanksgiving to God. For through the proof which this affords, many will give honour to God when they see how humbly you obey Him and how faithfully you confess the gospel of Christ; and will thank Him for your liberal contribution to their need and to the general good".

This gives the general drift of the argument, but only a detailed comparison with the Greek text will show up any metaphorical fancy in the minds of the translators (such as "it overflows in a flood"), and any words omitted no doubt on the grounds of style (such as "ministration" in verse 13).

The want of the saints in Jerusalem had been supplied, and believers there would already be rejoicing before God as a result of knowing of the "liberal distribution" made by the Corinthians because the gospel of Christ had so worked in their souls. The N.E.B. translators fancy that "many" will give honour to God, the "many" being distinct from the recipients, "God's people". This may well be true, since the circle of praise would grow. But the word "many" does not occur in the Greek; only the present participle (of course without a subject, neither "many" nor "they") of the verb "glory" appears. It would therefore seem to refer to the previous noun, namely "the saints" at Jerusalem, a word that the N.E.B. translators were apparently loath to use, no doubt not being "modern" enough.

For a better understanding of the verses, we must refer to the A.V., where the three words "administration", "service" and "ministration" occur. The first word "administration" (referring to Paul's own work in exhorting and acting as a go-between) and the third word "ministration" (referring to the Corinthian's liberality), are one and the same in the Greek, namely *diakonia*. This word is the common and general description of all spiritual and material service accomplished by believers for believers. The reader should examine the occurrences of this word in a concordance, both in its verbal form *diakoneo* and in its two noun-forms *diakonia* (service) and *diakonos* (servant). The root is the basis of the word *deacon*, referring to any believer who accomplishes anything in God's service. Note, as an *elder*, a man possesses a spiritual *charge*; as a *deacon*, he possesses a spiritual *gift*.

But the second word translated "service" in the A.V. is quite distinct; it is *litourgia*, appearing in the N.T. as a verb and in two noun-forms only about fifteen times. Its basic meaning is given to be public service discharged by a citizen at his own expense. It refers essentially to priestly service, so when used of material service the level of the latter is raised to the highest functioning of the saints. No wonder such activity brings forth praise to God ! The distinct uses of this word are as follows:

Priestly service:

Luke 1. 23, the days of the *ministration* of Zacharias.

Hebrews 8. 2, Christ, a *minister* of the sanctuary.

Hebrews 8. 6, having obtained a more excellent *ministry*.

Hebrews 9. 21, the vessels of the *ministry* of the tabernacle.

Hebrews 10. 11, the O.T. priests standing daily *ministering*.

Acts 13. 2, the prophets and teachers *ministered* to the Lord.

Spiritual service:

Romans 15. 16, Paul, a *minister* of Jesus Christ to the Gentiles.

Practical service:

Romans 15. 27, the Gentiles to *minister* to the Jews in carnal
   things (but in verse 25 the common word for service is used).

Philippians 2. 17, Paul offered upon the sacrifice and *service* of
   their faith.

Philippians 2. 25, Epaphroditus *ministered* to Paul's wants.

Philippians 2. 30, "to supply your lack of *service* toward me".

It is only through the grace of God that our own service can thus be designated. The realisation of this great truth should bring about greater zeal and faithfulness to the Lord.

In verse 13, the word "experiment" means *proof*. Acts of kindness, "any consolation in Christ, . . . any comfort of love, . . . any fellowship of the

Spirit, . . . any bowels and mercies", Phil. 2. 1, form an outward proof both
of general service and of higher priestly service. To the Jews, it was a proof
of the love of the Corinthians, and as such brought forth glory to God.
Their praise and prayers centred around the following features:

1. *"For your professed subjection unto the gospel of Christ"*. This means
   more than what we would call a confession of faith after a gospel
   meeting. It also implies a confession of devotion to Christ and
   adherence to His Word after a ministry meeting. The ministry of
   the Word to believers should bring forth fruit after its own kind,
   something little realised in ministry today. Spiritually minded
   saints do rejoice when they see this fruit particularly in younger
   believers. The Lord spoke of this when He said, "Let your light so
   shine before men, that they may see your good works, and glorify
   your Father which is in heaven", Matt. 5. 16.

2. *The liberal distribution to the saints in Jerusalem.* The Gospel had
   radiated out from Jerusalem, and now it returned through works
   meet for faith and repentance.

3. *Distribution to "all men".* This suggests that there were others
   helped by the collection.

4. *Prayer for the donors,* verse 14. Paul received much from the
   Philippians, Phil. 4. 15–20, leading to *praise* in verse 20 and
   prayer for the donors in 1. 3–6.

5. A *longing,* verse 14, namely an earnest desire after the
   Corinthians. The believers in Jerusalem could see the "exceeding
   grace of God in" them, or better, "the surpassing grace of God
   upon" them. The recipients would long to be able to manifest the
   same blessed features of grace, not for selfish reasons of increasing
   their own possessions, but to be able to glorify God as they had
   done in their early days in Acts 2–4, when "great grace was upon
   them all", Acts 4. 33.

15. Paul concludes the subject with suitable praise, "Thanks be unto
God for His unspeakable gift". Some expositors have understood this as
referring merely to the grace of being able to give freely to others. But
would this be called "unspeakable", or indescribable, incapable of verbal
explanation (a word occurring only once in the Greek N.T.)? One
expositor* has called such a suggestion "derogatory", and with this we
agree. Praise concerned with the grace of giving in material things which
perish, would be poor if the believer's heart was not moved more to
adoring praise to God for the gift of all gifts, the Son given.

The similar thought of "unspeakable" occurs in chapter 12 verse 4,
where "unspeakable" words refer to the fact that there was no permission
to repeat them. Also 1 Kings 10. 7 may be consulted, where words were of
no avail in themselves to describe the wisdom and prosperity of Solomon.

* *Notes on the Second Epistle to the Corinthians,* by W. Kelly; p. 182.

2 CORINTHIANS 10

Section 4.   The Example of the True Minister
Subject 1.   Apostolic Humility

Relationships of this Section

Paul now reaches the last section of this Epistle, a section that must have been for him the most difficult to write. The report that Titus had brought him from Corinth made the apostle *joyfully* aware that the assembly as a whole would receive him, but he was also *sorrowfully* aware that a small minority would not receive him. The first nine chapters would be appreciated only by those who would receive him. Chapters 3–6 deal with the exposition of true ministry, being designed to strengthen the many in Corinth who needed special help after having repented as a result of the first Epistle. In these chapters, Paul adopts the *language of fellowship*, using "we" throughout.

But the last four chapters are written essentially to the few who would not receive him; the subject is not *ministry* but the *minister*. Very humbly, Paul justifies his position and actions. He gives proof of his apostolic status to those few who sought to question it. At that time such teaching was necessary only for the *few*; nowadays it is necessary for the *many*. At the same time, Paul hesitates to write about himself; how much more pleasing to write about the glories of Christ, as in Eph. 1; Phil. 2. 5–11; Col. 1. 12–22. Indeed, Paul calls writing about himself "folly", asking that his readers should "bear with" him, 2 Cor. 11. 1. As a man saved by grace, Paul could not and would not commend himself, 10. 12; only those whom the Lord commends are worth listening to, v. 18. However, as we read these chapters, we look beyond the writings of Paul as such, and realise that it is the Lord commending His servant, since we are reading words which have been divinely inspired.

In these chapters, Paul adopts the *language of individuality*, using "I" throughout. There could not be full fellowship (as previously in the Epistle) with those who refused his authority. The fact that four chapters are necessary to deal with this subject contrasts strangely with the first Epistle. In spite of all the authority necessary to introduce the many corrections found there, Paul draws attention to his apostleship only briefly. In 1.1, we find his apostolic *authorship*; in 9. 1–3 his apostolic *liberty*; in 15. 9–10 his apostolic *calling*. But nowhere is the subject developed as it is here.

The authority of Paul the apostle is far from being similar to that of a dictator. Many kings in the O.T. had a character exactly the opposite to that of Paul. Such a character was prophesied for the first king over Israel, 1 Sam. 8. 11–18. Rehoboam said, "And now whereas my father did lade you with a heavy yoke, I will add to your yoke: my father hath chastised you with whips, but I will chastise you with scorpions", 1 Kings 12. 11.

Instead, Paul spoke of heart-felt humility and of the many circumstances opposing his ministry.

An outline of the four chapters is as follows:

10. 1–11:   Apostolic humility in warfare and authority.
10. 12–18: Apostolic service limited according to the will of God.
11. 1–4:   Objects of the apostle and false apostles.
11. 5–11:   Apostolic character for such objects.
11. 12–15: Character and intents of false apostles.
11. 16–33: Apostolic boasting in sufferings without and within.
12. 1–9:   Apostolic calling because of a granted vision.
12. 10–13: The chiefest apostle in suffering and signs.
12. 14–21: Paul's preparation for his visit to Corinth.
13. 1–14:   Paul approved because of his work accomplished in Corinth.

Exposition of 2 Cor. 10: Apostolic Humility

Verses 1–11: Apostolic Humility in Warfare and Authority

1 Now I Paul myself beseech you by the meekness and gentleness of Christ, who in presence *am* base among you, but being absent am bold toward you:

2 But I beseech *you*, that I may not be bold when I am present with that confidence, wherewith I think to be bold against some, which think of us as if we walked according to the flesh.

3 For though we walk in the flesh, we do not war after the flesh:

4 (For the weapons of our warfare *are* not carnal, but mighty through God to the pulling down of strong holds;)

5 Casting down imaginations, and every high thing that exalteth itself against the knowledge of God, and bringing into captivity every thought to the obedience of Christ;

6 And having in a readiness to revenge all disobedience, when your obedience is fulfilled.

7 Do ye look on things after the outward appearance? If any man trust to himself that he is Christ's, let him of himself think this again, that, as he *is* Christ's, even so *are* we Christ's.

8 For though I should boast somewhat more of our authority, which the Lord hath given us for edification, and not for your destruction, I should not be ashamed:

9 That I may not seem as if I would terrify you by letters.

10 For *his* letters, say they, *are* weighty and powerful; but *his* bodily presence *is* weak, and *his* speech contemptible.

11 Let such an one think this, that, such as we are in word by letters when we are absent, such *will we be* also in deed when we are present.

1. "I Paul myself" denotes that what follows is essentially personal; no one else could be sufficiently identified with him in these remarks and circumstances. Paul's method of beseeching (or, rather, exhorting) was by the same character of meekness and gentleness as found in Christ when He had to deal with those who had gone astray. The meekness of Christ is found in Matthew 11. 29, where the corresponding adjective occurs, "Take My yoke upon you, and learn of Me; for I am *meek* and lowly in heart". Here, the Lord is not referring to "the wise and prudent", v. 25, but to the "babes", those for whom a sinful life is a burden and who seek refuge in the Son. To such, the Lord does not correct from a superior position of strength, but He adopts the lowly *position of meekness* to attract the wayward soul. Earlier in the chapter, He pronounced judgment on Capernaum and the other cities, adopting an *upbraiding position*, v. 20. This would speak judgment to cities which would neither recognise His mighty works nor their own sin. Such men are not those "that labour and are heavy laden" to whom the Lord would reveal Himself in meekness.

Paul, following the example of the Master, is addressing himself to believers, albeit wayward ones. Practising this himself, Paul could exhort others in the same way, as "ye which are spiritual, restore such an one in the spirit of *meekness*", Gal. 6. 1, and "In *meekness* instructing those that oppose themselves; if God peradventure will give them repentance to the acknowledging of the truth", 2 Tim. 2. 25. The roots of both words "meekness and gentleness" appear in Titus 3. 2, where Titus has to instruct believers to be "*gentle*, shewing all *meekness* unto all men".

We must not think that meekness and gentleness are characteristic of a blindness that condones sin. In these chapters Paul is meek and gentle, but he does not mince matters and he goes straight to the point. Often these days, plain speaking has given place to powerless generalisations, supposedly in the spirit of grace. The consciences of the hearers, who would be rebuked and convicted by straight-forward preaching, find a measure of rest and satisfaction in such generalisations.

The word "gentleness", occurring in the Greek twice as a noun and five times as an adjective in the N.T., denotes the character of forbearance, fairness, considerateness in those in authority, where active love towards believers and those in need of repentance can display a self-forgetting humility. Consider how gently the Lord dealt with the woman taken in adultery, John 8. 3–11; how the Lord dealt with Peter as he confessed that he was a sinful man, Luke 5. 4–11; how there was no rebuke when He found His own asleep in the garden, Matt. 26. 40–46.

Moreover, Paul would be "base" when present among the Corinthians. This is the character of being humble, lowly, modest, the word sometimes used to describe the lowly circumstances of a brother in contrast to one who is rich, James 1. 9. Paul uses the root idea again in 2 Corinthians 11. 7, "Have I committed an offence in *abasing* myself?" The word is used of the Lord—the One "*lowly* in heart", Matt. 11. 29, contrasted to Capernaum as "exalted unto heaven". Again, He "*humbled* himself, and became obedient unto death", Phil. 2. 8, from whence He was "highly exalted" of God. This kind of character, whether seen in the Lord or in a believer, is something that grates unpleasantly upon the active unspiritual man. But this manifestation of character established Paul's calling, and justifies the believer who walks happily in it today.

Paul observes that he is "base" when present with the Corinthians, but that he is "bold" when absent. This boldness (meaning having confidence, or being courageous) occurs only six times in the N.T., five of which occur in this second Epistle; see 5. 6, 8; 7. 16; 10. 1, 2, and also Heb. 13. 6. Apostolic boldness is shown in the writings of Paul, because all his Epistles would be used by believers throughout the ages as a divinely inspired source of correction. Apostolic courage which struck at the conscience *then*, would be translated into the Spirit's action through His word *now*.

2. Although the A.V. uses the word "beseech" in both verses 1 and 2, in point of fact two different words are used in the original: "exhort" appears in verse 1 (as from a preacher in grace, but with a *superior* position), and "beseech" rightly appears in verse 2 (as from a brother in humility, with an *inferior* position). The two words "think" in this verse, referring to Paul and to some of the Corinthians, mean "reckon".

Paul's boldness towards these men in Corinth took upon itself different forms, depending on whether he was present with them or not. As absent, it was manifest in his letters, as verses 9–10; as present, it could be manifest by deeds rather than by words. Paul desired to manifest the first form only, fearing the consequences if he had to be bold in his attitude when present; see verses 20–21 of chapter 12. His accusers were men who reckoned that Paul walked according to the flesh. Paul writes to counter this, trusting that the Epistle would have a prior effect.

The inroads of the world, the flesh, and the devil can be disastrous, if the means of grace given by the ascended Lord pass unheeded, Eph. 4. 11–13, when believers can be like "children, tossed to and fro, and carried about with every wind of doctrine, by the sleight of men, and cunning craftiness, whereby they lie in wait to deceive", v. 14. Essentially,

the *world* refers to the influence of men outside;
the *flesh* refers to the influence and desires of men inside;
the *devil* refers to the influence of the powers of darkness.

In 1 Corinthians 3. 1, Paul previously had had to write to the assembly "as unto carnal", going on to say that they were walking "as men". The *flesh within* was copying the *world without*. But here the few in Corinth who had not repented were now accusing the apostle of walking "according to the flesh". This is the familiar dodge of self-justification, the flesh twists its own failures back in a worse form on to these who are more spiritual. Those in the wrong will often try to make light dark in others, going any length in order to do so. Those who are spiritual may find this very distasteful. The grace of patience may endure it, but the charges and accusations must be answered if the testimony of the assembly appears to be suffering by remaining patiently silent. Paul answers for himself here. In John 8. 44, the Lord had said to the Pharisees, "Ye are of your father the devil, and the lusts of your father ye will do", but they accused the Lord conversely of casting out devils through the prince of the devils, Matt. 9. 34; 12. 24. The Lord answered in no uncertain manner in the following verses 25–45. This was no time to be silent; His testimony and work depended upon it (contrast Matthew 27. 12; Luke 23. 9).

3. "For though we walk in the flesh, we do not war after the flesh" involves a great principle that Paul found it necessary to repeat. In verses 2 and 3, the word "flesh" occurs in conjunction with three distinct ideas:

Walk according to the flesh. This refers to the conduct of the unspiritual believer.

Walk in the flesh. By this, Paul merely means his daily life as lived in the body; it is a physical concept. "I live in the flesh", Paul wrote elsewhere, Phil. 1. 22, and of the Lord it is written that "the Word was made flesh", John 1. 14. This is a fact of creation, and nothing unspiritual is implied.

Warfare according to the flesh. In the context Paul is referring, not to overcoming his own temptations, but to his position as a soldier of Christ to keep out the enemy. The Corinthians, cut to their conscience, accused Paul of adopting methods according to the flesh in his manner of approach to them. In verses 4–6, however, the apostle shows that his methods and objects were entirely spiritual. Such experiences enabled Paul later to write to Timothy, "Thou therefore endure hardness, as a good soldier of Jesus Christ. No man that warreth entangleth himself with the affairs of this life; that he may please him who hath chosen him to be a soldier", 2 Tim. 2. 3–4. Paul, as he recalled to Timothy, had dealt spiritually with Phygellus and Hermogenes, 1. 15, Hymenaeus and Philetus, 2. 17. Elsewhere, he mentions Hymenaeus and Alexander and the experience of warring a good warfare, 1 Tim. 1. 18–20. See examples in Numbers 14. 40–45; 2 Chronicles 32. 8.

Romans 8 is the great chapter showing the contrast between the flesh and the Spirit. The principle is embodied in verse 9, "But ye are not in the flesh, but in the Spirit". This is a settled fact of grace, an outcome of conversion; it cannot be changed. Physically, of course, the believer is in the flesh; that is a different matter. But spiritually, *he is not in the flesh*; that is the province of unbelievers. On the other hand, *the flesh can still be in us*, demonstrating weakness and practical carnality. Romans 8 does not deal with that side of things, but rather shows something for the believer to enjoy, namely not being in the flesh but in the Spirit. The flesh in us is not something to enjoy, but to be corrected and mortified. Galatians 5 deals with this.

4. This verse states Paul's *method* in warfare, while verses 5–6 show his *objects*. The passage refers to the method Paul used in dealing with the Corinthian assembly. The Word of God for correction and discipline, is the only effective weapon that believers have. There can be no question of "taking the law into one's own hands" or of seeking redress via unbelieving judges outside the assembly. Likewise personal abuse would be objectionable to God. The power of the written and preached Word is God's available method for warfare.

In Ephesians 6. 13–17, all the armour mentioned is *defensive*, except in verse 17, where one weapon for the *offensive* is mentioned, "the sword of the Spirit, which is the word of God". Elsewhere such a weapon is described as "the word of God . . . quick, and powerful, and sharper than any two-edged sword", Heb. 4. 12. The Lord had "cast out the spirits with His *word*", Matt. 8. 16; in Capernaum, "His *word* was with power", Luke 4. 32.

In the O.T., the strongholds of Jericho, Josh. 6. 20, and of Zion, 2 Sam. 5. 7, were taken by means approved of God. But the strong-holds that Paul has in mind are the rigid minds of men, in particular of believers, who resist the truth of God, closing their minds to His authority, by preferring their own ways and their own thoughts. The nation of Israel, in its various phases of unbelief, constituted such a stronghold, as the following verses witness:

> Isaiah 6. 9, "Hear ye indeed, but understand not; and see ye indeed, but perceive not".
>
> Matthew 23. 37, "O Jerusalem, Jerusalem, . . . how often would I have gathered thy children together, . . . and ye would not".
>
> Romans 10. 21, "All day long I have stretched forth My hands unto a disobedient and gainsaying people".

5. In Paul's warfare, things of negative value had to be cast out, while things of positive value had to be retained and developed.

The first negative thing is what is translated "imaginations", or *reasonings*. This refers to the rational mind apart from faith, in its arguments and in its preferences. This word is used of the rational Gentiles in Romans 2. 15, who "shew the work of the law written in their hearts, their conscience also bearing witness, and their *thoughts* the mean while accusing or else excusing one another". Such rationalism is manifested, not only in unbelievers seeking thus to justify themselves, but also in believers particularly when religious matters are in question. The Corinthians had reasoned about morality, 1 Cor. 5, about doctrine, ch. 15, and about the financial affairs of the apostle, ch. 9.

The second negative thing is what Paul calls "every high thing that exalteth itself against the knowledge of God". Pride in the religious heart refuses to detach itself from such a pedestal. Capernaum was thus elevated, and would not descend until brought down to hell, Matt. 11. 23. The Corinthians had elevated their liberty in Christ, 1 Cor. 8, 10; through boasting they had falsely elevated their gifts received through grace, 1 Cor. 14; they had "reigned as kings", 4. 8. Attachment to such things is the ruin of the Roman church, the established church, the non-conformist churches, and of much evangelical witness today. Men and organisations will not have spiritual simplicity, but desire things which ultimately will be proved to be but chaff.

The positive thing that Paul sought in his warfare was that every thought should be brought into captivity to the obedience of Christ. This is a very *pleasant* captivity. Elsewhere, there is a captivity that *can not be called pleasant*. For example, the Jews would "be led away captive into all nations", Luke 21. 24; Paul, looking at "the body of this death" prior to deliverance through the Lord Jesus Christ recalls another law in his members warring against the law of his mind, bringing him "into captivity to the law of sin" in his members, Rom. 7. 23.

A believer is not to have a will of his own. He is not his own because he has been bought with a price, and is therefore a bondservant unto the Lord. Every thought is involved, regarding Christ, doctrine, conduct, and service. The Word of God is capable of producing this blessed effect. His servants should preach to this end, allowing the Word to have this influence upon the souls who listen. The engrafted Word is to be received with meekness, not like those who hear but are not doers, James 1. 21–22.

Every thought is to be brought into the "obedience of Christ". This does not refer specifically to the obedience of the Lord to His Father and God while in this world, although this can be the believer's example. Rather Paul refers to christian obedience in Christ, as distinct from obeying one's own thoughts and motives. Paul had received grace and apostleship that such "obedience to the faith" should be found among all nations. Of the Jews, a great number of the priests were "obedient to the faith", Acts 6. 7. Of the Gentiles, their "obedience is come abroad unto all men", Rom. 16. 19, relating to the doctrine they had learned and to the fact that they served the Lord Jesus Christ.

6. Even when the obedience of the majority in Corinth was thus developed, Paul was still ready to deal with the disobedience of the minority. The apostle knew that he laboured to "present every man perfect in Christ Jesus", Col. 1. 28, and that the apostolic and other gifts were given "for the perfecting of the saints", Eph. 4. 12. Therefore Paul was not likely to sit back and remain unconcerned abut disobedience that reflected immaturity in the minority. If necessary, Paul would go beyond correction and exhortation; with a governmental position he was ready "to revenge all disobedience". Though painful, this was necessary from time to time, as we note in various references:

Romans 16.17, "avoid them";
1 Corinthians 5. 13, "put away . . . that wicked person";
1 Timothy 1. 20, "I have delivered unto Satan";
1 Timothy 5. 20, "them that sin rebuke before all";
2 Timothy 3. 5, "from such turn away";
2 Timothy 4. 14, "the Lord reward him according to his works".

7. These men in Corinth, instead of concentrating upon the spiritual means that Paul used, and upon the objects before him were so carnal that they merely beheld the outward appearance. In fact, they sought to find in Paul what they would regard as base things, unlike Samuel who had sought out the most *attractive* features while also looking on the outward appearance, 1 Sam. 16. 7. The Corinthians tried to argue that Paul was different when absent than when present. His letters were regarded as powerful, but his bodily presence and speech as weak and contemptible. They tried to use this as an excuse to undermine his authority in the Lord and to question his apostleship. No doubt there was a difference, but the error was to interpret this in a carnal way. The spiritual man would see that the *power behind the writings* of Paul when absent, would be translated into *power in deeds* when present. Physical peculiarities, so catching to the eye, were entirely irrelevant, and indeed showed up the spiritual state of those foolish enough to be occupied with them.

But this verse goes further; it appears that some of the Corinthians were suggesting that Paul did not even belong to Christ. Chapter 9 of the previous Epistle has a bearing on this. Paul would not live of the Gospel, even though this liberty was decreed of the Lord; hence these men would argue that Paul did not belong to the Lord. Paul deals with this insinuation in a simple way. He observes that if they felt that they were Christians, so too must he be a Christian, since they had derived all their original faith through him. He was their one father, 1 Cor. 4. 15. In other words, an unbeliever could never accomplish any christian work in a soul; like can only produce like; a seed reproduces after its own kind. An evangelist with a zeal for souls will gain souls; a teacher with a desire for the building up of the saints will see this accomplished. A teacher who talks with no zeal or purpose is not likely to make any impression upon his hearers. Hence the argument is weighty "as he is Christ's, even so are we Christ's". Paul uses this same idea in chapter 13 verses 5–6; the Corinthians being approved show that Paul is not reprobate; he is as they are, and his work in them proves the fact.

8. Each believer stands on the same footing as being the possession of the Lord. But in other respects believers differ, and each believer should cultivate the ability to discern what God has done in others. These men in Corinth were minimising the servant of God who had worked among them. But in the distinction which God had wrought, he possessed something they lacked, namely authority unto edification. This goes beyond the fact of being the Lord's possession; it embraces *how the Lord chooses to use* His possession. Moreover, in the verse, Paul is not ashamed to boast of this authority for edification, such boasting being not in self-attainment but in the purpose of the Lord. It is interesting to note that Paul uses this verb "to boast" (or "glory" as it is sometimes translated) more times in chapters 10–12 than in any other epistle. It occurs eighteen times in these three chapters.

Paul's authority, held in humility, was for *edification* (see later) and not to *destruction*. This word destruction, *kathairesis*, occurs only three times in the N.T., namely, in the present verse 8, in verse 4, "to the *pulling down* of strong holds", and in 13. 10, "the power which the Lord hath given me to edification, and not to *destruction*". As a verb, it appears in verse 5 of the present chapter, "*casting down* imaginations". In the context, the word contains an element of force, to overthrow, demolish. Elsewhere, extreme and fond care may be involved, since the same verb is used when they took the body of Jesus down from the cross, Mark 15. 46, Luke 23. 53; Acts 13. 29. Note that Paul states that religious rigidity and rationalism (strong holds and imaginations) are thrown down, *not* believers themselves. Note also that Paul uses the plural in this verse, "*our* authority", "given *us* for edification". This is something characteristic of all servants of God even if they do not attain to the apostolic calling.

The great truth that service is unto edification, needs amplification. Later, Paul writes, "we do all things, dearly beloved, for your edifying", 2 Cor. 12. 19. Previously he had written, "Let all things be done unto edifying", 1 Cor. 14. 26. Essentially,

God-ward, we do all things for His glory;

sinner-ward, we do all things for their salvation;

saint-ward, we do all things for their edification.

A concordance will show the occurrence of this word in the N.T. Note, however, that in 1 Timothy 1. 4, "godly edifying" should read "God's dispensation" (or administration); the difference arises through the correct Greek letter *n* in the word being wrongly changed to *d* in some manuscripts.

Edification refers to the act of building, but care is necessary in understanding what kind of activity is involved. In Acts 9. 31 we find that the churches throughout all Judaea, Galilee, and Samaria had rest, that they "were edified" and also "multiplied". Through the conversion of Saul, the persecutors were without a leader, so the church had rest. This verse shows that *edification* is not the same as *multiplication*, or growth in numbers. The brickwork and roof of a house are finished *before* a start is made on the internal fittings and decorations. The concrete frame of a skyscraper is constructed *before* the rooms are inserted between the floors. In 1 Kings 5–6, great stones, costly stones, and hewed stones for the foundations and walls were placed in position *before* the interior was covered with cedar, fir wood and gold, and the oracle with pure gold.

The book of the Acts uses the words "add" and "multiply" for the increase in numbers of the "living stones":

"The Lord added . . . daily", 2. 47;

"There were added unto them about three thousand souls", 2. 41;

"Believers were the more added to the Lord", 5. 14;

"When the number . . . was multiplied", 6. 1.

Adding is the work of the Lord through evangelistic endeavour; multiplication is the following sign of life shown by the saints. A building is added to, but plants in the garden multiply.

Edification, however, is a process that commences once believers are in a local assembly. It deals with individual character, with spirituality, growth in grace, in learning of Christ and of His ways in the church. God uses evangelists for adding, but pastors and teachers deal with edification. Clearly believers can only edify others if they have the pattern set before them. The details of the *interior* of the tabernacle and temple were given by the Lord just as much as their *exterior* fundamental framework. Believers engaged in edification must have a vision before them of what God requires to be accomplished in a soul.

We can collate here various verses containing details of the process of edification.

1. SERVANTS USED IN EDIFICATION

   Motives of the servant

   "Let every one of us please his neighbour for his good to edification", Rom.15. 2.

   "Seek that ye may excel to the edifying of the church", 1 Cor. 14. 12.

   One's heart is directed to the coming of the Lord, and in the light of that, believers comfort themselves "together, and edify one another", 1 Thess. 5. 11.

   Ability of the servant

   Authority and power come from the Lord, 2 Cor. 10. 8; 13. 10.

   In Exodus 31. 2–6, Bezaleel and Aholiab were granted the ability of the Spirit in all manner of workmanship in the building of the tabernacle.

   Conduct of the servant

   "Knowledge puffeth up, but charity edifieth", 1 Cor 8. 1.

   "All things are lawful, but all things are not expedient: all things are lawful, but all things edify not", 1 Cor. 10. 23. (The phrase "for me" should twice be omitted in this verse.)

2. SERVICE THAT EDIFIES

   Reason why gifts are given

   "for the edifying of the body of Christ", Eph. 4. 12, that is to embellish the saints with the likeness of Christ.

   "Maketh increase of the body unto the edifying of itself in love", Eph. 4. 16.

   The church is the object

   "He that prophesieth edifieth the church", 1 Cor. 14. 4.

   "That the church may receive edifying", 1 Cor. 14. 5.

   All service embraced

   "Let all things be done unto edifying", 1 Cor. 14. 26. This relates to what is done in a meeting. Are certain things done because of custom, to fill in time, to please men? See also 2 Cor. 12. 19.

Responsibility of the saints
"Let us therefore follow after . . . things wherewith one may edify another", Rom. 14. 19.
Means God uses
The Word preached and taught, "He that prophesieth speaketh unto men to edification, and exhortation, and comfort", 1 Cor. 14. 3.

3. DANGER IN SERVICE NOT EDIFYING
Gifts being used in an invalid manner
"For thou verily giveth thanks well, but the other is not edified", 1 Cor. 14. 17. In the context, this refers to the boastful display of being able to speak in another language when the assembly as a whole cannot understand it.
Corrupt talk
"Let no corrupt communication proceed out of your mouth, but that which is good to the use of edifying, that it may minister grace unto the hearers", Eph. 4. 29. A sermon may, alas, give out sweet and bitter water mixed.

These quotations serve to show that God expects a high standard in all that is done for edification. We must examine ourselves and our service, lest we fall from the precepts of Scripture and from the example of the apostle.

9–10. Paul now returns to the comments made on his Epistles by these men in Corinth. This minority was not affected unto repentance, but they were affected in another direction, namely that of fear. They sought unjust arguments to justify themselves in not taking heed to these letters. Note that the expression "say they" should be "saith he", the same as "such an one" in verse 11; Paul addresses himself to each believer individually.

In verse 10, Paul exposes the criticism of these Corinthians concerning his letters and bodily presence, showing that he is not ignorant of these criticisms circulated behind his back. Paul has no fear of criticism; only unspiritual men are rebuffed by criticism.

Two words are used to describe his letters, and two further words relate to his presence.

Weighty. The letters are so impressive, that a man cannot overlook or neglect them, even if he would desire to do so. The Word of God is always effective in one way or another, either drawing men to it or driving them from it, John 6. 63–69. These men in Corinth found Paul's writings weighty on the conscience, or else they would not have taken their wayward stand. The same root meaning occurs in such contexts as "they bind *heavy* burdens and grievous to be borne", Matt. 23. 4; "after my departing shall *grievous* wolves enter in among you", Acts 20. 29.

Powerful. The Scriptures are strong and mighty, and cannot be broken, Heb. 4. 12. It is possible for believers, to recognise the powerful effect of preaching or the reading of the Word, and yet to remain indifferent to its claim upon the heart and mind, as these men did. "The scripture cannot be broken", said the Lord in John 10. 35, relating to its power, yet the Pharisees would use every attempt to thwart it, ultimately without success. The Corinthians would claim its power, yet their attitude and deeds would show that their claim was but make-believe. A large bridge across an estuary may be weighty and mighty, yet some foolish man may prefer to use a small rowing boat which would cause him much trouble in a storm.

Bodily presence weak, (contrasting with powerful). This word is used of the sick, in the Gospel records; of the Corinthians themselves, "many are *weak* and sickly among you", 1 Cor. 11. 30; and of the wife "as unto the *weaker* vessel", 1 Pet. 3. 7. No doubt this was true of Paul, since he had the thorn in the flesh to contend with. The Corinthians were cunningly seeking to use this weakness to try and show some spiritual inconsistency in the apostle.

Speech contemptible, or "naught", (opposite to weighty). The idea was spread abroad that the apostle's speech was not worth anything. The reason was that Paul preached spiritual things *without* outward show, 1 Cor. 1–2. An unspiritual man, whether a believer or an unbeliever, would be unable to perceive value in such preaching on account of his deafness and blindness. This is characteristic of many today, yet the corrective influence of the Word is the only way of dealing with them. One must certainly not attempt to pacify them by descending to their state, by changing a spiritual message or discourse into something more appealing to their tastes. None should attempt to please men, 1 Thess. 2. 4, even if the preaching is criticised. The same idea occurs as "despised" in Galatians 4. 14, and "set at naught" in Acts 4. 11 relating to man's treatment of the Stone now become the Head of the corner.

11. Paul answers the charges justly. The letters demonstrated the aspirations and sensitivities of his heart expressed verbally. Men could not know the reality of his heart; such inner feelings and motives are only known to the Lord. All that men can know are words that they can read when the writer is absent, and deeds that they can see when he is present. In fact, his testimony when present is greater than when absent. The apostle acted according to the truth of the inspired letters, showing that he really believed what was written.

God seeks a response to His Word, both in the heart and in conduct. The lesson for today is that we should be imitators of Paul, our deeds being in keeping with the Epistles. The importance of knowing the Epistles cannot be over-emphasised, so that we may act according to the ways of

Christ revealed in them.

A man who fails to appreciate the necessity of works is a poor ambassador for Christ. Faith comes first by the Word of God, and the "work of faith" follows, 1 Thess. 1. 3. Paul behaved "holily and justly and unblameably", 2. 10; James would show his faith by his works, James 2. 18; John would love "in deed and in truth", 1 John 3. 18. Paul, at least, intended to demonstrate this to the full when he arrived in Corinth. Could they argue against his conduct? Observing his works would strengthen their faith in deeper things, John 10. 38.

Verses 12–18: Apostolic Service Limited according to the Will of God

12 For we dare not make ourselves of the number, or compare ourselves with some that commend themselves: but they measuring themselves by themselves, and comparing themselves among themselves, are not wise.

13 But we will not boast of things without *our* measure, but according to the measure of the rule which God hath distributed to us, a measure to reach even unto you.

14 For we stretch not ourselves beyond *our measure,* as though we reached not unto you: for we are come as far as to you also in *preaching* the gospel of Christ:

15 Not boasting of things without *our* measure, *that is,* of other men's labours; but having hope, when your faith is increased, that we shall be enlarged by you according to our rule abundantly,

16 To preach the gospel in the *regions* beyond you, *and* not to boast in another man's line of things made ready to our hand.

17 But he that glorieth, let him glory in the Lord.

18 For not he that commendeth himself is approved, but whom the Lord commendeth.

12. Although on occasions Paul must assert his apostolic authority, yet with what apostolic wisdom he discerned when it was proper and when it was improper to do so! For example, in the opening verse of Philippians, he would not draw attention to himself as an apostle. At the same time, even to these wayward Corinthians, he would not commend himself as an apostle, "For not he that commendeth himself is approved, but whom the Lord commendeth", 2 Cor. 10. 18. We should notice various verses where the idea of commendation occurs:

Acts 14. 26, "Antioch, from whence they had been *recommended* to the grace of God for the work which they fulfilled". This refers to the Lord's people commending a brother for work he had been called to by a specific intervention of God.

2 Corinthians 4. 2, "by manifestation of the truth *commending* ourselves to every man's conscience in the sight of God". Paul had no hesitation in commending himself by a walk manifesting truth. This really displayed the grace of Christ in effecting such a change in the chief of sinners.

2 Corinthians 6. 4, "in all things *approving* ourselves as the ministers

of God". Here it is a question of his character displaying the graces of Christ.

2 Corinthians 12. 11. Paul asserts that the Corinthians should have commended him for the work done; instead he had to boast of reproach and infirmities for Christ's sake.

Even though the processes of divine inspiration would have the apostle speak of himself in these verses, Paul would not adopt a carnal attitude in the matter. The unspiritual would measure themselves by themselves, and would compare themselves among themselves. Such men were not wise (or lacked the ability to comprehend thoroughly the principles of humility involved).

Measuring themselves would involve a boastful spirit of recognising that they could do this or that. It is the opposite to the spirit of the servants who confessed that they were unprofitable when they had done their duty.

Comparing themselves would involve the boastful spirit of scorn and defiance, recognising that they could do something which others could not. It is the spirit of seeking who should be the greatest.

13. Paul's outlook would not focus on any self-ability or on any self-calling. Only that which was of God in himself was worthy to be considered or boasted in. The general trend of teaching in verses 13–16 is evident, but the two words "measure" and "rule" occur. The former deals with the question "How much?" and the latter with the question "Of what sort?"

Rule. This is the translation of the Greek word *kanon*, from which the English word canon comes, used to describe the authoritative collection of O.T. and N.T. books. Physically the word means a rule, and hence spiritually and metaphorically it means a principle of action and service, of conduct and doctrine. Referring to service, it implies the field of service that God would have us take up. In verse 14, Paul explains what the rule was in his case, "preaching the gospel of Christ". Each believer develops according to the rule "which God hath distributed" to him.

Other examples of the use of this word in the N.T. are: (a) Galatians 6. 16, the rule for one's walk. Either one believes that one is a "new creature" boasting only in the cross of the Lord Jesus Christ, or one has no true christian rule at all, always digressing to Jewish or other ritual, v. 15. (b) Philippians 3. 16 gives another rule for one's walk, namely all to be likeminded in pressing towards heavenly things.

Measure. This refers to how far the rule is to be taken, where it is to be exercised. Paul would not preach anywhere, anyhow, but only where and how God would choose. Paul could boast in this, since it reflected the purposes of God and not the intentions of an unsanctified heart. Paul was exercised, of course, about these things, but his desire as an evangelist was dovetailed with the plan of God.

The idea of *measure* must be distinguished from that of *need*. There is need everywhere for the gospel to be preached, but if evangelists recognised this as a sole criterion for service, their movements would be erratic and haphazard in the extreme. In the present context, Paul's measure was the Macedonian coast extending round into Achaia and Corinth. Recognition of the measure of one's service comes from perceiving the will of God in the matter, as many scriptures demonstrate:

> Acts 10. 20, Peter went to Caesarea following his vision and the instruction by the Spirit.
>
> Acts 13. 1–4, Paul embarked on his first journey by the leading of the Holy Spirit.
>
> Acts 16.10, Paul crossed into Macedonia only because the Lord had called them to preach the gospel there.
>
> Acts 18. 21, Paul went to Ephesus on his third journey only because it was the will of God that he should.

In other words, the Lord thrusts labourers into His harvest field where He wills, Matt. 9. 37–38. This is the measure by which every servant of Christ should abide.

14. Paul now applies this principle to his own movements. "We stretch not ourselves beyond" means that he would not go beyond the will of God in his location of service. "As though we reached not unto you" suggests avoiding the appearance of being interested elsewhere in service. But Paul was quite clear in what he was doing, "We are come as far as to you also in preaching the gospel of Christ". The phrase "as far as" refers to the "measure", and the words "preaching the gospel" to the "rule". In other words, the apostle limited his service to the sphere of God.

The phrase "gospel of God" occurs six times in the Epistles, and "gospel of Christ" eight times. Essentially, the former is in relation to the unsaved, as 2 Cor. 11. 7, while the latter relates to the saved or to the preacher, 9. 13. Again, the former relates to the origin and authority of the gospel, while the latter to its foundation and the channel through which it is brought. Elsewhere, we find the expression "our gospel", 1 Thess. 1. 5; 2 Thess. 2. 14, relating to the possession of the preacher and to the responsibility of the believer to propagate it.

15. Paul would not boast or meddle with the service of other brethren, to which the Spirit had not led him. Even in Corinth, Paul had had his particular work of planting, 1 Cor. 3. 6, and would not boast in another man's work as if it were his own (for example, that of Apollos, who watered). The apostle would recognise the faithful labours of other servants of God; they had their measure and their rule while Paul had his. He would not build on or boast in another man's foundation, as he wrote in Romans 15. 17–20, "I have therefore whereof I may glory through Jesus Christ in those things which pertain to God. For I will not dare to speak of any of those things which Christ hath not wrought by me, to make the

Gentiles obedient, by word and deed, through mighty signs and wonders, by the power of the Spirit of God; I have fully preached the gospel of Christ. Yea, so have I striven to preach the gospel, not where Christ was named, lest I should build upon another man's foundation". Today, believers may be too systematised for such independent work, but it is good to abide by the limitations of one's own calling to service.

Paul's exercise was to break new ground with the gospel message, but he would not neglect a work already established in order to do so. He laboured among the Corinthians, both in epistles when absent and in preaching when present, until "your faith is increased". Only then would the apostle allow himself to be "enlarged" as he explains in the next verse. If possible, Paul would not move on from an evangelistic centre until the believers there were standing on their own spiritual feet. Again, once they were established, he would not tarry merely to repeat work already done, by going over the same ground again. His rule, the gospel, could be enlarged under these circumstances. Today, an evangelist may appear to be more organised, with arrangements made for him to move rapidly from one centre to another. Others may appear to be less organised, as Paul was, with few prior engagements and preparations, enabling them to tarry in a fruitful field in the will of God. Each servant of God should know before the Lord how his measure is delineated, avoiding the mechanical and seeking the spiritual in discerning the will of the Lord.

16. The extension of Paul's service would be to preach the gospel in the regions beyond Corinth, his object being to "see Rome", Acts 19. 21, and Spain, Rom. 15. 24. But wherever he went, he would "not boast in another man's line (that is, rule) of things made ready to our hand". If the fundamentals of the gospel had been preached at Rome with converts obtained already, then Paul would extend the scope of this work, and not sit down comfortably in a work previously started by others. In fact, Paul had already written to the Romans, knowing that salvation had visited that city through other workers. When he arrived there, his purpose was to build on what was already laid, as an apostle seeking to "impart unto you some spiritual gift, to the end ye may be established", Rom. 1. 11; this was still part of the gospel, v. 15. This desire to build up a work already started, should be contrasted with the verse already quoted from Romans 15. 20. In that verse it is a question of pioneering evangelistic endeavour (relating to his proposed visit to Spain), but in chapter 1 it is a question of pastoral care of an established assembly.

17. *Conclusion.* Paul had appeared to boast in his own calling to service in order to make his position clear to the Corinthians. But having written this paragraph, he directs attention to the proper quarter, "But he that glorieth, let him glory in the Lord" (the word "glory" here properly means "boast"). Such an attitude of heart would also place verses 22–33 of the following chapter in a proper perspective.

Paul had made the same quotation at the end of chapter 1 in the first Epistle. There was no room for self-boasting in any servant of God. Paul is quoting from Jeremiah 9. 23–24. Natural wisdom, might and riches form no ground for legitimate boasting; no flesh can glory in His presence. But the ground for glorying is the fact that the Lord delights in exercising loving kindness, judgment, and righteousness. This removes self and makes Christ all in all.

18. Paul returns to the thoughts of verse 12; commendation and approval come only from the Lord. Such approval is recognised by how the Lord takes up service rendered. It was proved in Paul's case, and these few in Corinth could not gainsay the apostle's arguments. This is exemplified by how the Lord Jesus showed His approval of the publican but not of the Pharisee, Luke 18. 14.

2 CORINTHIANS 11

Section 4.   The Example of the True Minister
Subject 2.   True and False Apostles

Background of this Subject

Paul continues his arguments to provide proof of his apostolic status for those who would not accept him in Corinth. Throughout these chapters, he hesitates to write about himself, but God had control of His servant and by divine inspiration this was written. As a man, Paul regards it as "folly" to write about himself, 11. 1, asking even these men in Corinth to bear with him. He felt that this was foolishness, v. 17, since he had no desire to commend himself, 10. 12, accepting only the commendation of God, v. 18.

In this chapter, Paul introduces the contrasts between himself as a true apostle of the Lord Jesus Christ, and certain other men whom he designates as "false apostles". In verses 1–2, he declares the true apostolic *object*, the presentation of the saints to Christ. Verses 3–4 give the counter-object of the false apostles and teachers. Then in verses 5–11, he describes the apostolic *character* suitable for such a blessed task, but he does not touch upon his divinely given authority for this work. Again by way of contrast, in verses 12–15 the apostle describes the character and intents of the false apostles. Finally, in verses 16–33, we find the detailed account of the true apostle's boasting in his *sufferings* for Christ's sake, both within and without the assembly. This is plain speaking, and none but a man called of God would sustain such privations and tribulations, thereby losing his natural life but gaining his spiritual reward. This description continues to verse 11 of chapter 12, concluding with the open testimony "Truly the signs of an apostle were wrought among you in all patience, in signs, and wonders, and mighty deeds", v. 12.

It is verse 13 that contains the description "false". Paul would warn every believer against complacency. It is not a wise thing to submit oneself to the supposed and apparent service of others without question or discernment. To do so would be equivalent to the neglect of the many warnings given in Scripture against false men of every kind. It is possible for men to do things apparently in the name of the Lord, yet not to be owned by the Lord since they do not do God's will, and are instead workers of iniquity, Matt. 7. 21–23. The apostle John would exhort us to "try the spirits whether they are of God", 1 John 4. 1. One method of discerning the difference is that the world will listen to false men but not to the true servant of God, "Hereby know we the spirit of truth, and the spirit of error", vv. 5–6. The Lord warned, "Take heed what ye hear", Mark 4. 24.

This subject is so relevant to the testimony today that a detailed look at the variety of such false men is of value.

False Christs

Matthew 24. 23–24, "Then if any man shall say unto you, Lo, here

is Christ, or there; believe it not. For there shall arise false Christs
. . . and shall shew great signs and wonders".

1 John 2. 18, "as ye have heard that antichrist shall come, even now
are there many antichrists".

False apostles

2 Corinthians 11. 13, "False apostles, deceitful workers,
transforming themselves into the apostles of Christ".

Revelation 2. 2, written to Ephesus, "thou hast tried them which say
they are apostles, and are not, and hast found them liars".

False prophets

Deuteronomy 13. 1–5, "Thou shalt not hearken unto the words of
that prophet"; "that prophet . . . shall be put to death".

Isaiah 30. 10, "Prophesy not unto us right things, speak unto us
smooth things, prophesy deceits".

Ezekiel 13. 16–17, "the prophets of Israel . . . which prophesy out of
their own heart".

Matthew 7. 15, "Beware of false prophets, which come to you in
sheep's clothing, but inwardly they are ravening wolves".

Matthew 24. 11, "And many false prophets shall rise, and shall
deceive many".

Matthew 24. 24, "there shall arise . . . false prophets".

2 Peter 2. 1, "there were false prophets also among the people".

1 John 4. 1, "many false prophets are gone out into the world."

False evangelists

2 Corinthians 11. 4, "if he that cometh preacheth another Jesus,
whom we have not preached".

Acts 15. 1, "And certain men . . . taught . . . Except ye be
circumcised after the manner of Moses, ye cannot be saved".

Galatians 1. 7, "another gospel, which is not another; but there be
some that trouble you, and would pervert the gospel of God".

False teachers

2 Peter 2. 1, "there shall be false teachers among you, who privily
shall bring in damnable heresies, even denying the Lord".

1 Timothy 4. 1–5, "some shall depart from the faith. . . ."

Jude 4, "there are certain men crept in unawares . . . denying the
only Lord God, and our Lord Jesus Christ".

False pastors

Ezekiel 34. 1–10 provides a dreadful description of such men.

False elders

Acts 20. 30, "of your own selves (that is, of the elders of the
Ephesian church to whom Paul was speaking) shall men arise,
speaking perverse things, to draw away disciples after them". This
can be a real danger, since elders, having authority and leadership,
are sometimes automatically followed by the flock.

False brethren

Galatians 2. 4, "false brethren unawares brought in, who came in privily to spy out our liberty which we have in Christ Jesus".

2 Corinthians 11. 26, Paul is found amongst "false brethren", which he describes as a "peril".

This is an impressive list, showing that the Lord's people must be alive to the dangers involved. It should be noticed that both *gifts* (namely the five given in Ephesians 4. 11) and *local charge* are included in the list. Everything that God has ordained in the assembly is liable to attack locally. At the same time, we rejoice that "greater is he that is in you, than he that is in the world", 1 John 4. 4, and that "the gates of hell shall not prevail against" the church of Christ, Matt. 16. 18.

Exposition of 2 Cor. 11: True and False Apostles

Verses 1–4: Objects of the Apostle and False Apostles

1 Would to God ye could bear with me a little in *my* folly: and indeed bear with me.
2 For I am jealous over you with godly jealousy: for I have espoused you to one husband, that I may present *you as* a chaste virgin to Christ.
3 But I fear, lest by any means, as the serpent beguiled Eve through his subtilty, so your minds should be corrupted from the simplicity that is in Christ.
4 For if he that cometh preacheth another Jesus, whom we have not preached, or *if* ye receive another spirit, which ye have not received, or another gospel, which ye have not accepted, ye might well bear with *him.*

1. The A.V. phrase "Would to God" translates a single word in the Greek text, and strictly speaking any reference to God in the phrase is absent. The word is an interjection, meaning "O that", or "would that". The word occurs again in Galatians 5. 12, where it is more properly rendered as "I would". The phenomenon of inserting the divine name is not restricted to this particular phrase. The familiar exclamation "God forbid", Rom. 6. 2; Gal. 6. 14, really contains no reference to God. This expression merely means "May it not be that", "Far be it from"—an expression of a wish that something should not be.

Paul requests the Corinthians to bear with him a little in his folly, in the necessity of having to speak about himself. This word "folly" is translated "foolishly" in verses 17 and 21, derived from the word "fool" occurring in verses 16 and 19, referring to an unwise and inconsiderate person. Paul thus perpetuates this humble thought about himself throughout this section, concluding with "I am become a *fool* in glorying", 12. 11. Although in the apostle's argument it is necessary to refer to himself so much, yet he hastens in verse 2 to show the blessed object of his service in reference to Christ. The *reason* of the Corinthians is reached in verse 1, while their *heart* is attained in verse 2.

2. The sensitivities of Paul's heart and the object before him, are laid bare when he declares "I am jealous over you with godly jealousy", or more

literally, "with the jealousy of God". This word translated "jealousy" has both a good and a bad sense in the N.T.; the context must decide which meaning is implied in any given case.

In *a good sense*, the word means *zeal* and *ardour in behalf of.* It is used of the Lord in John 2. 17, "The *zeal* of Thine house hath eaten Me up", and of Israel when Paul witnessed that "they have a *zeal* of God, but not according to knowledge", Rom. 10. 2. It is in this good sense that Paul employs the word in the verse under consideration.

In *a bad sense*, the word means *envy*. For example, the Jews in Antioch were "filled with *envy*" when they saw the multitudes coming together to hear the Word of God, Acts 13. 45.

The phrase "with the zeal of God" is remarkable, in that the desires and ardour of a servant can resemble those of the Master. It shows the heights to which the expectancy of a brother engaged in service should rise. It takes formality and routine out of service, maintaining freshness and spirituality. A similar thought occurs in Numbers 25. 11, where Phinehas, the son of Eleazar the son of Aaron, was *zealous with the zeal of God* when he used a javelin to purge evil from the congregation. As a result of this, to the family of Phinehas was granted the "covenant of an everlasting priesthood", a subject that occupies such a prominent place in the history of Samuel, Saul, David, and Solomon. The high priests Eli, Ahimelech, and Abiathar were not high priests in the family of Phinehas, but through another son of Aaron, namely Ithamar. The proper list of the "everlasting priesthood" occurs in 1 Chronicles 6. 4–8, where Zadok was re-established by Solomon as high priest *alone*, 1 Kings 2. 26, 27, 35. The zeal of Phinehas is recalled in Psalm 106. 30–31 . This zeal sought to function in the sanctuary, but this was not possible until the unsanctified inroads described in Numbers 25 were dealt with. Likewise, in Paul's case, he describes many in 2 Corinthians 11 who would hinder the workings of his own zeal, but once sanctified service alone is dominant, there can be no end to the blessings in Christ that the saints can enjoy.

The care that Paul bestowed upon the saints befitted the holy position into which they had been brought. Even now believers have been espoused to one husband, presented as a chaste virgin to Christ. This word "espoused" is distinct from that occurring in Matthew 1. 18; Mary was originally espoused to Joseph in the sense of having been asked in marriage, but before they came together, Matt.1. 18; Luke 1. 34. But in 2 Corinthians 11. 2, the word implies "to fit together" and "united in marriage". Paul had brought the Corinthians into intimate contact with the Lord by faith. He had initiated their affection for Christ and he had enabled them to dwell with Him in their hearts.

It must be realised that Paul is dealing essentially with practical matters. It is as a local assembly in affection and service that they have thus been presented to Christ. The fact that Paul expressed his fears in verse 3 that they might be corrupted, is sufficient to show that the apostle is writing about their *state* and not their *standing*. His exercise had been to maintain the believers chaste after their conversion, by keeping them unspotted from the world and from the inroads of error. This contrasts with the universal aspect of the bride, decreed by the Lord, which refers to the believers' standing that nothing can mar.

The Song of Solomon in the O.T. presents both sides of the picture, namely the state and the standing of the bride. This does not refer specifically to the church of the present dispensation, but principles relating to grace and responsibility are found there. The affections of the bride had waned in chapter 3; she sought her beloved but found him not, showing that her state did not answer to her standing. She regains appreciation of the grace of her standing in her great confession of the beauties of Christ, 5. 10–16, and His answer in 6. 4 to 7. 9 confirms that He sees her through eyes of divine affection and grace.

Israel as a nation in the O.T. waxed and waned in this truth. Jehovah could recall the original "kindness of thy youth, the love of thine espousals", Jer. 2. 2, but this had been corrupted, since "as a wife treacherously departeth from her husband, so have ye dealt treacherously with Me, O house of Israel", 3. 20. Yet what promise of restored affections is held out for a future day ! "I will betroth thee unto Me for ever, . . . in righteousness, and in judgment, and in lovingkindness, and in mercies . . . in faithfulness", Hos. 2. 19, 20. The Maker of the nation shall be their husband, Isa. 54. 5 and "as the bridegroom rejoiceth over the bride, so shall thy God rejoice over thee", 62. 5.

Paul's zeal was to present the saints to Christ. All those who abide in the apostle's teaching are similarly presented. The idea of presentation is found in many different aspects in the N.T.

Presentation by oneself
Romans 6. 13, "Yield (present) yourselves unto God".
Romans 12. 1, "I beseech you . . . that ye present your bodies a living sacrifice, holy, acceptable unto God".

Presentation by the apostle
2 Corinthians 11. 2, "that I may present you as a chaste virgin to Christ".
Colossians 1. 28, "that we may present every man perfect in Christ Jesus".

Presentation by the Lord
2 Corinthians 4. 14, "He . . . shall present us with you".
Ephesians 5. 27, "That He may present it to Himself a glorious church".
Colossians 1. 22, "reconciled . . . to present you holy and unblameable and unreproveable in His sight".
Hebrews 2. 13, "Behold I and the children which God hath given Me".
Jude 24 "Now unto Him that is able . . . to present you faultless before the presence of His glory with exceeding joy."

3. Such blessedness, however, is always likely to be disturbed, and Paul's fear is recorded that all may take heed. The original method of the enemy of souls is still today the chief disturbing influence among the people of God. The serpent is the form the enemy takes when he seeks to make error seem reasonable. This is no open temptation to idolatry or to the denial of Christ and Him crucified. In fact, by such cunning craftiness nothing may seem to be wrong to those whose minds and hearts are not solely taken up with the Word of God.

The lesson of Genesis 3 is hard to learn, seemingly irrelevant to those who do not want to be warned. Eve was beguiled (that is, *deceived*) by a question, "Yea, hath God said, Ye shall not eat of every tree of the garden", v. 1, and by deliberately twisting the very words of God, "Ye shall not surely die", v. 4, when God had said ". . . thou shalt surely die", 2. 17. This is the method of those wanting to make black white, the powers of darkness appearing to be angels of light. Sin had *deceived* Paul in his unconverted days, Rom. 7. 11. Those who cause divisions and offences contrary to the doctrine that we have learned are to be marked and avoided, since "by good words and fair speeches *deceive* the hearts of the simple", Rom. 16. 17, 18. The Thessalonians were *deceived* regarding the day of Christ, and Paul beseeched them not to be troubled by spirit, word, letter or by "any means", 2 Thess. 2. 2, 3. All these examples tell the same story, namely wrong justifying itself to be right, and of course "subtilty" has to be used to gain access to the mind and heart.

This word "subtilty" means craftiness, a word occurring only five times in the N.T. For example, in Luke 20. 23, Jesus "perceived their craftiness", when the chief priests and scribes tempted Him regarding the tribute money to Caesar. These men had arranged "spies, which should feign themselves just men, that they might take hold of His words", thereby demonstrating the spirit of craftiness. Such temptation may come the way of believers if they are not watchful. The Lord had the divine insight to recognise this craftiness; He saw the hearts of those who feigned themselves just men. Believers today have no such insight, and are cast wholly upon the Word of God.

Paul knew that the Corinthians had been "corrupted from the simplicity that is in Christ". Simplicity means a singleness of heart, as Ephesians 6. 5 and Colossians 3. 22. It is the attitude of faith that has one object before the heart upon the narrow path leading to life. Paul had written the first Epistle to the Corinthians because he had known that they had been corrupted. Its corrective influence worked then for their good. Under the control of the Spirit of God the Word may still have its original influence on us today.

4. Paul finally outlines the objects before the false apostles, described as him "that cometh". Craftily they sought to change the very truth held by the Corinthians. It appears that they had endured such teachers before their repentance upon reading the first Epistle; they had been bearing with it (not "with him" as the A.V. reads).

Another Jesus, that is, *allos*, another of the same kind. The same man
Christ Jesus was proclaimed, but different and wrong things were
said about Him. Some would say that Christ was in the wrong place,
Matt. 24. 23; others would preach "Christ of contention, not
sincerely", Phil. 1. 16. Men today would preach another Jesus. They
would display Him as an example, teacher, as a good man and a
martyr; they would explain away His miracles and His resurrection;
His divine nature would be denied. He is declared to be one who
loves but does not judge, as the one whose death provided no
availing sacrifice. These are "damnable heresies, even denying the
Lord", 2 Pet. 2. 1.

Another spirit, that is, *heteros*, another of a different kind. John exhorts
us to "believe not every spirit, but try the spirits", 1 John 4. 1. One
test is whether a confession is made that Jesus Christ is come in the
flesh, v. 2; another test is whether the world hears them, v. 5. Such
a test would embrace every truth surrounding "God . . . manifest in
the flesh", 1 Tim. 3. 16. These other spirits make havoc of the true
Spirit's activity, as, for example, in 1 Corinthians 14.

Another gospel, that is, *heteros*, another of a different kind. The name
of Jesus may be used, but the gospel may be entirely different from
the one by which believers know they have been saved. One can
turn from the true grace of Christ to "another gospel" (of a different
kind), Gal. 1. 6, "which is not another" (of the same kind), v. 7.
Such men pervert the gospel of Christ by introducing law,
circumcision, good works, the wisdom and methods of men, 1 Cor.
1, and the variety of foreign concepts promulgated today.

Verses 5–11: Apostolic Character for such Objects

5 For I suppose I was not a whit behind the very chiefest apostles.
6 But though *I be* rude in speech, yet not in knowledge; but we have been
throughly made manifest among you in all things.
7 Have I commited an offence in abasing myself that ye might be exalted,
because I have preached to you the gospel of God freely?
8 I robbed other churches, taking wages *of them,* to do you service.
9 And when I was present with you, and wanted, I was chargeable to no
man: for that which was lacking to me the brethren which came from
Macedonia supplied: and in all *things* I have kept myself from being
burdensome unto you, and *so* will I keep *myself.*
10 As the truth of Christ is in me, no man shall stop me of this boasting in
the regions of Achaia.
11 Wherefore? because I love you not? God knoweth.

5. Paul always realised that he was distinct from the other apostles. Yet
he "was not a whit behind the very chiefest apostles". He had no less
authority than John, who had even heard, seen, looked upon, and handled
the Word of life, 1 John 1.1. He had no less authority than Peter, who had
been a "witness of the sufferings of Christ", 1 Pet. 5. 1. And why? Because

he had seen the Lord in ascension glory. If the other disciples had been called by the Lord in the days of His flesh, Matt. 10. 1, 2, then Paul had been called by the Lord in the eternal days of His exaltation. It had pleased God to reveal His Son in Paul, Gal. 1. 16; he had been called to be an apostle by the will of God, 1 Cor. 1. 1; it is by Christ that he "received grace and apostleship", Rom. 1. 5; authority and power had been given him by the Lord, 2 Cor. 10. 8; 13. 10.

At the same time, humility shone through his calling and success. He felt that he was the least of the apostles, not meet to be called an apostle, because he persecuted the church of God, 1 Cor. 15. 9. By contrast, he laboured more abundantly than the others, v. 10, which Paul ascribed to the grace of God which was with him. He was least because of his *previous works*, but he was greatest because of the *divine purpose*. The other apostles had seen the Lord with their eyes, but God would demonstrate that the greatest work is done by those who appreciate the Lord by faith on ascension ground. The principle that the least shall be greatest is vividly portrayed here .

6. Paul now outlines a few features of his character as an apostle. *Firstly* he states the contrast that he was rude in speech but not in knowledge. Paul was painfully aware that he suffered some defect in his speech which would not commend itself to a carnal mind. God had caused His servant to prosper in spite of this. Paul knew this, of course, but these wayward men in Corinth could not understand the supremacy of the power of God over the natural weaknesses of the flesh. Hence here Paul contrasts his speech with his apostolic *knowledge* of divine truth, while in 10. 10–11, he contrasts his bodily presence and his speech with his deeds.

Secondly Paul records the fact that he had been thoroughly manifested among the Corinthians in all things. In 12. 12, he recalls the signs, wonders and mighty deeds wrought among the saints in Corinth; in Romans 15. 19 he recalls similar works that Christ had wrought by him among the Gentiles; in Acts 20. 18–21 he dwells on his service in the early days at Ephesus; in 1 Thessalonians 2. 2–12 he records his conduct before the young Christians in Thessalonica; in 2 Timothy 3. 10 he writes to Timothy of his "doctrine, manner of life, purpose, faith" which were fully known. Every servant of God should humbly be able to recall the manifestation of conduct, holiness, dependence, trust, and adherence to the Word. Much more is manifest to the Lord, who says, "I know thy works", Rev. 2. 2.

7. *Thirdly*, Paul deals with preaching "the gospel of God freely". That is to say, he would not "live of the gospel", 1 Cor. 9. 14. God had given liberty to His full-time servants to be sustained in their material needs by His people, but Paul would labour with his hands to supply his own needs, Acts 20. 34. Time and again the Corinthians held this against the apostle, since from the beginning he had thus conducted himself in Corinth, 18. 3.

Paul had devoted the whole of 1 Corinthians 9 to this subject. The majority in Corinth had been convinced by the apostle's argument, but the few still held this against Paul. It is a serious thing for a believer not to be convinced by a whole chapter in the Word of God. A second warning may be given as in the present case, but one cannot play with and ignore divine truth indefinitely.

Paul regarded this policy as abasing himself—the vessel and the channel being lost sight of—in order that the converts should be "exalted", namely raised to a high spiritual standing in Christ. He humbled himself in poverty, hunger, suffering and necessity, Phil. 4. 12. God will take care of all His servants, and will reverse such abasement in a coming day, as many Scriptures declare:

Abasement

John 3. 30, "He must increase, but I must decrease".

1 Corinthians 4. 9, "God hath set forth us the apostles last, as it were appointed to death".

2 Corinthians 6. 9, "as unknown".

Contrast Acts 8. 9, where Simon gave out that he was a great one.

Exaltation

Luke 14. 11, "he that humbleth himself shall be exalted". In the assembly, a believer should do nothing for the advancement of self or self-interests; one should take the lowest room until the Lord leads him "up higher".

1 Peter 5. 6, "Humble yourselves therefore under the mighty hand of God, that He may exalt you in due time". See also Phil. 2. 9. and James 4. 10

8. How was Paul maintained in his service? He "robbed other churches", in the sense that only the Philippians communicated with him when he went to Corinth, Phil. 4. 15. This word "rob", occurring only once in the N.T., means the "right of seizing goods of a merchant for payment". It need hardly be remarked that the reference to "churches" is to local assemblies; it has no reference to buildings where thieves may break through and steal, Matt. 6. 19. Indeed, the author has heard this given as a justification for calling a *hall* where the local assembly meets by the name of *church*.

9. Here, Paul outlines in more detail what robbing other churches meant to him. Paul had worked as a tentmaker in Corinth, but it appears that this had not been sufficient for his needs. The brethren from Macedonia supplied his lack. They had done this previously when Paul was at Thessalonica, Phil. 4. 16, and also later when he was in Rome, v. 10. In Corinth, where Paul was dealing with quite a different kind of man from that in Macedonia, he would be "chargeable to no man" and would keep himself "from being burdensome". His policy was that children should not lay up for the parents but the parents for the children, 2 Cor.

12. 14. But the Corinthians were rich, 1 Cor. 4. 8, and the unspiritual were touchy that Paul would not accept their support. Paul knew that such would not be a savour acceptable to God, "Should I accept this of your hand? saith the Lord", Mal. 1. 13. By contrast, the Philippians' gift was "an odour of a sweet smell, a sacrifice acceptable, wellpleasing to God", Phil. 4. 18. Hence the Corinthians rejected his apostleship. This, alas, often happens; the pride of some becomes touchy, so they reject the teaching and spirituality of others.

10. But the majority in Corinth could not stop Paul's boasting, since he followed Christ.

11. Paul would boast because he loved the Corinthians; his boasting was designed to help and correct them. If he had not boasted in what the Lord had done through him, this minority would then have had the opportunity of continuing in their own course. Paul would have created an opportunity or the flesh to dominate. But the motives of Paul were known to God, "God knoweth". The apostle wrote everything for *their help* and not for *his gain*.

Verses 12–15: Character and Intents of False Apostles

> 12 But what I do, that I will do, that I may cut off occasion from them which desire occasion; that wherein they glory, they may be found even as we.
> 13 For such *are* false apostles, deceitful workers, transforming themselves into the apostles of Christ.
> 14 And no marvel; for Satan himself is transformed into an angel of light.
> 15 Therefore *it is* no great thing if his ministers also be transformed as the ministers of righteousness; whose end shall be according to their works.

12. Paul was absolutely dogmatic in his intentions to deal with the opportunists in Corinth, who sought to discredit him and substitute themselves, though without humility and sufferings. He would remove the very opportunities that they sought to use. We find in these verses the rise of evil ways which would give birth to a clerical class and system, the gifts and calling of Christ being abandoned in favour of a mockery of apostolic succession. In verse 2, we have already commented upon a similar situation in the O.T. Regarding the O.T. priesthood, men's ways and thoughts were not God's ways and thoughts. The true line through Eleazar and Phinehas was discarded by opportunists of Ithamar's family, who established themselves in the high-priestly line. This occasion was only cut off by Solomon at the beginning of his reign when he removed Abiathar and allowed Zadok alone to be high priest, 1 Kings 2. 27, 35. Similarly over the years since Paul's day, tradition has not died hard, but has survived and multiplied. The ecclesiastical heirarchy is an established feature of the great denominations of Christendom, showing how an opportunity for departure from the Word was taken and developed. Such systems cannot

be eliminated, but they can be cut off by individual believers, judging such in their hearts and seeking to be separated by following the gifts and calling of Christ in local assemblies.

13. These men transformed themselves into the apostles of Christ. They had a desire for an authority they did not possess, and for doctrine not in keeping with the Scriptures. True apostles were given by Christ, Eph. 4. 11, and not made by self. Today, the desire to do something, to be something, to say something opposite to what Paul did, was, or said, is equivalent to speaking "great swelling words of vanity", 2 Pet. 2. 18.

In our verse, it would appear that the men Paul has in mind are brethren in the assembly, but in verse 15, the thought goes further, where "his ministers" must refer to men outside assembly fellowship. Believers today cannot afford to be complacent about these dangers which Paul put on record for all time. As we outlined in the background to this chapter, every phase of assembly service can be undermined by such insidious activity of unholy men. The apostle would say to our own hearts, "Take heed therefore unto yourselves", Acts 20. 28, "looking diligently lest any man fail of the grace of God", Heb. 12. 15.

14. That such unholiness should ever mar the local testimony of God's people is not to be wondered at, since the same transformation is seen in Satan himself. He appears in two forms:
1.   *as a serpent*, in deceit, openly suggesting rebellion; perhaps in power as a roaring lion seeking whom he may devour, 1 Pet. 5. 8;
2.   *in light*, thereby to dazzle and confuse the satisfied, rich and proud heart. Scripture refers in several places to this side of Satan's history and activity:

Luke 10. 18, "I beheld Satan as lightning fall from heaven".

Isaiah 14. 12–14, Satan is seen as Lucifer, the day star, the son of the morning, the one who thought in his heart to exalt his throne above the throne of God.

Ezekiel 28. 17, "Thine heart was lifted up because of thy beauty, thou hast corrupted thy wisdom by reason of thy brightness".

15. The character of Satan reflects upon the character of those who are "his ministers". This word *minister* is the same as the familiar word "deacon", namely any believer who serves in the local assembly, and which occurs so many times in the N.T. Satan has his counterfeits among men. To be a minister of Satan is a strong description, and it is suggested that it refers to men outside the assembly, although physically they may be attached to it. The idea of being a servant of Satan goes deeper in Romans 6. 16, "Know ye not, that to whom ye yield yourselves servants to obey, his servants ye are to whom ye obey; whether of sin unto death, or of obedience unto righteousness?" The word servant here means bondservant. Again we find two exactly opposite manifestations of loyalty.

The idea of copying is involved—servants or bond-servants either of the powers of darkness or of the Lord Jesus Christ. The Saviour warned of such men who would come in "sheep's clothing, but inwardly they are ravening wolves", Matt. 7.15. Outwardly they appear beautiful, as whited sepulchres, but within they are full of "dead men's bones, and of all uncleanness", Matt. 23. 27. Similarly, Jacob appeared as Esau to Isaac his father, by means of a false make-up. Believers are warned to discern the spirits of men, whether they are of God or whether they are of antichrist. Believers may be beguiled in their unwary moments because antichrists may appear to be transformed into spirits from God.

Bad works, however, have a bad end for those who continue in them. For believers, before the judgment seat of Christ, that which is wood, hay and stubble will be burnt up. They will suffer loss of reward thereby, but they will be saved, 1 Cor. 3. 12–15. For unbelievers, who have defiled the temple of God, their end before the great white throne will be to be destroyed. For believers, the Lord shall come quickly; His reward shall be with Him to give every man according as his work shall be, Rev. 22. 12. But for unbelievers, the Lord shall be revealed from heaven with His mighty angels, in flaming fire "taking vengeance on them that know not God, and that obey not the gospel of our Lord Jesus Christ: who shall be punished with everlasting destruction from the presence of the Lord, and from the glory of his power", 2 Thess. 1. 7–9. The Lord's people should be instructed by these solemn pronouncements.

Verses 16–33: Apostolic Boasting in Sufferings Without and Within

16 I say again, Let no man think me a fool; if otherwise, yet as a fool receive me, that I may boast myself a little.

17 That which I speak, I speak, I speak *it* not after the Lord, but as it were foolishly, in this confidence of boasting.

18 Seeing that many glory after the flesh, I will glory also.

19 For ye suffer fools gladly, seeing ye *yourselves* are wise.

20 For ye suffer, if a man bring you into bondage, if a man devour *you,* if a man take *of you,* if a man exalt himself, if a man smite you on the face.

21 I speak as concerning reproach, as though we had been weak. Howbeit whereinsoever any is bold, (I speak foolishly), I am bold also.

22 Are they Hebrews? so *am* I. Are they Israelites? so *am* I. Are they the seed of Abraham? so *am* I.

23 Are they ministers of Christ? (I speak as a fool) I *am* more; in labours more abundant, in stripes above measure, in prisons more frequent, in deaths oft.

24 Of the Jews five times received I forty *stripes* save one.

25 Thrice was I beaten with rods, once was I stoned, thrice I suffered shipwreck, a night and a day I have been in the deep;

26 In journeyings often, *in* perils of waters, *in* perils of robbers, *in* perils by *mine own* countrymen, *in* perils by the heathen, *in* perils in the city, *in* perils in the wilderness, *in* perils in the sea, *in* perils among false brethren;

27 In weariness and painfulness, in watchings often, in hunger and thirst, in

fastings often, in cold and nakedness.

28 Beside those things that are without, that which cometh upon me daily, the care of all the churches.

29 Who is weak, and I am not weak? who is offended, and I burn not?

30 If I must needs glory, I will glory of the things which concern mine infirmities.

31 The God and Father of our Lord Jesus Christ, which is blessed for evermore, knoweth that I lie not.

32 In Damascus the governor under Aretas the king kept the city of the Damascenes with a garrison, desirous to apprehend me:

33 And through a window in a basket was I let down by the wall, and escaped his hands.

16–21. In these strange six verses, Paul prepares the ground for the following paragraph. Still with the intention of proving his apostolic calling, he is going to speak of his personal experiences, something that he hesitates greatly to do.

As we read these verses, we are constrained to ask, is this really the apostle Paul writing? For the writer claims that he is not speaking "after the Lord", v. 17, but "after the flesh", v. 18. Elsewhere, he had written, "That no flesh should glory in His presence",1 Cor. 1. 29, and "we . . . have no confidence in the flesh", Phil. 3. 3. Here, the flesh refers to the regenerate or unregenerate mind dealing with the things of God.

The point is that in these verses, Paul, is deliberately *adopting the point of view held by the Corinthians*; he is reflecting their thoughts when they would read the Epistle. He knew their attitude well, and could use it to his advantage. He knew that they believed themselves to be superior in many things; they were able to "suffer" (that is, to bear with) the indignities described in verse 20, indignities that Paul designates as "reproach" (that is, dishonour), v. 21. They were thus able also to suffer, or bear with, fools. If this, then, was their outlook, Paul would adopt a position that they could suffer. From *their* point of view, he would write as a fool, and "after the flesh". But from *his* point of view—and from *God's*—he would really be writing "after the Lord". Writing "after the flesh" would gain their *ear* and their *reason*, but writing "after the Lord" would gain their *heart* and their *response unto repentance.*

22. The details which Paul now gives of himself show the true character of his heart. The Lord had said that He was the good Shepherd; He turned not from the pathway set before Him, a pathway of sufferings leading to glory. Other men may be "thieves and robbers", John 10. 8; the hireling, seeing danger drawing near, "leaveth the sheep, and fleeth . . . because he . . . careth not for the sheep", vv. 12, 13. Those with designs upon their own gain and importance have no interest in the well-being of the people of God. When danger threatens, those with no calling from God will rapidly abandon any pretence to such a calling. But Paul went forward in the footsteps of the Master, thereby proving his calling to divine service.

Paul's long list conveniently divides itself into various groups.

Verses 22–23a: personal details;
Verses 23b-25a: sufferings caused by men;
Verse 25b: sufferings caused by nature;
Verse 26: sufferings in his journeys;
Verse 27: physical privations;
Verse 28: anxieties regarding the local assemblies;
Verses 32–33: sufferings at the hands of political and religious
    opponents.

Paul now asks four questions about "they", this referring, we presume, to the other apostles, as in verse 5. The references to Hebrews, Israelites, Abraham, and Christ go backwards in time.

Hebrews. Paul restricts himself to the same personal details that the other apostles possessed. Thus he does not mention the fact that he was a "Hebrew of the Hebrews" and a Pharisee, as in Phil. 3. 5, where Paul was showing that any confidence in the flesh was counted loss for Christ, vv. 4, 7. Such national differences are of no importance among believers, since "There is neither Jew nor Greek, . . . for ye are all one in Christ Jesus", Gal. 3. 28. Elsewhere, Paul records his personal details, saying or implying that he was a Jew, Acts 22. 3; 26. 4. In the N.T., a Hebrew means a Hebrew-speaking Jew, distinguished in Acts 6. 1 from Greek-speaking Jews. The Jews were the descendants of the southern kingdom consisting of Judah and Benjamin. In the O.T. however, the implication of a Hebrew is far wider (although the order adopted by Paul suggests that he is not referring to this). The name refers to a descendant of Eber of Shem, Gen. 10. 21; 11. 15. Thus Abram was called a Hebrew, 14. 13. Later in O.T. terminology, the word applies essentially to the twelve tribes in Egypt, Exod. 2. 6, namely to the descendants of Jacob.

Israelites. Paul goes backwards, from the Hebrew-speaking descendants of Judah inhabiting Palestine, to the wider term Israelites, meaning all the descendants of Jacob, including the northern kingdom of Samaria taken into captivity in 2 Kings 17, and who never returned to the land. See Romans 11. 1.

The seed of Abraham. Paul goes further backwards, passing over Isaac. He refers to Abraham *according to the flesh*, for all believers are of Abraham's seed *spiritually according to promise*, Gal. 3. 29.

Ministers of Christ, that is, servants or deacons of Christ. Paul goes backwards to the eternal Christ, who had said, "Before Abraham was, I am", John 8. 58.

Whereas concerning the first three questions, Paul and the other apostles were on the same footing, "so am I", yet for the last question Paul is different, "I am more". The following list shows in what way he was a minister of Christ more than the others. This was an indisputable proof of his apostleship.

23. It should be noticed that Paul restricts his list describing his "labours more abundant". In fact, he makes mention only of the *physical* consequences of his *spiritual* labours. Paul was very conscious that it was God who accomplished his spiritual work: "I laboured more abundantly than they all: yet not I, but *the grace of God* which was with me", 1 Cor. 15. 10; "Whereunto I also labour, striving according to *His working*, which worketh in me mightily", Col. 1. 29. Hence Paul would not mention the achievements of his three missionary journeys, and the numerous churches established, which had been the work of God. This would, of course, have been sufficient to demonstrate his apostleship, but these men in Corinth were not sufficiently spiritual to have appreciated it.

The physical sufferings of Paul were a direct consequence of the statement made by God when he was converted, "I will shew him how great things he must suffer for My name's sake", Acts 9. 16. What the *unconverted* Saul had sown, that he had to reap in his *converted* life. The many things that he had done "contrary to the *name* of Jesus of Nazareth", Acts 26. 9, had to be translated into suffering "for My *name's* sake". Although painful to the flesh, Paul rejoiced and boasted in these things, if it served the cause of edification in any way.

23–27. Not all these vicissitudes of service have their place in the record of the apostle's service and movements in the book of Acts. The reason is obvious. In the Acts they are not necessary; the book being given essentially for those who are spiritual. The Spirit would keep the spiritual side rather than the physical side to the fore. But here, in 2 Corinthians 11, the original intention of the passage was that the understanding of the unspiritual should be furthered.

> *In stripes above measure.* The apostle followed in the footsteps of the Master, "with His stripes we are healed", Isa. 53. 5. The apostle could not forget such cruelty, recalling such stripes in 2 Corinthians 6. 5. Many stripes had been laid upon him in Philippi, Acts 16. 23, but works meet for repentance were brought forth by the jailor, who "washed their stripes", v. 33, his baptism signifying such a change of heart and life.

> *In prisons more frequent.* The familiar occasion was in Philippi, Acts 16. 23, prior to writing this Epistle. Afterwards, he knew that "bonds" awaited him, 20. 23; 21. 11. In Caesarea, he was kept in prison for two years, 24. 26, 27; 25. 14. Paul wrote his later Epistles from prison in Rome, Phil. 1. 13; 2 Tim. 1. 16; Philem. 9. But in prison, the Lord comforted His servant, Acts 23. 11, saying "Be of good cheer". He was the One who, according to His will, could set at liberty, Luke 4. 18; Acts 5. 19; 12. 7.

> *In deaths oft.* Paul had the sentence of death in himself, but was delivered by God "from so great a death", 2 Cor. 1. 9, 10. His persecutions were such that he described them with the words, "I die daily", 1 Cor. 15. 31. Certainly in Lystra, when they stoned Paul,

they thought that he had been dead, Acts 14. 19. Paul was thereby following others who had passed that way before him, as Stephen and James, 12. 2; see Matthew 23. 34–35. The exercise of the apostle was that Christ should be magnified in his body, whether by life or by death, Phil. 1. 20.

Forty stripes save one from the Jews five times. The Lord had warned that such scourging and beating would take place in the synagogues, by those who were fanatical in the Jews' religion without Christ, Matt. 10. 17; Mark 13. 9. The law was explicit in Deuteronomy 25; forty stripes must not be exceeded. The Jews kept the law formally in employing only thirty-nine stripes, but how cold and unrighteous were their hearts. Prior to the administration of such stripes the judges were meant to "justify the righteous, and condemn the wicked", vv. 1–3. The Jews were not capable of judging righteous judgment with the stumbling block of Christ crucified before them, so five times Paul had to suffer at their hands. By this they made a mockery of the law of God.

Thrice beaten with rods. In these verses, Paul is referring to events prior to Acts 20. 2, when the Epistle was written. One such event was in Philippi, 16. 22, where the heathen magistrates "commanded to beat them". Even by heathen standards, this was unlawful, since Paul was a Roman and uncondemned, v. 37. Both Jewish law and the heathen law were violated by the custodians of it, in their antagonism against the preachers of the gospel.

Once stoned. The Lord had told of stoning in His parable, Matt. 21. 35. He Himself escaped stoning since His hour had not yet come, John 8. 59. Stephen had been stoned to death, Acts 7. 59 and Paul had been stoned and left as dead at Lystra, 14. 19. Such practices brought out the depths of faith in those who thus suffered, Heb. 11. 37.

The various references to the sea, "thrice I suffered shipwreck", "a night and a day I have been in the deep", "in perils of waters", "in perils in the sea", augment the record in the Acts. We must not read the later journey to Rome and the shipwreck on the island of Malta into this account by Paul, since the journey in Acts 27 took place over two years later. The events must have occurred during the sea voyages connecting up the various stages of his missionary journeys, Acts 13. 4, 13; 14. 26; 16. 11; 18. 18, 21. During such trials, the presence of the Lord was assured, since He had been the One to calm the sea to give rest to the troubled souls of His disciples, Matt. 8. 26. See Psalm 107. 23–31.

The various references to his journeys over land, "in journeyings often", "in perils of robbers", "in perils by mine own countrymen", "in perils by the heathen", "in perils in the city", "in perils in the wilderness", "in perils among false brethren", all tend to augment the record of the Acts. But the children of Israel had been sustained by their God during their wilderness wanderings, in spite of enemies on every side. Of the movements of the

Lord Jesus it had been written, "For He shall give His angels charge over Thee, to keep Thee in all Thy ways", Ps. 91. 11. He had been preserved as He traversed the same journey as the man who went down from Jerusalem to Jericho and fell among thieves, Luke 10. 30. Paul, too, was journeying according to the will of God. Ultimate safety was guaranteed as long as God had work for His servant to accomplish.

The privations of the body, described in verse 27, are those of one who had learnt the lesson of what he preached, "Look not every man on his own things, but every man also on the things of others", Phil. 2. 4. In that chapter, the examples of Christ and of His followers Paul,Timothy, and Epaphroditus demonstrate various phases of this truth. "In weariness and painfulness" more properly should read "in labour and toil". The verbal form of the first word carries the meaning of weariness through labour, as in the Lord's case, John 4. 6. The Acts is remarkably silent concerning the physical effects of such service and journeys on the stamina of the apostle, yet our verse 27 shows that God was not unmindful of such conditions in His servant. In his "watchings often", he had worked day and night for three years in Ephesus, Acts 20. 31 No wonder, then, we read of a welcome break of seven days in Troas, 20. 6, of another seven days at Tyre, 21. 4, of Paul refreshing himself with his friends in Sidon, 27. 3, of another seven days rest at Puteoli, 28. 14, and of fellowship shown by brethren at Appii forum, 28. 15, enabling Paul to take courage. The Lord's people today, who give themselves over to much service, cannot serve effectively if the mind and body are tired without appropriate rest. The construction of mind and body, and their inter-relationship under conditions of service and stress, the rising and falling of the frail human form (see 2 Cor. 1. 8–10) are all things ordained of God, as is the necessity of suitable rest (every seventh day under the O.T. economy). Any servant of God would be unwise to continue throughout life in defiance of these principles that God has established in His own creation.

28. The sufferings thus far listed are sufferings "without" namely incidentals to the evangelistic and pastoral labours of Paul. In this verse we find things that are within the scope of such spiritual labours. "That which cometh upon me daily" means a *crowding* of calls daily upon the attention and thoughts of the apostle. The majority of the editors of the Greek text suppress two letters in the word for "crowding", thereby transforming the meaning into "my anxiety". The word "care" means *anxious interest*; it occurs as a verb in Philippians 4. 6, "*Be careful for nothing*". There, it seems to refer to one's possessions, interests, and well-being, as in Matthew 6. 25 where the Lord said, " *Take no thought* for your life, what ye shall eat, or what ye shall drink; . . ." But such anxious interest about the well-being of the Lord's people is not excluded; Paul's heart was daily occupied with them. Today, the deeper the sincerity of a labourer concerning what he knows to be the truth, the more will his heart be taken up with anxious interest in the saints. Sleepless nights may result;

the mind may find no rest as it turns the problems over in prayer. On the other hand, the more mechanical the service and with little insight into the mind of God concerning His ways among His people, the less will the labourer show anxious interest in the saints. He will tend to sleep peacefully wondering what all the fuss is about in others, his fellow-labourers.

Paul's daily interest in the many assemblies about which he was concerned manifested itself in different ways:

> *In constant prayer*: for the Romans, Rom. 1. 9; for the Corinthians, 1 Cor. 1. 4; for the Ephesians, Eph 1. 16; for the Philippians, Phil. 1. 4; for the Colossians, Col 1. 3; for the Thessalonians, 1 Thess. 1. 2–3; 2 Thess. 1. 3; for Timothy, 2 Tim. 1. 3.

> Paul's care caused him to *return* to Lystra, the city of his persecution, to confirm "the souls of the disciples", Acts 14. 21.

> His care produced the exercise to *visit* the brethren in every city where he had previously preached the Word of God, Acts 15. 36.

> He had *warned* the Ephesians day and night for three years with tears, knowing the dangers to come, Acts 20. 31.

> He had *no rest in his spirit* in Troas, on account of his anxiety for the Corinthians, 2 Corinthians 2. 13.

> He was willing to travail in birth again for the Galatians, until Christ was formed in them, Galatians 4. 19.

> His anxiety in Athens caused him to *send* Timothy back to Thessalonica to establish and comfort them, 1 Thessalonians 3. 1, 2, 5, 7.

29. If any one is weak, if any of the other apostles are weak, that is, in sustaining sufferings for the testimony of Christ, then Paul is weaker. Was not Christ "crucified through weakness", 2 Cor. 13. 4, that is, at the hands of men? In spite of outward appearances, He now lives by the power of God, v. 4, manifested openly to believers through His resurrection, Eph. 1. 19, 20. A similar conclusion in Paul's case would be drawn later, 2 Cor. 12. 11, 12.

Similarly with the second question; are there any among the Corinthians offended at Paul? Yet his desire burns deeply for them. A burning spirit in spite of opposition is no mark of an unspiritual man, who would have given up long ago, turning his efforts elsewhere. But the very spiritual persistence of Paul proved his character.

30. Still perpetuating the theme of personal boasting, the apostle keeps only his infirmities before him. In such a context there can be no room for boasting in the Lord's successes through him; he mentions this later in 13. 3, but not in the context of boasting. Salvation through his preaching of Christ, the establishment of churches, and their growth in grace through his ministry, were the works of God. Happy the servant of Christ today who can speak in similar tones !

31. But has Paul told the truth? Has there been a tendency to exaggerate? Can the Corinthians be certain as to the facts? Paul's experiences were unique compared with anything that they had heard before. Unique events are not to be taken lightly or without question. Hence Paul names as witness "The God and Father of our Lord Jesus Christ, which is blessed for evermore". God, who cannot lie, Titus 1. 2, cannot be a witness of a man who is a liar. In the ungodly, this sin has such a dreadful end, Rev. 21. 8. Had not Moses, after having placed before the people the details of life and death, of blessing and cursing, called "heaven and earth to record" against them, Deut. 30. 19? In other words, all personal conversation and writing, all preaching and ministry, should be accomplished under the principle of "Yea, yea; Nay, nay", Matt. 5. 37, with the realisation that God above knows the hearts and thoughts.

32–33. The experience in Damascus after many days following his conversion, when the Jews took counsel to kill Paul, Acts 9. 1–25 was evidently worse than what Luke recorded in the Acts. The fact that it has its place here in Paul's list shows how it had impressed itself upon his mind. Acts 9. 23–24 shows that it was the Jews who were behind the plot, because Paul was proving "that this is very Christ", v. 22. But in his letter the apostle states that it was the "governor under Aretas the king" who was "desirous to apprehend" him. Paul writes that he escaped "his" hands, rather than from the Jews. Taken together, we see that it was a politico-religious plot against the testimony of Christ. It had been the same when men crucified the Lord of glory; the chief priests had been instant in seeking His death, while the kings and rulers, Herod and Pilate, were intimately concerned, Acts 4. 26, 27. This is characteristic of a religious system attached to the state, which will be headed up in the appearance of the political and religious beasts of Revelation 13. 1–7. The marriage of church and state has no part in the counsels of God for the church. No good thing can come from such a union although this figures high in the counsels of men. The experience of Paul (and of history) shows that when evil men gain control in either sphere then believers suffer persecution. Lack of persecution, however, should not cause believers to smile complacently upon such a union.

2 CORINTHIANS 12

Section 4.   The Example of the True Minister
Subject 3.   Preparation For Service

Background of this Subject

Paul continues his arguments, by them seeking to effect the repentance of those in Corinth who were not amenable to his apostolic authority. The first part of the chapter deals with "visions and revelations of the Lord", while the latter part deals with Paul's intentions to visit Corinth. Taken together, the subject of *preparation* pervades the chapter:

Verses 1–13 show Paul's *general preparation*—that which is preparatory to all service, the grounding of his soul in the ways of God both unto exaltation and unto humiliation.

Verses 14–21 deal with Paul's *special preparation*—relating to his proposed visit to Corinth.

The former without the latter would show a lack of *works*, while the latter without the former would show a lack of *faith*. God's method for His servant was one of perfect balance.

Exposition of 2 Cor. 12: Preparation for Service

Verses 1–9: Visions and Revelations of the Lord

1 It is not expedient for me doubtless to glory. I will come to visions and revelations of the Lord.
2 I knew a man in Christ above fourteen years ago, (whether in the body, I cannot tell; or whether out of the body, I cannot tell: God knoweth;) such an one caught up to the third heaven.
3 And I knew such a man, (whether in the body, or out of the body, I cannot tell: God knoweth;)
4 How that he was caught up into paradise, and heard unspeakable words, which it is not lawful for a man to utter.
5 Of such an one will I glory: yet of myself I will not glory, but in mine infirmities.
6 For though I would desire to glory, I shall not be a fool; for I will say the truth: but *now* I forbear, lest any man should think of me above that which he seeth me *to be*, or *that* he heareth of me.
7 And lest I should be exalted above measure through the abundance of the revelations, there was given to me a thorn in the flesh, the messenger of Satan to buffet me, lest I should be exalted above measure.
8 For this thing I besought the Lord thrice, that it might depart from me.
9 And he said unto me, My grace is sufficient for thee: for my strength is made perfect in weakness. Most gladly therefore will I rather glory in my infirmities, that the power of Christ may rest upon me.

1. Paul now comes to the greatest manifestation of his apostolic calling—something that transcends human suffering and spiritual labour on earth, by taking one into the heavenlies. If Paul hesitated to boast in his physical sufferings, and if he touched very lightly upon his spiritual labours, how much more would it not be expedient (or profitable) for him to boast before the Corinthians, as a result of the following vision. Paul had a deep exercise regarding the desirability of describing this vision; the pros and cons are given in verse 6.

There is a difference between *vision* and *revelation*.

Vision. This is the means that God sometimes used to communicate with men. Oftentimes it had an effect upon the human eye, but not always so. The communication usually referred to matters relating to daily life and service. For example, Zacharias had a vision in the temple relating to the birth of his son, Luke 1. 11–22. Ananias had a vision relating to visiting the newly-converted Saul of Tarsus, Acts 9. 10. Both Cornelius and Peter had visions in Acts 10. 3, 17, relating to their being brought together for the preaching of the gospel. In Paul's case in 2 Corinthians 12, it was a vision because he saw and heard things, and because there would be practical repercussions in apostolic service.

Revelation. This is an unfolding, an uncovering of what had previously been hidden. For example, in Matthew 16. 16, 17, Peter's confession of the Christ as the Son of the living God, is stated by the Lord to be a result of revelation from the Father. Again, the knowledge of "these things" is kept from the wise and prudent, and revealed to babes, Matt. 11. 25. Similarly, the Father is known from revelation by the Son, v. 27. Thus revelation concerns the knowledge of divine Persons, and of doctrinal truth. *Revelation* is given for the heart and for *faith*, while *visions* are given for the *mind* and for *works*.

Paul was a man of varying visions for the circumstances of life, and a man of revelation for his apostolic duty in declaring the new truth of the assembly. A brief review of his visions is not without interest.

1. Acts 9. 3, the vision of *conversion*. Paul loved to recall this later in his life during times of trial, both in Jerusalem, 22. 6, and in Caesarea, 26. 13. The apostle describes this affecting experience as a "heavenly vision", v. 19.

2. Acts 9. 12, the vision of *restoration*. This concerned the coming of Ananias, that Paul might receive restoration of his physical eyesight, and that he might be baptized, 22. 16, demonstrating restoration from past sin unto a life lived for Christ.

3. Acts 22. 17, the vision of *purpose*. The divine will to send Paul "far hence unto the Gentiles" was declared.

4. Acts 16. 9, the vision of *guidance*. Paul, and only Paul, saw the man of Macedonia calling for help, thereby explaining why the Spirit had not allowed them to tarry in Asia, in the previous verses.

5. Acts 18. 9–10, the vision of *assembly formation*. The Lord had "much people" in Corinth, and Paul would labour for a year and a half to establish the assembly there.

6. Acts 23. 11, the vision for *future testimony*. Paul had testified and suffered in Jerusalem, and the Lord would inform His servant that he must also bear witness at Rome.
7. Acts 27. 23, the vision for *safety*. In the storm on the way to Rome, the angel of God would speak to Paul alone, telling him that all would be saved.
8. 2 Corinthians 12. 2–4, the vision for *apostolic authority*.

2. "I knew a man in Christ" should read "I know", a verb in the present tense. Paul is relating his present knowledge of the experience of the past, as did Peter in 2 Peter 1. 15–19.

Paul's description of this vision and revelation is quite different from that of Peter, who openly states that "we" were eyewitnesses of the majesty of Christ, 2 Pet. 1. 16. Paul, on the other hand, writes merely of "a man in Christ". This clearly refers to himself according to verse 7 where he mentions that he had received "the abundance of the revelations". Paul writes as he does to gain the understanding of backsliders. Peter writes to believers to prevent them from becoming backsliders.

In Galatians 2. 1, one period of fourteen years in the life of the apostle is given—namely from the time of his return from Arabia, Gal. 1. 17, to the time between the first and second missionary journeys when he went up to Jerusalem, Acts 15. 2–4. The second period of fourteen years recorded in our verse 2 is usually taken to refer to the time between the end of his first journey at Lystra, Acts 14. 19, and the writing of this second Epistle from Macedonia, 20.1. Some expositors lay stress on numbers; fourteen equals seven multiplied by two, seven being the number of perfection or completion, while two is the number of testimony, John 8. 17. Hence this recorded period of time after the vision suggests perfect testimony of what was witnessed in the vision. This was necessary so as to speak the truth and not to exaggerate, and to instruct the gainsayers in Corinth with an honest testimony that could not be refuted.

Some have suggested that the vision took place between Paul's conversion on the Damascus road and the time three days later when Ananias came to Paul, Acts 9. 9. But the only physical defect that Paul had then was blindness, and the description "whether in the body, I cannot tell; or whether out of the body, I cannot tell: God knoweth" hardly appears to fit. Paul was doubtful about the matter, and would not speculate. But the occasion in Lystra, when the people "having stoned Paul, drew him out of the city, supposing he had been dead", Acts 14. 19, would appear more appropriate. If this is the occasion, it is interesting to note that men moved him *outside the city*, but that God moved His servant *out of the world*. This contrasts with the experience of Stephen, Acts 7. 58, where they first cast him out of the city and then stoned him. When the text says that the people "drew" Paul out of the city, supposing he had been dead, the word carries the meaning of "drag", as in John 21. 8, "dragging the net with fishes". Such an experience suggests that Paul was not conscious physically. He was therefore in a state where God could take him up spiritually in a special way. Consciously, Paul writes that he did not know what happened; the connection of the vision with his body was outside his knowledge. The unconscious state had been used by God to special purpose. Moreover, it was not only a vision; it was a movement, similar to what Ezekiel had experienced as he was transported from the river Chebar (in captivity) to Jerusalem, "and the spirit lifted me up between the earth and the heaven, and brought me in the visions of God to Jerusalem, to the door of the inner gate . . .", Ezek. 8. 3. See also Ezek. 37. 1; 40. 1, 4.

The "third heaven" is not exactly defined in Scripture; mythology should best be avoided in interpreting the expression. The implication is that there are a first and a second heaven. This is a phenomenon both of creation and of the phraseology of many languages. In English, the words "sky" and "the skies", tend to convey a different meaning from the words "heaven" and "the heavens". The former refer to the physical creation, while the latter have a spiritual sense, at least to the believer. In a more poetical sense, the latter words still have the same meaning as the former. But in other languages, as French, German, and N.T. Greek, two sets of words do not exist, and the one word (and its plural form) *ciel, Himmel, ouranos*, must refer both to the physical and the spiritual. We need not be surprised, therefore, at the existence of several heavens.

First heaven. This refers to the local atmosphere surrounding the earth. In Noah's day, the "windows of heaven were opened", Gen. 7. 11, referring to the physical origin of the waters of the flood. It is in this connection that Satan is described as "the prince of the power of the air", Eph. 2. 2, having fallen as lightning from a higher sphere, Luke 10. 18. It is here the disciples saw the Lord ascend, Acts 1. 9, a cloud hiding His further movements from their eyes. It is here that believers will first meet their Lord at His coming again, 1 Thess. 4. 17. Elisha saw Elijah taken "up by a whirlwind into heaven", 2 Kings 2. 11. This reflects only on what Elisha could see physically. It cannot refer to the higher heaven, in keeping with the words of the Lord, "no man hath ascended up to heaven, but He that came down from heaven, even the Son of man which is in heaven", John 3 . 13.

Second heaven. This refers to the stellar heavens, seen in part with the naked eye, but in greater detail through astronomical telescopes and photography. The heaven was created in the beginning, Gen. 1.1. The psalmist spoke of this in many places in his song, "who hast set Thy glory above the heavens", Ps. 8. 1; "Thy heavens, the work of Thy fingers, the moon and the stars, which Thou hast ordained", v. 3; "The heavens declare the glory of God", 19. 1. Revelation 21. 1 refers to this, "I saw a new heaven and a new earth: for the first heaven and the first earth were passed away". The word "first" in this verse refers to the first in time, not to the sequence in character described here. Solomon seems to refer to this in his prayer of dedication of the temple, "the heaven and heaven of heavens cannot contain Thee", 1 Kings 8. 27. As He rose, Jesus the Son of God as a great High Priest "passed *through* the heavens", Heb. 4. 14 R.V., *en route* for the "throne of the majesty in the heavens", 8. 1. No doubt it is from this sphere that Satan is cast in Revelation 12. 7–10.

Third heaven. The spiritual now transcends the physical; this refers to the proper dwelling place of God. Christ entered "into heaven itself, now to appear in the presence of God for us", Heb. 9. 24. The house "not made with hands, eternal in the heavens", 2 Cor. 5. 1, obviously refers to this, since the physical side of things is ruled out by the very thought Paul is expounding in that verse.

3. In our judgment, it would have been more appropriate if the phrase "How that he was caught up into paradise", v. 4, had been incorporated in verse 3. It appears that verse 3 "And I knew such a man, (whether in the body, or out of the body, I cannot tell: God knoweth;)" merely repeats the previous verse 2. This indeed is so, showing the stress that the apostle put upon such a strange yet vital experience. But what is important to note is that each of these two statements has a conclusion, namely "such an one caught up into the third heaven", v. 2, and "that he was caught up into paradise", v. 4. The former represents the *place*, while the latter represents the *character* of the place.

4. The actual word "paradise" means "garden with a wall". Confusion will arise if we think that all occurrences of this word in the N.T. refer to the same place. Rather, the character of the places thus designated is the same, and may simply be expressed as a place *where the Lord is* at one particular time, as the following thoughts show. It is necessary to consider the place of the departed dead throughout the ages in the economy of God, and in this connection we repeat a few of the thoughts given on the opening verses of 2 Corinthians 5.

At death, bodies were placed in the grave, but "hades" (translated "hell" in the A.V.) was the place for departed spirits. In the O.T., the corresponding Hebrew word is often translated "grave"; this is a great error, and a concordance must be consulted if proper sense is to be preserved. The N.T. provides abundant evidence that hades was divided into two parts, embracing those waiting for "the resurrection of life" and those waiting for "the resurrection of damnation (that is, judgment)", John 5 . 29. Before the death of the Lord Jesus, the abode of the blessed was termed "Abraham's bosom", Luke 16. 22, the place where Lazarus was, and the place of rest for all the O.T. saints, including those men of faith listed in Hebrews 11. There was Moses, ready to appear at the transfiguration of the Lord, Luke 9. 30, although his body had been buried in a valley in Moab, Deut. 34. 6, unknown to man but contended for by

Satan, Jude 9. The place is also called "paradise" by the Lord Jesus when on the cross, the place to which both He and the repentant malefactor would go in death, Luke 23. 43. Peter affirms in Acts 2. 31 that the soul of the blessed Lord had been in hell (that is, this particular part of hades) while His body was in the tomb. This is quoted from Psalm 16. 10, while elsewhere, this place is termed "the lower parts of the earth", Eph. 4. 9, as the place to which the Lord descended before He ascended. See Matthew 12. 40; Jonah 2. 6.

But unrepentant sinners also have their place in hades, although in a part characterised by such different and awful conditions. The rich man's body was buried, but "in hell (hades) he lift up his eyes, being in torments", Luke 16. 23. The same name "hades" is used, but there was a great gulf fixed between these two portions of hades, a gulf that the senses of sight and hearing could traverse, although no soul could pass from one part to the other. This is the place of waiting for the resurrection of judgment, namely for the great white throne, Rev. 20. 11. Hades will be emptied for this to take place, "death and hell delivered up the dead which were in them", v. 13. The lake of fire, distinct from hades, will be the portion of those whose names are not found written in the book of life. The beast and the prophet will pass there directly without entering the intermediate place hades, Rev. 19. 20. This final abode of the wicked was first "prepared for the devil and his angels", Matt. 25. 41, described elsewhere as "the blackness of darkness for ever", Jude 13 . Further information is provided in 2 Peter 2. 4, where we read that "God spared not the angels that sinned, but cast them down to hell, and delivered them into chains of darkness, to be reserved unto judgment"; see also Jude 6. One cannot be dogmatic whether this refers to the second part of hades (where the souls of men await judgment) or to the lake of fire already in use for the angels but not for men. In the Greek, the word "hell" does not occur explicitly in this verse. The R.V. follows the A.V., but its margin gives "Tartarus". J. N. D. translates the phrase as "having cast them down to the deepest pit of gloom". The reader may well wonder why there is such a variation in the translation. The reason is that in the Greek there is only one word (a verb) standing for this phrase. It is the verbal form for the noun Tartarus, which in ancient mythology was the name given to the place where the wicked were confined and tormented. Peter does not embrace mythology by using the word. Words of all kinds and from various sources have to be used to express divine truth, and the only meaning that can be placed upon them is what is found elsewhere in Scripture. If the exact shade of meaning is not clear to us now (although no doubt clear to Peter's readers who would have been taught in these things), it ill becomes an expositor to be too dogmatic. Readers may be exercised themselves concerning the subject.

The Lord entered hades during the three days in which His body was in the tomb—the place being called "paradise", a place where the Lord was. Then the Lord was raised; He "ascended up far above all heavens", Eph. 4. 10. The saints in hades with Him rose also with Him, not of course as to their bodies (Matthew 27. 52–53 excepted); but the Lord "led captivity captive", Eph. 4. 8, as He led a multitude heavenward. Now, saints who pass from this scene of their labours no longer enter hades (or "paradise"), but they go to "be with Christ; which is far better", Phil. 1. 23. As such, they are not in the body, since that would be in the grave. Rather they are "found naked", "unclothed", "absent from the body", 2 Cor. 5. 3–8. But at His coming again, spirit soul and body will be reunited in resurrection. They will come with Jesus, 1 Thess. 4. 14, to be united to their bodies which shall rise first, v. 16. Then will be formed the "building of God", a "house which is from heaven", a body "clothed upon", 2 Cor. 5. 1–4; then mortality shall be "swallowed up of life".

It is now easy to see the implication of "paradise" to which Paul was taken. It was not hades as in Luke 16; rather it was to the place where the Lord was after His ascension, namely to the "third heaven". This phrase denotes the place, whereas the name "paradise" delineates the character of the place, specified by the presence of the Lord. It is therefore distinct from the place to which the Lord went after the cross, also named "paradise". Paul went up, but the Lord went down, Eph. 4. 9. The only other occasion this word occurs in the N.T. is in Revelation 2. 7, referring to the blessings promised to the overcomers in Ephesus. This also has a future implication; it does not look backwards.

It is not out of place to mention how 1 Peter 3. 19 fits into God's plan, namely "By which (Spirit) also He went and preached unto the spirits in prison; which sometimes were disobedient...." It is sometimes suggested that the Lord in death preached to the *wicked* in hell. In the light of the above, this cannot be so. The Lord went to paradise, while the wicked destroyed in the time of Noah were in a different section of hell. Rather the verse means that the Lord went and preached (in Noah's day) to the spirits (now) in prison— the same applying to the similar verse in 1 Peter 4. 6. The longsuffering of God waited in the days of Noah, the Spirit of God striving with men before the flood, Gen. 6. 3. This was the preaching of Christ through the Spirit.

In paradise Paul "heard unspeakable words, which it is not lawful for a man to utter". Paul did not break the silence enjoined upon him, as others had done before. For example, the Lord had asked the man cleansed of his leprosy to say nothing to any man, but he "began to publish it much, and to blaze abroad the matter", Mark 1. 45. On the other hand, elsewhere John had heard the words of heaven, and recorded them for the churches, Rev. 5. 9–14. When to speak and when not to speak; what to speak and what not to speak; these demand exercise and obedience in those who seek to say a word for the Lord in testimony.

Paul's experience shows that the Word of God does not embrace every possible truth—no doubt the highest features of heaven could not be expressed in words of a human language. Rather, the Word as we have it represents the selection that God wants us to possess; see John 21. 25. Curiosity may go outside the Word, and philosophy may speculate behind the truth as revealed, but believers who stand by the Word as *given* are nearest to the mind of God. Moreover, we have the divine example in the matter. The mystery of the "same body" had not been made known in O.T. times, Eph. 3. 5. The Spirit of prophecy had remained silent since it had not been in the divine plan to speak of such things then. The Lord Jesus had remained silent regarding the meaning of the parables of the kingdom. It was not given to the wise and the prudent to know, Matt. 13. 11, but the truth was made known only to His own, vv. 12, 16, 18, 36. The Lord's servant John knew later how to follow in his Master's steps. He was about to write the words of the "seven thunders", when he heard a voice from heaven saying, "Seal up those things . . . and write them not", Rev. 10. 4.

5. Paul will boast of such a one *in the past*, but as *in the present* he will not boast openly of a privilege not given to others. Rather he will boast in the common lot of all believers, namely in his infirmities, which in his special case were of apostolic severity.

6. Ever since this vision over fourteen years previously, Paul had had the desire to boast in it, yet he had remained silent in his writings and in his recorded oral ministry. It is best not to dwell upon experiences peculiar to oneself; others are bound to misunderstand if it is something outside their own experience. Paul would not be a fool by dwelling unnecessarily upon the event, particularly to unsympathetic readers. In fact, Paul wanted men to see him as he was under ordinary circumstances, not as he was in the vision, "lest any man should think of me above that which he seeth me to be, or that he heareth of me". The seeing appears to refer to the fact that Paul *saw* in the vision, and the hearing to the fact that he *heard* words in the vision. The vision indeed provided Paul with the knowledge behind his apostolic authority, but he would impart this knowledge by the affliction of persecution and toil. Any "show" in service is objectionable to God, but a humble disposition is well-pleasing unto Him, reflecting as it does the life of Christ lived here for His glory. "Tell the vision to no man" the Lord commanded as He descended the mount of transfiguration, Matt. 17. 9, appearing shortly afterwards with no money to pay tribute, v. 27.

7. The *old man Saul* would still be active unless the *new man Paul* always reckoned himself "to be dead unto sin, but alive unto God through Jesus Christ our Lord", Rom. 6. 11. The previous verses have shown where the apostle sought to hold himself; but God would also keep His servant low, lest he should be exalted above measure through "the abundance of the revelations". At his conversion in Acts 9, Paul was brought low by God, and in one way or another he was kept there during the years of his service. Sufferings followed many of his visions. The vision of the man of Macedonia in Acts 16. 9 soon led to afflictions in Philippi and Thessalonica. The vision in Corinth, 18. 9, soon led to the Jews making insurrection with one accord against Paul. The vision on the ship, 27. 23, soon led to his sufferings in Rome. The glory on the mount, Luke 9. 29, led to a conversation about the Lord's decease. But conversely, glory follows such sufferings according to the promise of God, 1 Pet. 1 . 11; Luke 24. 26; 2 Tim. 2. 12; 2 Cor. 4. 17.

There is a danger of the flesh exalting itself in divine privilege, so oftentimes the flesh physically is kept low in one kind of infirmity or another. This may be apparent to others, as in Paul's case, or it may be hidden from public knowledge. In this case the brother or sister concerned, having discerned the mind of the Lord, must remain spiritually content in knowing that it is for his or her good under the hand of God. Such may not be joyous in the present, but "afterward it yieldeth the peaceable fruit of righteousness unto them which are exercised thereby", Heb. 12. 11.

There has been speculation on the nature of Paul's "thorn in the flesh", based on a few scattered verses and phrases throughout his Epistles; see Gal. 4. 15; 2 Cor. 10. 10. Expositors suggest that the thorn related to his eyesight, a deficiency introducing weakness and an unbecoming appearance. Indeed, one manuscript existing in Greek and Coptic, known as the *Apocryphal Acts of Paul*, and written about AD 160 by an orthodox Christian, gives the following description:*

> "And he saw Paul coming, a man little of stature, thin-haired upon the head, crooked in the legs, of good state of body, with eyebrows joining, and nose somewhat hooked, full of grace: for sometimes he appeared like a man, and sometimes he had the face of an angel".

This is, of course, of passing interest only. We can be certain that when Scripture is silent as to details, then its balm of comfort reaches all souls with different afflictions, yet with the same object in view.

The thorn in the flesh was something allowed by God, coming from the outside, but not directly produced by God Himself, for Paul describes it as "the messenger of Satan". The permissive will of God, and the activity of Satan, are likewise seen in Job's case, Job 2. 6. The patience of this man shows that the Lord is very pitiful and of tender mercy, James 5. 11 . The failure of bodily functions is, of course, a consequence of sin, but not necessarily as a result of one's own sin. It is a harsh contempt of God's ways with His own to judge a brother on account of some illness or physical defect, thinking that this is God's governmental hand upon him for some sin committed. Compare John 9. 3, where the Lord explained that the man was born blind, not because of any particular sin, but "that the works of God should be made manifest in him". Likewise the sickness of Lazarus was for the glory of God, John 11. 4.

8. Paul prayed three times that this thorn in the flesh might depart. It was irksome to him and no doubt he felt that it was damaging to his testimony for Christ. Three times were sufficient for Paul to know what the mind of the Lord was. There is nothing mechanical in praying three

---

* Acts of Paul 2. 3, in the *Apocryphal New Testament*, translated by Montague Rhodes James, Oxford.

times when such prayer comes from the heart; the Lord had prayed three times in Gethsemane, Matt. 26. 44. This has no connection with the vain repetitions of the heathen, Matt. 6. 7, and with the multitudes of formal prayers that have been read in identical form for hundreds of years, obviously with no discernment as to whether or not God would answer the prayer, else such prayers would either cease or would turn into thanksgiving. In 2 Corinthians 11. 28, we noted Paul's constant and daily prayers for the churches, but for himself he would only pray three times. He was in touch with God to know that that was enough.

The various N.T. conditions for prayer to be answered form an important study for the believer. Some are as follows:

Matthew 7. 11, a good thing asked;

Matthew 18. 19, two or three agreeing;

Matthew 21. 21, "doubt not";

Mark 11. 24, "believe that ye receive them";

Luke 17. 6, "if ye had faith";

John 14. 13, asking in His name;

John 15. 7, "if ye abide in Me, and My words abide in you";

John 15. 16, if we bring forth lasting fruit;

James 5.16, "the effectual fervent prayer of a righteous man";

1 John 3 . 22, keeping His commandments, and doing things that are pleasing in His sight;

1 John 5.14, asking according to His will.

The blending of the believer's side and of God's side would give greater intelligence and confidence in prayer; coldness and formality are removed as one approaches before the throne of grace.

9. God's will was manifest to His servant, "My grace is sufficient for thee: for My strength is made perfect in weakness". Grace is sufficient; His strength is independent of human weakness. This message from God enabled Paul to continue in his service in spite of contrary conditions. The apostle bowed to the Lord's will; Paul would boast in his infirmities, realising the divine object in them. The power of Christ upon him was far more satisfying to the soul than all the prosperity and ability of the physical body. The flesh can do little else than displace the power of God. The flesh can do nothing spiritual—it cannot build with gold, silver and precious stones, 1 Cor. 3. 12. Paul had been among the Corinthians with weakness, fear and much trembling, lest the energy of the flesh should dominate to the exclusion of the power of God, 1 Cor. 2. 3–5. Later, Paul could write, "I can do all things through Christ which strengtheneth me", Phil. 4. 13. This was the lesson of his life, finally bearing fruit when he was in prison in Rome.

The children of Israel ran counter to this experience of Paul, as we find in Isaiah 30. 1–3, "Woe to the rebellious children . . . that take counsel, but not of Me; . . . that they may add to their sin: that walk to go down into Egypt, and have not asked at My mouth; to strengthen themselves in the strength of Pharaoh, and to trust in the shadow of Egypt ! Therefore shall the strength of Pharaoh be your shame, and the trust in the shadow of Egypt your confusion". See also Isaiah 40. 31.

Verses 10–13: The Chiefest Apostle in Suffering and Signs

> 10 Therefore I take pleasure in infirmities, in reproaches, in necessities, in persecutions, in distresses for Christ's sake: for when I am weak, then am I strong.
> 11 I am become a fool in glorying; ye have compelled me: for I ought to have been commended of you: for in nothing am I behind the very chiefest apostles, though I be nothing.
> 12 Truly the signs of an apostle were wrought among you in all patience, in signs, and wonders, and mighty deeds.
> 13 For what is it wherein ye were inferior to other churches, except *it be* that I myself was not burdensome to you? forgive me this wrong.

10. Paul finally provides a brief conclusion to his arguments from chapter 10 onwards. It should be observed that verse 10 is often associated with the previous paragraph dealing with Paul's vision; see the R.V. and J.N.D.'s version.

Paul takes pleasure in everything that magnifies the power of God. If his own weakness provides a channel for God's power, then this is the proper path for him. Was not Christ crucified through weakness, yet now lives by the power of God?, 2 Cor. 13. 4. Paul lists five features of his own weakness:

Infirmities: the physical deficiencies of the body, thereby avoiding glorying in the vessel;

Reproaches: the verbal attacks of men because his teaching was of Christ and Him crucified;

Necessities: the apostle's daily wants that were not always met for the convenience of the flesh;

Persecutions: the physical harm he endured for his faith in Christ;

Distresses: the anguish of soul he often felt for his brethren in Christ. The apostle endured these "for Christ's sake", because the cause of Christ was maintained and extended by them. At the same time, Paul was strong because of the delivering power of God. In chapter 1, he had stressed the deliverance which God accomplishes in those who have the "sentence of death" in themselves, vv. 9–10. The Lord is never unmindful of the circumstances of His servants, and even at the end of his life, Paul still experienced the same grace, "Notwithstanding the Lord stood with me, and strengthened me", 2 Tim 4. 17.

11. Paul again dwells on his dislike of speaking about himself, but circumstances necessitated it. Compare Acts 26, where he had to speak of himself at great length to king Agrippa. It is as if Paul had to write his own letter of commendation to the Corinthians, although he was so well known to them through his previous visit. Only the apostle can do this, under the control of the Spirit of divine inspiration. For a brother today to write his own letter of commendation, dwelling on his character and service, would savour of pride. It would show that he hardly had the fellowship and confidence of his brethren who only would have the proper authority and ability to write the letter.

Rather, Paul should have been commended by the Corinthians— they should have recognised the fullness of the apostolic character and service, and should have been able to point this out to others. He had dwelt on this previously, 2 Cor. 3. 1. In fact, Paul, being what he was, needed no letter from the Corinthians to another assembly, nor did he need a letter from another assembly to the Corinthians. They themselves were Paul's letter, and he uses this particular form of argument again throughout chapter 13. The apostle's work was a far better letter!

A letter of commendation is not a formal thing, and replicated a hundred times. A letter is a written description of service and character, recognised by commending brethren locally, and intended to give confidence to the receiving assembly. It leaves no room for a display of the flesh and for glorying in pride. Romans 16. 1–2 should also be read in this connection. Paul commends Phebe to the believers in Rome, dwelling on her character and service, and on her needs that should be met by the saints in Rome. The receiving assembly will then have sufficient grounds to act on Romans 15. 7, "Wherefore receive ye one another, as Christ also received us to the glory of God". The assembly and the one received will then be of one mind so that with "one mouth" they glorify God, v. 6.

Paul's letter demonstrated that he was in nothing "behind the very chiefest apostles", though he were nothing. Originally, he was the chief of sinners, 1 Tim. 1. 15; now he was the chiefest of the apostles. Such a transformation is a pattern to all believers, v. 16. Aaron was raised from the depth of idolatry, Exod. 32. 1–6, to the spiritual heights of the high priesthood.

Paul accomplished all that Peter and John did, and more. They were essentially apostles of the circumcision, but Paul's horizons were widened to the uncircumcised. Peter had been a witness of the sufferings of Christ, 1 Pet. 5. 1, but Paul was a partaker of them, Phil. 3. 10. Paul was allowed of God to accomplish miracles; he was granted the knowledge of the church, and of its peculiar hope based on the return of the Lord for His own.

12. The achievements of the apostles were not those of an ordinary believer; their special abilities marked them out, thereby giving them a unique position among the believers. For example, when Paul was in Ephesus, "God wrought special miracles by the hands of Paul", Acts 19. 11, 12. When writing to Rome, Paul could testify that "mighty signs and wonders, by the power of the Spirit of God" had accompanied the preaching of the gospel. Moreover, Paul recalls that when this was manifest among the Corinthians, it was "in all patience", namely with endurance, as if he were conscious of the presence of opposition at all stages of the work. Note that

signs affect the conscience (as in John's Gospel);

wonders affect the intellect;

mighty deeds affect the body.

The recognition of the apostleship of Paul, together with the implementation of his teaching, would remove all error and disunity among the people of God. Paul has arrived at this conclusion in order to unite these few in Corinth with the rest of the assembly. It certainly is a means for dealing with a split assembly—to note that the Lord gave His chosen vessel this special authority, and that those who are spiritual are bound to recognise it. The careful reading of these chapters 10–13 would provide a solid basis for dealing with disharmony in a local gathering. One could then approach the more practical and doctrinal parts of Paul's epistles with greater intelligence and humility.

13. If Paul is not inferior to the other apostles, then neither are the churches that he founded. No one local assembly can be inferior to others if it is founded on the one foundation, 1 Cor. 3. 11; if it is growing into the one Head, Eph. 2. 21; 4. 15; if it is based on the same Scriptures, having the same hope. The universal appeal of these two Epistles to the Corinthians (see the designation "all" saints in 1 Cor. 1. 2; 2 Cor. 1. 1) shows that no assembly thus founded can be inferior to any other. Differences there may be, and this caused the difficulty to the Corinthian mind. Paul "was not burdensome"; that is, he would not take financial gifts which the rich wished to bestow. Paul would only accept gifts when the motive in giving was a "sweet smell", Phil. 4. 18. This was lacking on the part of the Corinthians, 1 Cor. 16. 17.

Verses 14–21: Paul's Preparation for his Visit to Corinth

14 Behold, the third time I am ready to come to you; and I will not be burdensome to you; for I seek not yours, but you: for the children ought not to lay up for the parents, but the parents for the children.

15 And I will very gladly spend and be spent for you; though the more abundantly I love you, the less I be loved.

16 But be it so, I did not burden you: nevertheless, being crafty, I caught you with guile.

17 Did I make a gain of you by any of them whom I sent unto you?

18 I desired Titus, and with him I sent a brother. Did Titus make a gain of you? walked we not in the same spirit? walked we not in the same steps?

19 Again, think ye that we excuse ourselves unto you? we speak before God in Christ: but we do all things, dearly beloved, for your edifying.

20 For I fear, lest, when I come, I shall not find you such as I would, and that I shall be found unto you such as ye would not: lest there be debates, envyings, wraths, strifes, backbitings, whisperings, swellings, tumults:

21 And lest, when I come again, my God will humble me among you, and that. I shall bewail many which have sinned already, and have not repented of the uncleanness and fornication and lasciviousness which they have committed.

14. Paul was writing this Epistle during the time when he was going over the parts of Macedonia, giving them much exhortation, Acts 20. 2. Shortly afterwards he would journey down the coast to Corinth, so he could write "Behold, the third time I am ready to come to you". Later, he writes "This is the third time I am coming to you", 2 Cor. 13. 1. There are different opinions regarding the interpretation of this verse.

1.   Paul is writing about the three times he *intended* to visit Corinth. Firstly, it was on his second missionary journey that he evangelised Corinth, Acts 18. 1. Secondly, when in Ephesus, he purposed "in the spirit", Acts 19. 21, to visit Achaia, visiting the Corinthians first before passing into Macedonia, 2 Cor. 1. 16. This did not take place; the apostle passed through Troas and went directly to Macedonia. It is here that he formulates his third intention.

2.   Others suggest that Paul, while at Ephesus for three years during his third journey, actually paid a brief visit to Corinth after having written the first Epistle. Reliable works of a more theological kind must be consulted for further details.*

What is not in doubt, and hence something more important for faith, is that Paul's movements were accomplished in a spiritual frame of mind, namely "in the spirit", Acts 19. 21; "if the Lord permit", 1 Cor. 16. 7; no purpose "according to the flesh", 2 Cor. 1. 17.

Paul repeats his policy—he will not be burdensome to them. He still will not take gifts although he knew that this policy stirred up opposition in the minds of some who were rich. If this Epistle could not correct these men, then sinking to their whims was no legitimate substitute. We therefore presume that Paul was as good as his word, for *afterwards* he was still in the good of the truth of the Lord's words. "It is more blessed to give than to receive", Acts 20. 35.

Paul writes, "I seek not yours, but you", namely, he was interested in their souls and not their material possessions. How often had this been the burden of the apostle's heart, and it is a good example for those who have the well-being of the saints at heart today. For example,

1 Thessalonians 2. 8, "We were willing to have imparted unto you, not the gospel of God only, but also our own souls, because ye were dear unto us".

Colossians 1. 9, "to desire that ye might be filled with the knowledge of His will in all wisdom and spiritual understanding".

Romans 1. 11, "For I long to see you, that I may impart unto you some spiritual gift, to the end that ye may be established".

By this means Paul would lay up for his children in the faith; they had but one father in the gospel, 1 Cor. 4. 15. Paul uses the figure of the family circle, whether in the human, bird, or animal kingdoms. Life itself is transferred from the parents, and later their material possessions are also transferred to the children in their upbringing. What unselfish care and affection Paul had for his children, a care that young converts should

---

* See pages 255–257, *The New Bible Dictionary*, The Inter-Varsity Fellowship.

receive from those responsible for bringing them to the Lord.

15. By the idea "I will very gladly spend and be spent for you", Paul regards himself as that which is being transferred to them. He would either spend his time, zeal, and energy for them, or he would allow his physical, mental, and spiritual self to be spent even unto weariness and ill-health on their behalf.

But Paul recognises a great principle that applies when a spiritual man has to do with an unspiritual or carnal believer. A love that seeks the well-being of others is not received if the others will not appreciate it. Love does not always do what is desired or expected by those loved. The Lord had loved sinners in the world, but they had mocked Him to scorn because they wanted love to be manifested in another way. Elsewhere Paul had written, "Ye are not straitened in us (that is, Paul's affection for them was not restricted) but ye are straitened in your own bowels (that is, their own love was restricted)", 2 Cor. 6. 12.

16. Paul's own holy conduct of not being burdensome to the Corinthians, is twisted by these men to the charge made against him that he caught them with guile. (The last phrase must be construed as a quotation made by Paul of their accusations.) The word "guile" is employed in a bad sense, meaning an insidious artifice, a bait or a piece of apparatus for entrapping. The Corinthians were suggesting that the apostle obtained financial help in a cunning way, through Titus or someone else. But this could not be so, as verses 17–18 go on to show; Paul was not alone in his policy of not being burdensome.

17–18. The other brethren sent to Corinth adopted the same attitude as Paul. Neither he nor Titus made any gain as a result of their work and stay in Corinth. Titus received no gifts directly, and Paul received no gifts indirectly through any third person whom he may send. What Paul was when present, so he was when absent; he was not double-faced, but walking with a single heart before his God.

It is a good thing when brethren who work together have the same outlook on matters relating to Christian liberty (not, only doctrinally, as would be expected in any case). Titus walked "in the same spirit", having a common outlook, and "in the same steps", in common deeds. Previously, Paul had described Titus as "my partner and fellowhelper concerning you", 2 Cor. 8. 23, "partner" referring to a common outlook, and "fellowhelper" to common deeds. Human nature being what it is, this is a unity hard to attain, but when attained, "how good and how pleasant it is for brethren to dwell together in unity ! It is like the precious ointment upon the head, that ran down upon the beard, even Aaron's beard: that went down to the skirts of his garments", Ps. 133. 1, 2.

It is interesting to observe that the word "steps" in our verse occurs elsewhere only twice in the N.T. Romans 4. 12 speaks of those "who also walk in the *steps* of that faith of our father Abraham, which he had being yet uncircumcised", while 1 Peter 2. 21 reminds us that "Christ also suffered for us, leaving us an example, that ye should follow His *steps*". We have, then, three sets of steps,

1. the steps of *fellowship*;
2. the steps of *faith*;
3. the steps of *suffering*.

19. Paul is not acting and writing to defend himself against their unjust charges. Rather, (a) he is speaking before the divine gaze, and (b) he is doing all things for their edifying. Paul's motives were God-ward and saint-ward. Some service today that seems so uninspiring, so light, so lacking in substance, so profitless for edification, would either be discarded or be transformed if these two points were borne in mind. Some seek to speak because they are asked to do so, yet knowing that they have no gift in that direction. Others speak because they are asked to do so by brethren who exercise no discrimination as to whether the proposed speaker is gifted or not. Such a state of affairs is playing with divine principles, but Paul's recipe is the basis for assembly progress and prosperity.

See 2 Corinthians 10. 8 for notes on the subject of edification.

20. In these last two verses, Paul opens his heart to his fear that some in Corinth would not repent even as a result of reading this second Epistle. It is possible for hearts to be persistently stubborn even in the face of the most powerful word. In verse 21, Paul would be humbled among them and would mourn over many, but in verse 20, he would appear as one "such as ye would not", namely using apostolic authority with a rod and with sharpness, 13. 10.

Paul wished to avoid the following things:

Debates: that is, contentions, as in 1 Corinthians 1. 11 where they took sides with particular servants of God.

Envyings: that is jealousy, as in Acts 13. 45 where the Jews, seeing the multitudes, were filled with envy.

Wraths: as in Luke 4. 28 where they were filled with wrath, their consciences having been convicted by the Word.

Strifes: that is, the forceful attitude of a party, as in Philippians 1. 16, where some preached Christ of contention.

Backbitings: that is, evil speaking, as 1 Peter 2. 12, where some spoke evil of the saints.

Whisperings: that is, subtle planning behind the back of truth; see Romans 1. 29.

Swellings: that is, puffing up, elated with pride. This word occurs six times in 1 Corinthians as a verb.

Tumults: that is, disorder. But God is not the author of confusion, 1 Cor. 14. 33.

21. Paul lastly seems to refer to various weaknesses dealt with in the first Epistle, concerning which "many . . . have sinned already, and have not repented". Such men were apparently contented that Paul knew of these things, but they did not reckon with the Lord walking amongst His own as in Revelation 2–3. These moral disorders may be taken at their face value, but the words may also have implications concerning assembly conduct and practice.

> *Uncleanness* would refer to evil things allowed within the assembly, such as false doctrine, 1 Cor. 15.
>
> *Fornication* would refer to contact with evil outside the assembly, as 1 Cor. 5, 6.
>
> *Lasciviousness* would refer to the lustful and wrong use of spiritual things within the assembly, such as the gift of speaking with tongues, 1 Cor. 14.

2 CORINTHIANS 13

Section 4.   The Example of the True Minister
Subject 4.   Approval of the Apostle

Background of this Subject

Paul now puts the finishing touches to this letter, prior to his visit to Corinth shortly afterwards. Verses 1–10 conclude this section that started at chapter 10. Verses 11–14 conclude the Epistle for all believers in Corinth. The *general* conclusion, vv. 11–14, has spiritual unity as its theme, while the *particular* conclusion, vv. 1–10, stresses Paul's own apostolic work in Corinth during his first visit. As another* has written,

> "He then puts an end to the question about his ministry by presenting an idea which ought to confound them utterly. If Christ had not spoken by him, Christ did not dwell in them. If Christ was in them, He must have spoken by the apostle, for he had been the means of their conversion."

The argument may be followed by noticing that the words "proof", v. 3, "prove", v. 5, "reprobates", vv. 5, 6, 7, "approved", v. 7, all contain the same root (positively or negatively). The basic idea is one of *approval* or of *probate*. When a deceased person has made a will, the executor obtains a "grant of probate". This is an authorisation of approval of the will by the registrar of a probate registry, and enables the executor to put the will into effect. Is probate granted to the apostolic service and to the Corinthian believers? Is his service and is their faith approved? Paul shows that *both he and they must be approved together.*

Exposition of 2 Cor. 13: Approval of the Apostle

1 This *is* the third *time* I am coming to you. In the mouth of two or three witnesses shall every word be established.
2 I told you before, and foretell you, as if I were present, the second time; and being absent now I write to them which heretofore have sinned, and to all other, that, if I come again, I will not spare:
3 Since ye seek a proof of Christ speaking in me, which to you-ward is not weak, but is mighty in you.
4 For though he was crucified through weakness, yet he liveth by the power of God. For we also are weak in him, but we shall live with him by the power of God toward you.
5 Examine yourselves, whether ye be in the faith; prove your own selves. Know ye not your own selves, how that Jesus Christ is in you, except ye be reprobates?
6 But I trust that ye shall know that we are not reprobates.
7 Now I pray to God that ye do no evil; not that we should appear approved, but that ye should do that which is honest, though we be as reprobates.
8 For we can do nothing against the truth, but for the truth.
9 For we are glad, when we are weak, and ye are strong: and this also we wish, *even* your perfection..

* Chapter 13 of 2 Corinthians, *Synopsis of the Books of the Bible*, volume 4, J.N.D.

10 Therefore I write these things being absent, lest being present I should use sharpness, according to the power which the Lord hath given me to edification, and not to destruction.

11 Finally, brethren, farewell. Be perfect, be of good comfort, be of one mind, live in peace; and the God of love and peace shall be with you.

12 Greet one another with an holy kiss.

13 All the saints salute you.

14 The grace of the Lord Jesus Christ, and the love of God, and the communion of the Holy Ghost, *be* with you all. Amen.

1. Paul again mentions the fact that it is the "third time"; see 12. 14. However one views the matter, it is true that there are three occasions on which Paul was in the process of coming to Corinth. In 12. 14 he mentions that he was ready to come; here that he was actually coming. In Acts 18. 1 he was coming to Corinth; as he left Ephesus he was actually en route for Corinth; and finally, as he was leaving Macedonia having written this second Epistle, he was on his journey to Corinth.

There could be no gainsaying the veracity of Paul's testimony; "in the mouth of two or three witnesses shall every word be established". Some suggest that Paul's three comings would provide three distinct, yet consistent, spheres of testimony. On the other hand the plurality of witnesses may be implied *in fact*, rather than *figuratively*. No doubt Timothy, who was also writing the Epistle, would be with Paul; so would some of the Macedonians, 9. 4. There were also others accompanying the apostle, and Acts 20. 4 provides a list of names. These would all speak the same things, having a common outlook on spiritual matters, since "can two walk together, except they be agreed?" Amos 3. 3.

God's plan for the authentication of testimony pervades the Scriptures. The Lord has said, "The testimony of two men is true", John 8. 17, referring to Deuteronomy 17. 6. The ninth commandment, "Thou shalt not bear false witness", Exod. 20. 16, had prepared the ground for this principle to be introduced. Such a safeguard was deliberately abandoned by the two false witnesses in Matthew 26. 59–62.

For example, the principle is seen in the way in which God's mind concerning sin was made known. The ten commandments were spoken *twice*, by God in Exodus 20. 1 and by Moses in Deuteronomy 5. 1–21; *twice* they were given on stones, Exod. 31. 18; 34. 28; there were *two* stones written on *two* sides, Exod. 32. 15; there were *two* arks in which they were successively placed, Deut. 10. 1–5; Exod. 40. 20; there are *two* great commandments, Matt. 22. 38–40.

The truth of the Lord's Person was made known according to the same principle, although the Lord needed not the testimony of man. The Lord Jesus made it clear that His own testimony counted as one, and that of the Father counted as another, John 8. 18. The Lord had properly announced His own person in verses such as John 4. 26; 9. 37; Mark 14. 61–62. Then quite apart from the witness of His own works, and that of John the Baptist, John 5. 32–36, there was the witness rendered by the Father, 5. 37; Matt. 3. 17; 17. 5. If men will not heed the double witness of the divine voice, will they heed the voice of men? If men will not heed the double witness of "Moses and the prophets", would they be persuaded through a miracle, Luke 16. 31?

Similarly with Paul; he needed not a "cloud of witnesses", Heb. 12. 1. In our chapter, he provides only his own witness together with the unrealised witness of the Corinthians themselves. They would have to "examine yourselves", 2 Cor. 13. 5 to discover that there was a witness in themselves.

2. The purely physical side of Paul's movements, "I told you before, and foretell you, as if I were present, the second time", seems to be capable of being construed in two ways.

> *Either* "the second time" refers to a previous visit, in which case, prior to his third visit, he repeats in writing the warnings already given on his second visit;
>
> *Or* "the second time" refers to his forthcoming visit, and he foretells them in writing what he will tell them verbally, and what he had already told them either in his Epistles or else during his first visit.

Dare we say regarding a point in the Scriptures, "does it really matter which is intended?" The lesson is obvious; Paul would not spare them that had sinned, and by drawing attention to the fact that he was repeating this warning, we see that Paul was perfectly consistent over the years regarding the conduct that he knew was comely in the people of God. In Ephesus, he had consistently warned everyone night and day "by the space of three years", Acts 20. 31. Today, it is a damage to the testimony if brethren start to droop from a consistent, steadfast position in Christ, allowing inconsistency and waywardness to come into their own lives, into the lives of others, and into the local assembly over which they may even be overseers.

The carnal believers in Corinth might object if Paul came with a rod to correct and not to spare; he therefore pens these last words to gain their ear.

3. Having dwelt so long on his weaknesses in the previous chapters, Paul would think that these men in Corinth might like to see something powerful and mighty. He had spoken of the "power of Christ" resting upon him, 12. 9; the outward "signs, and wonders, and mighty works", v. 12, could easily be forgotten. The Corinthians would want facts and up-to-date experiences. The "proof of Christ speaking in" Paul was neither something ethereal nor a make-believe. The "demonstration of the Spirit and of power", 1 Cor. 2. 4, can be perceived by all believers if they know the right direction in which to look. The Corinthians had to look to themselves; something mighty through Paul had been accomplished in them. Let all believers look to themselves to perceive that which is powerful and mighty accomplished in them, not through apostles, but humble servants likewise called of God to their own particular calling.

Note that the portion from "which to you-ward is not weak . . ." to the end of verse 4 is a parenthesis.

4. The example of Christ, occurring in the parenthesis, is recorded because it is so note-worthy and similar that Paul cannot afford to overlook it.

> *In Christ's case,* "He was crucified through weakness". He had no intrinsic weakness of His own, although He was manifest in flesh. It refers to the weaknesses pressing in from the outside. He sustained the spitting, the buffeting and the smiting, Matt. 26. 67; He was scourged and suffered the pain of the crown of thorns, 27. 26, 29; physical weakness prevented Him from carrying His own cross all the way, v. 32. The physical condition of the blessed Saviour is described in Psalm 22. 14–17; His strength was dried up and His mouth was dry as He was brought into the dust of death. But now He lives, and that "by the power of God" that was wrought in Christ "when He raised Him from the dead", Eph. 1. 20.

> *In Paul's case,* he was "weak in Him", namely in Christ. Paul does not refer to any sinful tendencies, since such could not be described as "in Him". Rather Paul is referring to the external toils and perils of service that brought great physical strain upon his stamina. In Galatians 2. 20, he lives through the *faith* of the Son of God; here he lives through the *power* of God taking up the frail vessel, a power, Paul stresses, that was directed even to the Corinthians.

5. Paul now returns to verse 3, "Since ye seek a proof of Christ speaking in me". How? By looking inwards, *not* introspectively by pondering the old man and his deeds, *but* upon Christ dwelling there, Eph. 3. 17. They had to examine themselves and notice that, in spite of all the errors and obstinacy of their hearts, grace reigned unto righteousness through faith. After all, they were so different from the heathen around, not because of their works, but because God had worked within. Recognising this, they found themselves approved. They could not be "reprobates", or rejected, or not approved, except of course in the exceptional circumstances of one or another not being saved, but masquerading as a trouble maker in the assembly. All this contrasts with God's proof of Israel, Jud. 3. 1; they were proved and found wanting.

6. Whence came their blessed experience and standing in Christ? Originally by the work of Paul! If their blessings were a result of Paul's labours, then *since* they were approved, *so also* was the labourer approved. It could not be otherwise; the Lord had intimated the same thing in another way, "A good tree cannot bring forth evil fruit, neither can a corrupt tree bring forth good fruit. Every tree that bringeth not forth good fruit is hewn down, and cast into the fire. Wherefore by their fruits ye shall know them", Matt. 7. 18–20. Paul trusts that the Corinthians, recognising the force of this argument, would know that Paul was not reprobate, but that he was approved—certainly by God, but also by themselves.

7. Paul places these men before the Lord, that they should do no evil, by repenting of their sins and doing that which is honest. The apostle realises that if grace works to repentance in these men, then their attitude to him would automatically rectify itself. But Paul wants a higher motive than that to govern their repentance. Simply to change in outlook, so that Paul "should appear approved" would be far from satisfactory. That would merely be looking to man, albeit to an apostle. Repentance and service should have in view the higher motive of pleasing God. Paul would well leave himself counted as a reprobate if the Corinthians would turn to please God.

8. The word "can" here means "to have power", the same root occurring in the word "power" twice in verse 4. Paul observes that saints have no power against the truth, only for the truth. In spite of all the scheming of the Corinthians against Paul, any effects were but illusory and apparent. They could only do something for the truth when repentance gripped their hearts before God.

9. Paul would gladly remain weak, so that the power of God may again be seen openly amongst the saints. His desire was even their "perfection". This noun occurs only once in the N.T., but the corresponding verb occurs thirteen times. This means to *adjust thoroughly*, to bring into its *proper condition*. The nets were *mended*, Matt. 4. 21; praise was *perfected*, 21. 16; those overtaken with a fault should be *restored*, Gal. 6. 1; the worlds had been *framed* by the Word of God, Heb. 11. 3 . Previously Paul had desired that the Corinthians should be *"perfectly joined together"*, 1 Cor. 1. 10. He now expresses his wish that these men in Corinth should be restored to their same happy, spiritual condition that they had enjoyed during his original stay with them. This is a prayer and a wish for today, the blessed regaining of the holy things that the apostle stood for, and which can so easily be lost by the glitter and attraction of more material and ceremonial things.

10. As John explained the reason for the writing of his Gospel, John 20. 31, so Paul explains in this verse why he has written these last chapters. He wanted the written word and not the spoken word of severity to do its work in their hearts. The Corinthians may care to think that his speech was "contemptible", 2 Cor. 10. 10, but Paul knew that his authority (not "power") was unto edification and not to destruction; see 10. 8; 12. 19. The word "destruction" here means "pulling down", "overthrowing", as 2 Cor. 10. 4; Acts 19. 27. It is, as it were, that the apostle half feared that the use of "sharpness" might exceed the bounds of edification, resulting instead in an overthrow. How careful the apostle was, so that in all things only the works of God should flow through him.

11. Finally, Paul addresses all the saints, calling them brethren and bidding them "farewell", a word that means "rejoice" in the same sense as in Philippians 4. 4.

His other exhortations are of immediate application:

Be perfect: this is the verbal form of the word "perfection" occurring in verse 9. The apostle desired all the saints to be adjusted spiritually so as to be in accord with their standing in Christ Jesus.

Be of good comfort: that is, be encouraged. The saints needed this in the light of the divided atmosphere which the trouble makers caused to pervade the assembly.

Be of one mind: this word is dominant in the Philippians, occurring over ten times. There, Paul reminds them of the danger of some minding "earthly things", 3. 19, and shows them the blessedness of the revelation of God, which grants a oneness of mind and desire to be imitators of Paul and of *all* others who thus walk, vv. 15–17.

Live in peace: the Lord similarly exhorted His own, Mark 9. 50, while Paul likewise instructed the Romans and Thessalonians, Rom. 12. 18; 1 Thess. 5. 13. Peace may seem hard to attain when a few seek to maintain trouble, but the Lord Jesus promised that He would leave His peace with His people, John 14. 27. A mind at peace with God is also at peace with the saints, even though outward circumstances seem contrary. The presence of the God of love and peace cannot be lost by those who are spiritual. This is complementary to the presence of the Lord Jesus, 2 Cor. 13. 5, and to the presence of the Holy Spirit 1 Cor. 6. 19.

12–13. There two verses show the unity of relations between all the people of God. "Greet" and "salute" are one and the same word. *Externally*, the Macedonians greeted the Corinthians, while *internally* believers were to sanctify the customary form of greeting, namely the kiss was to be transformed into the "holy kiss". Unsanctified forms of greeting merely give licence to the flesh.

14. The unity of manifestation of the Godhead is a fitting thought to conclude an Epistle dealing with a background of disunity. We have already noticed such a unity in verse 11. Here are other cases for meditation, where the Father, Son and Holy Spirit are seen:

The Lord's baptism. Matthew 3. 16, 17.

The Lord's death. Hebrews 9. 14.

Believer's baptism. Matthew 28. 19–20.

Believer's benediction. 2 Corinthians 13. 14.

Giving of the Spirit. John 14. 16, 26; 15. 26; Acts 2. 33.

Dwelling in the saints. The Spirit dwells within, John 14. 17; 1 John 2. 27; 1 Cor. 6. 19. The Lord Jesus dwells in our hearts, John 14. 20;

17. 23; Eph. 3. 17. The Father Himself dwells within, John 14. 23; Eph. 2. 22.

In worship. Galatians 4. 6.

Giving of spiritual gifts. Romans 12. 3; Ephesians 4. 7; 1 Corinthians 12. 11 .

Divine interest in service. 1 Corinthians 12. 4–6.

Divine intervention in hard hearts. Isaiah 6. 10 is often quoted. In Isaiah 6 it is the voice of the Lord; in John 12. 39–41 the glory is that of Christ; in Acts 28. 25 the voice is that of the Holy Spirit.

Anointing of the Lord. In Isaiah 61. 1–3 it is the voice of the Lord; in 42. 1–4 it is the voice of God; in 11. 1–9 it is the voice of the Spirit of prophecy.

In our verse, can we see a glimpse of the unity of the boards of the tabernacle? The silver sockets may correspond to the grace of the Lord Jesus Christ, the bars to the communion of the Holy Spirit, and the overlaid gold to the love of God. Such grace is to "you all"; none is omitted, even though some were walking far from the light. Only grace could bear with such wayward believers.

Conclusion. As far as the divine record of inspiration is concerned, there is no conclusion to this Epistle. It had been written from Macedonia, and after its despatch Paul had followed it soon afterwards on his visit to Corinth, Acts 20. 2–3. We do not know the effects of this Epistle or of his visit, upon the majority in Corinth who would receive him. Similarly we do not know the effects of this Epistle on the minority who would not receive him, or the steps that Paul had to take during his visit to correct or deal with these men. The Epistle to the Romans was written during this visit, and verses such as Romans 15. 26–27; 16. 22–23 may tend to show a happier disposition in his heart.

Generally speaking, this lack of any recorded results suggests that the Epistle is deliberately left like an open-ended trumpet, the voice from which is not reflected back from a wall nearby, but rather propagates outwards to reach the people of God in all times and places. In other words, the Spirit of God causes it to reach even to us; its power undiminished, its authority unchallenged (except by men who are of no account), its value abundantly precious, and its sanctifying and correcting influence widely applicable. Studying the Epistle should bring us more into line with Paul's ways which were in Christ Jesus.

Although outside the scope of Scripture, it is interesting to note that when Clement later wrote his letter to Corinth from Rome, he was able to appeal to the authority of the apostle Paul without fear of contradiction. This means that the group of men who were contending with Paul had either been silenced by his coming with severity, or else they had left the assembly at Corinth, not, of course, to join with any other assembly elsewhere. Believers should take courage that God is still on the throne, and that Christ is still the Head of His church.